AUTOMOTIVE ENGINES
THEORY AND SERVICING

EIGHTH EDITION

James D. Halderman

PEARSON

Boston   Columbus   Indianapolis   New York   San Francisco   Upper Saddle River
Amsterdam   Cape Town   Dubai   London   Madrid   Milan   Munich   Paris   Montreal
Toronto   Delhi   Mexico City   Sao Paulo   Sydney   Hong Kong   Seoul   Singapore   Taipei

Editor-in-Chief: Vernon Anthony
Senior Acquisitions Editor: Lindsey
 Prudhomme Gill
Team Lead for Program Management:
 Laura Weaver
Director of Marketing: David Gesell
Marketing Manager: Stacey Martinez
Senior Marketing Coordinator: Alicia
 Wozniak
Marketing Assistant: Les Roberts

Production Manager: Holly Shufeldt
Cover Art Director: Jayne Conte
Cover Designer: Suzanne Behnke
**Full-Service Project Management and
 Composition:** Integra Software Services, Ltd.
Printer/Binder: R.R. Donnelley/Willard
Cover Printer: Lehigh-Phoenix
 Color/Hagerstown
Text Font: Helvetica Neue

Library of Congress Cataloging-in-Publication Data
Halderman, James D.,
  Automotive engines: theory and servicing/James D. Halderman. —Eighth edition.
    p. cm
  Includes index.
  ISBN-13: 978-0-13-351500-8 (alk. paper)
  ISBN-10: 0-13-351500-1 (alk. paper)
  1. Automobiles—Motors. 2. Automobiles—Motors—Maintenance and repair. I. Title.
TL210.H29 2015
629.25'040288—dc23

                                         2013028873

1 2 3 4 5 6 7 8 9 10 V003 17 16 15 14 13

ISBN 10:   0-13-351500-1
ISBN 13: 978-0-13-351500-8

PREFACE

PROFESSIONAL TECHNICIAN SERIES Part of Pearson Automotive's Professional Technician Series, the eighth edition of *Automotive Engines: Theory and Servicing* represents the future of automotive textbooks. The series is a full-color, media-integrated solution for today's students and instructors. The series includes textbooks that cover all 8 areas of ASE certification, plus additional titles covering common courses.

The series is also peer reviewed for technical accuracy.

UPDATES TO THE EIGHTH EDITION

- All content is correlated to the latest NATEF tasks.
- A dramatic, new full-color design enhances the subject material.
- Many new full-color line drawing and photos have been added to help bring the subject to life.
- Infection control precautions have been added (Chapter 1).
- New OSHA standards information added (Chapter 2).
- Additional information on security and external Torx drivers (Chapter 4).
- Updated content on service information (Chapter 8).
- New content on the Atkinson cycle engine design (Chapter 10).
- New content on engine power rated in kilowatts (Chapter 10).
- Updated information on the role of the PCM and spark timing (Chapter 18).
- New content on pressure relief valves on intake manifolds (Chapter 23).
- Updated information on best practices when pre-lubing an engine (Chapter 34).
- Many new color photos and line drawings have been added to this edition.
- Content has been streamlined for easier reading and comprehension.

- This text is fully integrated with MyAutomotiveKit, an online supplement for homework, quizzing, testing, multimedia activities, and videos.
- Unlike other textbooks, this book is written so that the theory, construction, diagnosis, and service of a particular component or system is presented in one location. There is no need to search through the entire book for other references to the same topic.

NATEF CORRELATED NATEF certified programs need to demonstrate that they use course material that covers NATEF tasks. All Professional Technician textbooks have been correlated to the appropriate NATEF task lists. These correlations can be found in an appendix to the book.

A COMPLETE INSTRUCTOR AND STUDENT SUPPLEMENTS PACKAGE All Professional Technician textbooks are accompanied by a full set of instructor and student supplements. Please see page vi for a detailed list of supplements.

A FOCUS ON DIAGNOSIS AND PROBLEM SOLVING The Professional Technician Series has been developed to satisfy the need for a greater emphasis on problem diagnosis. Automotive instructors and service managers agree that students and beginning technicians need more training in diagnostic procedures and skill development. To meet this need and demonstrate how real-world problems are solved, "Real World Fix" features are included throughout and highlight how real-life problems are diagnosed and repaired.

The following pages highlight the unique core features that set the Professional Technician Series book apart from other automotive textbooks.

IN-TEXT FEATURES

chapter 1 — SHOP SAFETY

LEARNING OBJECTIVES: After studying this chapter, the reader should be able to: • Describe the personal protective equipment used by technicians. • Explain the safety tips for technicians and the cleaning methods and processes used in vehicle service. • Discuss shop safety procedures. • Discuss the purpose of fire extinguishers, fire blankets, and first aid and eye wash stations.

KEY TERMS: ANSI 2 • Bump cap 2 • Decibel (dB) 3 • Eye wash station 8 • Fire blankets 7 • Microbes 5 • "PASS" 6 • Personal protective equipment (PPE) 2 • Spontaneous combustion 4

PERSONAL PROTECTIVE EQUIPMENT

Safety is not just a buzzword on a poster in the work area. Safe work habits can reduce accidents and injuries, ease the workload, and keep employees pain free.

SAFETY GLASSES The most important **personal protective equipment (PPE)** a technician should wear all the time are safety glasses, which meet standard **ANSI Z87.1**. ● **SEE FIGURE 1–1**.

STEEL-TOED SHOES Steel-toed safety shoes are also a good investment. ● **SEE FIGURE 1–2**. If safety shoes are not available, then leather-topped shoes offer more protection than canvas or cloth covered shoes.

GLOVES Wear gloves to protect your hands from rough or sharp surfaces. Thin rubber gloves are recommended when working around automotive liquids such as engine oil, antifreeze, transmission fluid, or any other liquids that may be hazardous. Several types of gloves and their characteristics include:

- **Latex surgical gloves.** These gloves are relatively inexpensive, but tend to stretch, swell, and weaken when exposed to gas, oil, or solvents.
- **Vinyl gloves.** These gloves are also inexpensive and are not affected by gas, oil, or solvents. ● **SEE FIGURE 1-3**.
- **Polyurethane gloves.** These gloves are more expensive, yet very strong. Even though these gloves are also not affected by gas, oil, or solvents, they tend to be slippery.
- **Nitrile gloves.** These gloves are exactly like latex gloves, but are not affected by gas, oil, or solvents, yet they tend to be expensive.

FIGURE 1–1 Safety glasses should be worn at all times when working on or around any vehicle or servicing any component.

FIGURE 1–2 Steel-toed shoes are a worthwhile investment to help prevent foot injury due to falling objects. Even these well-worn shoes can protect the feet of this service technician.

SHOP SAFETY 1

OBJECTIVES AND KEY TERMS appear at the beginning of each chapter to help students and instructors focus on the most important material in each chapter. The chapter objectives are based on specific ASE and NATEF tasks.

 **TECH TIP**

It Just Takes a Second

Whenever removing any automotive component, it is wise to screw the bolts back into the holes a couple of threads by hand. This ensures that the right bolt will be used in its original location when the component or part is put back on the vehicle.

TECH TIPS feature real-world advice and "tricks of the trade" from ASE-certified master technicians.

 SAFETY TIP

Shop Cloth Disposal

Always dispose of oily shop cloths in an enclosed container to prevent a fire. ● **SEE FIGURE 1–69**. Whenever oily cloths are thrown together on the floor or workbench, a chemical reaction can occur, which can ignite the cloth even without an open flame. This process of ignition without an open flame is called **spontaneous combustion**.

SAFETY TIPS alert students to possible hazards on the job and how to avoid them.

 REAL WORLD FIX

Valve Springs Can Vary

A technician was building a small block Chevrolet V-8 engine at home and was doing the final detailed checks, and found that many of the valve springs did not have the same tension. Using a borrowed valve spring tester, the technician visited a local parts store and measured all of the valve springs that the store had in stock. The technician selected and purchased the 16 valve springs that were within specification and within a very narrow range of tension. Although having all valve springs equal may or may not affect engine operation, the technician was pleased that all of the valve springs were equal.

REAL WORLD FIXES present students with actual automotive scenarios and shows how these common (and sometimes uncommon) problems were diagnosed and repaired.

 FREQUENTLY ASKED QUESTION

How Many Types of Screw Heads Are Used in Automotive Applications?

There are many, including Torx, hex (also called Allen), plus many others used in custom vans and motor homes. ● **SEE FIGURE 1–9**.

FREQUENTLY ASKED QUESTIONS are based on the author's own experience and provide answers to many of the most common questions asked by students and beginning service technicians.

NOTE: Most of these "locking nuts" are grouped together and are commonly referred to as *prevailing torque nuts*. This means that the nut will hold its tightness or torque and not loosen with movement or vibration.

NOTES provide students with additional technical information to give them a greater understanding of a specific task or procedure.

CAUTION: *Never* use hardware store (nongraded) bolts, studs, or nuts on any vehicle steering, suspension, or brake component. Always use the exact size and grade of hardware that is specified and used by the vehicle manufacturer.

CAUTIONS alert students about potential damage to the vehicle that can occur during a specific task or service procedure.

☠ **WARNING**

Do not use incandescent trouble lights around gasoline or other flammable liquids. The liquids can cause the bulb to break and the hot filament can ignite the flammable liquid which can cause personal injury or even death.

WARNINGS alert students to potential dangers to themselves during a specific task or service procedure.

THE SUMMARY, REVIEW QUESTIONS, AND CHAPTER QUIZ at the end of each chapter help students review the material presented in the chapter and test themselves to see how much they've learned.

HOISTING THE VEHICLE   **STEP BY STEP**

1. The first step in hoisting a vehicle is to properly align the vehicle in the center of the stall.
2. Most vehicles will be correctly positioned when the left front tire is centered on the tire pad.
3. The arms can be moved in and out and most pads can be rotated to allow for many different types of vehicle construction.
4. Most lifts are equipped with short pad extensions that are often necessary to use to allow the pad to contact the frame of a vehicle without causing the arm of the lift to hit and damage parts of the body.
5. Tall pad extensions can also be used to gain access to the frame of a vehicle. This position is needed to safely hoist many pickup trucks, vans, and sport utility vehicles.
6. An additional extension may be necessary to hoist a truck or van equipped with running boards to give the necessary clearance.
7. Position the pads under the vehicle under the recommended locations.
8. After being sure all pads are correctly positioned, use the electromechanical controls to raise the vehicle.
9. With the vehicle raised one foot (30 cm) off the ground, push down on the vehicle to check to see if it is stable on the pads. If the vehicle rocks, lower the vehicle and reset the pads. The vehicle can be raised to any desired working level. Be sure the safety is engaged before working on or under the vehicle.
10. If raising a vehicle without a frame, place the flat pads under the pinch weld seam to spread the load. If additional clearance is necessary, the pads can be raised as shown.
11. When the service work is completed, the hoist should be raised slightly and the safety released before using the hydraulic to lower the vehicle.
12. After lowering the vehicle, be sure all arms of the lift are moved out of the way before driving the vehicle out of the work area.

64   CHAPTER 6   VEHICLE LIFTING AND HOISTING   65

STEP BY STEP photo sequences show in detail the steps involved in performing a specific task or service procedure.

RESOURCES IN PRINT AND ONLINE
Automotive Engines

Name of Supplement	Print	Online	Audience	Description
Instructor Resource Manual 0-13-351617-2		✔	Instructors	NEW! The Ultimate teaching aid: Chapter summaries, key terms, chapter learning objectives, lecture resources, discuss/demonstrate classroom activities, MyAutomotiveLab correlation, and answers to the in text review and quiz questions.
TestBank 0-13-351599-0		✔	Instructors	Test generation software and test bank for the text.
PowerPoint Presentation 0-13-351615-6		✔	Instructors	Slides include chapter learning objectives, lecture outline of the test, and graphics from the book.
Image Bank 0-13-351584-2		✔	Instructors	All of the images and graphs from the text-book to create customized lecture slides.
Instructors Resource CD-ROM 0-13-351622-9	✔			Take your instructor resources with you! This convenient CD houses the text PowerPoint presentation, Image Bank, instructors manual, and TestGen.
NATEF Correlated Task Sheets – for instructors 0-13-351616-4		✔	Instructors	Downloadable NATEF task sheets for easy customization and development of unique task sheets.
NATEF Task Sheets – For Students 0-13-351623-7	✔		Students	Study activity manual that correlates NATEF Automobile Standards to chapters and pages numbers in the text. Available to students at a discounted price when packaged with the text.
CourseSmart eText 0-13-351614-8		✔	Students	An alternative to purchasing the print text-book, students can subscribe to the same content online and save up to 50% off the suggested list price of the print text. Visit **www.coursesmart.com**

All online resources can be downloaded from the Instructor's Resource Center: **www.pearsonighered.com/irc**

ACKNOWLEDGMENTS

A large number of people and organizations have cooperated in providing the reference material and technical information used in this text. The author wishes to express sincere thanks to the following organizations for their special contributions:

ASE
Automotion, Inc.
Society of Automotive Engineers (SAE)

TECHNICAL AND CONTENT REVIEWERS

The following people reviewed the manuscript before production and checked it for technical accuracy and clarity of presentation. Their suggestions and recommendations were included in the final draft of the manuscript. Their input helped make this textbook clear and technically accurate while maintaining the easy-to-read style that has made other books from the same author so popular.

Jim Anderson
Greenville High School

Victor Bridges
Umpqua Community College

Darrell Deeter
Saddleback College

Dr. Roger Donovan
Illinois Central College

A. C. Durdin
Moraine Park Technical College

Herbert Ellinger
Western Michigan University

Al Engledahl
College of Dupage

Larry Hagelberger
Upper Valley Joint Vocational School

Oldrick Hajzler
Red River College

Betsy Hoffman
Vermont Technical College

Richard Krieger
Michigan Institute of technology

Steven T. Lee
Lincoln Technical Institute

Carlton H. Mabe, Sr.
Virginia Western Community College

Roy Marks
Owens Community College

Tony Martin
University of Alaska Southeast

Kerry Meier
San Juan College

Fritz Peacock
Indiana Vocational Technical College

Dennis Peter
NAIT (Canada)

Kenneth Redick
Hudson Valley Community College

Mitchell Walker
St. Louis Community College at Forest Park

Jennifer Wise
Sinclair Community College

Special thanks to instructional designer **Alexis I. Skriloff James**

PHOTO SEQUENCES

The author wishes to thank Blaine Heeter, Mike Garblik, and Chuck Taylor of Sinclair Community College in Dayton, Ohio, and James (Mike) Watson who helped with many of the photos. A special thanks to Dick Krieger for his detailed and thorough reviews of the manuscript before publication.

Most of all, I wish to thank Michelle Halderman for her assistance in all phases of manuscript preparation.

—James D. Halderman

ABOUT THE AUTHOR

JIM HALDERMAN brings a world of experience, knowledge, and talent to his work. His automotive service experience includes working as a flat-rate technician, a business owner, and a professor of automotive technology at a leading U.S. community college for more than 20 years.

He has a Bachelor of Science Degree from Ohio Northern University and a Masters Degree in Education from Miami University in Oxford, Ohio. Jim also holds a U.S. Patent for an electronic transmission control device. He is an ASE certified Master Automotive Technician and Advanced Engine Performance (L1) ASE certified.

Jim is the author of many automotive textbooks all published by Prentice Hall.

Jim has presented numerous technical seminars to national audiences including the California Automotive Teachers (CAT) and the Illinois College Automotive Instructor Association (ICAIA). He is also a member and presenter at the North American Council of Automotive Teachers (NACAT). Jim was also named Regional Teacher of the Year by General Motors Corporation and an outstanding alumnus of Ohio Northern University.

Jim and his wife, Michelle, live in Dayton, Ohio. They have two children. You can reach Jim at

jim@jameshalderman.com

BRIEF CONTENTS

CONTENTS

chapter 10
GASOLINE ENGINE OPERATION, PARTS, AND SPECIFICATIONS   91

chapter 11
DIESEL ENGINE OPERATION AND DIAGNOSIS   105

chapter 12
GASOLINE, ALTERNATIVE FUELS, AND DIESEL FUELS   126

chapter 1

SHOP SAFETY

LEARNING OBJECTIVES: **After studying this chapter, the reader should be able to:** • Describe the personal protective equipment used by technicians. • Explain the safety tips for technicians and the cleaning methods and processes used in vehicle service. • Discuss shop safety procedures. • Discuss the purpose of fire extinguishers, fire blankets, and first aid and eye wash stations.

KEY TERMS: ANSI 1 • Bump cap 2 • Decibel (dB) 2 • Eye wash station 7 • Fire blankets 6 • Microbes 4 • "PASS" 5 • Personal protective equipment (PPE) 1 • Spontaneous combustion 3

PERSONAL PROTECTIVE EQUIPMENT

Safety is not just a buzzword on a poster in the work area. Safe work habits can reduce accidents and injuries, ease the workload, and keep employees pain free.

SAFETY GLASSES   The most important **personal protective equipment (PPE)** a technician should wear all the time are safety glasses, which meet standard **ANSI** Z87.1. ● **SEE FIGURE 1–1.**

STEEL-TOED SHOES   Steel-toed safety shoes are also a good investment. ● **SEE FIGURE 1–2.** If safety shoes are not available, then leather-topped shoes offer more protection than canvas or cloth covered shoes.

GLOVES   Wear gloves to protect your hands from rough or sharp surfaces. Thin rubber gloves are recommended when

working around automotive liquids such as engine oil, antifreeze, transmission fluid, or any other liquids that may be hazardous. Several types of gloves and their characteristics include:

- **Latex surgical gloves.** These gloves are relatively inexpensive, but tend to stretch, swell, and weaken when exposed to gas, oil, or solvents.
- **Vinyl gloves.** These gloves are also inexpensive and are not affected by gas, oil, or solvents. ● **SEE FIGURE 1-3.**
- **Polyurethane gloves.** These gloves are more expensive, yet very strong. Even though these gloves are also not affected by gas, oil, or solvents, they tend to be slippery.
- **Nitrile gloves.** These gloves are exactly like latex gloves, but are not affected by gas, oil, or solvents, yet they tend to be expensive.

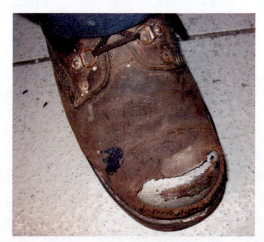

FIGURE 1–2 Steel-toed shoes are a worthwhile investment to help prevent foot injury due to falling objects. Even these well-worn shoes can protect the feet of this service technician.

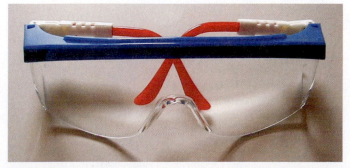

FIGURE 1–1 Safety glasses should be worn at all times when working on or around any vehicle or servicing any component.

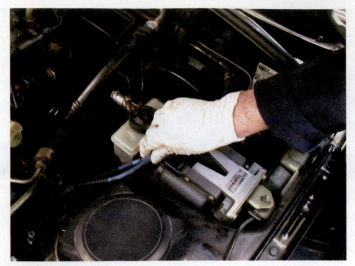

FIGURE 1–3 Protective gloves such as these vinyl gloves are available in several sizes. Select the size that allows the gloves to fit snugly. Vinyl gloves last a long time and often can be worn all day to help protect your hands from dirt and possible hazardous materials.

FIGURE 1–4 One version of a bump cap is this padded plastic insert that is worn inside a regular cloth cap.

- **Mechanic's gloves.** These gloves are usually made of synthetic leather and spandex and provide thermo protection, as well as protection from dirt and grime.

BUMP CAP Service technicians working under a vehicle should wear a **bump cap** to protect the head against under-vehicle objects and the pads of the lift. ● SEE FIGURE 1–4.

HANDS, JEWELRY, AND CLOTHING Remove jewelry that may get caught on something or act as a conductor to an exposed electrical circuit. ● SEE FIGURE 1–5.

Take care of your hands. Keep your hands clean by washing with soap and hot water that is at least 110°F (43°C). Avoid loose or dangling clothing. Also, ear protection should be worn

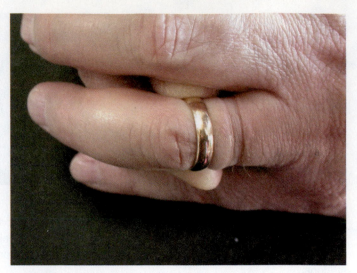

FIGURE 1–5 Remove all jewelry before performing service work on any vehicle.

TECH TIP

Professional Behavior in the Shop Is a Must

To be respected as a professional service technician and for safety, always behave in a professional manner. These behaviors include, but are not limited to the following:

- Show respect to other technicians and employees. For example, the shop owner or service manager may not always be right, but they are always the boss.
- Avoid horseplay or practical jokes.
- Act as if a customer is observing your behavior at all times because this is often the case.

if the sound around you requires that you raise your voice (sound level higher than 90 **decibels [dB]**).

NOTE: A typical lawnmower produces noise at a level of about 110 dB. This means that everyone who uses a lawnmower or other lawn or garden equipment should wear ear protection.

SAFETY TIPS FOR TECHNICIANS

- When lifting any object, get a secure grip with solid footing. Keep the load close to your body to minimize the strain. Lift with your legs and arms, not your back.
- Do not twist your body when carrying a load. Instead, pivot your feet to help prevent strain on the spine.

FIGURE 1–6 Always connect an exhaust hose to the tailpipe of the engine of a vehicle to be run inside a building.

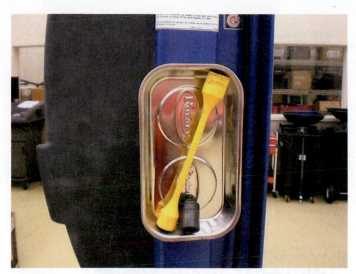

FIGURE 1–7 A magnetic tray is a helpful item to keep tools needed up where they can be easily reached without having to bend over saving time and energy over the course of a long day in the shop.

- Ask for help when moving or lifting heavy objects.
- Push a heavy object rather than pull it. (This is opposite to the way you should work with tools—never push a wrench! If you do and a bolt or nut loosens, your entire weight is used to propel your hand(s) forward. This usually results in cuts, bruises, or other painful injury.)
- Always connect an exhaust hose to the tailpipe of any running vehicle to help prevent the buildup of carbon monoxide (CO) inside a closed garage space. ● SEE FIGURE 1–6.
- When standing, keep objects, parts, and tools with which you are working between chest height and waist height. If seated, work at tasks that are at elbow height. ● SEE FIGURE 1–7.

FIGURE 1–8 An electric pusher used to push vehicles into or around the shop.

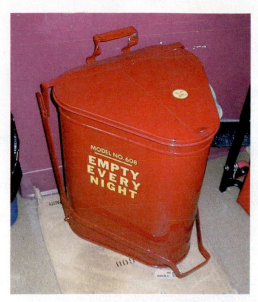

FIGURE 1–9 All oily shop cloths should be stored in a metal container equipped with a lid to help prevent spontaneous combustion.

+ SAFETY TIP

Shop Cloth Disposal

Always dispose of oily shop cloths in an enclosed container to prevent a fire. ● SEE FIGURE 1–9. Whenever oily cloths are thrown together on the floor or workbench, a chemical reaction can occur which can ignite the cloth even without an open flame. This process of ignition without an open flame is called **spontaneous combustion.**

- Always be sure the hood is securely held open.
- Ask for help when pushing a vehicle or use a motorized pusher. ● SEE FIGURE 1–8.

TECH TIP

Pound with Something Softer

If you must pound on something, be sure to use a tool that is softer than what you are about to pound on to avoid damage. Examples are given in the following table.

The Material Being Pounded	What to Pound With
Steel or cast iron	Brass or aluminum hammer or punch
Aluminum	Plastic or rawhide mallet or plastic-covered dead-blow hammer
Plastic	Rawhide mallet or plastic dead-blow hammer

CLEANING METHODS AND PROCESSES

There are four basic types of cleaning methods and processes used in vehicle service.

POWER WASHING   Power washing uses an electric- or gasoline-powered compressor to increase the pressure of water and force it out of a nozzle. The pressure of the water itself is usually enough to remove dirt, grease, and grime from vehicle components. Sometimes a chemical cleaner, such as a detergent, is added to the water to help with cleaning.

SAFE USE OF POWER WASHERS.   Because water is being sprayed at high pressure, a face shield should be worn when using a power washer to protect not only the eyes but also the face in the event of the spray being splashed back toward the technician. Also use a pressure washer in an area where the runoff from the cleaning will not contaminate local groundwater or cause harm to plants or animals.

CHEMICAL/MICROBE CLEANING   Chemical cleaning involves one of several cleaning solutions, including detergent, solvents, or small, living microorganisms called **microbes** that eat oil and grease. The microbes live in water and eat the hydrocarbons that are the basis of grease and oil.

SAFE USE OF CHEMICAL CLEANING.   A face shield should be worn when cleaning parts using a chemical cleaner. Avoid spilling the cleaner on the floor to help prevent slipping accidents. Clean and replace the chemical cleaner regularly.

ABRASIVE CLEANING   Abrasive cleaning is used to clean disassembled parts, such as engine blocks. The abrasives used include steel shot, ground walnut shells, or in the case of cleaning paint from a vehicle body, baking soda can be used.

SAFE USE OF ABRASIVE CLEANERS.   Always wear a protective face shield and protective clothing, including gloves, long sleeves, and long pants.

THERMAL OVENS   Thermal cleaning uses heat to bake off grease and dirt with special high-temperature ovens. This method of cleaning requires the use of expensive equipment but does not use any hazardous chemicals and is environmentally safe.

SAFE USE OF THERMAL OVENS.   Because thermal ovens operate at high temperatures, often exceeding 600°F (315°C), the oven should be turned off and allowed to cool overnight before removing the parts from the oven to avoid being exposed to the high temperature.

ELECTRICAL CORD SAFETY

Use correctly grounded three-prong sockets and extension cords to operate power tools. Some tools use only two-prong plugs. Make sure these are double insulated and repair or replace any electrical cords that are cut or damaged to prevent the possibility of an electrical shock. When not in use, keep electrical cords off the floor to prevent tripping over them. Tape the cords down if they are placed in high foot traffic areas.

JUMP-STARTING AND BATTERY SAFETY

To jump-start another vehicle with a dead battery, connect good-quality copper jumper cables as indicated in ● **FIGURE 1–10** or use a jump box. The last connection made should always be on the engine block or an engine bracket as far from the battery as possible. It is normal for a spark to be created when the jumper cables finally complete the jumper cable connections, and this spark could cause an explosion of the gases around the battery. Many newer vehicles have special ground connections built away from the battery just for the purpose of jump-starting. Check the owner manual or service information for the exact location.

Batteries contain acid and should be handled with care to avoid tipping them greater than a 45-degree angle. Always remove jewelry when working around a battery to avoid the

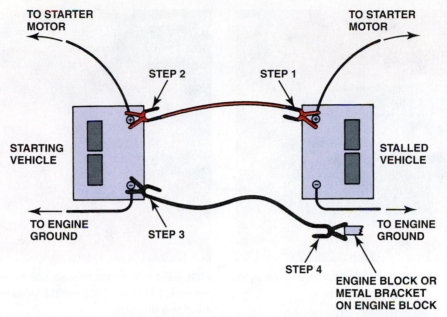

FIGURE 1–10 Jumper cable usage guide.

Compressed Air Safety

Improper use of an air nozzle can cause blindness or deafness. Compressed air must be reduced to less than 30 PSI (206 kPa). ● **SEE FIGURE 1–11**. If an air nozzle is used to dry and clean parts, make sure the air stream is directed away from anyone else in the immediate area. Always use an OSHA-approved nozzle with side slits that limit the maximum pressure at the nozzle to 30 PSI. Coil and store air hoses when they are not in use.

FIGURE 1–11 The air pressure going to the nozzle should be reduced to 30 PSI or less.

possibility of electrical shock or burns, which can occur when the metal comes in contact with a 12 volt circuit and ground, such as the body of the vehicle.

FIRE EXTINGUISHERS

There are four classes of fire extinguishers. Each class should be used on specific fires only.

- *Class A* is designed for use on general combustibles, such as cloth, paper, and wood.
- *Class B* is designed for use on flammable liquids and greases, including gasoline, oil, thinners, and solvents.
- *Class C* is used only on electrical fires.

- *Class D* is effective only on combustible metals such as powdered aluminum, sodium, or magnesium.

The class rating is clearly marked on the side of every fire extinguisher. Many extinguishers are good for multiple types of fires. ● **SEE FIGURE 1–12**.

When using a fire extinguisher, remember the word **"PASS."**

P = Pull the safety pin.

A = Aim the nozzle of the extinguisher at the base of the fire.

S = Squeeze the lever to actuate the extinguisher.

S = Sweep the nozzle from side to side.

● **SEE FIGURE 1–13**.

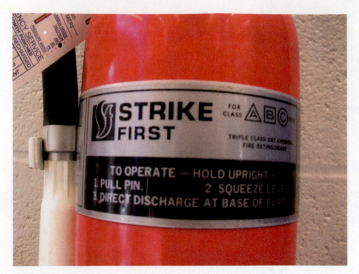

FIGURE 1–12 A typical fire extinguisher designed to be used on type class A, B, or C fires.

FIGURE 1–14 A treated wool blanket is kept in this easy-to-open wall-mounted holder and should be placed in a centralized location in the shop.

FIGURE 1–13 A CO_2 fire extinguisher being used on a fire set in an open steel drum during a demonstration at a fire department training center.

FIRE BLANKETS

Fire blankets are required to be available in the shop areas. If a person is on fire, a fire blanket should be removed from its storage bag and thrown over and around the victim to smother the fire. ● **SEE FIGURE 1–14** showing a typical fire blanket.

FIRST AID AND EYE WASH STATIONS

All shop areas must be equipped with a first aid kit and an eye wash station centrally located and kept stocked with emergency supplies.

TYPES OF FIRE EXTINGUISHERS Types of fire extinguishers include the following:

- **Water.** A water fire extinguisher, usually in a pressurized container, is good to use on Class A fires by reducing the temperature to the point where a fire cannot be sustained.
- **Carbon dioxide (CO_2).** A carbon dioxide fire extinguisher is good for almost any type of fire, especially Class B or Class C materials. A CO_2 fire extinguisher works by removing the oxygen from the fire and the cold CO_2 also helps reduce the temperature of the fire.
- **Dry chemical (yellow).** A dry chemical fire extinguisher is good for Class A, B, or C fires by coating the flammable materials, which eliminates the oxygen from the fire. A dry chemical fire extinguisher tends to be very corrosive and will cause damage to electronic devices.

FIRST AID KIT A first aid kit should include:

- Bandages (variety)
- Gauze pads
- Roll gauze
- Iodine swab sticks
- Antibiotic ointment
- Hydrocortisone cream
- Burn gel packets
- Eye wash solution
- Scissors
- Tweezers
- Gloves
- First aid guide

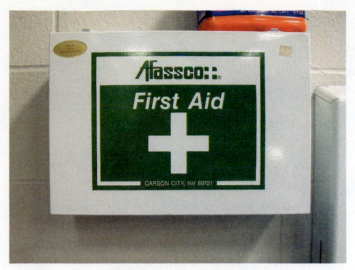

FIGURE 1–15 A first aid box should be centrally located in the shop and kept stocked with the recommended supplies.

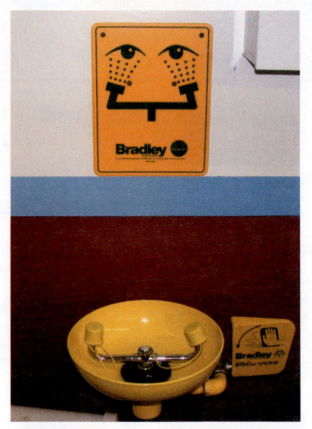

FIGURE 1–16 A typical eye wash station. Often a thorough flushing of the eyes with water is the best treatment in the event of eye contamination.

● **SEE FIGURE 1–15.** Every shop should have a person trained in first aid. If there is an accident, call for help immediately.

EYE WASH STATION
An **eye wash station** should be centrally located and used whenever any liquid or chemical gets into the eyes. If such an emergency does occur, keep eyes in a constant stream of water and call for professional assistance. ● **SEE FIGURE 1–16.**

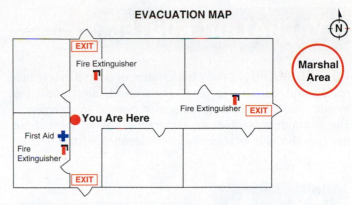

EVACUATION MAP

FIGURE 1–17 The evacuation routes from where you are in the building is shown on maps that are attached to the walls in schools and commercial buildings.

FIGURE 1–18 A properly marked aisle using yellow paint strips leading to an exit.

SAFETY TIP

Infection Control Precautions
Working on a vehicle can result in personal injury including the possibility of being cut or hurt enough to cause bleeding. Some infections such as hepatitis B, HIV (which can cause acquired immunodeficiency syndrome, or AIDS), and hepatitis C virus are transmitted through blood. These infections are commonly called blood-borne pathogens. Report any injury that involves blood to your supervisor and take the necessary precautions to avoid coming in contact with blood from another person.

EVACUATION ROUTES

POSTED MAPS Check the location of posted evacuation routes and be sure to read, understand, and follow the instructions for evacuating the area in case of an emergency. The evacuation routes are commonly posted throughout the building and often include the location of the nearest fire extinguisher and other safety related items. ● **SEE FIGURE 1–17.**

AISLE MARKINGS Aisles leading to the emergency exist must be marked with yellow paint or tape at least 2 inches (5 cm) wide. The aisles should also be 40 to 48 inches (102 to 122 cm) wide. Aisles should lead to exits as directly as possible. ● **SEE FIGURE 1–18.**

SUMMARY

1. All service technicians should wear safety glasses that meet standard ANSI Z87.1.
2. Ear protection should be worn anytime the noise level is at 90 decibels (dB) or higher.
3. Safety should be exercised when working with electrical cords or when jump-starting another vehicle.
4. If a fire extinguisher is needed, remember: Pull the safety pin, aim the nozzle, squeeze the lever, and sweep the nozzle from side-to-side.

REVIEW QUESTIONS

1. List four items that are personal protective equipment (PPE).
2. What are the types of fire extinguishers and their usage?
3. What items are included in a typical first aid box?

CHAPTER QUIZ

1. What do you call the service technician's protective head cover?
   - a. Cap
   - b. Hat
   - c. Bump cap
   - d. Helmet
2. All safety glasses should meet the standards set by _____.
   - a. ANSI
   - b. SAE
   - c. ASE
   - d. DOT
3. When washing hands, the water should be at what temperature?
   - a. 98°F (37°C)
   - b. 110°F (43°C)
   - c. 125°F (52°C)
   - d. 135°F (57°C)
4. Hearing protection should be worn anytime the noise level exceeds _____.
   - a. 60 dB
   - b. 70 dB
   - c. 80 dB
   - d. 90 dB
5. Two technicians are discussing the safe use of a wrench. Technician A says that a wrench should be pulled toward you. Technician B says that a wrench should be pushed away from you. Which technician is correct?
   - a. Technician A only
   - b. Technician B only
   - c. Both Technicians A and B
   - d. Neither Technician A nor B
6. Exhaust hoses should be used because one of the exhaust gases is deadly in high concentration. This gas is _____.
   - a. Carbon monoxide (CO)
   - b. Carbon dioxide (CO_2)
   - c. Hydrocarbons (HC)
   - d. Oxides of nitrogen (NO_X)
7. The process of combustion occurring without an open flame is called _____.
   - a. Direct ignition
   - b. Non-open flame combustion
   - c. Spontaneous combustion
   - d. Cold fusion
8. When using a fire extinguisher, what word can be used to remember what to do?
   - a. PASS
   - b. FIRE
   - c. RED
   - d. LEVER
9. Which type of fire extinguisher can create a corrosive compound when discharged?
   - a. CO_2
   - b. Dry chemical
   - c. Water
   - d. CO
10. Which item is usually *not* included in a first aid kit?
    - a. Eye wash solution
    - b. Antibiotic cream
    - c. Fire blanket
    - d. Bandages

chapter 2
ENVIRONMENTAL AND HAZARDOUS MATERIALS

LEARNING OBJECTIVES: **After studying this chapter, the reader should be able to:** • Identify hazardous waste materials in accordance with federal and state laws. • Discuss asbestos hazards and asbestos handling guidelines. • Explain the storage and disposal of brake fluid, used oil, coolants, lead-acid batteries, used tires, and air-conditioning refrigerant oil. • Explain the characteristics of hazardous solvents, fuel safety and storage, and airbag handling.

KEY TERMS: Aboveground storage tank (AGST) 12 • Asbestosis 11 • BCI 15 • CAA 10 • CFR 9 • EPA 9 • Hazardous waste material 9 • HEPA vacuum 11 • Mercury 17 • MSDS 10 • OSHA 9 • RCRA 10 • Right-to-know laws 10 • Solvent 11 • Underground storage tank (UST) 12 • Used oil 12 • WHMIS 10

HAZARDOUS WASTE

DEFINITION OF HAZARDOUS WASTE **Hazardous waste materials** are chemicals, or components, that the shop no longer needs that pose a danger to the environment and people if they are disposed of in ordinary garbage cans or sewers. However, no material is considered hazardous waste until the shop has finished using it and is ready to dispose of it.

PERSONAL PROTECTIVE EQUIPMENT (PPE) When handling hazardous waste material, one must always wear the proper protective clothing and equipment detailed in the right-to-know laws. This includes respirator equipment. All recommended procedures must be followed accurately. Personal injury may result from improper clothing, equipment, and procedures when handling hazardous materials.

FEDERAL AND STATE LAWS

OCCUPATIONAL SAFETY AND HEALTH ACT The United States Congress passed the **Occupational Safety and Health Act (OSHA)** in 1970. This legislation was designed to assist and encourage the citizens of the United States in their efforts to assure:

- Safe and healthful working conditions by providing research, information, education, and training in the field of occupational safety and health.

- Safe and healthful working conditions for working men and women by authorizing enforcement of the standards developed under the Act.

Because about 25% of workers are exposed to health and safety hazards on the job, the OSHA standards are necessary to monitor, control, and educate workers regarding health and safety in the workplace.

EPA The **Environmental Protection Agency (EPA)** publishes a list of hazardous materials that is included in the **Code of Federal Regulations (CFR)**. The EPA considers waste hazardous if it is included on the EPA list of hazardous materials, or it has one or more of the following characteristics:

- **Reactive.** Any material that reacts violently with water or other chemicals is considered hazardous.

- **Corrosive.** If a material burns the skin, or dissolves metals and other materials, a technician should consider it hazardous. A pH scale is used, with the number 7 indicating neutral. Pure water has a pH of 7. Lower numbers indicate an acidic solution and higher numbers indicate a caustic solution. If a material releases cyanide gas, hydrogen sulfide gas, or similar gases when exposed to low pH acid solutions, it is considered hazardous.

- **Toxic.** Materials are hazardous if they leak one or more of eight different heavy metals in concentrations greater than 100 times the primary drinking water standard.

- **Ignitable.** A liquid is hazardous if it has a flash point below 140°F (60°C), and a solid is hazardous if it ignites spontaneously.

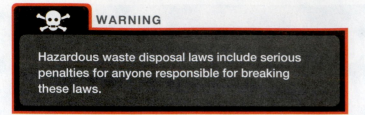
- **Radioactive.** Any substance that emits measurable levels of radiation is radioactive. When individuals bring containers of a highly radioactive substance into the shop environment, qualified personnel with the appropriate equipment must test them.

RIGHT-TO-KNOW LAWS

The **right-to-know laws** state that employees have a right to know when the materials they use at work are hazardous. Under the right-to-know laws, the employer has responsibilities regarding the handling of hazardous materials by their employees. All employees must be trained about the types of hazardous materials they will encounter in the workplace.

MATERIAL SAFETY DATA SHEETS (MSDS). All hazardous materials must be properly labeled, and information about each hazardous material must be posted on **material safety data sheets (MSDS)** now called Safety Data Sheets (SDS) available from the manufacturer. In Canada, MSDS information is called **Workplace Hazardous Materials Information Systems (WHMIS).**

The employer has a responsibility to place MSDS information where they are easily accessible by all employees.

The manufacturer must supply all warning and precautionary information about hazardous materials. This information must be read and understood by the employee before handling the material. ● **SEE FIGURE 2–1.**

RESOURCE CONSERVATION AND RECOVERY ACT (RCRA)

Federal and state laws control the disposal of hazardous waste materials and every shop employee must be familiar with these laws. Hazardous waste disposal laws include the **Resource Conservation and Recovery Act (RCRA).** This law states that hazardous material users are responsible for hazardous materials from the time they become a waste until the proper waste disposal is completed. Many shops hire an independent hazardous waste hauler to dispose of hazardous waste material. The shop owner, or manager, should have a written contract with the hazardous waste hauler. The RCRA controls the following types of automotive waste:

- Paint and body repair products waste
- Solvents for parts and equipment cleaning
- Batteries and battery acid
- Mild acids used for metal cleaning and preparation
- Waste oil, and engine coolants or antifreeze
- Air-conditioning refrigerants and oils
- Engine oil filters

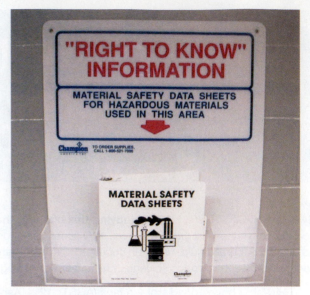

FIGURE 2–1 Safety Data Sheets (SDS) should be readily available for use by anyone in the area who may come into contact with hazardous materials.

FIGURE 2–2 Tag identify that the power has been removed and service work is being done.

LOCKOUT/TAGOUT

According to OSHA Title 29, code of Federal Regulations (CPR), part 1910.147, machinery must be locked out to prevent injury to employees when maintenance or repair work is being performed. Any piece of equipment that should not be used must be tagged and the electrical power disconnected to prevent it from being used. Always read, understand, and follow all safety warning tags. ● **SEE FIGURE 2–2.**

CLEAN AIR ACT

Air-conditioning (A/C) systems and refrigerants are regulated by the **Clean Air Act (CAA)**, Title VI, Section 609. Technician certification and service equipment is also regulated. Any technician working on automotive A/C systems must be certified. A/C refrigerants must not be released or vented into the atmosphere, and used refrigerants must be recovered.

ASBESTOS HAZARDS

Friction materials such as brake and clutch linings often contain asbestos. While asbestos has been eliminated from most original equipment friction materials, the automotive service technician cannot know whether the vehicle being serviced is or is not equipped with friction materials containing asbestos. It is important that all friction materials be handled as if they do contain asbestos.

Asbestos exposure can cause scar tissue to form in the lungs. This condition is called **asbestosis.** It gradually causes increasing shortness of breath, and the scarring to the lungs is permanent.

Even low exposures to asbestos can cause *mesothelioma*, a type of fatal cancer of the lining of the chest or abdominal cavity. Asbestos exposure can also increase the risk of *lung cancer* as well as cancer of the voice box, stomach, and large intestine. It usually takes 15 to 30 years or more for cancer or asbestos lung scarring to show up after exposure. Scientists call this the *latency period.*

Government agencies recommend that asbestos exposure be eliminated or controlled to the lowest level possible. These agencies have developed recommendations and standards that the automotive service technician and equipment manufacturer should follow. These U.S. federal agencies include the National Institute for Occupational Safety and Health (NIOSH), Occupational Safety and Health Administration (OSHA), and Environmental Protection Agency (EPA).

ASBESTOS OSHA STANDARDS

The Occupational Safety and Health Administration (OSHA) has established three levels of asbestos exposure. Any vehicle service establishment that does either brake or clutch work must limit employee exposure to asbestos to less than 0.2 fibers per cubic centimeter (cc) as determined by an air sample.

If the level of exposure to employees is greater than specified, corrective measures must be performed and a large fine may be imposed.

NOTE: Research has found that worn asbestos fibers such as those from automotive brakes or clutches may not be as hazardous as first believed. Worn asbestos fibers do not have sharp flared ends that can latch onto tissue, but rather are worn down to a dust form that resembles talc. Grinding or sawing operations on unworn brake shoes or clutch discs *will* contain *harmful* asbestos fibers. To limit health damage, always use proper handling procedures while working around any component that may contain asbestos.

ASBESTOS EPA REGULATIONS

The federal Environmental Protection Agency (EPA) has established procedures for the removal and disposal of asbestos. The EPA procedures require that products containing asbestos

FIGURE 2–3 All brakes should be moistened with water or solvent to help prevent brake dust from becoming airborne.

be "wetted" to prevent the asbestos fibers from becoming airborne. According to the EPA, asbestos-containing materials can be disposed of as regular waste. Only when asbestos becomes airborne is it considered to be hazardous.

ASBESTOS HANDLING GUIDELINES The air in the shop area can be tested by a testing laboratory, but this can be expensive. Tests have determined that asbestos levels can easily be kept below the recommended levels by using a liquid, like water, or a special vacuum.

NOTE: The service technician cannot tell whether the old brake pads, shoes, or clutch discs contain asbestos. Therefore, to be safe, the technician should assume that all brake pads, shoes, or clutch discs contain asbestos.

HEPA VACUUM. A special **high-efficiency particulate air (HEPA)** vacuum system has been proven to be effective in keeping asbestos exposure levels below 0.1 fibers per cubic centimeter.

SOLVENT SPRAY. Many technicians use an aerosol can of brake cleaning solvent to wet the brake dust and prevent it from becoming airborne. A **solvent** is a liquid that is used to dissolve dirt, grime, or solid particles. Commercial brake cleaners are available that use a concentrated cleaner that is mixed with water. ● **SEE FIGURE 2–3.** The waste liquid is filtered, and when dry, the filter can be disposed of as solid waste.

DISPOSAL OF BRAKE DUST AND BRAKE SHOE. The hazard of asbestos occurs when asbestos fibers are airborne. Once the asbestos has been wetted down, it is then considered to be solid waste, rather than hazardous waste. Old brake shoes and pads should be enclosed, preferably in a plastic bag, to help prevent any of the brake material from becoming airborne. *Always follow current federal and local laws concerning disposal of all waste.*

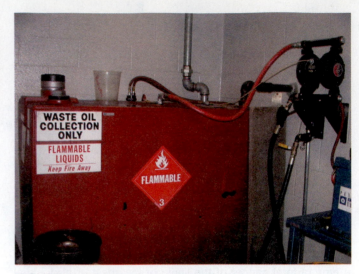

FIGURE 2–4 A typical aboveground oil storage tank.

USED BRAKE FLUID

Most brake fluid is made from polyglycol, is water soluble, and can be considered hazardous if it has absorbed metals from the brake system.

STORAGE AND DISPOSAL OF BRAKE FLUID

- Collect brake fluid in a container clearly marked to indicate that it is designated for that purpose.
- If the waste brake fluid is hazardous, be sure to manage it appropriately and use only an authorized waste receiver for its disposal.
- If the waste brake fluid is nonhazardous (such as old, but unused), determine from your local solid waste collection provider what should be done for its proper disposal.
- Do not mix brake fluid with used engine oil.
- Do not pour brake fluid down drains or onto the ground.
- Recycle brake fluid through a registered recycler.

USED OIL

Used oil is any petroleum-based or synthetic oil that has been used. During normal use, impurities such as dirt, metal scrapings, water, or chemicals can get mixed in with the oil. Eventually, this used oil must be replaced with virgin or re-refined oil. The EPA's used oil management standards include a three-pronged approach to determine if a substance meets the definition of *used oil*. To meet the EPA's definition of used oil, a substance must meet each of the following three criteria.

- **Origin.** The first criterion for identifying used oil is based on the oil's origin. Used oil must have been refined from crude oil or made from synthetic materials. Animal and vegetable oils are excluded from the EPA's definition of used oil.
- **Use.** The second criterion is based on whether and how the oil is used. Oils used as lubricants, hydraulic fluids, heat transfer fluids, and for other similar purposes are considered used oil. The EPA's definition also excludes products used as cleaning agents, as well as certain petroleum-derived products like antifreeze and kerosene.

- **Contaminants.** The third criterion is based on whether the oil is contaminated with either physical or chemical impurities. In other words, to meet the EPA's definition, used oil must become contaminated as a result of being used. This aspect of the EPA's definition includes residues and contaminants generated from handling, storing, and processing used oil.

NOTE: The release of only 1 gallon of used oil (a typical oil change) can make 1 million gallons of fresh water undrinkable.

If used oil is dumped down the drain and enters a sewage treatment plant, concentrations as small as 50 to 100 parts per million (ppm) in the wastewater can foul sewage treatment processes. Never mix a listed hazardous waste, gasoline, wastewater, halogenated solvent, antifreeze, or an unknown waste material with used oil. Adding any of these substances will cause the used oil to become contaminated, which classifies it as hazardous waste.

STORAGE AND DISPOSAL OF USED OIL
Once oil has been used, it can be collected, recycled, and used over and over again. An estimated 380 million gallons of used oil are recycled each year. Recycled used oil can sometimes be used again for the same job or can take on a completely different task. For example, used engine oil can be re-refined and sold at some discount stores as engine oil or processed for furnace fuel oil. After collecting used oil in an appropriate container such as a 55 gallon steel drum, the material must be disposed of in one of two ways.

- Shipped offsite for recycling
- Burned in an onsite or offsite EPA-approved heater for energy recovery

Used oil must be stored in compliance with an existing **underground storage tank (UST)** or an **aboveground storage tank (AGST)** standard, or kept in separate containers. ● **SEE FIGURE 2–4.** Containers are portable receptacles, such as a 55 gallon steel drum.

KEEP USED OIL STORAGE DRUMS IN GOOD CONDITION. This means that they should be covered, secured from vandals, properly labeled, and maintained in compliance with local fire codes. Frequent inspections for leaks, corrosion, and spillage are an essential part of container maintenance.

NEVER STORE USED OIL IN ANYTHING OTHER THAN TANKS AND STORAGE CONTAINERS. Used oil may also be stored in units that are permitted to store regulated hazardous waste.

USED OIL FILTER DISPOSAL REGULATIONS. Used oil filters contain used engine oil that may be hazardous. Before an oil filter is placed into the trash or sent to be recycled, it must be drained using one of the following hot-draining methods approved by the EPA.

- Puncture the filter antidrainback valve or filter dome end and hot drain for at least 12 hours
- Hot draining and crushing
- Dismantling and hot draining
- Any other hot-draining method, which will remove all the used oil from the filter

After the oil has been drained from the oil filter, the filter housing can be disposed of in any of the following ways.

- Sent for recycling
- Picked up by a service contract company
- Disposed of in regular trash

SOLVENTS

The major sources of chemical danger are liquid and aerosol brake cleaning fluids that contain chlorinated hydrocarbon solvents. Several other chemicals that do not deplete the ozone, such as heptane, hexane, and xylene, are now being used in nonchlorinated brake cleaning solvents. Some manufacturers are also producing solvents they describe as environmentally responsible, which are biodegradable and noncarcinogenic (not cancer causing).

There is no specific standard for physical contact with chlorinated hydrocarbon solvents or the chemicals replacing them. All contact should be avoided whenever possible. The law requires an employer to provide appropriate protective equipment and ensure proper work practices by an employee handling these chemicals.

EFFECTS OF CHEMICAL POISONING The effects of exposure to chlorinated hydrocarbon and other types of solvents can take many forms. Short-term exposure at low levels can cause symptoms such as:

- Headache
- Nausea
- Drowsiness

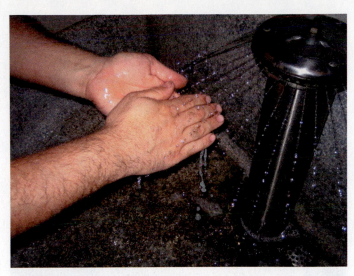

FIGURE 2–5 Washing hands and removing jewelry are two important safety habits all service technicians should practice.

- Dizziness
- Lack of coordination
- Unconsciousness

It may also cause irritation of the eyes, nose, and throat, and flushing of the face and neck. Short-term exposure to higher concentrations can cause liver damage with symptoms such as yellow jaundice or dark urine. Liver damage may not become evident until several weeks after the exposure.

HAZARDOUS SOLVENTS AND REGULATORY STATUS

Most solvents are classified as hazardous wastes. Other characteristics of solvents include the following:

- Solvents with flash points below 140°F (60°C) are considered flammable and, like gasoline, are federally regulated by the Department of Transportation (DOT).
- Solvents and oils with flash points above 60°C are considered combustible and, like engine oil, are also regulated by the DOT. All flammable items must be stored in a fireproof container. ● **SEE FIGURE 2–6.**

FIGURE 2–6 Typical fireproof flammable storage cabinet.

FREQUENTLY ASKED QUESTION

How Can You Tell If a Solvent Is Hazardous?
If a solvent or any of the ingredients of a product contains "fluor" or "chlor" then it is likely to be hazardous. Check the instructions on the label for proper use and disposal procedures.

It is the responsibility of the repair shop to determine if its spent solvent is hazardous waste. Solvent reclaimers are available that clean and restore the solvent so it lasts indefinitely.

USED SOLVENTS Used or spent solvents are liquid materials that have been generated as waste and may contain xylene, methanol, ethyl ether, and methyl isobutyl ketone (MIBK). These materials must be stored in OSHA-approved safety containers with the lids or caps closed tightly. Additional requirements include the following:

- Containers should be clearly labeled "Hazardous Waste" and the date the material was first placed into the storage receptacle should be noted.
- Labeling is not required for solvents being used in a parts washer.
- Used solvents will not be counted toward a facility's monthly output of hazardous waste if the vendor under contract removes the material.
- Used solvents may be disposed of by recycling with a local vendor, such as SafetyKleen®, to have the used solvent removed according to specific terms in the vendor agreement.

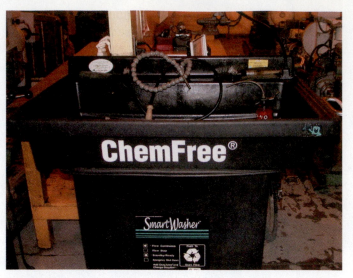

FIGURE 2–7 Using a water-based cleaning system helps reduce the hazards from using strong chemicals.

- Use aqueous-based (nonsolvent) cleaning systems to help avoid the problems associated with chemical solvents. ● **SEE FIGURE 2–7**.

COOLANT DISPOSAL

Coolant is a mixture of antifreeze and water. New antifreeze is not considered to be hazardous even though it can cause death if ingested. Used antifreeze may be hazardous due to dissolved metals from the engine and other components of the cooling system. These metals can include iron, steel, aluminum, copper, brass, and lead (from older radiators and heater cores). Coolant should be disposed of in one of the following ways:

- Coolant should be recycled either onsite or offsite.
- Used coolant should be stored in a sealed and labeled container. ● **SEE FIGURE 2–8**.
- Used coolant can often be disposed of into municipal sewers with a permit. Check with local authorities and obtain a permit before discharging used coolant into sanitary sewers.

LEAD-ACID BATTERY WASTE

About 70 million spent lead-acid batteries are generated each year in the United States alone. Lead is classified as a toxic metal and the acid used in lead-acid batteries is highly corrosive. The vast majority (95% to 98%) of these batteries are recycled through lead reclamation operations and secondary lead smelters for use in the manufacture of new batteries.

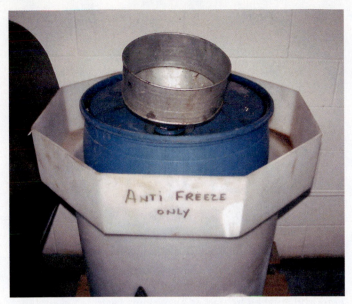

FIGURE 2–8 Used antifreeze coolant should be kept separate and stored in a leakproof container until it can be recycled or disposed of according to federal, state, and local laws. Note that the storage barrel is placed inside another container to catch any coolant that may spill out of the inside barrel.

BATTERY DISPOSAL Used lead-acid batteries must be reclaimed or recycled in order to be exempt from hazardous waste regulations. Leaking batteries must be stored and transported as hazardous waste. Some states have more strict regulations, which require special handling procedures and transportation. According to the **Battery Council International (BCI)**, battery laws usually include the following rules.

1. Lead-acid battery disposal is prohibited in landfills or incinerators. Batteries are required to be delivered to a battery retailer, wholesaler, recycling center, or lead smelter.

2. All retailers of automotive batteries are required to post a sign that displays the universal recycling symbol and indicates the retailer's specific requirements for accepting used batteries.

3. Battery electrolyte contains sulfuric acid, which is a very corrosive substance capable of causing serious personal injury, such as skin burns and eye damage. In addition, the battery plates contain lead, which is highly poisonous. For this reason, disposing of batteries improperly can cause environmental contamination and lead to severe health problems.

BATTERY HANDLING AND STORAGE Batteries, whether new or used, should be kept indoors if possible. The storage location should be an area specifically designated for battery storage and must be well ventilated (to the outside). If outdoor storage is the only alternative, a sheltered and secured area with acid-resistant secondary containment is strongly recommended. It is also advisable that acid-resistant secondary containment be used for indoor storage. In addition, batteries should be placed on acid-resistant pallets and never stacked.

FIGURE 2–9 This red gasoline container holds about 30 gallons of gasoline and is used to fill vehicles used for training.

FUEL SAFETY AND STORAGE

Gasoline is a very explosive liquid. The expanding vapors that come from gasoline are extremely dangerous. These vapors are present even in cold temperatures. Vapors formed in gasoline tanks on many vehicles are controlled, but vapors from gasoline storage may escape from the can, resulting in a hazardous situation. Therefore, place gasoline storage containers in a well-ventilated space. Although diesel fuel is not as volatile as gasoline, the same basic rules apply to diesel fuel and gasoline storage. These rules include the following:

1. Use storage cans that have a flash-arresting screen at the outlet. These screens prevent external ignition sources from igniting the gasoline within the can when someone pours the gasoline or diesel fuel.

2. Use only a red approved gasoline container to allow for proper hazardous substance identification. ● **SEE FIGURE 2–9**.

3. Do not fill gasoline containers completely full. Always leave the level of gasoline at least 1 in. from the top of the container. This action allows expansion of the gasoline at higher temperatures. If gasoline containers are completely full, the gasoline will expand when the temperature increases. This expansion forces gasoline from the can and creates a dangerous spill. If gasoline or diesel fuel

containers must be stored, place them in a designated storage locker or facility.

4. Never leave gasoline containers open, except while filling or pouring gasoline from the container.

5. Never use gasoline as a cleaning agent.

6. Always connect a ground strap to containers when filling or transferring fuel or other flammable products from one container to another to prevent static electricity that could result in explosion and fire. These ground wires prevent the buildup of a static electric charge, which could result in a spark and disastrous explosion.

AIRBAG HANDLING

Airbag modules are pyrotechnic devices that can be ignited if exposed to an electrical charge or if the body of the vehicle is subjected to a shock. Airbag safety should include the following precautions.

1. Disarm the airbag(s) if you will be working in the area where a discharged bag could make contact with any part of your body. Consult service information for the exact procedure to follow for the vehicle being serviced.

2. If disposing of an airbag, the usual procedure is to deploy the airbag using a 12 volt power supply, such as a jump-start box, using long wires to connect to the module to ensure a safe deployment.

3. Do not expose an airbag to extreme heat or fire.

4. Always carry an airbag pointing away from your body.

5. Place an airbag module facing upward.

6. Always follow the manufacturer's recommended procedure for airbag disposal or recycling, including the proper packaging to use during shipment.

7. Wear protective gloves if handling a deployed airbag.

8. Always wash your hands or body well if exposed to a deployed airbag. The chemicals involved can cause skin irritation and possible rash development.

USED TIRE DISPOSAL

Used tires are an environmental concern because of several reasons, including the following:

1. In a landfill, they tend to "float" up through the other trash and rise to the surface.

2. The inside of tires traps and holds rainwater, which is a breeding ground for mosquitoes. Mosquito-borne diseases include encephalitis, malaria and dengue fever.

3. Used tires present a fire hazard and, when burned, create a large amount of black smoke that contaminates the air.

FIGURE 2–10 Air-conditioning refrigerant oil must be kept separated from other oils because it contains traces of refrigerant and must be treated as hazardous waste.

Used tires should be disposed of in one of the following ways.

1. Used tires can be reused until the end of their useful life.

2. Tires can be retreaded.

3. Tires can be recycled or shredded for use in asphalt.

4. Derimmed tires can be sent to a landfill (most landfill operators will shred the tires because it is illegal in many states to landfill whole tires).

5. Tires can be burned in cement kilns or other power plants where the smoke can be controlled.

6. A registered scrap tire handler should be used to transport tires for disposal or recycling.

AIR-CONDITIONING REFRIGERANT OIL DISPOSAL

Air-conditioning refrigerant oil contains dissolved refrigerant and is therefore considered to be hazardous waste. This oil must be kept separated from other waste oil or the entire amount of oil must be treated as hazardous. Used refrigerant oil must be sent to a licensed hazardous waste disposal company for recycling or disposal. ● **SEE FIGURE 2–10**.

WASTE CHART All automotive service facilities create some waste and while most of it is handled properly, it is important that all hazardous and nonhazardous waste be accounted for and properly disposed. ● **SEE CHART 2–1** for a list of typical wastes generated at automotive shops, plus a checklist for keeping track of how these wastes are handled.

WASTE STREAM	TYPICAL CATEGORY IF NOT MIXED WITH OTHER HAZARDOUS WASTE	IF DISPOSED IN LANDFILL AND NOT MIXED WITH A HAZARDOUS WASTE	IF RECYCLED
Used oil	Used oil	Hazardous waste	Used oil
Used oil filters	Nonhazardous solid waste, if completely drained	Nonhazardous solid waste, if completely drained	Used oil, if not drained
Used transmission fluid	Used oil	Hazardous waste	Used oil
Used brake fluid	Used oil	Hazardous waste	Used oil
Used antifreeze	Depends on characterization	Depends on characterization	Depends on characterization
Used solvents	Hazardous waste	Hazardous waste	Hazardous waste
Used citric solvents	Nonhazardous solid waste	Nonhazardous solid waste	Hazardous waste
Lead-acid automotive batteries	Not a solid waste if returned to supplier	Hazardous waste	Hazardous waste
Shop rags used for oil	Used oil	Depends on used oil characterization	Used oil
Shop rags used for solvent or gasoline spills	Hazardous waste	Hazardous waste	Hazardous waste
Oil spill absorbent material	Used oil	Depends on used oil characterization	Used oil
Spill material for solvent and gasoline	Hazardous waste	Hazardous waste	Hazardous waste
Catalytic converter	Not a solid waste if returned to supplier	Nonhazardous solid waste	Nonhazardous solid waste
Spilled or unused fuels	Hazardous waste	Hazardous waste	Hazardous waste
Spilled or unusable paints and thinners	Hazardous waste	Hazardous waste	Hazardous waste
Used tires	Nonhazardous solid waste	Nonhazardous solid waste	Nonhazardous solid waste

CHART 2–1

Typical wastes generated at auto repair shops and typical category (hazardous or nonhazardous) by disposal method.

TECH TIP

Remove Components That Contain Mercury

Some vehicles have a placard near the driver's side door that lists the components that contain the heavy metal, mercury. **Mercury** can be absorbed through the skin and is a heavy metal that once absorbed by the body does not leave. ● **SEE FIGURE 2–11**.

These components should be removed from the vehicle before the rest of the body is sent to be recycled to help prevent releasing mercury into the environment.

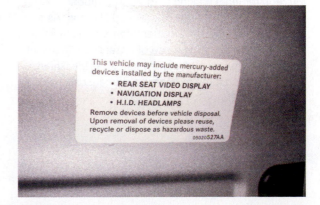

FIGURE 2–11 Placard near driver's door, including what devices in the vehicle contain mercury.

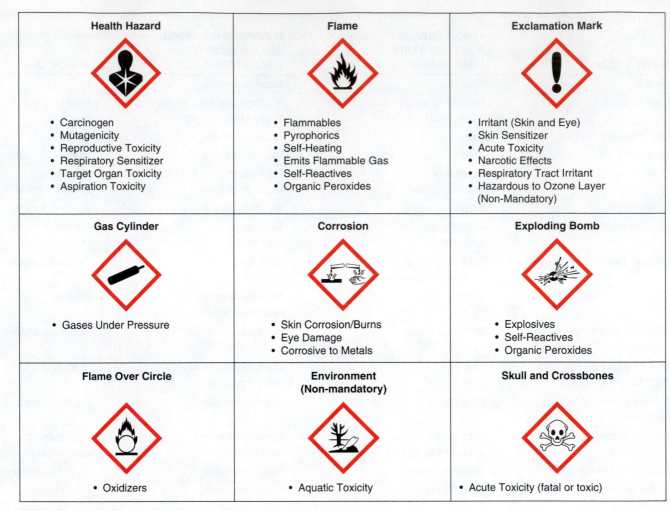

Health Hazard	Flame	Exclamation Mark
• Carcinogen • Mutagenicity • Reproductive Toxicity • Respiratory Sensitizer • Target Organ Toxicity • Aspiration Toxicity	• Flammables • Pyrophorics • Self-Heating • Emits Flammable Gas • Self-Reactives • Organic Peroxides	• Irritant (Skin and Eye) • Skin Sensitizer • Acute Toxicity • Narcotic Effects • Respiratory Tract Irritant • Hazardous to Ozone Layer (Non-Mandatory)
Gas Cylinder	Corrosion	Exploding Bomb
• Gases Under Pressure	• Skin Corrosion/Burns • Eye Damage • Corrosive to Metals	• Explosives • Self-Reactives • Organic Peroxides
Flame Over Circle	Environment (Non-mandatory)	Skull and Crossbones
• Oxidizers	• Aquatic Toxicity	• Acute Toxicity (fatal or toxic)

FIGURE 2–12 The OSHA global hazardous materials labels.

 TECH TIP

What Every Technician Should Know

OSHA has adopted new hazardous chemical labeling requirements making it agree with global labeling standards established by the United Nations. As a result, workers will have better information available on the safe handling and use of hazardous chemicals, allowing them to avoid injuries and possible illnesses related to exposures to hazardous chemicals. ● **SEE FIGURE 2–12.**

1. Hazardous materials include common automotive chemicals, liquids, and lubricants, especially those whose ingredients contain *chlor* or *fluor* in their name.

2. Right-to-know laws require that all workers have access to material safety data sheets (MSDS).

3. Asbestos fibers should be avoided and removed according to current laws and regulations.

4. Used engine oil contains metals worn from parts and should be handled and disposed of properly.

5. Solvents represent a serious health risk and should be avoided as much as possible.

6. Coolant should be disposed of properly or recycled.

7. Batteries are considered to be hazardous waste and should be discarded to a recycling facility.

REVIEW QUESTIONS

1. List five common automotive chemicals or products that may be considered hazardous materials.

2. The Resource Conservation and Recovery Act (RCRA) controls what types of automotive waste?

CHAPTER QUIZ

1. Hazardous materials include all of the following *except* _____.
   a. Engine oil
   b. Asbestos
   c. Water
   d. Brake cleaner

2. To determine if a product or substance being used is hazardous, consult _____.
   a. A dictionary
   b. An MSDS
   c. SAE standards
   d. EPA guidelines

3. Exposure to asbestos dust can cause what condition?
   a. Asbestosis
   b. Mesothelioma
   c. Lung cancer
   d. All of the above

4. Wetted asbestos dust is considered to be _____.
   a. Solid waste
   b. Hazardous waste
   c. Toxic
   d. Poisonous

5. An oil filter should be hot drained for how long before disposing of the filter?
   a. 30 to 60 minutes
   b. 4 hours
   c. 8 hours
   d. 12 hours

6. Used engine oil should be disposed of by all *except* the following methods.
   a. Disposed of in regular trash
   b. Shipped offsite for recycling
   c. Burned onsite in a waste oil-approved heater
   d. Burned offsite in a waste oil-approved heater

7. All of the following are the proper ways to dispose of a drained oil filter *except* _____.
   a. Sent for recycling
   b. Picked up by a service contract company
   c. Disposed of in regular trash
   d. Considered to be hazardous waste and disposed of accordingly

8. Which act or organization regulates air-conditioning refrigerant?
   a. Clean Air Act (CAA)
   b. MSDS
   c. WHMIS
   d. Code of Federal Regulations (CFR)

9. Gasoline should be stored in approved containers that include what color(s)?
   a. A red container with yellow lettering
   b. A red container
   c. A yellow container
   d. A yellow container with red lettering

10. What automotive devices may contain mercury?
    a. Rear seat video displays
    b. Navigation displays
    c. HID headlights
    d. All of the above

chapter 3

FASTENERS AND THREAD REPAIR

LEARNING OBJECTIVES: **After studying this chapter, the reader should be able to:** • Identify bolts and explain the strength ratings of threaded fasteners. • Discuss the purpose of nuts, taps, dies, and washers. • Discuss how snap rings and clips are used. • Explain how to avoid broken fasteners. • Compare the different types of thread repair inserts.

KEY TERMS: Bolts 20 • Cap screws 20 • Capillary action 27 • Christmas tree clips 26 • Cotter pins 26 • Crest 20 • Die 23 • Grade 21 • Helical insert 28 • Heli-Coil® 28 • Jam nut 27 • Metric bolts 21 • Pal nut 27 • Penetrating oil 27 • Pitch 20 • Pop rivet 26 • Prevailing torque nuts 23 • Self-tapping screw 25 • Snap ring 25 • Stud 20 • Tap 23 • Tensile strength 22 • Threaded insert 29 • UNC (Unified National Coarse) 20 • UNF (Unified National Fine) 20 • Washers 25

THREADED FASTENERS

Most of the threaded fasteners used on vehicles are cap screws. They are called **cap screws** when they are threaded into a casting. Automotive service technicians usually refer to these fasteners as **bolts,** regardless of how they are used. In this chapter, they are called bolts. Sometimes, studs are used for threaded fasteners. A **stud** is a short rod with threads on both ends. Often, a stud will have coarse threads on one end and fine threads on the other end. The end of the stud with coarse threads is screwed into the casting. A nut is used on the opposite end to hold the parts together.

The fastener threads *must* match the threads in the casting or nut. The threads may be measured either in fractions of an inch (called fractional) or in metric units. The size is measured across the outside of the threads, called the **crest** of the thread. ● **SEE FIGURE 3–1**.

Fractional threads are either coarse or fine. The coarse threads are called **Unified National Coarse (UNC),** and the fine threads are called **Unified National Fine (UNF).** Standard combinations of sizes and number of threads per inch (called **pitch**) are used. Pitch can be measured with a thread pitch gauge as shown in ● **FIGURE 3–2**.

Bolts are identified by their diameter and length as measured from below the head, and not by the size of the head or the size of the wrench used to remove or install the bolt. Bolts and screws have many different-shaped heads. ● **SEE FIGURE 3–3**.

Fractional thread sizes are specified by the diameter in fractions of an inch and the number of threads per inch. Typical UNC thread sizes would be 5/16-18 and 1/2-13. Similar UNF thread sizes would be 5/16-24 and 1/2-20. ● **SEE CHART 3–1**.

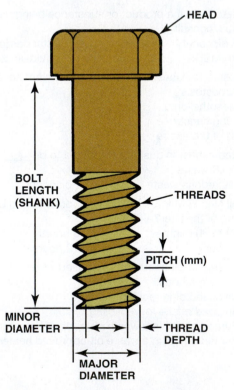

FIGURE 3–1 The dimensions of a typical bolt showing where sizes are measured. The major diameter is called the crest.

FIGURE 3–2 Thread pitch gauge used to measure the pitch of the thread. This bolt has 13 threads to the inch.

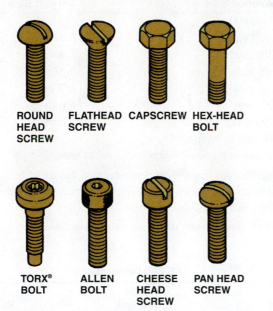

| ROUND HEAD SCREW | FLATHEAD SCREW | CAPSCREW | HEX-HEAD BOLT |
| TORX® BOLT | ALLEN BOLT | CHEESE HEAD SCREW | PAN HEAD SCREW |

FIGURE 3–3 Bolts and screws have many different heads which determine what tool must be used.

METRIC BOLTS

The size of a **metric bolt** is specified by the letter *M* followed by the diameter in millimeters (mm) across the outside (crest) of the threads. Typical metric sizes would be M8 and M12. Fine metric threads are specified by the thread diameter followed by *X* and the distance between the threads measured in millimeters (M8 × 1.5). ● **SEE FIGURE 3–4.**

GRADES OF BOLTS

Bolts are made from many different types of steel, and for this reason some are stronger than others. The strength or classification of a bolt is called the **grade.** The bolt heads are marked to indicate their grade strength. Graded bolts are commonly used in the suspension parts of the vehicle but can be used almost anywhere in the vehicle.

| | THREADS PER INCH | | OUTSIDE DIAMETER INCHES |
| | NC UNC | NF UNF | |
SIZE			
0	. .	80	0.0600
1	64	. .	0.0730
1	. .	72	0.0730
2	56	. .	0.0860
2	. .	64	0.0860
3	48	. .	0.0990
3	. .	56	0.0990
4	40	. .	0.1120
4	. .	48	0.1120
5	40	. .	0.1250
5	. .	44	0.1250
6	32	. .	0.1380
6	. .	40	0.1380
8	32	. .	0.1640
8	. .	36	0.1640
10	24	. .	0.1900
10	. .	32	0.1900
12	24	. .	0.2160
12	. .	28	0.2160
1/4	20	. .	0.2500
1/4	. .	28	0.2500
5/16	18	. .	0.3125
5/16	. .	24	0.3125
3/8	16	. .	0.3750
3/8	. .	24	0.3750
7/16	14	. .	0.4375
7/16	. .	20	0.4375
1/2	13	. .	0.5000
1/2	. .	20	0.5000
9/16	12	. .	0.5625
9/16	. .	18	0.5625
5/8	11	. .	0.6250
5/8	. .	18	0.6250
3/4	10	. .	0.7500
3/4	. .	16	0.7500
7/8	9	. .	0.8750
7/8	. .	14	0.8750

CHART 3-1

The American national system is one method of sizing fasteners.

The actual grade of bolts is two more than the number of lines on the bolt head. Metric bolts have a decimal number to indicate the grade. More lines or a higher grade number indicate a stronger bolt. Higher grade bolts usually have threads that are rolled rather than cut, which also makes them stronger. ● **SEE FIGURE 3–5.** In some cases, nuts and machine screws have similar grade markings.

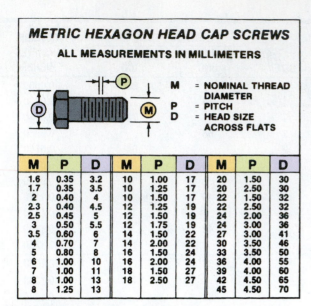

METRIC HEXAGON HEAD CAP SCREWS

ALL MEASUREMENTS IN MILLIMETERS

M = NOMINAL THREAD DIAMETER
P = PITCH
D = HEAD SIZE ACROSS FLATS

M	P	D	M	P	D	M	P	D
1.6	0.35	3.2	10	1.00	17	20	1.50	30
1.7	0.35	3.5	10	1.25	17	20	2.50	30
2	0.40	4	10	1.50	17	22	1.50	32
2.3	0.40	4.5	12	1.25	19	22	2.50	32
2.5	0.45	5	12	1.50	19	24	2.00	36
3	0.50	5.5	12	1.75	19	24	3.00	36
3.5	0.60	6	14	1.50	22	27	3.00	41
4	0.70	7	14	2.00	22	30	3.50	46
5	0.80	8	16	1.50	24	33	3.50	50
6	1.00	10	16	2.00	24	36	4.00	55
7	1.00	11	18	1.50	27	39	4.00	60
8	1.00	13	18	2.50	27	42	4.50	65
8	1.25	13				45	4.50	70

FIGURE 3–4 The metric system specifies fasteners by diameter, length, and pitch.

ROLLING THREADS

FIGURE 3–5 Stronger threads are created by cold-rolling a heat-treated bolt blank instead of cutting the threads using a die.

CAUTION: *Never* use hardware store (nongraded) bolts, studs, or nuts on any vehicle steering, suspension, or brake component. Always use the exact size and grade of hardware that is specified and used by the vehicle manufacturer.

TENSILE STRENGTH

Graded fasteners have a higher tensile strength than nongraded fasteners. **Tensile strength** is the maximum stress used under tension (lengthwise force) without causing failure of the fastener. Tensile strength is specified in pounds per square inch (PSI). See the following chart that shows the grade and specified tensile strength.

The strength and type of steel used in a bolt is supposed to be indicated by a raised mark on the head of the bolt. The type of mark depends on the standard to which the bolt was manufactured. Most often, bolts used in machinery are made to SAE Standard J429.

Metric bolt tensile strength property class is shown on the head of the bolt as a number, such as 4.6, 8.8, 9.8, and 10.9; the higher the number, the stronger the bolt. ● **SEE FIGURE 3–6.**

A 1/2 Inch Wrench Does Not Fit a 1/2 Inch Bolt

A common mistake made by persons new to the automotive field is to think that the size of a bolt or nut is the size of the head. The size of the bolt or nut (outside diameter of the threads) is usually smaller than the size of the wrench or socket that fits the head of the bolt or nut. Examples are given in the following table.

Wrench Size	Thread Size
7/16 inch	1/4 inch
1/2 inch	5/16 inch
9/16 inch	3/8 inch
5/8 inch	7/16 inch
3/4 inch	1/2 inch
10 mm	6 mm
12 mm or 13 mm*	8 mm
14 mm or 17 mm*	10 mm

*European (Système International d"Unités-SI) metric.

NOTE: An open-end wrench can be used to gauge bolt sizes. A 3/8 inch wrench will fit the threads of a 3/8 inch bolt.

SAE Bolt Designations

SAE Grade No.	Size Range	Tensile Strength, PSI	Material	Head Marking
1	1/4 through 1-1/2	60,000	Low or medium carbon steel	
2	1/4 through 3/4	74,000		
	7/8 through 1-1/2	60,000		
5	1/4 through 1	120,000	Medium carbon steel, quenched & tempered	
	1-1/8 through 1-1/2	105,000		
5.2	1/4 through 1	120,000	Low carbon martensite steel*, quenched & tempered	
7	1/4 through 1-1/2	133,000	Medium carbon alloy steel, quenched & tempered	
8	1/4 through 1-1/2	150,000	Medium carbon alloy steel, quenched & tempered	
8.2	1/4 through 1	150,000	Low carbon Martensite steel*, quenched & tempered	

*Martensite steel is steel that has been cooled rapidly, thereby increasing its hardness. It is named after a German metallurgist, Adolf Martens.

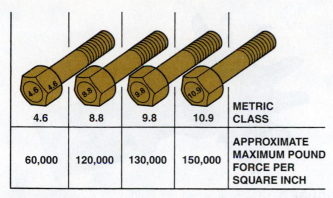

4.6	8.8	9.8	10.9	METRIC CLASS
60,000	120,000	130,000	150,000	APPROXIMATE MAXIMUM POUND FORCE PER SQUARE INCH

FIGURE 3–6 Metric bolt (cap screw) grade markings and approximate tensile strength.

FIGURE 3–7 Types of lock nuts. On the left, a nylon ring; in the center, a distorted shape; and on the right, a castle for use with a cotter key.

NUTS

Most nuts used on cap screws have the same hex size as the cap screw head. Some inexpensive nuts use a hex size larger than the cap screw head. Metric nuts are often marked with dimples to show their strength. More dimples indicate stronger nuts. Some nuts and cap screws use interference fit threads to keep them from accidentally loosening. This means that the shape of the nut is slightly distorted or that a section of the threads is deformed. Nuts can also be kept from loosening with a nylon washer fastened in the nut or with a nylon patch or strip on the threads. ● **SEE FIGURE 3–7.**

NOTE: Most of these "locking nuts" are grouped together and are commonly referred to as prevailing torque nuts. This means that the nut will hold its tightness or torque and not loosen with movement or vibration. Most prevailing torque nuts should be replaced whenever removed to ensure that the nut will not loosen during service. Always follow the manufacturer's recommendations. Anaerobic sealers, such as Loctite®, are used on the threads where the nut or cap screw must be both locked and sealed.

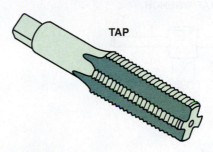

TAP

FIGURE 3–8 A typical bottoming tap used to create threads in holes that are not open, but stop in a casting, such as an engine block.

TAPS AND DIES

Taps and dies are used to cut threads. **Taps** are used to cut threads in holes drilled to an exact size depending on the size of the tap. A **die** is used to cut threads on round rods or studs. Most taps and dies come as a complete set for the most commonly used fractional and metric threads.

TAPS   There are two commonly used types of taps, including:

- **Taper tap.** This is the most commonly used tap and is designed to cut threads by gradually enlarging the threaded hole.
- **Bottoming tap.** This tap has a flat bottom instead of a tapered tip to allow it to cut threads to the bottom of a drilled hole. ● **SEE FIGURE 3–8.**

1/2-20 USA DRILL 29/64

FIGURE 3–9 Many taps, especially larger ones, have the tap drill size printed on the top.

All taps must be used in the proper size hole called a "tap drill size." This information is often stamped on the tap itself or in a chart that is included with a tap and die tool set. ● **SEE FIGURE 3–9.**

DIES   A die is a hardened steel round cutter with teeth on the inside of the center hole. ● **SEE FIGURE 3–10.** A die is rotated using a die handle over a rod to create threads.

PROPER USE OF TAPS AND DIES   Taps and dies are used to cut threads on rods in the case of a die or in a hole for a tap. A small tap can be held using a T-handle tap wrench but for larger taps a tap handle is needed to apply the needed force to cut threads. ● **SEE FIGURES 3–11A AND 3–11B.**

DIE

FIGURE 3–10 A die is used to cut threads on a metal rod.

FIGURE 3–13 A typical metric thread pitch gauge.

T-HANDLE
TAP WRENCH

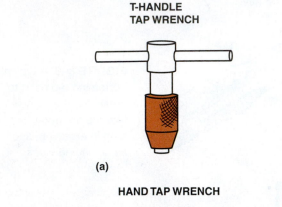

(a)

HAND TAP WRENCH

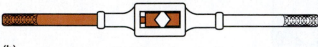

(b)

FIGURE 3–11 (a) A T-handle is used to hold and rotate small taps. (b) A tap wrench is used to hold and drive larger taps.

FIGURE 3–14 A thread chaser is shown at the top compared to a tap on the bottom. A thread chaser is used to clean threads without removing metal.

DIE HANDLE

FIGURE 3–12 A die handle used to rotate a die while cutting threads on a metal rod.

THREAD PITCH GAUGE

A thread pitch gauge is a hand tool that has the outline of various thread sizes machined on stamped blades. To determine the thread pitch size of a fastener, the technician matches the thread of the thread pitch gauge to the threads of the fastener. ● SEE FIGURE 3–13

TAP USAGE. Be sure that the hole is the correct size for the tap and start by inserting the tap straight into the hole. Lubricate the tap using tapping lubricant. Rotate the tap about one full turn clockwise, then reverse the direction of the tap one-half turn to break the chip that was created. Repeat the procedure until the hole is completely threaded.

DIE USAGE. A die should be used on the specified diameter rod for the size of the thread. Install the die securely into the die handle. ● SEE FIGURE 3–12.

Lubricate the die and the rod and place the die onto the end of the rod to be threaded. Rotate the die handle one full turn clockwise, then reverse the direction and rotate the die handle about a half turn counterclockwise to break the chip that was created. Repeat the process until the threaded portion has been completed.

 FREQUENTLY ASKED QUESTION

What Is the Difference Between a Tap and a Thread Chaser?

A tap is a cutting tool and is designed to cut new threads. A thread chaser has more rounded threads and is designed to clean dirty threads without removing metal. Therefore, when cleaning threads, it is best to use a thread chaser rather than a tap to prevent the possibility of removing metal, which would affect the fit of the bolt being installed. ● SEE FIGURE 3–14.

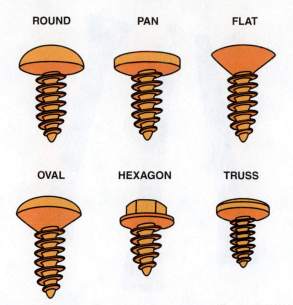

ROUND   PAN   FLAT

OVAL   HEXAGON   TRUSS

FIGURE 3–15 Sheet metal screws come with many head types.

SHEET METAL SCREWS

Sheet metal screws are fully threaded screws with a point for use in sheet metal. Also called **self-tapping screws,** they are used in many places on the vehicle, including fenders, trim, and door panels. ● SEE FIGURE 3–15.

These screws are used in unthreaded holes and the sharp threads cut threads as they are installed. This makes for a quick and easy installation when installing new parts, but the sheet metal screw can easily strip out the threads when used on the same part over and over, so care is needed.

When reinstalling self-tapping screws, first turn the screw lightly backwards until you feel the thread drop into the existing thread in the screw hole. Then, turn the screw in; if it threads in easily, continue to tighten the screw. If the screw seems to turn hard, stop and turn it backwards about another half turn to locate the existing thread and try again. This technique can help prevent stripped holes in sheet metal and plastic parts.

Sheet metal screws are sized according to their major thread diameter.

Size	Diameter Decimal (inch)	Diameter Nearest Fraction Inch
4	0.11	7/64
6	0.14	9/64
8	0.17	11/64
10	0.19	3/16
12	0.22	7/32
14	0.25	1/4

HEX NUT   JAM NUT   NYLON LOCK NUT   CASTLE NUT   ACORN NUT

FLAT WASHER   LOCK WASHER   STAR WASHER   STAR WASHER

FIGURE 3–16 Various types of nuts (top) and washers (bottom) serve different purposes and all are used to secure bolts or cap screws.

WASHERS

Washers are often used under cap screw heads and under nuts. ● SEE FIGURE 3–16.

Plain flat washers are used to provide an even clamping load around the fastener. Lock washers are added to prevent accidental loosening. In some accessories, the washers are locked onto the nut to provide easy assembly.

Flat washers are placed underneath a nut to spread the load over a wide area and prevent gouging of the material. However, flat washers do not prevent a nut from loosening.

Lock washers are designed to prevent a nut from loosening. Spring-type lock washers resemble a loop out of a coil spring. As the nut or bolt is tightened, the washer is compressed. The tension of the compressed washer holds the fastener firmly against the threads to prevent it from loosening. Lock washers should not be used on soft metal such as aluminum. The sharp ends of the steel washers would gouge the aluminum badly, especially if they are removed and replaced often.

Another type of locking washer is the star washer. The teeth on a star washer can be external or internal, and they bite into the metal because they are twisted to expose their edges. Star washers are used often on sheet metal or body parts. They are seldom used on engines. The spring steel lock washer also uses the tension of the compressed washer to prevent the fastener from loosening. The waves in this washer make it look like a distorted flat washer.

SNAP RINGS AND CLIPS

SNAP RINGS   Snap rings are not threaded fasteners, but instead attach with a springlike action. Snap rings are constructed of spring steel and are used to attach parts without using a threaded fastener. There are several different types of snap rings and most require the use of a special pair of pliers,

EXPANDING OR INTERNAL | EXPANDING OR EXTERNAL | E-CLIP | EXPANDING OR INTERNAL | CONTRACTING OR EXTERNAL | C-CLIP

FIGURE 3–17 Some different types of snap rings. An internal snap ring fits inside of a housing or bore, into a groove. An external snap ring fits into a groove on the outside of a shaft or axle. An E-clip fits into a groove in the outside of a shaft. A C-clip shown is used to retain a window regulator handle on its shaft.

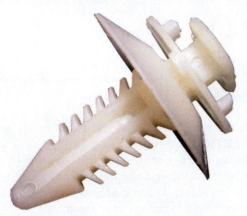

FIGURE 3–18 A typical door panel retaining clip.

called snap ring pliers, to release or install. The types of snap rings include:

- Expanding (internal)
- Contracting (external)
- E-clip
- C-clip
- Holeless snap rings in both expanding and contracting styles

● **SEE FIGURE 3–17.**

DOOR PANEL CLIPS Interior door panels and other trim pieces are usually held in place with plastic clips. Due to the tapered and fluted shape, these clips are often called **Christmas tree clips.** ● **SEE FIGURE 3–18.**

A special tool is often used to remove interior door panels without causing any harm. ● **SEE FIGURE 3–19.**

CAUTION: Use extreme care when removing panels that use plastic or nylon clips. It is very easy to damage the door panel or clip during removal.

PINS **Cotter pins,** also called a cotter key, are used to keep linkage or a threaded nut in place or to keep it retained. The word *cotter* is an Old English verb meaning "to close or fasten." There are many other types of pins used in vehicles, including clevis pins, roll pins, and hair pins. ● **SEE FIGURE 3–20.**

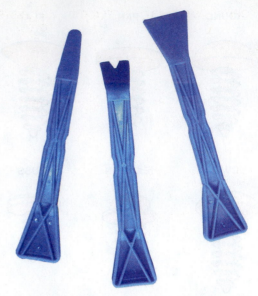

FIGURE 3–19 Plastic or metal trim tools are available to help the technician remove interior door panels and other trim without causing harm.

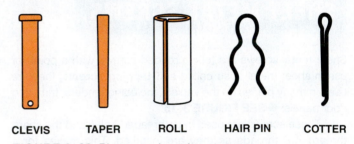

CLEVIS | TAPER | ROLL | HAIR PIN | COTTER

FIGURE 3–20 Pins come in various types.

Pins are used to hold together shafts and linkages, such as shift linkages and cable linkages. The clevis pin is held in place with a cotter pin, while the taper and roll pins are driven in and held by friction. The hair pin snaps into a groove on a shaft.

RIVETS Rivets are used in many locations to retain components, such as window mechanisms, that do not require routine removal and/or do not have access to the back side for a nut. A drill is usually used to remove a rivet and a rivet gun is needed to properly install a rivet. Some rivets are plastic and are used to hold some body trim pieces. The most common type of rivet is called a **pop rivet** because as the rivet tool applies a force to the shaft of the pop rivet, it causes the rivet to expand and tighten the two pieces together. When the shaft of the rivet, which looks like a nail, is pulled to its maximum, the shaft breaks, causing a "pop" sound.

Rivets may be used in areas of the vehicle where a semi-permanent attachment is needed and in places where there is no access to the back side of the workpiece. They are installed using a rivet gun or by peening with a ball-peen hammer. ● **SEE FIGURE 3–21.**

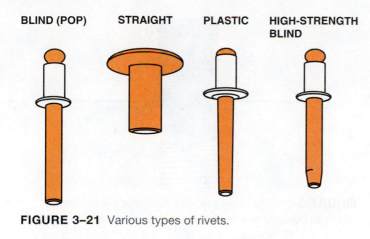

FIGURE 3–21 Various types of rivets.

BLIND (POP) STRAIGHT PLASTIC HIGH-STRENGTH BLIND

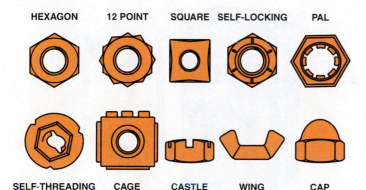

HEXAGON 12 POINT SQUARE SELF-LOCKING PAL

SELF-THREADING CAGE CASTLE WING CAP

FIGURE 3–22 All of the nuts shown are used by themselves except for the pal nut, which is used to lock another nut to a threaded fastener so they will not be loosened by vibration.

Both types of blind rivets require the use of a rivet gun to install. The straight rivet is placed through the workpieces and then peened over with a ball-peen hammer or an air-operated tool. The plastic rivet is used with a rivet gun to install some body trim parts.

LOCKING NUTS Some nuts, called jam nuts, are used to keep bolts and screws from loosening. **Jam nuts** screw on top of a regular nut and jam against the regular nut to prevent loosening. A jam nut is so called because of its intended use, rather than a special design. Some jam nuts are thinner than a standard nut. Jam nuts are also called **pal nuts.** ● SEE FIGURE 3–22.

There are also self-locking nuts of various types. Some have threads that are bent inward to grip the threads of the bolt. Some are oval-shaped at one end to fit tightly on a bolt. Fiber lock nuts have a fiber insert near the top of the nut or inside it; this type of nut is also made with a plastic or nylon insert. When the bolt turns through the nut, it cuts threads in the fiber or plastic. This puts a drag on the threads that prevents the bolt from loosening.

One of the oldest types of retaining nuts is the castle nut. It looks like a small castle, with slots for a cotter pin. A castellated nut is used on a bolt that has a hole for the cotter pin. ● SEE FIGURE 3–23.

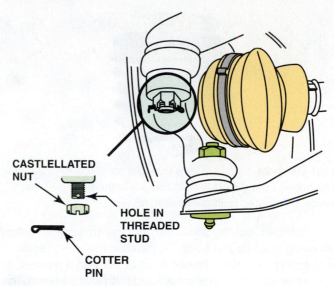

CASTLELLATED NUT
HOLE IN THREADED STUD
COTTER PIN

FIGURE 3–23 A castellated nut is locked in place with a cotter pin.

HOW TO AVOID BROKEN FASTENERS

Try not to break, strip, or round off fasteners in the first place. There are several ways that you can minimize the number of fasteners you damage. First, never force fasteners loose during disassembly. Taking a few precautionary steps will often prevent damage. If a bolt or nut will not come loose with normal force, try tightening it in slightly and then backing it out. Sometimes turning the fastener the other way will break corrosion loose, and the fastener will then come out easily. Another method that works well is to rest a punch on the head of a stubborn bolt and strike it a sharp blow with a hammer. Often this method will break the corrosion loose.

LEFT-HANDED THREADS Although rare, left-handed fasteners are occasionally found on engine assemblies. These fasteners will loosen when you turn them clockwise, and tighten when you turn them counterclockwise. Left-handed fasteners are used to fasten parts to the ends of rotating assemblies that turn counterclockwise, such as crankshafts and camshafts. Most automobile engines do not use left-handed threads; however, they will be found on many older motorcycle engines. Some left-handed fasteners are marked with an "L" on the bolt head for easy identification, others are not. Left-handed threads are also found inside some transaxles.

PENETRATING OIL **Penetrating oil** is a lightweight lubricant similar to kerosene, which soaks into small crevices in the threads by **capillary action.** The chemical action of penetrating oils helps to break up and dissolve rust and corrosion. The oil forms a layer of boundary lubrication on the threads to reduce friction and make the fastener easier to turn.

FIGURE 3–24 Helical inserts look like small, coiled springs. The outside is a thread to hold the coil in the hole, and the inside is threaded to fit the desired fastener.

FIGURE 3–25 The insert provides new, stock-size threads inside an oversize hole so that the original fastener can be used.

For best results, allow the oil time to soak in before removing the nuts and bolts. To increase the effectiveness of penetrating oil, tap on the bolt head or nut with a hammer, or alternately work the fastener back and forth with a wrench. This movement weakens the bond of the corrosion and lets more of the lubricant work down into the threads.

PROPER TIGHTENING   Proper tightening of bolts and nuts is critical for proper clamping force, as well as to prevent breakage. All fasteners should be tightened using a torque wrench. A torque wrench allows the technician to exert a known amount of torque to the fasteners. However, rotating torque on a fastener does not mean clamping force because up to 80% of the torque used to rotate a bolt or nut is absorbed by friction by the threads. Therefore, for accurate tightening, two things must be performed:

- The threads must be clean and lubricated if service information specifies that they be lubricated.

- Always use a torque wrench to not only ensure proper clamping force, but also to ensure that all fasteners are tightened the same.

THREAD REPAIR INSERTS

Thread repair inserts are used to replace the original threaded hole when it has become damaged beyond use. The original threaded hole is enlarged and tapped for threads and a threaded insert is installed to restore the threads to the original size.

HELICAL INSERTS   A **helical insert** looks like a small, stainless-steel spring. ● SEE FIGURE 3–24.

To install a helical insert, a hole must be drilled to a specified oversize, and then it is tapped with a special tap designed for the thread inserts. The insert is then screwed into the hole. ● SEE FIGURE 3–25.

The insert stays in the casting as a permanent repair and bolts can be removed and replaced without disturbing the insert. One advantage of a helical insert is that the original bolt can be used because the internal threads are the same size. When correctly installed, an insert is often stronger than the original threads, especially in aluminum castings. Some vehicle manufacturers, such as BMW, specify that the threads be renewed using

FIGURE 3–26 Heli-Coil® kits, available in a wide variety of sizes, contain everything needed to repair a damaged hole back to its original size.

an insert if the cylinder head has to be removed and reinstalled. Plus many high-performance engine rebuilders install inserts in blocks, manifolds, and cylinder heads as a precaution.

One of the best known of the helical fasteners is the **Heli-Coil®,** manufactured by Heli-Coil® Products. To install Heli-Coil® inserts, you will need to have a thread repair kit. The kit includes a drill bit, tap, installation mandrel, and inserts. Repair kits are available for a wide variety of diameters and pitch to fit both American Standard and metric threads. A simple kit contains the tooling for one specific thread size. Master kits that cover a range of sizes are also available. Installing an insert is similar to tapping new threads. A summary of the procedures includes:

1. Select the Heli-Coil® kit designed for the specific diameter and thread pitch of the hole to be repaired. ● SEE FIGURE 3–26.

2. Use the drill bit supplied with the kit. The drill size is also specified on the Heli-Coil® tap, to open up the hole to the necessary diameter and depth.

3. Tap the hole with the Heli-Coil® tap, being sure to lubricate the tap. Turn it in slowly and rotate counterclockwise occasionally to break the chip that is formed.

4. Thread an insert onto the installation mandrel until it seats firmly. Apply a light coating of the recommended thread locking compound to the external threads of the insert.

5. Use the mandrel to screw the insert into the tapped hole. Once started, spring tension prevents the insert from unscrewing. Stop when the top of the insert is 1/4 to 1/2 turn below the surface.

6. Remove the mandrel by unscrewing it from the insert, and then use a small punch or needle-nose pliers to break off the tang at the base of the insert. Never leave the tang in the bore. The finished thread is ready for use immediately.

THREADED INSERTS   **Threaded inserts** are tubular, case-hardened, solid steel wall pieces that are threaded inside and outside. The inner thread of the insert is sized to fit the original fastener of the hole to be repaired. The outer thread design will vary. These may be self-tapping threads that are installed in a blank hole, or machine threads that require the hole to be tapped. Threaded inserts return a damaged hole to original size by replacing part of the surrounding casting so drilling is required. Most inserts fit into three categories.

- Self-tapping
- Solid-bushing
- Key-locking

SELF-TAPPING INSERTS   The external threads of a self-tapping insert are designed to cut their own way into a casting. This eliminates the need of running a tap down the hole. To install a typical self-tapping insert, follow this procedure.

1. Drill out the damaged threads to open the hole to the proper size, using the specified size drill bit.

2. Select the proper insert and mandrel. As with Heli-Coils®, the drill bit, inserts, and mandrel are usually available as a kit.

3. Thread the insert onto the mandrel. Use a tap handle or wrench to drive the insert into the hole. Because the insert will cut its own path into the hole, it may require a considerable amount of force to drive the insert in.

4. Thread the insert in until the nut or flange at the bottom of the mandrel touches the surface of the workpiece. This is the depth stop to indicate the insert is seated.

5. Hold the nut or flange with a wrench, and turn the mandrel out of the insert. The threads are ready for immediate use.

SOLID-BUSHING INSERTS   The external threads of solid-bushing inserts are ground to a specific thread pitch, so you will have to run a tap into the hole. ● SEE FIGURE 3–27.

Some inserts use a machine thread so a standard tap can be used; others have a unique thread and you have to use a special tap. The thread inserts come with a matching installation kit. ● SEE FIGURE 3–28.

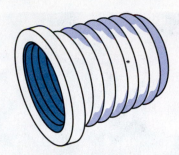

FIGURE 3–27 This solid-bushing insert is threaded on the outside, to grip the workpiece. The inner threads match the desired bolt size.

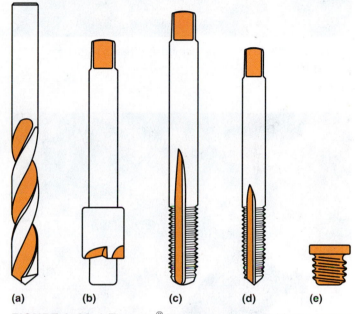

(a)   (b)   (c)   (d)   (e)

FIGURE 3–28 A Timesert® kit includes the drill (a), the recess cutter (b), a special tap (c), the installer (d), and the Timesert® threaded bushing (e).

To install threaded inserts, follow this procedure.

1. Drill out the damaged threads to open the hole to the proper size. The drill bit supplied with the kit must be the one used because it is properly sized to the tap. ● SEE FIGURE 3–29.

2. Cut the recess in the top of the hole with the special tool, then clean the hole with a brush or compressed air.

3. Use the previously detailed tapping procedures to thread the hole. ● SEE FIGURE 3–30. Be sure to tap deep enough; the top of the insert must be flush with the casting surface.

4. Thread the insert onto the installation driver, using the driver to screw the insert into the hole. Some inserts require that a thread-locking compound be applied; others go in dry.

5. Remove the installation driver, and the new threads are ready for service with the original fastener.

FIGURE 3–29 Drill out the damaged threads with the correct bit.

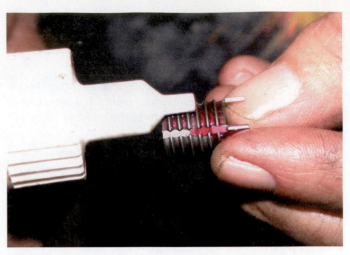

FIGURE 3–31 Put some thread-locking compound on the insert.

FIGURE 3–30 Use a special tap for the insert.

FIGURE 3–32 Use the driver to drive the keys down flush with the surface of the workpiece.

KEY-LOCKING INSERTS Key-locking inserts are similar to solid-bushing inserts, but are held in place by small keys. After the insert has been installed, the keys are driven into place—perpendicular to the threads—to keep the insert from turning out. A typical installation procedure includes the following steps.

1. Drill out the damaged thread with the specified drill size.

2. Tap the drilled hole with the specified tap.

3. After putting thread locking compound on the insert, use the mandrel to screw the insert into the tapped hole until it is slightly below the surface. ● **SEE FIGURE 3–31**. The keys act as a depth stop and prevent the insert from turning.

4. Drive the keys down using the driver supplied with the insert kit. Be sure the keys are flush with the top of the insert. ● **SEE FIGURES 3–32** and **3–33**.

FIGURE 3–33 The insert and insert locks should be below the surface of the workpiece.

1. The most common type of fastener is a threaded one often referred to as a bolt. A nut or threaded hole is used at the end of a bolt to fasten two parts together.

2. The size of threaded fasteners includes the diameter, length, and pitch of the threads, as well as the shape of the head of the bolt.

3. Metric bolts are labeled with an "M," and the diameter across the threads is in millimeters followed by the distance between the threads measured in millimeters, such as M8 × 1.5.

4. Graded bolts are hardened and are capable of providing more holding force than nongraded bolts.

5. Many nuts are capable of remaining attached to the bolt regardless of vibration. These types of nuts are often called prevailing torque nuts.

6. Other commonly used fasteners in the automotive service industry include sheet metal screws, snap rings and clips, door panel clips, cotter pins, and rivets.

7. Threads can be repaired using a Heli-Coil® or threaded insert.

REVIEW QUESTIONS

1. What is the difference between a bolt and a stud?

2. How is the size of a metric bolt expressed?

3. What is meant by the grade of a threaded fastener?

4. How do prevailing torque nuts work?

5. How are threaded inserts installed?

CHAPTER QUIZ

1. The thread pitch of a bolt is measured in what units?
   a. Millimeters
   b. Threads per inch
   c. Fractions of an inch
   d. Both a and b

2. Technician A says that the diameter of a bolt is the same as the wrench size used to remove or install the fastener. Technician B says that the length is measured from the top of the head of the bolt to the end of the bolt. Which technician is correct?
   a. Technician A only
   b. Technician B only
   c. Both Technicians A and B
   d. Neither Technician A nor B

3. The grade of a fastener, such as a bolt, is a measure of its _____.
   a. Tensile strength
   b. Hardness
   c. Finish
   d. Color

4. Which of the following is a metric bolt?
   a. 5/16 – 18
   b. 1/2 – 20
   c. M12 × 1.5
   d. 8 millimeter

5. A bolt that is threaded into a casting is often called a _____.
   a. Stud
   b. Cap screw
   c. Block bolt
   d. Crest bolt

6. The marks (lines) on the heads of bolts indicate _____.
   a. Size
   b. Grade
   c. Tensile strength
   d. Both b and c

7. A bolt that requires a 1/2 inch wrench to rotate is usually what size when measured across the threads?
   a. 1/2 inch
   b. 5/16 inch
   c. 3/8 inch
   d. 7/16 inch

8. A screw that can make its own threads when installed is called a _____ screw.
   a. Sheet metal
   b. Tapered
   c. Self-tapping
   d. Both a and c

9. All of the following are types of clips except _____.
   a. E-clip
   b. Cotter
   c. C-clip
   d. Internal

10. What type of fastener is commonly used to retain interior door panels?
    a. Christmas tree clips
    b. E-clips
    c. External clips
    d. Internal clips

LEARNING OBJECTIVES: **After studying this chapter, the reader should be able to:** • Compare the different types of wrenches. • Discuss the purpose of ratchets, sockets, and extensions, and screwdrivers. • Discuss the purpose of hammers, mallets, and pliers. • Explain the characteristics of cutters, punches, chisels, removers, and hacksaws. • Identify the different types of electrical hand tools. • Discuss the safety tips for using hand tools and hand tool maintenance.

KEY TERMS: Adjustable wrench 32 • Aviation tin snips 40 • Beam-type torque wrench 35 • Box-end wrench 32 • Breaker bar (flex handle) 34 • Cheater bar 46 • Chisel 41 • Clicker-type torque wrench 34 • Cold chisel 41 • Combination wrench 32 • Crowfoot socket 34 • Dead-blow hammer 38 • Diagonal (side-cut or dike) pliers 39 • Double-cut file 40 • Drive size 34 • Easy out 42 • Extension 34 • Files 40 • Fitting wrench 33 • Flare-nut wrench 33 • Flat-tip (straight blade) screwdriver 36 • Hacksaw 43 • Locking pliers 39 • Multigroove adjustable pliers 38 • Needle-nose pliers 39 • Nut splitter 42 • Open-end wrench 32 • Punch 41 • Ratchet 34 • Removers 41 • Screwdriver 36 • Seal driver 45 • Seal puller 45 • Single-cut file 40 • Slip-joint pliers 38 • Snap-ring pliers 40 • Socket 34 • Socket adapter 36 • Straight cut aviation snip 40 • Stud removal tool 41 • Stud remover 41 • Tin snips 40 • Torque wrench 34 • Tube-nut wrench 33 • Universal joint 34 • Utility knife 40 • Vise-Grip® 39 • Water pump pliers 38 • Wrench 32

WRENCHES

Wrenches are the most used hand tool by service technicians. Most wrenches are constructed of forged alloy steel, usually chrome-vanadium steel. ● **SEE FIGURE 4–1.**

After the wrench is formed, it is hardened, tempered to reduce brittleness, and then chrome plated. Wrenches are available in both fractional and metric sizes. There are several types of wrenches.

OPEN-END WRENCH An **open-end wrench** is often used to loosen or tighten bolts or nuts that do not require a lot of torque. An open-end wrench can be easily placed on a bolt or nut with an angle of 15 degrees, which allows the wrench to be

FIGURE 4–1 A forged wrench after it has been forged but before the flashing, extra material around the wrench, has been removed.

flipped over and used again to continue to rotate the fastener. The major disadvantage of an open-end wrench is the lack of torque that can be applied due to the fact that the open jaws of the wrench only contact two flat surfaces of the fastener. An open-end wrench has two different sizes, one at each end. ● **SEE FIGURE 4–2.**

BOX-END WRENCH A **box-end wrench** is placed over the top of the fastener and grips the points of the fastener. A box-end wrench is angled 15 degrees to allow it to clear nearby objects. ● **SEE FIGURE 4–3.**

Therefore, a box-end wrench should be used to loosen or to tighten fasteners. A box-end wrench is also called a **close-end** wrench. A box-end wrench has two different sizes, one at each end. ● **SEE FIGURE 4–4.**

COMBINATION WRENCH Most service technicians purchase **combination wrenches**, which have the open end at one end and the same size box end on the other. ● **SEE FIGURE 4–5.**

A combination wrench allows the technician to loosen or tighten a fastener using the box end of the wrench, turn it around, and use the open end to increase the speed of rotating the fastener.

ADJUSTABLE WRENCH An **adjustable wrench** is often used where the exact size wrench is not available or when a large nut, such as a wheel spindle nut, needs to be rotated but

FIGURE 4–2 A typical open-end wrench. The size is different on each end and notice that the head is angled 15 degrees at each end.

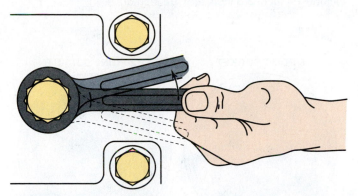

FIGURE 4–3 A typical box-end wrench is able to grip the bolt or nut at points completely around the fastener. Each end is a different size.

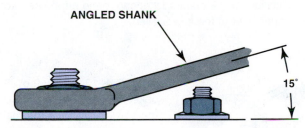

ANGLED SHANK

15°

FIGURE 4–4 The end of a box-end wrench is angled 15 degrees to allow clearance for nearby objects or other fasteners.

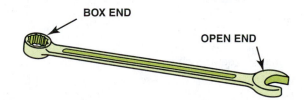

BOX END

OPEN END

FIGURE 4–5 A combination wrench has an open end at one end and a box end at the other with the same size at each end.

not tightened. An adjustable wrench should not be used to loosen or tighten fasteners because the torque applied to the wrench can cause the movable jaws to loosen their grip on the fastener, causing it to become rounded. ● SEE FIGURE 4–6.

LINE WRENCHES
Line wrenches are also called **flare-nut wrenches**, **fitting wrenches**, or **tube-nut wrenches** and are designed to grip almost all the way around a nut used to retain

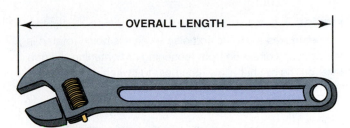

OVERALL LENGTH

FIGURE 4–6 An adjustable wrench. Adjustable wrenches are sized by the overall length of the wrench and not by how far the jaws open. Common sizes of adjustable wrenches include 8, 10, and 12 inch.

FIGURE 4–7 The end of a typical line wrench, which shows that it is capable of grasping most of the head of the fitting.

a fuel or refrigerant line, and yet be able to be installed over the line. ● SEE FIGURE 4–7.

SAFE USE OF WRENCHES. Wrenches should be inspected before use to be sure they are not cracked, bent, or damaged. All wrenches should be cleaned after use before being returned to the toolbox. Always use the correct size of wrench for the fastener being loosened or tightened to help prevent the rounding of the flats of the fastener. When attempting to loosen a fastener, pull a wrench-do not push a wrench. If a wrench is pushed, your knuckles can be hurt when forced into another object if the fastener breaks loose.

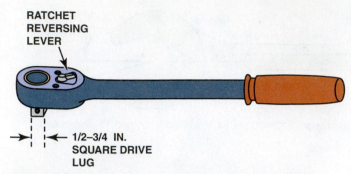

FIGURE 4–8 A typical ratchet used to rotate a socket. A ratchet makes a ratcheting noise when it is being rotated in the opposite direction from loosening or tightening. A knob or lever on the ratchet allows the user to switch directions.

FIGURE 4–9 A typical flex handle used to rotate a socket, also called a breaker bar because it usually has a longer handle than a ratchet and, therefore, can be used to apply more torque to a fastener than a ratchet.

RATCHETS, SOCKETS, AND EXTENSIONS

A **socket** fits over the fastener and grips the points and/or flats of the bolt or nut. The socket is rotated (driven) using either a long bar called a **breaker bar (flex handle)** or a **ratchet**. ● SEE FIGURES 4–8 AND 4–9.

A ratchet turns the socket in only one direction and allows the rotating of the ratchet handle back and forth in a narrow space. Socket **extensions** and **universal joints** are also used with sockets to allow access to fasteners in restricted locations.

Sockets are available in various **drive sizes**, including 1/4 inch, 3/8 inch, and 1/2 inch sizes for most automotive use. ● SEE FIGURES 4–10 AND 4–11.

Many heavy-duty truck and/or industrial applications use 3/4 inch and 1 inch sizes. The drive size is the distance of each side of the square drive. Sockets and ratchets of the same size are designed to work together.

CROWFOOT SOCKETS
A **crowfoot socket** is a socket that is an open-end or line wrench to allow access to fasteners that cannot be reached using a conventional wrench. ● SEE FIGURE 4–12.

Crowfoot sockets are available in the following categories.

- Fractional inch open-end wrench
- Metric open-end wrench

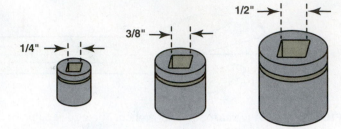

FIGURE 4–10 The most commonly used socket drive sizes include 1/4 inch, 3/8 inch, and 1/2 inch drive.

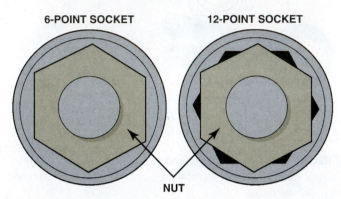

FIGURE 4–11 A 6-point socket fits the head of the bolt or nut on all sides. A 12-point socket can round off the head of a bolt or nut if a lot of force is applied.

FIGURE 4–12 A crowfoot socket is designed to reach fasteners using a ratchet or breaker bar with an extension.

- Fractional line wrench
- Metric line wrench

TORQUE WRENCHES
Torque wrenches are socket turning handles that are designed to apply a known amount of force to the fastener. There are two basic types of torque wrenches.

1. A **clicker-type torque wrench** is first set to the specified torque and then it "clicks" when the set torque value has been reached. When force is removed from the torque wrench handle, another click is heard. The setting on a clicker-type torque wrench should be set back to zero after use and checked for proper calibration regularly. ● SEE FIGURE 4–13.

FIGURE 4–13 Using a torque wrench to tighten connecting rod nuts on an engine.

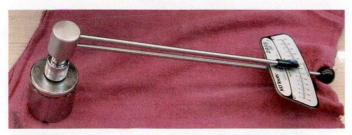

FIGURE 4–14 A beam-type torque wrench that displays the torque reading on the face of the dial. The beam display is read as the beam deflects, which is in proportion to the amount of torque applied to the fastener.

TECH TIP

Right to Tighten

It is sometimes confusing which way to rotate a wrench or screwdriver, especially when the head of the fastener is pointing away from you. To help visualize while looking at the fastener, say "righty tighty, lefty loosey."

2. A **beam- or dial-type torque wrench** is used to measure torque, but instead of presetting the value, the actual torque is displayed on the dial of the wrench as the fastener is being tightened. Beam-type torque wrenches are available in 1/4 inch, 3/8 inch, and 1/2 inch drives and both English and metric units. ● SEE FIGURE 4–14.

SAFE USE OF SOCKETS AND RATCHETS. Always use the proper size socket that correctly fits the bolt or nut. All sockets and ratchets should be cleaned after use before being placed back into the toolbox. Sockets are available in short and deep well designs. ● SEE FIGURE 4–16.

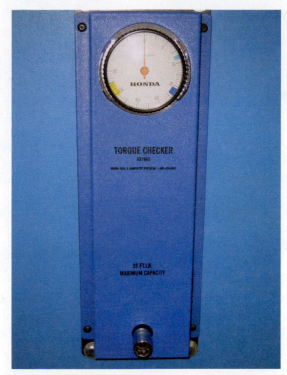

FIGURE 4–15 Torque wrench calibration checker.

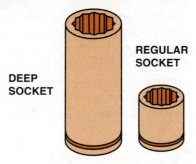

FIGURE 4–16 Deep sockets allow access to the nut that has a stud plus other locations needing great depth, such as spark plugs.

TECH TIP

Check Torque Wrench Calibration Regularly

Torque wrenches should be checked regularly. For example, Honda has a torque wrench calibration setup at each of their training centers. It is expected that a torque wrench be checked for accuracy before every use. Most experts recommend that torque wrenches be checked and adjusted as needed at least every year and more often if possible. ● SEE FIGURE 4–15.

Also select the appropriate drive size. For example, for small work, such as on the dash, select a 1/4 inch drive. For most general service work, use a 3/8 inch drive and for suspension and steering and other large fasteners, select a 1/2 inch drive. When loosening a fastener, always pull the ratchet toward you rather than push it outward.

FREQUENTLY ASKED QUESTION

Is It lb-ft or ft-lb of Torque?

The unit for torque is expressed as a force times the distance (leverage) from the object. Therefore, the official unit for torque is lb-ft (pound-feet) or newton-meters (a force times a distance). However, it is commonly expressed in ft-lb and even some torque wrenches are labeled with this unit.

TECH TIP

Double-Check the Specifications

Misreading torque specifications is easy to do but can have serious damaging results. Specifications for fasteners are commonly expressed pound-feet. Many smaller fasteners are tightened to specifications expressed in pound-inch

$$1 \text{ lb-ft} = 12 \text{ lb-in.}$$

Therefore, if a fastener were to be accidentally tightened to 24 pound-feet instead of 24 pound-inch, the actual torque applied to the fastener will be 288 lb-inch instead of the specified 24 pound-inch.

This extra torque will likely break the fastener, but it could also warp or distort the part being tightened. Always double-check the torque specifications.

TECH TIP

Use Socket Adapters with Caution

Socket adapters are available and can be used for different drive size sockets on a ratchet. Combinations include:

- 1/4 inch drive—3/8 inch sockets
- 3/8 inch drive—1/4 inch sockets
- 3/8 inch drive—1/2 inch sockets
- 1/2 inch drive—3/8 inch sockets

Using a larger drive ratchet or breaker bar on a smaller size socket can cause the application of too much force to the socket, which could crack or shatter. Using a smaller size drive tool on a larger socket will usually not cause any harm, but would greatly reduce the amount of torque that can be applied to the bolt or nut.

TECH TIP

Avoid Using "Cheater Bars"

Whenever a fastener is difficult to remove, some technicians will insert the handle of a ratchet or a breaker bar into a length of steel pipe. The extra length of the pipe allows the technician to exert more torque than can be applied using the drive handle alone. However, the extra torque can easily overload the socket and ratchet, causing them to break or shatter, which could cause personal injury.

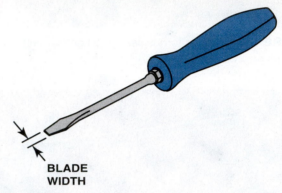

FIGURE 4–17 A flat-tip (straight blade) screwdriver. The width of the blade should match the width of the slot in the fastener being loosened or tightened.

SCREWDRIVERS

Many smaller fasteners are removed and installed by using a **screwdriver**. Screwdrivers are available in many sizes and tip shapes. The most commonly used screwdriver is called a **flat tip** or **straight blade**.

Flat-tip screwdrivers are sized by the width of the blade and this width should match the width of the slot in the screw. ● **SEE FIGURE 4–17**.

CAUTION: Do not use a screwdriver as a pry tool or as a chisel. Always use the proper tool for each application.

Another type of commonly used screwdriver is called a Phillips screwdriver, named for Henry F. Phillips, who invented the crosshead screw in 1934. Due to the shape of the crosshead screw and screwdriver, a Phillips screw can be driven with more torque than can be achieved with a slotted screw.

A Phillips head screwdriver is specified by the length of the handle and the size of the point at the tip. A #1 tip has a sharp point, a #2 tip is the most commonly used, and a #3 tip is blunt and is only used for larger sizes of Phillips head fasteners. For example, a #2 × 3 inch Phillips screwdriver would typically measure 6 inch from the tip of the blade to the end of the handle (3 inch long handle and 3 inch long blade) with a #2 tip.

FIGURE 4–18 Two stubby screwdrivers that are used to access screws that have limited space above. A straight blade is on top and a #2 Phillips screwdriver is on the bottom.

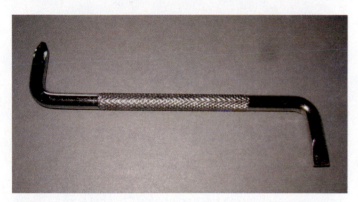

FIGURE 4–19 An offset screwdriver is used to install or remove fasteners that do not have enough space above to use a conventional screwdriver.

Both straight blade and Phillips screwdrivers are available with a short blade and handle for access to fasteners with limited room. ● **SEE FIGURE 4–18.**

OFFSET SCREWDRIVERS Offset screwdrivers are used in places where a conventional screwdriver cannot fit. An offset screwdriver is bent at the ends and is used similar to a wrench. Most offset screwdrivers have a straight blade at one end and a Phillips end at the opposite end. ● **SEE FIGURE 4–19.**

IMPACT SCREWDRIVER An impact screwdriver is used to break loose or tighten a screw. A hammer is used to strike the end after the screwdriver holder is placed in the head of the screw and rotated in the desired direction. The force from the hammer blow does two things: It applies a force downward holding the tip of the screwdriver in the slot and then applies a twisting force to loosen (or tighten) the screw. ● **SEE FIGURE 4–20.**

SAFE USE OF SCREWDRIVERS. Always use the proper type and size screwdriver that matches the fastener. Try to avoid pressing down on a screwdriver because if it slips, the screwdriver tip could go into your hand, causing serious personal injury. All screwdrivers should be cleaned after use. Do not use a screwdriver as a pry bar; always use the correct tool for the job.

FIGURE 4–20 An impact screwdriver used to remove slotted or Phillips head fasteners that cannot be broken loose using a standard screwdriver.

FIGURE 4–21 A typical ball-peen hammer.

? **FREQUENTLY ASKED QUESTION**

What is a Torx?
TORX–A Torx is a six-pointed star shaped tip that was developed by Camcar (formerly Textron) to offer higher loosening and tightening torque than is possible with a straight (flat tip) or Phillips. Torx is very commonly used in the automotive field for many components.

Commonly used Torx sizes from small to large include: T15, T20, T25, and T30. Some Torx fasteners include a round projection in the center requiring that a special version of a Torx bit be used. These are called security Torx bits that have a hole in the center to be used on these fasteners. External Torx fasteners are also used mostly as engine fasteners and are labeled E instead of T plus the size, such as E45.

HAMMERS AND MALLETS

HAMMERS Hammers and mallets are used to force objects together or apart. The shape of the back part of the hammer head (called the *peen*) usually determines the name. For example, a ball-peen hammer has a rounded end like a ball and it is used to straighten oil pans and valve covers, using the hammer head, and for shaping metal, using the ball peen. ● **SEE FIGURE 4–21.**

FIGURE 4–22 A rubber mallet used to deliver a force to an object without harming the surface.

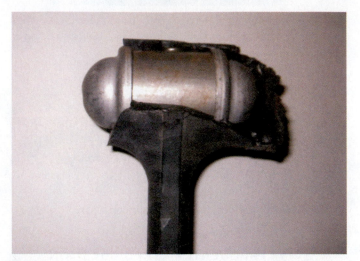

FIGURE 4–23 A dead-blow hammer that was left outside in freezing weather. The plastic covering was damaged, which destroyed this hammer. The lead shot is encased in the metal housing and then covered.

NOTE: A claw hammer has a claw used to remove nails and is not used for automotive service.

A hammer is usually sized by the weight of the head of the hammer and the length of the handle. For example, a commonly used ball-peen hammer has an 8 oz head with an 11 inch handle.

MALLETS Mallets are a type of hammer with a large striking surface, which allows the technician to exert force over a larger area than a hammer, so as not to harm the part or component. Mallets are made from a variety of materials including rubber, plastic, or wood. ● **SEE FIGURE 4–22.**

A shot-filled plastic hammer is called a **dead-blow hammer**. The small lead balls (shot) inside a plastic head prevent the hammer from bouncing off of the object when struck. ● **SEE FIGURE 4–23.**

SAFE USE OF HAMMERS AND MALLETS. All mallets and hammers should be cleaned after use and not exposed to extreme temperatures. Never use a hammer or mallet that is damaged in any way and always use caution to avoid doing damage to the components and the surrounding area. Always follow the hammer manufacturer's recommended procedures and practices.

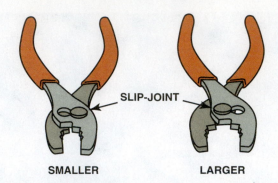

FIGURE 4–24 Typical slip-joint pliers, which are also common household pliers. The slip joint allows the jaws to be opened to two different settings.

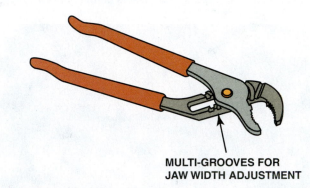

FIGURE 4–25 Multigroove adjustable pliers are known by many names, including the trade name Channel Locks.

PLIERS

SLIP-JOINT PLIERS Pliers are capable of holding, twisting, bending, and cutting objects and are an extremely useful classification of tools. The common household type of pliers is called the **slip-joint pliers**. There are two different positions where the junction of the handles meets to achieve a wide range of sizes of objects that can be gripped. ● **SEE FIGURE 4–24.**

MULTIGROOVE ADJUSTABLE PLIERS For gripping larger objects, a set of **multigroove adjustable pliers** is a commonly used tool of choice by many service technicians. Originally designed to remove the various size nuts holding rope seals used in water pumps, the name **water pump pliers** is also used. ● **SEE FIGURE 4–25.**

LINESMAN'S PLIERS Linesman's pliers are specifically designed for cutting, bending, and twisting wire. While commonly used by construction workers and electricians, linesman's pliers are very useful tools for the service technician who deals with wiring. The center parts of the jaws are designed to grasp round objects such as pipe or tubing without slipping. ● **SEE FIGURE 4–26.**

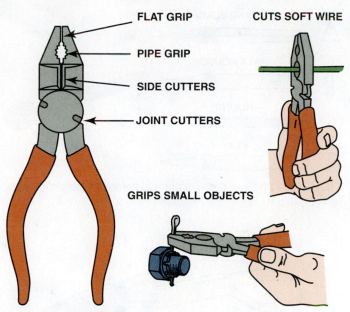

FLAT GRIP
PIPE GRIP
SIDE CUTTERS
JOINT CUTTERS

CUTS SOFT WIRE

GRIPS SMALL OBJECTS

FIGURE 4–26 A linesman's pliers are very useful because they can help perform many automotive service jobs.

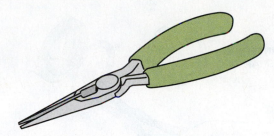

FIGURE 4–28 Needle-nose pliers are used where there is limited access to a wire or pin that needs to be installed or removed.

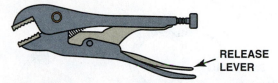

RELEASE LEVER

FIGURE 4–29 Locking pliers are best known by their trade name Vise-Grip®.

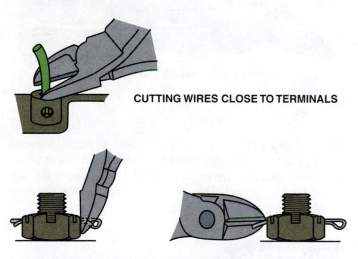

CUTTING WIRES CLOSE TO TERMINALS

PULLING OUT AND SPREADING COTTER PIN

FIGURE 4–27 Diagonal-cut pliers are another common tool that has many names.

🔧 **TECH TIP**

Brand Name Versus Proper Term

Technicians often use slang or brand names of tools rather than the proper term. This results in some confusion for new technicians. Some examples are given in the following table.

Brand Name	Proper Term	Slang Name
Crescent wrench	Adjustable wrench	Monkey wrench
Vise Grip	Locking pliers	
Channel Locks	Water pump pliers or multigroove adjustable pliers	Pump pliers
	Diagonal cutting pliers	Dikes or side cuts

DIAGONAL PLIERS **Diagonal pliers** are designed for cutting only. The cutting jaws are set at an angle to make it easier to cut wires. Diagonal pliers are also called **side cuts** or **dikes.** These pliers are constructed of hardened steel and they are used mostly for cutting wire. ● SEE FIGURE 4–27.

NEEDLE-NOSE PLIERS **Needle-nose pliers** are designed to grip small objects or objects in tight locations. Needle-nose pliers have long, pointed jaws, which allow the tips to reach into narrow openings or groups of small objects. ● SEE FIGURE 4–28.

Most needle-nose pliers have a wire cutter located at the base of the jaws near the pivot. There are several variations of

needle-nose pliers, including right angle jaws or slightly angled to allow access to certain cramped areas.

LOCKING PLIERS **Locking pliers** are adjustable pliers that can be locked to hold objects from moving. Most locking pliers also have wire cutters built into the jaws near the pivot point. Locking pliers come in a variety of styles and sizes and are commonly referred to by their trade name **Vise-Grip®**. The size is the length of the pliers, not how far the jaws open. ● SEE FIGURE 4–29.

SAFE USE OF PLIERS. Pliers should not be used to remove any bolt or other fastener. Pliers should only be used when specified for use by the vehicle manufacturer.

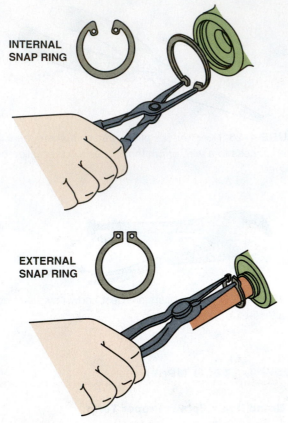

INTERNAL SNAP RING

EXTERNAL SNAP RING

FIGURE 4–30 Snap-ring pliers are also called lock-ring pliers and are designed to remove internal and external snap rings (lock rings).

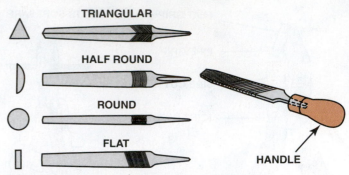

TRIANGULAR

HALF ROUND

ROUND

FLAT

HANDLE

FIGURE 4–31 Files come in many different shapes and sizes. Never use a file without a handle.

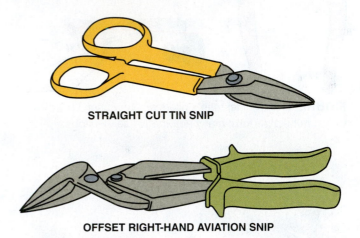

STRAIGHT CUT TIN SNIP

OFFSET RIGHT-HAND AVIATION SNIP

FIGURE 4–32 Tin snips are used to cut thin sheets of metal or carpet.

TECH TIP

Use Chalk

Often soft metal particles can become stuck in a file, especially when using it to file aluminum or other soft metals. Rub some chalk into the file before using it to prevent this from happening.

SNAP-RING PLIERS **Snap-ring pliers** are used to remove and install snap rings. Many snap-ring pliers are designed to be able to remove and install inward, as well as outward, expanding snap rings. Snap-ring pliers can be equipped with serrated-tipped jaws for grasping the opening in the snap ring, while others are equipped with points, which are inserted into the holes in the snap ring. ● **SEE FIGURE 4–30.**

FILES **Files** are used to smooth metal and are constructed of hardened steel with diagonal rows of teeth. Files are available with a single row of teeth called a **single-cut file**, as well as two rows of teeth cut at an opposite angle called a **double-cut file**. Files are available in a variety of shapes and sizes from small flat files, half-round files, and triangular files. ● **SEE FIGURE 4–31.**

SAFE USE OF FILES. Always use a file with a handle. Because files only cut when moved forward, a handle must be attached to prevent possible personal injury. After making a forward strike, lift the file and return the file to the starting position; avoid dragging the file backward.

CUTTERS

SNIPS Service technicians are often asked to fabricate sheet metal brackets or heat shields and need to use one or more types of cutters available. The simplest is called **tin snips**, which are designed to make straight cuts in a variety of materials, such as sheet steel, aluminum, or even fabric. A variation of the tin snips is called **aviation tin snips**. There are three designs of aviation snips including one designed to cut straight (called a **straight cut aviation snip**), one designed to cut left (called an **offset left aviation snip**), and one designed to cut right (called an offset right aviation snip). The handles are color coded for easy identification. These include yellow for straight, red for left, and green for right. ● **SEE FIGURE 4–32.**

UTILITY KNIFE A **utility knife** uses a replaceable blade and is used to cut a variety of materials such as carpet, plastic, wood, and paper products, such as cardboard. ● **SEE FIGURE 4–33.**

FIGURE 4–33 A utility knife uses replaceable blades and is used to cut carpet and other materials.

FIGURE 4–34 A punch used to drive pins from assembled components. This type of punch is also called a pin punch.

PIN

FIGURE 4–35 Warning stamped in the side of a punch warning that goggles should be worn when using this tool. Always follow safety warnings.

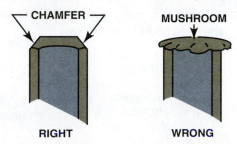

CHAMFER   MUSHROOM

RIGHT   WRONG

FIGURE 4–36 Use a grinder or a file to remove the mushroom material on the end of a punch or chisel.

SAFE USE OF CUTTERS. Whenever using cutters, always wear eye protection or a face shield to guard against the possibility of metal pieces being ejected during the cut. Always follow recommended procedures.

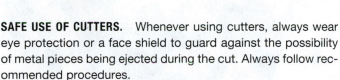

PUNCHES AND CHISELS

PUNCHES A **punch** is a small diameter steel rod that has a smaller diameter ground at one end. A punch is used to drive a pin out that is used to retain two components. Punches come in a variety of sizes, which are measured across the diameter of the machined end. Sizes include 1/16 inch, 1/8 inch, 3/16 inch, and 1/4 inch ● **SEE FIGURE 4–34.**

CHISELS A **chisel** has a straight, sharp cutting end that is used for cutting off rivets or to separate two pieces of an assembly. The most common design of chisel used for automotive service work is called a **cold chisel**.

SAFE USE OF PUNCHES AND CHISELS. Always wear eye protection when using a punch or a chisel because the hardened steel is brittle and parts of the punch could fly off and cause serious personal injury. See the warning stamped on the side of this automotive punch in ● **SEE FIGURE 4–35.**

Punches and chisels can also have the top rounded off, which is called "mushroomed." This material must be ground off to help avoid the possibility that the overhanging material is loosened and becomes airborne during use. ● **SEE FIGURE 4–36.**

REMOVERS

Removers are tools used to remove damaged fasteners. A remover tool is not normally needed during routine service unless the fastener is corroded or has been broken or damaged by a previous attempt to remove the bolt or nut.

To help prevent the need for a remover tool, all rusted and corroded fasteners should be sprayed with penetrating oil. Penetrating oil is a low viscosity oil that is designed to flow in between the threads of a fastener or other small separation between two parts. Commonly used penetrating oils include WD-40®, Kroil®, and CRC 5-56.

CAUTION: Do not use penetrating oil as a lubricating oil because it is volatile and will evaporate soon after usage leaving little lubricant behind for protection.

Removers are a classification of tool used to remove stuck or broken fasteners. Over time, rust and corrosion can cause the threads of the fastener to be attached to the nut or the casting making it very difficult to remove. There are several special tools that can be used to remove damaged fasteners. Which one to use depends on the type of damage.

DAMAGED HEADS If the bolt head or a nut becomes damaged or rounded, there are two special tools that can be used, including:

- **Stud remover.** A **stud removal tool** grips the part of the stud above the surface and uses a cam or wedge to grip

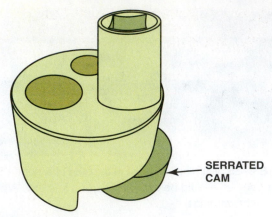

FIGURE 4–37 A stud remover uses an offset serrated wheel to grasp the stud so it will be rotated when a ratchet or breaker bar is used to rotate the assembly.

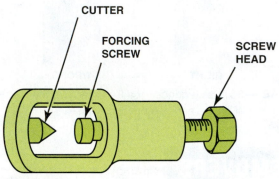

FIGURE 4–38 A nut splitter is used to split a nut that cannot be removed. After the nut has been split, a chisel is then used to remove the nut.

the stud as it is being rotated by a ratchet or breaker bar. ● **SEE FIGURE 4–37.**

- **Nut splitter.** A **nut splitter** is used to remove the nut by splitting it from the bolt. A nut splitter is used by inserting the cutter against a flat of the nut and tightening the threaded bolt of the splitter. The nut will be split away from the bolt and can then be removed. ● **SEE FIGURE 4–38.**

CAUTION: Do not rotate the entire nut splitter or damage to the cutting wedge will occur.

BROKEN BOLTS, STUDS, OR SCREWS
Often, bolts, studs, or screws break within the surface, making stud removal tools impossible to use. Bolt extractors are commonly called **easy outs**. An easy out is constructed of hardened steel with flutes or edges ground into the side in an opposite direction of most threads. ● **SEE FIGURE 4–39.**

NOTE: Always select the largest extractor that can be used to help avoid the possibility of breaking the extractor while attempting to remove the bolt.

A hole is drilled into the center of a broken bolt. Then, the extractor (easy out) is inserted into the hole and rotated

FIGURE 4–39 A set of bolt extractors, commonly called easy outs.

FIGURE 4–40 Removing plugs or bolts is easier if the plug is first heated to cherry red color, using a torch, and then applying wax. During cooling, the wax flows in between the threads, making it easier to remove.

TECH TIP

The Wax Trick

Many times rusted fasteners can be removed by using heat to expand the metal and break the rust bond between the fastener and the nut or casting. Many technicians heat the fastener using a torch and then apply paraffin wax or a candle to the heated fastener. ● **SEE FIGURE 4–40.** The wax will melt and as the part cools, will draw the liquid wax down between the threads. After allowing the part to cool, attempt to remove the fastener. It will often be removed without any trouble.

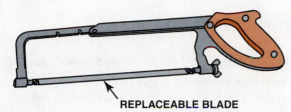

REPLACEABLE BLADE

FIGURE 4–41 A typical hacksaw that is used to cut metal. If cutting sheet metal or thin objects, a blade with more teeth should be used.

 FREQUENTLY ASKED QUESTION

I Broke Off an Easy Out—Now What?

An extractor (easy out) is hardened steel and removing this and the broken bolt is now a job for a professional machine shop. The part, which could be as large as an engine block, needs to be removed from the vehicle and taken to a machine shop that is equipped to handle this type of job. One method involves using an electrical discharge machine (EDM). An EDM uses a high amperage electrical current to produce thousands of arcs between the electrode and the broken tool. The part is submerged in a non-conducting liquid and each tiny spark vaporizes a small piece of the broken tool.

counterclockwise using a wrench. As the extractor rotates, the grooves grip tighter into the wall of the hole drilled in the broken bolt. As a result, most extractors are capable of removing most broken bolts.

HACKSAWS

A **hacksaw** is used to cut metals, such as steel, aluminum, brass, or copper. The cutting blade of a hacksaw is replaceable and the sharpness and number of teeth can be varied to meet the needs of the job. Use 14 or 18 teeth per inch (tpi) for cutting plaster or soft metals, such as aluminum and copper. Use 24 or 32 teeth per inch for steel or pipe. Hacksaw blades should be installed with the teeth pointing away from the handle. This means that a hacksaw cuts while the blade is pushed in the forward direction, and then pressure should be released as the blade is pulled rearward before repeating the cutting operation. ● **SEE FIGURE 4–41**.

SAFE USE OF HACKSAWS. Check that the hacksaw is equipped with the correct blade for the job and that the teeth are pointed away from the handle. When using a hacksaw, move the hacksaw slowly away from you, then lift slightly and return for another cut.

BASIC HAND TOOL LIST

Hand tools are used to turn fasteners (bolts, nuts, and screws). The following is a list of hand tools every automotive technician should possess. Specialty tools are not included.

Safety glasses

Tool chest

1/4 inch drive socket set (1/4 to 9/16 inch standard and deep sockets; 6 to 15 mm standard and deep sockets)

1/4 inch drive ratchet

1/4 inch drive 2 inch extension

1/4 inch drive 6 inch extension

1/4 inch drive handle

3/8 inch drive socket set (3/8 to 7/8 inch standard and deep sockets; 10 to 19 mm standard and deep sockets)

3/8 inch drive Torx set (T40, T45, T50, and T55)

3/8 inch drive 13/16 inch plug socket

3/8 inch drive 5/8 inch plug socket

3/8 inch drive ratchet

3/8 inch drive 1 1/2 inch extension

3/8 inch drive 3 inch extension

3/8 inch drive 6 inch extension

3/8 inch drive 18 inch extension

3/8 inch drive universal

1/2 inch drive socket set (1/2 to 1 inch standard and deep sockets; 9 to 19 mm standard and deep metric sockets)

1/2 inch drive ratchet

1/2 inch drive breaker bar

1/2 inch drive 5 inch extension

1/2 inch drive 10 inch extension

3/8 to 1/4 inch adapter

1/2 to 3/8 inch adapter

3/8 to 1/2 inch adapter

Crowfoot set (fractional inch)

Crowfoot set (metric)

3/8 through 1 inch combination wrench set

10 through 19 mm combination wrench set

1/16 through 1/4 inch hex (Allen) wrench set

2 through 12 mm hex (Allen) wrench set

3/8 inch hex socket

13 to 14 mm flare nut wrench

15 to 17 mm flare nut wrench

5/16 to 3/8 inch flare nut wrench

7/16 to 1/2 inch flare nut wrench

1/2 to 9/16 inch flare nut wrench

Diagonal pliers

Needle pliers

Hide Those from the Boss

An apprentice technician started working for a dealership and put his top tool box on a workbench. Another technician observed that, along with a complete set of good-quality tools, the box contained several adjustable wrenches. The more experienced technician said, "Hide those from the boss." If any adjustable wrench is used on a bolt or nut, the movable jaw often moves or loosens and starts to round the head of the fastener. If the head of the bolt or nut becomes rounded, it becomes that much more difficult to remove.

TECH TIP

Need to Borrow a Tool More than Twice? Buy It!

Most service technicians agree that it is okay for a beginning technician to borrow a tool occasionally. However, if a tool has to be borrowed more than twice, then be sure to purchase it as soon as possible. Also, whenever a tool is borrowed, be sure that you clean the tool and let the technician you borrowed the tool from know that you are returning the tool. These actions will help in any future dealings with other technicians.

Adjustable-jaw pliers

Locking pliers

Snap-ring pliers

Stripping or crimping pliers

Ball-peen hammer

Rubber hammer

Dead-blow hammer

Five-piece standard screwdriver set

Four-piece Phillips screwdriver set

#15 Torx screwdriver

#20 Torx screwdriver

File

Center punch

Pin punches (assorted sizes)

Chisel

Utility knife

Valve core tool

Filter wrench (large filters)

Filter wrench (smaller filters)

Test light

Feeler gauge

Scraper

Magnet

FIGURE 4–42 A typical beginning technician tool set that includes the basic tools to get started.

TOOL SETS AND ACCESSORIES

A beginning service technician may wish to start with a small set of tools before spending a lot of money on an expensive, extensive tool box. See ● **SEE FIGURES 4–42 AND 4–43**.

FIGURE 4–43 A typical large tool box, showing just one of many drawers.

TECH TIP

The Valve Grinding Compound Trick

Apply a small amount of valve grinding compound to a Phillips or Torx screw or bolt head. The gritty valve grinding compound "grips" the screwdriver or tool bit and prevents the tool from slipping up and out of the screw head. Valve grinding compound is available in a tube from most automotive parts stores.

FIGURE 4–44 A seal puller being used to remove a seal from a rear axle.

SEAL PULLERS AND DRIVERS

SEAL PULLERS Grease seals are located on many automotive components, including brake rotors, transmission housings, and differentials. A **seal puller** is used to properly remove grease seals, as shown in ● **SEE FIGURE 4–44**.

SEAL DRIVERS A **seal driver** can be either plastic or metal, usually aluminum, and is used to seat the outer lip of a grease seal into the grease seal pocket. A seal is usually driven into position using a plastic mallet and a seal driver that is the same size as the outside diameter of the grease seal retainer. ● **SEE FIGURE 4–45**.

ELECTRICAL HAND TOOLS

TEST LIGHTS A test light is used to test for electricity. A typical automotive test light consists of a clear plastic screwdriver-like handle that contains a light bulb. A wire is attached to one terminal of the bulb, which the technician connects to a clean metal part of the vehicle. The other end of the bulb is attached to a point that can be used to test for electricity at a connector or wire. When there is power at the point and a good connection at the other end, the light bulb lights. ● **SEE FIGURE 4–46**.

SOLDERING GUNS
- **Electric soldering gun.** This type of soldering gun is usually powered by 110 volt AC and often has two power settings expressed in watts. A typical electric soldering gun will produce from 85 to 300 watts of heat at the tip, which is more than adequate for soldering. ● **SEE FIGURE 4–47**.
- **Electric soldering pencil.** This type of soldering iron is less expensive and creates less heat than an electric

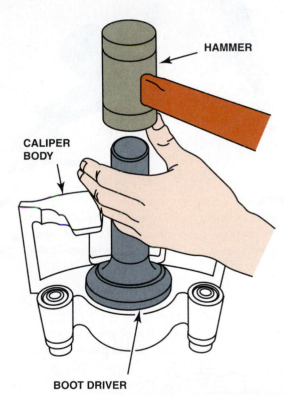

FIGURE 4–45 A seal driver or installer is usually plastic and is designed to seat the seal.

soldering gun. A typical electric soldering pencil (iron) creates 30 to 60 watts of heat and is suitable for soldering smaller wires and connections.
- **Butane-powered soldering iron.** A butane-powered soldering iron is portable and very useful for automotive service work because an electrical cord is not needed. Most butane-powered soldering irons produce about 60 watts of heat, which is enough for most automotive soldering.

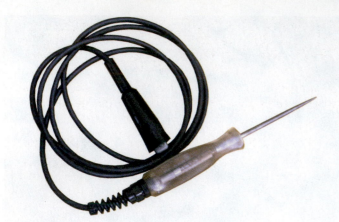

FIGURE 4–46 A typical 12 volt test light.

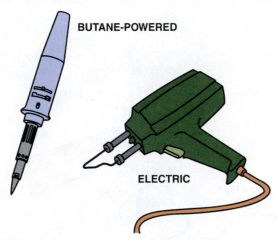

BUTANE-POWERED

ELECTRIC

FIGURE 4–47 An electric soldering gun used to make electrical repairs. Soldering guns are sold by the wattage rating. The higher the wattage, the greater amount of heat created. Most solder guns used for automotive electrical work usually fall within the 60 to 160 watt range.

In addition to a soldering iron, most service technicians who do electrical-related work should have the following:

- Wire cutters
- Wire strippers
- Wire crimpers
- Heat gun

A digital meter is a necessary tool for any electrical diagnosis and troubleshooting. A digital multimeter, abbreviated DMM, is usually capable of measuring the following units of electricity.

- DC volts
- AC volts
- Ohms
- Amperes

TECH TIP

It Just Takes a Second

Whenever removing any automotive component, it is wise to screw the bolts back into the holes a couple of threads by hand. This ensures that the right bolt will be used in its original location when the component or part is put back on the vehicle. Often, the same diameter of fastener is used on a component, but the length of the bolt may vary. Spending just a couple of seconds to put the bolts and nuts back where they belong when the part is removed can save a lot of time when the part is being reinstalled. Besides making certain that the right fastener is being installed in the right place, this method helps prevent bolts and nuts from getting lost or kicked away. How much time have you wasted looking for that lost bolt or nut?

SAFETY TIPS FOR USING HAND TOOLS

The following safety tips should be kept in mind whenever you are working with hand tools.

- Always *pull* a wrench toward you for best control and safety. Never push a wrench.
- Keep wrenches and all hand tools clean to help prevent rust and to allow for a better, firmer grip.
- Always use a six-point socket or a box-end wrench to break loose a tight bolt or nut.
- Use a box-end wrench for torque and an open-end wrench for speed.
- Never use a pipe extension or other type of "**cheater bar**" on a wrench or ratchet handle. If more force is required, use a larger tool or use penetrating oil and/or heat on the frozen fastener. (If heat is used on a bolt or nut to remove it, always replace it with a new part.)
- Always use the proper tool for the job. If a specialized tool is required, use the proper tool and do not try to use another tool improperly.
- Never expose any tool to excessive heat. High temperatures can reduce the strength ("draw the temper") of metal tools.
- Never use a hammer on any wrench or socket handle unless you are using a special "staking face" wrench designed to be used with a hammer.
- Replace any tools that are damaged or worn.

FIGURE 4–48 A binder clip being used to keep a fender cover from falling.

HAND TOOL MAINTENANCE

Most hand tools are constructed of rust-resistant metals but they can still rust or corrode if not properly maintained. For best results and long tool life, the following steps should be taken.

- Clean each tool before placing it back into the tool box.
- Keep tools separated. Moisture on metal tools will start to rust more readily if the tools are in contact with another metal tool.
- Line the drawers of the tool box with a material that will prevent the tools from moving as the drawers are opened and closed. This helps to quickly locate the proper tool and size.
- Release the tension on all "clicker-type" torque wrenches after use.
- Keep the tool box secure.

 TECH TIP

Use a Binder Clip

A binder clip (size 1 1/4 inch wide) is used by wise technicians to help keep fender covers in place.
● **SEE FIGURE 4–48.** Binder clips are found at office supply stores.

SUMMARY

1. Wrenches are available in open end, box end, and combination open and box end.
2. An adjustable wrench should only be used where the proper size is not available.
3. Line wrenches are also called flare-nut wrenches, fitting wrenches, or tube-nut wrenches and are used to remove fuel or refrigerant lines.
4. Sockets are rotated by a ratchet or breaker bar, also called a flex handle.
5. Torque wrenches measure the amount of torque applied to a fastener.
6. Screwdriver types include straight blade (flat tip) Torx, and Phillips.
7. Hammers and mallets come in a variety of sizes and weights.
8. Pliers are a useful tool and are available in many different types, including slip-joint, multigroove, linesman's, diagonal, needle-nose, and locking pliers.
9. Other common hand tools include snap-ring pliers, files, cutters, punches, chisels, and hacksaws.

REVIEW QUESTIONS

1. Why are wrenches offset 15 degrees?
2. What are the other names for a line wrench?
3. What are the standard automotive drive sizes for sockets?
4. Which type of screwdriver requires the use of a hammer or mallet?
5. What is inside a dead-blow hammer?
6. What type of cutter is available in left and right cutters?

1. When working with hand tools, always _____.
   a. Push the wrench—don't pull toward you
   b. Pull a wrench—don't push a wrench

2. The proper term for Channel Locks is _____.
   a. Vise Grips
   b. Crescent wrench
   c. Locking pliers
   d. Multigroove adjustable pliers

3. The proper term for Vise Grips is _____.
   a. Locking pliers
   b. Slip-joint pliers
   c. Side cuts
   d. Multigroove adjustable pliers

4. Which tool listed is a brand name?
   a. Locking pliers
   b. Monkey wrench
   c. Side cutters
   d. Vise Grips

5. Two technicians are discussing torque wrenches. Technician A says that a torque wrench is capable of tightening a fastener with more torque than a conventional breaker bar or ratchet. Technician B says that a torque wrench should be calibrated regularly for the most accurate results. Which technician is correct?
   a. Technician A only
   b. Technician B only
   c. Both Technicians A and B
   d. Neither Technician A nor B

6. What type of screwdriver should be used if there is very limited space above the head of the fastener?
   a. Offset screwdriver
   b. Stubby screwdriver
   c. Impact screwdriver
   d. Robertson screwdriver

7. Where is the "peen" of the hammer?
   a. The striking face
   b. The handle
   c. The back part opposite the striking face
   d. The part that connects to the handle

8. What type of hammer is plastic coated, has a metal casing inside, and is filled with small lead balls?
   a. Dead-blow hammer
   b. Soft-blow hammer
   c. Sledge hammer
   d. Plastic hammer

9. Which type of pliers is capable of fitting over a large object?
   a. Slip-joint pliers
   b. Linesman's pliers
   c. Locking pliers
   d. Multigroove adjustable pliers

10. Which tool has a replaceable cutting edge?
    a. Side-cut pliers
    b. Tin snips
    c. Utility knife
    d. Aviation snips

chapter 5

POWER TOOLS AND SHOP EQUIPMENT

LEARNING OBJECTIVES: After studying this chapter, the reader should be able to: • Describe the purpose of the air compressor, and other air and electrically operated tools. • Compare the different types of trouble lights. • Describe the purpose of the bench/pedestal grinder and the bench vise. • Discuss the purpose of hydraulic presses, portable crane and chain hoist, and engine stands.

KEY TERMS: Air-blow gun 51 • Air compressor 49 • Air drill 51 • Air ratchet 50 • Bearing splitter 53 • Bench grinder 52 • Bench vise 52 • Die grinder 51 • Engine stand 54 • Hydraulic press 53 • Impact wrench 50 • Incandescent light 51 • Light-emitting diode (LED) 52 • Portable crane 53 • Stone wheel 52 • Trouble light 51 • Wire brush wheel 52 • Work light 51

AIR COMPRESSOR

A shop air compressor is usually located in a separate room or an area away from the customer area of a shop. An **air compressor** is powered by a 220 V AC electric motor and includes a storage tank and the compressor itself, as well as the pressure switches, which are used to maintain a certain minimum level of air pressure in the system. The larger the storage tank, expressed in gallons, the longer an air tool can be operated in the shop without having the compressor start operating. ● **SEE FIGURE 5–1.**

SAFE USE OF COMPRESSED AIR. Air under pressure can create dangerous situations. For example, an object, such as a small piece of dirt, could be forced out of an air hose blow gun with enough force to cause serious personal injury. All OSHA-approved air nozzles have air vents drilled around the outside of the main discharge hole to help reduce the force of the air blast. Also, the air pressure used by an air nozzle (blow gun) must be kept to 30 PSI (207 kPa) or less. ● **SEE FIGURE 5–2.**

FIGURE 5–1 A typical shop compressor. It is usually placed out of the way, yet accessible to provide for maintenance to the unit.

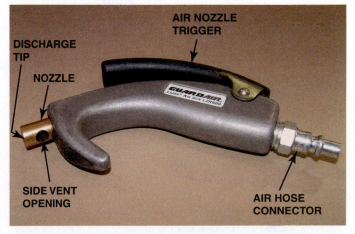

FIGURE 5–2 Always use an air nozzle that is OSHA approved. The openings in the side are used to allow air to escape if the nozzle tip were to become clogged.

In Figure 5–2, the labeled parts are:
- AIR NOZZLE TRIGGER
- DISCHARGE TIP
- NOZZLE
- SIDE VENT OPENING
- AIR HOSE CONNECTOR

FIGURE 5–3 A typical 1/2 inch drive impact wrench.

FIGURE 5–5 A typical battery-powered 3/8 inch drive impact wrench.

FIGURE 5–4 This impact wrench features a variable torque setting using a rotary knob. The direction of rotation can be changed by pressing the button at the bottom.

FIGURE 5–6 A black impact socket. Always use impact-type sockets whenever using an impact wrench to avoid the possibility of shattering the socket, which can cause personal injury.

AIR AND ELECTRICALLY OPERATED TOOLS

IMPACT WRENCH An **impact wrench**, either air (pneumatic) or electrically powered, is a tool that is used to remove and install fasteners. The air-operated 1/2 inch drive impact wrench is the most commonly used unit. ● SEE FIGURE 5–3.

The direction of rotation is controlled by a switch. ● SEE FIGURE 5–4.

Electrically powered impact wrenches commonly include:

- Battery-powered units. ● SEE FIGURE 5–5.
- 110-volt AC-powered units. This type of impact wrench is very useful, especially if compressed air is not readily available.

CAUTION: Always use impact sockets with impact wrenches, and be sure to wear eye protection in case the socket or fastener shatters. Impact sockets are thicker walled and constructed with premium alloy steel. They are hardened with a black oxide finish to help prevent corrosion and distinguish them from regular sockets. ● SEE FIGURE 5–6.

AIR RATCHET An **air ratchet** is used to remove and install fasteners that would normally be removed or installed using a ratchet and a socket. An air ratchet is much faster, yet has an air hose attached, which reduces accessibility to certain places. ● SEE FIGURE 5–7.

FIGURE 5–7 An air ratchet is a very useful tool that allows fast removal and installation of fasteners, especially in areas that are difficult to reach or do not have room enough to move a hand ratchet wrench.

 Real World Fix

The Case of the Rusty Air Impact Wrenches

In one busy shop, it was noticed by several technicians that water was being pumped through the air compressor lines and out of the vents of air impact wrenches whenever they were used. It is normal for moisture in the air to condense in the air storage tank of an air compressor. One of the routine service procedures is to drain the water from the air compressor. The water had been drained regularly from the air compressor at the rear of the shop, but the problem continued. Then someone remembered that there was a second air compressor mounted over the parts department. No one could remember ever draining the tank from that compressor. After that tank was drained, the problem of water in the lines was solved. The service manager assigned a person to drain the water from both compressors every day and to check the oil level. The oil in the compressor is changed every six months to help ensure long life of the expensive compressors.

DIE GRINDER A **die grinder** is a commonly used air-powered tool, which can also be used to sand or remove gaskets and rust. ● **SEE FIGURE 5–8.**

AIR DRILL An **air drill** is a drill that rotates faster than electric drills (up to 20,000 RPM). Air drills are commonly used in auto body work when many holes need to be drilled for plug welding.

AIR-BLOW GUN An **air-blow gun** is used to clean equipment and other purposes where a stream of air would be needed. Automotive air-blow guns should meet OSHA requirements and include passages to allow air to escape outward at the nozzle, thereby relieving pressure if the nozzle were to become blocked.

FIGURE 5–8 This typical die grinder surface preparation kit includes the air-operated die grinder, as well as a variety of sanding discs for smoothing surfaces or removing rust.

AIR-OPERATED GREASE GUN An air-operated grease gun uses shop air to operate a plunger, which then applies a force to the grease cartridge. Most air-operated grease guns use a 1/4 inch air inlet and operate on 90 PSI of air pressure.

BATTERY-POWERED GREASE GUN Battery-powered grease guns are more expensive than air-operated grease guns but offer the convenience of not having an air hose attached, making use easier. Many use rechargeable 14 to 18 volt batteries and use standard grease cartridges.

TROUBLE LIGHTS

INCANDESCENT **Incandescent lights** use a filament that produces light when electric current flows through the bulb. This was the standard **trouble light**, also called a **work light** for many years until safety issues caused most shops to switch to safer fluorescent or LED lights. If incandescent light bulbs are used, try to locate bulbs that are rated "rough service," which is designed to withstand shock and vibration more than conventional light bulbs.

 WARNING

Do not use incandescent trouble lights around gasoline or other flammable liquids. The liquids can cause the bulb to break and the hot filament can ignite the flammable liquid.

FIGURE 5–9 A fluorescent trouble light operates cooler and is safer to use in the shop because it is protected against accidental breakage where gasoline or other flammable liquids would happen to come in contact with the light.

FLUORESCENT A trouble light is an essential piece of shop equipment, and for safety, should be fluorescent rather than incandescent. Incandescent light bulbs can scatter or break if gasoline were to be splashed onto the bulb creating a serious fire hazard. Fluorescent light tubes are not as likely to be broken and are usually protected by a clear plastic enclosure. Trouble lights are usually attached to a retractor, which can hold 20 to 50 ft of electrical cord. ● **SEE FIGURE 5–9.**

LED TROUBLE LIGHT **Light-emitting diode (LED)** trouble lights are excellent to use because they are shock resistant, long lasting, and do not represent a fire hazard. Some trouble lights are battery powered and therefore can be used in places where an attached electrical cord could present problems.

BENCH/PEDESTAL GRINDER

A grinder can be mounted on a workbench or on a stand-alone pedestal.

BENCH- OR PEDESTAL-MOUNTED GRINDER These high-powered grinders can be equipped with a wire brush wheel and/or a stone wheel.

- A **wire brush wheel** is used to clean steel or sheet metal parts.
- A **stone wheel** is used to grind metal or to remove the mushroom from the top of punches or chisels. ● **SEE FIGURE 5–10.**

FIGURE 5–10 A typical pedestal grinder with a wire wheel on the left side and a stone wheel on the right side. Even though this machine is equipped with guards, safety glasses or a face shield should always be worn when using a grinder or wire wheel.

CAUTION: Always wear a face shield when using a wire wheel or a grinder. Also keep the part support ledge (table), also called a throat plate, within 1/16 inch (2 mm) of the stone.

Most **bench grinders** are equipped with a grinding wheel (stone) on one side and a wire brush wheel on the other side. A bench grinder is a very useful piece of shop equipment and the wire wheel end can be used for the following:

- Cleaning threads of bolts
- Cleaning gaskets from sheet metal parts, such as steel valve covers

CAUTION: Use a steel wire brush only on steel or iron components. If a steel wire brush is used on aluminum or copper-based metal parts, it can remove metal from the part.

The grinding stone end of the bench grinder can be used for the following:

- Sharpening blades and drill bits
- Grinding off the heads of rivets or parts
- Sharpening sheet metal parts for custom fitting

BENCH VISE

A **bench vise** is used to hold components so that work can be performed on the unit. The size of a vise is determined by the width of the jaws. Two common sizes of vises are 4 inch and 6 inch models. The jaws of most vises are serrated and can cause damage to some components unless protected. Many types of protection can be used, including aluminum or copper jaw covers or by simply placing wood between the vise jaws and the component being held. ● **SEE FIGURE 5–11.**

FIGURE 5–11 A typical vise mounted to a workbench.

SAFE USE OF VISES. The jaws of vises can cause damage to the part or component being held. Use pieces of wood or other soft material between the steel jaws and the workpiece to help avoid causing damage. Many vises are sold with optional aluminum jaw covers. When finished using a vise, be sure to close the jaws and place the handle straight up and down to help avoid personal injury to anyone walking near the vise.

HYDRAULIC PRESSES

Hydraulic presses are hand-operated hydraulic cylinders mounted to a stand and designed to press bearings on or off of shafts, as well as other components. To press off a bearing, a unit called a **bearing splitter** is often required to apply force to the inner race of a bearing. Hydraulic presses use a pressure gauge to show the pressure being applied. Always follow the operating instructions supplied by the manufacturer of the hydraulic press. ● SEE FIGURE 5–12.

PORTABLE CRANE AND CHAIN HOIST

A **portable crane** is used to remove and install engines and other heavy vehicle components. Most portable cranes use a hand-operated hydraulic cylinder to raise and lower a boom that is equipped with a nylon strap or steel chain. At the end of the strap or chain is a steel hook that is used to attach around a bracket or auxiliary lifting device. ● SEE FIGURE 5–13.

SAFE USE OF PORTABLE CRANES. Always be sure to attach the hook(s) of the portable crane to a secure location on the unit being lifted. The hook should also be attached to the center of the weight of the object so it can be lifted straight up without tilting.

FIGURE 5–12 A hydraulic press is usually used to press bearings on and off of rear axles and transmissions.

FIGURE 5–13 A typical portable crane used to lift and move heavy assemblies, such as engines and transmissions.

🔧 **TECH TIP**

Cover Work While Pressing

Whenever pressing on a bearing or other component, use an old brake drum over the shaft and the bearing. In the event the bearing shatters during the pressing operation, the brake drum will prevent the parts of the bearing from flying outward where they could cause serious personal injury.

FIGURE 5–14 Two engines on engine stands. The plastic bags over the engines help keep dirt from getting onto these engines and engine parts.

CAUTION: Always keep feet and other body parts out from underneath the engine or unit being lifted. Always work around a portable crane as if the chain or strap could break at any time.

ENGINE STANDS

An **engine stand** is designed to safely hold an engine and to allow it to be rotated. This allows the technician to easily remove, install, and perform service work to the engine. ● **SEE FIGURE 5–14.**

Most engine stands are constructed of steel and supported by four casters to allow easy movement. There are two basic places where an engine stand attaches to the engine depending on the size of the engine. For most engines and stands, the retaining bolts attach to the same location as the bell housing at the rear of the engine.

On larger engines, such as the 5.9 Cummins inline 6-cylinder diesel engine, the engine mounts to the stand using the engine mounting holes in the block. ● **SEE FIGURE 5–15.**

SAFE OPERATION OF AN ENGINE STAND. When mounting an engine to an engine stand, be sure that the engine is being supported by a portable crane. Be sure the attaching bolts are

FIGURE 5–15 An engine stand that grasps the engine from the sides rather than the end.

grade 5 or 8 and the same thread size as the threaded holes in the block. Check that there is at least 1/2 inch (13 mm) of bolt thread engaged in the threaded holes in the engine block. Be sure that all attaching bolts are securely tightened before releasing the weight of the engine from the crane. Use caution when loosening the rotation retaining bolts because the engine could rotate rapidly, causing personal injury.

CARE AND MAINTENANCE OF SHOP EQUIPMENT

All shop equipment should be maintained in safe working order. Maintenance of shop equipment usually includes the following operations or procedures.

- **Keep equipment clean.** Dirt and grime can attract and hold moisture, which can lead to rust and corrosion. Oil or grease can attract dirt.
- **Keep equipment lubricated.** While many bearings are sealed and do not require lubrication, always check the instructions for the use of the equipment for suggested lubrication and other service procedures.

CAUTION: Always follow the instructions from the equipment manufacturer regarding proper use and care of the equipment.

1 Inspect the cart and make sure the tanks are chained properly before moving it to the work location.

2 Start by attaching the appropriate work tip to the torch handle. The fitting should only be tightened hand tight. Make sure the valves on the torch handle are closed at this time.

3 Each tank has a regulator assembly with two gauges. The high pressure gauge shows tank pressure, and the low pressure gauge indicates working pressure.

4 Open the oxygen tank valve fully open, and open the acetylene tank valve 1/2 turn.

5 Open the oxygen valve on the torch handle 1/4 turn in preparation for adjusting oxygen gas pressure.

6 Turn the oxygen regulator valve clockwise and adjust oxygen gas pressure to 20 PSI. Close the oxygen valve on the torch handle.

CONTINUED ▶

7 Open the acetylene valve on the torch handle 1/4 turn and adjust acetylene gas pressure to 7 PSI. Close the acetylene valve on the torch handle.

8 Open the oxygen valve on the torch handle 1/4 turn and use an appropriate size tip cleaner to clean the tip orifice. Finish by closing the oxygen valve.

9 Put on leather gloves and open the acetylene valve on the torch handle 1/4 turn. Use a flint striker to ignite the acetylene gas exiting the torch tip.

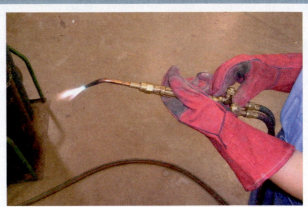

10 Adjust the acetylene valve until the base of the flame just touches the torch tip. Slowly open the oxygen valve on the torch handle and adjust for a neutral flame (blue cone is well-defined).

11 Once work is complete, extinguish the flame by quickly closing the acetylene valve on the torch handle. Be prepared to hear a loud "pop" when the flame goes out. Close the oxygen valve on the torch handle.

12 Close the valves on both tanks and turn the regulator handles CCW until they no longer contact the internal springs. Open the gas valves briefly on the torch handle to release gas pressure from the hoses. Close the gas valves on the torch handle and put away the torch assembly.

13 Heating attachments include ordinary heating tips, middle and right and a "rosebud" (left). Ordinary heating tips work fine for most purposes, but occasionally the rosebud is utilized when a great deal of heat is needed.

14 Note that while acetylene tank pressures are relatively low, the oxygen tank can be filled to over 2,000 PSI. This can represent a serious hazard if precautions are not taken. Be absolutely certain that the tanks are chained properly to the cart before attempting to move it!

15 Any time heating or cutting operations are being performed, be sure that any flammables have been removed from the immediate area. A fire blanket may be placed over floor drains or other objects to prevent fires. A fire extinguisher should be on hand in case of an emergency.

16 Be sure to wear appropriate personal protective equipment during heating and cutting operations.

17 Note that heating operations should be performed over steel or firebrick. Never heat or cut steel close to concrete, as it could cause the concrete to explode.

18 When heating steel, move the torch in a circular pattern to prevent melting of the metal. Don't hold the torch too close to the work as this will cause a "snapping" or "backfire" that can extinguish the flame.

CONTINUED ▶

19 Affix the cutting attachment to the torch handle. Note that the cutting attachment has a cutting handle and a separate oxygen valve.

20 Fully open the oxygen valve on the torch handle. Oxygen flow will now be controlled with the valve on the cutting attachment.

21 Oxygen gas pressure should be adjusted to 30 PSI whenever using the cutting attachment. Acetylene pressure is kept at 7 PSI.

22 Open the acetylene valve on the torch handle 1/4 turn and light the torch. Adjust the flame until its base just touches the cutting tip. Slowly open the oxygen valve on the cutting attachment and adjust the flame until the blue cone is well-defined.

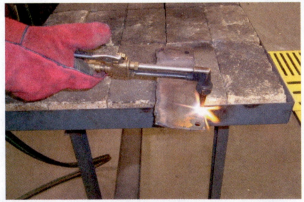

23 Direct the flame onto a thin spot or sharp edge of the metal to be cut. This will build the heat quicker in order to get the cut started.

24 When the metal glows red, depress the cutting handle and move the torch to advance the cut. You will need to move the torch faster when cutting thinner pieces of steel. On thicker pieces, point the cutting tip into the direction of the cut.

SUMMARY

1. Most shops are equipped with a large air compressor that supplies pressurized air to all stalls for use by the technician.

2. An air impact wrench is the most commonly used power tool in the shop. It is used mostly to remove fasteners. Caution should be exercised not to overtighten a fastener, using an air impact wrench.

3. Other air-operated tools include an air ratchet and a die grinder.

4. A bench or pedestal grinder usually has both a grinding stone and a wire brush wheel.

5. Trouble lights should be fluorescent or LED for maximum safety in the shop.

6. A hydraulic press is used to remove bearings from shafts and other similar operations.

7. A portable crane is used to remove and install engines or engine/transmission assemblies from vehicles.

8. Engine stands are designed to allow the technician to rotate the engine to get access to the various parts and components.

REVIEW QUESTIONS

1. List the tools used by service technicians that use compressed air?

2. Which trouble light design(s) is (are) the recommended type for maximum safety?

3. What safety precautions should be adhered to when working with a vise?

4. When using a blow gun, what precautions need to be taken?

CHAPTER QUIZ

1. When using compressed air and a blow gun, what is the maximum allowable air pressure?
   a. 10 PSI
   b. 20 PSI
   c. 30 PSI
   d. 40 PSI

2. Which air impact drive size is the most commonly used?
   a. 1/4 inch
   b. 3/8 inch
   c. 1/2 inch
   d. 3/4 inch

3. What type of socket should be used with an air impact wrench?
   a. Black
   b. Chrome
   c. 12 point
   d. Either a or b

4. What can be used to cover the jaws of a vise to help protect the object being held?
   a. Aluminum
   b. Wood
   c. Copper
   d. All of the above

5. Technician A says that impact sockets have thicker walls than conventional sockets. Technician B says that impact sockets have a black oxide finish. Which technician is correct?
   a. Technician A only
   b. Technician B only
   c. Both Technicians A and B
   d. Neither Technician A nor B

6. Two technicians are discussing the use of a typical bench/pedestal-mounted grinder. Technician A says that a wire brush wheel can be used to clean threads. Technician B says that the grinding stone can be used to clean threads. Which technician is correct?
   a. Technician A only
   b. Technician B only
   c. Both Technicians A and B
   d. Neither Technician A nor B

7. A hydraulic press is being used to separate a bearing from a shaft. What should be used to cover the bearing during the pressing operation?
   a. Shop cloth
   b. Brake drum
   c. Fender cover
   d. Paper towel

8. Which type of trouble light is recommended for use in the shop?
   a. Incandescent
   b. Fluorescent
   c. LED
   d. Either b or c

9. When mounting an engine to an engine stand, what grade of bolt should be used?
   a. 5 or 8
   b. 4 or 7
   c. 3 or 5
   d. 1 or 4

10. Proper care of shop equipment includes _____.
    a. Tuning up every six months
    b. Keeping equipment clean
    c. Keeping equipment lubricated
    d. Both b and c

chapter 6

VEHICLE LIFTING AND HOISTING

LEARNING OBJECTIVES: After studying this chapter, the reader should be able to: • Discuss the purpose of floor jacks and creepers. • Describe vehicle hoists and drive-on ramps, and discus the proper methods to follow to safely hoist a vehicle.

KEY TERMS: Creeper 60 • Floor jack 60 • Jack stands 60 • Safety stands 60

FLOOR JACK

A **floor jack** is a hand-operated hydraulic device that is used to lift vehicles or components, such as engines, transmissions, and rear axle assemblies. Most floor jacks use four casters, which allow the jack to be easily moved around the shop. ● **SEE FIGURE 6-1.**

SAFE USE OF FLOOR JACKS. Floor jacks are used to lift a vehicle or major vehicle component, but they are not designed to hold a load. Therefore **safety stands**, also called **jack stands** should always be used to support the vehicle. After the floor jack has lifted the vehicle, safety stands should be placed under the vehicle, and then, using the floor jack, lowered onto the safety stands. The floor jack can be lifted in position as another safety device but the load should be removed from the floor jack. If a load is retained on the floor jack, hydraulic fluid can leak past seals in the hydraulic cylinders, which would lower the vehicle, possibly causing personal injury. ● **SEE FIGURE 6-2.**

CREEPERS

When working underneath a vehicle, most service technicians use a **creeper**, which consists of a flat or concaved surface equipped with low-profile casters. A creeper allows the technician to maneuver under the vehicle easily.

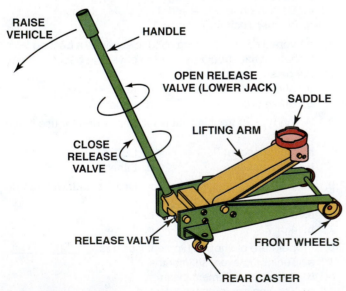

FIGURE 6-1 A hydraulic hand-operated floor jack.

FIGURE 6-2 Safety stands are being used to support the rear of this vehicle. Notice a creeper also.

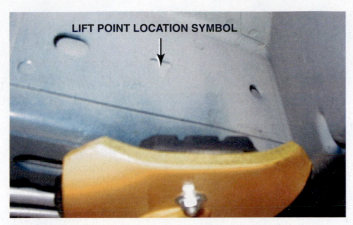

LIFT POINT LOCATION SYMBOL

FIGURE 6–3 Most newer vehicles have a triangle symbol indicating the recommended hoisting lift points.

SAFE USE OF CREEPERS Creepers can create a fall hazard if left on the floor. When a creeper is not being used, it should be picked up and placed vertically against a wall or tool box to help prevent accidental falls.

VEHICLE HOISTS

Vehicle hoists include older in ground pneumatic/hydraulic (air pressure over hydraulic) and above ground units. Most of the vehicle hoists used today use an electric motor to pressurize hydraulic fluid, which lifts the vehicle using hydraulic cylinders. Hoists are rated by the maximum weight that they can safely lift, such as 7,000 to 12,000 or more. Hoists can also have equal length arms or can be equipped with different length arms allowing the vehicle to be set so the doors can be opened and not hit the center support column. Many chassis and underbody service procedures require that the vehicle be hoisted or lifted off the ground. The simplest methods involve the use of drive-on ramps or a floor jack and safety (jack) stands, whereas in ground or surface-mounted lifts provide greater access.

SETTING THE PADS IS A CRITICAL PART OF THIS PROCEDURE

All automobile and light-truck service manuals include recommended locations to be used when hoisting (lifting) a vehicle. Some vehicles have a decal on the driver's door indicating the recommended lift points. The recommended standards for the lift points and lifting procedures are found in SAE Standard JRP-2184. ● **SEE FIGURE 6–3.**

These recommendations typically include the following points.

1. The vehicle should be centered on the lift or hoist so as not to overload one side or put too much force either forward or rearward. Use tall safety stands if a major component is

(a)

(b)

FIGURE 6–4 (a) Tall safety stands can be used to provide additional support for a vehicle while on a hoist. (b) A block of wood should be used to avoid the possibility of doing damage to components supported by the stand.

going to be removed from the vehicle, such as the engine, to help support the vehicle. ● **SEE FIGURE 6–4.**

2. The pads of the lift should be spread as far apart as possible to provide a stable platform.

3. Each pad should be placed under a portion of the vehicle that is strong and capable of supporting the weight of the vehicle.

   a. Pinch welds at the bottom edge of the body are generally considered to be strong.

FIGURE 6–5 This training vehicle fell from the hoist when the pads were not set correctly. No one was hurt, but the vehicle was damaged.

CAUTION: Even though pinch weld seams are the recommended location for hoisting many vehicles with unitized bodies (unit-body), care should be taken not to place the pad(s) too far forward or rearward. Incorrect placement of the vehicle on the lift could cause the vehicle to be imbalanced, and the vehicle could fall. This is exactly what happened to the vehicle in ● SEE FIGURE 6–5.

   b. Boxed areas of the body are the best places to position the pads on a vehicle without a frame. Be careful to note whether the arms of the lift might come into contact with other parts of the vehicle before the pad touches the intended location. Commonly damaged areas include the following:

   1. Rocker panel moldings
   2. Exhaust system (including catalytic converter)
   3. Tires or body panels. ● SEE FIGURES 6–6 AND 6–7.

(a)

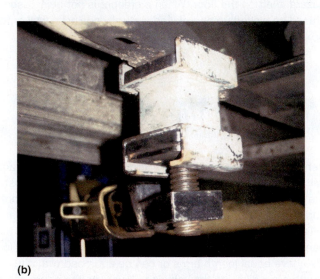

(b)

FIGURE 6–6 (a) An assortment of hoist pad adapters that are often necessary to safely hoist many pickup trucks, vans, and sport utility vehicles. (b) A view from underneath a Chevrolet pickup truck showing how the pad extensions are used to attach the hoist lifting pad to contact the frame.

(a)

(b)

FIGURE 6–7 (a) In this photo the pad arm is just contacting the rocker panel of the vehicle. (b) This photo shows what can occur if the technician places the pad too far inward underneath the vehicle. The arm of the hoist has dented in the rocket panel.

4. As soon as the pads touch the vehicle, check for proper pad placement. The vehicle should be raised about 1 ft (30 cm) off the floor, then stopped and shaken to check for stability. If the vehicle seems to be stable when checked at a short distance from the floor, continue raising the vehicle and continue to view the vehicle until it has reached the desired height. The hoist should be lowered onto the mechanical locks, and then raised off of the locks before lowering.

CAUTION: Do not look away from the vehicle while it is being raised (or lowered) on a hoist. Often one side or one end of the hoist can stop or fail, resulting in the vehicle being slanted enough to slip or fall.

NOTE: Most hoists can be safely placed at any desired height as long as it is high enough for the safety latches to engage. For ease while working, the area in which you are working should be at chest level. When working on brakes or suspension components, it is not necessary to work on them down near the floor or over your head. Raise the hoist so that the components are at chest level.

5. Before lowering the hoist, the safety latch(es) must be released and the direction of the controls reversed. The speed downward is often adjusted to be as slow as possible for additional safety.

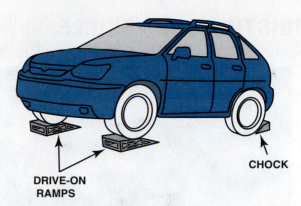

DRIVE-ON RAMPS

CHOCK

FIGURE 6–8 Drive-on-type ramps. The wheels on the ground level *must* be chocked (blocked) to prevent accidental movement down the ramp.

DRIVE-ON RAMPS

Ramps are an inexpensive way to raise the front or rear of a vehicle. ● **SEE FIGURE 6–8.** Ramps are easy to store, but they can be dangerous because they can "kick out" when driving the vehicle onto the ramps.

CAUTION: Professional repair shops do not use ramps because they are dangerous to use. Use only with extreme care.

HOISTING THE VEHICLE

1 The first step in hoisting a vehicle is to properly align the vehicle in the center of the stall.

2 Most vehicles will be correctly positioned when the left front tire is centered on the tire pad.

3 The arms can be moved in and out and most pads can be rotated to allow for many different types of vehicle construction.

4 Most lifts are equipped with short pad extensions that are often necessary to use to allow the pad to contact the frame of a vehicle without causing the arm of the lift to hit and damage parts of the body.

5 Tall pad extensions can also be used to gain access to the frame of a vehicle. This position is needed to safely hoist many pickup trucks, vans, and sport utility vehicles.

6 An additional extension may be necessary to hoist a truck or van equipped with running boards to give the necessary clearance.

7 Position the pads under the vehicle under the recommended locations.

8 After being sure all pads are correctly positioned, use the electromechanical controls to raise the vehicle.

9 With the vehicle raised one foot (30 cm) off the ground, push down on the vehicle to check to see if it is stable on the pads. If the vehicle rocks, lower the vehicle and reset the pads. The vehicle can be raised to any desired working level. Be sure the safety is engaged before working on or under the vehicle.

10 If raising a vehicle without a frame, place the flat pads under the pinch weld seam to spread the load. If additional clearance is necessary, the pads can be raised as shown.

11 When the service work is completed, the hoist should be raised slightly and the safety released before using the hydraulic to lower the vehicle.

12 After lowering the vehicle, be sure all arms of the lift are moved out of the way before driving the vehicle out of the work stall.

1. Whenever a vehicle is raised off the ground using a floor jack, it must be supported using safety stands.
2. Creepers should be stored vertically to prevent the possibility of stepping on it, which could cause a fall and personal injury.
3. Always adhere to the specified hoisting locations as found in service information.
4. Adapters or extensions are often needed when hoisting pickup trucks or vans.

REVIEW QUESTIONS

1. Why must safety stands be used after lifting a vehicle with a floor jack?
2. What precautions should be adhered to when storing a creeper?
3. What precautions should be adhered to when hoisting a vehicle?

CHAPTER QUIZ

1. A safety stand is also called a _____.
   a. Jack
   b. Jack stand
   c. Bottle jack
   d. Safety stool

2. A creeper should be stored _____.
   a. Vertically
   b. Under a vehicle
   c. Flat on the floor
   d. Upside down on the floor

3. The SAE standard for hoist location is _____.
   a. J-1980
   b. SAE-2009
   c. JRP-2184
   d. J-14302

4. Tall safety stands would be used to _____.
   a. Help support the vehicle when a major component is removed from the vehicle.
   b. Lift a vehicle
   c. Lift a component such as an engine high off the ground
   d. Both b and c

5. Commonly damaged areas of a vehicle during hoisting include _____.
   a. Rocker panels
   b. Exhaust systems
   c. Tires or body panels
   d. All of the above

6. Pad extensions may be needed when hoisting what type of vehicle?
   a. Small cars
   b. Pickup trucks
   c. Vans
   d. Either b or c

7. Technician A says that a hoist can be stopped at any level as long as the safety latch engages. Technician B says that the vehicle should be hoisted to the top of the hoist travel for safety. Which technician is correct?
   a. Technician A only
   b. Technician B only
   c. Both Technicians A and B
   d. Neither Technician A nor B

8. Before lowering the vehicle, what should the technician do?
   a. Be sure nothing is underneath the vehicle
   b. Raise the vehicle enough to release the safety latch
   c. Be sure no one will be walking under or near the vehicle
   d. All of the above

9. Technician A says that a creeper should be stored vertically. Technician B says that a creeper should be stored on its casters. Which technician is correct?
   a. Technician A only
   b. Technician B only
   c. Both Technicians A and B
   d. Neither Technician A nor B

10. When checking for stability, how high should the vehicle be raised?
    a. About 2 inch (5 cm)
    b. About 6 inch (15 cm)
    c. About 1 ft (30 cm)
    d. About 3 ft (91 cm)

chapter 7

MEASURING SYSTEMS AND TOOLS

LEARNING OBJECTIVES: **After studying this chapter, the reader should be able to:** • Compare the English customary measuring system and the metric system of measure. • Discuss the purpose of tape measures, micrometers, and depth micrometers. • Discuss the purpose of telescopic gauges, small-hole gauges, and vermier dial calipers. • Discuss the purpose of the straightedges, dial indicators, feeler gauges, and dial bore gauges.

KEY TERMS: Feeler gauge 73 • Sleeve 68 • Small-hole gauge 71 • Spindle 68 • Split-ball gauge 71 • Straightedge 73 • Thickness gauge 73 • Thimble 68

ENGLISH CUSTOMARY MEASURING SYSTEM

The English customary measuring system was established about A.D. 1100 in England during the reign of Henry I. The foot was determined to be 12 inches and was taken from the length of a typical foot. The yard (36 inches) was determined to be the length from King Henry's nose to the end of his outstretched hand. The mile came from Roman days and was originally defined as the distance traveled by a soldier in 1,000 paces or steps. Other English units, such as the pound (weight) and volume (gallon), evolved over the years from Roman and English measurements.

The Fahrenheit temperature scale was created by Gabriel Fahrenheit (1686–1736) and he used 100°F as the temperature of the human body, which he missed by 1.4 degrees (98.6°F is considered now to be normal temperature). On the Fahrenheit scale, water freezes at 32°F and water boils at 212°F.

METRIC SYSTEM OF MEASURE

Most of the world uses the metric system of measure. The metric system was created in the late 1700s in France and used the physical world for the basis of the measurements. For example, the meter was defined as being 1/40,000,000 of the circumference of the earth (the distance around the earth at the poles). The Celsius temperature scale developed by Anders

Celsius (1701–1744) used the freezing point of water as 0°C (32°F) and the boiling point of water as 100°C (212°F). Other units include a liter of water, which was then used as a standard of weight where 1 liter of water (about 1 quart) weighs 1 kilogram (1,000 grams). Units of measure are then divided or multiplied by 10,100, and 1,000 to arrive at usable measurements. For example, a kilometer is 1,000 meters and is the most commonly used metric measurement for distance for travel. Other prefixes include:

m = milli = 1/1,000
k = kilo = 1,000
M = mega = 1,000,000

LINEAR METRIC MEASUREMENTS

1 kilometer = 0.62 mile
1 meter = 39.37 inches
1 centimeter (1/100 meter) = 0.39 inch
1 millimeter (1/1,000 meter) = 0.039 inch

VOLUME MEASUREMENT

1 cc (cubic centimeter) = 0.06 cubic inch
1 liter = 0.26 U.S. gallon (about 1 quart)

WEIGHT MEASUREMENT

1 gram = 0.035 ounce
1 kilogram (1,000 grams) = 2.2 pounds

PRESSURE MEASUREMENTS

1 kilopascal (kPa) = 0.14 pound per square inch (6.9 kPa = 1 PSI)
1 bar = 14.5 pounds per square inch

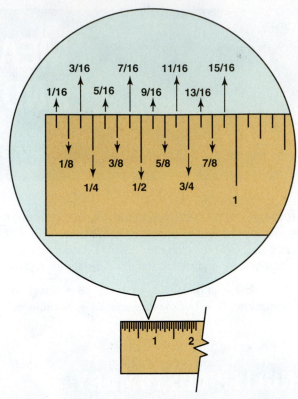

FREQUENTLY ASKED QUESTION

What Weighs a Gram?

To better understand the metric system measurements, it is often helpful to visualize a certain object and relate it to a metric unit of measure. For example, the following objects weigh about 1 gram.

- A dollar bill
- A small paper clip

FIGURE 7–1 A rule showing that the larger the division, the longer the line.

DERIVED UNITS All units of measure, except for the base units, are a combination of units that are referred to as derived units of measure. Some examples of derived units include:

Torque

Velocity

Density

Energy

Power

LINEAR MEASUREMENTS (TAPE MEASURE/RULE)

A tape measure or machinist rule divides inches into smaller units. Each smaller unit is drawn with a line shorter than the longer unit. The units of measure starting with the largest include:

1 inch

1/2 inch

1/4 inch

1/8 inch

1/16 inch

Some rules show 1/32 of an inch. ● **SEE FIGURE 7–1**.

A metric scale is also included on many tape measures and machinists rules. ● **SEE FIGURE 7–2**.

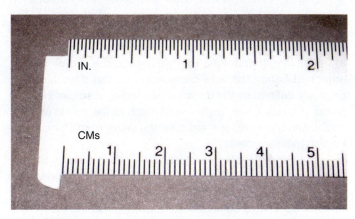

FIGURE 7–2 A plastic rule that has both inches and centimeters. Each line between the numbers on the centimeters represents 1 millimeter because there are 10 millimeters in 1 centimeter.

MICROMETER

A micrometer is the most used measuring instrument in engine-service and repair. ● **SEE FIGURE 7–3**.

The **thimble** rotates over the **sleeve** on a screw that has 40 threads per inch. Every revolution of the thimble moves the **spindle** 0.025 inch. The thimble is graduated into 25 equally spaced lines; therefore, each line represents 0.001 inch. Every micrometer should be checked for calibration on a regular basis. ● **SEE FIGURES 7–4 THROUGH 7–6**.

CRANKSHAFT MEASUREMENT Even though the connecting rod journals and the main bearing journals are usually different sizes, they both can and should be measured for out-of-round and taper. ● **SEE FIGURE 7–7**.

OUT-OF-ROUND. A journal should be measured in at least two positions across the diameter and every 120 degrees around the journal, as shown in ● **FIGURE 7–8**, for an example of the six readings. Calculate the out-of-round measurement by

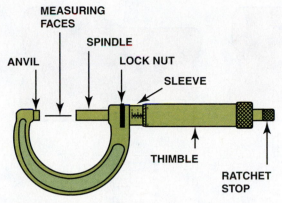

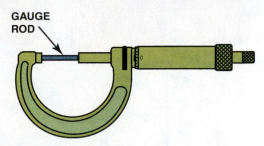

FIGURE 7–3 A typical micrometer showing the names of the parts. The sleeve may also be called the barrel or stock.

FIGURE 7–4 All micrometers should be checked and calibrated as needed using a gauge rod.

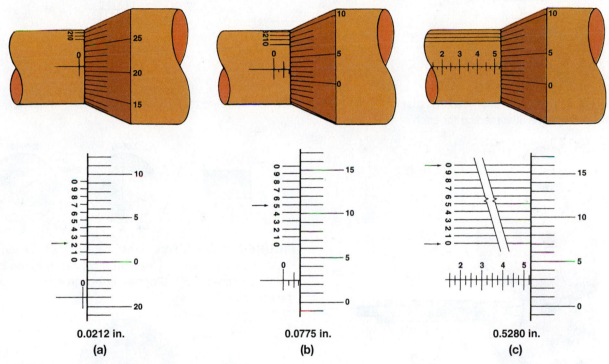

| 0.0212 in. | 0.0775 in. | 0.5280 in. |
| (a) | (b) | (c) |

FIGURE 7–5 The three micrometer readings are (a) 0.0212 inch; (b) 0.0775 inch; (c) 0.5280 inch. These measurements used the vernier scale on the sleeve to arrive at the ten-thousandth measurement. The number that is aligned represents the digit in the ten-thousandth place.

subtracting the lowest reading from the highest reading for both A and B positions.

Position A: 2.0000 – 1.9995 = 0.0005 inch

Position B: 2.0000 – 1.9989 = 0.0011 inch

The maximum out-of-round measurement occurs in position B (0.0011 inch), which is the measurement that should be used to compare against factory specifications to determine if any machining will be necessary.

TAPER. To determine the taper of the journal, compare the readings in the same place between A and B positions and subtract the lower reading from the higher reading.

For example:

Position A		Position B	
2.0000	-	2.0000	=0.0000
1.9999	-	1.9999	=0.0000
1.9995	-	1.9989	=0.0006

Use 0.0006 inch as the taper for the journal and compare with factory specifications.

CAMSHAFT MEASUREMENT The journal of the camshaft(s) can also be measured using a micrometer and compared with factory specifications for taper and out-of-round. ● **SEE FIGURE 7–9.**

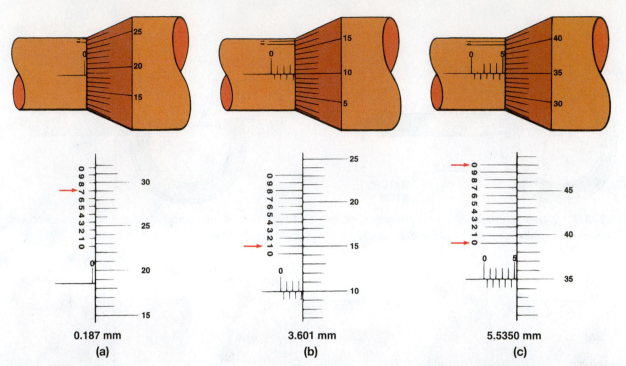

0.187 mm	3.601 mm	5.5350 mm
(a)	(b)	(c)

FIGURE 7–6 Metric micrometer readings that use the vernier scale on the sleeve to read to the nearest 0.001 millimeter. The arrows point to the final reading for each of the three examples.

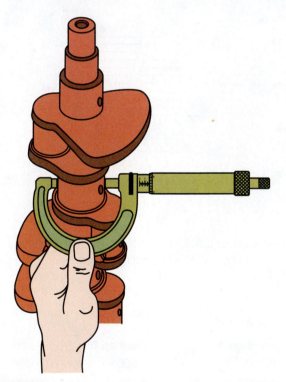

FIGURE 7–7 Using a micrometer to measure the connecting rod journal for out-of-round and taper.

NOTE: On overhead valve (pushrod) engines, the camshaft journal diameter often decreases slightly toward the rear of the engine. Overhead camshaft engines usually have the same journal diameter.

The cam lift can also be measured with a micrometer and compared with factory specifications, as shown in ●**FIGURE 7–10**.

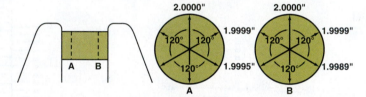

FIGURE 7–8 Crankshaft journal measurements. Each journal should be measured in at least six locations, but also in position A and position B and at 120-degree intervals around the journal.

FIGURE 7–9 Camshaft journals should be measured in three locations, 120 degrees apart, to check for out-of-round.

TELESCOPIC GAUGE

A telescopic gauge is used with a micrometer to measure the inside diameter of a hole or bore.

The cylinder bore can be measured by inserting a telescopic gauge into the bore and rotating the handle lock to allow the arms of the gauge to contact the inside bore of the cylinder. Tighten the handle lock and remove the gauge from the cylinder. Use a micrometer to measure the telescopic gauge. ●**SEE FIGURE 7–11**.

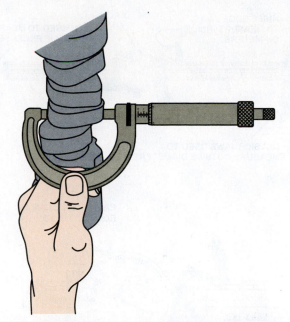

FIGURE 7–10 Checking a camshaft for wear by measuring the lobe height with a micrometer.

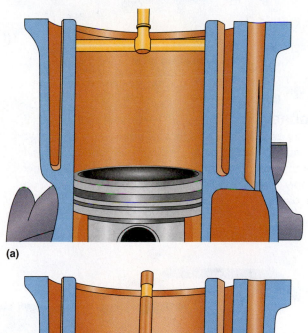

(a)

(b)

FIGURE 7–11 When the head is first removed, the cylinder taper and out-of-round should be checked below the ridge (a) and above the piston when it is at the bottom of the stroke (b).

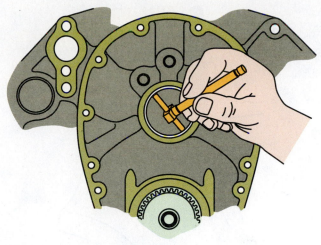

(a)

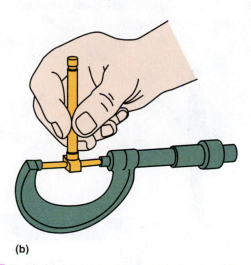

(b)

FIGURE 7–12 (a) A telescopic gauge being used to measure the inside diameter (ID) of a camshaft bearing. (b) An outside micrometer used to measure the telescopic gauge.

A telescopic gauge can also be used to measure the following:

- Camshaft bearing (● SEE FIGURE 7–12.)
- Main bearing bore (housing bore) measurement
- Connecting rod bore measurement

SMALL-HOLE GAUGE

A **small-hole gauge** (also called a **split-ball gauge**) is used with a micrometer to measure the inside diameter of small holes such as a valve guide in a cylinder head. ● SEE **FIGURES 7–13 AND 7–14.**

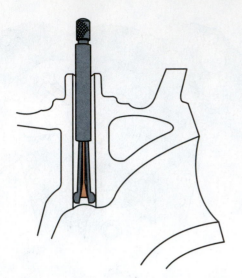

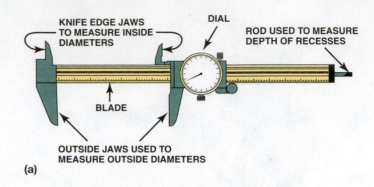

KNIFE EDGE JAWS TO MEASURE INSIDE DIAMETERS

DIAL

ROD USED TO MEASURE DEPTH OF RECESSES

BLADE

OUTSIDE JAWS USED TO MEASURE OUTSIDE DIAMETERS

(a)

FIGURE 7–13 Cutaway of a valve guide with a hole gauge adjusted to the hole diameter.

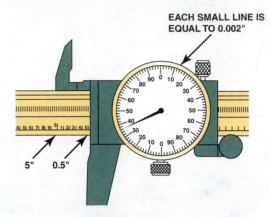

EACH SMALL LINE IS EQUAL TO 0.002"

5"   0.5"

ADD READING ON BLADE (5.5")
TO READING ON DIAL (0.036") TO
GET FINAL TOTAL MEASUREMENT (5.536")

(b)

FIGURE 7–15 (a) A typical vernier dial caliper. This is a very useful measuring tool for automotive engine work because it is capable of measuring inside, outside, and depth measurements. (b) To read a vernier dial caliper, simply add the reading on the blade to the reading on the dial.

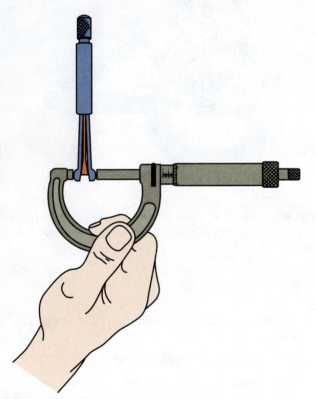

FIGURE 7–14 The outside of a hole gauge being measured with a micrometer.

VERNIER DIAL CALIPER

A vernier dial caliper is normally used to measure length, inside and outside diameters, and depth. ● **SEE FIGURE 7–15**.

FIGURE 7–16 A group of feeler gauges (also known as thickness gauges), used to measure between two parts. The long gauges on the bottom are used to measure the piston-to-cylinder wall clearance.

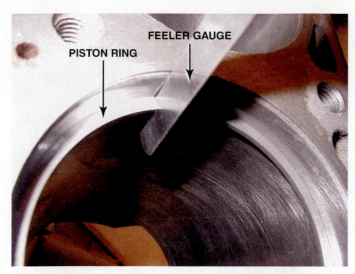

FIGURE 7–17 A feeler gauge, also called a thickness gauge, is used to measure the small clearances such as the end gap of a piston ring.

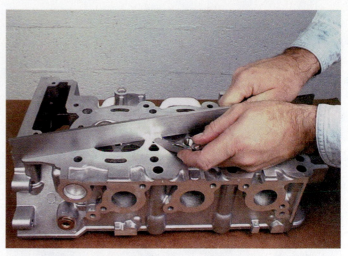

FIGURE 7–18 A straightedge is used with a feeler gauge to determine if a cylinder head is warped or twisted.

STRAIGHTEDGE

A **straightedge** is a precision ground metal measuring gauge that is used to check the flatness of engine components when used with a feeler gauge. A straightedge is used to check the flatness of the following:

- Cylinder heads (● **SEE FIGURE 7–18.**)
- Cylinder block deck
- Straightness of the main bearing bores (saddles)

DIAL INDICATOR

A dial indicator is a precision measuring instrument used to measure crankshaft end play, crankshaft runout, and valve guide wear. A dial indicator can be mounted three ways, including:

- **Magnetic mount.** This is a very useful method because a dial indicator can be attached to any steel or cast iron part.
- **Clamp mount.** A clamp-mounted dial indicator is used in many places where a mount could be clamped.
- **Threaded rod.** Using a threaded rod allows the dial indicator to be securely mounted, such as shown in ● **FIGURE 7–19.**

DIAL BORE GAUGE

A dial bore gauge is an expensive, but important, gauge used to measure cylinder taper and out-of-round as well as main bearing (block housing) bore for taper and out-of-round.

 FREQUENTLY ASKED QUESTION

What Is the Difference Between the Word *Gage* and *Gauge*?

The word *gauge* means "measurement or dimension to a standard of reference." The word *gauge* can also be spelled *gage.* Therefore, in most cases, the words mean the same.

INTERESTING NOTE: One vehicle manufacturing representative told me that *gage* was used rather than *gauge* because even though it is the second acceptable spelling of the word, it is correct and it saved the company a lot of money in printing costs because the word *gage* has one less letter! One letter multiplied by millions of vehicles with gauges on the dash and the word *gauge* used in service manuals adds up to a big savings to the manufacturer.

FEELER GAUGE

A **feeler gauge** (also known as a **thickness gauge**) is an accurately manufactured strip of metal that is used to determine the gap or clearance between two components. ● **SEE FIGURE 7–16.**

A feeler gauge can be used to check the following:

- Piston ring gap (● **SEE FIGURE 7–17.**)
- Piston ring side clearance
- Connecting rod side clearance
- Piston-to-wall clearance

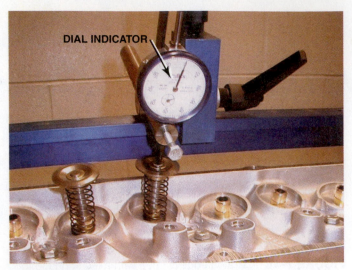

FIGURE 7-19 A dial indicator is used to measure valve lift during flow testing of a high-performance cylinder head.

● SEE FIGURE 7-20. A dial bore gauge has to be adjusted to a dimension, such as the factory specifications. The reading on the dial bore gauge then indicates plus (+) or minus (−) readings from the predetermined dimension. This is why a dial bore is best used to measure taper and out-of-round because it shows the difference in cylinder or bore rather than an actual measurement.

FIGURE 7-20 A dial bore gauge is used to measure cylinders and other engine parts for out-of-round and taper conditions.

DEPTH MICROMETER

A depth micrometer is similar to a conventional micrometer except that it is designed to measure the depth from a flat surface. ● SEE FIGURE 7-21.

FIGURE 7-21 A depth micrometer being used to measure the height of the rotor of an oil pump from the surface of the housing.

SUMMARY

1. A tape measure or machinist rule can be used to measure linear distances.

2. A micrometer can measure 0.001 inch by using a thimble that has 40 threads per inch. Each rotation of the thimble moves the thimble 0.025 inch. The circumference of the thimble is graduated into 25 marks, each representing 0.001 inch.

3. A micrometer is used to check the diameter of a crankshaft journal as well as the taper and out-of-round.

4. A camshaft bearing and lobe can be measured using a micrometer.

5. A telescopic gauge is used with a micrometer to measure the inside of a hole or bore, such as the big end of a connecting rod or a cylinder bore.

6. A small-hole gauge (also called a split-ball gauge) is used with a micrometer to measure small holes such as the inside diameter of a valve guide in a cylinder head.

7. A vernier dial caliper is used to measure the outside diameter of components such as pistons or crankshaft bearing journals as well as inside diameters and depth measurements.

8. A feeler gauge (also called a thickness gauge) is used to measure the gap or clearance between two components such as piston ring gap, piston-ring side clearance, and connecting rod side clearance. A feeler gauge is also used with a precision straightedge to measure the flatness of blocks and cylinder heads.

9. A dial indicator and dial bore gauge are used to measure differences in a component such as crankshaft end play (dial indicator) or cylinder taper (dial bore gauge).

REVIEW QUESTIONS

1. Explain how a micrometer is read.
2. Describe how to check a crankshaft journal for out-of-round and taper.
3. List engine components that can be measured with the help of a telescopic gauge.
4. List the gaps or clearances that can be measured using a feeler (thickness) gauge.
5. Explain why a dial bore gauge has to be set to a dimension before using.

CHAPTER QUIZ

1. The threaded movable part that rotates on a micrometer is called the _____.
   a. Sleeve
   b. Thimble
   c. Spindle
   d. Anvil

2. To check a crankshaft journal for taper, the journal should be measured in at least how many locations?
   a. One
   b. Two
   c. Four
   d. Six

3. To check a crankshaft journal for out-of-round, the journal should be measured in at least how many locations?
   a. Two
   b. Four
   c. Six
   d. Eight

4. A telescopic gauge can be used to measure a cylinder bore if what other measuring device is used to measure the telescopic gauge?
   a. Micrometer
   b. Feeler gauge
   c. Straightedge
   d. Dial indicator

5. To directly measure the diameter of a valve guide in a cylinder head, use a micrometer and a _____.
   a. Telescopic gauge
   b. Feeler gauge
   c. Small-hole gauge
   d. Dial indicator

6. Which of the following *cannot* be measured using a feeler gauge?
   a. Valve guide clearance
   b. Piston-ring gap
   c. Piston-ring side clearance
   d. Connecting rod side clearance

7. Which of the following *cannot* be measured using a straightedge and a feeler gauge?
   a. Cylinder head flatness
   b. Block deck flatness
   c. Straightness of the main bearing bores
   d. Straightness of the cylinder bore

8. Which measuring gauge needs to be set up (adjusted) to a fixed dimension before use?
   a. Dial indicator
   b. Dial bore gauge
   c. Vernier dial gauge
   d. Micrometer

9. The freezing point of water is _____.
   a. 0°C
   b. 32°F
   c. 0°F
   d. Both a and b

10. Which metric unit of measure is used for volume measurement?
    a. Meter
    b. cc
    c. Centimeter
    d. Millimeter

chapter 8

SERVICE INFORMATION

LEARNING OBJECTIVES: After studying this chapter, the reader should be able to: • Discuss the importance of vehicle service records, owner's manuals, lubrication guides, and labor guide manuals. • Discuss the importance of service manuals. • Discuss the advantages and disadvantages of hard copy versus electronic service information. • Explain electronic service information. • Explain hotline services, specialty repair manuals, and aftermarket supplies guides and catalogs.

KEY TERMS: Julian date 81 • Labor guides 79 • Service information 77 • Technical service bulletin (TSB) 80

VEHICLE SERVICE HISTORY RECORDS

Whenever service work is performed, a record of what was done is usually kept on file by the shop or service department for a number of years. The wise service technician will check the vehicle service history if working on a vehicle with an unusual problem. Often, a previous repair may indicate the reason for the current problem or it could be related to the same circuit or components. For example, a collision could have caused hidden damage that can affect the operation of the vehicle. Knowing that a collision had been recently repaired may be helpful to the technician.

OWNER'S MANUALS

It has been said by many automotive professional technicians and service advisors that the owner's manual is not read by many vehicle owners. Most owner's manuals contain all or most of the following information.

1. How to reset the maintenance reminder light
2. Specifications, including viscosity of oil needed and number of quarts (liters)
3. Tire pressures and standard as well as optional tire sizes
4. Maintenance schedule for all fluids, including coolant, brake fluid, automatic transmission fluid, and differential fluid

5. How to program the remote control as well as the power windows and door locks
6. How to reset the tire pressure monitoring system after a tire rotation ● **SEE FIGURE 8–1.**

LUBRICATION GUIDES

Lubrication guides, such as those published by Chek-Chart and Chilton, include all specifications for lubrication-related service including:

- Hoisting location
- Lubrication points
- Grease and oil specifications
- Capacities for engine oil, transmission fluid, coolant, and differential fluid

SERVICE MANUALS

Factory and aftermarket service manuals, also called shop manuals, contain specifications and service procedures. While factory service manuals cover just one year and one or more models of the same vehicle, most aftermarket service manuals cover multiple years and/or models in one manual.

FIGURE 8–1 The owner's manual has a lot of information pertaining to the operation as well as the maintenance and resetting procedures that technicians often need.

 REAL WORLD FIX

Owner's Manual Is the Key to Proper Operation

A customer purchased a used Pontiac Vibe and complained to a shop that the cruise control would disengage and had to be reset if driven below 25 mph (40 km/h). The service technician was able to verify that in fact this occurred, but did not know if this feature was normal or not. The technician checked the owner's manual and discovered that this vehicle was designed to operate this way. Unlike other cruise control systems, those systems on Toyota-based vehicles are designed to shut off below 25 mph, requiring the driver to reset the desired speed. The customer was informed that nothing could be done to correct this concern and the technician also learned something. Vehicles that use the Toyota cruise control system include all Toyotas, plus Lexus, Pontiac Vibe, and Chevrolet Prism.

NOTE: Some vehicle manufacturers offer owner's manuals on their website for a free download.

Included in most service manuals are the following:

- Capacities and recommended specifications for all fluids
- Specifications including engine and routine maintenance items
- Testing procedures
- Service procedures including the use of special tools when needed
- Component location information

 **TECH TIP**

Exploded Views

Exploded views of components such as engines and transmissions are available in shop manuals and electronic service information, as well as in parts and labor time guides. These views, showing all of the parts as if the assembly was blown apart, give the service technician a clear view of the various parts and their relationship to other parts in the assembly.

While some factory service manuals are printed in one volume, most factory **service information** is printed in several volumes due to the amount and depth of information presented. The typical factory service manual is divided into sections.

GENERAL INFORMATION   General information includes topics such as:

- Warnings and cautions
- Vehicle identification numbers on engine, transmission/transaxle, and body parts
- Lock cylinder coding
- Fastener information
- Decimal and metric equivalents
- Abbreviations and standard nomenclature used
- Service parts identification label and process code information

MAINTENANCE AND LUBRICATION INFORMATION
Maintenance and lubrication information includes topics such as:

- Schedule for "normal" as well as "severe" usage time and mileage charts
- Specified oil and other lubricant specifications
- Chassis lubrication points
- Tire rotation methods
- Periodic vehicle inspection services (items to check and time/mileage intervals)
- Maintenance item part numbers, such as oil and air filter numbers, and specifications, such as oil capacity and tire pressures

ENGINES

- Engine electrical diagnosis (battery, charging, cranking, ignition, and wiring)
- Engine mechanical diagnosis
- Specific engine information for each engine that may be used in the vehicle(s) covered by the service manual, including:
  - Engine identification
  - On-vehicle service procedures

- Description of the engine and the operation of the lubrication system
- Exploded views showing all parts of the engine
- Disassembly procedures
- Inspection procedures and specifications of the parts and subsystems
- Assembly procedures
- Torque specifications for all fasteners, including the torque sequence

AUTOMATIC TRANSMISSION/TRANSAXLE

- General information (identification and specifications)
- Diagnosis procedures, including preliminary checks and fluid level procedures
- General service, including leak detection and correction
- Cooler flushing procedures
- Unit removal procedures
- Unit disassembly procedures and precautions
- Unit assembly procedures and torque specifications

ELECTRICAL SYSTEMS

- Symbols used
- Troubleshooting procedures
- Repair procedures (wire repair, connectors, and terminals)
- Power distribution
- Ground distribution
- Component location views
- Harness routing views
- Individual electrical circuits, including circuit operation and schematics

HEATING, VENTILATION, AND AIR CONDITIONING

- Heater system
  - General description
  - Heater control assembly
  - Diagnosis, including heater electrical wiring and vacuum system
  - Blower motor and fan assembly diagnosis and servicing procedures
  - Air distribution values
  - Fastener torque specifications
- Air-conditioning system
  - General description and system components
  - Air-conditioning system diagnosis, including leakdetection
  - Air-conditioning and heater function tests
  - Air-conditioning service procedures
  - Refrigerant recovery, recycling, adding oil, evacuating procedures, and charging procedures
  - Troubleshooting guide

TECH TIP

Print It Out

It is often a benefit to have the written instructions or schematics (wiring diagrams) at the vehicle while diagnosing or performing a repair. One advantage of a hard copy service manual is that it can be taken to the vehicle and used as needed. However, dirty hands can often cause pages to become unreadable. The advantage of electronic format service information is that the material can be printed out and taken to the vehicle for easy access. This also allows the service technician to write or draw on the printed copy, which can be a big help when performing tests such as electrical system measurements. These notes can then be used to document the test results on the work order.

ENGINE PERFORMANCE (DRIVEABILITY AND EMISSIONS)

- Vehicle emission control information (VECI) label, visual/physical underhood inspection
- On-board diagnostic system
- Scan tool values
- Wiring harness service
- Symptom charts
- Diagnostic trouble code (DTC) information

ADVANTAGES OF HARD COPY VERSUS ELECTRONIC SERVICE INFORMATION

All forms of service information have some advantages, including:

HARD COPY	ELECTRONIC SERVICE INFORMATION
• Easy to use—no hardwareor expensive computers needed	• Information can be printed out and taken to the vehicle
• Can be taken to the vehicle for reference	• Has a search function for information
• Can view several pages easily for reference	• Internet or network access allows use at several locations in the shop

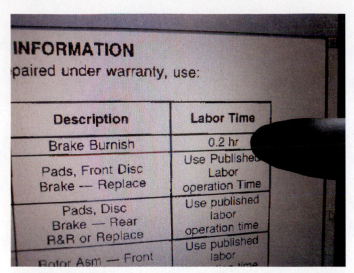

INFORMATION
paired under warranty, use:

Description	Labor Time
Brake Burnish	0.2 hr
Pads, Front Disc Brake — Replace	Use Published Labor operation Time
Pads, Disc Brake — Rear R&R or Replace	Use published labor operation time
Rotor Asm — Front	Use published labor

FIGURE 8–2 Some technical service bulletins also include the designated flat-rate time when specifying a repair procedure.

TECH TIP

Look for Severe Service Times

Many time guides provide additional time for vehicles that may be excessively rusted due to climate conditions or have been subjected to abuse. Be sure to quote the higher rate if any of these conditions are present on the customer's vehicle.

DISADVANTGES OF HARD COPY VERSUS ELECTRONIC SERVICE INFORMATION

All forms of service information have some disadvantages, including:

HARD COPY	ELECTRONIC SERVICE INFORMATION
• Can be lost or left in the vehicle	• Requires a computer and printer
• Cost is high for each manual	• Internet or network access can be a challenge
• Can get dirty and unreadable	• Cost can be high

LABOR GUIDE MANUALS

Labor guides, also called flat-rate manuals, list vehicle service procedures and the time it should take an average technician to complete the task. This flat-rate time is

then the basis for estimates and pay for technicians. Some manuals also include a parts list, including the price of the part to help service advisors create complete estimates for both labor and parts. These manuals are usually called "parts and time guides." Some guides include labor time only.
● **SEE FIGURE 8–2.**

Most experienced service technicians are paid by a method called **flat-rate**. The flat-rate method of pay is also called **incentive** or **commission pay**. "Flat-rate" means that the technician is paid a set amount of time (flat-rate) for every service operation. The amount of time allocated is published in a flat-rate manual. For example, if a bumper requires replacement, the flat-rate manual may call for 1.0 hour (time is always expressed in tenths of an hour). Each hour has 60 minutes. Each tenth of an hour is 1/10 of 60 or 6 minutes.

0.1 hour = 6 minutes

0.2 hour = 12 minutes

0.3 hour = 18 minutes

0.4 hour = 24 minutes

0.5 hour = 30 minutes

0.6 hour = 36 minutes

0.7 hour = 42 minutes

0.8 hour = 48 minutes

0.9 hour = 54 minutes

1.0 hour = 60 minutes

Many service operations are greater than 1 hour and are expressed as such:

2.4 hours = 2 hours and 24 minutes

3.6 hours = 3 hours and 36 minutes

The service technician would therefore get paid the flat-rate time regardless of how long it actually took to complete the job. Often, the technician can "beat flat-rate" by performing the operation in less time than the published time. It is therefore important that the technician not waste time and work efficiently to get paid the most for a day's work. The technician also has to be careful to perform the service procedure correctly because if the job needs to be done again due to an error, the technician does the repair at no pay. Therefore, the technician needs to be fast and careful at the same time. The vehicle manufacturer determines the flat-rate for each labor operation by having a team of technicians perform the operation several times. The average of all of these times is often published as the allocated time. The flat-rate method was originally developed to determine a fair and equitable way to pay dealerships for covered warranty repairs. Because the labor rate differs throughout the country, a fixed dollar amount would not be fair compensation. However, if a time could be established for each operation, then the vehicle manufacturer could reimburse the dealership for the set number of hours multiplied by the labor rate approved for that dealership. For example, if the approved labor rate is $60.00 per hour and:

Technician A performed 6.2 hours × $60.00 = $372.00

Technician B performed 4.8 hours × $60.00 = $288.00

The total paid to the dealership by the manufacturer = $660.00

This does not mean that the service technician gets paid $60.00 per hour. Sorry, no! This means that the dealership gets reimbursed for labor at the $60.00 per hour rate. The service technician usually gets paid a lot less than half of the total labor charge. Depending on the part of the country and the size of the dealership and community, the technician's flat-rate per hour income can vary from $7.00 to $20.00 or more per flat-rate hour. Remember, a high pay rate ($20 for example) does not necessarily mean that the service technician will be earning $800.00 per week (40 hours × $20.00 per hour = $800.00). If the dealership is not busy or it is a slow time of year, maybe the technician will only have the opportunity to "turn" 20 hours per week. So it is not really the pay rate that determines what a technician will earn but rather a combination of all of the following:

- Pay rate
- Number of service repairs performed
- Skill and speed of the service technician
- Type of service work (a routine brake service may be completed faster and easier than a difficult engine performance problem)

A service technician earns more at a busy dealership with a lower pay rate than at a smaller or less busy dealership with a higher pay rate.

ELECTRONIC SERVICE INFORMATION

There are many programs available that will provide electronic service information for the automotive industry. Sometimes the vehicle makers make information available on CDs or DVDs, but mostly it is available online. Most electronic service information has technical service bulletins (TSBs), wiring diagrams, and a main menu that includes the major components of the vehicle as a starting point. ● SEE FIGURE 8–3. ALLDATA and Mitchell On-Demand are commonly used software programs that include service information for many vehicles.

Service information and testing procedures should be closely followed including any symptom charts or flow charts. A sampleof a symptom information chart is shown ● CHART 8–1.

HOME SCREEN The Home screen is the first screen displayed when you start. It displays buttons that represent the major sections of the program. Access to the Home screen is available from anywhere within the program by clicking the Home button on the toolbar.

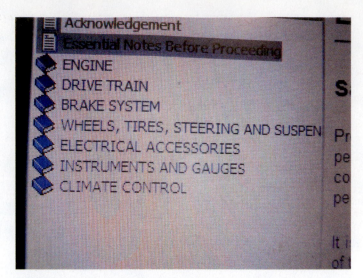

FIGURE 8–3 A main menu showing the major systems of the vehicle. Clicking on one of these major topics opens up another menu showing more detailed information.

TOOLBARS A main toolbar is displayed on most screens, providing quick access to certain functions. This toolbar varies somewhat, depending upon what information is being accessed.

ELECTRONIC SERVICE INFORMATION Electronic service information is available mostly by subscription and provides access to an Internet site where service manual–type information is available. Most vehicle manufacturers also offer electronic service information to their dealers and to most schools and colleges that offer corporate training programs.

TECHNICAL SERVICE BULLETINS **Technical service bulletins**, often abbreviated TSBs, are issued by the vehicle manufacturer to notify service technicians of a problem and include the necessary corrective action. Technical service bulletins are designed for dealership technicians but are republished by aftermarket companies and made available along with other service information to shops and vehicle repair facilities.

INTERNET The Internet has opened the field for information exchange and access to technical advice. One of the most useful websites is the International Automotive Technician's network at www.iatn.net. This is a free site but service technicians need to register to join. For a small monthly sponsor fee, the shop or service technician can gain access to the archives, which include thousands of successful repairs in the searchable database.

RECALLS AND CAMPAIGNS A recall or campaign is issued by a vehicle manufacturer and a notice is sent to all owners in the event of a safety- or emission-related fault or concern. While these faults may be repaired by independent shops, it is generally handled by a local dealer. Items that have

POSSIBLE CAUSE	REASON
Throttle-position (TP) sensor	• The TP sensor should be within the specified range at idle. If too high or too low, the computer may not provide a strong enough extra pulse to prevent a hesitation. • An open or short in the TP sensor can result in hesitation because the computer would not be receiving correct information regarding the position of the throttle.
Throttle-plate deposit buildup	An airflow restriction at the throttle plates creates not only less air reaching the engine but also swirling air due to the deposits. This swirling or uneven airflow can cause an uneven air-fuel mixture being supplied to the engine, causing poor idle quality and a sag or hesitation during acceleration.
Manifold absolute pressure (MAP) sensor fault	The MAP sensor detects changes in engine load and signals to the computer to increase the amount of fuel needed for proper operation. Check the vacuum hose and the sensor itself for proper operation.
Check the throttle linkage for binding	A kinked throttle cable or cruise (speed) control cable can cause the accelerator pedal to bind.
Contaminated fuel	Fuel contaminated with excessive amounts of alcohol or water can cause a hesitation or sag duringacceleration. **NOTE: To easily check for the presence of alcohol in gasoline, simply geta sample of the fuel and place it in a clean container. Add some water and shake. If no alcohol is in the gasoline, the water will settle to the bottom and be clear. If there is alcohol in the gasoline, the alcohol will absorb the water. The alcohol–water combination will settle to the bottom of thecontainer, but will be cloudy rather than clear.**
Clogged, shorted, or leaking fuel injectors	Any injector problem that results in less than an ideal amount of fuel being delivered to the cylinder scan result in a hesitation, a sag, or stumble during acceleration.
Spark plugs or spark plug wires	Any fault in the ignition system such as a defective spark plug wire or cracked spark plug can cause hesitation, a sag, or stumble during acceleration. At higher engine speeds, a defective spark plug wireis not as noticeable as it is at lower speeds, especially in vehicles equipped with a V-8 engine.
EGR valve operation	Hesitation, a sag, or stumble can occur if the EGR valve opens too soon or is stuck partially open.
False air	A loose or cracked intake hose between the mass airflow (MAF) sensor and the throttle plate can be the cause of hesitation.

CHART 8–1

A chart showing symptoms for hesitation while accelerating. These charts help the technician diagnose faults that do not set a diagnostic trouble code (DTC).

created recalls in the past have included potential fuel system leakage problems, exhaust leakage, or electrical malfunctions that could cause a possible fire or the engine to stall. Unlike technical service bulletins whose cost is only covered when the vehicle is within the warranty period, a recall or campaign is always done at no cost to the vehicle owner.

HOTLINE SERVICES

A hotline service provider is a subscription-based helpline to assist service technicians solve technical problems. While services vary, most charge a monthly fee for a certain amount of time each month to talk to an experienced service technician who has a large amount of resource materials available for reference. Often, the technician hired by the hotline services specializes in one vehicle make and is familiar with many of the pattern failures that are seen by other technicians in the field.

 FREQUENTLY ASKED QUESTION

What Is the Julian Date?

The **Julian date** (abbreviated JD) is the number of the day of the year. January 1 is day 001. The Julian date is named for Julius Caesar, who developed the current calendar. The Julian date is often mentioned in technical service bulletin where changes need to be made to certain component if the date of manufactured falls within the specified Julian dates.

Hotline services are an efficient way to get information on an as-needed basis.

Some examples of hotline automotive service providers include:

- Identifix
- Autohotlineusa

FIGURE 8–4 Whenever calling a hot line service be sure that you have all of the vehicle information ready and are prepared to give answers regarding voltage readings or scan tool data when talking to the vehicle specialist.

- Taylor Automotive Tech-Line
- Aspire
- ● **SEE FIGURE 8–4**.

SPECIALITY REPAIR MANUALS

Examples of specialty repair manuals include unit repair for assembled components, such as automatic transmission/transaxle, manual transmission/transaxle, differentials, and engines. Some specialty repair manuals cover older or antique vehicles, which may include unit repair sections.

AFTERMARKET SUPPLIES GUIDES AND CATALOGS

Aftermarket supplies guides and catalogs are usually free and often include expanded views of assembled parts along with helpful hints and advice. Sometimes the only place where this information is available is at trade shows associated with automotive training conferences and expos. Go to the following websites for examples of training conferences with trade shows.

- www.CARSevent.com
- www.avtechexpo.com
- www.visionkc.com (Vision Expo)

ADDITIONAL INFORMATION

FROM THE CUSTOMER   The service advisor or shop owner records the following information from the customer and about the vehicle:

1. Record the vehicle identification number (VIN) of the vehicle on the work order

2. Record the make, model, year, and mileage on the work order

3. Record what the customer's complaint (concern) is so that the service technician can verify the complaint and make the proper repair

4. Review the customer's vehicle history file and identifying additional required service

CHECK THE VEHICLE BEFORE WORK IS STARTED   As part of the work order writing process, the service advisor should look over the vehicle and make a written note of any body damage that may already exist. If any damage is noted it should be mentioned to the customer and noted on the work order. Often the customer is not aware of any damage especially on the passenger side and thus would blame the shop for the damage after the service work was performed.

SPECIAL SERVICE TOOLS   Automotive dealerships have tool rooms that are supposed to have all the special service tools that are recommended by the factory. These tool rooms are for the use of the dealership technicians so that they have access to the tools needed to work on the vehicle being serviced. The tools are often sorted by content area and are identified by a tool number. ● **SEE FIGURE 8–5**.

Special service tools are made primarily by a small group of manufacturers.

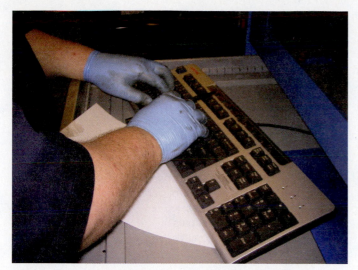

FIGURE 8–5 When accessing service information, always check what special service tools are required to perform the job.

FIGURE 8–6 The special tool number is printed or stamped on the tool for easy identification.

The majority of these tools are made by the SPX, who was recently acquired by the Bosch Automotive Service Solutions. They make the following special service tools (SST):

- Miller Special Tools (Chrysler)
- Rotunda Tools (Ford, Mazda, Jaguar, Land Rover)
- Kent-Moore Tools (Detroit Diesel, General Motors, Hyundai, Lexus, Mitsubishi, Nissan, Saab, Subaru, Volvo, Kia, Toyota, Isuzu). ● SEE FIGURE 8–6.

Other Manufacturers of Special Service Tools include:

- Sir Tools
- Assenmacher
- Baum Tools

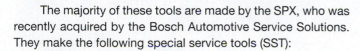

REVIEW QUESTIONS

1. What is included in the vehicle owner's manual that could be helpful for a service technician?
2. Lubrication service guides include what type of information?
3. Explain why factory service manuals or factory electronic service information are the most detailed of all service information.
4. Explain how flat-rate and parts guides are useful to customers.
5. List additional types of service manuals that are available.
6. Describe how hotline services and Internet sites assist service technicians.

CHAPTER QUIZ

1. What type of information is commonly included in the owner's manual that would be a benefit to service technicians?
   a. Maintenance reminder light reset procedures
   b. Tire pressure monitoring system reset procedures
   c. Maintenance items specifications
   d. All of the above
2. Two technicians are discussing the need for the history of the vehicle. Technician A says that an accident could cause faults due to hidden damage. Technician B says that some faults could be related to a previous repair. Which technician is correct?
   a. Technician A only
   b. Technician B only
   c. Both Technicians A and B
   d. Neither Technician A nor B
3. The viscosity of engine oil is found where?
   a. Owner's manual
   b. Factory service manual or service information
   c. Lubrication guide
   d. All of the above

4. Wiring diagrams are usually found where?
   a. Owner's manuals
   b. Factory service manuals
   c. Unit repair manuals
   d. Lubrication guides

5. What type of manual includes time needed to perform service procedures?
   a. Flat-rate manuals
   b. Owner's manuals
   c. Factory service manuals
   d. Parts guide

6. Component location can be found in _____.
   a. Factory service manuals
   b. Owner's manuals
   c. Component location manuals
   d. Both a and c

7. Aftermarket service information is available in what format?
   a. Manuals
   b. CDs or DVDs
   c. Internet
   d. All of the above

8. Hotline services are _____.
   a. Free
   b. Available for a service fee
   c. Available on CD or DVD format
   d. Accessed by the Internet

9. Aftermarket parts catalogs can be a useful source of information and they are usually _____.
   a. Free
   b. Available by paid subscription
   c. Available on CD or DVD
   d. Available for a fee on a secured Internet site

10. Which type of manual or service information includes the flat-rate time and the cost of parts?
   a. Parts and time guides
   b. Factory service manuals
   c. Component location guides
   d. Free Internet sites

chapter 9

VEHICLE IDENTIFICATION AND EMISSION RATINGS

LEARNING OBJECTIVES: **After studying this chapter, the reader should be able to:** • Discuss the parts of a vehicle, and differentiate between front-wheel drive and rear-wheel drive. • Explain vehicle identification, vehicle safety certification label, and the VECI label. • Discuss emission standards in the United States. • Explain calibration codes and casting numbers.

KEY TERMS: Bin number 88 • Calendar year (CY) 85 • Calibration codes 89 • California Air Resources Board (CARB) 87 • Casting numbers 89 • Country of origin 85 • Environmental Protection Agency (EPA) 87 • Gross axle weight rating (GAWR) 86 • Gross vehicle weight rating (GVWR) 86 • Model year (MY) 85 • Tier 87 • Vehicle emissions control information (VECI) 86 • Vehicle identification number (VIN) 85

PARTS OF A VEHICLE

The names of the parts of a vehicle are based on the location and purpose of the component.

LEFT SIDE OF THE VEHICLE—RIGHT SIDE OF THE VEHICLE Both of these terms refer to the left and right as if the driver is sitting behind the steering wheel. Therefore, the left side (including components under the hood) is on the driver's side.

FRONT AND REAR The proper term for the back portion of any vehicle is rear (e.g. left rear tire).

FRONT-WHEEL DRIVE VERSUS REAR-WHEEL DRIVE

Front-wheel drive (FWD) means that the front wheels are being driven by the engine, as well as turned by the steering wheel. Rear-wheel drive (RWD) means that the rear wheels are driven by the engine. If the engine is in the front, it can be either front- or rear-wheel drive. In many cases, a front engine vehicle can also drive all four wheels called four-wheel drive (4WD) or all-wheel drive (AWD). If the engine is located at the rear of the vehicle, it can be rear-wheel drive or four-wheel (AWD) drive.

VEHICLE IDENTIFICATION

All service work requires that the vehicle, including the engine and accessories, be properly identified. The most common identification is the make, model, and year of the vehicle.

Make: e.g., Chevrolet
Model: e.g., Trailblazer
Year: e.g., 2007

The year of the vehicle is often difficult to determine exactly. A model may be introduced as the next year's model as soon as January of the previous year. Typically, a new **model year** (abbreviated **MY**) starts in September or October of the year prior to the actual new year, but not always. This is why the **vehicle identification number**, usually abbreviated **VIN**, is so important. ● **SEE FIGURE 9–1.**

Since 1981, all vehicle manufacturers have used a VIN that is 17 characters long. Although every vehicle manufacturer assigns various letters or numbers within these 17 characters, there are some constants, including:

- The first number or letter designates the **country of origin**. ● **SEE CHART 9–1.**
- The model of the vehicle is commonly the fourth and/or fifth character.
- The eighth character is often the engine code. (Some engines cannot be determined by the VIN number.)
- The tenth character represents the **calendar year** (abbreviated **CY**) on all vehicles. ● **SEE CHART 9–2.**

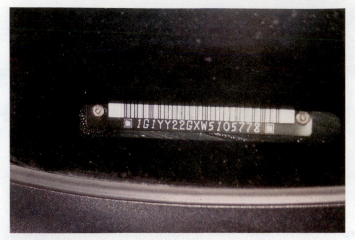

FIGURE 9–1 Typical vehicle identification number (VIN) as viewed through the windshield.

FIGURE 9–2 A VECI label on a 2008 Ford.

1 = United States	9 = Brazil	U = Romania
2 = Canada	J = Japan	V = France
3 = Mexico	K = Korea	W = Germany
4 = United States	L = China	X = Russia
5 = United States	R = Taiwan	Y = Sweden
6 = Australia	S = England	Z = Italy
8 = Argentina	T = Czechoslovakia	

CHART 9–1

The first number or letter designates the country of origin.

A = 1980/2010	L = 1990/2020	Y = 2000/2030
B = 1981/2011	M = 1991/2021	1 = 2001/2031
C = 1982/2012	N = 1992/2022	2 = 2002/2032
D = 1983/2013	P = 1993/2023	3 = 2003/2033
E = 1984/2014	R = 1994/2024	4 = 2004/2034
F = 1985/2015	S = 1995/2025	5 = 2005/2035
G = 1986/2016	T = 1996/2026	6 = 2006/2036
H = 1987/2017	V = 1997/2027	7 = 2007/2037
J = 1988/2018	W = 1998/2028	8 = 2008/2038
K = 1989/2019	X = 1999/2029	9 = 2009/2039

CHART 9–2

VIN year chart (*The pattern repeats every 30 years*)

VEHICLE SAFETY CERTIFICATION LABEL

A vehicle safety certification label is attached to the left side pillar post on the rearward-facing section of the left front door. This label indicates the month and year of manufacture as well as the **gross vehicle weight rating (GVWR)**, the **gross axle weight rating (GAWR)**, and the vehicle identification number (VIN).

VECI LABEL

The **vehicle emissions control information (VECI)** label under the hood of the vehicle shows informative settings and emission hose routing information. ● **SEE FIGURE 9–2.**

The VECI label (sticker) can be located on the bottom side of the hood, the radiator fan shroud, the radiator core support, or the strut towers. The VECI label usually includes the following information.

- Engine identification
- Emissions standard that the vehicle meets
- Vacuum hose routing diagram
- Base ignition timing (if adjustable)
- Spark plug type and gap
- Valve lash
- Emission calibration code

EMISSION STANDARDS IN THE UNITED STATES

In the United States, emissions standards are managed by the **Environmental Protection Agency (EPA)** as well as some U.S. state governments. Some of the strictest standards in the world are formulated in California by the **California Air Resources Board (CARB)**.

TIER 1 AND TIER 2 Federal emission standards are set by the Clean Air Act Amendments (CAAA) of 1990 grouped by **tier.** All vehicles sold in the United States must meet **Tier** 1 standards that went into effect in 1994 and are the least stringent. Additional Tier 2 standards have been optional since 2001, and were completely adopted in 2009. The current Tier 1 standards are different between automobiles and light trucks (SUVs, pickup trucks, and minivans), but Tier 2 standards are the same for both types.

There are several ratings that can be given to vehicles, and a certain percentage of a manufacturer's vehicles must meet different levels in order for the company to sell its products in affected regions. Beyond Tier 1, and in order by stringency, are the following levels.

- **TLEV—Transitional Low-Emission Vehicle.** More stringent for HC than Tier 1.

- **LEV—(also known as LEV I)—Low-Emission Vehicle.** An intermediate California standard about twice as stringent as Tier 1 for HC and NO_X.

- **ULEV—(also known as ULEV I).** Ultra-Low-Emission Vehicle. A stronger California standard emphasizing very low HC emissions.

- **ULEV II—Ultra-Low-Emission Vehicle.** A cleaner-than-average vehicle certified under the Phase II LEV standard. Hydrocarbon and carbon monoxide emissions levels are nearly 50% lower than those of a LEV II-certified vehicle. ● **SEE FIGURE 9–3.**

- **SULEV—Super-Ultra-Low-Emission Vehicle.** A California standard even tighter than ULEV, including much lower HC and NO_X emissions; roughly equivalent to Tier 2 Bin 2 vehicles.

- **ZEV—Zero-Emission Vehicle.** A California standard prohibiting any tailpipe emissions. The ZEV category is largely restricted to electric vehicles and hydrogen-fueled vehicles. In these cases, any emissions that are created are produced at another site, such as a power plant or hydrogen reforming center, unless such sites run on renewable energy.

NOTE: A battery-powered electric vehicle charged from the power grid will still be up to 10 times cleaner than even the cleanest gasoline vehicles over their respective lifetimes.

The current California ZEV regulation allows manufacturers a choice of two options for meeting the ZEV requirements.

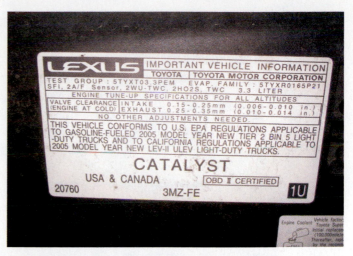

FIGURE 9–3 The underhood decal showing that this Lexus RX-330 meets both national (Tier 2; BIN 5) and California LEV-II (ULEV) regulation standards.

1. Vehicle manufacturers can meet the ZEV obligations by meeting standards that are similar to the ZEV rule as it existed in 2001. This means using a formula allowing a vehicle mix of 2% pure ZEVs, 2% AT-PZEVs (vehicles earning advanced technology partial ZEV credits), and 6% PZEVs (extremely clean conventional vehicles). The ZEV obligation is based on the number of passenger cars and small trucks a manufacturer sells in California.

2. Manufacturers may also choose a new alternative ZEV compliance strategy of meeting part of the ZEV requirement by producing the sales-weighted market share of approximately 250 fuel-cell vehicles. The remainder of the ZEV requirements could be achieved by producing 4% AT-PZEVs and 6% PZEVs. The required number of fuel-cell vehicles will increase to 2,500 from 2009 to 2011, 25,000 from 2012 through 2020, and 50,000 from 2015 through 2017. Manufacturers can substitute battery electric vehicles for up to 50% of the fuel-cell vehicle requirements.

   - **PZEV—Partial-Zero-Emission Vehicle.** Compliant with the SULEV standard; additionally has near-zero evaporative emissions and a 15-year/150,000-mile warranty on its emission control equipment.

Tier 2 standards are even more stringent. Tier 2 variations are appended with "II," such as LEV II or SULEV II. Other categories have also been created.

- **ILEV—Inherently Low-Emission Vehicle.**

- **AT-PZEV—Advanced Technology Partial-Zero-Emission Vehicle.** If a vehicle meets the PZEV standards and is using high-technology features, such as an electric motor or high-pressure gaseous fuel tanks for compressed natural gas, it qualifies as an AT-PZEV. Hybrid electric vehicles such as the Toyota Prius can qualify, as can internal combustion engine vehicles that run on natural gas (CNG), such as the Honda Civic GX. These vehicles are classified as "partial" ZEV because they receive partial

		NMOG Grams (Mile)	CO Grams (Mile)	NOx Grams (Mile)
LEV I (Cars)	TLEV	0.125 (0.156)	3.4 (4.2)	0.4 (0.6)
	LEV	0.075 (0.090)	3.4 (4.2)	0.2 (0.3)
	ULEV	0.040 (0.055)	1.7 (2.1)	0.2 (0.3)
LEV II (Cars and Trucks less than 8,500 lbs)	LEV	0.075 (0.090)	3.4 (4.2)	0.05 (0.07)
	ULEV	0.040 (0.055)	1.7 (2.1)	0.05 (0.07)
	SULEV	–(0.010)	–(1.0)	–(0.02)

CHART 9–3

LEV Standard Categories

NOTE: Numbers in parentheses are 100,000 mile standards for LEV I, and 120,000 mile standards for LEV II. NMOG means non-methane organic gases, which includes alcohol. CO means carbon monoxide. NOx means oxides of nitrogen. Data compiled from California Environmental Protection Agency—Air Resource Board (CARB) documents.

Certification Level	NMOG (g/ml)	CO (g/ml)	NOx (g/ml)
LEV II	0.090	4.2	0.07
ULEV II	0.055	2.1	0.07
SULEV II	0.010	1.0	0.02

CHART 9–4

California LEV II 120,000 Mile Tailpipe Emissions Limits

NOTE: Numbers in parentheses are 100,000 mile standards for LEV I, and 120,000 mile standards for LEV II. NMOG means non-methane organic gases, which includes alcohol. CO means carbon monoxide. NOx means oxides of nitrogen. The specification is in grams per mile (g/ml). Data compiled from California Environmental Protection Agency—Air Resources Board (CARB) documents.

Certification Level	NMOG (g/ml)	CO (g/ml)	NOx (g/ml)
Bin 1	0.0	0.0	0.0
Bin 2	0.010	2.1	0.02
Bin 3	0.055	2.1	0.03
Bin 4	0.070	2.1	0.04
Bin 5	0.090	4.2	0.07
Bin 6	0.090	4.2	0.10
Bin 7	0.090	4.2	0.15
Bin 8a	0.125	4.2	0.20
Bin 8b	0.156	4.2	0.20
Bin 9a	0.090	4.2	0.30
Bin 9b	0.130	4.2	0.30
Bin 9c	0.180	4.2	0.30
Bin 10a	0.156	4.2	0.60
Bin 10b	0.230	6.4	0.60
Bin 10c	0.230	6.4	0.60
Bin 11	0.230	7.3	0.90

CHART 9–5

EPA Tier 2—120,000 Mile Tailpipe Emission Limits

NOTE: The bin number is determined by the type and weight of the vehicle. The highest bin allowed for vehicles built after January 1, 2007, is Bin 8. Data compiled from the Environmental Protection Agency (EPA).

U.S. EPA VEHICLE INFORMATION PROGRAM (THE HIGHER THE SCORE, THE LOWER THE EMISSIONS)	
Selected Emissions Standards	Score
Bin 1 and ZEV	10
PZEV	9.5
Bin 2	9
Bin 3	8
Bin 4	7
Bin 5 and LEV II cars	6
Bin 6	5
Bin 7	4
Bin 8	3
Bin 9a and LEV I cars	2
Bin 9b	2
Bin 10a	1
Bin 10b and Tier 1 cars	1
Bin 11	0

CHART 9–6

Air Pollution Score
Courtesy of the Environmental Protection Agency (EPA).

credit for the number of ZEV vehicles that automakers would otherwise be required to sell in California.

- **NLEV—National Low-Emission Vehicle.** All vehicles nationwide must meet this standard, which started in 2001. ● **SEE CHARTS 9–3 AND 9–4.**

FEDERAL EPA BIN NUMBER The higher the tier number, the newer the regulation; the lower the **bin number**, the cleaner the vehicle. The 2004 Toyota Prius is a very clean Bin 3, while the Hummer H2 is a dirty Bin 11. Examples include:

- Tier 1: The former federal standard; carried over to model year 2004 for those vehicles not yet subject to the phase-in.
- Tier 2, Bin 1: The cleanest federal Tier 2 standard; a zero-emission vehicle (ZEV).
- Tier 2, Bins 2–4: Cleaner than the average standard.
- Tier 2, Bin 5: "Average" of new Tier 2 standards, roughly equivalent to a LEV II vehicle.
- Tier 2, Bins 6–9: Not as clean as the average requirement for a Tier 2 vehicle.

- Tier 2, Bin 10: Least-clean Tier 2 bin applicable to passenger vehicles.

  ● **SEE CHARTS 9–5 AND 9–6.**

FIGURE 9–4 A typical computer calibration sticker on the case of the controller. The information on the sticker is often needed when ordering parts or a replacement controller.

FIGURE 9–5 Engine block identification number cast into the block is used for identification.

CALIBRATION CODES

Calibration codes are usually located on powertrain control modules (PCMs) or other controllers. Some calibration codes are only accessible with a scan tool. Whenever diagnosing an engine operating fault, it is often necessary to know the calibration code to be sure that the vehicle is the subject of a technical service bulletin or other service procedure. ● **SEE FIGURE 9–4.**

CASTING NUMBERS

Whenever an engine part such as a block is cast, a number is put into the mold to identify the casting. ● **SEE FIGURE 9–5.** These **casting numbers** can be used to check dimensions such as the cubic inch displacement and other information. Sometimes changes are made to the mold, yet the casting number is not changed. Most often the casting number is the best piece of identifying information that the service technician can use for identifying an engine.

SUMMARY

1. The front, rear, left, and right side of a vehicle are as viewed from the driver's seat.
2. The vehicle identification number (VIN) is very important as it includes when the vehicle was built, as well as the engine code and many other details about the vehicle.
3. The VECI label under the hood often needs to be checked by the technician to properly service the vehicle.
4. Other vehicle information that the technician may need for a service or repair include calibration codes, casting numbers, and emissions rating.

REVIEW QUESTIONS

1. From what position are the terms left and right determined?
2. What are the major pieces of information that are included in the vehicle identification number (VIN)?
3. What information is included on the VECI label under the hood?
4. What does Tier 2 Bin 5 mean?

1. The passenger side is called the _____.
   a. Right side
   b. Left side
   c. Either right or left side, depending on how the vehicle is viewed
   d. Both a and b

2. A vehicle with the engine in the front can be _____.
   a. Front-wheel drive
   b. Rear-wheel drive
   c. Four-wheel drive
   d. All of the above

3. The vehicle identification number (VIN) is how many characters long?
   a. 10
   b. 12
   c. 17
   d. 21

4. The tenth character represents the year of the vehicle. If the tenth character is a "Y," what year is the vehicle?
   a. 1998
   b. 2000
   c. 2002
   d. 2004

5. The first character of the vehicle identification number is the country of origin. Where was the vehicle built that has a "5" as the first character?
   a. United States
   b. Canada
   c. Mexico
   d. Japan

6. The VECI label includes all *except* _____.
   a. Engine identification
   b. Horsepower and torque rating of the engine
   c. Spark plug type and gap
   d. Valve lash

7. The vehicle safety certification label includes all *except* _____.
   a. VIN
   b. GVWR
   c. Tire pressure recommendation
   d. GAWR

8. What are the characters that are embedded in most engine blocks and are used for identification?
   a. VIN
   b. Calibration codes
   c. Bin number
   d. Casting number

9. If the first character of the VIN is an "S," where was the vehicle made?
   a. United States
   b. Mexico
   c. Canada
   d. England

10. Technician A says that the lower the bin number is, the cleaner. Technician B says that SULEV has cleaner standards than ULEV. Which technician is correct?
   a. Technician A only
   b. Technician B only
   c. Both Technicians A and B
   d. Neither Technician A nor B

chapter 10

GASOLINE ENGINE OPERATION, PARTS, AND SPECIFICATIONS

LEARNING OBJECTIVES: After studying this chapter, the reader should be able to: • Discuss engine construction, purpose and function of an engine, and energy and power of an engine. • Explain engine parts and systems. • Explain four-stroke cycle operation. • Discuss engine classification and construction. • Explain engine measurement. • Discuss compression ratio, torque, and horsepower.

KEY TERMS: Block 91 • Bore 99 • Bottom dead center (BDC) 94 • Boxer 94 • Cam-in-block design 96 • Camshaft 96 • Combustion 91 • Combustion chamber 91 • Compression ratio (CR) 100 • Connecting rod 94 • Crankshaft 94 • Cycle 94 • Cylinder 94 • Displacement 100 • Double overhead camshaft (DOHC) 96 • Exhaust valve 94 • External combustion engine 91 • Four-stroke cycle 94 • Intake valve 94 • Internal combustion engine 91 • Mechanical force 91 • Mechanical power 91 • Naturally aspirated 98 • Nonprincipal end 98 • Oil galleries 93 • Overhead valve (OHV) 96 • Pancake 94 • Piston stroke 94 • Principal end 98 • Pushrod engine 96 • Rotary engine 97 • Single overhead camshaft (SOHC) 96 • Stroke 99 • Supercharger 98 • Top dead center (TDC) 94 • Turbocharger 98 • Wankel engine 97

PURPOSE AND FUNCTION

The purpose and function of an engine is to convert the heat energy of burning fuel into mechanical energy. In a typical vehicle, mechanical energy is then used to perform the following:

- Propel the vehicle
- Power the air-conditioning system and power steering
- Produce electrical power for use throughout the vehicle

ENERGY AND POWER

Engines use energy to produce power. The chemical energy in fuel is converted to heat energy by the burning of the fuel at a controlled rate. This process is called **combustion.** If engine combustion occurs within the power chamber, the engine is called an **internal combustion engine.**

NOTE: An external combustion engine burns fuel outside of the engine itself, such as a steam engine.

Engines used in automobiles are internal combustion heat engines. They convert the chemical energy of the gasoline into heat within a power chamber that is called a **combustion chamber.** Heat energy released in the combustion chamber raises the temperature of the combustion gases within the chamber. The increase in gas temperature causes the pressure of the gases to increase. The pressure developed within the combustion chamber is applied to the head of a piston to produce a usable **mechanical force,** which is then converted into useful **mechanical power.**

ENGINE CONSTRUCTION OVERVIEW

BLOCK All automotive and truck engines are constructed using a solid frame, called a **block.** A block is constructed of cast iron or aluminum and provides the foundation for most of the engine components and systems. The block is cast and then machined to very close tolerances to allow other parts to be installed.

ROTATING ASSEMBLY Pistons are installed in the block and move up and down during engine operation. Pistons are connected to connecting rods, which connect the pistons to the crankshaft. The crankshaft converts the up-and-down motion of the piston to rotary motion, which is then transmitted to the drive wheels and propels the vehicle. ● **SEE FIGURE 10–1.**

FIGURE 10–1 The rotating assembly for a V-8 engine that has eight pistons and connecting rods and one crankshaft.

FIGURE 10–2 A cylinder head with four valves per cylinder, two intake valves (larger) and two exhaust valves (smaller).

? **FREQUENTLY ASKED QUESTION**

What Is a Flat-Head Engine?

A flat-head engine is an older type engine design that has the valves in the block. The valves are located next to the cylinders and the air-fuel mixture, and exhaust flows through the block to the intake and exhaust manifolds. Because the valves are in the block, the heads are flat and, therefore, are called flat-head engines. The most commonly known was the Ford flat-head V-8 produced from 1932 until 1953. Typical flat-head engines included:

- Inline 4-cylinder engines (many manufacturers)
- Inline 6-cylinder engines (many manufacturers)
- Inline 8-cylinder engines (many manufacturers)
- V-8s (Cadillac and Ford)
- V-12s (Cadillac and Lincoln)

FIGURE 10–3 The coolant temperature is controlled by the thermostat, which opens and allows coolant to flow to the radiator when the temperature reaches the rating temperature of the thermostat.

CYLINDER HEADS All engines use a cylinder head to seal the top of the cylinders, which are in the engine block. The cylinder head also contains both intake valves that allow air and fuel into the cylinder and exhaust valves, which allow the hot gases left over to escape from the engine. Cylinder heads are constructed of cast iron or aluminum and are then machined for the valves and other valve-related components.
● **SEE FIGURE 10–2.**

ENGINE PARTS AND SYSTEMS

INTAKE AND EXHAUST MANIFOLDS Air and fuel enter the engine through an intake manifold and exit the engine through the exhaust manifold. Intake manifolds operate cooler than exhaust manifolds and are therefore constructed of nylon-reinforced plastic or aluminum. Exhaust manifolds must be able to withstand hot exhaust gases, so most are constructed from cast iron or steel tubing.

COOLING SYSTEM All engines must have a cooling system to control engine temperatures. While some older engines were air cooled, all current production passenger vehicle engines are cooled by circulating antifreeze coolant through passages in the block and cylinder head. The coolant picks up the heat from the engine and after the thermostat opens, the water pump circulates the coolant through the radiator where the excess heat is released to the outside air, cooling the coolant. The coolant is continuously circulated through the cooling system and the temperature is controlled by the thermostat. ● **SEE FIGURE 10–3.**

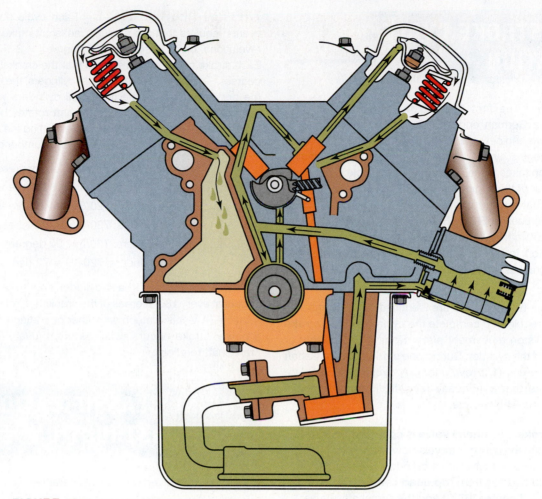

FIGURE 10-4 A typical lubrication system, showing the oil pan, oil pump, oil filter, and oil passages.

LUBRICATION SYSTEM

All engines contain moving and sliding parts that must be kept lubricated to reduce wear and friction. The oil pan, bolted to the bottom of the engine block, holds 4 to 7 quarts (4 to 7 liters) of oil. An oil pump, which is driven by the engine, forces the oil through the oil filter and then into passages in the crankshaft and block. These passages are called **oil galleries**. The oil is also forced up to the valves and then falls down through openings in the cylinder head and block, then back into the oil pan. ● **SEE FIGURE 10-4.**

FUEL SYSTEM AND IGNITION SYSTEM

All engines require both a fuel system to supply fuel to the cylinders and an ignition system to ignite the air-fuel mixture in the cylinders. The fuel system includes the following components.

- Fuel tank, where fuel is stored and where most fuel pumps are located
- Fuel filter and lines, which transfer the fuel for the fuel tank to the engine
- Fuel injectors, which spray fuel into the intake manifold or directly into the cylinder, depending on the type of system used

The ignition system is designed to take 12 volts from the battery and convert it to 5,000 to 40,000 volts needed to jump the gap of a spark plug. Spark plugs are threaded into the cylinder head of each cylinder, and when the spark occurs, it ignites the air-fuel mixture in the cylinder creating pressure and forcing the piston down in the cylinder. The following components are part of the ignition system.

- **Spark plugs.** Provide an air gap inside the cylinder where a spark occurs to start combustion
- **Sensor(s).** Includes crankshaft position (CKP) and camshaft position (CMP) sensors, used by the powertrain control module (PCM) to trigger the ignition coil(s) and the fuel injectors
- **Ignition coils.** Increase battery voltage to 5,000 to 40,000 volts
- **Ignition control module (ICM).** Controls when the spark plug fires
- **Associated wiring.** Electrically connects the battery, ICM, coil, and spark plugs

FOUR-STROKE CYCLE OPERATION

PRINCIPLES The first **four-stroke cycle** engine was developed by a German engineer, Nickolaus Otto, in 1876. Most automotive engines use the four-stroke cycle of events. The process begins by the starter motor rotating the engine until combustion takes place. The four-stroke cycle is repeated for each cylinder of the engine. ● **SEE FIGURE 10–5.**

A piston that moves up and down, or reciprocates, in a **cylinder** can be seen in **FIGURE 10–5.** The piston is attached to a **crankshaft** with a **connecting rod.** This arrangement allows the piston to reciprocate (move up and down) in the cyliner as the crankashaft rotates. ● **SEE FIGURE 10–6.**

OPERATION Engine cycles are identified by the number of piston strokes required to complete the cycle. A **piston stroke** is a one-way piston movement either from top to bottom or bottom to top of the cylinder. During one stroke, the crankshaft rotates 180 degrees (1/2 revolution). A **cycle** is a complete series of events that continually repeats. Most automobile engines use a four-stroke cycle.

- **Intake stroke.** The **intake valve** is open and the piston inside the cylinder travels downward, drawing a mixture of air and fuel into the cylinder. The crankshaft rotates 180 degrees from **top dead center (TDC)** to **bottom dead center (BDC)** and the camshaft rotates 90 degrees.

- **Compression stroke.** As the engine continues to rotate, the intake valve closes and the piston moves upward in the cylinder, compressing the air-fuel mixture. The crankshaft rotates 180 degrees from BDC to TDC and the camshaft rotates 90 degrees.

- **Power stroke.** When the piston gets near the top of the cylinder, the spark at the spark plug ignites the air-fuel mixture, which forces the piston downward. The crankshaft rotates 180 degrees from TDC to BDC and the camshaft rotates 90 degrees. The combustion pressure developed in the combustion chamber at the correct time will push the piston downward to rotate the crankshaft.

- **Exhaust stroke.** The engine continues to rotate, and the piston again moves upward in the cylinder. The exhaust valve opens, and the piston forces the residual burned gases out of the **exhaust valve** and into the exhaust manifold and exhaust system. The crankshaft rotates 180 degrees from BDC to TDC and the camshaft rotates 90 degrees.

This sequence repeats as the engine rotates. To stop the engine, the electricity to the ignition system is shut off by the ignition switch, which stops the spark to the spark plugs.

THE 720-DEGREE CYCLE Each cycle (four strokes) of events requires that the engine crankshaft make two complete revolutions, or 720 degrees (360 degrees × 2 = 720 degrees). Each stroke of the cycle requires that the crankshaft rotate 180 degrees. The greater the number of cylinders, the closer together the power strokes of the individual cylinders will occur. The number of degrees that the crankshaft rotates between power strokes can be expressed as an angle. To find the angle between cylinders of an engine, divide 720 by the number of cylinders.

Angle with 3 cylinders: 720/3 = 240 degrees

Angle with 4 cylinders: 720/4 = 180 degrees

Angle with 5 cylinders: 720/5 = 144 degrees

Angle with 6 cylinders: 720/6 = 120 degrees

Angle with 8 cylinders: 720/8 = 90 degrees

Angle with 10 cylinders: 720/10 = 72 degrees

This means that in a 4-cylinder engine, a power stroke occurs at every 180 degrees of the crankshaft rotation (every 1/2 rotation). A V-8 is a much smoother operating engine because a power stroke occurs twice as often (every 90 degrees of crankshaft rotation).

ENGINE CLASSIFICATION AND CONSTRUCTION

Engines are classified by several characteristics, including:

- **Number of strokes.** Most automotive engines use the four-stroke cycle.

- **Cylinder arrangement.** An engine with more cylinders is smoother operating because the power pulses produced by the power strokes are more closely spaced. An inline engine places all cylinders in a straight line. The 4-, 5-, and 6-cylinder engines are commonly manufactured inline engines. A V-type engine, such as a V-6 or V-8, has the number of cylinders split and built into a V shape. ● **SEE FIGURE 10–7.** Horizontally opposed 4- and 6-cylinder engines have two banks of cylinders that are horizontal, resulting in a low engine. This style of engine is used in Porsche and Subaru engines, and is often called the **boxer** or **pancake** engine design. ● **SEE FIGURE 10–8.**

- **Longitudinal and transverse mounting.** Engines may be mounted either parallel with the length of the vehicle (longitudinally) or crosswise (transversely). ● **SEE FIGURES 10–9 AND 10–10.** The same engine may be mounted in various vehicles in either direction.

NOTE: Although it might be possible to mount an engine in different vehicles both longitudinally and transversely, the engine component parts may *not* be interchangeable. Differences can include different engine blocks and crankshafts, as well as different water pumps.

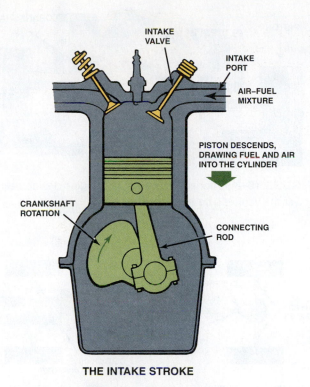

THE INTAKE STROKE

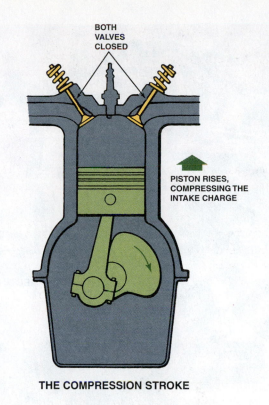

THE COMPRESSION STROKE

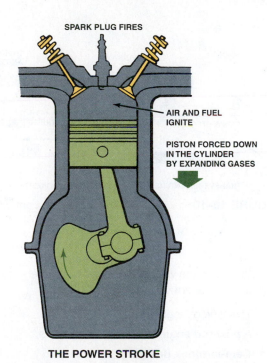

THE POWER STROKE

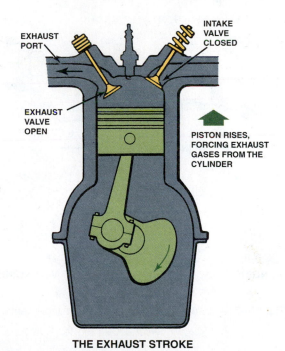

THE EXHAUST STROKE

FIGURE 10–5 The downward movement of the piston draws the air-fuel mixture into the cylinder through the intake valve on the intake stroke. On the compression stroke, the mixture is compressed by the upward movement of the piston with both valves closed. Ignition occurs at the beginning of the power stroke, and combustion drives the piston downward to produce power. On the exhaust stroke, the upward-moving piston forces the burned gases out the open exhaust valve.

FIGURE 10–6 Cutaway of an engine showing the cylinder, piston, connecting rod, and crankshaft.

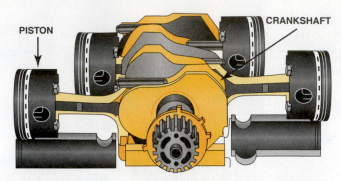

FIGURE 10–8 A horizontally opposed engine design helps to lower the vehicle's center of gravity.

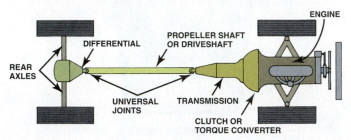

FIGURE 10–9 A longitudinally mounted engine drives the rear wheels through a transmission, driveshaft, and differential assembly.

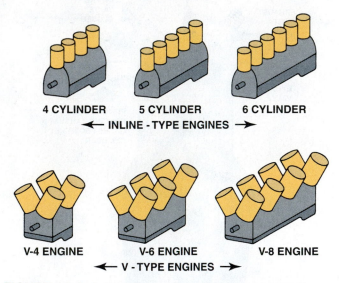

FIGURE 10–7 Automotive engine cylinder arrangements.

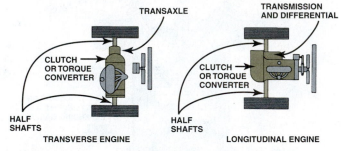

FIGURE 10–10 Two types of front-engine, front-wheel drive mountings.

- **Valve and camshaft number and location.** The number of valves per cylinder and the number and location of camshafts are major factors in engine operation. A typical older-model engine uses one intake valve and one exhaust valve per cylinder. Many newer engines use two intake and two exhaust valves per cylinder. The valves are opened by a **camshaft.** Some engines use one camshaft for the intake valves and a separate camshaft for the exhaust valves. When the camshaft is located in the block, the valves are operated by lifters, pushrods, and rocker arms.

This type of engine is called:

- A **pushrod engine**
- **Cam-in-block design**
- **Overhead valve (OHV),** because an overhead valve engine has the valves located in the cylinder head (● **SEE FIGURE 10–11.**)

When one overhead camshaft is used, the design is called a **single overhead camshaft (SOHC)** design. When two overhead camshafts are used, the design is called a **double overhead camshaft (DOHC)** design. ● **SEE FIGURES 10–12 AND 10–13.**

FIGURE 10–11 Cutaway of an overhead valve (OHV) V-8 engine showing the lifters, pushrods, roller rocker arms, and valves.

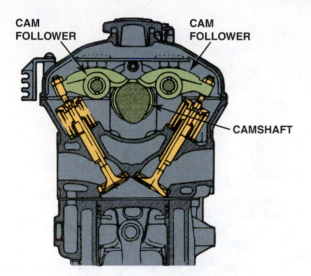

SINGLE OVERHEAD CAMSHAFT

CAM FOLLOWER — CAM FOLLOWER

CAMSHAFT

DOUBLE OVERHEAD CAMSHAFT

CAMSHAFT — LIFTER — CAMSHAFT

LIFTER

FIGURE 10–12 SOHC engines usually require additional components, such as a rocker arm, to operate all of the valves. DOHC engines often operate the valves directly.

FIGURE 10–13 A DOHC engine uses a camshaft for the intake valves and a separate camshaft for the exhaust valves in each cylinder head.

? FREQUENTLY ASKED QUESTION

What Is a Rotary Engine?

A successful alternative engine design is the **rotary engine**, also called the **Wankel engine** after its inventor, Felix Heinrich Wankel (1902–1988), a German inventor. The Mazda RX-7 and RX-8 represent the only long-term use of the rotary engine. The rotating combustion chamber engine runs very smoothly, and it produces high power for its size and weight.

The basic rotating combustion chamber engine has a triangular-shaped rotor turning in a housing. The housing is in the shape of a geometric figure called a two-lobed epitrochoid. A seal on each corner, or apex, of the rotor is in constant contact with the housing, so the rotor must turn with an eccentric motion. This means that the center of the rotor moves around the center of the engine. The eccentric motion can be seen in ● **FIGURE 10–14.**

NOTE: **A V-type engine uses two banks or rows of cylinders. An SOHC design, therefore, uses two camshafts but only one camshaft per bank (row) of cylinders. A DOHC V-6, therefore, has four camshafts, two for each bank.**

■ **Type of fuel.** Most engines operate on gasoline, whereas some engines are designed to operate on ethanol (E85), methanol (M85), natural gas, propane, or diesel fuel.

■ **Cooling method.** Most engines are liquid cooled, but some older models were air cooled. Air-cooled engines, such as the original VW Beatle, could not meet exhaust emission standards.

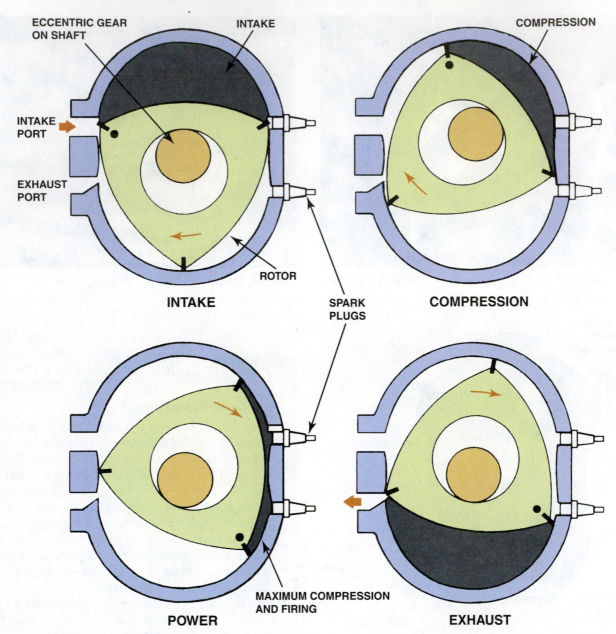

FIGURE 10–14 A rotary engine operates on the four-stroke cycle but uses a rotor instead of a piston and crankshaft to achieve intake, compression, power, and exhaust stroke.

- **Type of induction pressure.** If atmospheric air pressure is used to force the air-fuel mixture into the cylinders, the engine is called **naturally aspirated.** Some engines use a **turbocharger** or **supercharger** to force the air-fuel mixture into the cylinder for even greater power.

ENGINE ROTATION DIRECTION The SAE standard for automotive engine rotation is counterclockwise (CCW) as viewed from the flywheel end (clockwise as viewed from the front of the engine). The flywheel end of the engine is the end to which the power is applied to drive the vehicle. This is called the **principal end** of the engine. The **nonprincipal end** of the engine is opposite the principal end and is generally referred to as the *front* of the engine, where the accessory belts are used.
● **SEE FIGURE 10–15.**

Therefore, in most rear-wheel-drive vehicles, the engine is mounted longitudinally with the principal end at the rear of the engine. Most transversely mounted engines also adhere to the same standard for direction of rotation. Many Honda engines, and some marine applications, may differ from this standard.

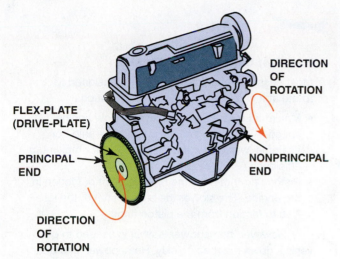

FIGURE 10–15 Inline 4-cylinder engine showing principal and nonprincipal ends. Normal direction of rotation is clockwise (CW) as viewed from the front or accessory belt (nonprincipal) end.

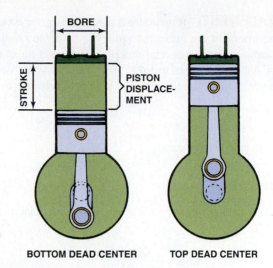

FIGURE 10–16 The bore and stroke of pistons are used to calculate an engine's displacement.

 FREQUENTLY ASKED QUESTION

What Is the Atkinson Cycle?

In 1882, James Atkinson, a British engineer, invented an engine that achieved a higher efficiency than the Otto cycle but produced lower power at low engine speeds. The Atkinson cycle engine was produced in limited numbers until 1890, when sales dropped, and the company that manufactured the engines finally went out of business in 1893.

However, the one key feature of the Atkinson cycle that remains in use today is that the intake valve is held open longer than normal to allow a reverse flow into the intake manifold. This reduces the effective compression ratio and engine displacement and allows the expansion to exceed the compression ratio while retaining a normal compression pressure. This is desirable for good fuel economy because the compression ratio in a spark ignition engine is limited by the octane rating of the fuel used, while a high expansion delivers a longer power stroke and reduces the heat wasted in the exhaust. This increases the efficiency of the engine because more work is being achieved. The Atkinson cycle engine design is commonly used in hybrid electric vehicles.

FIGURE 10–17 The distance between the centerline of the main bearing journal and the centerline of the connecting rod journal determines the stroke of the engine. This photo is a little unusual because it shows a V-6 with a splayed crankshaft used to even out the impulses on a 90-degree, V-6 engine design.

ENGINE MEASUREMENT

BORE The diameter of a cylinder is called the **bore**. The larger the bore, the greater the area on which the gases have to work. Pressure is measured in units, such as pounds per square inch (PSI). The greater the area (in square inches), the higher the force exerted by the pistons to rotate the crankshaft. ● SEE FIGURE 10–16.

STROKE The **stroke** of an engine is the distance the piston travels from top dead center (TDC) to bottom dead center (BDC). This distance is determined by the throw of the crankshaft. The throw is the distance from the centerline of the crankshaft to the centerline of the crankshaft rod journal. The throw is one-half of the stroke. ● SEE FIGURE 10–17.

The longer this distance is, the greater the amount of air-fuel mixture that can be drawn into the cylinder. The more air-fuel mixture inside the cylinder, the more force will result when the mixture is ignited.

NOTE: Changing the connecting rod length does *not* change the stroke of an engine. Changing the connecting rod only changes the position of the piston in the cylinder. Only the crankshaft determines the stroke of an engine.

DISPLACEMENT

Engine size is described as displacement. **Displacement** is the cubic inch (cu. in.) or cubic centimeter (cc) volume displaced or how much air is moved by all of the pistons. A liter (L) is equal to 1,000 cubic centimeters; therefore, most engines today are identified by their displacement in liters.

$$1 \text{ L} = 1,000 \text{ cc}$$
$$1 \text{ L} = 61 \text{ cu. inch}$$
$$1 \text{ cu. inch} = 16.4 \text{ cc}$$

CONVERSION

- To convert cubic inches to liters, divide cubic inches by 61.02.

$$\text{Liters} = \frac{\text{Cubic inches}}{61.02}$$

- To convert liters into cubic inches, multiply by 61.02.

$$\text{Cubic inches} = \text{Liters} \times 61.02$$

CALCULATING CUBIC INCH DISPLACEMENT

The formula to calculate the displacement of an engine is basically the formula for determining the volume of a cylinder multiplied by the number of cylinders.

The formula is:

Cubic inch displacement = π (pi) × R² × Stroke × Number of cyliners

R = Radius of the cylinder or one-half of the bore. The πR^2 part is the formula for the area of a circle.

Applying the formula to a 6-cylinder engine:

- Bore = 4.000 inch
- Stroke = 3.000 inch
- p = 3.14
- R = 2 inches
- R² = 4 (2^2 or 2 × 2)

Cubic inches = 3.14 × 4 (R²) × 3 (stroke) × 6 (number of cylinders).

Cubic inches = 226 cubic inches

Because 1 cubic inch equals 16.4 cubic centimeters, this engine displacement equals 3,706 cubic centimeters or, rounded to 3,700 cubic centimeters, 3.7 liters. ● **SEE CHART 10–1** for an example of engine sizes for a variety of bore and stroke measurements.

ENGINE SIZE CONVERSION

Many vehicle manufacturers will round the displacement so the calculated cubic inch displacement may not agree with the published displacement value. ● **SEE CHART 10–2**.

TECH TIP

How Fast Can an Engine Rotate?

Most passenger vehicle engines are designed to rotate at low speed for the following reasons.

- Maximum efficiency is achieved at low engine speed. A diesel engine used in a large ship, for example, will rotate at about 50 RPM for maximum efficiency.
- Piston ring friction is the highest point of friction in the engine. The slower the engine speed, the less loss to friction from the piston rings.

However, horsepower is what is needed to get a vehicle down the road quickly. Horsepower is torque times engine speed divided by 5,252. Therefore, a high engine speed usually indicates a high horsepower. For example, a Formula 1 race car is limited to 2.4 liter V-8 but uses a 1.6 inch (40 mm) stroke. This extremely short stroke means that the engine can easily achieve the upper limit allowed by the rules of 18,000 RPM while producing over 700 horsepower.

The larger the engine, the more power the engine is capable of producing. Several sayings are often quoted about engine size:

"There is no substitute for cubic inches."
"There is no replacement for displacement."

Although a large engine generally uses more fuel, making an engine larger is often the easiest way to increase power.

COMPRESSION RATIO

DEFINITION **Compression ratio (CR)** is the ratio of the difference in the cylinder volume when the piston is at the bottom of the stroke to the volume in the cylinder above the piston when the piston is at the top of the stroke. The compression ratio of an engine is an important consideration when rebuilding or repairing an engine. ● **SEE FIGURE 10–18.**

If Compression Is Lower	If Compression Is Higher
Lower power	Higher power possible
Poorer fuel economy	Better fuel economy possible
Easier engine cranking	Harder to crank engine, especially when hot
More advanced ignition timing possible without spark knock (detonation)	Less ignition timing required to prevent spark knock (detonation)

V-8 ENGINE					
Stroke	3.50	3.75	3.875	4.00	4.125
Bore	cu. in.	cu. in.	cu. in.	cu. in.	cu. in.
3.00	199	212	219	226	233
3.125	214	229	237	244	252
3.250	232	249	257	265	274
3.375	251	269	277	286	295
3.500	269	288	298	308	317
3.625	288	309	319	330	339
3.750	309	332	343	354	365
3.875	331	354	366	378	390
4.00	352	377	389	402	414
4.125	373	399	413	426	439
6-CYLINDER ENGINE					
Stroke	3.50	3.75	3.875	4.00	4.125
Bore	cu. in.	cu. in.	cu. in.	cu. in.	cu. in.
3.00	148	159	164	169	175
3.125	161	172	178	184	190
3.250	174	186	193	199	205
3.375	188	201	208	215	222
3.500	202	216	223	228	238
3.625	216	232	239	247	255
3.750	232	249	257	265	273
3.875	248	266	275	283	292
4.00	264	283	292	301	311
4.125	280	299	309	319	329
4-CYLINDER ENGINE					
Stroke	3.50	3.75	3.875	4.00	4.125
Bore	cu. in.	cu. in.	cu. in.	cu. in.	cu. in.
3.00	99	106	110	113	117
3.125	107	115	119	123	126
3.250	116	124	129	133	137
3.375	125	134	139	143	148
3.500	135	144	149	152	159
3.625	144	158	160	165	170
3.750	155	166	171	177	182
3.875	165	177	183	189	195
4.00	176	188	195	201	207
4.125	186	200	206	213	220

CHART 10-1

To find the cubic inch displacement, find the bore that is closest to the actual value, then go across to the closest stroke value.

		LITERS TO CUBIC INCHES			
LITERS	CUBIC INCHES	LITERS	CUBIC INCHES	LITERS	CUBIC INCHES
1.0	61	3.2	196	5.4	330
1.3	79	3.3	200 / 201	5.7	350
1.4	85	3.4	204	5.8	351
1.5	91	3.5	215	6.0	366 / 368
1.6	97 / 98	3.7	225	6.1	370
1.7	105	3.8	229 / 231 / 232	6.2	381
1.8	107 / 110 / 112	3.9	239 / 240	6.4	389 / 390 / 391
1.9	116	4.0	241 / 244	6.5	396
2.0	121 / 122	4.1	250 / 252	6.6	400
2.1	128	4.2	255 / 258	6.9	420
2.2	132 / 133 / 134 / 135	4.3	260 / 262 / 265	7.0	425 / 427 / 428 / 429
2.3	138 / 140	4.4	267	7.2	440
2.4	149	4.5	273	7.3	445
2.5	150 / 153	4.6	280 / 281	7.4	454
2.6	156 / 159	4.8	292	7.5	460
2.8	171 / 173	4.9	300 / 301	7.8	475 / 477
2.9	177	5.0	302 / 304 / 305 / 307	8.0	488
3.0	181 / 182 / 183	5.2	318	8.8	534
3.1	191	5.3	327		

CHART 10–2

Liters to cubic inches is often not exact and can result in representing several different engine sizes based on their advertised size in liters.

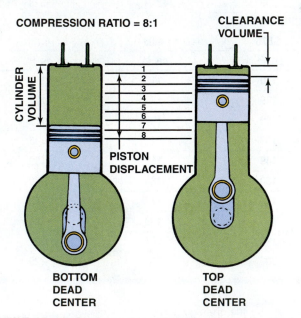

FIGURE 10–18 Compression ratio is the ratio of the total cylinder volume (when the piston is at the bottom of its stroke) to the clearance volume (when the piston is at the top of its stroke).

CALCULATING COMPRESSION RATIO The compression ratio (CR) calculation uses the formula:

$$CR = \frac{\text{Volume in cylinder with piston at bottom of cylinder}}{\text{Volume in cylinder with piston at top center}}$$

● **SEE FIGURE 10–19.**

For example: What is the compression ratio of an engine with 50.3 cu. in. displacement in one cylinder and a combustion chamber volume of 6.7 cu. in.?

$$CR = \frac{50.3 + 6.7 \text{ cu. inch}}{6.7 \text{ cu. inch}} = \frac{57.0}{6.7} = 8.5$$

CHANGING COMPRESSION RATIO Any time an engine is modified, the compression ratio should be checked to make sure it is either the same as it was originally or has been changed to match the diesel compression ratio. Factors that can affect compression ratio include:

- **Head gasket thickness.** A thicker than stock gasket will decrease the compression ratio and a thinner than stock gasket will increase the compression ratio.

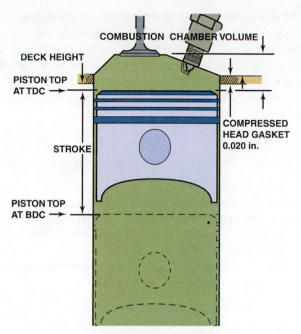

FIGURE 10–19 Combustion chamber volume is the volume above the piston with the piston is at top dead center.

- **Increasing the cylinder size.** If the bore or stroke is increased, a greater amount of air will be compressed into the combustion chamber, which will increase the compression ratio.

TORQUE AND HORSEPOWER

DEFINITION OF TORQUE Torque is the term used to describe a rotating force that may or may not result in motion. Torque is measured as the amount of force multiplied by the length of the lever through which it acts. If you use a 1 feet long wrench to apply 10 pounds (lb) of force to the end of the wrench to turn a bolt, then you are exerting 10 pound-feet (lb-ft) of torque. ● **SEE FIGURE 10–20.**

Torque is the twisting force measured at the end of the crankshaft and measured on a dynamometer. Engine torque is always expressed at a specific engine speed (RPM) or range of engine speeds where the torque is at the maximum. For example, an engine may be listed as producing 275 pound-feet @ 2,400 RPM.

The metric unit for torque is newton-meters, because the newton is the metric unit for force and the distance is expressed in meters.

1 pound-foot = 1.3558 newton-meters

1 newton-meter = 0.7376 pound-foot

DEFINITION OF POWER The term *power* means the rate of doing work. Power equals work divided by time. Work is achieved when a certain amount of mass (weight) is

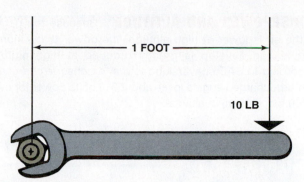

FIGURE 10–20 Torque is a twisting force equal to the distance from the pivot point times the force applied expressed in units called pound-feet (lb-ft) or newton-meters (N-m).

? FREQUENTLY ASKED QUESTION

Is Torque ft-lb or lb-ft?

The definition of torque is a force (lb) applied to an object times the distance from that object (ft). Therefore, based on the definition of the term, torque should be:

lb-ft (a force times a distance)

Newton-meter (N-m) (a force times a distance)

However, torque is commonly labeled, even on some torque wrenches as ft-lb.

? FREQUENTLY ASKED QUESTION

What's with these Kilowatts?

A watt is the electrical unit for *power*, the capacity to do work. It is named after a Scottish inventor, James Watt (1736–1819). The symbol for power is P. Electrical power is calculated as amperes times volts:

$$P \text{ (power)} = I \text{ (amperes)} \cdot E \text{ (volts)}$$

Engine power is commonly rated in watts or kilowatts (1,000 watts equal 1 kilowatt), because 1 horsepower is equal to 746 watts. For example, a 200 horsepower engine can be rated in the metric system, as having the power equal to 149,200 watts or 149.2 kilowatts (kW).

moved a certain distance by a force. If the object is moved in 10 seconds or 10 minutes does not make a difference in the amount of work accomplished, but it does affect the amount of power needed. Power is expressed in units of foot-pounds per minute and power also includes the engine speed (RPM) where the maximum power is achieved. For example, an engine may be listed as producing 280 hp @ 4,400 RPM.

HORSEPOWER AND ALTITUDE Because the density of the air is lower at high altitude, the power that a normal engine can develop is greatly reduced at high altitude. According to SAE conversion factors, a nonsupercharged or nonturbocharged engine loses about 3% of its power for every 1,000 feet (300 m) of altitude.

Therefore, an engine that develops 200 brake horsepower at sea level will only produce about 116 brake horsepower at the top of Pike's Peak in Colorado at 14,110 feet (4,300 m) (3% × 14 − 42%). Supercharged and turbocharged engines are not as greatly affected by altitude as normally aspirated engines, which are those engines that breathe air at normal atmospheric pressure.

SUMMARY

1. The four strokes of the four-stroke cycle are intake, compression, power, and exhaust.

2. Engines are classified by number and arrangement of cylinders and by number and location of valves and camshafts, as well as by type of mounting, fuel used, cooling method, and type of air induction.

3. Most engines rotate clockwise as viewed from the front (accessory) end of the engine. The SAE standard is counterclockwise as viewed from the principal (flywheel) end of the engine.

4. Engine size is called displacement and represents the volume displaced by all of the pistons.

REVIEW QUESTIONS

1. What are the strokes of a four stroke cycle?

2. If an engine at sea level produces 100 hp, how many horsepower would it develop at 6,000 ft of altitude?

CHAPTER QUIZ

1. All overhead valve engines _____.
   a. Use an overhead camshaft
   b. Have the valves located in the cylinder head
   c. Operate by the two-stroke cycle
   d. Use the camshaft to close the valves

2. An SOHC V-8 engine has how many camshafts?
   a. One   c. Three
   b. Two   d. Four

3. The coolant flow through the radiator is controlled by the _____.
   a. Size of the passages in the block
   b. Thermostat
   c. Cooling fan(s)
   d. Water pump

4. Torque is expressed in units of _____.
   a. Pound-feet
   b. Foot-pounds
   c. Foot-pounds per minute
   d. Pound-feet per second

5. Horsepower is expressed in units of _____.
   a. Pound-feet   c. Foot-pounds per minute
   b. Foot-pounds   d. Pound-feet per second

6. A normally aspirated automobile engine loses about _____ power per 1,000 ft of altitude.
   a. 1%   c. 5%
   b. 3%   d. 6%

7. One cylinder of an automotive four-stroke cycle engine completes a cycle every _____.
   a. 90 degrees
   b. 180 degrees
   c. 360 degrees
   d. 720 degrees

8. How many rotations of the crankshaft are required to complete each stroke of a four-stroke cycle engine?
   a. One-fourth
   b. One-half
   c. One
   d. Two

9. A rotating force is called _____.
   a. Horsepower
   b. Torque
   c. Combustion pressure
   d. Eccentric movement

10. Technician A says that a crankshaft determines the stroke of an engine. Technician B says that the length of the connecting rod determines the stroke of an engine. Which technician is correct?
   a. Technician A only
   b. Technician B only
   c. Both Technicians A and B
   d. Neither Technician A nor B

DIESEL ENGINE OPERATION AND DIAGNOSIS

LEARNING OBJECTIVES: **After studying this chapter, the reader should be able to:** • State the characteristics of diesel engines. • Describe the fuel tank and lift pump, injection pump, and engine-driven vacuum pump. • Explain the HEUI system. • Discuss the purpose of glow plugs, diesel fuel heaters, diesel injector nozzles, and accelerator pedal position sensors. • Explain the purpose of diesel engine turbochargers. • Discuss the purpose of the exhaust gas recirculation system, selective catalytic reduction, and diesel oxidation catalysts. • Explain diesel particulate matter, and discuss the function of diesel exhaust particulate filters. • Discuss diesel exhaust smoke diagnosis. • Discuss compression testing, glow plug resistance balance test, injector pop testing, and diesel emission testing.

KEY TERMS: Diesel exhaust fluid (DEF) 119 • Diesel exhaust particulate filter (DPF) 116 • Diesel oxidation catalyst (DOC) 116 • Differential pressure sensor (DPS) 117 • Direct injection (DI) 107 • Glow plug 112 • Heat of compression 105 • High-pressure common rail (HPCR) 109 • Hydraulic electronic unit injection (HEUI) 109 • Indirect injection (IDI) 107 • Injection pump 105 • Lift pump 108 • Pop tester 122 • Particulate matter (PM) 116 • Opacity 123 • Regeneration 117 • Selective catalytic reduction (SCR) 119 • Soot 116 • Urea 119 • Water-fuel separator 108

DIESEL ENGINES

FUNDAMENTALS   In 1892, a German engineer named Rudolf Diesel perfected the compression ignition engine that bears his name. The diesel engine uses heat created by compression to ignite the fuel, so it requires no spark ignition system.

The diesel engine requires compression ratios of 16:1 and higher. Incoming air is compressed until its temperature reaches about 1,000°F (540°C). This is called **heat of compression**. As the piston reaches the top of its compression stroke, fuel is injected into the cylinder, where it is ignited by the hot air. ● **SEE FIGURE 11–1**.

As the fuel burns, it expands and produces power. Because of the very high compression and torque output of a diesel engine, it is made heavier and stronger than the same size gasoline-powered engine.

A diesel engine uses a fuel system with a precision **injection pump** and individual fuel injectors. The pump delivers fuel to the injectors at a high pressure and at timed intervals. Each injector sprays fuel into the combustion chamber at the precise moment required for efficient combustion. ● **SEE FIGURE 11–2**.

ADVANTAGES AND DISADVANTAGES   A diesel engine has several advantages compared to a similar size gasoline-powered engine, including:

1. More torque output
2. Greater fuel economy
3. Long service life

A diesel engine has several disadvantages compared to a similar size gasoline-powered engine, including:

1. Engine noise, especially when cold and/or at idle speed
2. Exhaust smell
3. Cold weather startability
4. Vacuum pump that is needed to supply the vacuum needs of the heat, ventilation, and air-conditioning system

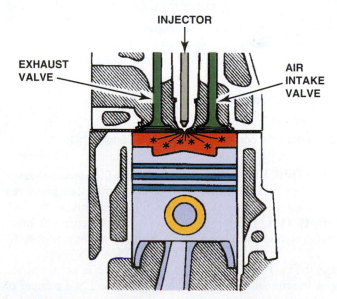

FIGURE 11–1 Diesel combustion occurs when fuel is injected into the hot, highly compressed air in the cylinder.

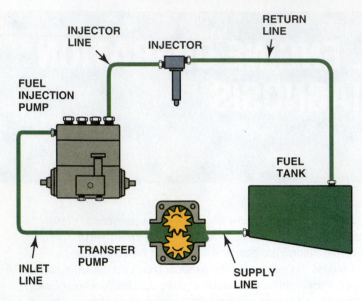

FIGURE 11–2 A typical injector pump type of automotive diesel fuel–injection system.

FIGURE 11–3 A Cummins diesel engine as found in a Dodge pickup truck. A high-pressure pump (up to 30,000 PSI) is used to supply diesel fuel to this common rail, which has tubes running to each injector. Note the thick cylinder walls and heavy-duty construction.

SYSTEM OR COMPONENT	DIESEL ENGINE	GASOLINE ENGINE
Block	Cast iron and heavy (● SEE FIGURE 11–3.)	Cast iron or aluminum and as light as possible
Cylinder head	Cast iron or aluminum	Cast iron or aluminum
Compression ratio	17:1–25:1	8:1–12:1
Peak engine speed	2000–2500 RPM	5000–8000 RPM
Pistons	Aluminum with combustion pockets and heavy-duty connecting rods (● SEE FIGURE 11–4.)	Aluminum, usually flat top or with valve relief but no combustion pockets

CHART 11-1

Comparison between a typical gasoline and a diesel engine.

5. Heavier than a gasoline engine

6. Fuel availability

7. Extra cost compared to a gasoline engine

CONSTRUCTION
Diesel engines must be constructed heavier than gasoline engines because of the tremendous pressures that are created in the cylinders during operation. ● SEE CHART 11-1. The torque output of a diesel engine is often double or more than the same size gasoline-powered engines.

AIR-FUEL RATIOS
In a diesel engine, air is not controlled by a throttle as in a gasoline engine. Instead, the amount of fuel injected is varied to control power and speed. The air-fuel

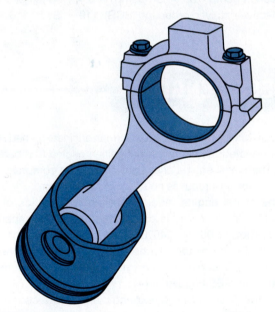

FIGURE 11–4 A rod/piston assembly from a 5.9 liter Cummins diesel engine used in a Dodge pickup truck.

mixture of a diesel engine can vary from as lean as 85:1 at idle to as rich as 20:1 at full load. This higher air-fuel ratio and the increased compression pressures make the diesel more fuel efficient than a gasoline engine, in part because diesel engines do not suffer from throttling losses. Throttling losses involve the power needed in a gasoline engine to draw air past a closed or partially closed throttle.

In a gasoline engine, the speed and power are controlled by the throttle valve, which controls the amount of air entering the engine. Adding more fuel to the cylinders of a gasoline engine without adding more air (oxygen) will not increase the speed or

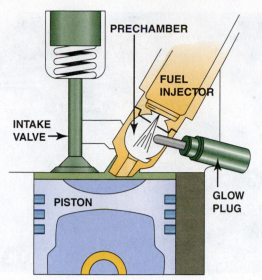

FIGURE 11–5 An indirect injection diesel engine uses a prechamber and a glow plug.

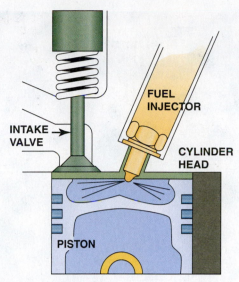

FIGURE 11–6 A direct injection diesel engine injects the fuel directly into the combustion chamber. Many designs do not use a glow plug.

power of the engine. In a diesel engine, speed and power are not controlled by the amount of air entering the cylinders because the engine air intake is always wide open. Therefore, the engine always has enough oxygen to burn the fuel in the cylinder and will increase speed (and power) when additional fuel is supplied.

NOTE: Many newer diesel engines are equipped with a throttle valve. This valve is used by the emission control system and is not designed to control the speed of the engine.

INDIRECT AND DIRECT INJECTION

In an **indirect injection** (abbreviated **IDI**) diesel engine, fuel is injected into a small prechamber, which is connected to the cylinder by a narrow opening. The initial combustion takes place in this prechamber. This has the effect of slowing the rate of combustion, which tends to reduce noise. ● **SEE FIGURE 11–5**.

All indirect injection diesel engines require the use of a glow plug which is an electrical heater that helps start the combustion process.

In a **direct injection** (abbreviated **DI**) diesel engine, fuel is injected directly into the cylinder. The piston incorporates a depression where initial combustion takes place. Direct injection diesel engines are generally more efficient than indirect injection engines, but have a tendency to produce greater amounts of noise. ● **SEE FIGURE 11–6**.

While some direct injection diesel engines use glow plugs to help cold starting and to reduce emissions, many direct injection diesel engines do not use glow plugs.

DIESEL FUEL IGNITION

Ignition occurs in a diesel engine by injecting fuel into the air charge, which has been heated by compression to a temperature greater than the ignition point of the fuel or about 1,000°F (538°C). The chemical reaction of burning the fuel creates heat, which causes the gases to expand, forcing the piston to rotate the crankshaft. A four-stroke diesel engine requires two rotations of the crankshaft to complete one cycle.

- On the intake stroke, the piston passes TDC, the intake valve(s) opens, and filtered air enters the cylinder, while the exhaust valve(s) remains open for a few degrees to allow all of the exhaust gases to escape from the previous combustion event.

- On the compression stroke, after the piston passes BDC, the intake valve(s) closes and the piston travels up to TDC (completion of the first crankshaft rotation).

- On the power stroke, the piston nears TDC on the compression stroke and diesel fuel is injected into the cylinder by the injectors. The ignition of the fuel does not start immediately but the heat of compression starts the combustion phases in the cylinder. During this power stroke, the piston passes TDC and the expanding gases force the piston down, rotating the crankshaft.

- On the exhaust stroke, as the piston passes BDC, the exhaust valve(s) opens and the exhaust gases start to flow out of the cylinder. This continues as the piston travels up to TDC, pumping the spent gases out of the cylinder. At TDC, the second crankshaft rotation is complete.

THREE PHASES OF COMBUSTION

There are three distinct phases or parts to the combustion in a diesel engine.

1. **Ignition delay.** Near the end of the compression stroke, fuel injection begins, but ignition does not begin immediately. This period is called *ignition delay*.

2. **Rapid combustion.** This phase of combustion occurs when the fuel first starts to burn, creating a sudden rise in cylinder pressure. It is this sudden and rapid rise in combustion

FIGURE 11–7 A fuel temperature sensor is being tested using an ice bath.

chamber pressure that causes the characteristic diesel engine knock.

3. **Controlled combustion.** After the rapid combustion occurs, the rest of the fuel in the combustion chamber begins to burn and injection continues. This process occurs in an area near the injector that contains fuel surrounded by air. This fuel burns as it mixes with the air.

FUEL TANK AND LIFT PUMP

PARTS INVOLVED A fuel tank used on a vehicle equipped with a diesel engine differs from the one used with a gasoline engine in the following ways.

- The filler neck is larger for diesel fuel. The nozzle size is 15/16 inch (24 mm) instead of 13/16 inch (21 mm) for gasoline filler necks. Truck stop diesel nozzles for large over-the-road truck are usually larger, 1.25 inch or 1.5 inch (32 mm or 38 mm) to allow for faster fueling of large-capacity fuel tanks.
- There are no evaporative emission control devices or a charcoal (carbon) canister. Diesel fuel is not as volatile as gasoline and, therefore, diesel vehicles do not have evaporative emission control devices.

The diesel fuel is usually drawn from the fuel tank by a separate pump, called a **lift pump** and delivers the fuel to the injection pump. Between the fuel tank and the lift pump is a **water-fuel separator.** Water is heavier than diesel fuel and sinks to the bottom of the separator. Part of normal routine maintenance on a vehicle equipped with a diesel engine is to drain the water from the water-fuel separator. A float is often used inside the separator, which is connected to a warning light on the dash that lights if the water reaches a level where

FIGURE 11–8 A typical distributor-type diesel injection pump showing the pump, lines, and fuel filter.

it needs to be drained. The water separator is often part of the fuel filter assembly. Both the fuel filter and the water separator are common maintenance items.

NOTE: Water can cause corrosive damage and wear to diesel engine parts because it is not a good lubricant. Water cannot be atomized by a diesel fuel injector nozzle and will often "blow out" the nozzle tip.

Many diesel engines also use a *fuel temperature sensor.* The computer uses this information to adjust fuel delivery based on the density of the fuel. ● SEE FIGURE 11–7.

INJECTION PUMP

NEED FOR HIGH-PRESSURE FUEL PUMP A diesel engine injection pump is used to increase the pressure of the diesel fuel from very low values from the lift pump to the extremely high pressures needed for injection.

- The lift pump is a *low-pressure, high-volume pump.*
- The high-pressure injection pump is a *high-pressure, low-volume pump.*

Injection pumps are usually driven by a gear off the camshaft at the front of the engine. As the injection pump shaft rotates, the diesel fuel is fed from a fill port to a high-pressure chamber. If a distributor-type injection pump is used, the fuel is forced out of the injection port to the correct injector nozzle through the high-pressure line. ● SEE FIGURE 11–8.

NOTE: Because of the very tight tolerances in a diesel engine, the smallest amount of dirt can cause excessive damage to the engine and to the fuel-injection system.

DISTRIBUTOR INJECTION PUMP A distributor diesel injection pump is a high-pressure pump assembly with lines leading to each individual injector. The high-pressure lines

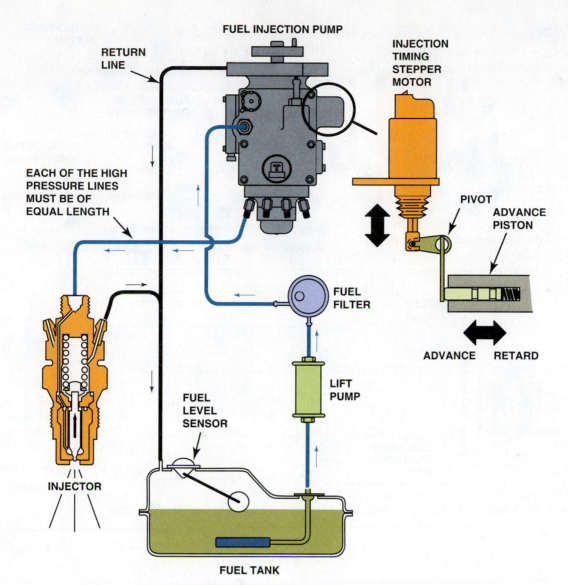

RETURN LINE

FUEL INJECTION PUMP

INJECTION TIMING STEPPER MOTOR

EACH OF THE HIGH PRESSURE LINES MUST BE OF EQUAL LENGTH

PIVOT

ADVANCE PISTON

FUEL FILTER

ADVANCE   RETARD

INJECTOR

FUEL LEVEL SENSOR

LIFT PUMP

FUEL TANK

FIGURE 11–9 A schematic of Standadyne diesel fuel–injection pump assembly showing all of the related components.

between the distributor and the injectors must be the exact same length to ensure proper injection timing. The high-pressure fuel causes the injectors to open. Due to the internal friction of the lines, there is a slight delay before fuel pressure opens the injector nozzle. The injection pump itself creates the injection advance needed for engine speeds above idle often by using a stepper motor attached to the advance piston, and the fuel is then discharged into the lines. ● SEE FIGURE 11–9.

NOTE: The lines expand during an injection event. This is how timing checks are performed. The pulsing of the injector line is picked up by a probe used to detect the injection event similar to a timing light used to detect a spark on a gasoline engine.

HIGH-PRESSURE COMMON RAIL Newer diesel engines use a fuel delivery system referred to as a **high-pressure common rail (HPCR)** design. Diesel fuel under high pressure, over 20,000 PSI (138,000 kPa), is applied to the

injectors, which are opened by a solenoid controlled by the computer. Because the injectors are computer controlled, the combustion process can be precisely controlled to provide maximum engine efficiency with the lowest possible noise and exhaust emissions. ● SEE FIGURE 11–10.

HEUI SYSTEM

PRINCIPLES OF OPERATION Ford 7.3, 6.0, and 6.4 liter (and Navistar) diesels use a system called a **hydraulic electronic unit injection** system, or **HEUI** system. The components used include:

- High-pressure engine oil pump and reservoir
- Pressure regulator for the engine oil
- Passages in the cylinder head for flow of fuel to the injectors

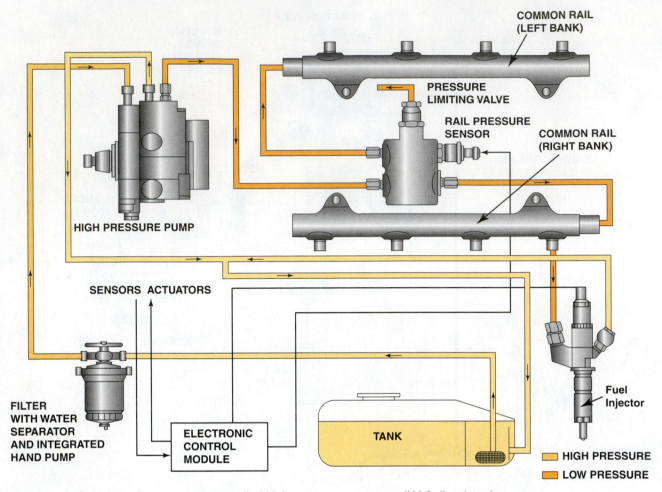

FIGURE 11–10 Overview of a computer-controlled high-pressure common rail V-8 diesel engine.

COMMON RAIL (LEFT BANK)

PRESSURE LIMITING VALVE

RAIL PRESSURE SENSOR

COMMON RAIL (RIGHT BANK)

HIGH PRESSURE PUMP

SENSORS ACTUATORS

Fuel Injector

FILTER WITH WATER SEPARATOR AND INTEGRATED HAND PUMP

ELECTRONIC CONTROL MODULE

TANK

■ HIGH PRESSURE
■ LOW PRESSURE

OPERATION The engine oil is pressurized to provide an opening pressure strong enough to overcome the fuel pressure when the solenoid is commanded to open by the PCM. The system functions as follows:

- Fuel is drawn from the tank by the tandem fuel pump, which circulates fuel at low pressure through the fuel filter/water separator/fuel heater bowl and then fuel is directed back to the fuel pump where fuel is pumped at high pressure into the cylinder head fuel galleries.

- The injectors, which are hydraulically actuated by engine oil pressure from the high-pressure oil pump, are then fired by the powertrain control module (PCM). The control system for the fuel injectors is the PCM, and the injectors are fired based on sensor inputs received by the PCM.
  ● SEE FIGURE 11–11.

HEUI injectors rely on O-rings to keep fuel and oil from mixing or escaping, causing performance problems or engine damage. HEUI injectors use five O-rings. The three external O-rings should be replaced with updated O-rings if they fail. The two internal O-rings are not replaceable and if these fail,

O-RING GROOVE

FIGURE 11–11 A HEUI injector from a Ford PowerStroke diesel engine. The O-ring grooves indicate the location of the O-rings that seal the fuel section of the injector from coolant and from the engine oil.

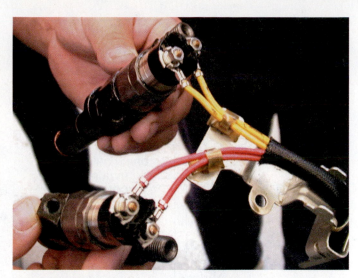

FIGURE 11–12 Typical computer-controlled diesel engine fuel injectors.

the injector(s) must be replaced. The most common symptoms of injector O-ring trouble include:

- Oil getting in the fuel
- The fuel filter element turning black
- Long cranking times before starting
- Sluggish performance
- Reduction in power
- Increased oil consumption (This often accompanies O-ring problems or any fault that lets fuel in the oil.)

DIESEL INJECTOR NOZZLES

PARTS INVOLVED Diesel injector nozzles are spring-loaded closed valves that spray fuel directly into the combustion chamber or precombustion chamber when the injector is opened. Injector nozzles are threaded or clamped into the cylinder head, one for each cylinder, and are replaceable as an assembly.

The tip of the injector nozzle has many holes to deliver an atomized spray of diesel fuel into the cylinder. Parts of a diesel injector nozzle include:

- **Heat shield.** This is the outer shell of the injector nozzle and may have external threads where it seals in the cylinder head.
- **Injector body.** This is the inner part of the nozzle and contains the injector needle valve and spring, and threads into the outer heat shield.
- **Diesel injector needle valve.** This precision machined valve and the tip of the needle seal against the injector body when it is closed. When the valve is open, diesel fuel is sprayed into the combustion chamber. This passage is controlled by a computer-controlled solenoid on diesel engines equipped with computer-controlled injection.
- **Injector pressure chamber.** The pressure chamber is a machined cavity in the injector body around the tip of the injector needle. Injection pump pressure forces fuel into this chamber, forcing the needle valve open.

DIESEL INJECTOR NOZZLE OPERATION The electric solenoid attached to the injector nozzle is computer controlled and opens to allow fuel to flow into the injector pressure chamber. ● **SEE FIGURE 11–12**.

The fuel flows down through a fuel passage in the injector body and into the pressure chamber. The high fuel pressure in the pressure chamber forces the needle valve upward, compressing the needle valve return spring and forcing the needle valve open.

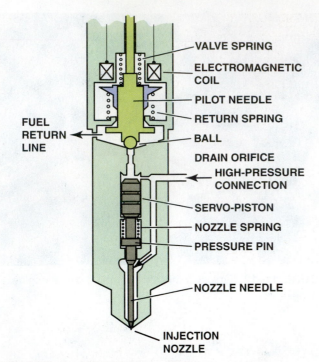

FIGURE 11–13 A Duramax injector showing all the internal parts.

When the needle valve opens, diesel fuel is discharged into the combustion chamber in a hollow cone spray pattern.

Any fuel that leaks past the needle valve returns to the fuel tank through a return passage and line. ● SEE FIGURE 11–13.

GLOW PLUGS

PURPOSE AND FUNCTION Glow plugs are always used in diesel engines equipped with a precombustion chamber and may be used in direct injection diesel engines to aid starting. A **glow plug** is a heating element that uses 12 volts from the battery and aids in the starting of a cold engine by providing heat to help the fuel to ignite. ● SEE FIGURE 11–14.

As the temperature of the glow plug increases, the resistance of the heating element inside increases, thereby reducing the current in amperes needed by the glow plugs.

OPERATION Most glow plugs used in newer vehicles are controlled by the Powertrain Control Module, which monitors coolant temperature and intake air temperature. The glow plugs are turned on or pulsed on or off depending on the temperature of the engine. The PCM will also keep the glow plug turned on after the engine starts, to reduce white exhaust smoke (unburned fuel) and to improve idle quality after starting. ● SEE FIGURE 11–15.

The "wait to start" lamp (if equipped) will light when the engine and the outside temperatures are low to allow time for the glow plugs to get hot.

FIGURE 11–14 A glow plug assortment showing the various types and sizes of glow plugs used. Always use the specified glow plugs.

HEATED INLET AIR Some diesel engines, such as the Dodge Cummins and the General Motors 6.6 liter Duramax V-8, use an electrical heater wire to warm the intake air to help in cold weather starting and running. ● SEE FIGURE 11–16.

ENGINE-DRIVEN VACUUM PUMP

Because a diesel engine is unthrottled, it creates very little vacuum in the intake manifold. Several engine and vehicle components operate using vacuum, such as the exhaust gas

 FREQUENTLY ASKED QUESTION

How Can You Tell If Gasoline Has Been Added to the Diesel Fuel by Mistake?

If gasoline has been accidentally added to diesel fuel and is burned in a diesel engine, the result can be very damaging to the engine. The gasoline can ignite faster than diesel fuel, which would tend to increase the temperature of combustion. This high temperature can harm injectors and glow plugs, as well as pistons, head gaskets, and other major diesel engine components. If contaminated fuel is suspected, first smell the fuel at the filler neck. If the fuel smells like gasoline, then the tank should be drained and refilled with diesel fuel. If the smell test does not indicate a gasoline or any rancid smell, then test a sample for proper specific gravity.

Note: Diesel fuel designed for on-road use should be green. Red diesel fuel (high sulfur) should only be found in off-road or farm equipment.

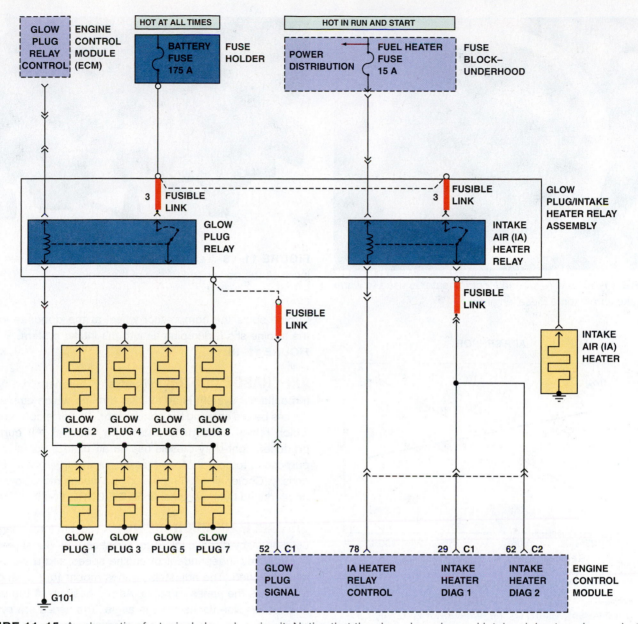

FIGURE 11–15 A schematic of a typical glow plug circuit. Notice that the glow plug relay and intake air heater relay are both computer controlled.

recirculation (EGR) valve and the heating and ventilation blend and air doors. Most diesels used in cars and light trucks are equipped with an engine-driven vacuum pump to supply the vacuum for these components.

DIESEL FUEL HEATERS

Diesel fuel heaters help prevent power loss and stalling in cold weather. The heater is placed in the fuel line between the tank and the primary filter. Some coolant heaters are thermostatically controlled, which allows fuel to bypass the heater once it has reached operating temperature.

ACCELERATOR PEDAL POSITION SENSOR

Some light-truck diesel engines are equipped with an electronic throttle to control the amount of fuel injected into the engine. Because a diesel engine does not use a throttle in the air intake, the only way to control engine speed is by controlling the amount of fuel being injected into the cylinders. Instead of a mechanical link from the accelerator pedal to the diesel injection pump, a throttle-by-wire system uses an accelerator pedal position (APP) sensor. To ensure safety, it consists of three separate sensors that change in voltage as the accelerator pedal is depressed. ● **SEE FIGURE 11–17.**

FIGURE 11–16 A wire-wound electric heater is used to warm the intake air on some diesel engines.

APP SENSOR

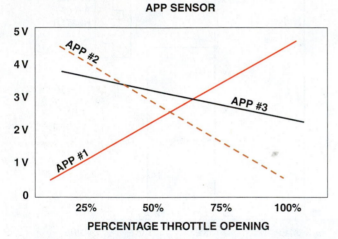

FIGURE 11–17 A typical accelerator pedal position (APP) sensor uses three different sensors in one package with each creating a different voltage as the accelerator is moved.

The computer checks for errors by comparing the voltage output of each of the three sensors inside the APP and compares them to what they should be if there are no faults. If an error is detected, the engine and vehicle speed are often reduced.

DIESEL ENGINE TURBOCHARGERS

TURBOCHARGED DIESELS A turbocharger greatly increases engine power by pumping additional compressed air into the combustion chambers. This allows a greater quantity of fuel to be burned in the cylinders resulting in greater power output. In a turbocharger, the turbine wheel spins as exhaust gas flows out of the engine and drives the turbine blades. The

FIGURE 11–18 A Cummins diesel turbocharger is used to increase the power and torque of the engine.

turbine spins the compressor wheel at the opposite end of the turbine shaft, pumping air into the intake system. ● **SEE FIGURE 11–18**.

AIR CHARGE COOLER The first component in a typical turbocharger system is an air filter through which ambient air passes before entering the compressor. The air is compressed, which raises its density (mass/unit volume). All currently produced light-duty diesels use an air charge cooler whose purpose is to cool the compressed air to further raise the air density. Cooler air entering the engine means more power can be produced by the engine. ● **SEE FIGURE 11–19**.

VARIABLE TURBOCHARGER A variable turbocharger is used on many diesel engines for boost control. Boost pressure is controlled independent of engine speed and a wastegate is not needed. The adjustable vanes mount to a unison ring that allows the vanes to move. As the position of the unison ring rotates, the vanes change angle. The vanes are opened to minimize flow at the turbine and exhaust back pressure at low engine speeds. To increase turbine speed, the vanes are closed. The velocity of the exhaust gases increases, as does the speed of the turbine. The unison ring is connected to a cam that is positioned by a rack-and-pinion gear. The turbocharger's vane position actuator solenoid connects to a hydraulic piston, which moves the rack to rotate the pinion gear and cam. ● **SEE FIGURE 11–20**.

The turbocharger vane position control solenoid valve is used to advance the unison ring's relationship to the turbine and thereby articulate the vanes. This solenoid actuates a spool valve that applies oil pressure to either side of a piston. Oil flow has three modes: apply, hold, and release.

- *Apply* moves the vanes toward a closed position.
- *Hold* maintains the vanes in a fixed position.
- *Release* moves the vanes toward the open position.

The turbocharger vane position actuation is controlled by the ECM, which can change turbine boost efficiency independent of

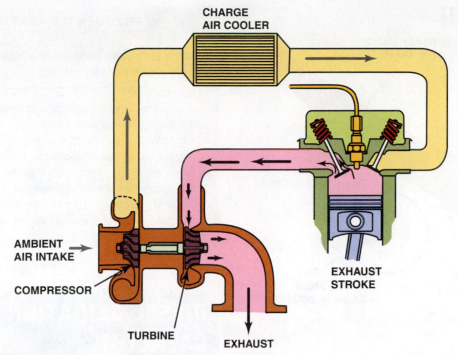

FIGURE 11–19 An air charge cooler is used to cool the compressed air.

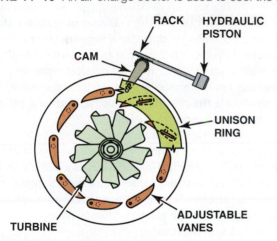

FIGURE 11–20 A variable vane turbocharger allows the boost to be controlled without the need of a wastegate.

engine speed. The ECM provides a control signal to the valve solenoid along with a low-side reference. A pulse-width-modulated signal from the ECM moves the valve to the desired position.

FIGURE 11–21 A cutaway showing the exhaust cooler. The cooler the exhaust is, the more effective it is in controlling NO_x emissions.

EXHAUST GAS RECIRCULATION

The EGR system recycles some exhaust gas back into the intake stream to cool combustion, which reduces oxides of nitrogen (NO_x) emissions. The EGR system includes:

- Plumbing that carries some exhaust gas from the turbocharger exhaust inlet to the intake ports

- EGR control valve
- Stainless steel cooling element used to cool the exhaust gases (● **SEE FIGURE 11–21.**)

The EGR valve is PCM controlled and often uses a DC stepper motor and worm gear to move the valve stem open. The gear is not attached to the valve and can only force it open. Return spring force closes the valve. The EGR valve and sensor assembly is a five-wire design. The PCM uses the position sensor to verify that valve action is as commanded.

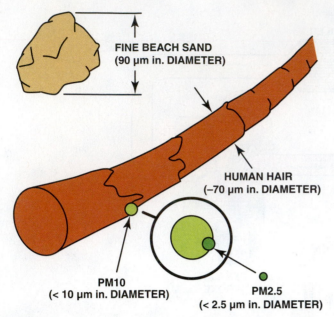

FINE BEACH SAND
(90 μm in. DIAMETER)

HUMAN HAIR
(−70 μm in. DIAMETER)

PM10
(< 10 μm in. DIAMETER)

PM2.5
(< 2.5 μm in. DIAMETER)

FIGURE 11–22 Relative size of particulate matter to a human hair.

? **FREQUENTLY ASKED QUESTION**

What Is the Big Deal for the Need to Control Very Small Soot Particles?

For many years soot or particulate matter (PM) was thought to be less of a health concern than exhaust emissions from gasoline engines. It was felt that the soot could simply fall to the ground without causing any noticeable harm to people or the environment. However, it was discovered that the small soot particulates when breathed in are not expelled from the lungs like larger particles but instead get trapped in the deep areas of the lungs where they accumulate.

DIESEL PARTICULATE MATTER

PARTICULATE MATTER STANDARDS **Particulate matter (PM),** also called **soot,** refers to tiny particles of solid or semisolid material suspended in the atmosphere. This includes particles between 0.1 and 50 microns in diameter. The heavier particles, larger than 50 microns, typically tend to settle out quickly due to gravity. Particulates are generally categorized as follows:

- **Total suspended particulate (TSP).** Refers to all particles between 0.1 and 50 microns. Up until 1987, the Environmental Protection Agency (EPA) standard for particulates was based on levels of TSP.

- **PM10.** Refers to particulate matter of 10 microns or less (approximately 1/6 the diameter of a human hair). EPA has a standard for particles based on levels of PM10.

- **PM2.5.** Refers to particulate matter of 2.5 microns or less (approximately 1/20 the diameter of a human hair), also called "fine" particles. In July 1997, the EPA approved a standard for PM2.5. ● **SEE FIGURE 11–22.**

SOOT CATEGORIES In general, soot particles produced by diesel combustion fall into the following categories.

- **Fine.** Less than 2.5 microns
- **Ultrafine.** Less than 0.1 micron, and make up 80% to 95% of soot

DIESEL OXIDATION CATALYST

PURPOSE AND FUNCTION **Diesel oxidation catalysts (DOC)** are used in all light-duty diesel engines, since 2007. They consist of a flow-through honeycomb-style substrate structure that is wash coated with a layer of catalyst materials, similar to those used in a gasoline engine catalytic converter. These materials include the precious metals platinum and palladium, as well as other base metal catalysts.

Catalysts chemically react with exhaust gas to convert harmful nitrogen oxide into nitrogen dioxide, and to oxidize absorbed hydrocarbons. The chemical reaction acts as a combustor for the unburned fuel that is characteristic of diesel compression ignition. The main function of the DOC is to start a regeneration event by converting the fuel-rich exhaust gases to heat.

The DOC also reduces:

- Carbon monoxide (CO)
- Hydrocarbons (HC)
- Odor-causing compounds such as aldehydes and sulfur
● **SEE FIGURE 11–23.**

DIESEL EXHAUST PARTICULATE FILTER

PURPOSE AND FUNCTION **Diesel exhaust particulate filters (DPFs)** are used in all light-duty diesel vehicles, since 2007, to meet the exhaust emissions standards. The heated exhaust gas from the DOC flows into the DPF, which captures diesel exhaust gas particulates (soot) to prevent them from being released into the atmosphere. This is done by forcing the

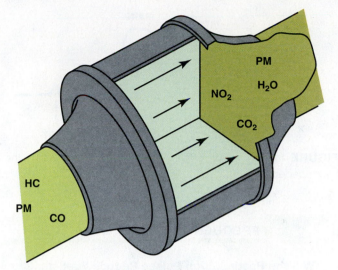

FIGURE 11–23 Chemical reaction within the DOC.

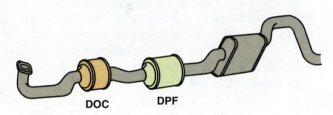

FIGURE 11–24 Aftertreatment of diesel exhaust is handled by the DOC and DPF.

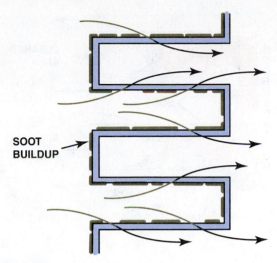

FIGURE 11–25 The soot is trapped in the passages of the DPF. The exhaust has to flow through the sides of the trap and exit.

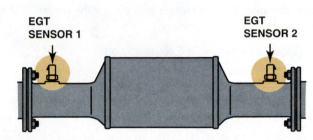

FIGURE 11–26 EGT 1 and EGT 2 are used by the PCM to help control after treatment.

exhaust through a porous cell which has a silicon carbide substrate with honeycomb-cell-type channels that trap the soot. The main difference between the DPF and a typical catalyst filter is that the entrance to every other cell channel in the DPF substrate is blocked at one end. So instead of flowing directly through the channels, the exhaust gas is forced through the porous walls of the blocked channels and exits through the adjacent open-ended channels. This type of filter is also referred to as a "wall-flow" filter. ● SEE FIGURE 11–24.

OPERATION
Soot particulates in the gas remain trapped on the DPF channel walls where, over time, the trapped particulate matter will begin to clog the filter. The filter must therefore be purged periodically to remove accumulated soot particles. The process of purging soot from the DPF is described as **regeneration.** When the temperature of the exhaust gas is increased, the heat incinerates the soot particles trapped in the filter and is effectively renewed. ● SEE FIGURE 11–25.

EXHAUST GAS TEMPERATURE SENSORS
The following two exhaust gas temperature sensors are used to help the PCM control the DPF.

- EGT sensor 1 is positioned between the DOC and the DPF where it can measure the temperature of the exhaust gas entering the DPF.

- EGT sensor 2 measures the temperature of the exhaust gas stream immediately after it exits the DPF.

The Powertrain Control Module monitors the signals from the EGT sensors as part of its calibrations to control DPF regeneration. Proper exhaust gas temperatures at the inlet of the DPF are crucial for proper operation and for starting the regeneration process. Too high a temperature at the DPF will cause the DPF substrate to melt or crack. Regeneration will be terminated at temperatures above 1,470°F (800°C). With too low a temperature, self-regeneration will not fully complete the soot-burning process. ● SEE FIGURE 11–26.

DPF DIFFERENTIAL PRESSURE SENSOR
The DPF **differential pressure sensor (DPS)** has two pressure sample lines.

- One line is attached before the DPF.
- The other is located after the DPF.

The exact location of the DPS varies by vehicle model type such as medium duty, pickup, or van. By measuring the exhaust supply (upstream) pressure from the DOC, and the post DPF (downstream) pressure, the PCM can determine differential pressure, also called "delta" pressure, across the DPF. Data from the DPF differential pressure sensor is used by the PCM to calibrate for controlling DPF exhaust system operation.

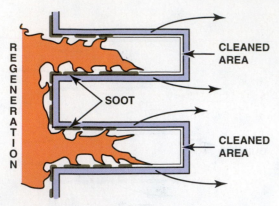

FIGURE 11–27 Regeneration burns the soot and renews the DPF.

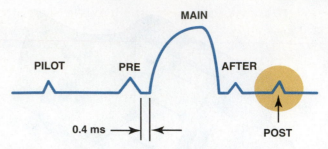

FIGURE 11–28 The post-injection pulse occurs to create the heat needed for regeneration.

DIESEL PARTICULATE FILTER REGENERATION The primary reason for soot removal is to prevent the buildup of exhaust back pressure. Excessive back pressure increases fuel consumption, reduces power output, and can potentially cause engine damage. Several factors can trigger the diesel PCM to perform regeneration, including:

- Distance since last DPF regeneration
- Fuel used since last DPF regeneration
- Engine run time since last DPF regeneration
- Exhaust differential pressure across the DPF

DPF REGENERATION PROCESS A number of engine components are required to function together for the regeneration process to be performed:

1. PCM controls that impact DPF regeneration include late post-injections, engine speed, and adjusting fuel pressure.
2. Adding late post-injection pulses provides the engine with additional fuel to be oxidized in the DOC, which increases exhaust temperatures entering the DPF to 900°F (500°C) or higher. **SEE FIGURE 11–27**.
3. The intake air valve acts as a restrictor that reduces air entry to the engine, which increases engine operating temperature.
4. The intake air heater may also be activated to warm intake air during regeneration.

TYPES OF DPF REGENERATION DPF regeneration can be initiated in a number of ways, depending on the vehicle application and operating circumstances. The two main regeneration types are as follows:

- **Passive regeneration.** During normal vehicle operation when driving conditions produce sufficient load and exhaust temperatures, passive DPF regeneration may occur. This passive regeneration occurs without input from the PCM or the driver. A passive regeneration may typically occur while the vehicle is being driven at highway speed or towing a trailer.

> **? FREQUENTLY ASKED QUESTION**
>
> **Will the Postinjection Pulses Reduce Fuel Economy?**
>
> Maybe. Due to the added fuel-injection pulses and late fuel-injection timing, an increase in fuel consumption may be noticed on the driver information center (DIC) during the regeneration time period. A drop in overall fuel economy should not be noticeable.
> **SEE FIGURE 11–28**.

- **Active regeneration.** Active regeneration is commanded by the PCM when it determines that the DPF requires it to remove excess soot buildup and conditions for filter regeneration have been met. Active regeneration is usually not noticeable to the driver. The vehicle needs to be driven at speeds above 30 mph for approximately 20 to 30 minutes to complete a full regeneration. During regeneration, the exhaust gases reach temperatures above 1,000°F (550°C). Active regeneration is usually not noticeable to the driver.

> **☠ WARNING**
>
> Tailpipe outlet exhaust temperature will be greater than 572°F (300°C) during service regeneration. To help prevent personal injury or property damage from fire or burns, keep vehicle exhaust away from any object and people.

ASH LOADING Regeneration will not burn off ash. Only the particulate matter (PM) is burned off during regeneration. Ash is a noncombustible by-product from normal oil consumption. Ash accumulation in the DPF will eventually cause a restriction in the particulate filter. To service an ash-loaded DPF, the DPF will need to be removed from the vehicle and cleaned or

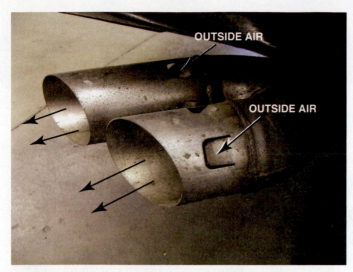

FIGURE 11–29 The exhaust is split into two outlets and has slits to help draw outside air in as the exhaust leaves the tailpipe. The end result is cooler exhaust gases exiting the tailpipe.

OUTSIDE AIR

OUTSIDE AIR

 FREQUENTLY ASKED QUESTION

What Is an Exhaust Air Cooler?

An exhaust air cooler is simply a section of tailpipe that has slits for air to enter. As hot exhaust rushes past the gap, outside air is drawn into the area which reduces the exhaust discharge temperature. The cooler significantly lowers exhaust temperature at the tailpipe from about 800°F (430°C) to approximately 500°F (270°C). ● SEE FIGURE 11–29.

replaced. Low ash content engine oil (API CJ-4) is required for vehicles with the DPF system. The CJ-4 rated oil is limited to 1% ash content.

SELECTIVE CATALYTIC REDUCTION

PURPOSE AND FUNCTION Selective catalytic reduction (SCR) is a method used to reduce NO_x emissions by injecting urea into the exhaust stream. Instead of using large amounts of exhaust gas recirculation (EGR), the SCR system uses a urea. **Urea** is used as a nitrogen fertilizer. It is colorless, odorless, and nontoxic. Urea is called **diesel exhaust fluid (DEF)** in North America and AdBlue in Europe: ● SEE FIGURE 11–30.

The urea is injected into the catalyst where it sets off a chemical reaction which converts nitrogen oxides (NO_x) into nitrogen (N_2) and water (H_2O). Vehicle manufacturers size the

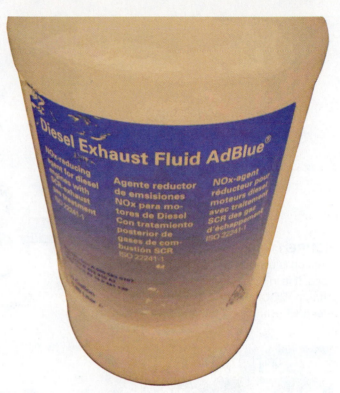

FIGURE 11–30 Diesel exhaust fluid cost $3 to $4 a gallon and is housed in a separate container that holds from 5 to 10 gallons, or enough to last until the next scheduled oil change in most diesel vehicles that use SCR.

onboard urea storage tank so that it needs to be refilled at about each scheduled oil change or every 7,500 miles (12,000 km). A warning light alerts the driver when the urea level needs to be refilled. If the warning light is ignored and the diesel exhaust fluid is not refilled, current EPA regulations require that the operation of the engine be restricted and may not start unless the fluid is refilled. This regulation is designed to prevent the engine from being operated without the fluid, which, if not, would greatly increase exhaust emissions. ● SEE FIGURE 11–31.

ADVANTAGES OF SCR Using urea injection instead of large amounts of EGR results in the following advantages.

- Potential higher engine power output for the same size engine
- Reduced NO_x emissions up to 90%
- Reduced HC and CO emissions up to 50%
- Reduced particulate matter (PM) by 50%

DISADVANTAGES OF SCR Using urea injection instead of large amounts of EGR results in the following disadvantages.

- Onboard storage tank required for the urea
- Difficult to find local sources of urea
- Increased costs to the vehicle owner due to having to refill the urea storage tank

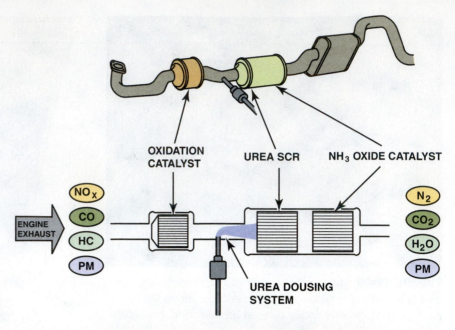

FIGURE 11–31 Urea (diesel exhaust fluid) injection is used to reduce NO_x exhaust emissions. It is injected after the diesel oxidation catalyst (DOC) and before the diesel particulate filter (DPF) on this 6.7 liter Ford diesel engine.

OXIDATION CATALYST   UREA SCR NH_3 OXIDE CATALYST

ENGINE EXHAUST

NO_x CO HC PM

N_2 CO_2 H_2O PM

UREA DOUSING SYSTEM

DIESEL EXHAUST SMOKE DIAGNOSIS

Although some exhaust smoke is considered normal operation for many diesel engines, especially older units, the cause of excessive exhaust smoke should be diagnosed and repaired.

BLACK SMOKE Black exhaust smoke is caused by incomplete combustion because of a lack of air or a fault in the injection system that could cause an excessive amount of fuel in the cylinders. Items that should be checked include the following:

- Injector balance test to locate faulty injectors using a scan tool
- Proper operation of the fuel rail pressure (FRP) sensor
- Restrictions in the intake or turbocharger
- Engine oil usage

WHITE SMOKE White exhaust smoke occurs most often during cold engine starts because the smoke is usually condensed fuel droplets. White exhaust smoke is also an indication of cylinder misfire on a warm engine. The most common causes of white exhaust smoke include:

- Inoperative glow plugs
- Low engine compression
- Incorrect injector spray pattern
- Coolant leak into the combustion chamber

GRAY OR BLUE SMOKE Blue exhaust smoke is usually due to oil consumption caused by worn piston rings, scored cylinder walls, or defective valve stem seals. Gray or blue smoke can also be caused by a defective injector(s).

DIESEL PERFORMANCE DIAGNOSIS

Always start the diagnosis of a diesel engine concern by checking the oil. Higher than normal oil level can indicate that diesel fuel has leaked into the oil. Diesel engines can be diagnosed using a scan tool in most cases, because most of the pressure sensors values can be displayed. Common faults include:

- Hard starting
- No start
- Extended cranking before starting
- Low power

Using a scan tool, check the sensor values in ● **CHART 11–2**. to help pin down the source of the problem. Also check the minimum pressures that are required to start the engine if a no-start condition is being diagnosed. ● **SEE FIGURE 11–32**.

COMPRESSION TESTING

A compression test is fundamental for determining the mechanical condition of a diesel engine. To test the compression on a diesel engine, the following will have to be done.

- Remove the glow plug (if equipped) or the injector.
- Use a diesel compression gauge, as the compression is too high to use a gasoline engine compression gauge.

A diesel engine should produce at least 300 PSI (2,068 kPa) of compression pressure and all cylinders should be within 50 PSI (345 kPa) of each other. ● **SEE FIGURE 11–33**.

DIESEL TROUBLESHOOTING CHART

5.9 DODGE CUMMINS 2003–2008

Low-pressure pump	8–12 PSI
Pump amperes	4 A
Pump volume	45 oz. inch 30 sec.
High-pressure pump	5,000–23,000 PSI
Idle PSI	5,600–5,700 PSI
Electronic Fuel Control (EFC) maximum fuel pressure	Disconnect EFC to achieve maximum pressure
Injector volts	90 V
Injector amperes	20 A
Glow plug amperes	60–80 A × 2 (120–160 A)
Minimum PSI to start	**5,000 PSI**

GM DURAMAX 2001–2008

Low-pressure pump vacuum	2–10 inch Hg
Pump amperes	NA
Pump volume	NA
High-pressure pump	5 K-2.3 K-2.6 K PSI
Idle PSI	5,000–6,000 PSI (30–40 MPa)
Fuel Rail Pressure Regulator (FRPR) maximum fuel pressure	Disconnect to achieve maximum pressure
Injector volts	48 V or 93 V
Injector amperes	20 A
Glow plug amperes	160 A
Minimum to start	**1,500 PSI (10 MPa)**

SPRINTER 2.7 2002–2006

Low-pressure pump	6–51 PSI
High-pressure pump	800–23,000 PSI
Idle PSI	4,900 PSI
Fuel Rail Pressure Control (FRPC) maximum fuel pressure	Apply power and ground to FRPC to achieve maximum pressure
Injector volts	80 V
Injector amperes	20 A
Glow plug amperes	17 A each (85–95 A total)
Minimum to start	**3,200 PSI (1–1.2 V to start)**

6.0 POWERSTROKE 2003–2008

Low-pressure pump	50–60 PSI
High-pressure pump	500–4,000 PSI
Idle PSI	500 PSI+
Injection Pressure Regulator (IPR) maximum fuel pressure	Apply power and ground to IPR
Injector volts	48 V
Injector amperes	20 A
Glow plug amperes	20–25 A each (160–200 A total)
Minimum to start	**500 PSI (0.85 V)**

CHART 11–2

The values can be obtained by using a scan tool and basic test equipment. Always follow the vehicle manufacturer's recommended procedures.

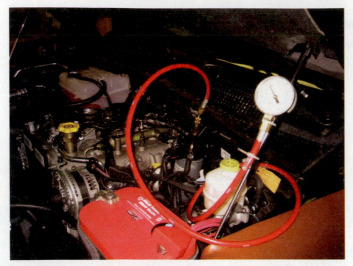

FIGURE 11–32 A pressure gauge checking the fuel pressure from the lift pump on a Cummins 6.7 liter diesel.

FIGURE 11–33 A compression gauge that is designed for the higher compression rate of a diesel engine should be used when checking the compression.

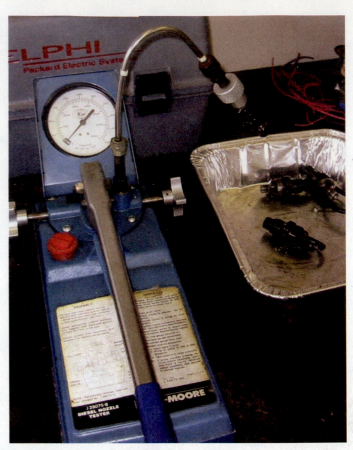

FIGURE 11–34 A typical pop tester used to check the spray pattern of a diesel engine injector.

GLOW PLUG RESISTANCE BALANCE TEST

Glow plugs increase in resistance as their temperature increases. All glow plugs should have about the same resistance when checked with an ohmmeter. A similar test of the resistance of the glow plugs can be used to detect a weak cylinder. This test is particularly helpful on a diesel engine that is not computer controlled. To test for even cylinder balance using glow plug resistance, perform the following on a warm engine.

1. Unplug, measure, and record the resistance of all glow plugs.
2. With the wires still removed from the glow plugs, start the engine.
3. Allow the engine to run for several minutes to allow the combustion inside the cylinder to warm the glow plugs.
4. Measure the plugs and record the resistance of all glow plugs.
5. The resistance of all glow plugs should be higher than at the beginning of the test. A glow plug that is in a cylinder that is not firing correctly will not increase in resistance as much as the others.
6. Another test is to measure exhaust manifold temperature at each exhaust port using an infrared thermometer or a pyrometer. Misfiring cylinders will run cold.

INJECTOR POP TESTING

A **pop tester** is a device used for checking a diesel injector nozzle for proper spray pattern. The handle is depressed and pop-off pressure is displayed on the gauge. ● **SEE FIGURE 11–34.**

TECH TIP

Always Use Cardboard to Check for High-Pressure Leaks

If diesel fuel is found on the engine, a high-pressure leak could be present. When checking for such a leak, wear protective clothing including safety glasses, a face shield, gloves, and a long-sleeved shirt. Then use a piece of cardboard to locate the high-pressure leak. When a Duramax diesel is running, the pressure in the common rail and injector tubes can reach over 20,000 PSI. At these pressures, the diesel fuel is atomized and cannot be seen but can penetrate the skin and cause personal injury. A leak will be shown as a dark area on the cardboard. When a leak is found, shut off the engine and find the exact location of the leak without the engine running.

CAUTION: Sometimes a leak can actually cut through the cardboard, so use extreme care.

The spray pattern should be a hollow cone, but will vary depending on design. The nozzle should also be tested for leakage (dripping of the nozzle) while under pressure. If the spray pattern is not correct, then cleaning, repairing, or replacing the injector nozzle may be necessary.

DIESEL EMISSION TESTING

OPACITY TEST The most common diesel exhaust emission test used in state or local testing programs is called the opacity test. **Opacity** means the percentage of light that is blocked by the exhaust smoke.

- A 0% opacity means that the exhaust has no visible smoke and does not block light from a beam projected through the exhaust smoke.
- A 100% opacity means that the exhaust is so dark that it completely blocks light from a beam projected through the exhaust smoke.
- A 50% opacity means that the exhaust blocks half of the light from a beam projected through the exhaust smoke. ● **SEE CHART 11-3.**

SNAP ACCELERATION TEST In a snap acceleration test, the vehicle is held stationary, with wheel chocks in place and brakes released as the engine is rapidly accelerated to high idle, with the transmission in neutral while smoke emissions are measured. This test is conducted a minimum of six times and the three most consistent measurements are averaged for a final score.

	20% opacity
	40% opacity
	60% opacity
	80% opacity
	100% opacity

CHART 11-3

An opacity test is sometimes used during a state emission test on diesel engines.

FIGURE 11-35 The letters on the side of this injector on a Cummins 6.7 liter diesel indicate the calibration number for the injector.

TECH TIP

Do Not Switch Injectors

In the past, it was common practice to switch diesel fuel injectors from one cylinder to another when diagnosing a dead cylinder problem. However, most high-pressure common rail systems used in new diesel engines utilize precisely calibrated injectors that should not be mixed up during service. Each injector has its own calibration number. ● **SEE FIGURE 11-35.**

ROLLING ACCELERATION TEST Vehicles with a manual transmission are rapidly accelerated in low gear from an idle speed to a maximum governed RPM while the smoke emissions are measured.

STALL ACCELERATION TEST Vehicles with automatic transmissions are held in a stationary position with the parking brake and service brakes applied while the transmission is placed in "drive." The accelerator is depressed and held momentarily while smoke emissions are measured.

The standards for diesels vary according to the type of vehicle and other factors, but usually include a 40% opacity or less.

SUMMARY

1. A diesel engine uses heat of compression to ignite the diesel fuel when it is injected into the compressed air in the combustion chamber.

2. There are two basic designs of combustion chambers used in diesel engines. Indirect injection (IDI) uses a pre-combustion chamber, whereas direct injection (DI) occurs directly into the combustion chamber.

3. The three phases of diesel combustion include:
   a. Ignition delay
   b. Rapid combustion
   c. Controlled combustion

4. The typical diesel engine fuel system consists of the fuel tank, lift pump, water-fuel separator, and fuel filter.

5. The engine-driven injection pump supplies high-pressure diesel fuel to the injectors.

6. The two most common types of fuel injection used in diesel engines are:
   a. Distributor-type injection pump
   b. Common rail design where all of the injectors are fed from the same fuel supply from a rail under high pressure

7. Injector nozzles are either opened by the high-pressure pulse from the distributor pump or electrically by the computer on a common rail design.

8. Glow plugs are used to help start a cold diesel engine and help prevent excessive white smoke during warm-up.

9. Emissions are controlled on newer diesel engines by using a diesel oxidation catalytic converter, a diesel exhaust particulate filter, exhaust gas recirculation, and a selective catalytic reduction system.

10. Diesel engines can be tested using a scan tool, as well as measuring the glow plug resistance or compression reading, to determine a weak or nonfunctioning cylinder.

REVIEW QUESTIONS

1. What is the difference between direct injection and indirect injection?

2. What are the three phases of diesel ignition?

3. What are the two most commonly used types of diesel injection systems?

4. Why are glow plugs kept working after the engine starts?

5. What exhaust aftertreatment is needed to achieve exhaust emission standards for vehicles 2007 and newer?

6. What are the advantages and disadvantages of SCR?

CHAPTER QUIZ

1. How is diesel fuel ignited in a warm diesel engine?
   a. Glow plugs
   b. Heat of compression
   c. Spark plugs
   d. Distributorless ignition system

2. Which type of diesel injection produces less noise?
   a. Indirect injection (IDI)
   b. Common rail
   c. Direct injection
   d. Distributor injection

3. Which diesel injection system requires the use of a glow plug?
   a. Indirect injection (IDI)
   b. High-pressure common rail
   c. Direct injection
   d. Distributor injection

4. The three phases of diesel ignition include _____.
   a. Glow plug ignition, fast burn, slow burn
   b. Slow burn, fast burn, slow burn
   c. Ignition delay, rapid combustion, controlled combustion
   d. Glow plug ignition, ignition delay, controlled combustion

5. What fuel system component is used in a vehicle equipped with a diesel engine that is seldom used on the same vehicle when it is equipped with a gasoline engine?
   a. Fuel filter
   b. Fuel supply line
   c. Fuel return line
   d. Water-fuel separator

6. The diesel injection pump is usually driven by a _____.
   a. Gear off the camshaft
   b. Belt off the crankshaft
   c. Shaft drive off the crankshaft
   d. Chain drive off the camshaft

7. Which diesel system supplies high-pressure diesel fuel to all of the injectors all of the time?
   a. Distributor
   b. Inline
   c. High-pressure common rail
   d. Rotary

8. Glow plugs should have high resistance when _____ and lower resistance when _____.
   a. Cold/warm
   b. Warm/cold
   c. Wet/dry
   d. Dry/wet

9. Technician A says that glow plugs are used to help start a diesel engine and are shut off as soon as the engine starts. Technician B says that the glow plugs are turned off as soon as a flame is detected in the combustion chamber. Which technician is correct?
   a. Technician A only
   b. Technician B only
   c. Both Technicians A and B
   d. Neither Technician A nor B

10. What part should be removed to test cylinder compression on a diesel engine?
   a. Injector
   b. Intake valve rocker arm and stud
   c. Glow plug
   d. Glow plug or injector

chapter 12

GASOLINE, ALTERNATIVE FUELS, AND DIESEL FUELS

LEARNING OBJECTIVES: **After studying this chapter, the reader should be able to:** • Discuss the characteristics of gasoline, refining of gasoline, and volatility of gasoline. • Explain air-fuel ratios, normal and abnormal combustion, and octane rating. • Discuss gasoline additives, gasoline blending, and testing gasoline for alcohol content. • Discuss general gasoline recommendations. • Explain alternative fuel vehicles, and discuss the safety procedures when working with alternative fuels. • Discuss E85, methanol, and propane fuel. • Discuss compressed natural gas, liquefied natural gas, and P-series fuels. • Discuss synthetic fuels. • Compare diesel fuel, biodiesel, and E-diesel fuel.

KEY TERMS: AFV 136 • Air-fuel ratio 128 • Antiknock index (AKI) 130 • API gravity 145 • ASTM 128 • B5 145 • B20 145 • Biodiesel 145 • Biomass 138 • Catalytic cracking 126 • Cetane number 144 • Cloud point 144 • Coal to liquid (CTL) 143 • Compressed natural gas (CNG) 139 • Cracking 126 • Detonation 129 • Diesohol 147 • Distillation 126 • E10 132 • E85 136 • E-diesel 147 • Ethanol 132 • Ethyl alcohol 136 • FFV 136 • Fischer-Tropsch 142 • Flex fuel 136 • FTD 142 • Fuel compensation sensor 137 • Fungible 127 • Gasoline 126 • Grain alcohol 136 • GTL 142 • Hydrocracking 127 • Liquified petroleum gas (LPG) 139 • LP gas 139 • M85 139 • Methanol 138 • Methanol to gasoline (MTG) 143 • NGV 139 • Octane rating 129 • Oxygenated fuels 131 • Petrodiesel 146 • Ping 129 • PPO 146 • Propane 139 • RVP 128 • Spark knock 129 • Stoichiometric 129 • SVO 146 • Syncrude 143 • Syn-gas 138 • UCO 146 • ULSD 145 • Underground coal gasification (UCG) 143 • Variable fuel sensor 137 • V-FFV 138 • Volatility 127 • WVO 146 • WWFC 134

INTRODUCTION

Using the proper fuel is important for the proper operation of any engine. Although gasoline is the most commonly used fuel today, there are several alternative fuels that can be used in some vehicles. Diesel fuel contains much lower amounts of sulfur than before 2007 and this allows the introduction of many new clean burning diesel engines.

GASOLINE

Gasoline is a term used to describe a complex mixture of various hydrocarbons refined from crude petroleum oil for use as a fuel in engines. Gasoline and air burns in the cylinder of the engine and produces heat and pressure which is transferred to rotary motion inside the engine and eventually powers the drive wheels of a vehicle. When the combustion process in the engine is perfect, all of the fuel and air are consumed and only carbon dioxide and water are produced.

REFINING

DISTILLATION In the late 1800s, crude was separated into different products by boiling in a process called **distillation**. Distillation works because crude oil is composed of hydrocarbons with a broad range of boiling points.

In a distillation column, the vapor of the lowest boiling hydrocarbons, propane and butane, rises to the top. The straight-run gasoline (also called naphtha), kerosene, and diesel fuel cuts are drawn off at successively lower positions in the column.

CRACKING **Cracking** is the process during which hydrocarbons with higher boiling points can be broken down (cracked) into lower boiling hydrocarbons by treating them to very high temperatures. This process, called *thermal cracking,* was used to increase gasoline production starting in 1913.

Today, instead of high heat, cracking is performed using a catalyst and is called **catalytic cracking**. A catalyst is a material that speeds up or otherwise facilitates a chemical reaction without undergoing a permanent chemical change itself. Catalytic cracking produces gasoline of higher quality than thermal cracking.

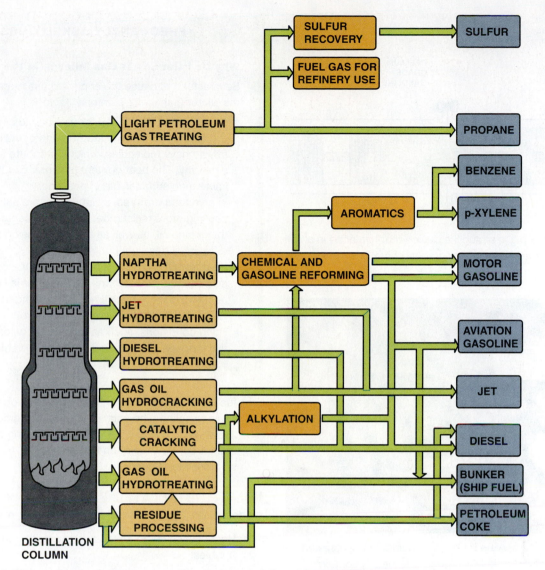

FIGURE 12–1 The crude oil refining process showing most of the major steps and processes.

Hydrocracking is similar to catalytic cracking in that it uses a catalyst, but the catalyst is in a hydrogen atmosphere. Hydrocracking can break down hydrocarbons that are resistant to catalytic cracking alone and it is used to produce diesel fuel rather than gasoline.

Other types of refining processes include:

- Reforming
- Alkylation
- Isomerization
- Hydrotreating
- Desulfurization

● **SEE FIGURE 12–1**.

SHIPPING The gasoline is transported to regional storage facilities by tank railway car or by pipeline. In the pipeline method, all gasoline from many refiners is often sent through the same pipeline and can become mixed. All gasoline is said to be **fungible,** meaning that it is capable of being interchanged because each grade is created to specification so there is no reason to keep the different gasoline brands separated except for grade. Regular grade, midgrade, and premium grades are separated by using a device, called a *pig,* in the pipeline and sent to regional storage facilities. ● **SEE FIGURE 12–2**.

It is at these regional or local storage facilities where the additives and dye (if any) are added and then shipped by truck to individual gas stations.

DEFINITION **Volatility** describes how easily the gasoline evaporates (forms a vapor). The definition of volatility assumes that the vapors will remain in the fuel tank or fuel line and will cause a certain pressure based on the temperature of the fuel.

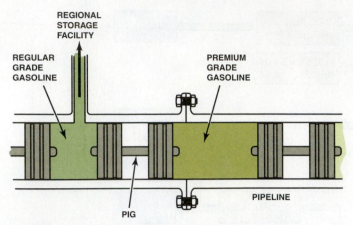

REGIONAL STORAGE FACILITY

REGULAR GRADE GASOLINE

PREMIUM GRADE GASOLINE

PIG

PIPELINE

FIGURE 12–2 A pig is a pluglike device that is placed in a pipeline to separate two types or grades of fuel.

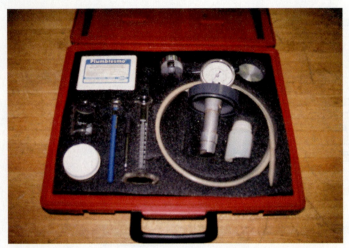

FIGURE 12–3 A gasoline testing kit, including an insulated container where water at 100°F is used to heat a container holding a small sample of gasoline. The reading on the pressure gauge is the Reid vapor pressure (RVP).

REID VAPOR PRESSURE **Reid vapor pressure (RVP)** is the pressure of the vapor above the fuel when the fuel is at 100°F (38°C). Increased vapor pressure permits the engine to start in cold weather. Gasoline without air will not burn. Gasoline must be vaporized (mixed with air) to burn in an engine. ● **SEE FIGURE 12–3**.

SEASONAL BLENDING Cold temperatures reduce the normal vaporization of gasoline; therefore, winter-blended gasoline is specially formulated to vaporize at lower temperatures for proper starting and driveability at low ambient temperatures.

- **Winter blend.** The **American Society for Testing and Materials (ASTM)** standards for winter-blend gasoline allow volatility of up to 15 pounds per square inch (PSI) RVP.
- **Summer blend.** At warm ambient temperatures, gasoline vaporizes easily. However, the fuel system (fuel pump,

? **FREQUENTLY ASKED QUESTION**

Why Do I Get Lower Gas Mileage in the Winter?

Several factors cause the engine to use more fuel in the winter than in the summer.

- Gasoline that is blended for use in cold climates is designed for ease of starting and contains fewer heavy molecules, which contribute to fuel economy. The heat content of winter gasoline is lower than summer-blend gasoline.
- In cold temperatures, all lubricants are stiff, causing more resistance. These lubricants include the engine oil, as well as the transmission and differential gear lubricants.
- Heat from the engine is radiated into the outside air more rapidly when the temperature is cold, resulting in longer run time until the engine has reached normal operating temperature.
- Road conditions, such as ice and snow, can cause tire slippage or additional drag on the vehicle.

fuel-injector nozzles, etc.) is designed to operate with liquid gasoline. The volatility of summer-grade gasoline should be about 7 PSI RVP. According to ASTM standards, the maximum RVP should be 10.5 PSI for summer-blend gasoline.

VOLATILITY-RELATED PROBLEMS If using winter-grade fuel during warm weather, the following may occur.

- Heat causes some fuel to evaporate, thereby causing bubbles.
- When the fuel is full of bubbles (sometimes called *vapor lock*), the engine is not being supplied with enough fuel and the engine runs lean. A lean engine will lead to the following:

1. Rough idle
2. Stalling
3. Hesitation on acceleration
4. Surging

If using summer-grade fuel in cold temperatures, then the engine will be hard to start (long cranking before starting) due to the lack of volatility to allow the engine to start easily.

AIR-FUEL RATIOS

DEFINITION The **air-fuel ratio** is the proportion by weight of air and gasoline that the injection system mixes as needed for engine combustion. Air-fuel ratios in which a gasoline engine can operate without stalling range from 8:1 to 18.5:1. ● **SEE FIGURE 12–4**.

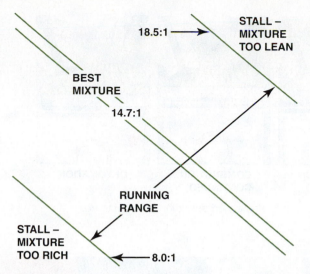

FIGURE 12-4 An engine will not run if the air-fuel mixture is either too rich or too lean.

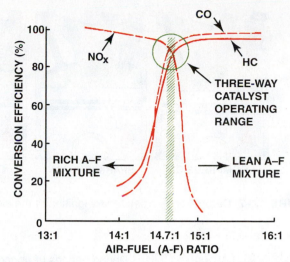

FIGURE 12-5 With a three-way catalytic converter, emission control is most efficient with an air-fuel ratio between 14.65:1 and 14.75:1.

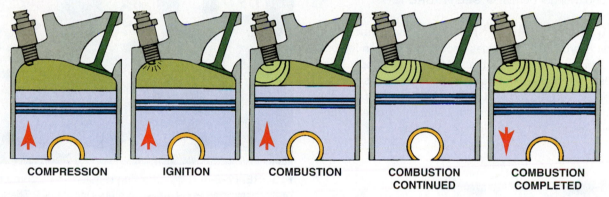

COMPRESSION   IGNITION   COMBUSTION   COMBUSTION CONTINUED   COMBUSTION COMPLETED

FIGURE 12-6 Normal combustion is a smooth, controlled burning of the air-fuel mixture.

These ratios are usually stated by weight, as follows:

- 8 parts of air by weight combined with 1 part of gasoline by weight (8:1), which is the richest mixture that an engine can tolerate and still fire reliably
- 18.5 parts of air mixed with 1 part of gasoline (18.5:1), which is the leanest practical ratio

Richer or leaner air-fuel ratios cause the engine to misfire badly or not run at all.

STOICHIOMETRIC AIR-FUEL RATIO
The ideal mixture or ratio at which all of the fuel combines with all of the oxygen in the air and burns completely is called the **stoichiometric** ratio, a chemically perfect combination. In theory, this ratio for gasoline is an air-fuel mixture of 14.7:1. The stoichiometric ratio is a compromise between maximum power and maximum economy. ● SEE FIGURE 12–5.

NORMAL AND ABNORMAL COMBUSTION

TERMINOLOGY The **octane rating** of gasoline is the measure of its antiknock properties. **Spark knock** (also called **detonation** or **ping**) is a metallic noise an engine makes, usually during acceleration, resulting from abnormal or uncontrolled combustion inside the cylinder. Normal combustion occurs smoothly and progresses across the combustion chamber from the point of ignition.
● SEE FIGURE 12–6.

Normal flame-front combustion travels between 45 and 90 mph (72 and 145 km/h). The speed of the flame front depends on air-fuel ratio, combustion chamber design (determining amount of turbulence), and temperature.

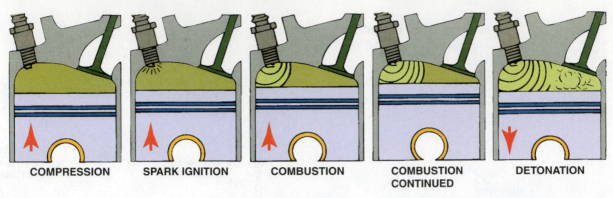

| COMPRESSION | SPARK IGNITION | COMBUSTION | COMBUSTION CONTINUED | DETONATION |

FIGURE 12–7 Detonation is a secondary ignition of the air-fuel mixture. It is also called spark knock or pinging.

ABNORMAL COMBUSTION   During periods of abnormal combustion, called spark knock or detonation, the combustion speed increases by up to 10 times to near the speed of sound. The increased combustion speed also causes increased temperatures and pressures, which can damage pistons, gaskets, and cylinder heads. ● **SEE FIGURE 12–7.**

CONTROLLING SPARK KNOCK   Spark knock was commonly heard in older engines especially when under load and in warm weather temperatures. Most engines built since the 1990s are equipped with a knock sensor that is used to signal the powertrain control module (PCM) to retard the ignition timing if knock is detected. Using the proper octane fuel helps to ensure that spark knock does not occur.

FIGURE 12–8 A pump showing regular with a pump octane of 87, plus rated at 89, and premium rated at 93. These ratings can vary with brand as well as in different parts of the country.

OCTANE RATING

RATING METHODS   The two basic methods used to rate gasoline for antiknock properties (octane rating) include the *Research method* and the *Motor method*.

Each uses a model of the special *cooperative fuel research* (CFR) single-cylinder engine to test the octane of a fuel sample, and the two methods use different engine settings. The research method typically results in readings that are 6 to 10 points higher than those of the motor method. For example, a fuel with a research octane number (RON) of 93 might have a motor octane number (MON) of 85.

GASOLINE GRADES   The octane rating posted on pumps in the United States is the average of the two methods and is referred to as R + M ÷ 2, meaning that, for the fuel used in the previous example, the rating posted on the pumps would be:

$$\frac{RON + MON}{2} = \frac{93 + 85}{2} = 89$$

This pump octane rating is often called the **antiknock index (AKI)**.
● **SEE FIGURE 12–8.**

Grades	Octane Rating
Regular	87
Midgrade (also called Plus)	89
Premium	91 or higher

CHART 12–1

The octane rating displayed on the fuel pumps can vary depending on climate.

Except in high-altitude areas, the grades and octane ratings are shown in ● **SEE CHART 12–1.**

OCTANE EFFECTS OF ALTITUDE   As the altitude increases, atmospheric pressure drops. The air is less dense because a pound of air takes more volume. The octane rating of fuel does not need to be as high because the engine cannot take in as much air. This process will reduce the combustion (compression) pressures inside the engine. In mountainous areas, gasoline (R + M) ÷ 2 octane ratings are two or more

What Grade of Gasoline Does the EPA Use When Testing Engines?

Due to the various grades and additives used in commercial fuel, the government (EPA) uses a liquid called indolene, which has a research method octane number of 96.5 and a motor method octane rating of 88, resulting in a (R + M) ÷ 2 rating of 92.25.

TECH TIP

Horsepower and Fuel Flow

To produce 1 hp, the engine must be supplied with 0.50 lb of fuel per hour (lb/hr). Fuel injectors are rated in pounds per hour. For example, a V-8 engine equipped with 25 lb/hr fuel injectors could produce 50 hp per cylinder (per injector) or 400 hp. Even if the cylinder head or block is modified to produce more horsepower, the limiting factor may be the injector flow rate.

The following are flow rates and resulting horsepower for a V-8 engine.

- 30 lb/hr: 60 hp per cylinder, or 480 hp
- 35 lb/hr: 70 hp per cylinder, or 560 hp
- 40 lb/hr: 80 hp per cylinder, or 640 hp

Of course, injector flow rate is only one of many variables that affect power output. Installing larger injectors without other major engine modifications could decrease engine output and drastically increase exhaust emissions.

numbers lower than normal (according to the SAE, about one octane number lower per 1,000 ft or 300 m in altitude). ● **SEE FIGURE 12–9**.

A second reason for the lowered octane requirement of engines running at higher altitudes is the normal enrichment of the air-fuel ratio and lower engine vacuum with the decreased air density. Some problems, therefore, may occur when driving out of high-altitude areas into lower areas where the octane rating must be higher. Most electronic fuel injection systems can compensate for changes in altitude and modify air-fuel ratio and ignition timing for best operation.

Because the combustion burn rate slows at high altitude, the ignition (spark) timing can be advanced to improve power. The amount of timing advance can be about 1 degree per 1,000 ft over 5,000 ft. Therefore, if driving at 8,000 ft of altitude, the ignition timing can be advanced 3 degrees.

VOLATILITY EFFECTS OF ALTITUDE
High altitude also allows fuel to evaporate more easily. The volatility of fuel should be reduced at higher altitudes to prevent vapor from forming in sections of the fuel system, which can cause driveability

FIGURE 12–9 The posted octane rating in most high-altitude areas shows regular at 85 instead of the usual 87.

and stalling problems. The extra heat generated in climbing to higher altitudes plus the lower atmospheric pressure at higher altitudes combine to cause possible driveability problems as the vehicle goes to higher altitudes.

GASOLINE ADDITIVES

DYE Dye is usually added to gasoline at the distributor to help identify the grade and/or brand of fuel. Fuels are required to be colored using a fuel soluble dye in many countries. In the United States and Canada, diesel fuel used for off-road use and not taxed is required to be dyed red for identification. Gasoline sold for off-road use in Canada is dyed purple.

OXYGENATED FUEL ADDITIVES Oxygenated fuels contain oxygen in the molecule of the fuel itself. Examples of oxygenated fuels include:

- **Methyl tertiary butyl ether (MTBE).** This fuel is manufactured by means of the chemical reaction of methanol and isobutylene. Unlike methanol, MTBE does not increase the volatility of the fuel, and is not as sensitive to water as are other alcohols. The maximum allowable volume level, according to the EPA, is 15% but is currently being phased out due to health concerns, as well as MTBE contamination of drinking water if spilled from storage tanks.

- **Tertiary-amyl methyl ether (TAME).** This fuel contains an oxygen atom bonded to two carbon atoms, and is added to gasoline to provide oxygen to the fuel. It is slightly soluble in water, very soluble in ethers and alcohol, and soluble in most organic solvents including hydrocarbons.

- **Ethyl tertiary butyl ether (ETBE).** This fuel is derived from ethanol. The maximum allowable volume level is

FIGURE 12–10 This fuel tank indicates that the gasoline is blended with 10% ethanol (ethyl alcohol) and can be used in any gasoline vehicle. E85 contains 85% ethanol and can only be used in vehicles specifically designed to use it.

FIGURE 12–11 A container with gasoline containing water and alcohol. Notice the separation line where the alcohol-water mixture separated from the gasoline and sank to the bottom.

17.2%. The use of ETBE is the cause of much of the odor from the exhaust of vehicles if using reformulated gasoline, as mandated for use in some parts of the country.

- **Ethanol.** Also called *ethyl alcohol,* **ethanol** is drinkable alcohol and is usually made from grain. Adding 10% ethanol (ethyl alcohol or grain alcohol) increases the $(R + M) \div 2$ octane rating by three points.

The alcohol added to the base gasoline, however, also raises the volatility of the fuel about 0.5 PSI. Most automobile manufacturers permit up to 10% ethanol if driveability problems are not experienced.

The oxygen content of a 10% blend of ethanol in gasoline, called **E10,** is 3.5% oxygen by weight. ● SEE FIGURE 12–10.

GASOLINE BLENDING

Gasoline additives, such as ethanol and dyes, are usually added to the fuel at the distributor. Adding ethanol to gasoline is a way to add oxygen to the fuel itself. There are three basic

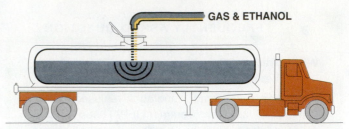

FIGURE 12–12 In-line blending is the most accurate method for blending ethanol with gasoline because computers are used to calculate the correct ratio.

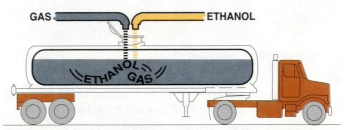

FIGURE 12–13 Sequential blending uses a computer to calculate the correct ratio as well as the prescribed order that the products are loaded.

? FREQUENTLY ASKED QUESTION

What Is Meant by "Phase Separation"?

All alcohols absorb water, and the alcohol-water mixture can separate from the gasoline and sink to the bottom of the fuel tank. This process is called phase separation. To help avoid engine performance problems, try to keep at least a quarter tank of fuel at all times, especially during seasons when there is a wide temperature span between daytime highs and nighttime lows. These conditions can cause moisture to accumulate in the fuel tank as a result of condensation of the moisture in the air. Keeping the fuel tank full reduces the amount of air and moisture in the tank. ● SEE FIGURE 12–11.

methods used to blend ethanol with gasoline to create E10 (10% ethanol, 90% gasoline).

1. **In-line blending.** Gasoline and ethanol are mixed in a storage tank or in the tank of a transport truck while it is being filled. Because the quantities of each can be accurately measured, this method is most likely to produce a well-mixed blend of ethanol and gasoline. ● SEE FIGURE 12–12.

2. **Sequential blending.** This method is usually performed at the wholesale terminal and involves adding a measured amount of ethanol to a tank truck followed by a measured amount of gasoline. ● SEE FIGURE 12–13.

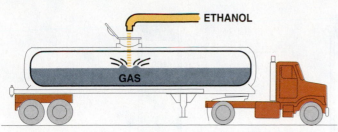
FIGURE 12–14 Splash blending occurs when the ethanol is added to a tanker with gasoline and is mixed as the truck travels to the retail outlet.

 FREQUENTLY ASKED QUESTION

Is Water Heavier than Gasoline?

Yes. Water weighs about 8 lb per gallon, whereas gasoline weighs about 6 lb per gallon. The density as measured by specific gravity includes:

Water = 1.000 (the baseline for specific gravity)

Gasoline = 0.730 to 0.760

This means that any water that gets into the fuel tank will sink to the bottom.

3. **Splash blending.** This method can be done at the retail outlet or distributor and involves separate purchases of ethanol and gasoline. In a typical case, a distributor can purchase gasoline, and then drive to another supplier and purchase ethanol. The ethanol is then added (splashed) into the tank of gasoline. This method is the least accurate method of blending and can result in ethanol concentration for E10 that should be 10% to range from 5% to over 20% in some cases. ● **SEE FIGURE 12–14.**

TESTING GASOLINE FOR ALCOHOL CONTENT

Take the following steps when testing gasoline for alcohol content.

 WARNING

Do not smoke or run the test around sources of ignition!

1. Pour suspect gasoline into a graduated cylinder.
2. Carefully fill the graduated cylinder to the 90 mL mark.
3. Add 10 mL of water to the graduated cylinder by counting the number of drops from an eyedropper.

4. Put the stopper in the cylinder and shake vigorously for one minute. Relieve built-up pressure by occasionally removing the stopper. Alcohol dissolves in water and will drop to the bottom of the cylinder.
5. Place the cylinder on a flat surface and let it stand for two minutes.
6. Take a reading near the bottom of the cylinder at the boundary between the two liquids.
7. For percentage of alcohol in gasoline, subtract 10 to get the percentage.

For example,

The reading is 20 mL: 20 − 10 = 10% alcohol

If the increase in volume is 0.2% or less, it may be assumed that the test gasoline contains no alcohol. ● **SEE FIGURE 12–15.**

Alcohol content can also be checked using an electronic tester. See the photo sequence at the end of the chapter.

GENERAL GASOLINE RECOMMENDATIONS

The fuel used by an engine is a major expense in the operation cost of the vehicle. The proper operation of the engine depends on clean fuel of the proper octane rating and vapor pressure for the atmospheric conditions.

To help ensure proper engine operation and keep fuel costs to a minimum, follow these guidelines.

1. Purchase fuel from a busy station to help ensure that it is fresh and less likely to be contaminated with water or moisture.
2. Keep the fuel tank above one-quarter full, especially during seasons in which the temperature rises and falls by more than 20°F between daytime highs and nighttime lows. This helps to reduce condensed moisture in the fuel tank and could prevent gas line freeze-up in cold weather.

NOTE: Gas line freeze-up occurs when the water in the gasoline freezes and forms an ice blockage in the fuel line.

3. Do not purchase fuel with a higher octane rating than is necessary. Try using premium high-octane fuel to check for operating differences. Most newer engines are equipped with a detonation (knock) sensor that signals the vehicle computer to retard the ignition timing when spark knock occurs. Therefore, an operating difference may not be noticeable to the driver when using a low-octane fuel, except for a decrease in power and fuel economy. In other words, the engine with a knock sensor will tend to operate knock free on regular fuel, even if premium, higher octane fuel is specified. Using premium fuel may result in more power

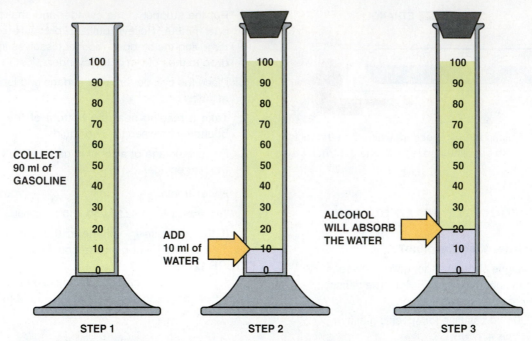

COLLECT
90 ml of
GASOLINE

100
90
80
70
60
50
40
30
20
10
0

STEP 1

ADD
10 ml of
WATER

100
90
80
70
60
50
40
30
20
10
0

STEP 2

ALCOHOL
WILL ABSORB
THE WATER

100
90
80
70
60
50
40
30
20
10
0

STEP 3

FIGURE 12–15 Checking gasoline for alcohol involves using a graduated cylinder and adding water to check if the alcohol absorbs the water.

FIGURE 12–16 The gas cap on a Ford vehicle notes that BP fuel is recommended.

and greater fuel economy. The increase in fuel economy, however, would have to be substantial to justify the increased cost of high-octane premium fuel. Some drivers find a good compromise by using midgrade (plus) fuel to benefit from the engine power and fuel economy gains without the cost of using premium fuel all the time.

4. Try to avoid using gasoline with alcohol in warm weather, even though many alcohol blends do not affect engine driveability. If warm-engine stumble, stalling, or rough idle occurs, change brands of gasoline.

5. Do not purchase fuel from a retail outlet when a tanker truck is filling the underground tanks. During the refilling procedure, dirt, rust, and water may be stirred up in the underground tanks. This undesirable material may be pumped into your vehicle's fuel tank.

6. Do not overfill the gas tank. After the nozzle clicks off, add just enough fuel to round up to the next dime. Adding additional gasoline will cause the excess to be drawn into the charcoal canister. This can lead to engine flooding and excessive exhaust emissions.

7. Be careful when filling gasoline containers. Always fill a gas can on the ground to help prevent the possibility of static electricity buildup during the refueling process. ● **SEE FIGURE 12–17**.

WARNING

STATIC ELECTRICITY SPARK EXPLOSION HAZARD

- DO NOT GET BACK IN YOUR VEHICLE WHILE REFUELING
- RE-ENTRY COULD CAUSE STATIC ELECTRICITY BUILD UP

- USE APPROVED CONTAINER
- PUT CONTAINER ON GROUND (NEVER ON OR IN A VEHICLE)
- KEEP NOZZLE IN CONTACT WITH CONTAINER

ELECTRONIC DEVICES HAZARD

KEEP CELLULAR PHONES OR OTHER DEVICES IN YOUR VEHICLE DURING REFUELING.

FIGURE 12–17 Many service stations have signs posted warning customers to place plastic fuel containers on the ground while filling. If placed in a trunk or pickup truck bed equipped with a plastic liner, static electricity could build up during fueling and discharge from the container to the metal nozzle, creating a spark and possible explosion. Some service stations have warning signs not to use cell phones while fueling to help avoid the possibility of an accidental spark creating a fire hazard.

 FREQUENTLY ASKED QUESTION

Why Should I Keep the Fuel Gauge Above One-Quarter Tank?

The fuel pickup inside the fuel tank can help keep water from being drawn into the fuel system unless water is all that is left at the bottom of the tank. Over time, moisture in the air inside the fuel tank can condense, causing liquid water to drop to the bottom of the fuel tank. (Recall that water is heavier than gasoline–about 8 pound per gallon for water and about 6 pound per gallon for gasoline.) If alcohol-blended gasoline is used, the alcohol can absorb the water and the alcohol-water combination can be burned inside the engine. However, when water combines with alcohol, a separation layer occurs between the gasoline at the top of the tank and the alcohol-water combination at the bottom. When the fuel level is low, the fuel pump will draw from this concentrated level of alcohol and water. Because alcohol and water do not burn as well as pure gasoline, severe driveability problems can occur such as stalling, rough idle, hard starting, and missing.

 **TECH TIP**

Do Not Overfill the Fuel Tank

Gasoline fuel tanks have an expansion volume area at the top. The volume of this expansion area is equal to 10% to 15% of the volume of the tank. This area is normally not filled with gasoline, but rather is designed to provide a place for the gasoline to expand into, if the vehicle is parked in the hot sun and the gasoline expands. This prevents raw gasoline from escaping from the fuel system. A small restriction is usually present to control the amount of air and vapors that can escape the tank and flow to the charcoal canister.

This volume area could be filled with gasoline if the fuel is slowly pumped into the tank. Since it can hold an extra 10% (2 gallons in a 20 gallon tank), some people deliberately try to fill the tank completely. When this expansion volume is filled, liquid fuel (rather than vapors) can be drawn into the charcoal canister. When the purge valve opens, liquid fuel can be drawn into the engine, causing an excessively rich air-fuel mixture. Not only can this liquid fuel harm vapor recovery parts, but overfilling the gas tank could also cause the vehicle to fail an exhaust emission test, particularly during an enhanced test when the tank could be purged while on the rollers.

TECH TIP

The Sniff Test

Problems can occur with stale gasoline from which the lighter parts of the gasoline have evaporated. Stale gasoline usually results in a no-start situation. If stale gasoline is suspected, sniff it. If it smells rancid, replace it with fresh gasoline.

NOTE: If storing a vehicle, boat, or lawnmower over the winter, put some gasoline stabilizer into the gasoline to reduce the evaporation and separation that can occur during storage. Gasoline stabilizer is frequently available at lawnmower repair shops or marinas.

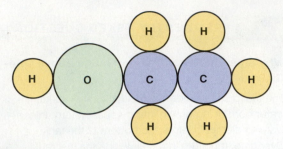

FIGURE 12–18 The ethanol molecule showing two carbon atoms, six hydrogen atoms, and one oxygen atom.

FIGURE 12–19 Some retail stations offer a variety of fuel choices, such as this station in Ohio where E10 and E85 are available.

E85

WHAT IS E85? Vehicle manufacturers have available vehicles that are capable of operating on gasoline plus ethanol or a combination of gasoline and ethanol called **E85,** composed of 85% ethanol and 15% gasoline. Ethanol is also called **ethyl alcohol** or **grain alcohol,** because it is usually made from grain and is the type of alcohol found in alcoholic drinks such as beer, wine, and distilled spirits like whiskey. Ethanol is composed of two carbon atoms and six hydrogen atoms with one added oxygen atom. ● **SEE FIGURE 12–18**.

Pure ethanol has an octane rating of about 113. E85, which contains 35% oxygen by weight, has an octane rating of 100 to 105. This compares to a regular unleaded gasoline which has a rating of 87. ● **SEE FIGURE 12–19**.

NOTE: The octane rating of E85 depends on the exact percentage of ethanol used, which can vary from 81% to 85%. It also depends on the octane rating of the gasoline used to make E85.

HEAT ENERGY OF E85 E85 has less heat energy than gasoline.

Gasoline: 114,000 BTUs per gallon

E85: 87,000 BTUs per gallon

This means that the fuel economy is reduced by 20% to 30% if E85 is used instead of gasoline.

Example: A Chevrolet Tahoe 5.3 liter V-8 with an automatic transmission has an EPA rating using gasoline of 15 mpg in the city and 20 mpg on the highway. If this same vehicle is fueled with E85, the EPA fuel economy rating drops to 11 mpg in the city and 15 mpg on the highway.

ALTERNATIVE FUEL VEHICLES

The 15% gasoline in the E85 blend helps the engine start, especially in cold weather. Vehicles equipped with this capability are commonly referred to as:

- **Alternative fuel vehicles (AFVs)**
- **Flex fuels**
- **Flexible fuel vehicles (FFVs)**

Using E85 in a flex fuel vehicle can result in a power increase of about 5%. For example, an engine rated at 200 hp using gasoline or E10 could produce 210 hp if using E85.

NOTE: E85 may test as containing less than 85% ethanol if tested because it is often blended according to outside temperature. A lower percentage of ethanol with a slightly higher percentage of gasoline helps engines start in cold climates.

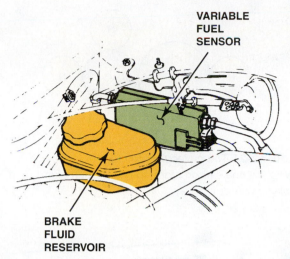

FIGURE 12–20 The location of the variable fuel sensor can vary, depending on the make and model of vehicle, but it is always in the fuel line between the fuel tank and the fuel injectors.

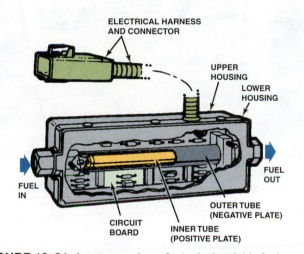

FIGURE 12–21 A cutaway view of a typical variable fuel sensor.

These vehicles are equipped with an electronic sensor in the fuel supply line that detects the presence and percentage of ethanol. The PCM then adjusts the fuel injector on-time and ignition timing to match the needs of the fuel being used.

E85 contains less heat energy, and therefore will use more fuel, but the benefits include a lower cost of the fuel and less environmental impact associated with using an oxygenated fuel.

General Motors, Ford, Chrysler, and Mazda are a few of the manufacturers offering E85 compatible vehicles. E85 vehicles use fuel system parts designed to withstand the additional alcohol content, modified driveability programs that adjust fuel delivery and timing to compensate for the various percentages of ethanol fuel, and a **fuel compensation sensor** that measures both the percentage of ethanol blend and the temperature of the fuel. This sensor is also called a **variable fuel sensor**. ● **SEE FIGURES 12–20 AND 12–21.**

E85 FUEL SYSTEM REQUIREMENTS
Most E85 vehicles are very similar to non-E85 vehicles. Fuel system components may be redesigned to withstand the effects

FIGURE 12–22 A flex fuel vehicle often has a yellow gas cap, which is labeled E85/gasoline.

FIGURE 12–23 This flexible fuel vehicle (FFV) vehicle emission control information (VECI) sticker located under the hood indicates that is can operate on either gasoline or ethanol.

of higher concentrations of ethanol. In addition, since the stoichiometric point for ethanol is 9:1 instead of 14.7:1 as for gasoline, the air-fuel mixture has to be adjusted for the percentage of ethanol present in the fuel tank.

The benefits of E85 vehicles include:

- Reduced pollution
- Less CO_2 production
- Less dependence on imported oil

FLEX FUEL VEHICLE IDENTIFICATION
Flexible fuel vehicles (FFVs) can be identified by:

- Emblems on the side, front, and/or rear of the vehicle
- Yellow fuel cap showing E85/gasoline (● **SEE FIGURE 12–22.**)
- Vehicle emission control information (VECI) label under the hood (● **SEE FIGURE 12–23.**)
- Vehicle identification number (VIN)

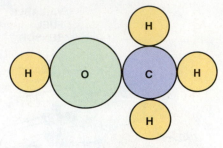

NOTE: For additional information on E85 and for the location of E85 stations in your area, go to www.e85fuel.com.

METHANOL

METHANOL TERMINOLOGY **Methanol,** also known as *methyl alcohol, wood alcohol,* or *methyl hydrate,* is a chemical compound formula that includes one carbon atom, four hydrogen atoms, and one oxygen atom. ● **SEE FIGURE 12–24.**

Methanol is a light, volatile, colorless, tasteless, flammable, poisonous liquid with a very faint odor. Methanol can be used in the following ways.

- As an antifreeze, a solvent, or a fuel
- To denature ethanol (to make undrinkable)

Methanol burns in air, forming CO_2 (carbon dioxide) and H_2O (water). A methanol flame is almost colorless. Methanol is often called wood alcohol because it was once produced

FIGURE 12–24 The molecular structure of methanol showing the one carbon atom, four hydrogen atoms, and one oxygen atom.

FIGURE 12–25 Sign on methanol pump shows that methyl alcohol is a poison and can cause skin irritation and other personal injury. Methanol is used in industry as well as being a fuel.

chiefly as a by-product of the destructive distillation of wood. ● **SEE FIGURE 12–25.**

PRODUCTION OF METHANOL The biggest source of methanol in the United States is coal. Using a simple reaction between coal and steam, a gas mixture called **syn-gas** (synthesis gas) is formed. The components of this mixture are carbon monoxide and hydrogen, which, through an additional chemical reaction, are converted to methanol.

Natural gas can also be used to create methanol and is reformed or converted to synthesis gas, which is later made into methanol.

Biomass can be converted to synthesis gas by a process called partial oxidation, and later converted to methanol. Biomass is organic material, and includes:

- Urban wood wastes
- Primary mill residues
- Forest residues
- Agricultural residues
- Dedicated energy crops (e.g., sugarcane and sugar beets) that can be made into fuel

FIGURE 12–26 Propane fuel storage tank in the trunk of a Ford taxi.

FIGURE 12–27 The blue sticker on the rear of this vehicle indicates that it is designed to use compressed natural gas. This Ford truck also has a sticker that allows it to be driven in the high occupancy vehicle (HOV) lane, even if there is just the driver, because it is a CNG vehicle.

Electricity can be used to convert water into hydrogen, which is then reacted with carbon dioxide to produce methanol.

Methanol is toxic and can cause blindness and death. It can enter the body by ingestion, inhalation, or absorption through the skin. Dangerous doses will build up if a person is regularly exposed to fumes or handles liquid without skin protection. If methanol has been ingested, a doctor should be contacted immediately. The usual fatal dose is 4 fl oz (100 to 125 mL).

M85 Some flexible fuel vehicles are designed to operate on 85% methanol and 15% gasoline, called **M85**. Methanol is very corrosive and requires that the fuel system components be constructed of stainless steel and other alcohol-resistant rubber and plastic components. The heat content of M85 is about 60% of that of gasoline.

PROPANE

Propane is the most widely used of all the alternative fuels mainly because of its use in fleets, which utilize a central refueling station. Propane is normally a gas but is easily compressed into a liquid and stored in inexpensive containers. When sold as a fuel, it is also known as **liquified petroleum gas (LPG)** or **LP gas,** because the propane is often mixed with about 10% of other gases, including:

- Butane
- Propylene
- Butylenes
- Mercaptan, to give the colorless and odorless propane a smell

Propane is nontoxic, but if inhaled can cause asphyxiation through lack of oxygen. Propane is heavier than air and lays near the floor if released into the atmosphere. Propane

is commonly used in forklifts and other equipment located inside warehouses and factories, because the exhaust from the engine using propane is not harmful. Propane is a by-product of petroleum refining of natural gas. In order to liquefy the fuel, it is stored in strong tanks at about 300 PSI (2,000 kPa). The heating value of propane is less than that of gasoline; therefore, more is required, which reduces the fuel economy. ● **SEE FIGURE 12–26.**

COMPRESSED NATURAL GAS

CNG VEHICLE DESIGN Another alternative fuel that is often used in fleet vehicles is **compressed natural gas (CNG).** Vehicles using this fuel are often referred to as **natural gas vehicles (NGVs).** Look for the blue CNG label on vehicles designed to operate on compressed natural gas. ● **SEE FIGURE 12–27.**

Because natural gas must be compressed to 3,000 PSI (20,000 kPa) or more, the weight and cost of the storage container are major factors when it comes to preparing a vehicle to run on CNG. The tanks needed for CNG are typically constructed of 0.5 inch (3 mm) thick aluminum reinforced with fiberglass. ● **SEE FIGURE 12–28.**

The octane rating of CNG is about 130 and the cost per gallon is roughly half of the cost of gasoline. However, the heat value of CNG is also less, and therefore more is required to produce the same power; and the miles per gallon is less.

FIGURE 12–28 A CNG storage tank from a Honda Civic GX shown with the fixture used to support it while it is being removed or installed in the vehicle. Honda specifies that three technicians be used to remove or install the tank through the rear door of the vehicle due to the size and weight of the tank.

FIGURE 12–29 The fuel injectors used on this Honda Civic GX CNG engine are designed to flow gaseous fuel instead of liquid fuel and cannot be interchanged with any other type of injector.

CNG COMPOSITION Compressed natural gas is a blend of the following:

- Methane
- Propane
- Ethane
- N-butane
- Carbon dioxide
- Nitrogen

Once it is processed, compressed natural gas is at least 93% methane. Natural gas is nontoxic, odorless, and colorless in its natural state. It is odorized during processing, using ethyl mercaptan ("skunk"), to allow for easy leak detection. Natural gas is lighter than air and will rise when released into the air. Since CNG is already a vapor, it does not need heat to vaporize before it will burn, which improves cold start-up and results in lower emissions during cold operation. However, because it is already in a gaseous state, it displaces some of the air charge in the intake manifold, leading to a 10% reduction in engine power as compared to an engine operating on gasoline. Natural gas also burns slower than gasoline; therefore, the ignition timing must be advanced more when the vehicle operates on natural gas. The stoichiometric ratio, the point at which all the air and fuel is used or burned, is 16.5:1 compared to 14.7:1 for gasoline. This means that more air is required to burn 1 pound of natural gas than is required to burn 1 pound of gasoline. ● **SEE FIGURE 12–29**.

The CNG engine is designed to include:

- Increased compression ratio
- Strong pistons and connecting rods
- Heat-resistant valves
- Fuel injectors designed for gaseous fuel instead of liquid fuel

CNG FUEL SYSTEMS When completely filled, the CNG tank has 3,600 PSI of pressure in the tank. When the ignition is turned on, the alternate fuel electronic control unit activates the high-pressure lock-off, which allows high-pressure gas to pass to the high-pressure regulator.

- The high-pressure regulator reduces the high-pressure CNG to approximately 150 to 170 PSI and sends it to the low-pressure lock-off. The low-pressure lock-off is also controlled by the alternate fuel electronic control unit and is activated at the same time as the high-pressure lock-off.

- From the low-pressure lock-off, the CNG is directed to the low-pressure regulator. This is a two-stage regulator that first reduces the pressure to approximately 4 to 6 PSI in the first stage and then to about 0.5 PSI in the second stage.

- From here, the low-pressure gas is delivered to the gas mass sensor/mixture control valve. This valve controls the air-fuel mixture. The CNG gas distributor adapter then delivers the gas to the intake stream.

CNG vehicles are designed for fleet use that usually have their own refueling capabilities. One of the drawbacks to using CNG is the time that it takes to refuel a vehicle. The ideal method of refueling is the slow-fill method. The slow filling method compresses the natural gas as the tank is being fueled. This method ensures that the tank will receive a full charge of CNG; however, this method can take three to five hours to accomplish. If more than one vehicle needs filling, the facility will need multiple CNG compressors to refuel the vehicles.

There are three commonly used CNG refilling station pressures.

P24: 2,400 PSI

P30: 3,000 PSI

P36: 3,600 PSI

Try to find and use a station with the highest refilling pressure. Filling at lower pressures will result in less compressed natural gas being installed in the storage tank, thereby reducing the driving range. ● SEE FIGURE 12–30.

The fast-fill method uses CNG that is already compressed. However, as the CNG tank is filled rapidly, the internal temperature of the tank will rise, which causes a rise in tank pressure.

FIGURE 12–30 This CNG pump is capable of supplying compressed natural gas at either 3,000 PSI or 3,600 PSI. The price per gallon is higher for the higher pressure.

Once the temperature drops in the CNG tank, the pressure in the tank also drops, resulting in an incomplete charge in the CNG tank. This refueling method may take only about five minutes, but it will result in an incomplete charge to the CNG tank, reducing the driving range. ● SEE CHART 12–2 for a comparison of the most frequently used alternative fuels.

ALTERNATE FUEL COMPARISON CHART					
CHARACTERISTIC	PROPANE	CNG	METHANOL	ETHANOL	REGULAR UNLEADED GAS
Octane	104	130	100	100	87–93
BTU per gallon	91,000	NA	70,000	83,000	114,000–125,000
Gallon equivalent	1.15	122 ft^3 – 1 gallon of gasoline	1.8	1.5	1
Onboard fuel storage	Liquid	Gas	Liquid	Liquid	Liquid
Miles/gallon as compared to gas	85%	Varies with pressure	55%	70%	100%
Relative tank size required to yield driving range equivalent to gas	Tank is 1.25 times larger	Tank is 3.5 times larger	Tank is 1.8 times larger	Tank is 1.5 times larger	
Pressure	200 PSI	3,000–3,600 PSI	NA	NA	NA
Cold weather capability	Good	Good	Poor	Poor	Good
Vehicle power	5%–10% power loss	10%–20% power loss	4% power increase	5% power increase	Standard
Toxicity	Nontoxic	Nontoxic	Highly toxic	Toxic	Toxic
Corrosiveness	Noncorrosive	Noncorrosive	Corrosive	Corrosive	Minimally corrosive
Source	Natural gas/petroleum refining	Natural gas/crude oil	Natural gas/coal	Sugar and starch crops/biomass	Crude oil

CHART 12–2 The characteristics of alternative fuels compared to regular unleaded gasoline show that all have advantages and disadvantages.

LIQUIFIED NATURAL GAS

Natural gas can be turned into a liquid if cooled to below -260°F (-127°C). The natural gas condenses into a liquid at normal atmospheric pressure and the volume is reduced by about 600 times. This means that the natural gas can be more efficiently transported over long distances where no pipelines are present when liquefied.

Because the temperature of liquefied natural gas (LNG) must be kept low, it is best used for fleets where a central LPG station can be used to refuel the vehicles.

P-SERIES FUELS

P-series alternative fuel is patented by Princeton University and is a nonpetroleum or natural gas based fuel suitable for use in flexible fuel vehicles or any vehicle designed to operate on E85 (85% ethanol, 15% gasoline). P-series fuel is recognized by the U.S. Department of Energy as being an alternative fuel, but is not yet available to the public. P-series fuels are blends of the following:

- Ethanol (ethyl alcohol)
- Methyltetrahydrofuron (MTHF)
- Natural gas liquids, such as pentanes
- Butane

The ethanol and MTHF are produced from renewable feedstocks, such as corn, waste paper, biomass, agricultural waste, and wood waste (scraps and sawdust). The components used in P-series fuel can be varied to produce regular grade, premium grade, or fuel suitable for cold climates. ● **SEE CHART 12–3** for the percentages of the ingredients based on fuel grade.

SYNTHETIC FUELS

INTRODUCTION Synthetic fuels can be made from a variety of products, using several different processes. Synthetic fuel must, however, make these alternatives practical only when conventional petroleum products are either very expensive or not available.

FISCHER-TROPSCH Synthetic fuels were first developed using the **Fischer-Tropsch** method, and have been in use since the 1920s to convert coal, natural gas, and other fossil fuel products into a fuel that is high in quality and clean burning. The process for producing Fischer-Tropsch fuels was patented by two German scientists, Franz Fischer and Hans Tropsch, during World War I. The Fischer-Tropsch method uses carbon monoxide and hydrogen (the same synthesis gas used to

COMPOSITION OF P-SERIES FUELS (BY VOLUME)			
Component	Regular Grade (%)	Premium Grade (%)	Cold Weather (%)
Pentanes plus	32.5	27.5	16
MTHF	32.5	17.5	26
Ethanol	35	55	47
Butane	0	0	11

CHART 12–3

P-series fuel varies in composition, depending on the octane rating and temperature.

? FREQUENTLY ASKED QUESTION

What Is a Tri-Fuel Vehicle?

In Brazil, most vehicles are designed to operate on ethanol or gasoline, or any combination of the two. In this South American country, ethanol is made from sugarcane, is commonly available, and is lower in price than gasoline. Compressed natural gas (CNG) is also being made available so many vehicle manufacturers in Brazil, such as General Motors and Ford, are equipping vehicles to be capable of using gasoline, ethanol, or CNG. These vehicles are called tri-fuel vehicles.

produce hydrogen fuel) to convert coal and other hydrocarbons to liquid fuels in a process similar to hydrogenation, another method for hydrocarbon conversion. The process using natural gas, also called **gas-to-liquid (GTL)** technology, uses a catalyst, usually iron or cobalt, and incorporates steam reforming to give off the by-products of carbon dioxide, hydrogen, and carbon monoxide. ● **SEE FIGURE 12–31.**

Whereas traditional fuels emit environmentally harmful particulates and chemicals, namely sulfur compounds, Fischer-Tropsch fuels combust with no soot or odors and emit only low levels of toxins. Fischer-Tropsch fuels can also be blended with traditional transportation fuels with little equipment modification, as they use the same engine and equipment technology as traditional fuels.

The fuels contain a very low sulfur and aromatic content and they produce virtually no particulate emissions. Researchers also expect reductions in hydrocarbon and carbon monoxide emissions. Fischer-Tropsch fuels do not differ in fuel performance from gasoline and diesel. At present, Fischer-Tropsch fuels are very expensive to produce on a large scale, although research is under way to lower processing costs. Diesel fuel created using the **Fischer-Tropsch diesel (FTD)** process is often called *GTL diesel*. GTL diesel can also be combined with petroleum diesel to produce a GTL blend. This fuel product is currently being sold in Europe and plans are in place to introduce it in North America.

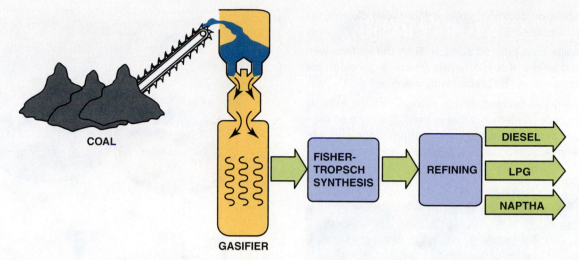

FIGURE 12–31 A Fischer-Tropsch processing plant is able to produce a variety of fuels from coal.

COAL TO LIQUID

Coal is very abundant in the United States and can be converted to a liquid fuel through a process called **coal to liquid (CTL)**. The huge cost of processing is the main obstacle to this type of fuel. The need to invest $1.4 billion per plant before it can make product is the reason no one has built a CTL plant yet in the United States. Investors need to be convinced that the cost of oil is going to remain high in order to get them to commit this kind of money.

A large plant might be able to produce 120,000 barrels of liquid fuel a day and would consume about 50,000 tons of coal per day. However, such a plant would create about 6,000 tons of CO_2 per day, which could contribute to global warming. With this factor and with the costs involved, CTL technology is not likely to expand.

Despite the limitations, two procedures can be used to convert CTL fuel.

1. **Direct method.** In the direct method, coal is broken down to create liquid products. First the coal is reacted with hydrogen (H_2) at high temperatures and pressure with a catalyst. This process creates a synthetic crude, called **syncrude,** which is then refined to produce gasoline or diesel fuel.

2. **Indirect method.** In the indirect method, coal is first turned into a gas and the molecules are reassembled to create the desired product. This process involves turning coal into syngas, which is then converted into liquid, using the Fischer-Tropsch diesel (FTD) process.

Russia has been using CTL by injecting air into the underground coal seams. Ignition is provided and the resulting gases are trapped and converted to liquid gasoline and diesel fuel through the Fischer-Tropsch process. This underground method is called **underground coal gasification (UCG).**

METHANOL TO GASOLINE

Exxon Mobil has developed a process for converting methanol (methyl alcohol) into gasoline in a process called **methanol to gasoline (MTG).** The MTG process was discovered by accident when a gasoline additive made from methanol was being created. The process instead created olefins (alkenes), paraffins (alkenes), and aromatic compounds, which in combination are known as gasoline. The process uses a catalyst and is currently being produced in New Zealand.

FUTURE OF SYNTHETIC FUELS

Producing gasoline and diesel fuels by other methods besides refining from crude oil has usually been more expensive. With the increasing cost of crude oil, alternative methods are now becoming economically feasible. Whether the diesel fuel or gasoline is created from coal, natural gas, or methanol, or created by refining crude oil, the transportation and service pumps are already in place. Compared to using compressed natural gas or other similar alternative fuels, synthetic fuels represent the lowest cost.

SAFETY PROCEDURES WHEN WORKING WITH ALTERNATIVE FUELS

All fuels are flammable and many are explosive under certain conditions. Whenever working around compressed gases of any kind (CNG, LNG, propane, or LPG), always wear personal protective equipment (PPE), including at least the following items.

1. Safety glasses and/or face shield

2. Protective gloves

3. Long-sleeve shirt and pants, to help protect bare skin from the freezing effects of gases under pressure in the event that the pressure is lost

If a spill should occur, take the following actions.

1. If any fuel gets on the skin, the area should be washed immediately.

2. If fuel spills on clothing, change into clean clothing as soon as possible.

3. If fuel spills on a painted surface, flush the surface with water and air dry. If simply wiped off with a dry cloth, the paint surface could be permanently damaged.

4. As with any fuel-burning vehicle, always vent the exhaust to the outside. If methanol fuel is used, the exhaust contains *formaldehyde,* which has a sharp odor and can cause severe burning of the eyes, nose, and throat.

> ☠ **WARNING**
>
> Do not smoke or have an open flame in the area when working around or refueling any vehicle.

DIESEL FUEL

FEATURES OF DIESEL FUEL Diesel fuel must meet an entirely different set of standards than gasoline. Diesel fuel contains 12% more heat energy than the same amount of gasoline. The fuel in a diesel engine is not ignited with a spark, but is ignited by the heat generated by high compression. The pressure of compression (400 to 700 PSI, or 2,800 to 4,800 kPa) generates temperatures of 1,200°F to 1,600°F (700°C to 900°C), which speeds the preflame reaction to start the ignition of fuel injected into the cylinder.

DIESEL FUEL REQUIREMENTS All diesel fuel must have the following characteristics.

- **Cleanliness.** It is imperative that the fuel used in a diesel engine be clean and free from water. Unlike the case with gasoline engines, the fuel is the lubricant and coolant for the diesel injector pump and injectors. Good-quality diesel fuel contains additives such as oxidation inhibitors, detergents, dispersants, rust preventatives, and metal deactivators.

- **Low-temperature fluidity.** Diesel fuel must be able to flow freely at all expected ambient temperatures. One specification for diesel fuel is its "pour point," which is the temperature below which the fuel would stop flowing.

- **Cloud point.** Another concern with diesel fuel at lower temperatures concerns **cloud point,** the low-temperature point when the waxes present in most diesel fuels tend to form crystals that can clog the fuel filter. Most diesel fuel suppliers distribute fuel with the proper pour point and cloud point for the climate conditions of the area.

CETANE NUMBER The cetane number for diesel fuel is the opposite of the octane number for gasoline. The **cetane number** is a measure of the ease with which the fuel can be ignited. The cetane rating of the fuel determines, to a great

(a)

(b)

FIGURE 12–32 (a) Regular diesel fuel on the left has a clear or greenish tint, whereas fuel for off-road use is tinted red for identification. (b) This fuel pump in a farming area clearly states the red diesel fuel is for off-road use only.

extent, its ability to start the engine at low temperatures and to provide smooth warmup and even combustion. The cetane rating of diesel fuel should be between 45 and 50. The higher the cetane rating, the more easily the fuel is ignited.

SULFUR CONTENT The sulfur content of diesel fuel is very important to the life of the engine. Sulfur in the fuel creates sulfuric acid during the combustion process, which can damage engine components and cause piston ring wear. Federal regulations are getting extremely tight on sulfur content to less than 15 parts per million (ppm). High-sulfur fuel contributes to acid rain.

DIESEL FUEL COLOR Diesel fuel intended for use on the streets and highways is either clear or green. Diesel fuel to be used on farms and off-road use is dyed red. ● **SEE FIGURE 12–32.**

GRADES OF DIESEL FUEL

ASTM also classifies diesel fuel by volatility (boiling range) into the following grades.

Grade 1	This grade of diesel fuel has the lowest boiling point and the lowest cloud and pour points, as well as a lower BTU content (less heat per pound of fuel). As a result, grade 1 is suitable for use during low-temperature (winter) operation. Grade 1 produces less heat per pound of fuel compared to grade 2, and may be specified for use in diesel engines involved in frequent changes in load and speed, such as those found in city buses and delivery trucks.
Grade 2	This grade has a higher boiling point, cloud point, and pour point as compared with grade 1. It is usually specified where constant speed and high loads are encountered, such as in long-haul trucking and automotive diesel applications.

DIESEL FUEL SPECIFIC GRAVITY TESTING

The density of diesel fuel should be tested whenever there is a driveability concern. The density or specific gravity of diesel fuel is measured in units of **API gravity,** which is an arbitrary scale expressing the gravity or density of liquid petroleum products devised jointly by the American Petroleum Institute and the National Bureau of Standards. The measuring scale is calibrated in terms of degrees API. Oil with the least specific gravity has the highest API gravity. The formula for determining API gravity is as follows:

$$\text{Degrees API gravity} = (141.5 \div \text{Specific gravity at } 60° \text{ F}) - 131.5$$

The normal API gravity for grade 1 diesel fuel is 39 to 44 (typically 40). The normal API gravity for grade 2 diesel fuel is 30 to 39 (typically 35). A hydrometer calibrated in API gravity units should be used to test diesel fuel. ● **SEE FIGURE 12–33.**

ULTRA-LOW-SULFUR DIESEL FUEL

Diesel fuel is used in diesel engines and is usually readily available throughout the United States, Canada, and Europe, where many more cars are equipped with diesel engines. Diesel engines manufactured to 2007 or newer standards must use **ultra-low-sulfur diesel (ULSD)** fuel containing less than 15 PPM of sulfur compared to the older, low-sulfur specification of 500 PPM. The purpose of the lower sulfur amount in diesel fuel is to reduce emissions of sulfur oxides (SOx) and particulate matter (PM) from heavy-duty highway engines and vehicles that use diesel fuel. The emission controls used on 2007 and newer diesel engines require the use of ULSD for reliable operation.

ULSD will eventually replace the current highway diesel fuel, low-sulfur diesel, which can have as much as 500 PPM of sulfur. ULSD is required for use in all model year 2007 and newer vehicles equipped with advanced emission control systems. ULSD looks lighter in color and has less smell than other diesel fuels.

FIGURE 12–33 Testing the API viscosity of a diesel fuel sample using a hydrometer.

 FREQUENTLY ASKED QUESTION

What Is JP-8 Fuel?

The three fuels used in U.S. military vehicles are:
1. Gasoline
2. DF-2 (diesel fuel grade 2)
3. JP-8 (jet propulsion grade 8)

Currently there is a mandate to convert all vehicles used in all branches of the U.S. military to use only one fuel: JP-8. JP-8 is similar to kerosene and is considered to be a "heavy" fuel. This means that all cars, trucks, tanks, and aircraft must use this one fuel. The advantages to the military would be huge, because regardless of the vehicle, only one fuel needs to be made available.

BIODIESEL

DEFINITION OF BIODIESEL

Biodiesel is a domestically produced, renewable fuel that can be manufactured from vegetable oils, animal fats, or recycled restaurant greases. Biodiesel is safe, biodegradable, and reduces serious air pollutants such as particulate matter (PM), carbon monoxide, and hydrocarbons. Biodiesel is defined as mono-alkyl esters of long-chain fatty acids derived from vegetable oils or animal fats which conform to ASTM D6751 specifications for use in diesel engines. Biodiesel refers to the pure fuel before blending with diesel fuel. ● **SEE FIGURE 12–34.**

Biodiesel blends are denoted as BXX, with the "XX" representing the percentage of biodiesel contained in the blend (i.e., **B20** is 20% biodiesel, 80% petroleum diesel). Blends of 5% biodiesel with 95% petroleum diesel, called **B5,** can generally be used in unmodified diesel engines. Some diesel-powered

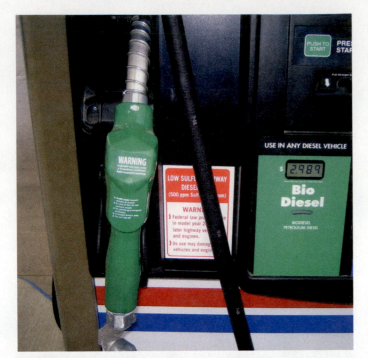

FIGURE 12–34 A biodiesel pump decal indicating that the diesel fuel is ultra-low-sulfur diesel (ULSD) and must be used in 2007 and newer diesel vehicles.

vehicles can use B20 (20% biodiesel). Dodge, for example, allows the use of B5 in all diesel vehicles and B20 only if the optional additional fuel filter is installed. Biodiesel can also be used in its pure form (B100), but it may require certain engine modifications to avoid maintenance and performance problems and may not be suitable for wintertime use. Users should consult their engine warranty statement for more information on fuel blends of greater than 20% biodiesel.

In general, B20 costs 30 to 40 cents more per gallon than conventional diesel. Although biodiesel costs more than regular diesel fuel, often called **petrodiesel,** fleet managers can make the switch to alternative fuels without purchasing new vehicles, acquiring new spare parts inventories, rebuilding refueling stations, or hiring new service technicians.

FEATURES OF BIODIESEL Biodiesel has the following characteristics.

1. Purchasing biodiesel in bulk quantities decreases the cost of fuel.
2. Biodiesel maintains similar horsepower, torque, and fuel economy.
3. Biodiesel has a higher cetane number than conventional diesel, which increases the engine's performance.
4. Biodiesel has a high flash point and low volatility so it does not ignite as easily as petrodiesel, which increases the margin of safety in fuel handling. In fact, it degrades four times faster than petrodiesel and is not particularly soluble in water.

? FREQUENTLY ASKED QUESTION

I Thought Biodiesel Was Vegetable Oil?

Biodiesel is vegetable oil with the glycerin component removed by means of reacting the vegetable oil with a catalyst. The resulting hydrocarbon esters are 16 to 18 carbon atoms in length, almost identical to the petroleum diesel fuel atoms. This allows the use of biodiesel fuel in a diesel engine with no modifications needed. Biodiesel-powered vehicles do not need a second fuel tank, whereas vehicles powered with vegetable oil do.

There are three main types of fuel used in diesel engines.

- Petroleum diesel, a fossil hydrocarbon with a carbon chain length of about 16 carbon atoms
- Biodiesel, a hydrocarbon with a carbon chain length of 16 to 18 carbon atoms
- Vegetable oil, a triglyceride with a glycerin component joining three hydrocarbon chains of 16 to 18 carbon atoms each, called **straight vegetable oil (SVO)**

Other terms used when describing vegetable oil include:

- **Pure plant oil (PPO),** a term most often used in Europe to describe SVO
- **Waste vegetable oil (WVO),** which could include animal or fish oils from cooking
- **Used cooking oil (UCO),** a term used when the oil may or may not be pure vegetable oil

Vegetable oil is not liquid enough at common ambient temperatures for use in a diesel engine fuel delivery system designed for the lower viscosity petroleum diesel fuel. Vegetable oil needs to be heated to obtain a similar viscosity to biodiesel and petroleum diesel. This means that a heat source needs to be provided before the fuel can be used in a diesel engine. This is achieved by starting on petroleum diesel or biodiesel fuel until the engine heat can be used to sufficiently warm a tank containing the vegetable oil. It also requires purging the fuel system of vegetable oil with petroleum diesel or biodiesel fuel prior to stopping the engine to avoid the vegetable oil thickening and solidifying in the fuel system away from the heated tank. The use of vegetable oil in its natural state does, however, eliminate the need to remove the glycerin component.

Many vehicle and diesel engine fuel system suppliers permit the use of biodiesel fuel that is certified as meeting testing standards. None permit the use of vegetable oil in its natural state.

5. It is nontoxic, which makes it safe to handle, transport, and store. Maintenance requirements for B20 vehicles and petrodiesel vehicles are the same.

6. Biodiesel acts as a lubricant, which can add to the life of the fuel system components.

NOTE: For additional information on biodiesel and the locations where it can be purchased, visit www. biodiesel.org.

E-DIESEL FUEL

DEFINITION   **E-diesel**, also called **diesohol** outside of the United States, is standard No. 2 diesel fuel that contains up to 15% ethanol. While E-diesel can have up to 15% ethanol by volume, typical blend levels are from 8% to 10%.

CETANE RATING OF E-DIESEL   The higher the cetane number, the shorter the delay between injection and ignition. Normal diesel fuel has a cetane number of about 50. Adding 15% ethanol lowers the cetane number. To increase the cetane number back to that of conventional diesel fuel, a cetane-enhancing additive is added to E-diesel. The additive used to increase the cetane rating of E-diesel is ethylhexylnitrate or ditertbutyl peroxide.

E-diesel has better cold-flow properties than conventional diesel. The heat content of E-diesel is about 6% less than conventional diesel, but the particulate matter (PM) emissions are reduced by as much as 40%, carbon monoxide by 20%, and oxides of nitrogen (NOx) by 5%.

Currently, E-diesel is considered to be experimental and can be used legally in off-road applications or in mass-transit buses with EPA approval. For additional information, visit www.e-diesel.org.

Fuel	Nozzle Diameter	Pump Handle Color (Varies–no established standard)
Gasoline	13/16 inch (21 mm)	Black, red, white, green, or blue
E10	13/16 inch (21 mm)	Black, red, white, green, or blue
E85	13/16 inch (21 mm)	Yellow or black
Diesel fuel	15/16 inch (24 mm)	Yellow, green, or black
Biodiesel	15/16 inch (24 mm)	Green
Truckstop diesel	1 1/14 or 1 1/2 inch (32 or 38 mm)	Varies

CHART 12–4

Fuel pump nozzle size is standardized except for use by over-the-road truckstops where high fuel volumes and speedy refills require larger nozzle sizes compared to passenger vehicle filling station nozzles.

?   FREQUENTLY ASKED QUESTION

What Are the Pump Nozzle Sizes?

Unleaded gasoline nozzles are smaller than those used for diesel fuel to help prevent fueling errors. However, it is still possible to fuel a diesel vehicle with gasoline.

● **SEE CHART 12–4** for the sizes and colors used for fuel pump nozzles.

TESTING FOR ALCOHOL CONTENT IN GASOLINE

1 A fuel composition tester (SPX Kent-Moore J-44175) is the recommended tool to use to test the alcohol content of gasoline.

2 This battery-powered tester uses light-emitting diodes (LEDs), meter lead terminals, and two small openings for the fuel sample.

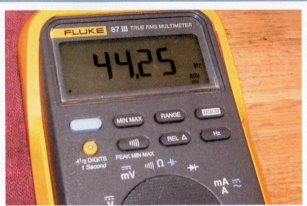

3 The first step is to verify the proper operation of the tester by measuring the air frequency by selecting AC hertz on the meter. The air frequency should be between 35 Hz and 48 Hz.

4 After verifying that the tester is capable of correctly reading the air frequency, gasoline is poured into the testing cell of the tool.

5 Record the AC frequency as shown on the meter and subtract 50 from the reading (e.g., 60.50 − 50.00 = 10.5). This number (10.5) is the percentage of alcohol in the gasoline sample.

6 Adding additional amounts of ethyl alcohol (ethanol) increases the frequency reading.

SUMMARY

1. Gasoline is a complex blend of hydrocarbons. Gasoline is blended for seasonal usage to achieve the correct volatility for easy starting and maximum fuel economy under all driving conditions.

2. Winter-blend fuel used in a vehicle during warm weather can cause a rough idle and stalling because of its higher Reid vapor pressure (RVP).

3. Abnormal combustion (also called detonation or spark knock) increases both the temperature and the pressure inside the combustion chamber.

4. Most regular grade gasoline today, using the (R + M) ÷ 2 rating method, is 87 octane; midgrade (plus) is 89 and premium grade is 91 or higher.

5. Oxygenated fuels contain oxygen to lower CO exhaust emissions.

6. Flexible fuel vehicles (FFVs) are designed to operate on gasoline or gasoline-ethanol blends up to 85% ethanol (E85).

7. E85 has fewer BTUs of energy per gallon compared with gasoline and will therefore provide lower fuel economy.

8. Methanol is also called methyl alcohol or wood alcohol and, while it can be made from wood, it is mostly made from natural gas.

9. Propane is the most widely used alternative fuel. Propane is also called liquefied petroleum gas (LPG).

10. Compressed natural gas (CNG) is available for refilling in several pressures, including 2,400 PSI, 3,000 PSI, and 3,600 PSI.

11. Safety procedures when working around alternative fuel include wearing the necessary personal protective equipment (PPE), including safety glasses and protective gloves.

12. Diesel fuel requirements include cleanliness, low-temperature fluidity, and proper cetane rating.

13. Emission control devices used on 2007 and newer engines require the use of ultra-low-sulfur diesel (ULSD) that has less than 15 parts per million (ppm) of sulfur.

14. Biodiesel is the blend of vegetable-based liquid with regular diesel fuel. Most diesel engine manufacturers allow the use of a 5% blend, called B5, without any changes to the fuel system or engine.

REVIEW QUESTIONS

1. What is the difference between summer-blend and winter-blend gasoline?

2. What is Reid vapor pressure?

3. What does the (R + M) ÷ 2 gasoline pump octane rating indicate?

4. What is stoichiometric?

5. How is a flexible fuel vehicle identified?

6. What other gases are often mixed with propane?

7. Why is it desirable to fill a compressed natural gas (CNG) vehicle with the highest pressure available?

8. P-series fuel is made of what products?

9. The Fischer-Tropsch method can be used to change what into gasoline?

10. Biodiesel blends are identified by what designation?

CHAPTER QUIZ

1. Winter-blend gasoline _____.
   a. Vaporizes more easily than summer-blend gasoline
   b. Has a higher RVP
   c. Can cause engine driveability problems if used during warm weather
   d. All of the above

2. Technician A says that spark knock, ping, and detonation are different names for abnormal combustion. Technician B says that any abnormal combustion raises the temperature and pressure inside the combustion chamber and can cause severe engine damage. Which technician is correct?
   a. Technician A only
   b. Technician B only
   c. Both Technicians A and B
   d. Neither Technician A nor B

3. Technician A says that the research octane number is higher than the motor octane number. Technician B says that the octane rating posted on fuel pumps is an average of the two ratings. Which technician is correct?
   a. Technician A only
   b. Technician B only
   c. Both Technicians A and B
   d. Neither Technician A nor B

4. Technician A says that in going to high altitudes, engines produce lower power. Technician B says that most engine control systems can compensate the air-fuel mixture for changes in altitude. Which technician is correct?
   a. Technician A only
   b. Technician B only
   c. Both Technicians A and B
   d. Neither Technician A nor B

5. Which method of blending ethanol with gasoline is the most accurate?
   a. In-line
   b. Sequential
   c. Splash
   d. All of the above

6. What can be used to measure the alcohol content in gasoline?
   a. Graduated cylinder
   b. Electronic tester
   c. Scan tool
   d. Both a and b

7. E85 means that the fuel is made from _____.
   a. 85% gasoline and 15% ethanol
   b. 85% ethanol and 15% gasoline
   c. Ethanol that has 15% water
   d. Pure ethyl alcohol

8. A flex fuel vehicle can be identified by _____.
   a. Emblems on the side, front, and/or rear of the vehicle
   b. VECI
   c. VIN
   d. All of the above

9. When refueling a CNG vehicle, why is it recommended that the tank be filled to a high pressure?
   a. The range of the vehicle is increased.
   b. The cost of the fuel is lower.
   c. Less of the fuel is lost to evaporation.
   d. Both a and c

10. What color is diesel fuel dyed if it is for off-road use only?
    a. Red
    b. Green
    c. Blue
    d. Yellow

chapter 13

COOLANT

LEARNING OBJECTIVES: **After studying this chapter, the reader should be able to:** • Discuss coolant fundamentals. • Compare the different types of coolant. • Discuss coolant freezing/boiling temperatures and water as coolant. • Discuss coolant testing and coolant replacement issues.

KEY TERMS: DEX-COOL 152 • Electrolysis 156 • Embittered coolant 153 • Ethylene glycol based coolant 152 • Galvanic activity 156 • Hybrid organic acid technology (HOAT) 152 • Inorganic additive technology (IAT) 152 • Organic acid technology (OAT) 152 • Passivation 157 • Phosphate hybrid organic acid technology (PHOAT) 153 • Refractometer 155

COOLANT FUNDAMENTALS

PURPOSE OF COOLANT
Coolant is used in the cooling system because it:

1. Transfers heat from the engine to the radiator
2. Protects the engine and the cooling system from rust and corrosion
3. Prevents freezing in cold climates

Coolant is a mixture of antifreeze and water. Water is able to absorb more heat per gallon than any other liquid coolant. Under standard conditions, the following occurs.

- Water boils at 212°F (100°C) at sea level.
- Water freezes at 32°F (0°C).
- When water freezes, it increases in volume by about 9%. The expansion of the freezing water can easily crack engine blocks, cylinder heads, and radiators.

A curve depicting freezing point as compared with the percentage of antifreeze mixture is shown in ● **FIGURE 13–1**.

FREEZING/BOILING TEMPERATURES
It should be noted that the freezing point increases as the antifreeze concentration is increased above 60%. The normal mixture is 50% antifreeze and 50% water. Ethylene glycol antifreeze contains:

- Anticorrosion additives
- Rust inhibitors
- Water pump lubricants

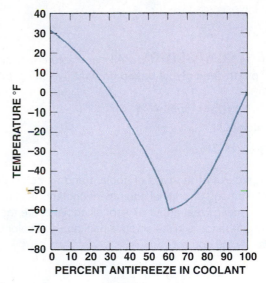

FIGURE 13–1 Graph showing the relationship of the freezing point of the coolant to the percentage of antifreeze used in the coolant.

At the maximum level of protection, an ethylene glycol concentration of 60% will absorb about 85% as much heat as will water. Ethylene glycol based antifreeze also has a higher boiling point than water. A curve depicting freezing point as compared with the percentage of antifreeze mixture is shown in ● **FIGURE 13–2**.

If the coolant boils, it vaporizes and does not act as a cooling agent because it is not in liquid form or in contact with the cooling surfaces.

All coolants have rust and corrosion inhibitors to help protect the metals in the engine and cooling systems.

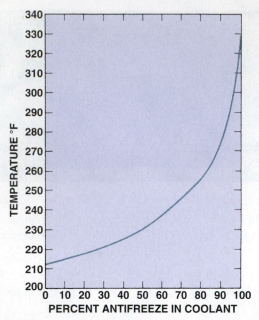

FIGURE 13–2 Graph showing how the boiling point of the coolant increases as the percentage of antifreeze in the coolant increases.

COOLANT COMPOSITION
All manufacturers recommend the use of **ethylene glycol based coolant**, which contains:

- Ethylene glycol (EG): 47%
- Water: 50%
- Additives: 3%

Regardless of the type of coolant and its color, the only difference among all original equipment coolants is in the additives. This means that about 97% of all coolants are the same. The only difference is in the additive package and color used to help identify the coolant.

TYPES OF COOLANT

INORGANIC ACID TECHNOLOGY
Inorganic additive technology (IAT) is conventional coolant that has been used for over 50 years. Most conventional green antifreeze contains inorganic salts such as:

- Sodium silicate (silicates)
- Phosphates
- Borates

Silicates have been found to be the cause of erosive wear to water pump impellers. The color of IAT coolant is green. Phosphates in these coolants can cause deposits to form if used with water that is hard (contains minerals). IAT coolants used in new vehicles were phased out in the mid-1990s.

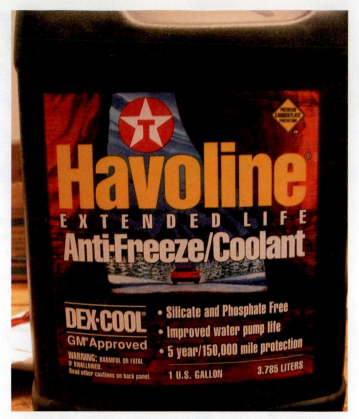

FIGURE 13–3 Havoline was the first company to make and market OAT coolant. General Motors uses the term DEX-COOL.

ORGANIC ACID TECHNOLOGY
Organic acid technology (OAT) coolant contains ethylene glycol, but does not contain silicates or phosphates. The color of this type of coolant is usually orange.

DEX-COOL, developed by Havoline, is just one brand of OAT coolant, which has been used in General Motors vehicles since 1996. ● **SEE FIGURE 13–3.**

DEX-COOL uses ethylhexanoic acid (2-EH) as a corrosive inhibitor. 2-EH is prone to damage plastics, such as Nylon 6.6 used in intake manifold gaskets and radiators. Other brands of OAT coolant that are also orange but do not contain 2-EH include:

- Zerex G30 or G05 OAT
- Peak Global OAT

These coolants are usually available in premix (with water) and pure coolant containers.

HYBRID ORGANIC ACID TECHNOLOGY
A newer variation of this technology is called **hybrid organic acid technology (HOAT).** It is similar to the OAT-type antifreeze as it uses organic acid salts (carboxylates) that are not abrasive to water pumps, yet provide the correct pH. The pH of the coolant is usually above 11. A pH of 7 is neutral, with lower numbers indicating an acidic solution and higher numbers indicating an alkaline solution. If the pH is too high, the coolant can cause scaling and reduce the heat transferability of the coolant. If the pH is too low, the resulting acidic solution could

? **FREQUENTLY ASKED QUESTION**

What Is a "G" Coolant?

The "G" coolants come from the trade name *Glysantin* of BASF in Europe and Valvoline (Zerex) in the United States. The following is a summary of the types listed by G number.

- G05: different from DEX-COOL in certain amounts of additives
- G30 and G34: nonsilicate and phosphate free
- G11: blue VW used before 1997
- G12: pink/red VW 1997+ (purple VW 2003+)
  - HOAT formulation
  - Phosphate free
- G48: low silicate and phosphate free
  - Blue
  - Nitrates, amines, phosphate (NAP) free

FIGURE 13–4 Coolant used in Fords that use Mazda engines and in Mazda vehicles. It requires the use of a PHOAT coolant which is dark green.

cause corrosion of the engine components exposed to the coolant.

HOAT coolants can be green, orange, yellow, gold, pink, red, or blue.

Samples of HOAT coolants include:

- **VW/Audi pink.** Contains some silicates and an organic acid, and is phosphate free
- **Mercedes/Ford yellow.** Contains low amounts of silicate and no phosphate
- **Ford yellow.** Contains low silicate, no phosphate, and is dyed yellow for identification
- **Honda blue.** Contains a special coolant with just one organic acid
- **European/Korean blue.** Contains low silicates and no phosphates
- **Asian red.** Contains no silicates but has some phosphate

PHOSPHATE HYBRID ORGANIC ACID TECHNOLOGY

Phosphate hybrid organic acid technology (PHOAT) is used in Mazda-based Fords (2008+), same as Mazda FL-22, and is ethylene glycol based. This coolant is available in a 55% coolant/45% water premix. ● **SEE FIGURE 13–4.**

- Concentration: 55%
- Boiling point (with 15 PSI pressure cap): 270°F (132°C)
- Freezing point: −47°F (−44°C)
- Color: Dark green
- Embittered (made to taste bitter so animals will not drink it)

The use of PHOAT coolant in these engines is required to be assured of proper protection of the material used in the engine. It is also only available in premix containers to ensure that the water used meets specifications.

? **FREQUENTLY ASKED QUESTION**

What Is "Pet Friendly" Antifreeze?

Conventional ethylene glycol antifreeze used by all vehicle manufacturers is attractive to pets and animals because it has a sweet taste. Ethylene glycol is fatal to any animal if swallowed, so any spill should be cleaned up quickly. There are two types of coolant that are safer for use around pets than the conventional type.

- **Propylene glycol (PG).** This type of antifreeze is *less* attractive to pets and animals because it is not as sweet, but it is still harmful if swallowed. This type of coolant, including the Sierra brand, should not be mixed with any other ethylene glycol based coolant.

CAUTION: Some vehicle manufacturers do not recommend the use of propylene glycol coolant. Check the recommendation in the owner manual or service information before using it in a vehicle.

- **Embittered coolant.** This coolant has a small amount of a substance that makes it taste bitter and therefore not appealing to animals. The embittering agent used in ethylene glycol (EG) antifreeze is usually denatonium benzoate, added at the rate of 30 PPM. Oregon and California require all coolant sold in these states since 2004 to be embittered. ● **SEE FIGURE 13–5.**

FIGURE 13-5 Not all embittered coolant is labeled embittered.

 REAL WORLD FIX

If 50% Is Good, 100% Must Be Better

A vehicle owner said that the cooling system of his vehicle would never freeze or rust. He said that he used 100% antifreeze (ethylene glycol) instead of a 50/50 mixture with water.

However, after the temperature dropped to –20°F (–29°C), the radiator froze and cracked. (Pure antifreeze freezes at about 0°F [–18°C].) After thawing, the radiator had to be repaired. The owner was lucky that the engine block did not also crack.

For best freeze protection with good heat transfer, use a 50/50 mixture of antifreeze and water. A 50/50 mixture of antifreeze and water is the best compromise between temperature protection and the heat transfer that is necessary for cooling system operation. Do not exceed 70% antifreeze (30% water). As the percentage of antifreeze increases, the boiling temperature increases, and freezing protection increases (up to 70% antifreeze), but the heat transfer performance of the mixture decreases.

UNIVERSAL COOLANT Universal coolant is usually a hybrid organic acid technology (HOAT), with extended life, and a low-silicate, phosphate-free antifreeze/coolant. It can be used in many vehicles, but cannot meet the needs for engines requiring a silicate-free formulation.

 **WATER**

INTRODUCTION Water is half of the coolant and can have an effect on the corrosion protection of coolant due to variations in its quality, which is often unknown. As a result,

 FREQUENTLY ASKED QUESTION

What Makes Some Water Bad for Coolant?

City water is treated with chloride, which, if the levels are high enough, can cause corrosion problems when used in coolants. Well water may contain iron or other minerals that can affect the coolant and may increase the corrosion or cause electrolysis. Due to the fact that the water quality is often unknown and could affect the engine, many vehicle manufacturers are specifying the use of pre-mixed coolant. In pre-mix coolant, the water is usually de-mineralized and meets the standards for use in coolant.

many vehicle manufacturers, such as Honda and Toyota, are specifying the use of premix coolants only. The main reason is that not only can the water/coolant ratio be maintained, but also the quality of the water can be controlled.

PROPERTIES Water is about half of the coolant and is used because of the following qualities.

1. It is inexpensive.
2. It is an efficient heat exchange fluid because of its excellent thermal conductivity (the ability of a material to conduct heat).
3. It has good specific heat capacity, meaning it takes more heat energy to increase the temperature, versus one with low specific heat capacity.
4. The boiling point is 212°F (100°C) (at sea level).
5. The freezing point is 32°F (0°C).

COOLANT FREEZING/ BOILING TEMPERATURES

FREEZING POINT An antifreeze and water mixture is an example wherein the freezing point differs from the freezing point of either pure antifreeze or pure water.

	Freezing Point
Pure water	32°F (0°C)
Pure antifreeze*	0°F (–18°C)
50/50 mixture	–34°F (–37°C)
70% antifreeze/30% water	–84°F (–64°C)

*Pure antifreeze is usually 95% ethylene glycol, 2% to 3% water, and 2% to 3% additives.

Depending on the exact percentage of water used, antifreeze (not premixed), as sold in containers, freezes at about 0°F (–18°C). Premixed coolant will freeze at about –34°F (–37°C).

Why Is Most Coolant 50/50 with Water?

According to the freezing point, it appears that the lowest freezing point of coolant is achieved when 70% antifreeze is used with 30% water. While the freezing temperature is lower, the high concentrate of antifreeze reduces the heat transferability of the coolant. Therefore, most vehicle manufacturers specify a 50/50 mixture of antifreeze and water to achieve the best balance between freeze protection and heat conductivity.

FIGURE 13–6 Checking the freezing temperature of the coolant using a hydrometer.

BOILING POINT

The boiling point of antifreeze and water is also a factor of mixture concentrations.

	Boiling Point at Sea Level	Boiling Point with 15 PSI Pressure Cap
Pure water	212°F (100°C)	257°F (125°C)
50/50 mixture	218°F (103°C)	265°F (130°C)
70/30 mixture	225°F (107°C)	276°F (136°C)

COOLANT TESTING

Normal coolant tests include:

- **Visual inspection.** Coolant should be clean and bright.
- **Freeze/boiling point.** A high freezing point or low boiling point indicates dilution (too much water).
- **pH.** The wrong pH indicates buffer loss, which is used to help maintain the pH level.
- **Coolant voltage.** A high voltage indicates the wrong pH or a stray current flow.

Various methods are used to test coolant.

HYDROMETER TESTING

Coolant can be checked using a coolant hydrometer. The hydrometer measures the density of the coolant. The higher the density, the more concentration of antifreeze in the water. Most coolant hydrometers read the freezing and boiling points of the coolant. ● **SEE FIGURE 13–6.**

If the engine is overheating and the hydrometer reading is near –50°F (–60°C), suspect that pure 100% antifreeze is present. For best results, the coolant should have a freezing point lower than –20°F (–29°C) and a boiling point above 234°F (112°).

REFRACTOMETER

A **refractometer** is a tester used to test the freezing point of coolant by placing a few drops of coolant on the prism surface. The technician then holds the unit up to light and looks through the eyepiece for the location of the shadow on the display.

Ignore the Wind Chill Factor

The wind chill factor is a temperature that combines the actual temperature and the wind speed to determine the overall heat loss effect on open skin. Because it is the heat loss factor for open skin, the wind chill temperature is *not* to be considered when determining antifreeze protection levels.

Although moving air makes it feel colder, the actual temperature is not changed by the wind, and the engine coolant will not be affected by the wind chill. If you are not convinced, try placing a thermometer in a room and wait until a stable reading is obtained. Now turn on a fan and have the air blow across the thermometer. The temperature will not change.

A refractometer measures the extent to which light is bent (refracted) to determine the index of refraction of a liquid sample. The refractive index is commonly used for the following:

- To identify or confirm the identity of a sample coolant
- To determine the purity of a coolant by comparing its refractive index to the value for the pure substance
- To determine the concentration of a solute in a solution by comparing the solution's refractive index to a standard curve

● **SEE FIGURE 13–7.**

PH The term *pH* comes from a French word, meaning "power of hydrogen," and is a measure of acidity or alkalinity of a solution.

- Less than 7 pH is considered acidic.
- Greater than 7 pH is considered alkaline.

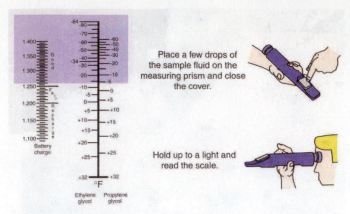

FIGURE 13–7 Using a refractometer is an accurate method to check the freezing point of coolant.

FIGURE 13–8 A meter that measures the actual pH of the coolant can be used for all coolants, unlike many test stripes that cannot be used to test the pH of red or orange coolants.

The pH of new coolant varies according to the type of coolant used. Typical pH values for new coolant include:

IAT: 9 to 10.5 new

OAT: 7.5 to 8.5 new (G30 and G34 designations)

HOAT: 7.5 to 8.5 new (G05, G48, G11, or G12 designation)

PHOAT: 7.5 to 8.5 new

When testing for pH, use either a test strip or a pH meter. If using a test strip be sure that it is calibrated to test the type of coolant being used in the vehicle.

Used coolant pH readings are usually lower than when the coolant is new and range between 7.5 and 10 for IAT and lower for used OAT, HOAT, and PHOAT coolants. For best results use a pH tester that measures the actual pH of the coolant. ● SEE FIGURE 13–8.

GALVANIC ACTIVITY
Galvanic activity is the flow of an electrical current as a result of two different metals in a liquid, which acts like a battery. Galvanic activity does *not* require an outside source of voltage. The two different metals, usually iron and aluminum, become the plates of the battery and the coolant is the electrolyte. The higher the electrical conductivity of the coolant, the greater is the amount of corrosion. ● SEE FIGURE 13–9.

ELECTROLYSIS
Electrolysis requires the use of an outside voltage source. The source is usually due to a poor electrical ground connection.

- Electrical flow through the cooling system may cause metal to flow into the coolant.
- This metal transfer can eat holes in a heater core or radiator.
- Electrolysis holes will usually start from the inside and have a dark coloration.

TESTING FOR GALVANIC ACTIVITY AND ELECTROLYSIS
A voltmeter set to read DC volts is used to test for galvanic activity and electrolysis. To check for

BI-METAL CORROSION

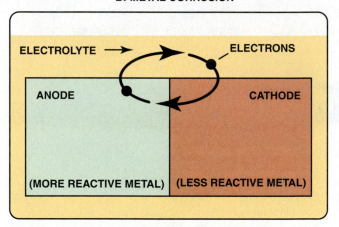

FIGURE 13–9 Galvanic activity is created by two dissimilar metals in contact with a liquid, in this case coolant.

excessive voltage caused by galvanic activity or electrolysis, perform the following steps.

STEP 1 Allow the engine to cool and then carefully remove the pressure cap from the radiator.

STEP 2 Set the voltmeter to DC volts and connect the black meter lead to a good engine ground.

STEP 3 Place the red meter lead into the coolant.

STEP 4 Read the meter. If the voltage is above 0.5 Volt, this indicates excessive galvanic activity. Normal readings should be less than 0.2 Volt (200 mV). Flush and refill the cooling system.

STEP 5 To test for excessive electrolysis, start the engine and turn on all electrical accessories, including the headlights on high beam.

STEP 6 Read the voltmeter. If the reading is higher than 0.5 Volt, check for improper body ground wires or connections. Normal readings should be less than 0.3 Volt (300 mV).

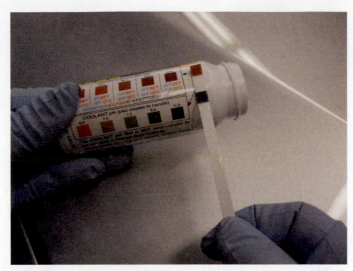

FIGURE 13–10 A test strip can be used to determine the pH and percentage of glycol of the coolant. The percentage of glycol determines the freezing and boiling temperatures, as shown on the bottle that contains the test strips.

TEST STRIP TESTING Test strips can be used to check one or more of the following:

- Freeze point
- Boiling point
- Level of pH

Test strips will change color when they are dipped into the coolant, and the color change is compared to the container. Test strips are fairly accurate, easy to use, and inexpensive.

For best results, use test strips that are new and have been stored in a sealed bottle. Using older test strips may affect the accuracy. ● **SEE FIGURE 13–10.**

COOLANT REPLACEMENT ISSUES

INTERVALS Coolant should be replaced according to the vehicle manufacturer's recommended interval.

- For most new vehicles using OAT or HOAT type coolant, this interval may be every five years or 150,000 miles (241,000 km), whichever occurs first.
- Japanese brand vehicles usually have a replacement interval of three years or 36,000 miles (58,000 km), whichever occurs first.
- If the coolant is changed from a long life to a conventional IAT coolant, the replacement interval needs to be changed to every two years or 24,000 miles (39,000 km), whichever occurs first.

PASSIVATION **Passivation** is a chemical reaction that takes place between coolant additives and the metal that it protects. This means that a chemical barrier is created between the coolant and the metals of the engine. When changing coolants, passivation can take from a few days to a few weeks.

- Each chemical package does its own passivation.
- If you change chemical packages, passivation has to start over.

Therefore, because of passivation concerns, most experts agree that for best results do not change types of coolants. Always use what the vehicle manufacturer recommends. Always check service information for the exact recommended replacement interval for the vehicle being serviced.

RECYCLING COOLANT Coolant (antifreeze and water) should be recycled. Used coolant may contain heavy metals, such as lead, aluminum, and iron, which are absorbed by the coolant during its use in the engine.

Recycle machines filter out these metals and dirt and reinstall the depleted acids. The recycled coolant, restored to be like new, can be reinstalled into the vehicle.

CAUTION: Most vehicle manufacturers warn that coolant should not be reused unless it is recycled and the acids restored. However, Mercedes lifetime coolant is very expensive, and according to Mercedes can be drained, filtered, and reused.

SUMMARY

1. All coolants are ethylene glycol based. Some aftermarket coolants use propylene glycol.
2. Used coolant should be recycled whenever possible.
3. The freezing temperature of the coolant can be tested using a hydrometer or refractometer.

4. Proper cooling system maintenance usually calls for replacing the coolant every two years or every 24,000 miles (36,000 km) for IAT coolant but longer for OAT, HOAT, and PHOAT coolants.

REVIEW QUESTIONS

1. What types of coolant are used in vehicles?
2. Why is a 50/50 mixture of antifreeze and water commonly used as a coolant?
3. What are the differences among IAT, OAT, HOAT, and PHOAT coolants?
4. What are some of the heavy metals that can be present in used coolant?
5. What is the difference between galvanic activity and electrolysis?

CHAPTER QUIZ

1. Coolant is water and _____.
   - a. Methanol
   - b. Glycerin
   - c. Kerosene
   - d. Ethylene glycol

2. As the percentage of antifreeze in the coolant increases, _____.
   - a. The freezing point decreases (up to a point)
   - b. The boiling point decreases
   - c. The heat transfer increases
   - d. All of the above

3. Adding a chemical to make ethylene glycol coolant bitter to the taste is called _____.
   - a. Passivation
   - b. Embittered
   - c. Refractometer
   - d. Electrolysis

4. Asian red coolant is what type?
   - a. IAT
   - b. OAT
   - c. HOAT
   - d. PHOAT

5. DEX-COOL is what type of coolant?
   - a. IAT
   - b. OAT
   - c. HOAT
   - d. PHOAT

6. PHOAT coolant is what color?
   - a. Dark green
   - b. Red
   - c. Orange
   - d. Blue

7. DEX-COOL is _____.
   - a. Propylene glycol
   - b. Ethylene glycol
   - c. Is silicate and phosphate free
   - d. Both b and c

8. Two technicians are discussing testing coolant for proper pH. Technician A says that coolant has a pH above 7 when new and becomes lower with use in an engine. Technician B says that OAT and HOAT coolants have a lower pH when new compared to the old green IAT coolant. Which technician is correct?
   - a. Technician A only
   - b. Technician B only
   - c. Both Technicians A and B
   - d. Neither Technician A nor B

9. Reusing old coolant is generally not approved by vehicle manufacturers except _____.
   - a. General Motors
   - b. Ford
   - c. Chrysler
   - d. Mercedes

10. A voltmeter was used to check the coolant and a reading of 0.2 volt with the engine off was measured. A reading of 0.8 volt was measured with the engine running and all electrical accessories turned on. Technician A says that the coolant should be flushed to solve the galvanic activity. Technician B says that the ground wires and connections should be inspected and repaired to solve the electrolysis problem. Which technician is correct?
   - a. Technician A only
   - b. Technician B only
   - c. Both Technicians A and B
   - d. Neither Technician A nor B

COOLING SYSTEM OPERATION AND DIAGNOSIS

LEARNING OBJECTIVES: **After studying this chapter, the reader should be able to:** • Explain the purpose and function of the cooling system, and cooling system operation. • Explain the purpose of thermostats, radiators, pressure caps, and water pumps. • Explain coolant flow in the engine and coolant recovery systems. • Explain the purpose of cooling fans and heater cores. • Describe cooling system testing and explain the purpose of coolant temperature warning light. • Explain cooling system inspection and cooling system service.

KEY TERMS: Bar 165 • Bleed holes 169 • Bypass 161 • Centrifugal pump 167 • Coolant recovery system 166 • Cooling fins 164 • Core tubes 164 • Impeller 167 • Parallel flow system 169 • Reverse cooling 167 • Scroll 167 • Series flow system 169 • Series-parallel flow system 169 • Silicone coupling 170 • Steam slits 169 • Surge tank 166 • Thermostatic spring 170

COOLING SYSTEM

PURPOSE AND FUNCTION Satisfactory cooling system operation depends on the design and operating conditions of the system. The design is based on heat output of the engine, radiator size, type of coolant, size of water pump (coolant pump), type of fan, thermostat, and system pressure. The cooling system must allow the engine to warm up to the required operating temperature as rapidly as possible and then maintain that temperature.

Peak combustion temperatures in the engine run from 4,000°F to 6,000°F (2,200°C to 3,300°C). The combustion temperatures will *average* between 1,200°F and 1,700°F (650°C and 925°C). Continued temperatures as high as this would weaken engine parts, so heat must be removed from the engine. The cooling system keeps the head and cylinder walls at a temperature that is within the range for maximum efficiency. The cooling system removes about one-third of the heat created in the engine. Another third escapes to the exhaust system.
● **SEE FIGURE 14–1.**

LOW-TEMPERATURE ENGINE PROBLEMS Engine operating temperatures must be above a minimum temperature for proper engine operation. If the coolant temperature does not reach the specified temperature as determined by the thermostat, then the following engine-related faults can occur.

▪ A P0128 diagnostic trouble code (DTC) can be set. This code indicates "coolant temperature below thermostat regulating temperature," which is usually caused by a defective thermostat staying open or partially open.

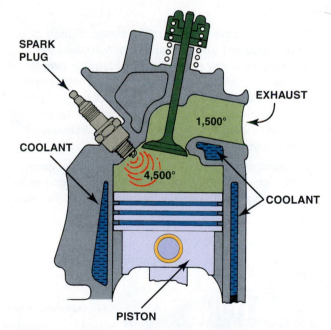

FIGURE 14–1 Typical combustion and exhaust temperatures.

▪ Moisture created during the combustion process can condense and flow into the oil. *For each gallon of fuel used, moisture equal to a gallon of water is produced.* The condensed moisture combines with unburned hydrocarbons and additives to form carbonic acid, sulfuric acid, nitric acid, hydrobromic acid, and hydrochloric acid.

To reduce cold engine problems and to help start engines in cold climates, most manufacturers offer block

Overheating Can Be Expensive

A faulty cooling system seems to be a major cause of engine failure. Engine rebuilders often have night-mares about seeing their rebuilt engine placed back in service in a vehicle with a clogged radiator. Most engine technicians routinely replace the water pump and all hoses after an engine overhaul or repair. The radiator should also be checked for leaks and proper flow whenever the engine is repaired or replaced. Overheating is one of the most common causes of engine failure.

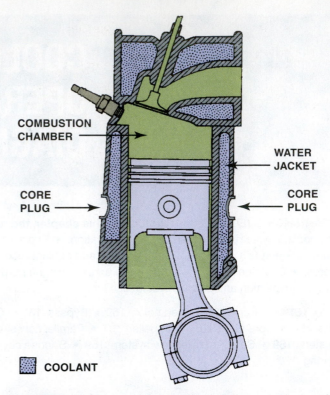

COOLANT

FIGURE 14–2 Coolant circulates through the water jackets in the engine block and cylinder head.

heaters as an option. These block heaters are plugged into household current (110 volts AC) and the heating element warms the coolant.

HIGH-TEMPERATURE ENGINE PROBLEMS Maximum temperature limits are required to protect the engine. Higher than normal temperatures can cause the following engine-related issues.

- High temperatures will oxidize the engine oil producing hard carbon and varnish. The varnish will cause the hydraulic valve lifter plungers to stick. Higher than normal temperatures will also cause the oil to become thinner (lower viscosity than normal). Thinned oil will also get into the combustion chamber by going past the piston rings and through valve guides to cause excessive oil consumption.

- The combustion process is very sensitive to temperature. High coolant temperatures raise the combustion temper-atures to a point that may cause detonation (also called spark knock or ping) to occur.

COOLING SYSTEM OPERATION

PURPOSE AND FUNCTION   Coolant flows through the engine, where it picks up heat. It then flows to the radiator, where the heat is given up to the outside air. The coolant continually recirculates through the cooling system, as illustrated in ● **FIGURES 14–2 AND 14–3.**

COOLING SYSTEM OPERATION   The temperature of the coolant rises as much as 15°F (8°C) as it goes through the engine and cools as it goes through the radiator. *The coolant flow rate may be as high as 1 gallon (4 liters) per minute for each horsepower the engine produces.*

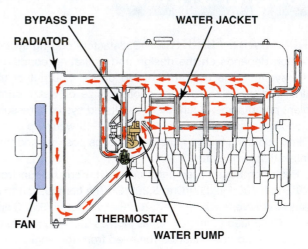

FIGURE 14–3 Coolant flow through a typical engine cooling system.

Hot coolant comes out of the thermostat housing on the top of the engine on most engines. The engine coolant outlet is connected to the radiator by the upper radiator hose and clamps. The coolant in the radiator is cooled by air flowing through the radiator. As the coolant moves through the radia-tor, it cools. The cooler coolant leaves the radiator through an outlet and the lower radiator hose, and then flows to the inlet side of the water pump, where it is recirculated through the engine.

NOTE: Some newer engine designs such as Chrysler's 4.7 liter V-8 and General Motor's 4.8, 5.3, 5.7, and

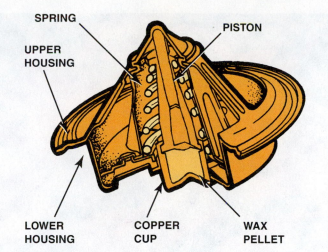

FIGURE 14–4 A cross section of a typical wax-actuated thermostat showing the position of the wax pellet and spring.

6.0 liter V-8s place the thermostat on the inlet side of the water pump. As the cooled coolant hits the thermostat, the thermostat closes until the coolant temperature again causes it to open. Placing the thermostat in the inlet side of the water pump therefore reduces the rapid temperature changes that could cause stress in the engine, especially if aluminum heads are used with a cast iron block.

Radiators are designed for the maximum rate of heat transfer using minimum space. Cooling airflow through the radiator is aided by a belt- or electric motor–driven cooling fan.

THERMOSTATS

PURPOSE AND FUNCTION There is a normal operating temperature range between low-temperature and high-temperature extremes. The thermostat controls the minimum normal temperature. The thermostat is a temperature-controlled valve placed at the engine coolant outlet on most engines.

THERMOSTAT OPERATION An encapsulated wax-based plastic pellet heat sensor is located on the engine side of the thermostatic valve. As the engine warms, heat swells the heat sensor. ● SEE FIGURE 14–4.

A mechanical link, connected to the heat sensor, opens the thermostat valve. As the thermostat begins to open, it allows some coolant to flow to the radiator, where it is cooled. The remaining part of the coolant continues to flow through the bypass, thereby bypassing the thermostat and flowing back through the engine. ● SEE FIGURE 14–5.

The rated temperature of the thermostat indicates the temperature at which the thermostat starts to open. The thermostat is fully open at about 20°F higher than its opening temperature. ● SEE CHART 14–1.

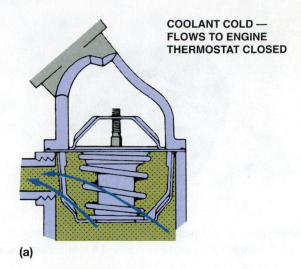

(a)

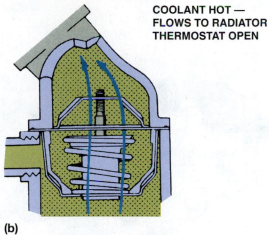

(b)

FIGURE 14–5 (a) When the engine is cold, the coolant flows through the bypass. (b) When the thermostat opens, the coolant can flow to the radiator.

THERMOSTAT TEMPERATURE RATING	STARTS TO OPEN	FULLY OPEN
180°F	180°F	200°F
195°F	195°F	215°F

CHART 14–1

The temperature of the coolant depends on the rating of the thermostat.

If the radiator, water pump, and coolant passages are functioning correctly, the engine should always be operating within the opening and fully open temperature range of the thermostat. ● SEE FIGURE 14–6.

NOTE: A bypass around the closed thermostat allows a small part of the coolant to circulate within the engine during warm-up. It is a small passage that leads from

FIGURE 14–6 A thermostat stuck in the open position caused the engine to operate too cold. If a thermostat is stuck closed, this can cause the engine to overheat.

FIGURE 14–8 A cutaway of a small block Chevrolet V-8 showing the passage from the cylinder head through the front of the intake manifold to the thermostat.

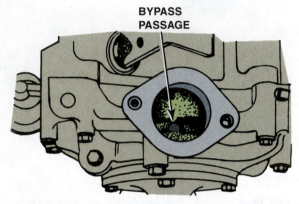

BYPASS PASSAGE

FIGURE 14–7 This internal bypass passage in the thermostat housing directs cold coolant to the water pump.

the engine side of the thermostat to the inlet side of the water pump. It allows some coolant to bypass the thermostat even when the thermostat is open. The bypass may be cast or drilled into the engine and pump parts.
● **SEE FIGURES 14–7 AND 14–8.**

The bypass aids in uniform engine warm-up. Its operation eliminates hot spots and prevents the building of excessive coolant pressure in the engine when the thermostat is closed.

THERMOSTAT TESTING There are three basic methods used to check the operation of the thermostat.

1. **Hot water method.** If the thermostat is removed from the vehicle and is closed, insert a 0.015 inch (0.4 mm) feeler gauge in the opening so that the thermostat will hang on the feeler gauge. The thermostat should then be suspended by the feeler gauge in a container of water or coolant along with a thermometer. The container should be heated until the thermostat opens enough to release and

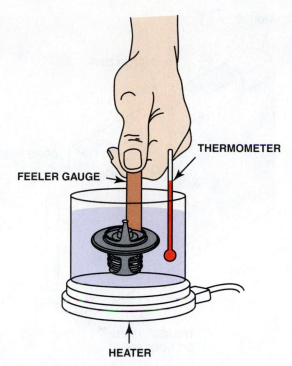

THERMOMETER

FEELER GAUGE

HEATER

FIGURE 14–9 Checking the opening temperature of a thermostat.

fall from the feeler gauge. The temperature at which the thermostat falls is the opening temperature of the thermostat. If it is within 5°F (4°C) of the temperature stamped on the thermostat, the thermostat is satisfactory for use. If the temperature difference is greater, the thermostat should be replaced. ● **SEE FIGURE 14–9.**

2. **Infrared thermometer method.** An infrared thermometer (also called a pyrometer) can be used to measure the temperature of the coolant near the thermostat. The area on the engine side of the thermostat should be at the highest temperature that exists in the engine. A properly operating cooling system should cause the pyrometer to read as follows:

- As the engine warms, the temperature reaches near thermostat opening temperature.
- As the thermostat opens, the temperature drops just as the thermostat opens, sending coolant to the radiator.
- As the thermostat cycles, the temperature should range between the opening temperature of the thermostat and 20°F (11°C) above the opening temperature.

NOTE: If the temperature rises higher than 20°F (11°C) above the opening temperature of the thermostat, inspect the cooling system for a restriction or low coolant flow. A clogged radiator could also cause the excessive temperature rise.

3. **Scan tool method.** A scan tool can be used on many vehicles to read the actual temperature of the coolant

FIGURE 14–10 Some thermostats are an integral part of the housing. This thermostat and radiator hose housing is serviced as an assembly. Some thermostats snap into the engine radiator fill tube underneath the pressure cap.

as detected by the engine coolant temperature (ECT) sensor. Although the sensor or the wiring to and from the sensor may be defective, at least the scan tool can indicate what the computer "thinks" is the engine coolant temperature.

THERMOSTAT REPLACEMENT Two important things about a thermostat include:

1. An overheating engine *may* result from a faulty thermostat.

2. An engine that does not get warm enough *always* indicates a faulty thermostat.

To replace the thermostat, coolant will have to be drained from the radiator drain petcock to lower the coolant level below the thermostat. It is not necessary to completely drain the system. The hose should be removed from the thermostat housing neck and then the housing removed to expose the thermostat. ● **SEE FIGURE 14–10.**

The gasket flanges of the engine and thermostat housing should be cleaned, and the gasket surface of the housing must be flat. The thermostat should be placed in the engine with the sensing pellet *toward* the engine. Make sure that the thermostat position is correct, and install the thermostat housing with a new gasket or O-ring.

CAUTION: Failure to set the thermostat into the recessed groove will cause the housing to become tilted when tightened. If this happens and the housing bolts are tightened, the housing will usually crack, creating a leak.

The upper hose should then be installed and the system refilled. Install the correct size of radiator hose clamp.

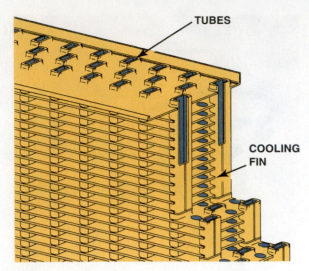

FIGURE 14–11 The tubes and fins of the radiator core.

RADIATORS

TYPES The two types of radiator cores in common use in most vehicles are:

- Serpentine fin core
- Plate fin core

In each of these types, the coolant flows through oval-shaped **core tubes**. Heat is transferred through the tube wall and soldered joint to **cooling fins**. The fins are exposed to the air that flows through the radiator, which removes heat from the radiator and carries it away. ● **SEE FIGURES 14–11 AND 14–12**.

Older automobile radiators were made from yellow brass. Since the 1980s, most radiators have been made from aluminum with nylon-reinforced plastic side tanks. These materials are corrosion resistant, have good heat transferability, and are easily formed.

Core tubes are made from 0.0045 to 0.012 inch (0.1 to 0.3 mm) sheet brass or aluminum, using the thinnest possible materials for each application. The metal is rolled into round tubes and the joints are sealed with a locking seam.

The two basic designs of radiators include:

1. **Down-flow radiators.** This design was used mostly in older vehicles, where the coolant entered the radiator at the top and flowed downward, exiting the radiator at the bottom.

2. **Cross-flow radiators.** Most radiators use a cross-flow design, where the coolant flows from one side of the radiator to the opposite side.

HOW RADIATORS WORK The main limitation of heat transfer in a cooling system is in the transfer from the radiator to the air. Heat transfers from the water to the fins as much as seven times faster than heat transfers from the fins to the air, assuming equal surface exposure. The radiator must be

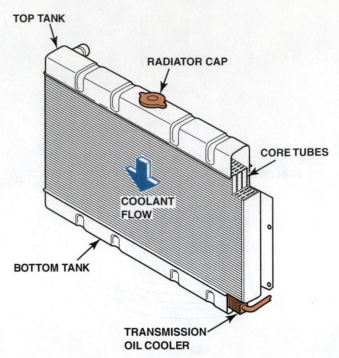

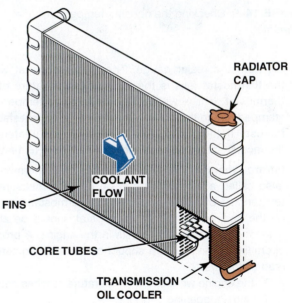

FIGURE 14–12 A radiator may be either a down-flow or a cross-flow type.

capable of removing an amount of heat energy approximately equal to the heat energy of the power produced by the engine. *Each horsepower is equivalent to 42 BTUs (10,800 calories) per minute.* As the engine power is increased, the heat-removing requirement of the cooling system is also increased.

With a given frontal area, radiator capacity may be increased by increasing the core thickness, packing more material into the same volume, or both. The radiator capacity may also be increased by placing a shroud around the fan so that more air will be pulled through the radiator.

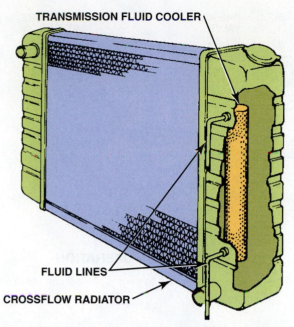

FIGURE 14–13 Many vehicles equipped with an automatic transmission use a transmission fluid cooler installed in one of the radiator tanks.

NOTE: The lower air dam in the front of the vehicle is used to help direct the air through the radiator. If this air dam is broken or missing, the engine may overheat, especially during highway driving due to the reduced airflow through the radiator.

When a transmission oil cooler is used in the radiator, it is placed in the outlet tank, where the coolant has the lowest temperature. ● SEE FIGURE 14–13.

PRESSURE CAPS

OPERATION On most radiators the filler neck is fitted with a pressure cap. The cap has a spring-loaded valve that closes the cooling system vent. This causes cooling pressure to build up to the pressure setting of the cap. At this point, the valve will release the excess pressure to prevent system damage. Engine cooling systems are pressurized to raise the boiling temperature of the coolant.

- *The boiling temperature will increase by approximately 3°F (1.6°C) for each pound of increase in pressure.*
- At sea level, water will boil at 212°F (100°C). With a 15 PSI (100 kPa) pressure cap, water will boil at 257°F (125°C), which is a maximum operating temperature for an engine.

FUNCTIONS The specified coolant system temperature serves two functions.

1. It allows the engine to run at an efficient temperature, close to 200°F (93°C), with no danger of boiling the coolant.

TECH TIP

Working Better Under Pressure

A problem that sometimes occurs with a high-pressure cooling system involves the water pump. For the pump to function, the inlet side of the pump must have a lower pressure than its outlet side. If inlet pressure is lowered too much, the coolant at the pump inlet can boil, producing vapor. The pump will then spin the coolant vapors and not pump coolant. This condition is called *pump cavitation.* Therefore, a radiator cap could be the cause of an overheating problem. A pump will not pump enough coolant if not kept under the proper pressure for preventing vaporization of the coolant.

2. The higher the coolant temperature, the more heat the cooling system can transfer. The heat transferred by the cooling system is proportional to the temperature difference between the coolant and the outside air. This characteristic has led to the design of small, high-pressure radiators that are capable of handling large quantities of heat. For proper cooling, the system must have the right pressure cap correctly installed.

A vacuum valve is part of the pressure cap and is used to allow coolant to flow back into the radiator when the coolant cools down and contracts. ● SEE FIGURE 14–14.

NOTE: The proper operation of the pressure cap is especially important at high altitudes. The boiling point of water is lowered by about 1°F for every 550 ft increase in altitude. Therefore, in Denver, Colorado (altitude 5,280 ft), the boiling point of water is about 202°F, and at the top of Pike's Peak in Colorado (14,110 ft) water boils at 186°F.

METRIC RADIATOR CAPS According to the *SAE Handbook,* all radiator caps must indicate their nominal (normal) pressure rating. Most original equipment radiator caps are rated at about 14 to 16 PSI (97 to 110 kPa).

However, many vehicles manufactured in Japan or Europe use radiator pressure indicated in a unit called a **bar.** One bar is the pressure of the atmosphere at sea level, or about 14.7 PSI. The conversions in ● CHART 14–2 can be used when replacing a radiator cap, to make certain it matches the pressure rating of the original.

NOTE: Many radiator repair shops use a 7 PSI (0.5 bar) radiator cap on a repaired radiator. A 7 PSI cap can still provide boil protection of 21°F (3°F × 7 PSI = 21°F) above the boiling point of the coolant. For example, if the boiling point of the antifreeze coolant is 223°F, then 21°F is added for the pressure cap, and boilover will not occur until about 244°F (223°F + 21°F = 244°F). Even though this lower pressure radiator cap provides some

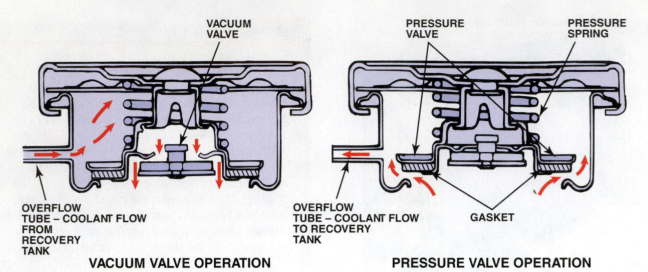

VACUUM VALVE OPERATION

PRESSURE VALVE OPERATION

FIGURE 14–14 The pressure valve maintains the system pressure and allows excess pressure to vent. The vacuum valve allows coolant to return to the system from the recovery tank.

BAR OR ATMOSPHERES	POUNDS PER SQUARE INCH (PSI)
1.1	16
1.0	15
0.9	13
0.8	12
0.7	10
0.6	9
0.5	7

CHART 14–2

Comparison showing the metric pressure as shown on the top of the cap to pounds per square inch (PSI).

protection and will also help protect the radiator repair, the coolant can still boil *before* the "hot" dash warning light comes on and, therefore, should not be used. In addition, the lower pressure in the cooling system could cause cavitation to occur and damage the water pump. For best results, always follow the vehicle manufacturer's recommended radiator cap.

COOLANT RECOVERY SYSTEMS

PURPOSE AND FUNCTION Excess pressure usually forces some coolant from the system through an overflow. Most cooling systems connect the overflow to a plastic reservoir to hold excess coolant while the system is hot. ● SEE FIGURE 14–15.

When the system cools, the pressure in the cooling system is reduced and a partial vacuum forms. This vacuum pulls the coolant from the plastic container back into the cooling system, keeping the system full. Because of this action, the system is

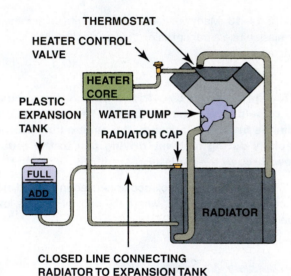

FIGURE 14–15 The level in the coolant recovery system raises and lowers with engine temperature.

called a **coolant recovery system**. A vacuum valve allows coolant to reenter the system as the system cools so that the radiator parts will not collapse under the partial vacuum.

SURGE TANK Some vehicles use a **surge tank**, which is located at the highest level of the cooling system and holds about 1 quart (1 liter) of coolant. A hose attaches to the bottom of the surge tank to the inlet side of the water pump. A smaller bleed hose attaches to the side of the surge tank to the highest point of the radiator. The bleed line allows some coolant circulation through the surge tank, and air in the system will rise below the radiator cap and be forced from the system if the pressure in the system exceeds the rating of the radiator cap. ● SEE FIGURE 14–16.

The Collapsed Radiator Hose Story

An automotive student asked the automotive instructor what brand of radiator hose is the best. Not knowing exactly what to say, the instructor asked if there was a problem with the brand hose used. The student had tried three brands and all of them collapsed when the engine cooled. The instructor then explained that the vehicle needed a new pressure cap and not a new upper radiator hose. The student thought that because the lower hose did not collapse that the problem *had* to be a fault with the hose. The instructor then explained that the lower radiator hose has a spring inside to keep the lower hose from collapsing due to the lower pressure created at the inlet to the water pump. The radiator cap was replaced and the upper radiator hose did not collapse when the engine cooled.

FIGURE 14–16 Some vehicles use a surge tank, which is located at the highest level of the cooling system, with a radiator cap.

WATER PUMPS

OPERATION The water pump (also called a coolant pump) is driven by one of two methods.

- Crankshaft belt
- Camshaft

Coolant recirculates from the radiator to the engine and back to the radiator. Low-temperature coolant leaves the radiator by the bottom outlet. It is pumped into the warm engine block, where it picks up some heat. From the block, the warm coolant flows to the hot cylinder head, where it picks up more heat.

NOTE: Some engines use reverse cooling. This means that the coolant flows from the radiator to the cylinder head(s) before flowing to the engine block.

Water pumps are not positive displacement pumps. The water pump is a **centrifugal pump** that can move a large volume of coolant without increasing the pressure of the coolant. The pump pulls coolant in at the center of the **impeller**. Centrifugal force throws the coolant outward so that it is discharged at the impeller tips. ● SEE FIGURE 14–17.

As engine speeds increase, more heat is produced by the engine and more cooling capacity is required. The pump impeller speed increases as the engine speed increases to provide extra coolant flow at the very time it is needed.

Coolant leaving the pump impeller is fed through a **scroll**. The scroll is a smoothly curved passage that changes the fluid flow direction with minimum loss in velocity. The scroll is connected to the front of the engine so as to direct the coolant into the engine block. On V-type engines, two outlets are often used, one for each cylinder bank. Occasionally, diverters are necessary

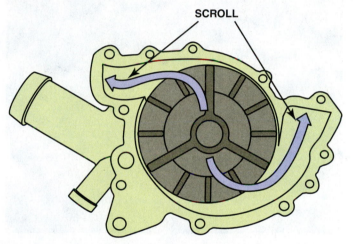

FIGURE 14–17 Coolant flow through the impeller and scroll of a coolant pump for a V-type engine.

? **FREQUENTLY ASKED QUESTION**

How Much Coolant Can a Water Pump Move?

A typical water pump can move a maximum of about 7,500 gallons (28,000 liters) of coolant per hour, or recirculate the coolant in the engine over 20 times per minute. This means that a water pump could be used to empty a typical private swimming pool in an hour! The slower the engine speed, the less power is consumed by the water pump. However, even at 35 mph (56 km/h), the typical water pump still moves about 2,000 gallons (7,500 liters) per hour or 0.5 gallon (2 liters) per second! ● SEE FIGURE 14–18.

FIGURE 14–18 A demonstration engine running on a stand, showing the amount of coolant flow that actually occurs through the cooling system.

FIGURE 14–20 The bleed weep hole in the water pump allows coolant to leak out of the pump and not be forced into the bearing. If the bearing failed, more serious damage could result.

FIGURE 14–19 This severely corroded water pump could not circulate enough coolant to keep the engine cool. As a result, the engine overheated and blew a head gasket.

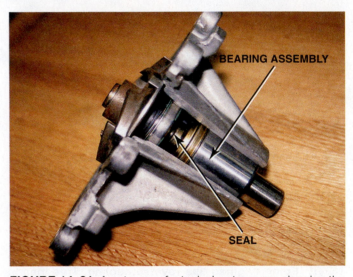

FIGURE 14–21 A cutaway of a typical water pump showing the long bearing assembly and the seal. The weep hole is located between the seal and the bearing. If the seal fails, then coolant flows out of the weep hole to prevent the coolant from damaging the bearing.

in the water pump scroll to equalize coolant flow between the cylinder banks of a V-type engine in order to equalize the cooling.

WATER PUMP SERVICE A worn impeller on a water pump can reduce the amount of coolant flow through the engine. ● **SEE FIGURE 14–19**.

If the seal of the water pump fails, coolant will leak out of the weep hole. The hole allows coolant to escape without getting trapped and forced into the water pump bearing assembly. ● **SEE FIGURE 14–20**.

The hole allows coolant to escape without getting trapped and forced into the water pump bearing assembly.

If the bearing is defective, the pump will usually be noisy and will have to be replaced. Before replacing a water pump

that has failed because of a loose or noisy bearing, check all of the following:

1. Drive belt tension
2. Bent fan
3. Fan for balance

If the water pump drive belt is too tight, excessive force may be exerted against the pump bearing. If the cooling fan is bent or out of balance, the resulting vibration can damage the water pump bearing. ● **SEE FIGURE 14–21**.

Release the Belt Tension Before Checking a Water Pump

The technician should release water pump belt tension before checking for water pump bearing looseness. To test a water pump bearing, it is normal to check the fan for movement; however, if the drive belt is tight, any looseness in the bearing will not be felt.

COOLANT PASSAGE

GAS VENT

FIGURE 14–22 A Chevrolet V-8 block that shows the large coolant holes and the smaller gas vent or bleed holes that must match the head gasket when the engine is assembled.

COOLANT FLOW IN THE ENGINE

TYPES OF SYSTEMS Coolant flows through the engine in one of the following ways.

- **Parallel flow system.** In the **parallel flow system**, coolant flows into the block under pressure and then crosses the head gasket to the head through main coolant passages beside *each* cylinder.

- **Series flow system.** In the **series flow system,** the coolant flows around all the cylinders on each bank. All the coolant flows to the *rear* of the block, where large main coolant passages allow the coolant to flow across the head gasket. The coolant then enters the rear of the heads. In the heads, the coolant flows forward to a crossover passage on the intake manifold outlet at the *highest point* in the engine cooling passage. This is usually located at the front of the engine. The outlet is either on the heads or in the intake manifold.

- **Series-parallel flow system.** Some engines use a combination of these two coolant flow systems and call it a **series-parallel flow system**. Any steam that develops will go directly to the top of the radiator. In series flow systems, **bleed holes** or **steam slits** in the gasket, block, and head perform the function of letting out the steam.

COOLANT FLOW AND HEAD GASKET DESIGN Most V-type engines use cylinder heads that are interchangeable side to side, but not all engines. Therefore, based on the design of the cooling system and flow through the engine, it is very important to double check that the cylinder head is matched to the block and that the head gasket is installed correctly (end for end) so that all of the cooling passages are open to allow the proper flow of coolant through the system. ● SEE **FIGURE 14–22.**

COOLING FANS

ELECTRONICALLY CONTROLLED COOLING FAN Two types of electric cooling fans used on many engines include:

- One two-speed cooling fan
- Two cooling fans (one for normal cooling and one for high heat conditions)

The PCM commands low-speed fans on under the following conditions.

- Engine coolant temperature (ECT) exceeds approximately 223°F (106°C).
- A/C refrigerant pressure exceeds 190 PSI (1,310 kPa).
- After the vehicle is shut off, the engine coolant temperature at key-off is greater than 284°F (140°C) and system voltage is more than 12 volts. The fan(s) will stay on for approximately three minutes.

The PCM commands the high-speed fan on under the following conditions.

- Engine coolant temperature (ECT) reaches 230°F (110°C).
- A/C refrigerant pressure exceeds 240 PSI (1,655 kPa).
- Certain diagnostic trouble codes (DTCs) set.

To prevent a fan from cycling on and off excessively at idle, the fan may not turn off until the ignition switch is moved to the off position or the vehicle speed exceeds approximately 10 mph (16 km/h).

Many rear-wheel-drive vehicles and all transverse engines drive the fan with an electric motor. ● SEE **FIGURE 14–23.**

NOTE: Most electric cooling fans are computer controlled. To save energy, most cooling fans are turned off whenever the vehicle is traveling faster than 35 mph (55 km/h). The ram air caused by the vehicle speed is enough to keep the radiator cool. Of course, if the computer senses that

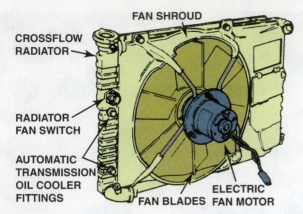

FAN SHROUD

CROSSFLOW
RADIATOR

RADIATOR
FAN SWITCH

AUTOMATIC
TRANSMISSION
OIL COOLER
FITTINGS

FAN BLADES

ELECTRIC
FAN MOTOR

FIGURE 14–23 A typical electric cooling fan assembly showing the radiator and related components.

THERMOSTATIC SPRING

FIGURE 14–24 A typical engine-driven thermostatic spring cooling fan.

> ☠ **WARNING**
>
> Some electric cooling fans can come on after the engine is off without warning. Always keep hands and fingers away from the cooling fan blades unless the electrical connector has been disconnected to prevent the fan from coming on. Always follow all warnings and cautions.

the temperature is still too high, the computer will turn on the cooling fan, to "high," if possible, in an attempt to cool the engine to avoid severe engine damage.

THERMOSTATIC FANS On some rear-wheel-drive vehicles, a thermostatic cooling fan is driven by a belt from the crankshaft. It turns faster as the engine turns faster. Generally, the engine is required to produce more power at higher speeds. Therefore, the cooling system will also transfer more heat. Increased fan speed aids in the required cooling. Engine heat also becomes critical at low engine speeds in traffic where the vehicle moves slowly. The thermostatic fan is designed so that it uses little power at high engine speeds and minimizes noise. Two types of thermostatic fans include:

1. **Silicone coupling.** The **silicone coupling** fan drive is mounted between the drive pulley and the fan.

   NOTE: When diagnosing an overheating problem, look carefully at the cooling fan. If silicone is leaking, then the fan may not be able to function correctly and should be replaced.

2. **Thermostatic spring.** A second type of thermal fan has a **thermostatic spring** added to the silicone coupling fan drive. The thermostatic spring operates a valve that allows the fan to freewheel when the radiator is cold. As the radiator warms to about 150°F (65°C), the air hitting the thermostatic spring will cause the spring to change its shape. The new shape of the spring opens a valve that allows the drive to operate like the silicone coupling drive. When the engine is very cold, the fan may operate at high

> 🔧 **TECH TIP**
>
> **Be Sure to Always Use a Fan Shroud**
>
> A fan shroud forces the fan to draw air through the radiator. If a fan shroud is not used, then air is drawn from around the fan and will reduce the airflow through the radiator. Many overheating problems are a result of not replacing the factory shroud after engine work or body repair work to the front of the vehicle.

speeds for a short time until the drive fluid warms slightly. The silicone fluid will then flow into a reservoir to let the fan speed drop to idle. ● **SEE FIGURE 14–24**.

The fan is designed to move enough air at the lowest fan speed to cool the engine when it is at its highest coolant temperature. The fan shroud is used to increase the cooling system efficiency.

HEATER CORES

PURPOSE AND FUNCTION Most of the heat absorbed from the engine by the cooling system is wasted. Some of this heat, however, is recovered by the vehicle heater. Heated coolant is passed through tubes in the small core of the heater. Air is passed across the heater fins and is then sent to the passenger compartment. In some vehicles, the heater and air conditioning work in series to maintain vehicle compartment temperature. ● **SEE FIGURE 14–25**.

FIGURE 14–25 A typical heater core installed in a heating, ventilation, and air-conditioning (HVAC) housing assembly.

FIGURE 14–26 A heavily corroded radiator from a vehicle that was overheating. A visual inspection discovered that the corrosion had eaten away many of the cooling fins, yet did not leak. This radiator was replaced and it solved the overheating problem.

HEATER PROBLEM DIAGNOSIS   When the heater does not produce the desired amount of heat, many owners and technicians replace the thermostat before doing any other troubleshooting. It is true that a defective thermostat is the reason for the *engine* not to reach normal operating temperature, but there are many other causes besides a defective thermostat that can result in lack of heat from the heater. To determine the exact cause, follow this procedure.

STEP 1   After the engine has been operated, feel the upper radiator hose. If the engine is up to proper operating temperature, the upper radiator hose should be too hot to hold. The hose should also be pressurized.
   a. If the hose is not hot enough, replace the thermostat.
   b. If the hose is not pressurized, test or replace the radiator pressure cap if it will not hold the specified pressure.
   c. If okay, see step 2.

STEP 2   With the engine running, feel both heater hoses. (The heater should be set to the maximum heat position.) Both hoses should be too hot to hold. If both hoses are warm (not hot) or cool, check the heater control valve for proper operation (if equipped). If one hose is hot and the other (return) is just warm or cool, remove both hoses from the heater core or engine and flush the heater core with water from a garden hose.

STEP 3   If both heater hoses are hot and there is still a lack of heating concern, then the fault is most likely due to an airflow blend door malfunction. Check service information for the exact procedure to follow.

NOTE: Heat from the heater that "comes and goes" is most likely the result of low coolant level. Usually with the engine at idle, there is enough coolant flow through the heater. At higher engine speeds, however, the lack of coolant through the heads and block prevents sufficient flow through the heater.

COOLING SYSTEM TESTING

VISUAL INSPECTION   Many cooling system faults can be found by performing a thorough visual inspection. Items that can be inspected visually include:

- Water pump drive belt for tension or faults
- Cooling fan for faults
- Heater and radiator hoses for condition and leaks
- Coolant overflow or surge tank coolant level
- Evidence of coolant loss
- Radiator condition ● **SEE FIGURE 14–26.**

PRESSURE TESTING   Pressure testing using a hand-operated pressure tester is a quick and easy cooling system test. The radiator cap is removed (engine cold!) and the tester is attached in the place of the radiator cap. By operating the plunger on the pump, the entire cooling system is pressurized. ● **SEE FIGURE 14–27.**

CAUTION: Do not pump up the pressure beyond that specified by the vehicle manufacturer. Most systems should not be pressurized beyond 14 PSI (100 kPa). If a greater pressure is used, it may cause the water pump, radiator, heater core, or hoses to fail.

If the cooling system is free from leaks, the pressure should stay and not drop. If the pressure drops, look for evidence of leaks anywhere in the cooling system, including:

1. Heater hoses
2. Radiator hoses
3. Radiator
4. Heater core

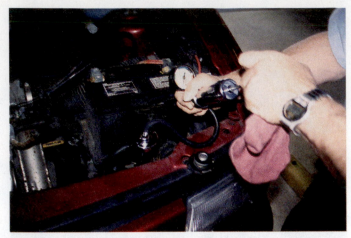

FIGURE 14–27 Pressure testing the cooling system. A typical hand-operated pressure tester applies pressure equal to the radiator cap pressure. The pressure should hold; if it drops, this indicates a leak somewhere in the cooling system. An adapter is used to attach the pump to the cap to determine if the radiator can hold pressure, and release it when pressure rises above its maximum rated pressure setting.

5. Cylinder head
6. Core plugs in the side of the block or cylinder head

Pressure testing should be performed whenever there is a leak or suspected leak. The pressure tester can also be used to test the radiator cap. An adapter is used to connect the pressure tester to the radiator cap. Replace any cap that will not hold pressure. ● SEE FIGURE 14–28.

COOLANT DYE LEAK TESTING   One of the best methods to check for a coolant leak is to use a fluorescent dye in the coolant, one that is specifically designed for coolant. Operate the vehicle with the dye in the coolant until the engine reaches normal operating temperature. Use a black light to inspect all areas of the cooling system. When there is a leak, it will be easy to spot because the dye in the coolant will be seen as bright green. ● SEE FIGURE 14–29.

COOLANT TEMPERATURE WARNING LIGHT

PURPOSE AND FUNCTION   Most vehicles are equipped with a heat sensor for the engine operating temperature indicator light. If the warning light comes on during driving (or the temperature gauge goes into the red danger zone), then the coolant temperature is about 250°F to 258°F (120°C to 126°C), which is still *below* the boiling point of the coolant (assuming a properly operating pressure cap and system). ● SEE FIGURE 14–30.

PRECAUTIONS   If the coolant temperature warning light comes on, follow these steps.

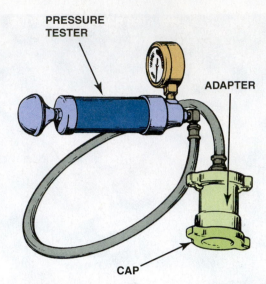

FIGURE 14–28 The pressure cap should be checked for proper operation using a pressure tester as part of the cooling system diagnosis.

FIGURE 14–29 Use dye specifically made for coolant when checking for leaks using a black light.

STEP 1   Shut off the air conditioning and turn on the heater. The heater will help rid the engine of extra heat. Set the blower speed to high.

STEP 2   If possible, shut the engine off and let it cool. (This may take over an hour.)

STEP 3   Never remove the radiator cap when the engine is hot.

STEP 4   Do *not* continue to drive with the hot light on, or serious damage to your engine could result.

STEP 5   If the engine does not feel or smell hot, it is possible that the problem is a faulty hot light sensor or gauge. Continue to drive, but to be safe, stop occasionally and check for any evidence of overheating or coolant loss.

FIGURE 14–30 When an engine overheats, often the coolant overflow container boils.

COMMON CAUSES OF OVERHEATING
Overheating can be caused by defects in the cooling system, such as the following:

1. Low coolant level
2. Plugged, dirty, or blocked radiator
3. Defective fan clutch or electric fan
4. Incorrect ignition timing (if adjustable)
5. Low engine oil level
6. Broken fan drive belt
7. Defective radiator cap
8. Dragging brakes
9. Frozen coolant (in freezing weather)
10. Defective thermostat
11. Defective water pump (the impeller slipping on the shaft internally)
12. Blocked cooling passages in the block or cylinder head(s)

COOLING SYSTEM INSPECTION

COOLANT LEVEL
The cooling system is one of the most maintenance-free systems in the engine. Normal maintenance involves an occasional check on the coolant level. It should also include a visual inspection for signs of coolant system leaks and for the condition of the coolant hoses and fan drive belts.

CAUTION: The coolant level should only be checked when the engine is cool. Removing the pressure cap from a hot engine will release the cooling system pressure while the coolant temperature is above its atmospheric boiling temperature. When the cap is removed, the

Highway Overheating

A vehicle owner complained of an overheating vehicle, but the problem occurred only while driving at highway speeds. The vehicle, equipped with a 4-cylinder engine, would run in a perfectly normal manner in city driving situations.

The technician flushed the cooling system and replaced the radiator cap and the water pump, thinking that restricted coolant flow was the cause of the problem. Further testing revealed coolant spray out of one cylinder when the engine was turned over by the starter with the spark plugs removed.

A new head gasket solved the problem. Obviously, the head gasket leak was not great enough to cause any problems until the engine speed and load created enough flow and heat to cause the coolant temperature to soar.

The technician also replaced the oxygen (O_2) sensor, because the IAT-type coolant contains phosphates and silicates that often contaminate the sensor. The deteriorated oxygen sensor could have contributed to the problem.

pressure will instantly drop to atmospheric pressure level, causing the coolant to boil immediately. Vapors from the boiling liquid will blow coolant from the system. Coolant will be lost, and someone may be injured or burned by the high-temperature coolant that is blown out of the filler opening.

ACCESSORY DRIVE BELT TENSION
Drive belt condition and proper installation are important for the proper operation of the cooling system.

There are four ways vehicle manufacturers specify that the belt tension is within factory specifications.

1. **Belt tension gauge.** A belt tension gauge is needed to achieve the specified belt tension. Install the belt and operate the engine with all of the accessories turned on, to run in the belt for at least five minutes. Adjust the tension of the accessory drive belt to factory specifications or use ● **CHART 14–3** for an example of the proper tension based on the size of the belt. Replace any serpentine belt that has more than three cracks in any one rib that appears in a 3 inch span.

2. **Marks on the tensioner.** Many tensioners have marks that indicate the normal operating tension range for the accessory drive belt. Check service information for the location of the tensioner mark. ● **SEE FIGURE 14–31.**

3. **Torque wrench reading.** Some vehicle manufacturers specify that a beam-type torque wrench be used to determine the torque needed to rotate the tensioner. If the

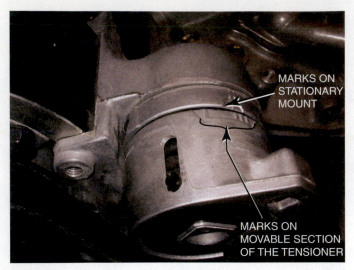

MARKS ON STATIONARY MOUNT

MARKS ON MOVABLE SECTION OF THE TENSIONER

FIGURE 14–31 Typical marks on an accessory drive belt tensioner.

NUMBER OF RIBS USED	TENSION RANGE (LB.)
3	45 to 60
4	60 to 80
5	75 to 100
6	90 to 125
7	105 to 145

CHART 14-3

The number of ribs determines the tension range of the belt.

 TECH TIP

The Water Spray Trick

Lower-than-normal alternator output could be the result of a loose or slipping drive belt. All belts (V and serpentine multigroove) use an interference angle between the angle of the Vs of the belt and the angle of the Vs on the pulley. A belt wears this interference angle off the edges of the V of the belt. As a result, the belt may start to slip and make a squealing sound even if tensioned properly.

A common trick to determine if the noise is from the belt is to spray water from a squirt bottle at the belt with the engine running. If the noise stops, the belt is the cause of the noise. The water quickly evaporates and therefore, water just finds the problem—it does not provide a short-term fix.

torque reading is below specifications, the tensioner must be replaced.

4. **Deflection.** Depress the belt between the two pulleys that are the farthest apart and the flex or deflection should be 1/2 inch.

COOLING SYSTEM SERVICE

FLUSHING COOLANT Flushing the cooling system includes the following steps.

STEP 1 Drain the system (dispose of the old coolant correctly).

STEP 2 Fill the system with clean water and flushing/cleaning chemical.

STEP 3 Start the engine until it reaches operating temperature with the heater on.

STEP 4 Drain the system and fill with clean water.

STEP 5 Repeat until drain water runs clear (any remaining flush agent will upset pH).

STEP 6 Fill the system with 50/50 antifreeze/water mix or pre-mixed coolant.

STEP 7 Start the engine until it reaches operating temperature with the heater on.

STEP 8 Adjust coolant level as needed.

Bleeding the air out of the cooling system is important because air can prevent proper operation of the heater and can cause the engine to overheat. Use a clear hose attached to the bleeder valve and the other end in a "suitable" container. This prevents coolant from getting on the engine and gives the technician a visual clue as to the color of coolant. ● **SEE FIGURE 14–32.**

Check service information for specific bleeding procedures and location of the air bleeder fittings.

COOLANT EXCHANGE MACHINE Many coolant exchange machines are able to perform one or more of the following operations.

- Exchange old coolant with new coolant
- Flush the cooling system
- Pressure or vacuum check the cooling system for leaks

The use of a coolant exchange machine pulls a vacuum on the cooling system which helps illuminate air pockets from forming during coolant replacement. If an air pocket were to occur, the following symptoms may occur.

1. **Lack of heat from the heater.** Air rises and can form in the heater core, which will prevent coolant from flowing.

2. **Overheating.** The engine can overheat due to the lack of proper coolant flow through the system.

Always follow the operating instructions for the coolant exchange machine being used. ● **SEE FIGURE 14–33.**

HOSE INSPECTION Coolant system hoses are critical to engine cooling. As the hoses get old, they become either soft or brittle and sometimes swell in diameter. Their condition depends on their material and on the engine service conditions. If

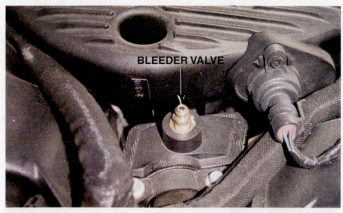

BLEEDER VALVE

(a)

(b)

FIGURE 14–32 (a) Many vehicle manufacturers recommend that the bleeder valve be opened whenever refilling the cooling system. (b) Chrysler recommends that a clear plastic hose (1/4 inch ID) be attached to the bleeder valve and directed into a suitable container to keep from spilling coolant onto the ground and on the engine and to allow the technician to observe the flow of coolant for any remaining oil bubbles.

TECH TIP

Always Replace the Pressure Cap

Replace the old radiator cap with a new cap with the same pressure rating. The cap can be located on the following:

1. Radiator
2. Coolant recovery reservoir
3. Upper radiator hose

WARNING: Never remove a pressure cap from a hot engine. When the pressure is removed from the system, the coolant will immediately boil and will expand upward, throwing scalding coolant in all directions. Hot coolant can cause serious burns.

FIGURE 14–33 Using a coolant exchange machine helps eliminate the problem of air getting into the system which can cause overheating or lack of heat due to air pockets getting trapped in the system.

a hose breaks while the engine is running, all coolant will be lost. A hose should be replaced any time it appears to be abnormal. ● **SEE FIGURE 14–34.**

NOTE: To make hose removal easier and to avoid possible damage to the radiator, use a utility knife and slit the hose lengthwise. Then simply peel the hose off.

The hose and hose clamp should be positioned so that the clamp is close to the bead on the neck. This is especially important on aluminum hose necks to avoid corrosion. When the hoses are in place and the drain petcock is closed, the cooling system can be refilled with the correct coolant mixture.

DISPOSING OF USED COOLANT Used coolant drained from vehicles should be disposed of according to state or local laws. Some communities permit draining into the sewer. Ethylene glycol will easily biodegrade. There could be problems with groundwater contamination, however, if coolant is spilled on open ground. Check with recycling companies authorized by local or state governments for the exact method recommended for disposal in your area.

CLEANING THE RADIATOR EXTERIOR Overheating can result from exterior and interior radiator plugging. External plugging is caused by dirt and insects. This type of plugging can be seen if you look straight through the radiator while a light is held behind it. It is most likely to occur on off-road vehicles. The plugged exterior of the radiator core can usually be cleaned with water pressure from a hose. The water is aimed at the *engine side* of the radiator. The water should flow freely through the core at all locations. If this does not clean the core, the radiator should be removed for cleaning at a radiator shop.

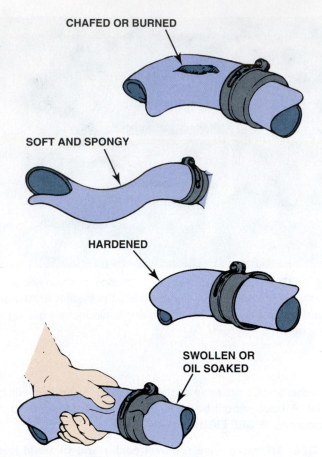

CHAFED OR BURNED

SOFT AND SPONGY

HARDENED

SWOLLEN OR
OIL SOAKED

FIGURE 14–34 All cooling system hoses should be checked for wear or damage.

FIGURE 14–35 The top 3/8 inch hose is designed for oil and similar liquids, whereas the 3/8 inch hose below is labeled "heater hose" and is designed for coolant.

TECH TIP

Quick and Easy Cooling System Problem Diagnosis

1. If overheating occurs in slow stop-and-go traffic, the usual cause is low airflow through the radiator. Check for airflow blockages or cooling fan malfunction.

2. If overheating occurs at highway speeds, the cause is usually a radiator or coolant circulation problem. Check for a restricted or clogged radiator.

TECH TIP

Always Use Heater Hoses Designed for Coolant

Many heater hoses are sizes that can also be used for other purposes such as oil lines. Always check and use hose that states it is designed for heater or cooling system use. ● **SEE FIGURE 14–35**.

SUMMARY

1. The purpose and function of the cooling system is to maintain proper engine operating temperature.

2. The thermostat controls engine coolant temperature by opening at its rated opening temperature to allow coolant to flow through the radiator.

3. Coolant fans are designed to draw air through the radiator to aid in the heat transfer process, drawing the heat from the coolant and transferring it to the outside air through the radiator.

4. The cooling system should be tested for leaks using a hand-operated pressure pump.

5. Water pumps are usually engine driven and circulate coolant through the engine and the radiator when the thermostat opens.

6. Coolant flows through the radiator hoses to and from the engine and through heater hoses to send heated coolant to the heater core in the passenger compartment.

1. What is normal operating coolant temperature?
2. Explain the flow of coolant through the engine and radiator.
3. Why is a cooling system pressurized?
4. What is the purpose of the coolant system bypass?
5. Describe how to perform a drain, flush, and refill procedure on a cooling system.
6. Explain the operation of a thermostatic cooling fan.
7. Describe how to diagnose a heater problem.
8. What are 10 common causes of overheating?

CHAPTER QUIZ

1. The upper radiator collapses when the engine cools. What is the most likely cause?
   a. Defective upper radiator hose
   b. Missing spring from the upper radiator hose, which is used to keep it from collapsing
   c. Defective thermostat
   d. Defective pressure cap

2. What can be done to prevent air from getting trapped in the cooling system when the coolant is replaced?
   a. Pour the coolant into the radiator slowly.
   b. Use a coolant exchange machine that draws a vacuum on the system.
   c. Open the air bleeder valves while adding coolant.
   d. Either b or c

3. Heat transfer is improved from the coolant to the air when the _____.
   a. Temperature difference is great
   b. Temperature difference is small
   c. Coolant is 95% antifreeze
   d. Both a and c

4. A water pump is a positive displacement type of pump.
   a. True
   b. False

5. Water pumps _____.
   a. Only work at idle and low speeds and are disengaged at higher speeds
   b. Use engine oil as a lubricant and coolant
   c. Are driven by the engine crankshaft or camshaft
   d. Disengage during freezing weather to prevent radiator failure

6. What diagnostic trouble code (DTC) could be set if the thermostat is defective?
   a. P0300   c. P0440
   b. P0171   d. P0128

7. Which statement is *true* about thermostats?
   a. The temperature marked on the thermostat is the temperature at which the thermostat should be fully open.
   b. Thermostats often cause overheating.
   c. The temperature marked on the thermostat is the temperature at which the thermostat should start to open.
   d. Both a and b

8. Technician A says that the radiator should always be inspected for leaks and proper flow before installing a rebuilt engine. Technician B says that overheating during slow city driving can only be due to a defective electric cooling fan. Which technician is correct?
   a. Technician A only
   b. Technician B only
   c. Both Technicians A and B
   d. Neither Technician A nor B

9. A customer complains that the heater works sometimes, but sometimes only cold air comes out while driving. Technician A says that the water pump is defective. Technician B says that the cooling system could be low on coolant. Which technician is correct?
   a. Technician A only
   b. Technician B only
   c. Both Technicians A and B
   d. Neither Technician A nor B

10. The normal operating temperature (coolant temperature) of an engine equipped with a 195°F thermostat is _____.
    a. 175°F to 195°F
    b. 185°F to 205°F
    c. 195°F to 215°F
    d. 175°F to 215°F

chapter 15

ENGINE OIL

LEARNING OBJECTIVES: After studying this chapter, the reader should be able to: • Explain the purpose of engine oil and engine oil additives. • Discuss the properties of engine oil. • Discuss SAE rating, API rating, ILSAC oil rating, European oil rating system, and Japanese oil rating. • Discuss synthetic oil and high mileage oils. • Discuss vehicle-specific specifications of oil. • Discuss the purpose and function of oil filters. • Describe the oil change procedure.

KEY TERMS: Additive package 181 • American Petroleum Institute (API) 179 • Antidrainback valve 185 • Association des Constructeurs Européens d'Automobiles (ACEA) 180 • Bypass valve 185 • HTHS 181 • International Lubricant Standardization and Approval Committee (ILSAC) 180 • Japanese Automobile Standards Organization (JASO) 181 • Miscible 178 • Pour point 178 • SAPS 181 • Society of Automotive Engineers (SAE) 178 • Viscosity index (VI) 178 • ZDDP 182

INTRODUCTION

Engine oil has a major effect on the proper operation and life of any engine. Engine oil provides the following functions in every engine.

- Lubricates moving parts
- Helps cool engine parts
- Helps seal piston rings
- Helps to neutralize acids created by the by-products of combustion
- Reduces friction in the engine
- Helps to prevent rust and corrosion

As a result of these many factors, the specified engine oil must be used and replaced at the specified mileage or time intervals.

PROPERTIES OF ENGINE OIL

The most important engine oil property is its thickness or viscosity.

- As oil is cooled, it gets thicker.
- As oil is heated, it gets thinner.

Therefore, its viscosity changes with temperature. The oil must not be too thick at low temperatures to allow the engine to start. The lowest temperature at which oil will pour is called its **pour point**. An index of the change in viscosity between the cold and hot extremes is called the **viscosity index (VI)**. All oils with a high viscosity index thin less with heat than do oils with a low viscosity index. Oils must also be **miscible**, meaning they are capable of mixing with other oils (brands and viscosities, for example) without causing any problems such as sludge.

SAE RATING

TERMINOLOGY   Engine oils are sold with a **Society of Automotive Engineers (SAE)** grade number, which indicates the viscosity range into which the oil fits. Oils tested at 212°F (100°C) have a number with no letter following. For example, SAE 30 indicates that the oil has only been checked at 212°F (100°C). This oil's viscosity falls within the SAE 30 grade number range when the oil is hot. Oils tested at 0°F (–18°C) are rated with a number and the letter *W*, which means *winter* and indicates that the viscosity was tested at 0°F, such as SAE 20W.

MULTIGRADE ENGINE OIL   An SAE 5W-30 multigrade oil meets the SAE 5W viscosity specification when cooled to 0°F (–18°C), and meets the SAE 30 viscosity specification when tested at 212°F (100°C).

Most vehicle manufacturers recommend the following multiviscosity engine oils.

- SAE 5W-30
- SAE 10W-30

● **SEE FIGURE 15–1.**

Oil with a high viscosity has a higher resistance to flow and is thicker than lower viscosity oil. Thick oil is not necessarily good oil and thin oil is not necessarily bad oil. Generally, the

FIGURE 15–1 The SAE viscosity rating required is often printed on the engine oil filler cap. Most hybrid electric vehicles specify either SAE 0W-20 or SAE 5W-20 engine oil.

following items can be considered in the selection of engine oil within the recommended viscosity range.

- Thinner oil
  1. Improved cold engine starting
  2. Improved fuel economy
- Thicker oil
  1. Improved protection at higher temperatures
  2. Reduced fuel economy

NOTE: Always use the specified viscosity engine oil.

API RATING

DEFINITION   The **American Petroleum Institute (API)**, working with the engine manufacturers and oil companies, has established an engine oil performance classification. Oils are tested and rated in production automotive engines. The oil container is printed with the API classification of the oil. The API performance or service classification and the SAE grade marking are the only information available to help determine which oil is satisfactory for use in an engine. ● SEE FIGURE 15–2 for a typical API oil container "doughnut."

GASOLINE ENGINE RATINGS   In gasoline engine ratings, the letter *S* means *service,* but can also indicate *s*park ignition engines. The rating system is open ended so that newer, improved ratings can be readily added as necessary (the letter *I* is skipped to avoid confusion with the number one).

    SA   Straight mineral oil (no additives), not suitable for use in any engine

The Case of the Wrong Oil Viscosity

A 2007 Dodge Durango 5.7 liter Hemi with a multiple displacement system (MDS) had the oil changed at a shop. SAE 10W-30 was used as this was the "standard" bulk oil in the shop. After the oil change, the vehicle was returned to the customer. Within a few minutes, however, the "check engine" light came on. The technician checked for diagnostic trouble codes (DTCs) and found a P0521 DTC stored. The technician checked service information and discovered that the code could be set if the incorrect viscosity engine oil had been used. The description of the P0521 read:

    "Oil pressure not reaching specified at 1250 RPM."

    The technician changed the oil and used the specified SAE 5W-20, then cleared the DTC. A test drive confirmed that the change to the correct viscosity oil solved the problem.

SB	Nondetergent oil with additives to control wear and oil oxidation
SC	Obsolete (1964)
SD	Obsolete (1968)
SE	Obsolete (1972)
SF	Obsolete (1980)
SG	Obsolete (1988)
SH	Obsolete (1993–1997)
SJ	Obsolete (1997–2001)
SL	2001–2003
SM	2004–2010
SN	2011+

NOTE: **Vehicles built since about 1996 that use roller valve lifers can use the newer, higher rated engine oil classifications where older, now obsolete ratings were specified. Newly overhauled antique cars or engines also can use the newer, improved oils, as the appropriate SAE viscosity grade is used for the anticipated temperature range. Engines older than about 1996 or those using flat-bottom lifters should use a zinc additive if using newer rated oil.**

DIESEL ENGINE RATINGS   Diesel classifications begin with the letter *C,* which stands for *commercial,* but can also indicate *c*ompression ignition or diesel engines.

CA	Obsolete
CB	Obsolete
CC	Obsolete
CD	Minimum rating for use in a diesel engine service

FIGURE 15–2 API doughnut for a SAE 5W-30, SM engine oil. When compared to a reference oil, the "energy conserving" designation indicates a 1.1% better fuel economy for SAE 10W-30 oils and 0.5% better fuel economy for SAE 5W-30 oils.

 TECH TIP

Three Oil Change Facts

Three facts that are important to know when changing oil are:

1. *Recommended SAE viscosity* (thickness) for the temperature range that is anticipated before the next oil change (such as SAE 5W-30)

2. *Quality rating* as recommended by the engine or vehicle manufacturer such as API SM and other specified rating such as the ILSAC and vehicle manufacturer's specifications

3. *Recommended oil change interval* (time or mileage) (usually every 5,000 miles or every six months)

CE	Designed for certain turbocharged or super-charged heavy-duty diesel engine service
CF	For off-road indirect injected diesel engine service
CF-2	Two-stroke diesel engine service
CF-4	High-speed four-stroke cycle diesel engine service
CG-4	Severe-duty high-speed four-stroke diesel engine service
CI-4	Severe-duty high-speed four-stroke diesel engine service
CJ-4	Required for use in all 2007 and newer diesels using ultra-low-sulfur diesel (ULSD) fuel

FIGURE 15–3 The International Lubricant Standardization and Approval Committee (ILSAC) starburst symbol. If this symbol is on the front of the container of oil, then it is acceptable for use in almost any gasoline engine.

ILSAC OIL RATING

DEFINITION The **International Lubricant Standardization and Approval Committee (ILSAC)** developed an oil rating that consolidates the SAE viscosity rating and the API quality rating. If an engine oil meets the standards, a "starburst" symbol is displayed on the *front* of the oil container. If the starburst is present, the vehicle owner and technician know that the oil is suitable for use in almost any gasoline engine. ● SEE **FIGURE 15–3**.

ILSAC RATINGS

- The original GF-1 (gasoline fueled) rating in 1993
- Updated to GF-2 in 1997
- Updated to GF-3 in 2000
- Updated to GF-4 in 2004
- Updated to GF-5 in 2010

For more information, visit www.gf-5.com.

EUROPEAN OIL RATING SYSTEM

DEFINITION The **Association des Constructeurs Européens d'Automobiles (ACEA)** rates the oil according to the following:

- Gasoline engine oils
  - ACEA A1 Low-friction low-viscosity oil (not suitable for some engines)

ACEA A2   General-purpose oil intended for normal oil change intervals; not suitable for some engines or extended oil drain intervals in any engine

ACEA A3   Designed for high-performance engines and/or extended oil drain intervals and under all temperature ranges

ACEA A4   Designed to meet the requirements for gasoline direct injection (GDI) engines

ACEA A5   Low-viscosity low-friction oil not suitable for some engines

- Diesel engine oils

ACEA B1   Low-viscosity oil designed for use in a passenger vehicle diesel engine that is equipped with an indirect injection system; not suitable for some diesel engines

ACEA B2   Designed for use in passenger vehicle diesel engines using indirect injection and using normal oil drain intervals

ACEA B3   Intended for use in a high-performance indirect injected passenger vehicle diesel engine and under extended oil drain interval conditions

ACEA B4   Intended for year-round use in direct injected passenger vehicle diesel engines; can be used in an indirect injected diesel engine

ACEA B5   Designed for extended oil drain intervals; not suitable for some engines

ACEA C1, C2, C3   Specifications for catalyst compatible oils, which have limits on the amount of sulfur, zinc, and other additives that could harm the catalytic converter

Starting in 2004, the ACEA began using combined ratings such as A1/B1, A3/B3, A3/B4, and A5/B5.

- ACEA oil also requires low levels of sulfated ash, phosphorous, and sulfur, abbreviated **SAPS**, and has a high temperature/high shear rate viscosity, abbreviated **HTHS**.

- C ratings are catalytic converter compatible oils and include:

  C1: basically A5/B5 oil with low SAPS, low HTHS

  C2: A5/B5 with low HTHS and mid-level SAPS

  C3: A5/B5 with high HTHS and mid-level SAPS

  C4: low SAPS; high HTHS

● SEE FIGURE 15–4.

JAPANESE OIL RATINGS

The **Japanese Automobile Standards Organization (JASO)** also publishes oil standards. The JASO tests use small Japanese engines, and their ratings require more stringent valve train wear standards than oil ratings in other countries. However, most Japanese brand vehicles specify SAE, API, and ILSAC rating standards for use in the engine.

FIGURE 15–4   ACEA ratings are included on the back of the oil container if it meets any of the standards. ACEA ratings apply to European vehicles only such as BMW, Mercedes, Audi, and VW.

FIGURE 15–5   Viscosity index (VI) improver is a polymer and feels like finely ground foam rubber. When dissolved in the oil, it expands when hot to keep the oil from thinning.

ENGINE OIL ADDITIVES

Oil producers are careful to check the compatibility of the oil additives they use. A number of chemicals that will help each other can be used for each of the additive requirements. The balanced additives are called an **additive package**.

ADDITIVES TO IMPROVE THE BASE OIL

- **Viscosity index (VI) improver.** Modifies the viscosity of the base fluid so that it changes less as the temperature rises; allows the lubricant to operate over a wider temperature range (● SEE FIGURE 15–5.)

- **Pour point depressant.** Keeps the lubricant flowing at low temperatures
- **Antifoam agents.** Foam reduces the effectiveness of a lubricant. The antifoam agents reduce/stop foaming when the oil is agitated or aerated.

ADDITIVES TO PROTECT THE BASE OIL

- **Antioxidants.** Slow the breakdown of the base fluid caused by oxygen (air) and heat (Oxidation is the main cause of lubricant degradation in service.)
- **Oxidants.** Prevent acid formation (corrosion) in the form of sludges, varnishes
- **Total base number (TBN).** The reserve alkalinity used to neutralize the acids created during the combustion process (Typical TBN levels are between 60 and 100, which is dependent on the fuel sulfur level. The higher the sulfur percentage in the fuel, the higher the TBN required. The higher the total base number of oil, the longer it can be used in an engine. Long-life oils usually have higher total base numbers than other oils.)

ADDITIVES TO PROTECT THE ENGINE

- **Rust inhibitor.** Inhibits the action of water on ferrous metal such as steel
- **Corrosion inhibitor.** Protects nonferrous metals such as copper
- **Antiwear additive.** Forms a protective layer on metal surfaces to reduce friction and prevent wear when no lubricant film is present
- **Extreme pressure additive.** Functions only when heavy loads and temperatures are occurring

OIL BRAND COMPATIBILITY

Many technicians and vehicle owners have their favorite brand of engine oil. The choice is often made as a result of marketing and advertising, as well as comments from friends, relatives, and technicians. If your brand of engine oil is not performing up to your expectations, then you may wish to change brands. For example, some owners experience lower oil pressure with a certain brand than they do with other brands with the same SAE viscosity rating.

- Most experts agree that the oil changes are the most important regularly scheduled maintenance for an engine.
- It is also wise to check the oil level regularly and add oil when needed.
- According to SAE standard J-357, all engine oils must be miscible (compatible) with all other brands of engine oil.
- Therefore, any brand of engine oil can be used as long as it meets the viscosity and API standards recommended by the vehicle manufacturer. Even though many people prefer a particular brand, be assured that, according to API and SAE, any major brand name engine oil can be used.

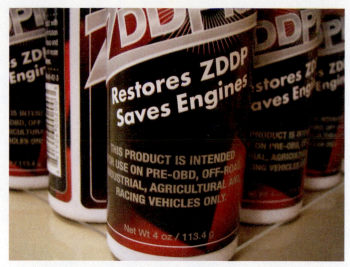

FIGURE 15–6 Using a zinc additive is important when using SM-rated oil in an engine equipped with a flat-bottom lifter, especially during the break-in period.

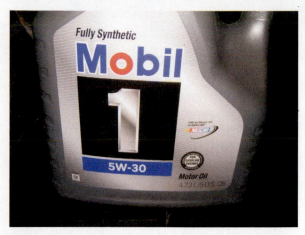

FIGURE 15–7 Mobil 1 synthetic engine oil is used by several vehicle manufacturers in new engines.

SYNTHETIC OIL

DEFINITION Synthetic engine oils have been available for years for military, commercial, and general public use. The term *synthetic* means that it is a manufactured product and not refined from a naturally occurring substance, as engine oil (petroleum base) is refined from crude oil. Synthetic oil is processed from several different base stocks using several different methods.

API GROUPS According to the American Petroleum Institute, engine oil is classified into the following groups.

- **Group I.** Mineral, nonsynthetic base oil with few if any additives; suitable for light lubricating needs and rust protection, not for use in an engine
- **Group II.** Mineral oil with quality additive packages; includes most conventional engine oils
- **Group III.** Hydrogenated (hydroisomerized) synthetic compounds commonly referred to as hydrowaxes or hydrocracked oil; the lowest costing synthetic engine oil; includes Castrol Syntec
- **Group IV.** Synthetic oils made from mineral oil and monomolecular oil called polyalpholefin (POA); includes Mobil 1 (● SEE FIGURE 15–7.)
- **Group V.** Nonmineral sources such as alcohol from corn called diesters or polyolesters; includes Red Line synthetic oil

Groups III, IV, and V are considered to be synthetic because the molecular structure of the finished product does not occur naturally, but is man-made through chemical processes. All synthetic engine oils perform better than group II (mineral) oils, especially when tested according to the Noack Volatility Test ASTM D-5800. This test procedure measures the ability of an oil to stay in grade after it has been heated

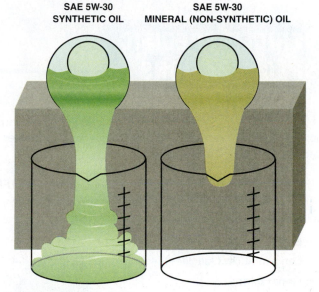

FIGURE 15–8 Both oils have been cooled to −20°F (−29°C). Notice that the synthetic oil on the left flows more freely than the mineral oil on the right even though both are SAE 5W-30.

to 300°F (150°C) for one hour. The oil is then measured for percentage of weight loss. As the lighter components boil off, the oil's viscosity will increase.

ADVANTAGES OF SYNTHETICS The major advantage of using synthetic engine oil is its ability to remain fluid at very low temperatures. ● SEE FIGURE 15–8.

This characteristic of synthetic oil makes it popular in colder climates where cold-engine cranking is important.

DISADVANTAGES OF SYNTHETICS The major disadvantage is cost. The cost of synthetic engine oils can be four to five times the cost of petroleum-based engine oils.

SYNTHETIC BLENDS A synthetic blend indicates that some synthetic oil is mixed with petroleum base engine oil; however, the percentage of synthetic used in the blend is unknown.

Use Synthetic Engine Oil in Lawn and Garden Equipment

Most four-cycle lawn and garden equipment engines are air cooled and operate hotter than many liquid-cooled engines. Lawn mowers and other small engines are often operated near or at maximum speed and power output for hours at a time. These operating conditions are hard on any engine oil. Try using synthetic oil. The cost is not as big a factor because most small four-cycle lawn mower engines require only about 1/2 quart (1/2 liter) of oil. The synthetic oil is able to perform under high temperatures better than conventional mineral oils.

FIGURE 15–9 European vehicle manufacturers usually specify engine oil with a broad viscosity range, such as SAE 5W-40, and their own unique standards, such as the Mercedes specification 229.51. Always use the oil specified by the vehicle manufacturer.

VEHICLE-SPECIFIC SPECIFICATIONS

BACKGROUND Some oils can meet industry specifications, such as SAE, API, and/or ILSAC ratings, but not pass the tests specified by the vehicle manufacturer.

VEHICLE MANUFACTURER–SPECIFIC OIL SPECIFICATIONS The oil used should meet the specifications of the vehicle manufacturer, which include the following:

- **BMW**
  Longlife-98 and longlife-01 (abbreviated LL-01), LL-04
- **General Motors**
  GM 6094M
  GM 4718M (synthetic oil specification)
  Dexos 1 (all GM gasoline engines, 2011+)
  Dexos 2 (all GM diesel engines, 2011+)
- **Ford**
  WSS-M2C153-H
  WSS-M2C929-A (low viscosity rating, SAE 5W-20)
  WSS-M2C930-A
  WSS-M2C931-A
  WSS-M2C934-A
- **Chrysler**
  MS-6395 (2005+ vehicles)
  MS-10725 (2004 and older)
- **Honda/Acura**
  HTO-06 (turbocharged engine only)
- **Mercedes**
  229.3, 229.5, 229.1, 229.3, 229.31, 229.5, and 229.51
  (● **SEE FIGURE 15–9.**)

- **Volkswagen (VW and Audi)**
  502.00, 505.00, 505.01, 503, 503.01, 505, 506 diesel, 506.1 diesel, and 507 diesel

Be sure to use the oil that meets all of the specifications, especially during the warranty period.

NOTE: Most Asian brand vehicle manufactures do not specify any specifications other than SAE, API, and ILSAC. These vehicles include:

- **Acura/Honda**
- **Toyota/Lexus/Scion**
- **Kia**
- **Hyundai**
- **Nissan/Infiniti**
- **Mitsubishi**
- **Mazda**
- **Suzuki**

HIGH MILEAGE OILS

DEFINITION A "high mileage oil" is sold for use in vehicles that have over 75,000 miles and are, therefore, nearing the eight-year, 80,000-mile catalytic converter warranty period.

Usually higher viscosity and lack of friction-reducing additives mean that most high mileage oils cannot meet ILSAC GF-4 rating and are, therefore, not recommended for use in most engines.

DIFFERENCES

- Esters are added to swell oil seals (main and valve-stem seals).
- The oil is used only in engines with higher than 75,000 miles.
- The oil usually does not have the energy rating of conventional oils (i.e., will not meet the specifications for use according to the owner manual in most cases).

FIGURE 15–10 A rubber diaphragm acts as an antidrainback valve to keep the oil in the filter when the engine is stopped and the oil pressure drops to zero.

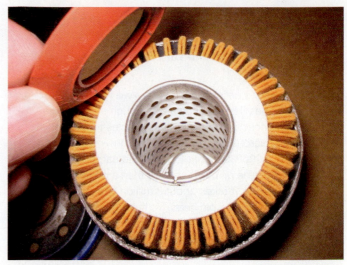

FIGURE 15–11 A cutaway of a typical spin-on oil filter. Engine oil enters the filter through the small holes around the center of the filter and flows through the pleated paper filtering media and out the large hole in the center of the filter. The center metal cylinder with holes is designed to keep the paper filter from collapsing under the pressure. The bypass valve can be built into the center on the oil filter or is part of the oil filter housing and located in the engine.

OIL FILTERS

CONSTRUCTION The oil within the engine is pumped from the oil pan through the filter before it goes into the engine lubricating system passages. The filter is made from either closely packed cloth fibers or a porous paper. Large particles are trapped by the filter. Microscopic particles will flow through the filter pores. These particles are so small that they can flow through the bearing oil film and not touch the surfaces, so they do no damage.

OIL FILTER VALVES Many oil filters are equipped with an **antidrainback valve** that prevents oil from draining out of the filter when the engine is shut off. ● **SEE FIGURE 15–10.**

This valve keeps oil in the filter and allows the engine to receive immediate lubrication as soon as the engine starts.

Either the engine or the filter is provided with a **bypass valve** that will allow the oil to go around the filter element. ● **SEE FIGURE 15–11.**

The bypass allows the engine to be lubricated with dirty oil, rather than having no lubrication, if the filter becomes plugged. The oil also goes through the bypass when the oil is cold and thick.

OIL FILTER DISPOSAL Oil filters should be crushed and/or drained of oil before discarding. After the oil has been drained, the filter can usually be disposed of as regular metal scrap. Always check and follow local, state, or regional oil filter disposal rules, regulations, and procedures. ● **SEE FIGURE 15–12.**

FIGURE 15–12 A typical filter crusher. The hydraulic ram forces out most of the oil from the filter. The oil is trapped underneath the crusher and is recycled.

OIL CHANGE

INTERVALS All vehicle and engine manufacturers recommend a maximum oil change interval. The recommended intervals are almost always expressed in terms of mileage or elapsed time (or hours of operation), whichever milestone is reached first.

Most vehicle manufacturers recommend an oil change interval of 7,500 to 12,000 miles (12,000 to 19,000 km) or every six months. If, however, *any one* of the conditions in the following list exists, the oil change interval recommendation drops to a more reasonable 2,000 to 3,000 miles (3,000 to 5,000 km) or every

FREQUENTLY ASKED QUESTION

Why Change Oil If the Oil Filter Can Trap All the Dirt?

Many persons believe that oil filters will remove all dirt from the oil being circulated through the filtering material. Most oil filters will filter particles that are about 10 to 20 microns in size. A micron is one-millionth of a meter or 0.000039 inch. Most dirt and carbon particles that turn engine oil black are less than a micron in size. In other words, it takes about 3 million of these carbon particles to cover a pin head. To help visualize the smallness of a micron, consider that a typical human hair is 60 microns in diameter. In fact, anything smaller than 40 microns is not visible to the human eye.

The dispersants added to engine oil prevent dirt from adhering together to form sludge. It is the same dispersant additive that prevents dirt from being filtered or removed by other means. If an oil filter could filter particles down to 1 micron, it would be so restrictive that the engine would not receive sufficient oil through the filter for lubrication. Oil recycling companies use special chemicals to break down the dispersants, which permit the dirt in the oil to combine into larger units that can be filtered or processed out of the oil.

FIGURE 15–13 Many vehicle manufacturers can display the percentage of oil life remaining, whereas others simply turn on a warning lamp when it has been determined that an oil change is required.

three months. The important thing to remember is that these are recommended *maximum* intervals and they should be shortened substantially if any of the following operating conditions exist.

1. Operating in dusty areas
2. Towing a trailer
3. Short-trip driving, especially during cold weather (The definition of a short trip varies among manufacturers, but it is usually defined as 4 to 15 miles (6 to 24 km) each time the engine is started.)
4. Operating in temperatures below freezing (32°F, 0°C)
5. Operating at idle speed for extended periods of time (such as normally occurs in police or taxi service)

Because most vehicles driven during cold weather are driven on short trips, technicians and automotive experts recommend changing the oil every 2,000 to 3,000 miles or every two to three months, whichever occurs first.

OIL LIFE MONITORS
Most vehicles built since the mid-1990s are equipped with a warning light that lets the driver know when the engine oil should be changed. The two basic types of oil change monitoring systems include:

- **Mileage only.** The service light will come on based on mileage only and may include a service "A" or "B" based on what service needs to be performed. The interval can be every 3,750 to 7,500 miles, or even longer in some cases where specialized engine oil is required.

TECH TIP

Follow the Seasons

Vehicle owners often forget when they last changed the oil. This is particularly true of the person who owns or is responsible for several vehicles. A helpful method for remembering when the oil should be changed is to change it at the start of each season of the year.

- Fall (September 21)
- Winter (December 21)
- Spring (March 21)
- Summer (June 21)

Remembering that the oil needs to be changed on these dates helps owners budget for the expense and the time needed.

- **Algorithm.** Computer programs contain algorithms that specify instructions a computer should perform (in a specific order) to carry out a task. This program uses the number of cold starts, the run time of the engine, and inputs from the engine coolant temperature (ECT) sensor to determine when the oil should be changed.

● **SEE FIGURE 15–13**.

OIL CHANGE PROCEDURE
An oil change includes the following steps.

STEP 1 Check the oil level on the dipstick before hoisting the vehicle. Document the work order and notify the owner if the oil level is low before changing the oil.

STEP 2 Safely hoist the vehicle.

STEP 3 Position a drain pan under the drain plug, then remove the plug with care to avoid contact with hot oil.

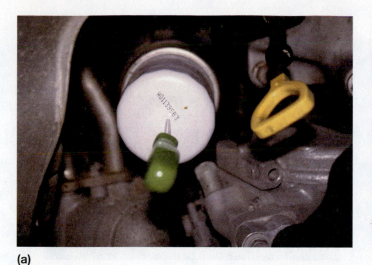
(a)

(b)

FIGURE 15-14 (a) A pick is pushed through the top of an oil filter that is positioned vertically. (b) When the pick is removed, a small hole allows air to get into the top of the filter which then allows the oil to drain out of the filter and back into the engine.

TECH TIP

The Pick Trick

Removing an oil filter that is installed upside down can be a real mess. When this design filter is loosened, oil flows out from around the sealing gasket. To prevent this from happening, use a pick to poke a hole in the top of the filter, as shown in ● **FIGURE 15-14**.

This small hole allows air to get into the filter, thereby allowing the oil to drain back into the engine rather than remain in the filter. After punching a hole in the filter, be sure to wait several minutes to allow time for the trapped oil to drain down into the engine before loosening the filter.

TECH TIP

Change Oil Every Friday?

A vehicle less than one year old came back to the dealer for some repair work. While writing the repair order, the service advisor noted that the vehicle had 88,000 miles on the odometer and was, therefore, out of warranty for the repair. Because the owner approved the repair anyway, the service advisor asked how he had accumulated so many miles in such a short time. The owner said that he was a traveling salesperson with a territory of "east of the Mississippi River."

Because the vehicle looked to be in new condition, the technician asked the salesperson how often he had the oil changed. The salesperson smiled and said proudly, "Every Friday."

Many fleet vehicles put on over 2,000 miles per week. How about changing their oil based on the time since last changed instead of by mileage?

CAUTION: Used engine oil has been determined to be harmful. Rubber gloves should be worn to protect the skin. If used engine oil gets on the skin, wash thoroughly with soap and water.

STEP 4 Allow the oil to drain freely so that the contaminants come out with the oil. It is not critically important to get every last drop of oil from the engine oil pan, because a quantity of used oil still remains in the engine oil passages and oil pump.

STEP 5 While the engine oil is draining, the oil plug gasket should be examined. If it appears to be damaged, it should be replaced.

NOTE: Honda/Acura recommends that the oil drain plug gasket be replaced at every oil change on many of their vehicles. The aluminum sealing gasket does not seal once it has been tightened. Always follow the vehicle manufacturer's recommendations.

STEP 6 When the oil stops running and starts to drip, reinstall and tighten the drain plug. Replace the oil filter.

STEP 7 Refill the engine with the proper type, grade, and quantity of oil. Restart the engine and allow the engine to idle until it develops oil pressure; then check the engine for leaks, especially at the oil filter.

OIL CHANGE

1 Before entering the customer's car for the first time, be sure to install a seat cover as well as a steering wheel cover to protect the vehicle's interior.

2 Run the engine until it is close to operating temperature. This will help the used oil drain more quickly and thoroughly.

3 Raise the vehicle on a hoist, and place the oil drain container in position under the oil drain plug. Be sure to wear protective gloves.

4 Remove the plug and allow the hot oil to drain from the engine. Use caution during this step as hot oil can cause painful burns!

5 While the engine oil continues to drain, remove the engine oil filter using a filter wrench. Some oil will drain from the filter, so be sure to have the oil drain container underneath when removing it.

6 Compare the new oil filter with the old one to be sure that it is the correct replacement.

CONTINUED ▶

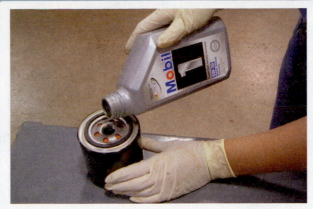

7 The wise service technician adds oil to the oil filter whenever possible. This provides faster filling of the filter during start-up and a reduced amount of time that the engine does not have oil pressure.

8 Apply a thin layer of clean engine oil to the gasket of the new filter. This oil film will allow the rubber gasket to slide and compress as the oil filter is being tightened.

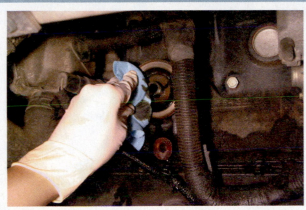

9 Clean the area where the oil filter gasket seats to be sure that no part of the gasket remains that could cause an oil leak if not fully removed.

10 Install the new oil filter and tighten it by hand. Do not use an oil filter wrench to tighten the filter! Most filters should be tightened 3/4 of a turn after the gasket contacts the engine.

11 Carefully inspect the oil drain plug and gasket. Replace the gasket as needed. Install the drain plug and tighten firmly but do not overtighten!

12 Lower the vehicle and clean around the oil fill cap before removing it.

OIL CHANGE (CONTINUED)

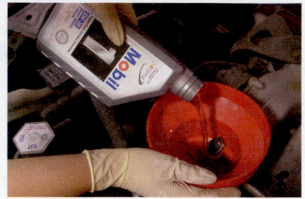

13 Use a funnel to add the specified amount of oil to the engine at the oil fill opening. When finished, replace the oil fill cap.

14 Start the engine and allow it to idle while watching the oil pressure gauge and/or oil pressure warning lamp. Oil pressure should be indicated within 15 seconds of starting the engine.

15 Stop the engine and let it sit for a few minutes to allow the oil to drain back into the oil pan. Look underneath the vehicle to check for any oil leaks at the oil drain plug(s) or oil filter.

16 Remove the oil-level dipstick and wipe it clean with a shop cloth.

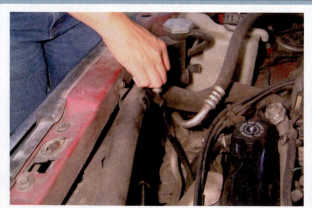

17 Reinstall the oil-level dipstick. Remove the dipstick a second time and read the oil level.

18 The oil level should be between the MIN and the MAX lines. In this case, the oil level should be somewhere in the cross-hatched area of the dipstick.

SUMMARY

1. Viscosity is the oil's thickness or resistance to flow.
2. SAE rating measures the viscosity of the oil.
3. API ratings reflect the quality of the oil.
4. The ILSAC rating symbol on the front of the container helps consumers find oil suitable for use in most gasoline engines.
5. Most vehicle manufacturers recommend use of SAE 5W-30 or SAE 10W-30 engine oil.
6. Many vehicle manufacturers provide specific oil standards for their vehicles.
7. Most vehicle manufacturers recommend changing the engine oil every six months or every 7,500 miles (12,000 km), whichever comes first. Most experts recommend changing the engine oil every 3,000 miles (5,000 km), or every three months, to help ensure long engine life.

REVIEW QUESTIONS

1. What property of oil does the SAE ratings reflect?
2. List the vehicle manufacturer's oil specifications.
3. Why is the oil filter bypassed when the engine oil is cold and thick?
4. What are the steps in performing an oil change?

CHAPTER QUIZ

1. The "W" in SAE 5W-20 means _____.
   a. Weight
   b. Winter
   c. With
   d. Without

2. Oil change intervals as specified by the vehicle manufacturer _____.
   a. Are *maximum* time and mileage intervals
   b. Are *minimum* time and mileage intervals
   c. Only include miles driven between oil changes
   d. Generally only include time between oil changes

3. Most conventional (mineral) oil is made from what API group?
   a. Group I
   b. Group II
   c. Group III
   d. Group IV or V

4. Which rating is the ACEA rating specified for use by many European vehicle manufacturers?
   a. SAE
   b. A3/B3
   c. SM
   d. GF-4

5. Technician A says that the engine oil used should be meet the vehicle manufacturer's standards. Technician B says that the specified viscosity of oil be used. Which technician is correct?
   a. Technician A only
   b. Technician B only
   c. Both Technicians A and B
   d. Neither Technician A nor B

6. Technician A says that some vehicle manufacturers recommend an ILSAC grade be used in the engine. Technician B says that an oil with the specified API rating *and* SAE viscosity rating should be used in an engine. Which technician is correct?
   a. Technician A only
   b. Technician B only
   c. Both Technicians A and B
   d. Neither Technician A nor B

7. Two technicians are discussing oil filters. Technician A says that the oil will remain perfectly clean if just the oil filter is changed regularly. Technician B says that oil filters can filter particles smaller than the human eye can see. Which technician is correct?
   a. Technician A only
   b. Technician B only
   c. Both Technicians A and B
   d. Neither Technician A nor B

8. The purpose of the oil filter bypass valve is to _____.
   a. Allow oil to bypass the filter if the filter becomes clogged
   b. Keep the oil from draining out of the filter when the engine is off and the oil pressure drops to zero
   c. Allows oil to bypass the oil filter when the oil is hot, to help cool the oil
   d. Both a and b

9. Different brands of oil can be used in a vehicle from one oil change to another if they meet the vehicle specifications, because all oil is _____.
   a. The same API group
   b. Miscible
   c. Of the same viscosity
   d. Both a and c

10. Older engines that use flat-bottom lifers should use oil (or an additive) that has enough _____.
    a. Viscosity
    b. ZDDP (zinc)
    c. Polyalpholefin (POA)
    d. Diesters

LUBRICATION SYSTEM OPERATION AND DIAGNOSIS

LEARNING OBJECTIVES: **After studying this chapter, the reader should be able to:** • Explain the purpose of the lubrication system, and state the lubrication principles. • Discuss engine lubrication systems. • Describe the purpose and function of oil pumps. • Discuss the purpose and function of oil passages. • Discuss oil pans, oil coolers, and the dry sump system.

KEY TERMS: Boundary lubrication 192 • Cavitate 195 • Dry sump 200 • Gallery 198 • Gerotor 194 • Hydrodynamic lubrication 192 • Positive displacement pumps 194 • Pressure regulating valve 195 • Sump 199 • Wet sump 200 • Windage tray 199

INTRODUCTION

Engine oil is the lifeblood of any engine. The purposes of a lubrication system include the following:

1. Lubricating all moving parts to prevent wear
2. Helping to cool the engine
3. Helping to seal piston rings
4. Cleaning, and holding dirt in suspension in the oil until it can be drained from the engine
5. Neutralizing acids that are formed as a result of the combustion process
6. Reducing friction
7. Preventing rust and corrosion

LUBRICATION PRINCIPLES

PURPOSE AND FUNCTION
Lubrication between two moving surfaces results from an oil film that separates the surfaces and supports the load. ● **SEE FIGURE 16–1**.

Although oil does not compress, it does leak out around the oil clearance between the shaft and the bearing. In some cases, the oil film is thick enough to keep the surfaces from seizing, but can allow some contact to occur. This condition is called **boundary lubrication**. The specified oil viscosity and oil clearances must be adhered to during service to help prevent boundary lubrication and wear from occurring, which usually happens when the engine is under a heavy load and low speeds. The movement of the shaft helps prevent contact with the bearing. If oil were put on a flat surface and a heavy block

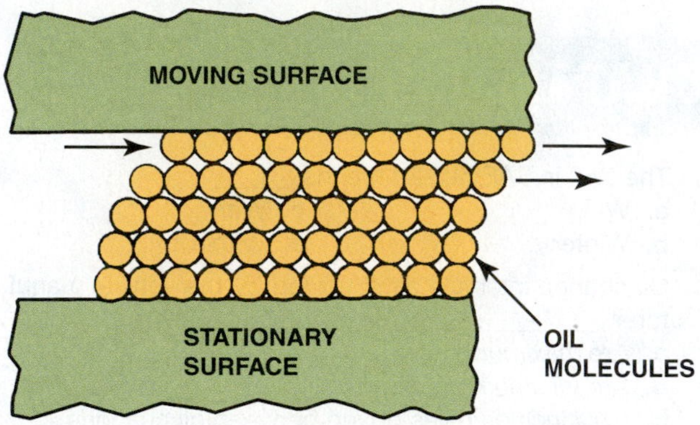

FIGURE 16–1 Oil molecules cling to metal surfaces but easily slide against each other.

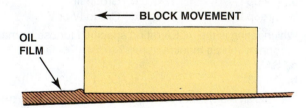

FIGURE 16–2 Wedge-shaped oil film developed below a moving block.

were pushed across the surface, the block would slide more easily than if it were pushed across a dry surface. The reason for this is that a wedge-shaped oil film is built up between the moving block and the surface, as illustrated in ● **FIGURE 16–2**.

HYDRODYNAMIC LUBRICATION
This wedging action is called **hydrodynamic lubrication**, and depends on the force applied to the rate of speed between the objects and the thickness of the oil. Thickness of oil is called the *viscosity,* and

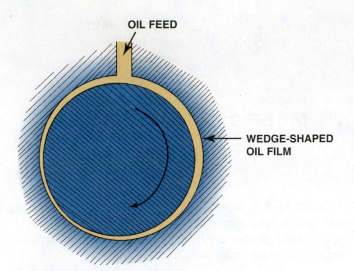

FIGURE 16–3 Wedge-shaped oil film curved around a bearing journal.

FIGURE 16–4 The dash oil pressure gauge may be a good indicator of engine oil pressure. If there is any concern about the oil pressure, always use a mechanical gauge to be sure.

is defined as the ability of the oil to resist flow. High-viscosity oil is thick and low-viscosity oil is thin.

- The prefix *hydro* refers to liquids, as in hydraulics.
- The term *dynamic* refers to moving materials.

Hydrodynamic lubrication occurs when a wedge-shaped film of lubricating oil develops between two surfaces that have relative motion between them. ● SEE FIGURE 16–3.

The engine oil pressure system feeds a continuous supply of oil into the lightly loaded part of the bearing oil clearance. Hydrodynamic lubrication takes over as the shaft rotates in the bearing to produce a wedge-shaped hydrodynamic oil film that is curved around the bearing. The pressure between the bearings and the crankshaft can exceed 1,000 PSI (6,900 kPa) due to hydrodynamic lubrication, as created by the wedging action between the bearing and the crankshaft journal. Most bearing wear occurs during the initial start-up, and continues until a hydrodynamic film is established.

ENGINE LUBRICATION SYSTEMS

PURPOSE AND FUNCTION The primary function of the engine lubrication system is to maintain a positive and continuous oil supply to the bearings. Engine oil pressure must be high enough to get the oil to the bearings with enough force to cause the oil flow that is required for proper cooling.

NORMAL OIL PRESSURE The normal engine oil pressure range is from 10 to 60 PSI (200 to 400 kPa) or 10 PSI per 1000 engine RPM. It is normal to see the following:

- Higher oil pressure when the engine is cold due to the oil being cold and at a higher viscosity
- Lower oil pressure when the engine is at normal operating temperature due to the oil

becoming thinner even though it is multiviscosity oil

- Lower oil pressures at idle and higher pressures at higher engine speeds because oil pumps are "positive displacement" pumps

The relatively low engine oil pressures obviously could not support these high bearing loads without hydrodynamic lubrication. Oil pressure measurements only show the oil pump pressure and not the pressure created between the bearings and the crankshaft journal due to hydrodynamic forces. ● SEE FIGURE 16–4.

OIL TEMPERATURE Excessive temperatures, either too low or too high, are harmful to any engine. If the oil is too cold, it could be too thick to flow through the oil passages and lubricate all engine parts. If the oil is too hot, it could become too thin to provide the film strength necessary to prevent metal-to-metal contact and wear. Estimated oil temperature can be determined with the following formula.

Estimated oil temperature = Outside air temperature + 120 F°

For example, 90°F outside air temperature + 120°F = 210°F estimated oil temperature.

During hard acceleration (or high-power demand activities such as trailer towing), the oil temperature will quickly increase. Oil temperature should not exceed 300°F (150°C).

OIL PUMPS

PURPOSE AND FUNCTION All production automobile engines have a full-pressure oil system. The oil pump is required to:

- Provide 3 to 6 gallons per minute of engine oil to lubricate the engine
- Maintain pressure, by forcing the oil into the lubrication system under pressure

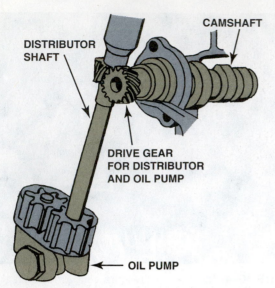

FIGURE 16–5 An oil pump driven by the camshaft.

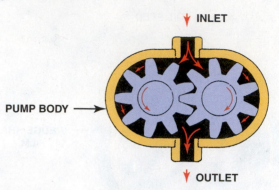

FIGURE 16–6 In an external gear-type oil pump, the oil flows through the pump around the outside of each gear. This is an example of a positive displacement pump, wherein everything entering the pump must leave the pump.

PARTS AND OPERATION In most engines that use a distributor, the distributor drive gear meshes with a gear on the camshaft, as shown in ●FIGURE 16–5.

The oil pump is driven from the end of the distributor shaft, often with a hexagon-shaped shaft. Some engines have a short shaft with a gear that meshes with the cam gear to drive both the distributor and oil pump. With a distributor-driven oil pump, the pump turns at one-half engine speed. On crankshaft-driven oil pump systems, the oil pump assembly is often made as part of the engine's front cover so that it turns at the same speed as the crankshaft.

TYPES OF OIL PUMPS All oil pumps are called **positive displacement pumps,** and each rotation of the pump delivers the same volume of oil; therefore, everything that enters must exit. Also a positive displacement pump will deliver more oil and higher pressure as the speed of the pump increases. Most automotive engines use one of two types of oil pumps, either gear or rotor.

- **External gear type.** A gear-type oil pump is usually driven by a shaft from the distributor, which is driven by the camshaft. As a result, this type of pump rotates at half engine (crankshaft) speed. The gear-type oil pump consists of two spur gears in a close-fit housing—one gear is driven while the other idles. As the gear teeth come out of mesh, they tend to leave a space, which is filled by oil drawn through the pump inlet. When the pump is pumping, oil is carried around the *outside* of each gear in the space between the gear teeth and the housing. As the teeth mesh in the center, oil is forced from the teeth into an oil passage, thus producing oil pressure. ●SEE FIGURE 16–6.
- **Internal/external gear type.** This type of oil pump is driven by the crankshaft and operates at engine speed. In this style of oil pump, two gears and a crescent stationary element are used. ●SEE FIGURE 16–7.

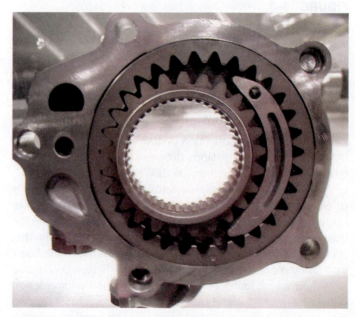

FIGURE 16–7 A typical internal/external oil pump mounted in the front cover of the engine that is driven by the crankshaft.

- **Rotor type.** This rotor-type oil pump is driven by the crankshaft and uses a special lobe-shape gear meshing with the inside of a lobed rotor. The center lobed section is driven and the outer section idles. As the lobes separate, oil is drawn in just as it is drawn into gear-type pumps. As the pump rotates, it carries oil around and between the lobes. As the lobes mesh, they force the oil out from between them under pressure in the same manner as the gear-type pump. The pump is sized so that it will maintain a pressure of at least 10 PSI (70 kPa) in the oil gallery when the engine is hot and idling. Pressure will increase because the engine-driven pump also rotates faster. ●SEE FIGURE 16–8.
- **Gerotor type.** This type of positive displacement oil pump uses an inner and an outer rotor. The term is derived from two words: "*gen*erated *rotor,*" or **gerotor.** The inner rotor has one fewer teeth than the outer rotor and both rotate. ●SEE FIGURE 16–9.

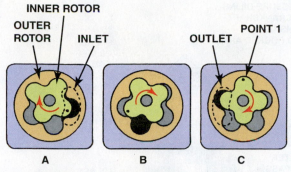

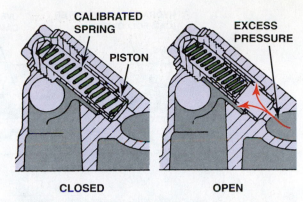

FIGURE 16-8 The operation of a rotor-type oil pump.

A. OIL IS PICKED UP IN LOBE OF OUTER ROTOR.
B. OIL IS MOVED IN LOBE OF OUTER ROTOR TO OUTLET.
C. OIL IS FORCED OUT OF OUTLET BECAUSE THE INNER AND OUTER ROTORS MESH TOO TIGHTLY AT POINT 1 AND THE OIL CANNOT PASS THROUGH.

FIGURE 16-10 Oil pressure relief valves are spring loaded. The stronger the spring tension, the higher the oil pressure.

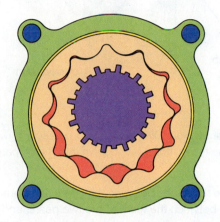

FIGURE 16-9 Gerotor-type oil pump driven by the crankshaft.

OIL PRESSURE REGULATION

In engines with a full-pressure lubricating system, maximum pressure is limited with a pressure *relief valve*. The relief valve (sometimes called the **pressure regulating valve**) is located at the outlet of the pump. The relief valve controls maximum pressure by bleeding off oil to the inlet side of the pump. ● SEE FIGURE 16-10.

The relief valve spring tension determines the maximum oil pressure. If a pressure relief valve is not used, the engine oil pressure will continue to increase as the engine speed increases. Maximum pressure is usually limited to the lowest pressure that will deliver enough lubricating oil to all engine parts that need to be lubricated.

The oil pump is made so that it is large enough to provide pressure at low engine speeds and small enough that it will not **cavitate** at high speed. Cavitation occurs when the pump tries to pull oil faster than it can flow from the pan to the pickup. When it cannot get enough oil, it will pull air. This puts air pockets or cavities in the oil stream. A pump is cavitating when it is pulling air or vapors.

NOTE: The reason for sheet metal covers over the pickup screen is to prevent cavitation. Oil is trapped under the cover, which helps prevent the oil pump from drawing in air, especially during sudden stops or during rapid acceleration.

After the oil leaves the pump, it first flows through the oil filter and then is delivered to the moving parts through drilled oil passages. ● SEE FIGURE 16-11.

FACTORS AFFECTING OIL PRESSURE Oil pressure can only be produced when the oil pump has a capacity larger than all the "leaks" in the engine.

- **Leaks.** The leaks are the clearances at end points of the lubrication system. The end points are at the edges of bearings, the rocker arms, the connecting rod spit holes, and so on. These clearances are designed into the engine and are necessary for its proper operation. As the engine parts wear and clearance becomes greater, more oil will leak out. In other words, worn main or rod bearings are often the cause of lower than normal oil pressure.

- **Oil pump capacity.** The oil pump must supply extra oil for any leaks. The capacity of the oil pump results from its size, rotating speed, and physical condition. When the pump is rotating slowly as the engine idles, oil pump capacity is low. *If the leaks are greater than the pump capacity, engine oil pressure is low.* As the engine speed increases, the pump capacity increases and the pump tries to force more oil out of the leaks. This causes the pressure to rise until it reaches the regulated maximum pressure.

NOTE: A clogged oil pump pickup screen can cause lower than normal oil pressure because the amount of oil delivered by the pump is reduced by the clogged screen.

- **Viscosity of the engine oil.** The viscosity of the oil affects both the pump capacity and the oil leakage. Thin oil or oil of very low viscosity slips past the edges of the pump and flows freely from the leaks. Hot oil has a low viscosity, and therefore, a hot engine often has low oil pressure. Cold oil is more viscous (thicker) than hot oil. This results in higher pressures, even with the cold engine idling. High oil pressure occurs with a cold engine, because the oil relief valve must open farther to release excess oil than is necessary with a hot engine. This larger opening increases the spring compression force, which in turn increases the oil pressure. Putting higher viscosity oil

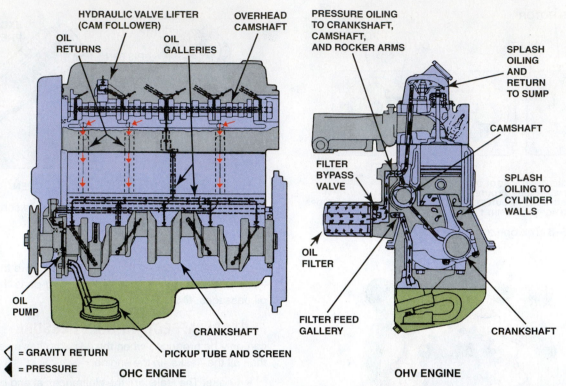

HYDRAULIC VALVE LIFTER (CAM FOLLOWER)
OVERHEAD CAMSHAFT
PRESSURE OILING TO CRANKSHAFT, CAMSHAFT, AND ROCKER ARMS
OIL RETURNS
OIL GALLERIES
SPLASH OILING AND RETURN TO SUMP
CAMSHAFT
FILTER BYPASS VALVE
SPLASH OILING TO CYLINDER WALLS
OIL FILTER
OIL PUMP
CRANKSHAFT
FILTER FEED GALLERY
CRANKSHAFT
 = GRAVITY RETURN
PICKUP TUBE AND SCREEN
= PRESSURE
OHC ENGINE
OHV ENGINE

FIGURE 16–11 A typical engine design that uses both pressure and splash lubrication. Oil travels under pressure through the galleries (passages) to reach the top of the engine. Other parts are lubricated as the oil flows back down into the oil pan or is splashed onto parts.

? FREQUENTLY ASKED QUESTION

Is a High-Pressure or High-Volume Oil Pump Needed?

No. Engine parts need pressure after the oil reaches the parts that are to be lubricated. The oil film between the parts is developed and maintained by hydrodynamic lubrication. Excessive oil pressure requires more horsepower and provides no better lubrication than the minimum effective pressure. A high-volume pump is physically larger and pumps more oil with each revolution. A high-volume pump is used mostly in race engines where the main and rod bearing clearances are much greater than normal and therefore would need a great volume of oil to make up for the oil leaking from the wide clearances.

in an engine will raise the engine oil pressure to the regulated setting of the relief valve at a lower engine speed.

OIL PUMP CHECKS   The cover is removed to check the condition of the oil pump.

- **Visual inspection.** The gears and housing are examined for scoring. If the gears and housing are heavily scored, the entire pump should be replaced. ● **SEE FIGURE 16–12**.

- **Measurements.** If they are lightly scored, the clearances in the pump should be measured. These clearances

include the space between the gears and housing, the space between the teeth of the two gears, and the space between the side of the gear and the pump cover. A feeler gauge is often used to make these measurements. Gauging plastic can be used to measure the space between the side of the gears and the cover. The oil pump should be replaced when excessive clearance or scoring is found.

On most engines, the oil pump should be replaced as part of any engine work, especially if the cause for the repair is lack of lubrication.

NOTE: The oil pump is the "garbage pit" of the entire engine. Any and all debris is often forced through the gears and housing of an oil pump. ● SEE FIGURE 16–13.

Always refer to the manufacturer's specifications when checking the oil pump for wear. Typical oil pump clearances include the following:

1. End plate clearance: 0.0015 inch (0.04 mm)
2. Side (rotor) clearance: 0.012 inch (0.30 mm)
3. Rotor tip clearance: 0.010 inch (0.25 mm)
4. Gear end play clearance: 0.004 inch (0.10 mm)

All parts should also be inspected closely for wear. Check the relief valve for scoring and check the condition of the spring. When installing the oil pump, coat the sealing surfaces with engine assembly lubricant. This lubricant helps draw oil from the oil pan on initial start-up.

(a)

(b)

FIGURE 16–12 (a) A visual inspection indicated that this pump cover was worn. (b) An embedded particle of something was found on one of the gears, making this pump worthless except for scrap metal.

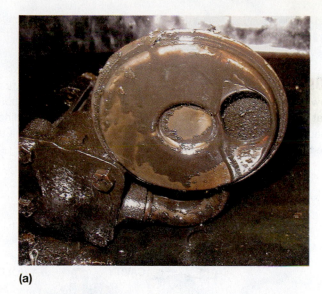

(a)

(b)

FIGURE 16–13 (a) The oil pump is the only part in an engine that gets unfiltered engine oil. The oil is drawn up from the bottom of the oil pan and is pressurized before flowing to the oil filter. (b) If debris gets into an oil pump, the drive or distributor shaft can twist and/or break. When this occurs, the engine will lose all oil pressure.

OIL PASSAGES

PURPOSE AND FUNCTION

Oil from the oil pump first flows through the oil filter then goes through a drilled hole that intersects with a drilled main oil **gallery,** or longitudinal header. This is a long hole drilled from the front of the block to the back.

- Inline engines use one oil gallery.
- V-type engines may use two or three galleries.

Passages drilled through the block bulkheads allow the oil to go from the main oil gallery to the main and cam bearings. ● SEE FIGURE 16–14.

In some engines, oil goes to the cam bearings first, and then to the main bearings. It is important that the oil holes in the bearings match with the drilled passages in the bearing saddles so that the bearing can be properly lubricated. Over a long period of use, bearings will wear. This wear causes excess clearance. The excess clearance will allow too much oil to leak from the side of the bearing. When this happens, there will be little or no oil left for bearings located farther downstream in the lubricating system. This is a major cause of bearing failure. To aid in

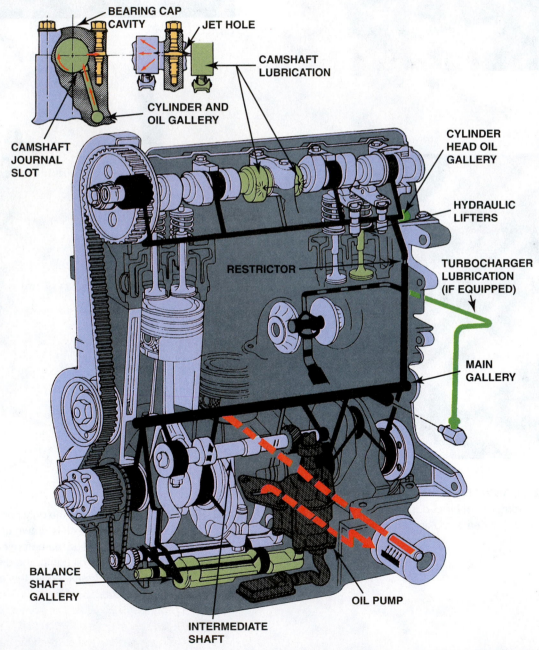

FIGURE 16–14 An intermediate shaft drives the oil pump on this overhead camshaft engine. Note the main gallery and other drilled passages in the block and cylinder head.

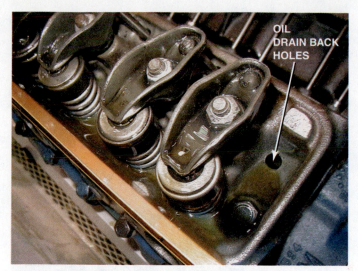

FIGURE 16–15 Oil is sent to the rocker arms on this Chevrolet V-8 engine through the hollow pushrods. The oil returns to the oil pan through the oil drainback holes in the cylinder head.

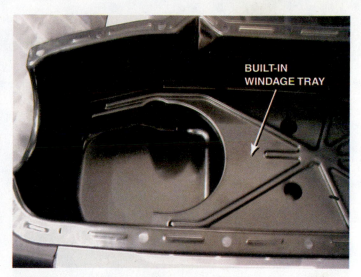

FIGURE 16–16 A typical oil pan with a built-in windage tray used to keep oil from being churned up by the rotating crankshaft.

bearing failure diagnosis, on most engines, the last rod bearing to receive oil pressure is typically the bearing farthest from the oil pump. If this bearing fails, then suspect low oil pressure as the probable cause.

VALVE TRAIN LUBRICATION The oil gallery may intersect or have drilled passages to the valve lifter bores to lubricate the lifters. When hydraulic lifters are used, the oil pressure in the gallery keeps refilling them. On some engines, oil from the lifters goes up the center of a hollow pushrod to lubricate the pushrod ends, the rocker arm pivot, and the valve stem tip. In other engines, an oil passage is drilled from either the gallery or a cam bearing to the block deck, where it matches with a head gasket hole and a hole drilled in the head to carry the oil to a rocker arm shaft. Some engines use an enlarged bolt hole to carry lubrication oil around the rocker shaft cap screw to the rocker arm shaft.

Holes in the bottom of the rocker arm shaft allow lubrication of the rocker arm pivot. Rocker arm assemblies need only a surface coating of oil, so the oil flow to the rocker assembly is minimized using restrictions or metered openings. The restriction or metering disk is in the lifter when the rocker assembly is lubricated through the pushrod. Oil that seeps from the rocker assemblies is returned to the oil pan through drain holes. These oil drain holes are often placed so that the oil drains on the camshaft or cam drive gears to lubricate them. Oil drain holes can be either machined or cast into the cylinder heads and block. ● SEE FIGURE 16–15.

Some engines have means of directing a positive oil flow to the cam drive gears or chain. This may include either of the following:

- Nozzle
- Chamfer on a bearing parting surface, which allows oil to spray on the loaded portion of the cam drive mechanism

TECH TIP

The New Hemi Engine Oiling System

The Chrysler Hemi V-8 engine uses a unique oiling system because the valve lifters are fed oil from the top of the cylinder heads and through the pushrods. While it is normal to have oil flowing through hollow pushrods, it is unique that in the Hemi V-8 the oil flows backward from normal and from the head *down* the hollow pushrods to the lifters. Be sure to use the specified viscosity of oil, as this is critical for proper lubrication of the valve lifters.

OIL PANS

PURPOSE AND FUNCTION The oil pan is where engine oil is used for lubricating the engine. Another name for the oil pan is a **sump.** As the vehicle accelerates, brakes, or turns rapidly, the oil tends to move around in the pan. Pan baffles and oil pan shapes are often used to keep the oil inlet under the oil at all times. As the crankshaft rotates, it acts like a fan and causes air within the crankcase to rotate with it. This can cause a strong draft on the oil, churning it so that air bubbles enter the oil, which then causes oil foaming. Oil with air will not lubricate like liquid oil, so oil foaming can cause bearings to fail. A baffle or **windage tray** is sometimes installed in engines to eliminate the oil churning problem. This may be an added part, as shown in ● FIGURE 16–16, or it may be a part of the oil pan.

Windage trays have the good side effect of reducing the amount of air disturbed by the crankshaft, so that less power is drained from the engine at high crankshaft speeds.

Why Is It Called a Windage Tray?

A windage tray is a plate or baffle installed under the crankshaft and is used to help prevent aeration of the oil. Where does the wind come from? Pistons push air down into the crankcase as they move from top dead center to bottom dead center. The pistons also draw air and oil upward when moving from bottom dead center to top dead center. At high engine speeds, this causes a great deal of airflow, which can easily aerate the oil. Therefore, a windage tray is used to help prevent this movement of air (wind) from affecting the oil in the pan. Try the following:

- Take an oil pan and add a few quarts (liters) of oil.
- Then take an electric hair dryer and use it to blow air into the oil pan.

Oil will be thrown everywhere, which helps illustrate why windage trays are used in all newer engines.

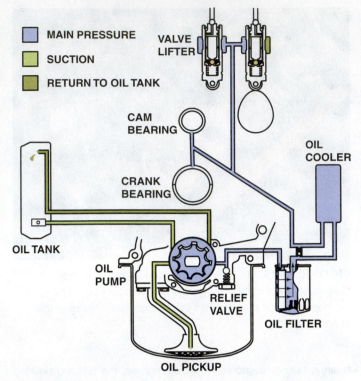

FIGURE 16–17 A dry sump system as used in a Chevrolet Corvette.

DRY SUMP SYSTEM

CONSTRUCTION AND OPERATION   The term *sump* is used to describe a location where oil is stored or held. In most engines, oil is held in the oil pan and the oil pump draws the oil from the bottom. This type of system is called a **wet sump** oil system. In a **dry sump** system, the oil pan is shallow and the oil is pumped into a remote reservoir. In this reservoir, the oil is cooled and any trapped air is allowed to escape before being pumped back to the engine. A dry sump system uses an externally mounted oil reservoir.

ADVANTAGES   The advantages of a dry sump system are as follows:

1. A shallow oil pan allows the engine to be mounted lower in the vehicle to improve cornering.

2. The oil capacity can be greatly expanded because the size of the reservoir is not limited. A larger quantity of oil means that the oil temperature can be controlled.

3. A dry sump system allows the vehicle to corner and brake for long periods, which is not able to be done with a wet sump system due to the oil being thrown to one side and away from the oil pickup.

4. A dry sump system also allows the engine to develop more power as the oil is kept away from the moving crankshaft.

DISADVANTAGES   A dry sump system has the following disadvantages.

1. The system is expensive as it requires components and plumbing not needed in a wet sump system.

2. The system is complex because the plumbing and connections, plus the extra components, result in more places where oil leaks can occur and change the way routine maintenance is handled. A dry sump oil system is used in most motor sport vehicles and is standard on certain high-performance production vehicles, such as some models of the Chevrolet Corvette, Porsche, and BMW. ● **SEE FIGURE 16–17**.

OIL COOLERS

Oil temperature must be controlled on many high-performance or turbocharged engines. A larger capacity oil pan helps to control oil temperature. Some engines use remote mounted oil coolers. Coolant flows through the oil cooler to help warm the oil when the engine is cold and cool the oil when the engine is hot. Oil temperature should be:

- Above 212°F (100°C) to boil off any accumulated moisture
- Below 280°F to 300°F (138°C to 148°C)

● **SEE FIGURE 16–18**.

❓ FREQUENTLY ASKED QUESTION

What Is Acceptable Oil Consumption?

There are a number of opinions regarding what is acceptable oil consumption. Most vehicle owners do not want their engine to use any oil between oil changes even if they do not change it more often than every 7,500 miles (12,000 km). Engineers have improved machining operations and piston ring designs to help eliminate oil consumption.

Many stationary or industrial engines are not driven on the road, so they do not accumulate miles but still may consume excessive oil.

A general rule for "acceptable" oil consumption is that it should be about 0.002 to 0.004 pound per horsepower per hour. To figure, use the following:

$$\frac{1.82 \times \textbf{Quarts used}}{\textbf{Operating hp} \times \textbf{Total hours}} = \textbf{Pound/hp/hr}$$

Therefore, oil consumption is based on the amount of work an engine performs. Although the formula may not be viable for vehicle engines used for daily transportation, it may be for the marine or industrial engine builder. Generally, oil consumption that is greater than 1 quart for every 600 miles (1 liter per 1,000 km) is considered to be excessive with a motor vehicle.

OIL COOLER

OIL FILTER

FIGURE 16–18 Oil is cooled by the flow of coolant through the oil filter adaptor.

SUMMARY

1. Viscosity is the oil's thickness or resistance to flow.
2. Normal engine oil pump pressure ranges from 10 to 60 PSI (200 to 400 kPa) or 10 PSI for every 1000 engine RPM.
3. Hydrodynamic oil pressure around engine bearings is usually over 1,000 PSI (6,900 kPa).
4. The oil pump is driven directly by the crankshaft or by a gear or shaft from the camshaft.

REVIEW QUESTIONS

1. What causes a wedge-shaped film to form in the oil?
2. What is hydrodynamic lubrication?
3. Explain why internal engine leakage affects oil pressure.
4. Describe how the oil flows from the oil pump, through the filter and main engine bearings, to the valve train.
5. What is the purpose of a windage tray?

1. Normal oil pump pressure in an engine is _____ PSI.
   a. 3 to 7
   b. 10 to 60
   c. 100 to 150
   d. 180 to 210

2. Two technicians are discussing oil pumps. Technician A says that many oil pumps are driven directly off the front of the crankshaft. Technician B says that some are driven from the distributor if the engine uses a distributor-type ignition system. Which technician is correct?
   a. Technician A only
   b. Technician B only
   c. Both Technicians A and B
   d. Neither Technician A nor B

3. A typical oil pump can pump how many gallons per minute?
   a. 3 to 6 gallons
   b. 6 to 10 gallons
   c. 10 to 60 gallons
   d. 50 to 100 gallons

4. In typical engine lubrication systems, what components are the last to receive oil and the first to suffer from a lack of oil or oil pressure?
   a. Main bearings
   b. Rod bearings
   c. Valve train components
   d. Oil filters

5. Hydrodynamic lubricants, created by the wedging action of oil between the crankshaft journal and the bearing, can be as high as _____ PSI.
   a. 60
   b. 120
   c. 500
   d. 1,000

6. What type of oil pump is driven by the crankshaft?
   a. Gerotor
   b. Internal/external gear
   c. External gear
   d. Both a and b

7. Lower than specified oil pressure is measured on a high mileage engine. Technician A says that worn main or rod bearings could be the cause. Technician B says that a clogged oil pump pickup screen could be the cause. Which technician is correct?
   a. Technician A only
   b. Technician B only
   c. Both Technicians A and B
   d. Neither Technician A nor B

8. Oil passages in an engine block are usually called _____.
   a. Galleries
   b. Holes
   c. Runners
   d. Pathways

9. Why is a dry sump system used in some high-performance vehicles?
   a. It allows the vehicle to corner or brake for long periods
   b. It allows the engine to develop more power
   c. It allows for a greater oil capacity so that oil temperatures can be controlled
   d. All of the above

10. Engine oil cooler uses what to cool the oil?
    a. Coolant
    b. Air
    c. Air-conditioning evaporator output
    d. Automatic transmission fluid after it flows through the radiator

LEARNING OBJECTIVES: After studying this chapter, the reader should be able to: • Explain the purpose and function of a battery, and discuss battery ratings. • Discuss battery service and battery service safety considerations. • Discuss battery voltage test, battery load testing, and conductance testing. • Explain how to safely jump start a battery, and discuss battery charging and charging circuit. • Explain the battery electrical drain test. • Describe the cranking circuit, and discuss how to diagnose starter problems using visual inspection. • Explain starter testing on a vehicle and how to test a starter using a scan tool. • Discuss voltage drop testing and how to check charging system voltage. • Discuss the need for proper starter drive-to-flywheel clearance. • Discuss how to test an alternator using a scan tool and using a scope. • Discuss AC ripple voltage check and AC current check. • Explain charging system voltage drop testing and alternator output test.

KEY TERMS: AC ripple voltage 221 • Alternator 203 • Ampere-hour 204 • Battery 203 • Battery electrical drain test 209 • Battery voltage correction factor 204 • CA 203 • Capacity test 207 • CCA 203 • Charging circuit 203 • Conductance tester 207 • Cranking circuit 203 • DE 219 • ELD 223 • IOD 209 • Load test 207 • LRC 223 • MCA 203 • Neutral safety switch 213 • Open-circuit battery voltage test 205 • Parasitic load 209 • Reserve capacity 204 • Ripple current 222 • SRE 219 • State of charge 208 • Surface charge 205 • Voltage drop test 215

Just as in the old saying "If Mother isn't happy—no one is happy," the battery, the starter, and the charging system have to function correctly for the engine performance to be satisfactory.

PURPOSE AND FUNCTION OF A BATTERY

The primary purpose of an automotive **battery** is to provide a source of electrical power for starting and for electrical demands that exceed alternator output. The battery also acts as a voltage stabilizer for the entire electrical system. The battery is a voltage stabilizer because it acts as a reservoir where large amounts of current (amperes) can be removed quickly during starting and replaced gradually by the **alternator** during charging. The battery *must* be in good (serviceable) condition before the charging system and the cranking system can be tested. For example, if a battery is discharged, the **cranking circuit** (starter motor) could test as being defective because the battery voltage might drop below specifications. The **charging circuit** could also test as being defective because of a weak or discharged battery. It is important to test the vehicle battery before further testing of the cranking or charging system.

BATTERY RATINGS

Batteries are rated according to the amount of current they can produce under specific conditions.

COLD-CRANKING AMPERES Every automotive battery must be able to supply electrical power to crank the engine in cold weather and still provide voltage high enough to operate the ignition system for starting. The cold-cranking power of a battery is the number of amperes that can be supplied at 0°F (–18°C) for 30 seconds while the battery still maintains a voltage of 1.2 volts per cell or higher. This means that the battery voltage would be 7.2 volts for a 12 volt battery and 3.6 volts for a 6 volt battery. The cold-cranking performance rating is called **cold-cranking amperes (CCA)**. Try to purchase a battery that offers the highest CCA for the money.

CRANKING AMPERES Cranking amperes (CA) are not the same as CCA, but are often advertised and labeled on batteries. The designation CA refers to the number of amperes that can be supplied by the battery at 32°F (0°C). This rating results in a higher number than the more stringent rating of CCA. ● SEE FIGURE 17–1.

MARINE CRANKING AMPERES Marine cranking amperes (MCA) rating is similar to the cranking amperes (CA) rating and is tested at 32°F (0°C).

FIGURE 17–1 This battery shows a large "1000" on the front panel but this is the CA rating and not the more important CCA rating. Always compare batteries with the same rating.

AMPERE-HOUR RATING   The **ampere-hour (Ah)** is how many amperes can be discharged from the battery before dropping to 10.5 volts over a 20 hour period. A battery that is able to supply 3.75 amperes for 20 hours has a rating of 75 ampere-hours (3.75 × 20 = 75).

RESERVE CAPACITY   The **reserve capacity** rating for batteries is *the number of minutes* for which the battery can produce 25 amperes and still have a battery voltage of 1.75 volts per cell (10.5 volts for a 12 volt battery). This rating is actually a measurement of the time for which a vehicle can be driven in the event of a charging system failure.

? FREQUENTLY ASKED QUESTION

How Can a Defective Battery Affect Engine Performance?

A weak or discharged battery should be replaced as soon as possible. A weak battery causes a constant load on the alternator that can cause the stator windings to overheat and fail. Low battery voltage also affects the electronic fuel-injection system. The computer senses low battery voltage and increases the fuel injector on-time to help compensate for the lower voltage to the fuel pump and fuel injectors. This increase in injector pulse time is added to the calculated pulse time and is sometimes called the **battery voltage correction factor**. Reduced fuel economy could therefore be the result of a weak or defective battery.

? FREQUENTLY ASKED QUESTION

Should Batteries Be Kept Off of Concrete Floors?

All batteries should be stored in a cool, dry place when not in use. Many technicians have been warned not to store or place a battery on concrete. According to battery experts, it is the temperature difference between the top and the bottom of the battery that causes a difference in the voltage potential between the top (warmer section) and the bottom (colder section). It is this difference in temperature that causes self-discharge to occur.

In fact, submarines cycle seawater around their batteries to keep all sections of the battery at the same temperature to help prevent self-discharge.

Therefore, always store or place batteries up off the floor and in a location where the entire battery can be kept at the same temperature, avoiding extreme heat and freezing temperatures. Concrete cannot drain the battery directly, because the case of the battery is a very good electrical insulator.

? FREQUENTLY ASKED QUESTION

What Can Cause a Battery to Explode?

Batteries discharge hydrogen and oxygen gases when being charged. If there happens to be a flame or spark, the hydrogen will burn. The oxygen can also help contribute to an explosion of a small pocket of hydrogen.

BATTERY SERVICE SAFETY CONSIDERATIONS

Batteries contain acid and release explosive gases (hydrogen and oxygen) during normal charging and discharging cycles. To help prevent physical injury or damage to the vehicle, always adhere to the following safety procedures.

1. Whenever working on any electrical component on a vehicle, disconnect the negative battery cable from the battery. When the negative cable is disconnected, all electrical circuits in the vehicle will be open, which will prevent accidental electrical contact between an electrical component and ground. Any electrical spark has the potential to cause explosion and personal injury.

2. Wear eye protection whenever working around any battery.

3. Wear protective clothing to avoid skin contact with battery acid.

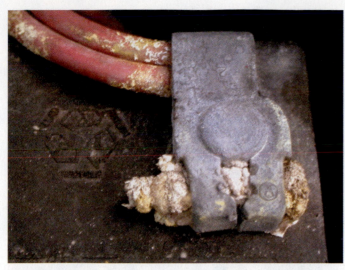

FIGURE 17–2 Corrosion on a battery cable could be an indication that the battery is either being overcharged or is sulfated, creating a lot of gassing of the electrolyte.

4. Always adhere to all safety precautions as stated in the service procedures for the equipment used for battery service and testing.

5. Never smoke or use an open flame around any battery.

BATTERY VISUAL INSPECTION

The battery and battery cables should be included in the list of items checked during a thorough visual inspection. Check the battery cables for corrosion and tightness. ● SEE FIGURE 17–2.

NOTE: On side post batteries, grasp the battery cable near the battery and attempt to rotate the cable in a clockwise direction in an attempt to tighten the battery connection.

If possible, remove the covers and observe the level of the electrolyte. ● SEE FIGURE 17–3.

BATTERY VOLTAGE TEST

Testing the battery voltage with a voltmeter is a simple method for determining the state of charge of any battery. ● SEE FIGURE 17–4. The voltage of a battery does not necessarily indicate whether the battery can perform satisfactorily, but it does indicate to the technician more about the battery's condition than a simple visual inspection. A battery that *looks* good may not be good. This test is commonly called an **open-circuit battery voltage test** because it is conducted with an open circuit—with no current flowing and no load applied to the battery.

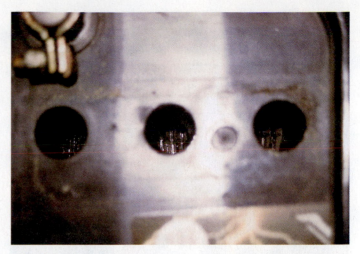

FIGURE 17–3 A visual inspection on this battery showed that the electrolyte level was below the plates in all cells.

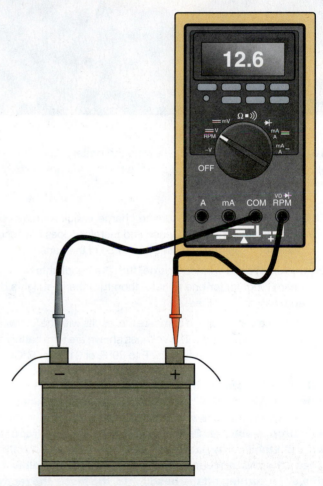

FIGURE 17–4 Using a DMM to measure the open-circuit voltage of a battery.

1. Connect a voltmeter to the positive (+) and negative (–) terminals of the battery. Set the voltmeter to read DC volts.

2. If the battery has just been charged or the vehicle has recently been driven, it is necessary to remove the surface charge from the battery before testing. A **surface charge** is a charge of higher-than-normal voltage that is only on the surface of

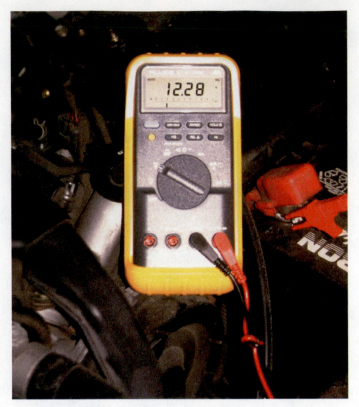

(a)

(b)

FIGURE 17–5 (a) Voltmeter showing the battery voltage when the headlights were on (engine off) for one minute. (b) Headlights were turned off and the battery voltage quickly recovered to indicate 12.6 volts.

the battery plates. The surface charge is quickly removed whenever the battery is loaded and therefore does not accurately represent the true state of charge of the battery.

3. To remove the surface charge, turn the headlights on high beam (brights) for one minute, then turn the headlights off and wait two minutes.

4. Read the voltmeter and compare the results with the following state-of-charge chart. The voltages shown are for a battery at or near room temperature (70°F to 80°F, or 21°C to 27°C).

NOTE: Watch the voltmeter when the headlights are turned on. A new good battery will indicate a gradual drop in voltage, whereas a weak battery will indicate a more rapid drop in voltage. Soon the voltage will stop dropping and will stabilize. A good new battery will likely stabilize above 12 volts. A weak older battery may drop below 11 volts. After turning off the headlights, the faster the recovery, generally, the better the battery. ● SEE FIGURE 17–5.

Battery voltage (V)	State of charge
12.6 or higher	100% charged
12.4	75% charged
12.2	50% charged
12.0	25% charged
11.9 or lower	Discharged

 **TECH TIP**

Use a Scan Tool to Check the Battery, Starter, and Alternator!

General Motors and Chrysler vehicles as well as selected others that can display data to a scan tool can be easily checked for proper operating voltage. Most scan tools can display battery or system voltage and engine speed in RPM (revolutions per minute). Connect a scan tool to the data link connector (DLC) and perform the following while watching the scan tool display ●
SEE FIGURE 17–6.

Many scan tools are also capable of recording or graphing engine data while cranking including:

• The RPM during cranking should be 80 to 250 RPMs.

• Battery voltage during cranking should be above 9.6 volts.

Note: Normal readings for a good battery and starter would be 10.5 to 11.5 volts.

• Battery voltage after engine starts should be 13.5 to 15 volts.

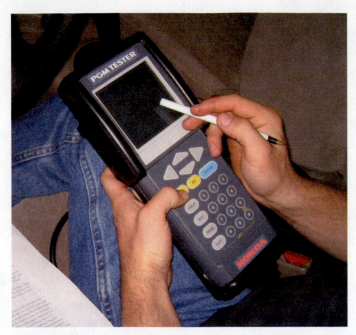

FIGURE 17–6 Using a scan tool to check battery voltage.

FIGURE 17–7 A Bear Automotive starting and charging tester. This tester automatically loads the battery for 15 seconds to remove the surface charge, waits 30 seconds to allow the battery to recover, and then loads the battery again. The LCD indicates the status of the battery.

BATTERY LOAD TESTING

One method to determine the condition of any battery is the **load test**, also known as a **capacity test**. Most automotive starting and charging testers use a carbon pile to create an electrical load on the battery. The amount of the load is determined by the original capacity of the battery being tested. The capacity is measured in cold-cranking amperes (CCA), which is the number of amperes that a battery can supply at 0°F (–18°C) for 30 seconds. An older type of battery rating is called the ampere-hour rating. The proper electrical load to be used to test a battery is one-half of the CCA rating or three times the ampere-hour rating, with a minimum of a 150 A load. Apply the load for a full 15 seconds and observe the voltmeter at the end of the 15 second period while the battery is still under load. A good battery should indicate above 9.6 V.

NOTE: This test is sometimes called the *one-minute test,* because many battery manufacturers recommend performing the load test twice, using the first load period (15 seconds) to remove the surface charge on the battery, then waiting for 30 seconds to allow time for the battery to recover, and then loading the battery again for 15 seconds. Total time required is 60 seconds (15 + 30 + 15 = 60 seconds or 1 minute). This method provides a true indication of the condition of the battery.
● **SEE FIGURES 17–7 AND 17–8.**

If the battery fails the load test, recharge the battery and retest. If the battery fails the load test again, replace the battery.

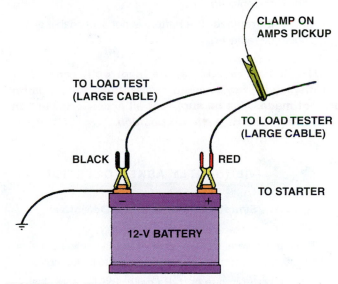

FIGURE 17–8 This shows a typical battery load tester hookup.

CONDUCTANCE TESTING

General Motors Corporation, Chrysler Corporation, Ford, and other vehicle manufacturers specify that a **conductance tester** be used to test batteries in vehicles still under factory warranty. The tester uses its internal electronic circuitry to determine the state of charge and capacity of the battery by measuring the voltage and conductance of the plates.
● **SEE FIGURE 17–9.**

Connect the unit to the positive and negative terminals of the battery, and after entering the CCA rating (if known),

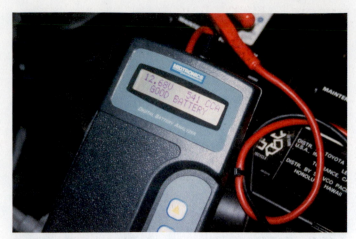

FIGURE 17–9 An electronic battery tester.

push the arrow keys. The tester determines one of the following:

- **Good battery.** The battery can return to service.
- **Charge and retest.** Fully recharge the battery and return it to service.
- **Replace the battery.** The battery is not serviceable and should be replaced.
- **Bad cell—replace.** The battery is not serviceable and should be replaced.

CAUTION: Test results can be incorrectly reported on the display if proper, clean connections to the battery are not made. Also be sure that all accessories and the ignition switch are in the off position.

 FREQUENTLY ASKED QUESTION

What Are Symptoms of a Weak or Defective Battery?

There are several warning signs that may indicate that a battery is near the end of its useful life, including:

- **Uses water in one or more cells.** This indicates that the plates are sulfated and that, during the charging process, the water in the electrolyte is being turned into separate hydrogen and oxygen gases.
- **Excessive corrosion on battery cables or connections.** Corrosion is more likely to occur if the battery is sulfated, creating hot spots on the plates. When the battery is being charged, the acid fumes are forced out of the vent holes and get onto the battery cables, connections, and even on the tray underneath the battery.
- **Slower-than-normal engine cranking.** When the capacity of the battery is reduced due to damage or age, it is less likely to supply the necessary current for starting the engine, especially during cold weather.

JUMP STARTING

To safely jump start a vehicle without doing any harm, use the following procedure.

1. Be certain the ignition switch is off on both vehicles.
2. Connect good-quality copper jumper cables as indicated in the guide in ● **FIGURE 17–10.**
3. Start the vehicle with the good battery and allow it to run for 5 to 10 minutes. This allows the alternator of the good vehicle to charge the battery on the disabled vehicle.
4. Start the disabled vehicle and, after the engine is operating smoothly, disconnect the jumper cables in the reverse order of step 2.

NOTE: To help prevent accidental touching of the jumper cables, simply separate them into two cables and attach using wire (cable) ties or tape so that the clamps are offset from each other, making it impossible for them to touch.

BATTERY CHARGING

If the **state of charge** of a battery is low, it must be recharged. It is best to slow-charge any battery to prevent possible overheating damage to the battery. Remember, it may take eight hours or more to charge a fully discharged battery. The initial charge rate should be about 35 amperes for 30 minutes to help start the charging process. Fast-charging a battery increases the temperature of the battery and can cause warping of the plates inside the battery. Fast-charging also increases the amount of gassing (release of hydrogen and oxygen), which can create a health and fire hazard. The battery temperature should not exceed 125°F (hot to the touch). Most batteries should be charged at a rate equal to 1% of the battery's CCA rating. ● **SEE FIGURE 17–11.**

Fast charge: 15 amperes maximum

Slow charge: 5 amperes maximum

● **SEE CHART 17–1** for battery charging times at various battery voltages and charging rates.

BATTERY SERVICE

Before returning the vehicle to the customer, check and service the following items as necessary.

1. Neutralize and clean any corrosion from the battery terminals with a solution of baking soda and water.
2. Carefully inspect the battery cables by visual inspection. ● **SEE FIGURE 17–12.**
3. Check the tightness and cleanliness of all ground connections.

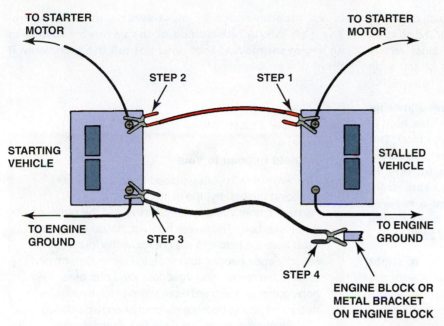

TO STARTER MOTOR

TO STARTER MOTOR

STEP 2

STEP 1

STARTING VEHICLE

STALLED VEHICLE

TO ENGINE GROUND

TO ENGINE GROUND

STEP 3

STEP 4

ENGINE BLOCK OR METAL BRACKET ON ENGINE BLOCK

FIGURE 17–10 Jumper cable usage guide.

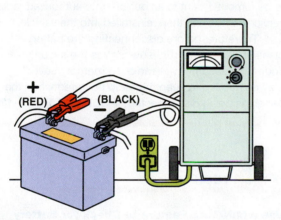

+ (RED)   − (BLACK)

FIGURE 17–11 To use a battery charger, make sure the charger is connected to the battery before plugging in the charger.

FIGURE 17–12 This battery cable was found corroded underneath. The corrosion had eaten through the insulation yet was not noticeable without careful inspection. This cable should be replaced.

OPEN CIRCUIT VOLTAGE, V	STATE OF CHARGE, %	CHARGING TIME (MIN) TO FULL CHARGE AT 80°F (27°C)*					
		at 60 A	at 50 A	at 40 A	at 30 A	at 20 A	at 10 A
12.6	100	Full Charge					
12.4	75	15	20	27	35	48	90
12.2	50	35	45	55	75	95	180
12.0	25	50	65	85	115	145	280
11.8	0	65	85	110	150	195	370

CHART 17–1

A chart that can be used to estimate the charging time based on battery voltage and charging rate.

*If colder, allow additional time.

BATTERY ELECTRICAL DRAIN TEST

The **battery electrical drain test** determines if some component or circuit in a vehicle or truck is causing a drain on the battery when everything is off. This test is also called the **ignition off-draw (IOD)** or **parasitic load** test. This test should be performed whenever one of the following conditions exists.

1. Whenever a battery is being charged or replaced (a battery drain could have been the cause for charging or replacing the battery)

2. Whenever the battery is suspected of being drained

Normal battery drain on a vehicle equipped with electronic radio, climate control, computerized fuel injection, and so forth, is usually about 20 to 30 mA (0.02 to 0.03 A). Most vehicle manufacturers recommend repairing the cause of any drain that exceeds 50 mA (0.05 A).

NOTE: Some manufacturers relate maximum allowable parasitic load to the size of the battery. The higher the battery capacity, the greater the allowable load. The maximum allowable drain on a battery can be calculated by dividing the reserve capacity of the battery in minutes by four to get the maximum allowable drain in milliamps. For example, if a battery had a reserve capacity of 100 minutes, it would have a maximum allowable parasitic load of 25 mA (100 ÷ 4 = 25 mA).

NOTE: Many electronic components draw a slight amount of current from the battery all the time with the ignition off. These components include:

1. **Digital clocks**
2. **Electronically tuned radios for station memory and clock circuits (if the vehicle is so equipped)**
3. **The engine control computer (if the vehicle is so equipped), through slight diode leakage**
4. **The alternator, through slight diode leakage**

These components may cause a voltmeter to read full battery voltage if it is connected between the negative battery terminal and the removed end of the negative battery cable. Using a voltmeter to measure battery drain is *not* **recommended by most vehicle manufacturers. The high internal resistance of the voltmeter results in an irrelevant reading that does not tell the technician if there is a problem.**

FREQUENTLY ASKED QUESTION

How Should I Connect a Battery Charger So as Not to Harm the Vehicle?

Most vehicle manufacturers recommend disconnecting both battery cables from the battery before charging the battery. Side post batteries require adapters or bolts with nuts attached to permit sufficient surface area around the battery terminal for proper current flow. The following steps will ensure a safe method of connecting a battery charger.

1. Make certain the battery charger is unplugged from the electrical outlet and the charger control is off.
2. Connect the leads of the charger to the battery— the red lead to the positive (+) terminal and the black lead to the negative (–) terminal.
3. Plug the charger into the electrical outlet.
4. Set the controls to the fast (high) rate for about 30 minutes or until the battery starts to take a charge. After 30 minutes, reduce the charge rate to about 1% of the CCA rating of the battery until the battery is charged.

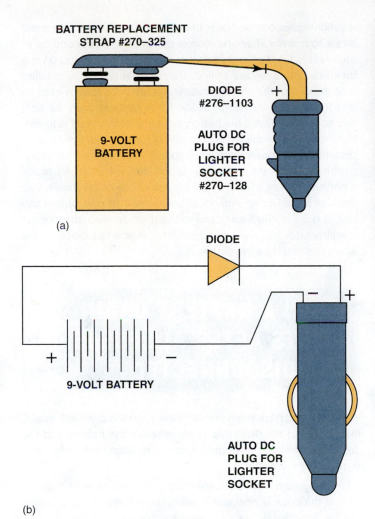

(a)

(b)

FIGURE 17–13 (a) Memory saver. The part numbers represent components from Radio Shack®. (b) A schematic drawing of the same memory saver.

BATTERY ELECTRICAL DRAIN TESTING USING AN AMMETER

The ammeter method is the most accurate way to test for a possible battery drain. Connect an ammeter in series between the battery terminal (post) and the disconnected cable. (Normal battery drain is 0.020 to 0.030 A and any drain greater than 0.050 A should be found and corrected.) Many digital multimeters have an ammeter scale that can be used to safely and accurately test for an abnormal parasitic drain.

CAUTION: Some vehicle manufacturers recommend that a test light be used before connecting an ammeter when checking for a battery drain. If the drain is large enough to light a test light, the ammeter may be damaged. Be certain to use an ammeter that is rated to read the anticipated amperage.

FIGURE 17–14 This mini clamp-on DMM is being used to measure the amount of battery electrical drain that is present. In this case, a reading of 20 mA (displayed on the meter as 00.02 A) is within the normal range of 20 to 30 mA. Be sure to clamp around all of the positive battery cables or all of the negative battery cables, whichever is easiest to clamp.

PROCEDURE FOR BATTERY ELECTRICAL DRAIN TEST

The fastest and easiest method to measure battery electrical drain is to connect an inductive DC ammeter that is capable of measuring low current (10 mA). ● SEE FIGURE 17–14 for an example of a clamp-on digital multimeter being used to measure battery drain.

Following is the procedure for performing the battery electrical drain test using an ammeter.

1. Make certain that all lights, accessories, and the ignition are off.

2. Check all vehicle doors to be certain that the interior courtesy (dome) lights are off.

3. Disconnect the *negative* (–) battery cable and install a parasitic load tool as shown in ● FIGURE 17–15.

4. Start the engine and drive the vehicle about 10 minutes, being sure to turn on all the lights and accessories, including the radio.

5. Turn off the engine and all of the accessories, including the underhood light.

6. Connect an ammeter across the parasitic load tool switch and wait 10 minutes or longer for all computers to go to sleep and circuits to shut down.

7. Open the switch on the load tool and read the battery electrical drain on the meter display.

   Results: Normal = 10 to 30 mA (0.02 to 0.03 A)

   Maximum allowable = 50 mA (0.05 A) (Industry standards—some vehicle manufacturers' specifications can vary)

   Be sure to reset the clock and antitheft radio, if equipped.

● SEE FIGURE 17–16.

FIGURE 17–15 After connecting the shutoff tool, start the engine and operate all accessories. Stop the engine and turn off everything. Connect the ammeter across the shut-off switch in parallel. Wait 20 minutes. This time allows all electronic circuits to "time out" or shut down. Open the switch—all current now will flow through the ammeter. A reading greater than specified, usually greater than 50 mA (0.05 A), indicates a problem that should be corrected.

FIGURE 17–16 The battery was replaced in this Acura and the radio displayed "code" when the replacement battery was installed. Thankfully, the owner had the five-digit code required to unlock the radio.

FINDING THE SOURCE OF THE DRAIN

If there is a drain, check and temporarily disconnect the following components.

1. Cell phone or MP3 player still connected to the vehicle
2. Glove compartment light
3. Trunk light

If after disconnecting these components the battery drain can still light the test light or draw more than 50 mA (0.05 A), disconnect one fuse at a time from the fuse box until the test light goes out or the ammeter reading drops. If the drain drops to normal after one fuse is disconnected, the source of the drain is located in that particular circuit, as labeled on the fuse box. As fuses are pulled, they should not be reinstalled until the end of the test. Reinstalling a fuse can reset a module and foul up the test. Start at the fuses farthest from the battery and work toward the battery until the faulty circuit is found. Note that many vehicles have multiple fuse boxes. Continue to disconnect the *power-side* wire connectors from each component included in that particular circuit until the ammeter reads a normal amount of draw. The source of the battery drain can then be traced to an individual component or part of one circuit. If none of the fuses causes the drain to stop, disconnect the alternator (alternator) output lead. A shorted diode in the alternator could be the cause.

WHEN A BATTERY DRAIN EXISTS AFTER ALL FUSES ARE DISCONNECTED

If all the fuses have been disconnected and the drain still exists, the source of the drain has to be between the battery and the fuse box. The most common sources of drain under the hood include the following:

1. **The alternator.** Disconnect the alternator wires and retest. If the draw is now within acceptable limits, the problem is a defective diode(s) in the alternator.
2. **The starter solenoid (relay) or wiring near its components.** These are also a common source of battery drain, due to high current flows and heat, which can damage the wire or insulation.

CRANKING CIRCUIT

The cranking circuit includes those mechanical and electrical components required to crank the engine for starting. The cranking force in the early 1900s was the driver's arm. Modern cranking circuits include the following:

1. **Starter motor.** The starter is normally a 0.5 to 2.6 hp (0.4 to 2 kilowatts) electric motor that can develop nearly 8 hp (6 kilowatts) for a very short time when first cranking a cold engine.
2. **Battery.** The battery must be of the correct capacity and be at least 75% charged to provide the necessary current and voltage for correct operation of the starter.
3. **Starter solenoid or relay.** The high current required by the starter must be able to be turned on and off. A large switch would be required if the current were controlled by the driver directly. Instead, a small current switch (ignition switch) operates a solenoid or relay that controls the high starter current.

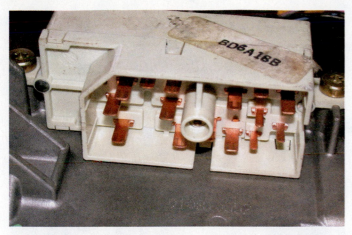

FIGURE 17–17 A typical ignition switch showing all of the electrical terminals after the connector has been removed.

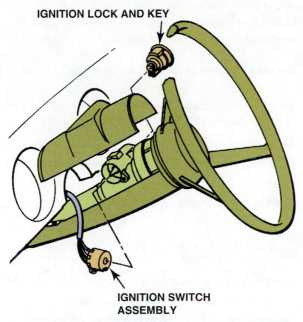

IGNITION LOCK AND KEY

IGNITION SWITCH ASSEMBLY

FIGURE 17–18 Some column-mounted ignition switches act directly on the contact points, whereas others use a link from the lock cylinder to the ignition switch.

4. **Starter drive.** The starter drive uses a small gear that contacts the engine flywheel gear and transmits starter motor power to rotate the engine.

5. **Ignition switch.** The ignition switch and safety control switches control the starter motor operation. ● **SEE FIGURES 17–17 AND 17–18.**

The engine is cranked by an electric motor that is controlled by a key-operated ignition switch or the PCM on vehicles equipped with electronic starting. The ignition switch will not operate the starter unless the automatic transmission is in neutral or park. This is to prevent an accident that might result from the vehicle moving forward or backward when the engine is started. Many automobile manufacturers use a **neutral safety switch or a clutch switch** that opens the circuit between the ignition switch and the starter to prevent starter motor operation unless the gear selector is in neutral or park. The safety switch can either be attached to the steering

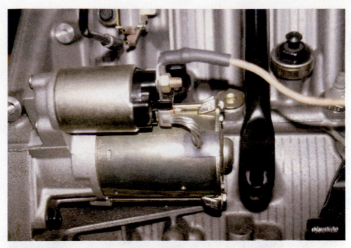

FIGURE 17–19 A typical solenoid-operated starter.

FIGURE 17–20 Carefully inspect all battery terminals for corrosion.

column inside the vehicle near the floor or on the side of the transmission/transaxle. According to vehicle manufacturing engineers, starters can be expected to start an engine 25,000 times during normal life of the vehicle. ● **SEE FIGURE 17–19.**

DIAGNOSING STARTER PROBLEMS USING VISUAL INSPECTION

For proper operation, all starters require that the vehicle battery be at least 75% charged and that both power-side and ground-side battery cables be free from excessive voltage drops. The following should be carefully checked as part of a thorough visual inspection.

- Carefully check the battery cables for tightness both at the battery and at the starter, and block connections. ● **SEE FIGURE 17–20.**
- Check to see if the heat shield (if equipped) is in place.

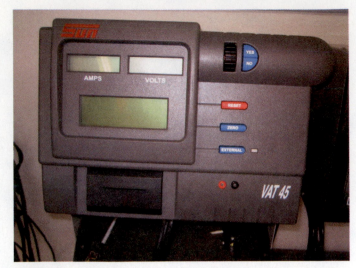

FIGURE 17–21 When connecting a starter tester such as a Sun VAT 45 to the vehicle, make certain that the inductive probe is placed over all of the cables or wires from the battery.

- Check for any nonstock add-on accessories or equipment that may drain the battery such as a sound system or extra lighting.
- Crank the engine. Feel the battery cables and connections. If any cables or connections are hot to the touch, then an excessive voltage drop is present or the starter is drawing too much current. The engine itself could be binding. Repair or replace the components or connections as needed.

STARTER TESTING ON THE VEHICLE

CHECK BATTERY Before performing a starter amperage test, be certain that the battery is sufficiently charged (75% or more) and capable of supplying adequate starting current.

STARTER AMPERAGE TEST A starter amperage test should be performed whenever the starter fails to operate normally (is slow in cranking) or as part of a routine electrical system inspection. Some service manuals specify normal starter amperage for starter motors being tested on the vehicle; however, most service manuals only give the specifications for bench-testing a starter without a load applied. These specifications are helpful in making certain that a repaired starter meets exact specifications, but they do not apply to starter testing on the vehicle. If exact specifications are not available, the following can be used as general maximum specifications for testing a starter on the vehicle. ● **SEE FIGURE 17–21.** Any ampere reading lower than these are acceptable:

- 4-cylinder engines = 150 to 185 (normally less than 100 A)
- 6-cylinder engines = 160 to 200 (normally less than 125 A)
- 8-cylinder engines = 185 to 250 (normally less than 150 A)

FIGURE 17–22 Always check the battery, using a conductance or load tester. A battery showing a green charge indicator does not mean that the battery is good.

Excessive current draw may indicate one or more of the following:

1. Low battery voltage (discharged or defective battery) ● **SEE FIGURE 17–22.**
2. Binding of starter armature as a result of worn bushings
3. Oil too thick (viscosity too high) for weather conditions
4. Shorted or grounded starter windings or cables
5. Tight or seized engine

 REAL WORLD FIX

The Case of the No Crank

A 4-cylinder engine would not crank. Previously the customer said that once in a while, the starter seemed to lock up when the vehicle sat overnight but would then finally crank. The problem only occurred in the morning and the engine would crank and start normally the rest of the day.

The vehicle finally would not start and was towed to the shop. The service technician checked the current draw of the starter and it read higher than the scale on the ammeter. The technician then attempted to rotate the engine by hand and found that the engine would not rotate. Based on this history of not cranking normally in the morning, the technician removed the spark plugs and attempted to crank the engine. This time the engine cranked and coolant was seen shooting from cylinders 2 and 3. Apparently coolant leaked into the cylinders, due to a fault with the head gasket, causing the engine to hydrolock, or not rotate due to liquid being trapped on top of the piston. Replacing the bad gasket solved the cranking problems in the morning.

TESTING A STARTER USING A SCAN TOOL

A scan tool can be used on most vehicles to check the cranking system. Follow these steps:

1. Connect the scan tool according to the manufacturer's instructions.
2. Select battery voltage and engine RPM on the scan tool.
3. Select "snapshot" and start recording or graphing if the scan tool is capable.
4. Crank the engine. Stop the scan tool recording.
5. Retrieve the scan data and record cranking RPM and battery voltage during cranking. Cranking RPM should be between 80 and 250 RPM. Battery voltage during cranking should be higher than 9.6 volts.

TECH TIP

Watch the Dome Light

When diagnosing any starter-related problem, open the door of the vehicle and observe the brightness of the dome or interior light(s). The brightness of any electrical lamp is proportional to the voltage.

Normal operation of the starter results in a slight dimming of the dome light.

- *If the light remains bright,* the problem is usually an open circuit in the control circuit.
- *If the light goes out or almost goes out,* the problem could include a discharged battery, a shorted or grounded armature, or field coils inside the starter.

A poor electrical connection that opens under load could also be the cause.

VOLTAGE DROP TESTING

PURPOSE OF VOLTAGE DROP TESTING **Voltage drop** is the drop in voltage that occurs when current is flowing through a resistance. For example, a voltage drop is the difference between voltage at the source and voltage at the electrical device to which it is flowing. The higher the voltage drop, the greater the resistance in the circuit. Even though voltage drop testing can be performed on any electrical circuit, the most common areas of testing include the cranking circuit and the charging circuit wiring and connections.

RESULTS OF EXCESSIVE VOLTAGE DROP A high voltage drop (high resistance) in the cranking circuit wiring can cause slow engine cranking with less-than-normal starter

TECH TIP

Don't Hit That Starter!

In the past, it was common to see service technicians hitting a starter in their effort to diagnose a no-crank condition. Often the shock of the blow to the starter aligned or moved the brushes, armature, and bushings. Many times, the starter functioned after being hit—even if only for a short time.

However, most of today's starters use permanent magnet fields, and the magnets can be easily broken if hit. A magnet that is broken becomes two weaker magnets. Some early permanent magnet (PM) starters used magnets that were glued or bonded to the field housing. If struck with a heavy tool, the magnets could be broken, with parts of the magnet falling onto the armature and into the bearing pockets, making the starter impossible to repair or rebuild.

? FREQUENTLY ASKED QUESTION

Is Voltage Drop the Same as Resistance?

Many technicians have asked the question: Why measure voltage drop when the resistance can be easily measured using an ohmmeter? Think of a battery cable with all the strands of the cable broken, except for one. If an ohmmeter is used to measure the resistance of the cable, the reading would be very low, probably less than 1 ohm. However, the cable is not capable of conducting the amount of current necessary to crank the engine. In less severe cases, several strands can be broken and affect the operation of the starter motor. Although the resistance of the battery cable will not indicate any increased resistance, the restriction to current flow will cause heat and a drop in the voltage available at the starter. Because resistance is not effective until current flows, measuring the voltage drop (differences in voltage between two points) is the most accurate method of determining the true resistance in a circuit.

How much is too much? According to Bosch Corporation, all electrical circuits should have a maximum of 3% loss of the voltage of the circuit to resistance. Therefore, in a 12 volt circuit, the maximum loss of voltage in cables and connections should be 0.36 volt ($12 \times 0.03 = 0.36$ volt). The remaining 97% of the circuit voltage (11.64 volts) is available to operate the electrical device (load). Just remember:

- **Low voltage drop = low resistance**
- **High voltage drop = high resistance**

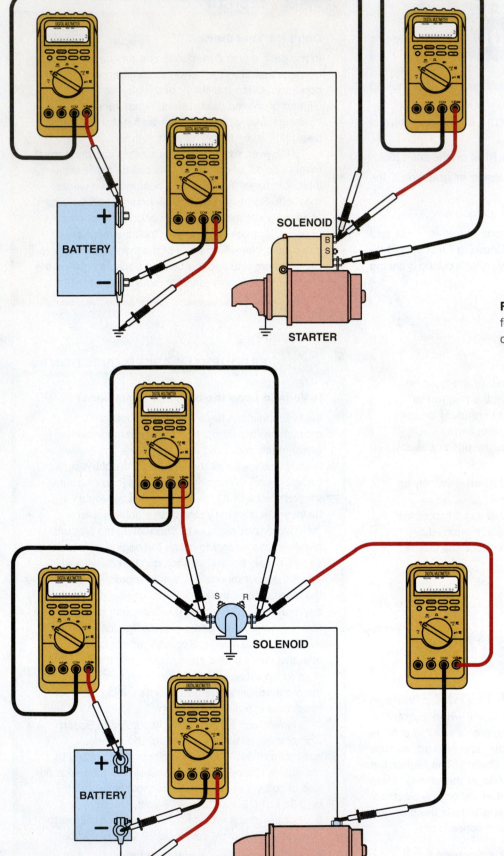

FIGURE 17–23 Voltmeter hookups for voltage drop testing of a GM-type cranking circuit.

FIGURE 17–24 Voltmeter hookups for voltage drop testing of a Ford-type cranking circuit.

FIGURE 17–25 Using the voltmeter leads from a starting and charging test unit to measure the voltage drop between the battery terminal (red lead) and the cable end (black lead). The engine must be cranked to cause current to flow through this connection.

amperage drain as a result of the excessive circuit resistance. If the voltage drop is high enough, such as could be caused by dirty battery terminals, the starter may not operate. A typical symptom of low battery voltage or high resistance in the cranking circuit is a "clicking" of the starter solenoid.

PERFORMING A VOLTAGE DROP TEST Voltage drop testing of the wire involves connecting any voltmeter (on the low scale) to the suspected high-resistance cable ends and cranking the engine. ● **SEE FIGURES 17–23 THROUGH 17–25.**

NOTE: Before a difference in voltage (voltage drop) can be measured between the ends of a battery cable, current must be flowing through the cable. *Resistance is not effective unless current is flowing.* **If the engine is not being cranked, current is not flowing through the battery cables and the voltage drop cannot be measured.**

Crank the engine with a voltmeter connected to the battery and record the reading. Crank the engine with the voltmeter connected across the starter and record the reading. If the difference in the two readings exceeds 0.5 volt, perform the following steps to determine the exact location of the voltage drop.

1. Connect the positive voltmeter test lead to the most positive end of the cable being tested. The most positive end of a cable is the end closest to the positive terminal of the battery.

2. Connect the negative voltmeter test lead to the other end of the cable being tested. With no current flowing through the cable, the voltmeter should read zero because there is the same voltage at both ends of the cable.

3. Crank the engine. The voltmeter should read less than 0.2 volt.

4. Evaluate the results. If the voltmeter reads zero, the cable being tested has no resistance and is good. If the voltmeter reads higher than 0.2 volt, the cable has excessive resistance and should be replaced. However, before

replacing the cable, make certain that the connections at both ends of the cable being tested are clean and tight. ● **SEE FIGURE 17–26.**

STARTER DRIVE-TO-FLYWHEEL CLEARANCE

NEED FOR PROPER CLEARANCE For the proper operation of the starter and absence of abnormal starter noise, there must be a slight clearance between the starter pinion and the engine flywheel ring gear. Many General Motors starters use shims (thin metal strips) between the flywheel and the engine block mounting pad to provide the proper clearance. ● **SEE FIGURE 17–27.**

NOTE: Some manufacturers use shims under the starter drive end housings during production. Other manufacturers *grind* **the mounting pads at the factory for proper starter pinion gear clearance. If** *any* **GM starter is replaced, the starter pinion** *must* **be checked and corrected as necessary to prevent starter damage and excessive noise.**

If the clearance is too great, the starter will produce a high-pitched whine *during* cranking. If the *clearance is too small,* the starter will produce a high-pitched whine *after* the engine starts, just as the ignition key is released.

NOTE: The major cause of broken drive-end housings on starters is too small a clearance. If the clearance cannot be measured, it is better to put a shim between the

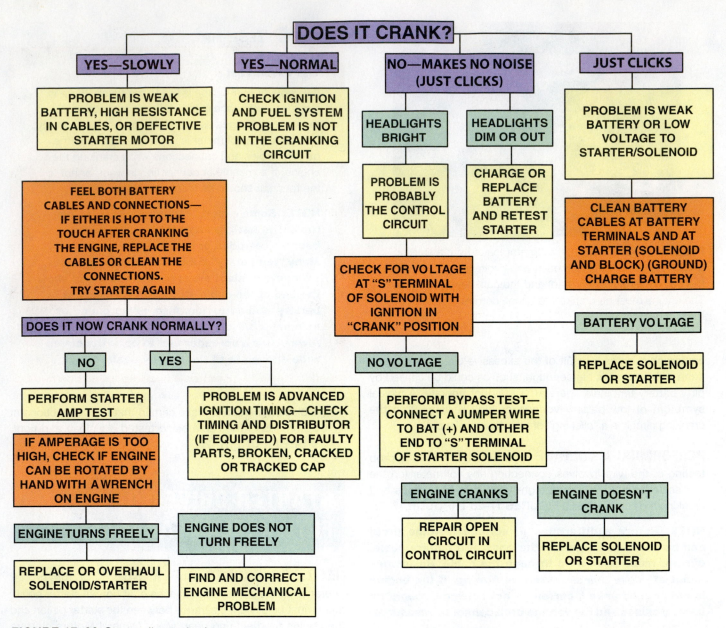

FIGURE 17–26 Starter diagnosis chart.

engine block and the starter than to leave one out and chance breaking a drive-end housing.

CHECKING FOR PROPER CLEARANCE
To be sure that the starter is shimmed correctly, use the following procedure:

STEP 1 Place the starter in position and finger-tighten the mounting bolts.

STEP 2 Use a 1/8 inch diameter drill bit (or gauge tool) and insert between the armature shaft of the starter and a tooth of the engine flywheel.

STEP 3 If the gauge tool cannot be inserted, use a full-length shim across both mounting holes, which moves the starter away from the flywheel.

STEP 4 Remove a shim or shims if the gauge tool is loose between the shaft and the tooth of the engine flywheel.

STEP 5 If no shims have been used and the fit of the gauge tool is too loose, add a half shim to the outside pad only. This moves the starter closer to the teeth of the engine flywheel.

CHARGING CIRCUIT

ALTERNATOR CONSTRUCTION
An alternator is constructed of a two-piece cast-aluminum housing. Aluminum is used because of its lightweight, nonmagnetic properties and

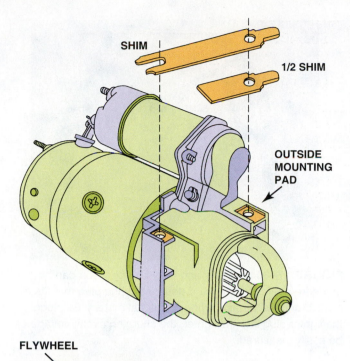

FIGURE 17–27 A shim (or half shim) may be needed to provide the proper clearance between the flywheel teeth of the engine and the pinion teeth of the starter.

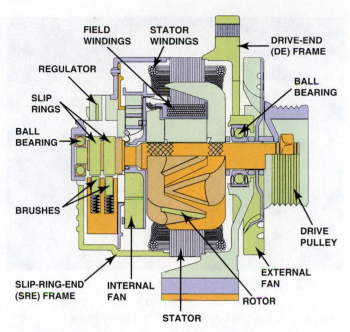

FIGURE 17–28 Cutaway view of a typical AC alternator.

heat transfer properties which are needed to help keep the alternator cool. A front ball bearing is pressed into the front housing (called the **drive-end [DE]** housing) to provide the support and friction reduction necessary for the belt-driven rotor assembly. The rear housing (called the **slip-ring-end [SRE]**) usually contains a roller-bearing support for the rotor and mounting for the brushes, diodes, and internal voltage regulator (if the alternator is so equipped). ● **SEE FIGURE 17–28.**

FREQUENTLY ASKED QUESTION

How Many Horsepower Does an Alternator Require to Operate?

Many technicians are asked how much power certain accessories require. A 100 A alternator requires about 2 hp from the engine, and 1 hp is equal to 746 watts (W). Watts are calculated by multiplying amperes times volts.

$$\text{Power in W} = 100\ A \times 14.5\ V$$
$$= 1{,}450\ W$$
$$1\ hp = 746\ W$$

Therefore, 1,450 W is about 2 hp.

Allowing about 20% for mechanical and electrical losses adds another 0.4 hp. Therefore, when anyone asks how much power it takes to produce 100 A from an alternator, the answer is about 2.4 hp.

TECH TIP

The Dead Rat Smell Test

When checking for the root cause of an alternator failure, the wise technician should sniff (smell) the alternator! If the alternator smells like a dead rat (rancid), the stator windings have been overheated by trying to charge a discharged or defective battery. If the battery voltage is continuously low, the voltage regulator will continue supplying full-field current to the alternator. The voltage regulator is designed to cycle on and off to maintain a narrow charging system voltage range.

If the battery voltage is continually below the cutoff point of the voltage regulator, the alternator is continually producing current in the stator windings. This constant charging can often overheat the stator and burn the insulating varnish covering the stator windings. If the alternator fails the sniff test, the technician should replace the alternator *and* replace or recharge and test the battery.

FIGURE 17–29 The digital multimeter should be set to read DC volts and the red lead connected to the battery positive (+) terminal and the black meter lead connected to the negative (−) battery terminal.

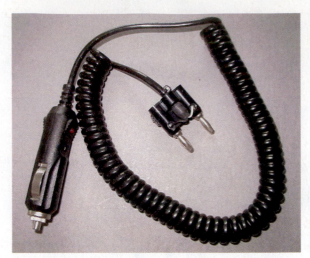

FIGURE 17–30 A simple and easy-to-use tester can be made from a lighter plug and double banana plug that fits the "COM" and "V" terminals of most digital meters. By plugging the lighter plug into the lighter, the charging circuit voltage can be easily measured.

CHECKING CHARGING SYSTEM VOLTAGE

DIGITAL MULTIMETER CONNECTIONS The charge indicator light on the dash should be on with the ignition on, engine off (KOEO), but should be off when the engine is running (KOER). If the charge light remains on with the engine running, check the charging system voltage. To measure charging system voltage, connect the test leads of a digital multimeter to the positive (+) and negative (−) terminals of the battery. Set the multimeter to read DC volts.

CHARGING SYSTEM VOLTAGE SPECIFICATIONS Most alternators are designed to supply between 13.5 and 15 volts at 2000 engine RPM. Be sure to check the vehicle manufacturer's specifications. For example, most General Motors Corporation vehicles specify a charging voltage of 14.7 volts ± 0.5 (or between 14.2 and 15.2 volts) at 2000 RPM and no load.

CHARGING SYSTEM VOLTAGE TEST PROCEDURE Charging system voltage tests should be performed on a vehicle with a battery at least 75% charged. If the battery is discharged (or defective), the charging voltage may be below specifications. To measure charging system voltage, follow these steps.

1. Connect the voltmeter as shown in ● **FIGURE 17–29.**
2. Set the meter to read DC volts.
3. Start the engine and raise to a fast idle (about 2000 RPM).

TECH TIP

The Lighter Plug Trick
Battery voltage measurements can be read through the lighter socket. ● **SEE FIGURE 17–30.** Simply construct a test tool using a lighter plug at one end of a length of two-conductor wire and the other end connected to a double banana plug. The double banana plug will fit most meters in the common (COM) terminal and the volt terminal of the meter.

4. Read the voltmeter and compare with specifications. If lower than specifications, charge the battery and test for excessive charging circuit voltage drop and for a possible open in the sensing wire before replacing the alternator.

NOTE: If the voltmeter reading rises, then becomes lower as the engine speed is increased, the alternator drive (accessory drive) belt is loose or slipping.

TESTING AN ALTERNATOR USING A SCAN TOOL

A scan tool can be used on most General Motors and Chrysler Corporation vehicles and others that have datastream information. Follow these steps:

1. Connect the scan tool according to the manufacturer's instructions.

2. Select battery voltage and engine RPM on the scan tool.

3. Start the engine and operate at 2000 RPM.

4. Observe the battery voltage. This voltage should be between 13.5 and 15 volts (or within the manufacturer's specifications).

NOTE: The scan tool voltage should be within 0.5 volt of the charging voltage as tested at the battery. If the scan tool indicates a voltage lower than actual battery voltage by more than 0.5 volt, check all power and ground connections at the computer for corrosion or defects.

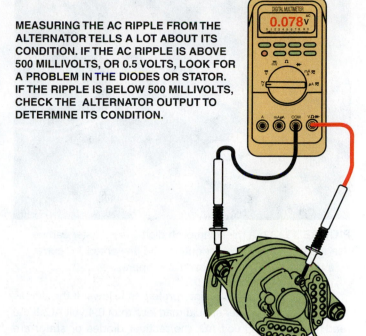

MEASURING THE AC RIPPLE FROM THE ALTERNATOR TELLS A LOT ABOUT ITS CONDITION. IF THE AC RIPPLE IS ABOVE 500 MILLIVOLTS, OR 0.5 VOLTS, LOOK FOR A PROBLEM IN THE DIODES OR STATOR. IF THE RIPPLE IS BELOW 500 MILLIVOLTS, CHECK THE ALTERNATOR OUTPUT TO DETERMINE ITS CONDITION.

FIGURE 17–31 AC ripple at the output terminal of the battery is more accurate than testing at the battery due to the resistance of the wiring between the alternator and the battery. Set the meter to read AC volts. The reading shown on the meter is only 78 millivolts (0.078 V), far below what the reading would be if a diode were defective.

🔧 TECH TIP

The Hand Cleaner Trick

Lower-than-normal alternator output could be the result of a loose or slipping drive belt. All belts (V and serpentine multigroove) use an interference angle between the angle of the V of the belt and the angle of the V on the pulley. A belt wears this interference angle off the edges of the V of the belt. As a result, the belt may start to slip and make a squealing sound even if tensioned properly.

A common trick used to determine if the noise is belt related is to use grit-type hand cleaner or scouring powder. With the engine off, sprinkle some powder onto the pulley side of the belt. Start the engine. The excess powder will fly into the air, so get away from under the hood when the engine starts. If the belts are now quieter, you know that it was the glazed belt that made the noise.

NOTE: Often, the noise sounds exactly like a noisy bearing. Therefore, before you start removing and replacing parts, try the hand cleaner trick.

The grit from the hand cleaner will often remove the glaze from the belt and the noise will not return. If the belt is worn or loose, however, the noise will return and the belt should be replaced. A fast, alternative method to check for belt noise is to spray water from a squirt bottle at the belt with the engine running. If the noise stops, the belt is the cause of the noise. The water quickly evaporates and therefore, unlike the gritty hand cleaner, water simply finds the problem—it does not provide a short-term fix.

AC RIPPLE VOLTAGE CHECK

A good alternator should produce only a small amount of AC voltage. It is the purpose of the diodes in the alternator to rectify AC voltage into DC voltage. **AC ripple voltage** is the AC part of the DC charging voltage produced by the alternator. If the AC ripple voltage is higher than 0.5 volt this can cause engine performance problems because the AC voltage can interfere with sensor signals. The procedure to check for AC voltage includes the following steps.

1. Set the digital meter to read AC volts.

2. Start the engine and operate it at 2000 RPM (fast idle).

3. Connect the voltmeter leads to the positive and negative battery terminals.

4. Turn on the headlights to provide an electrical load on the alternator.

NOTE: A higher, more accurate reading can be obtained by touching the meter lead to the output terminal of the alternator as shown in ● FIGURE 17–31.

FIGURE 17–32 A mini clamp-on digital multimeter can be used to measure alternator output and unwanted AC current by switching the meter to read DC amperes.

The results should be interpreted as follows: If the diodes are good, the voltmeter should read *less* than 0.4 volt AC. If the reading is *over* 0.5 volt AC, the rectifier diodes or stator are defective indicating that the alternator should be replaced.

NOTE: This test will *not* test for a defective diode trio, which is used in some alternators to power the field circuit internally and to turn off the dash charge light.

AC CURRENT CHECK

The amount of AC current (also called **ripple current**) in amperes flowing from the alternator to the battery can be measured using a clamp-on digital multimeter set to read AC amperes. Attach the clamp of the meter around the alternator output wire or all of the positive or negative battery cables if the output wire is not accessible. Start the engine and turn on all lights and accessories to load the alternator and read the meter display. The maximum allowable AC current (amperes) from the alternator is less than 10% of the rated output of the alternator. Because most newer alternators produce about 100 amperes DC, the maximum allowable AC amperes would be 10 amperes. If the reading is above 10 A (or 10%), this indicates that the rectifier diodes or a fault with the stator windings is present. ● **SEE FIGURE 17–32.**

CHARGING SYSTEM VOLTAGE DROP TESTING

PURPOSE OF CHARGING SYSTEM VOLTAGE DROP TESTING For the proper operation of any charging system, there must be good electrical connections between the battery positive terminal and the alternator output terminal. The alternator must also be properly grounded to the engine block.

Many vehicle manufacturers run the lead from the output terminal of the alternator to other connectors or junction blocks that are electrically connected to the positive terminal of the battery. If there is high resistance (a high voltage drop) in these connections or in the wiring itself, the battery will not be properly charged.

CHARGING SYSTEM VOLTAGE DROP TESTING PROCEDURE When there is a suspected charging system problem (with or without a charge indicator light on), simply follow these steps to measure the voltage drop of the insulated (power-side) charging circuit.

1. Start the engine and run it at a fast idle (about 2000 engine RPM).
2. Turn on the headlights to ensure an electrical load on the charging system.
3. Using any voltmeter, connect the positive test lead (usually red) to the output terminal of the alternator. Attach the negative test lead (usually black) to the positive post of the battery.

The results should be interpreted as follows:

1. If there is less than a 0.4 volt reading, then all wiring and connections are satisfactory.
2. If the voltmeter reads higher than 0.4 volt, there is excessive resistance (voltage drop) between the alternator output terminal and the positive terminal of the battery.
3. If the voltmeter reads battery voltage (or close to battery voltage), there is an open circuit between the battery and the alternator output terminal (look for a positive open fusible link).

To determine whether the alternator is correctly grounded, maintain the engine speed at 2000 RPM with the headlights on. Connect the positive voltmeter lead to the case of the alternator and the negative voltmeter lead to the negative terminal of the battery. The voltmeter should read less than 0.2 volt if the alternator is properly grounded. If the reading is over 0.2 volt, connect one end of an auxiliary ground wire to the case of the alternator and the other end to a good engine ground. ● **SEE FIGURE 17–33.**

TECH TIP

"2 to 4"

Most voltage drop specifications range between 0.2 and 0.4 volt. Generally, if the voltage loss (voltage drop) in a circuit exceeds 0.5 volt (1/2 volt), the wiring in that circuit should be repaired or replaced. During automotive testing, it is sometimes difficult to remember the exact specification for each test; therefore, the technician can simply remember "2 to 4" and that any voltage drop over that may indicate a problem.

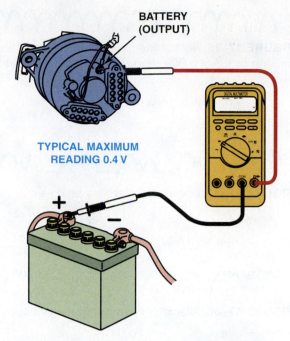

BATTERY
(OUTPUT)

TYPICAL MAXIMUM
READING 0.4 V

VOLTAGE DROP - INSULATED CHARGING CIRCUIT

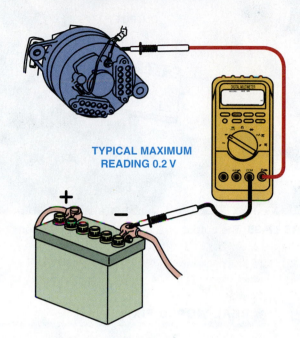

ENGINE AT 2000 RPM
CHARGING SYSTEM
LOADED TO 20 A

TYPICAL MAXIMUM
READING 0.2 V

VOLTAGE DROP - CHARGING GROUND CIRCUIT

FIGURE 17–33 Voltmeter hookup to test the voltage drop of the charging circuit.

ALTERNATOR OUTPUT TEST

A charging circuit may be able to produce correct charging circuit voltage, but not be able to produce adequate amperage output. If in doubt about charging system output, first check the condition of the alternator drive belt. With the engine off, attempt to rotate the fan of the alternator by hand. Replace tensioner or tighten drive belt if the alternator fan can be rotated by hand. ● **SEE FIGURE 17–34** for typical test equipment hookup.

The testing procedure for alternator output is as follows:

1. Connect the starting and charging test leads according to the manufacturer's instructions.

2. Turn the ignition switch on (engine off) and observe the ammeter. This is the ignition circuit current, and it should be about 2 to 8 amperes.

3. Start the engine and operate it at 2000 RPM (fast idle). Turn the load increase control slowly to obtain the highest reading on the ammeter scale while maintaining a battery voltage of at least 13 volts. Note the ampere reading.

4. Total the amperes from steps 2 and 3. Results should be within 10% (or 15 amperes) of the rated output. Rated output may be stamped on the alternator as shown in ● **FIGURE 17–35.**

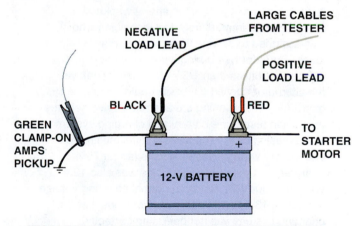

TEST LEAD CONNECTIONS FOR TESTING THE STARTING SYSTEM, CHARGING SYSTEM, VOLTAGE REGULATOR, AND DIODE STATOR.

FIGURE 17–34 Typical hookup of a starting and charging tester.

NOTE: Almost all vehicle manufacturers are now using some load response control (LRC) also called electronic load detector (ELD), in the control of the voltage output (voltage regulators) of the alternator. This means that the regulator does not react immediately to a load change, but rather slowly increases the load on the alternator to avoid engine idle problems. This gradual increase of voltage may require as long as 15 seconds. This delay has convinced some technicians that a problem exists in the alternator/regulator or computer control of the alternator.

FIGURE 17–35 The output on this alternator is printed on a label.

FIGURE 17–36 Normal alternator scope pattern. This AC ripple is on top of a DC voltage line. The ripple should be less than 0.50 V high.

FIGURE 17–37 Alternator pattern indicating a shorted diode.

FIGURE 17–38 Alternator pattern indicating an open diode.

 REAL WORLD FIX

The Two Minute Alternator Repair

A Chevrolet pickup truck was brought to a dealer for routine service. The owner stated that the battery required a jump start after a weekend of sitting. Almost immediately, the technician who was assigned to service the truck found a slightly loose alternator belt during a visual inspection. The belt felt tight (less than 1/2 inch of deflection), yet the alternator cooling fan blade could be turned by hand. After retensioning the alternator drive belt, the technician tested the battery and charging system voltage using a small handheld digital multimeter. The battery voltage was 12.4 volts (about 75% charged), but the charging voltage was also 12.4 volts at 2000 RPM. Because normal charging voltage should be 13.5 to 15 volts, it was obvious that the charging system was not operating correctly.

The technician checked the dash and found that the "charge" light was not on even though the rear bearing was not magnetized, indicating that the voltage regulator was not working. Before removing the alternator for service, the technician checked the wiring connection on the alternator. When the lead regulator connector was removed, the connector was discovered to be rusty. After the contacts were cleaned, the charging system was restored to normal operation. The technician had learned that the simple things should always be checked first before tearing into a big (or expensive) repair.

NOTE: When applying a load to the battery with a carbon pile tester during an alternator output test, do not permit the battery voltage to drop below 13 volts. Most alternators will produce their maximum output (in amperes) above 13 volts.

TESTING AN ALTERNATOR USING A SCOPE

Defective diodes and open or shorted stators can be detected on an ignition scope. Connect the scope leads as usual, *except* for the coil negative connection, which attaches to the alternator output ("BAT") terminal. With the pattern selection set to "raster" (stacked), start the engine and run to approximately 1000 RPM (slightly higher-than-normal idle speed). The scope should show an even ripple pattern reflecting the slight alternating up-and-down level of the alternator output voltage.

If the alternator is controlled by an electronic voltage regulator, the rapid on-and-off cycling of the field current can create vertical spikes evenly throughout the pattern. These spikes are normal. If the ripple pattern is jagged or uneven, a defective diode (open or shorted) or a defective stator is indicated. ● **SEE FIGURES 17–36 THROUGH 17–38.** If the alternator scope pattern does not show even ripples, the alternator should be replaced.

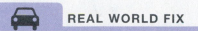

The Start/Stall/Start/Stall Problem

A Chevrolet 4-cylinder engine would stall every time it was started. The engine cranked normally and the engine started quickly. It would just stall once it had run for about 1 second. After hours of troubleshooting, it was discovered that if the "gages" fuse was removed, the engine would start and run normally. Because the alternator was powered by the "gages" fuse, the charging voltage was checked and found to be over 16 volts just before the engine stalled. Replacing the alternator fixed the problem. The computer shut down to prevent damage when the voltage exceeded 16 volts.

NOTE: A shorted throttle-body injector on a similar vehicle had the same characteristic problem. In this case, the lower resistance caused an increase in current flow (amperes) through the injector and through the computer switching transistor. To protect the transistor, the computer limited current to the injector after the engine started and the charging voltage increased to above 14 volts. As long as the alternator was disconnected, the current flow through the injector was okay and the engine ran when the alternator was disconnected.

SUMMARY

1. Batteries can be tested with a voltmeter to determine the state of charge. A battery load test loads the battery to one-half of its CCA rating. A good battery should be able to maintain above 9.6 volts for the entire 15 second test period.

2. A battery drain test should be performed if the battery runs down.

3. Proper operation of the starter motor depends on the battery being at least 75% charged and the battery cables being of the correct size (gauge) and having no more than a 0.2 volt drop.

4. Cranking system voltage drop testing includes cranking the engine, measuring the drop in voltage from the battery to the starter, and measuring the drop in voltage from the negative terminal of the battery to the engine block.

5. The cranking circuit should be tested for proper amperage draw.

6. An open in the control circuit can prevent starter motor operation.

7. Charging system testing requires that the battery be at least 75% charged to be assured of accurate test results. The charge indicator light should be on with the ignition switch on, but should go out whenever the engine is running. Normal charging voltage (at 2000 engine RPM) is 13.5 to 15 volts.

8. To check for excessive resistance in the wiring between the alternator and the battery, perform a voltage drop test.

REVIEW QUESTIONS

1. Describe the results of a voltmeter battery state-of-charge test.

2. List the steps for performing a battery load test.

3. Explain how to perform a battery drain test.

4. Explain how to perform a voltage drop test of the cranking circuit.

5. Describe how to test the voltage drop of the charging circuit.

6. Discuss how to measure the maximum amperage output of an alternator.

1. A battery high-rate discharge (load capacity) test is being performed on a 12 volt battery. Technician A says that a good battery should have a voltage reading of higher than 9.6 volts while under load at the end of the 15 second test. Technician B says that the battery should be discharged (loaded to two times its CCA rating). Which technician is correct?
   a. Technician A only
   b. Technician B only
   c. Both Technicians A and B
   d. Neither Technician A nor B

2. Normal battery drain (parasitic drain) on a vehicle with many computer and electronic circuits is _____.
   a. 20 to 30 milliamperes
   b. 2 to 3 amperes
   c. 150 to 300 milliamperes
   d. None of the above

3. When jump starting, _____.
   a. The last connection should be the positive post of the dead battery
   b. The last connection should be the engine block of the dead vehicle
   c. The alternator must be disconnected on both vehicles
   d. Both a and c

4. Technician A says that a discharged battery (lower-than-normal battery voltage) can cause solenoid clicking. Technician B says that a discharged battery or dirty (corroded) battery cables can cause solenoid clicking. Which technician is correct?
   a. Technician A only
   b. Technician B only
   c. Both Technicians A and B
   d. Neither Technician A nor B

5. Slow cranking can be caused by all of the following *except* _____.
   a. A low or discharged battery
   b. Corroded or dirty battery cables
   c. Engine mechanical problems
   d. An open neutral safety switch

6. If the starter turns slowly when engaged, a possible cause is _____.
   a. A worn or defective starter
   b. A defective solenoid
   c. A disconnected battery cable
   d. An open ignition switch

7. An acceptable charging circuit voltage on a 12 volt system is _____.
   a. 13.5 to 15 volts
   b. 12.6 to 15.6 volts
   c. 12 to 14 volts
   d. 14.9 to 16.1 volts

8. Technician A says that a voltage drop test of the charging circuit should only be performed when current is flowing through the circuit. Technician B says to connect the leads of a voltmeter to the positive and negative terminals of the battery to measure the voltage drop of the charging system. Which technician is correct?
   a. Technician A only
   b. Technician B only
   c. Both Technicians A and B
   d. Neither Technician A nor B

9. Testing the electrical system through the lighter plug using a digital meter can test _____.
   a. Charging system current
   b. Charging system voltage
   c. Cranking system current
   d. All of the above

10. The maximum acceptable AC ripple voltage is _____.
    a. 0.010 Volt (10 mV)
    b. 0.050 Volt (50 mV)
    c. 0.100 Volt (100 mV)
    d. 0.400 Volt (400 mV)

chapter 18

IGNITION SYSTEM OPERATION AND DIAGNOSIS

LEARNING OBJECTIVES: **After studying this chapter, the reader should be able to:** • Describe the purpose and function of the ignition system. • Discuss ignition switching and triggering. • Explain the purpose and function of distributor ignition systems. • Discuss waste-spark ignition systems and coil-on-plug ignition systems. • Discuss the purpose and function of knock sensors. • Explain ignition system diagnosis. • Explain spark plug construction, service, and how to conduct a spark plug wire inspection. • Explain ignition timing, and discuss the symptoms of a faulty ignition system.

KEY TERMS: Coil-on-plug (COP) system 228 • Companion cylinders 234 • Detonation 238 • Distributor ignition (DI) 228 • Electronic ignition (EI) 228 • EMI 228 • Firing order 233 • Hall effect 230 • ICM 229 • Ignition coil 228 • Ignition timing 248 • Ion-sensing ignition 238 • Iridium spark plugs 245 • Knock sensors 238 • Magnetic pulse alternator 230 • Pickup coil 230 • Ping 238 • Platinum spark plugs 245 • Primary ignition circuit 229 • Primary winding 228 • Schmitt trigger 231 • Secondary ignition circuit 229 • Secondary winding 228 • Spark knock 238 • Spark plugs 245 • Spark tester 240 • Switching 229 • Track 243 • Transistor 230 • Trigger 230 • Turns ratio 228 • Waste-spark system 228

IGNITION SYSTEM

PURPOSE AND FUNCTION The ignition system includes components and wiring necessary to create and distribute a high voltage (up to 40,000 volts or more) and send to the spark plug. A high-voltage arc occurs across the gap of a spark plug inside the combustion chamber. The spark raises the temperature of the air-fuel mixture and starts the combustion process inside the cylinder.

BACKGROUND All ignition systems apply battery voltage (close to 12 volts) to the positive side of the ignition coil(s) and pulse the negative side to ground.

- **Early ignition systems.** Before the mid-1970s, ignition systems used a mechanically opened set of contact points to make and break the electrical connection to ground. A cam lobe, located and driven by the distributor, opened the points. There was one lobe for each cylinder. The points used a rubbing block that was lubricated by applying a thin layer of grease on the cam lobe at each service interval. Each time the points opened, a spark was created in the ignition coil. The high-voltage spark then traveled to each spark plug through the distributor cap and rotor. The distributor was used twice in the creation of the spark, as follows:

  1. It was connected to the camshaft which rotated the distributor cam, causing the points to open and close.

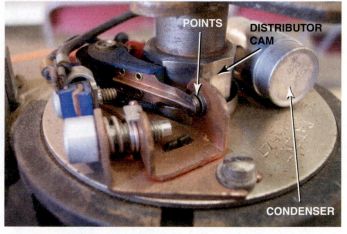

FIGURE 18–1 A point-type distributor from a hot rod being tested on a distributor machine.

  2. It used a rotor to send the high-voltage spark from the coil entering the center of the distributor cap to inserts connected to spark plug wires to each cylinder.
  ● **SEE FIGURE 18–1.**

- **Electronic ignition.** Since the mid-1970s, ignition systems have used sensors, such as a pickup coil and reluctor (trigger wheel), to trigger or signal an electronic module that switches the primary ground circuit of the ignition coil. **Distributor ignition (DI)** is the term specified by the Society of Automotive Engineers (SAE) for an ignition system that uses a distributor. **Electronic ignition (EI)** is the term specified by the SAE for an ignition system that does not use a distributor. Electronic ignition system types include:

1. **Waste-spark system**. This type of system uses one ignition coil to fire the spark plugs for two cylinders at the same time.

2. **Coil-on-plug (COP) system**. This type of system uses a single ignition coil for each cylinder with the coil placed above or near the spark plug.

IGNITION COIL CONSTRUCTION

The heart of any ignition system is the **ignition coil**. When the coil negative lead is grounded, the primary (low-voltage) circuit of the coil is complete and a magnetic field is created around the coil windings. When the circuit is opened, the magnetic field collapses and induces a high voltage in the secondary winding of the ignition coil.

The coil creates a high-voltage spark by electromagnetic induction. Many ignition coils contain two separate but electrically connected windings of copper wire. Other coils are true transformers in which the primary and secondary windings are not electrically connected. ● **SEE FIGURE 18–2.**

The center of an ignition coil contains a core of laminated soft iron (thin strips of soft iron). This core increases the magnetic strength of the coil.

- **Secondary coil winding.** Surrounding the laminated core are approximately 20,000 turns of fine wire (approximately 42 gauge). The winding is called the **secondary winding**.

- **Primary coil winding.** Surrounding the secondary windings are approximately 150 turns of heavy wire (approximately 21 gauge). The winding is called the **primary winding**. The secondary winding has about 100 times the number of turns of the primary winding, referred to as the **turns ratio** (approximately 100:1).

In older coils, these windings are surrounded with a thin metal shield and insulating paper and placed into a metal container filled with transformer oil to help cool the coil windings. Other coil designs use an air-cooled, epoxy-sealed E coil. The *E coil* is so named because the laminated, soft iron core is E shaped, with the coil wire turns wrapped around the center "finger" of the E and the primary winding wrapped inside the secondary winding. ● **SEE FIGURES 18–3 AND 18–4.**

IGNITION COIL OPERATION

All ignition systems use electromagnetic induction to produce a high-voltage spark from the ignition coil. **Electromagnetic induction (EMI)** means that a current can be created in a conductor (coil winding) by a moving magnetic field. The magnetic field in an ignition coil is produced by current flowing through the primary winding of the

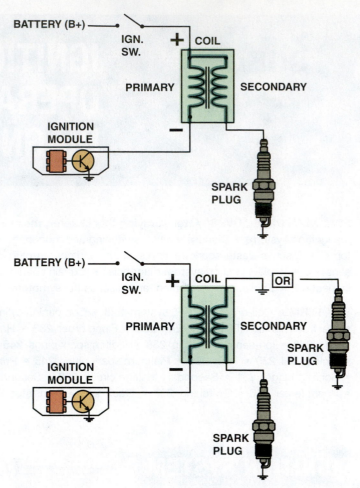

FIGURE 18–2 Some ignition coils are electrically connected, called married (top figure), whereas others use separate primary and secondary windings, called divorced (lower figure). The polarity (positive or negative) of a coil is determined by the direction in which the coil is wound.

FIGURE 18–3 The steel lamination used in an E coil helps increase the magnetic field strength, which helps the coil produce higher energy output for a more complete combustion in the cylinders.

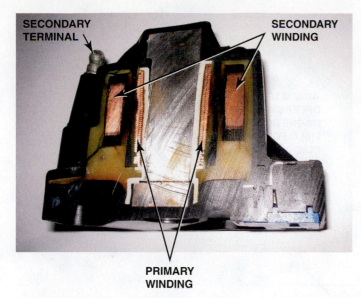

FIGURE 18–4 The primary windings are inside the secondary windings on this General Motors coil.

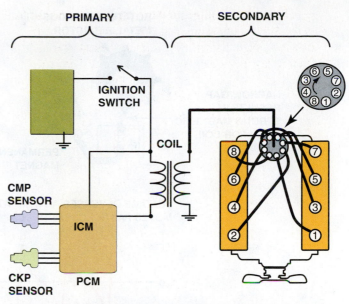

FIGURE 18–5 The primary ignition system is used to trigger and therefore create the secondary (high-voltage) spark from the ignition coil.

coil. An ignition coil is able to increase battery voltage to 40,000 volts or more in the following way.

- Battery voltage is applied to the primary winding.
- A ground is provided to the primary winding by the **ignition control module (ICM)**, igniter, or PCM.
- Current (approximately 2 to 6 amperes) flows in the primary coil creating a magnetic field.
- When the ground is opened by the ICM, the built-up magnetic field collapses.
- The movement of the collapsing magnetic field induces a voltage of 250 to 400 volts in the primary winding and 20,000 to 40,000 volts or more in the secondary winding with a current of 0.020 to 0.080 ampere.
- The high voltage created in the secondary winding is high enough to jump the air gap at the spark plug.
- The electrical arc at the spark plug ignites the air-fuel mixture in the combustion chamber of the engine.
- For each spark that occurs, the coil must be charged with a magnetic field and then discharged.

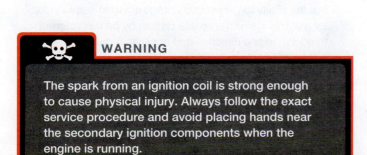

☠ **WARNING**

The spark from an ignition coil is strong enough to cause physical injury. Always follow the exact service procedure and avoid placing hands near the secondary ignition components when the engine is running.

The ignition components that regulate the current in the coil primary winding by turning it on and off are known collectively as the **primary ignition circuit**. When the primary circuit is carrying current, the secondary circuit is off. When the primary circuit is turned off, the secondary circuit has high voltage. The components necessary to create and distribute the high voltage produced in the secondary windings of the coil are called the **secondary ignition circuit**. ● SEE FIGURE 18–5.

These circuits include the following components.

- Primary ignition circuit
  1. Battery
  2. Ignition switch
  3. Primary windings of coil
  4. Pickup coil (crankshaft position sensor)
  5. Ignition module (igniter)
- Secondary ignition circuit
  1. Secondary windings of coil
  2. Distributor cap and rotor (if the vehicle is so equipped)
  3. Spark plug wires
  4. Spark plugs

IGNITION SWITCHING AND TRIGGERING

SWITCHING For any ignition system to function, the primary current must be turned on to charge the coil and off to allow the coil to discharge, creating a high-voltage spark. This turning on and off of the primary circuit is called **switching**. The unit that does the

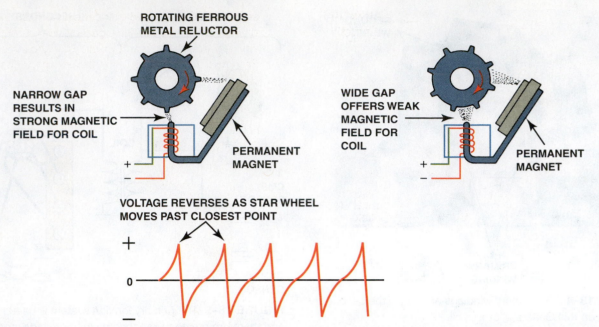

FIGURE 18–6 Operation of a typical pulse alternator (pickup coil). At the bottom is a line drawing of a typical scope pattern of the output voltage of a pickup coil. The module receives this voltage from the pickup coil and opens the ground circuit to the ignition coil when the voltage starts down from its peak (just as the reluctor teeth start moving away from the pickup coil).

switching is an electronic switch, such as a power transistor. This power transistor can be found in the following locations.

- Ignition control module (ICM) or igniter
- PCM (computer)

NOTE: On some coil-on-plug systems, the ICM is part of the ignition coil itself and is serviced as an assembly.

TRIGGERING The device that signals the switching of the coil on and off or just on in most instances is called the **trigger**. A trigger is typically a pickup coil in some distributor-type ignitions and a crankshaft position sensor (CKP) on electronic systems (waste spark and coil on plug). There are three types of devices used for triggering.

1. Magnetic sensor
2. Hall-effect switch
3. Optical sensor

PRIMARY CIRCUIT OPERATION To get a spark out of an ignition coil, the primary coil circuit must be turned on and off. The primary circuit current switching is controlled by a **transistor** (electronic switch) inside the ignition module (or igniter) and is controlled by one of several devices, including:

- **Magnetic sensor.** A simple and common ignition electronic switching device is the magnetic pulse alternator system. This is a type of magnetic sensor, often called a **magnetic pulse alternator** or **pickup coil**, and is installed in the distributor housing. The pulse alternator consists of a trigger wheel (reluctor) and a pickup coil. The pickup coil consists of an iron core wrapped with fine wire, in a coil at one end and attached to a permanent magnet at the other end. The center of the coil is called the pole piece. The pickup coil signal triggers the

transistor inside the module and is also used by the PCM for piston position information and engine speed (RPM). The reluctor is shaped so that the magnetic strength changes enough to create a usable varying signal for use by the module to trigger the coil. ● **SEE FIGURE 18–6.**

Magnetic crankshaft position sensors use the changing strength of the magnetic field surrounding a coil of wire to signal the module and computer. This signal is used by the electronics in the module and computer to determine piston position and engine speed (RPM). This sensor operates similarly to the distributor magnetic pickup coil. The crankshaft position sensor uses the strength of the magnetic field surrounding a coil of wire to signal the ICM. The rotating crankshaft has notches cut into it that trigger the magnetic position sensor, which change the strength of the magnetic field as the notches pass by the position sensor. ● **SEE FIGURE 18–7.**

- **Hall-effect switch.** This switch also uses a stationary sensor and rotating trigger wheel (shutter). Unlike the magnetic pulse alternator, the Hall-effect switch requires a small input voltage to generate an output or signal voltage. **Hall effect** has the ability to generate a voltage signal in semiconductor material (gallium arsenate crystal) by passing current through it in one direction and applying a magnetic field to it at a right angle to its surface. If the input current is held steady and the magnetic field fluctuates, an output voltage is produced that changes in proportion to field strength. Most Hall-effect switches in distributors have the following:

1. Hall element or device
2. Permanent magnet
3. Rotating ring of metal blades (shutters) similar to a trigger wheel (Another method uses a stationary sensor with a rotating magnet.) ● **SEE FIGURE 18–8.**

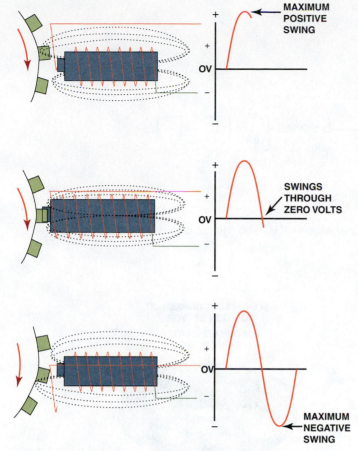

MAXIMUM
POSITIVE
SWING

OV

+

−

+

OV

+

−
SWINGS
THROUGH
ZERO VOLTS

+

OV

+

−

MAXIMUM
NEGATIVE
SWING

FIGURE 18–7 A magnetic sensor uses a permanent magnet surrounded by a coil of wire. The notches of the crankshaft (or camshaft) create a variable magnetic field strength around the coil. When a metallic section is close to the sensor, the magnetic field is stronger because metal is a better conductor of magnetic lines of force than air.

Some blades are designed to hang down, typically found in Bosch and Chrysler systems, while others may be on a separate ring on the distributor shaft, typically found in General Motors and Ford Hall-effect distributors.

▪ When the shutter blade enters the gap between the magnet and the Hall element, it creates a magnetic shunt that changes the field strength through the Hall element.

▪ This analog signal is sent to a **Schmitt trigger** inside the sensor itself, which converts the analog signal into a digital signal. A digital (on or off) voltage signal is created at a varying frequency to the ignition module or onboard computer.
● **SEE FIGURE 18–9.**

▪ **Optical sensors.** These use light from an LED and a phototransistor to signal the computer. An interrupter disc between the LED and the phototransistor has slits that allow the light from the LED to trigger the phototransistor on the other side of the disc. Most optical

sensors (usually located inside the distributor) use two rows of slits to provide individual cylinder recognition (low resolution) and precise distributor angle recognition (high resolution) signals that are used for cylinder misfire detection. ● **SEE FIGURE 18–10.**

🔧 **TECH TIP**

Optical Distributors Do Not Like Light

Optical distributors use the light emitted from LEDs to trigger phototransistors. Most optical distributors use a shield between the distributor rotor and the optical interrupter ring. Sparks jump the gap from the rotor tip to the distributor cap inserts. This shield blocks the light from the electrical arc from interfering with the detection of the light from the LEDs.

If this shield is not replaced during service, the light signals are reduced and the engine may not operate correctly. ● **SEE FIGURE 18–11.**

This can be difficult to detect because nothing looks wrong during a visual inspection. Remember that all optical distributors must be shielded between the rotor and the interrupter ring.

🔧 **TECH TIP**

The Tachometer Trick

When diagnosing a no-start or intermediate missing condition, check the operation of the tachometer. If the tachometer does not indicate engine speed (no-start condition) or drops toward zero (engine missing), then the problem is due to a defect in the *primary* ignition circuit. The tachometer gets its signal from the pulsing of the primary winding of the ignition coil. The following components in the primary circuit could cause the tachometer to not work when the engine is cranking.

• Pickup coil
• Crankshaft position sensor
• Ignition module (igniter)
• Coil primary wiring

If the vehicle is not equipped with a tachometer, use a scan tool to look at engine RPM. The results are as follows:

• No or an unstable engine RPM reading means the problem is in the primary ignition circuit.
• A steady engine RPM reading means the problem is in the secondary ignition circuit or is a fuel-related problem.

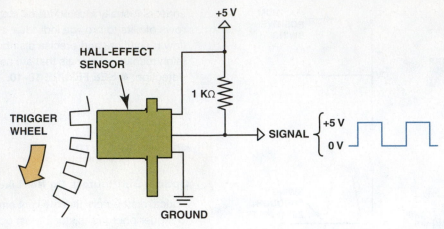

FIGURE 18–8 A Hall-effect sensor produces an on-off voltage signal whether it is used with a blade or a notched wheel.

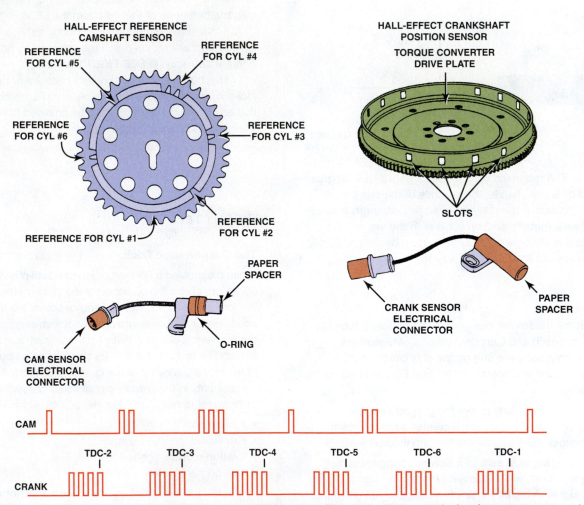

FIGURE 18–9 Some Hall-effect sensors look like magnetic sensors. This Hall-effect camshaft reference sensor and crankshaft position sensor have an electronic circuit built in that creates a 0 to 5 volt signal as shown at the bottom. These Hall-effect sensors have three wires: a power supply (8 volts) from the computer (controller), a signal (0 to 5 volts), and a signal ground.

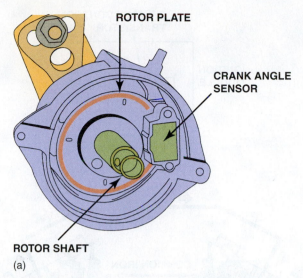

ROTOR PLATE

CRANK ANGLE SENSOR

ROTOR SHAFT

(a)

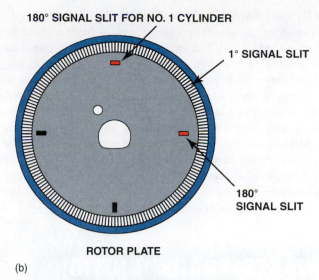

180° SIGNAL SLIT FOR NO. 1 CYLINDER

1° SIGNAL SLIT

180° SIGNAL SLIT

ROTOR PLATE

(b)

FIGURE 18–10 (a) Typical optical distributor. (b) Cylinder I slit signals the computer the piston position for cylinder I. The 1-degree slits provide accurate engine speed information to the PCM.

FIGURE 18–11 A light shield being installed before the rotor is attached.

DISTRIBUTOR IGNITION (DI)

PURPOSE AND FUNCTION The purpose of a distributor is to distribute the high-voltage spark from the output terminal of the ignition coil to the spark plugs for each cylinder. A gear or shaft drives the distributor that is connected to the camshaft and is driven at camshaft speed. Most distributor ignition systems also use a sensor to trigger the ignition control module. These triggering devices used in distributor ignition systems include:

- Magnetic pulse alternators, also called pickup coils
- Hall-effect sensors located in the distributor
- Optical sensors located in the distributor

FIGURE 18–12 The firing order is cast or stamped on the intake manifold on most engines that have a distributor ignition.

OPERATION OF DISTRIBUTOR IGNITION The distributor is used twice in most ignition systems that use a distributor.

- First, to trigger the ignition control module by the use of the rotating distributor shaft
- Second, by rotating the rotor to distribute the high-voltage spark to the individual spark plugs

FIRING ORDER **Firing order** means the order that the spark is distributed to the correct spark plug at the right time. The firing order of an engine is determined by crankshaft and camshaft design. The firing order is determined by the location of the spark plug wires in the distributor cap of an engine equipped with a distributor. The firing order is often cast into the intake manifold for easy reference. ● **SEE FIGURE 18–12.**

Service information also shows the firing order and the direction of the distributor rotor rotation, as well as the location of the spark plug wires on the distributor cap.

CAUTION: Ford V-8s use two different firing orders depending on whether the engine is high output (HO) or standard. Using the incorrect firing order can cause the engine to backfire and could cause engine damage or personal injury. General Motors V-6 engines use different firing orders and different locations for cylinder 1 between the 60-degree V-6 and the 90-degree V-6. Using the incorrect firing order or cylinder number location chart could result in poor engine operation or a no start. Firing order is also important for waste-spark-type ignition systems. The spark plug wire can often be installed on the wrong coil pack, which can create a no-start condition or poor engine operation.

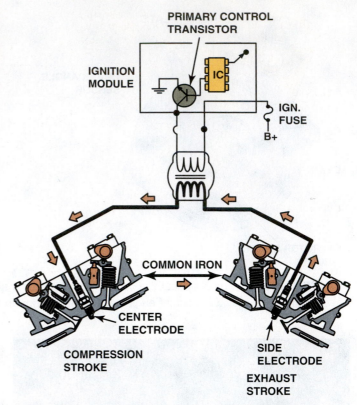

FIGURE 18–13 A waste-spark system fires one cylinder while its piston is on the compression stroke and into paired or companion cylinders while it is on the exhaust stroke. In a typical engine, it requires only about 2 to 3 kV to fire the cylinder on the exhaust stroke. The remaining coil energy is available to fire the spark plug under compression (typically about 8 to 12 kV).

WASTE-SPARK IGNITION SYSTEMS

PARTS INVOLVED Waste-spark ignition is another name for distributorless ignition system (DIS) or electronic ignition (EI). Waste-spark ignition was introduced in the mid-1980s and uses the ignition control module (ICM) and/or the powertrain control module (PCM) to fire the ignition coils. A 4-cylinder engine uses two ignition coils and a 6-cylinder engine uses three ignition coils. Each coil is a true transformer because the primary winding and secondary winding are not electrically connected. Each end of the secondary winding is connected to a cylinder exactly opposite the other in the firing order, which is called a **companion (paired) cylinder.** ● SEE FIGURE 18–13.

? **FREQUENTLY ASKED QUESTION**

How Can You Determine the Companion Cylinder?

Companion cylinders are two cylinders in the same engine that both reach top dead center (TDC) at the same time.

- One cylinder is on the compression stroke.
- The other cylinder is on the exhaust stroke.

To determine which two cylinders are companion cylinders in the engine, follow these steps.

STEP 1   Determine the firing order (such as 165432 for a typical V-6 engine).

STEP 2   Write the firing order and then place the second half under the first half.

$$\frac{165}{432}$$

STEP 3   The cylinder numbers above and below each other are companion or paired cylinders.

In this case 1 and 4, 6 and 3, and 5 and 2 are companion cylinders.

🔧 **TECH TIP**

Odds Fire Straight

Waste-spark ignition systems fire two spark plugs at the same time. Most vehicle manufacturers use a waste-spark system that fires the odd number cylinders (1, 3, and 5) by straight polarity (current flow from the top of the spark plug through the gap and to the ground electrode). The even number cylinders (2, 4, and 6) are fired reverse polarity, meaning that the spark jumps from the side electrode to the center electrode. Some vehicle manufacturers equip their vehicles with platinum plugs that have the expensive platinum alloy on only one electrode, as follows:

- On odd number cylinders (1, 3, 5), the platinum is on the center electrode.
- On even number cylinders (2, 4, 6), the platinum is on the ground electrode.

Replacement spark plugs use platinum on both electrodes (double platinum) and, therefore, can be placed in any cylinder location.

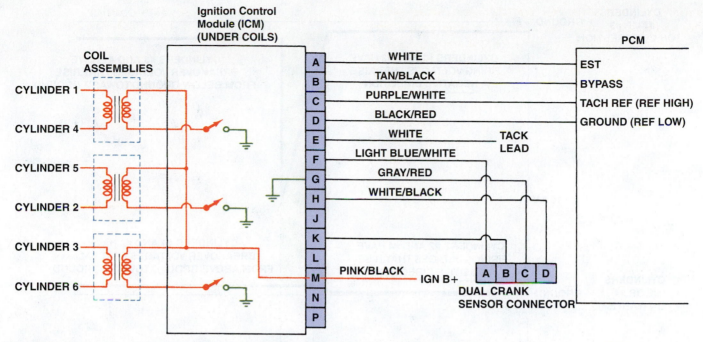

FIGURE 18–14 Typical wiring diagram of a V-6 waste-spark ignition system. The Powertrain Control Module (PCM) controls the actual firing time of the spark plugs through the "EST" circuit signal to the ignition control module (ICM).

WASTE-SPARK SYSTEM OPERATION
Both spark plugs fire at the same time (within nanoseconds of each other).

- When one cylinder (for example, cylinder number 6) is on the compression stroke, the other cylinder (number 3) is on the exhaust stroke.
- The spark that occurs on the exhaust stroke is called the *waste spark,* because it does no useful work and is only used as a ground path for the secondary winding of the ignition coil. The voltage required to jump the spark plug gap on cylinder 3 (the exhaust stroke) is only 2 to 3 kV.
- The cylinder on the compression stroke uses the remaining coil energy.
- One spark plug of each pair always fires straight polarity and the other cylinder always fires reverse polarity. Spark plug life is not greatly affected by the reverse polarity. If there is only one defective spark plug wire or spark plug, two cylinders may be affected.

The coil polarity is determined by the direction the coil is wound (left-hand rule for conventional current flow) and cannot be changed.

Each spark plug for a particular cylinder always will be fired either with straight or reversed polarity, depending on its location in the engine and how the coils are wired. However, the compression and waste-spark condition flip-flops. When one cylinder is on compression, such as cylinder 1, then the paired cylinder (number 4) is on the exhaust stroke. During the next rotation of the crankshaft, cylinder 4 is on the compression stroke and cylinder 1 is on the exhaust stroke.

Cylinder 1   Always fires straight polarity (from the center electrode to the ground electrode), one time, requiring 10 to 12 kV, and one time, requiring 3 to 4 kV.

Cylinder 4   Always fires reverse polarity (from the ground electrode to the center electrode), one time, requiring 10 to 12 kV, and one time, requiring 3 to 4 kV.

Waste-spark ignitions require a sensor (usually a crankshaft sensor) to trigger the coils at the correct time. ● **SEE FIGURE 18–14.**

The crankshaft sensor cannot be moved to adjust ignition timing, because ignition timing is not adjustable. The slight adjustment of the crankshaft sensor is designed to position the sensor exactly in the middle of the rotating metal disc for maximum clearance.

COMPRESSION-SENSING WASTE-SPARK IGNITION
Some waste-spark ignition systems, such as those used on Saturns and others, use the slight difference (about 5 microseconds) between the actual firing of the two spark plugs that are triggered by the ignition control module (ICM). It requires a higher voltage to fire a spark plug under compression than it does when the spark plug is being fired on the exhaust stroke. The electronics in the coil and the PCM can detect which of the two companion (paired) cylinders that are triggered at the same time requires the higher voltage, and therefore indicates the cylinder that is on the compression stroke. For example, a typical 4-cylinder engine equipped with a waste-spark ignition system will fire both cylinders 1 and 4. If cylinder 4 requires a higher voltage to fire, as determined by the electronics connected to the coil, then the PCM

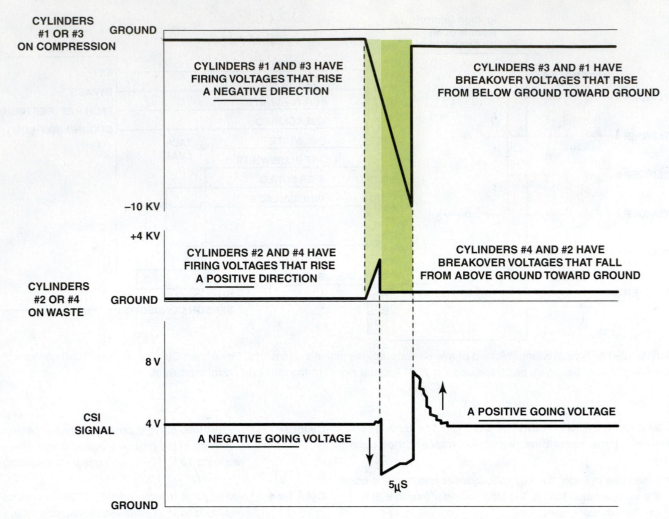

CYLINDERS #1 OR #3 ON COMPRESSION — GROUND

CYLINDERS #1 AND #3 HAVE FIRING VOLTAGES THAT RISE A NEGATIVE DIRECTION

CYLINDERS #3 AND #1 HAVE BREAKOVER VOLTAGES THAT RISE FROM BELOW GROUND TOWARD GROUND

−10 KV

+4 KV

CYLINDERS #2 AND #4 HAVE FIRING VOLTAGES THAT RISE A POSITIVE DIRECTION

CYLINDERS #4 AND #2 HAVE BREAKOVER VOLTAGES THAT FALL FROM ABOVE GROUND TOWARD GROUND

CYLINDERS #2 OR #4 ON WASTE — GROUND

8 V

CSI SIGNAL — 4 V

A NEGATIVE GOING VOLTAGE

A POSITIVE GOING VOLTAGE

5µS

GROUND

FIGURE 18–15 The slight (5 microsecond) difference in the firing of the companion cylinders is enough time to allow the PCM to determine which cylinder is firing on the compression stroke.

assumes that cylinder 4 is on the compression stroke. Engines equipped with compression-sensing ignition systems do not require the use of a camshaft position sensor to determine specific cylinder numbers. ● **SEE FIGURE 18–15.**

COIL-ON-PLUG IGNITION

TERMINOLOGY Coil-on-plug (COP) ignition uses one ignition coil for each spark plug. This system is also called *coil-by-plug, coil-near-plug,* or *coil-over-plug ignition.* ● **SEE FIGURES 18–16 AND 18–17.**

ADVANTAGES The coil-on-plug system eliminates the spark plug wires that are often the source of electromagnetic interference (EMI) that can cause problems to some computer signals. The vehicle computer controls the timing of the spark. Ignition timing also can be changed (retarded or advanced) on a cylinder-by-cylinder basis for maximum performance and to respond to knock sensor signals.

TYPES OF COP SYSTEMS There are two basic types of coil-on-plug ignition systems.

- **Two primary wires.** This design uses the vehicle computer to control the firing of the ignition coil. The two wires include the ignition voltage feed and the pulse ground wire, which is controlled by the computer. The ignition control module is located in the PCM, which handles all ignition timing and coil on-time control.

- **Three primary wires.** This design includes an ignition module at each coil. The three wires include:
  - Ignition voltage
  - Ground
  - Pulse from the computer to the built-in ignition module
  Vehicles use a variety of coil-on-plug-type ignition systems, including:

- Many General Motors V-8 engines use a coil-near- plug system with individual coils and modules for each individual cylinder that are placed on the valve covers. Short secondary ignition spark plug wires are used to connect the output terminal of the ignition coil to the

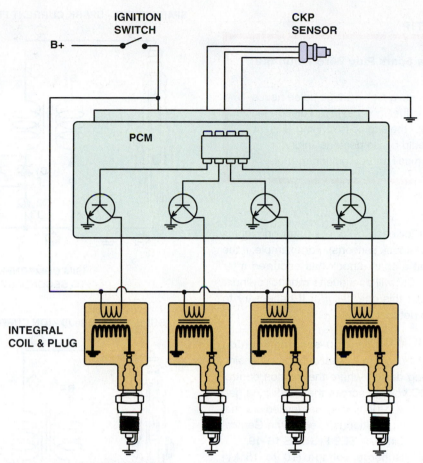

FIGURE 18–16 A typical coil-on-plug ignition system showing the triggering and the switching being performed by the PCM from input from the crankshaft position sensor.

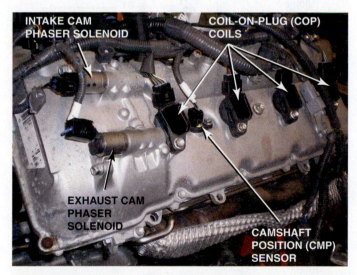

FIGURE 18–17 An overhead camshaft engine equipped with variable valve timing on both the intake and exhaust camshafts and coil-on-plug ignition.

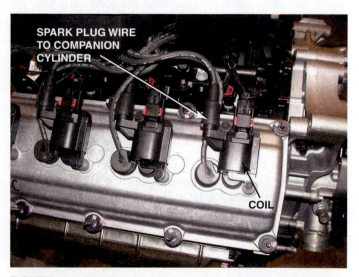

FIGURE 18–18 A Chrysler Hemi V-8 that has two spark plugs per cylinder. The coil on top of one spark fires that plug plus, through a spark plug wire, fires a plug in the companion cylinder.

spark plug; and therefore this system is called a *coil-near-plug* system.

■ In a combination of coil-on-plug and waste-spark systems, the systems fire a spark plug attached to the coil plus use a spark plug wire attached to the other secondary terminal

of the coil to fire another spark plug of the companion cylinder. This type of system is used in some Chrysler Hemi V-8 and Toyota V-6 engines. ● **SEE FIGURE 18–18.**

Most new engines use coil-over-plug-type ignition systems. Each coil is controlled by the PCM, which can vary the

ignition timing separately for each cylinder based on signals the PCM receives from the knock sensor(s). For example, if the knock sensor detects that a spark knock has occurred after firing cylinder 3, then the PCM will continue to monitor cylinder 3 and retard timing on just this one cylinder if necessary to prevent engine-damaging detonation.

ION-SENSING IGNITION In an **ion-sensing ignition** system, the spark plug itself becomes a sensor. An ion-sensing ignition uses a coil-on-plug design where the ignition control module (ICM) applies a DC voltage across the spark plug gap *after* the ignition event to sense the ionized gases (called plasma) inside the cylinder. Ion-sensing ignition is used in the General Motors EcoTec 4-cylinder engines. ● **SEE FIGURE 18–19.**

The secondary coil discharge voltage (10 to 15 kV) is electrically isolated from the ion-sensing circuit. The combustion flame is ionized and will conduct some electricity, which can be accurately measured at the spark plug gap. The purpose of this circuit includes:

- Misfire detection (required by OBD-II regulations)
- Knock detection (eliminates the need for a knock sensor)
- Ignition timing control (to achieve the best spark timing for maximum power with lowest exhaust emissions)
- Exhaust gas recirculation (EGR) control
- Air-fuel ratio control on an individual cylinder basis

Ion-sensing ignition systems still function the same as conventional coil-on-plug designs, but the engine does not need to be equipped with a camshaft position sensor for misfire detection, or a knock sensor, because both of these faults are achieved using the electronics inside the ignition control circuits.

KNOCK SENSORS

PURPOSE AND FUNCTION **Knock sensors** are used to detect abnormal combustion, often called **ping**, **spark knock**, or **detonation**. Whenever abnormal combustion occurs, a rapid pressure increase occurs in the cylinder, creating a vibration

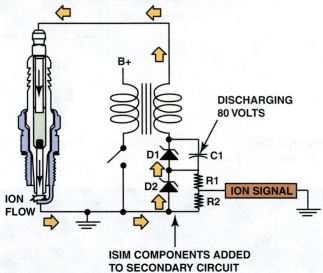

FIGURE 18–19 A DC voltage is applied across the spark plug gap after the plug fires and the circuit can determine if the correct air-fuel ratio was present in the cylinder and if knock occurred. The applied voltage for ion-sensing does not jump the spark plug gap, but determines the conductivity of the ionized gases left over from the combustion process.

in the engine block. It is this vibration that is detected by the knock sensor. The signal from the knock sensor is used by the PCM to retard the ignition timing until the knock is eliminated, thereby reducing the damaging effects of the abnormal combustion on pistons and other engine parts.

Inside the knock sensor is a piezoelectric element that is a type of crystal that produces a voltage when pressure or a vibration is applied to the unit. The knock sensor is tuned to the engine knock frequency, which is a range from 5 to

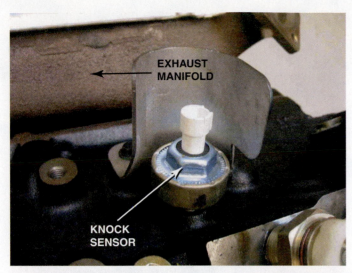

FIGURE 18–20 A typical knock sensor on the side of the block. Some are located in the "V" of a V-type engine and are not noticeable until the intake manifold has been removed.

A 50 V AC 1:1 PROBE B 200 mV OFF 1:1 PROBE
500 µS / DIV SINGLE TRIG:A⌐ -2DIV

A⌐

A

⬍ZOOM
HOLD

SINGLE FREE CAPTURE MIN MAX TRIGGER
RECURRENT RUN 10 20 DIV ON A AT 50%

FIGURE 18–21 A typical waveform from a knock sensor during a spark knock event. This signal is sent to the computer which in turn retards the ignition timing. This timing retard is accomplished by an output command from the computer to either a spark advance control unit or directly to the ignition module.

10 kHz, depending on the engine design. The voltage signal from the knock sensor is sent to the PCM. The PCM retards the ignition timing until the knocking stops. ● **SEE FIGURE 18–20.**

DIAGNOSING THE KNOCK SENSOR If a knock sensor diagnostic trouble code (DTC) is present, follow the specified testing procedure in the service information. A scan tool can be used to check the operation of the knock sensor, using the following procedure.

STEP 1 Start the engine and connect a scan tool to monitor ignition timing and/or knock sensor activity.

STEP 2 Create a simulated engine knocking sound by tapping on the engine block or cylinder head with a soft faced mallet.

STEP 3 Observe the scan tool display. The vibration from the tapping should have been interpreted by the knock sensor as a knock, resulting in a knock sensor signal and a reduction in the spark advance.

A knock sensor also can be tested using a digital storage oscilloscope. ● **SEE FIGURE 18–21.**

NOTE: Some engine computers are programmed to ignore knock sensor signals when the engine is at idle speed to avoid having the noise from a loose accessory drive belt, or other accessory, interpreted as engine knock. Always follow the vehicle manufacturer's recommended testing procedure.

REPLACING A KNOCK SENSOR If replacing a knock sensor, be sure to purchase the exact replacement needed, because they often look the same, but the frequency range can

---

🚗 **REAL WORLD FIX**

The Low Power Toyota

A technician talked about the driver of a Toyota who complained about poor performance and low fuel economy. The technician checked everything, and even replaced all secondary ignition components. Then the technician connected a scan tool and noticed that the knock sensor was commanding the timing to be retarded. Careful visual inspection revealed a "chunk" missing from the serpentine belt which caused a "noise" similar to a spark knock. Apparently the knock sensor was "hearing" the accessory drive belt noise and kept retarding the ignition timing. After replacing the accessory drive belt, a test drive confirmed that normal engine power was restored.

Other items that can fool the knock sensor to retard the ignition timing include:
- Loose valve lifter adjustment
- Engine knocks
- Loose accessory brackets such as air-conditioning compressor, power steering pumps, or alternator

vary according to engine design and location on the engine. Always tighten the knock sensor using a torque wrench and tighten to the specified torque to avoid causing damage to the piezoelectric element inside the sensor.

FIGURE 18–22 A spark tester looks like a regular spark plug with an alligator clip attached to the shell. This tester has a specified gap that requires at least 25,000 volts (25 kV) to fire.

FIGURE 18–23 A close-up showing the recessed center electrode on a spark tester. It is recessed 3/8 inch into the shell and the spark must then jump another 3/8 inch to the shell for a total gap of 3/4 inch.

IGNITION SYSTEM DIAGNOSIS

CHECKING FOR SPARK In the event of a no-start condition, the first step should be to check for secondary voltage out of the ignition coil or to the spark plugs. If the engine is equipped with a separate ignition coil, remove the coil wire from the center of the distributor cap, install a **spark tester**, and crank the engine. See the Tech Tip, "Always Use a Spark Tester." A good coil and ignition system should produce a blue spark at the spark tester. ● **SEE FIGURES 18–22 AND 18–23.**

If the ignition system being tested does not have a separate ignition coil, disconnect any spark plug wire from a spark plug and, while cranking the engine, test for spark available at the spark plug wire, again using a spark tester.

NOTE: An intermittent spark should be considered a no-spark condition.

Typical causes of a no-spark (intermittent spark) condition include the following:

1. Weak ignition coil
2. Low or no voltage to the primary (positive) side of the coil
3. High resistances, open coil wire, or spark plug wire
4. Negative side of the coil not being pulsed by the ignition module
5. Defective pickup coil or crankshaft position sensor
6. Defective ignition control module (ICM)
7. Defective main relay (can be labeled Main, EFI, ASD on Chrysler products; EEC on Ford vehicle relays)

The triggering sensor has to work to create a spark from the ignition coil(s). If there is a no-spark condition, check for triggering by using a scan tool and check for engine RPM while cranking the engine.

- If the engine speed (RPM) shows zero or almost zero while cranking, the most likely cause is a defective triggering sensor or sensor circuit fault.
- If the engine speed (RPM) is shown on the scan tool while cranking the engine, then the triggering sensor is working (in most cases).

Check service information for the exact procedure to follow for testing triggering sensors.

IGNITION COIL TESTING USING AN OHMMETER If an ignition coil is suspected of being defective, a simple ohmmeter check can be performed to test the resistance of the primary and secondary windings inside the coil. For accurate resistance measurements, the wiring to the coil should be removed before testing. To test the primary coil winding resistance, take the following steps. ● **SEE FIGURE 18–24.**

STEP 1 Set the meter to read low ohms.

STEP 2 Measure the resistance between the positive terminal and the negative terminal of the ignition coil. Most coils will give a reading between less than 1 and 3 ohms. Check the manufacturer's specifications for the exact resistance values.

To test the secondary coil winding resistance, follow these steps.

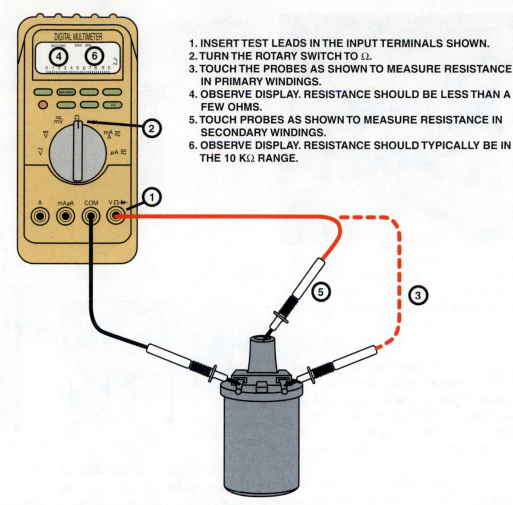

1. INSERT TEST LEADS IN THE INPUT TERMINALS SHOWN.
2. TURN THE ROTARY SWITCH TO Ω.
3. TOUCH THE PROBES AS SHOWN TO MEASURE RESISTANCE IN PRIMARY WINDINGS.
4. OBSERVE DISPLAY. RESISTANCE SHOULD BE LESS THAN A FEW OHMS.
5. TOUCH PROBES AS SHOWN TO MEASURE RESISTANCE IN SECONDARY WINDINGS.
6. OBSERVE DISPLAY. RESISTANCE SHOULD TYPICALLY BE IN THE 10 KΩ RANGE.

FIGURE 18–24 Checking an ignition coil using a multimeter set to read ohms.

TECH TIP

Always Use a Spark Tester

A spark tester looks like a spark plug except it has a recessed center electrode and no side electrode. The tester commonly has an alligator clip attached to the shell so that it can be clamped on a good ground connection on the engine. A good ignition system should be able to cause a spark to jump this wide gap at atmospheric pressure. Without a spark tester, a technician might assume that the ignition system is okay, because it can spark across a normal, grounded spark plug. The voltage required to fire a standard spark plug when it is out of the engine and not under pressure is about 3,000 volts or less. An electronic ignition spark tester requires a minimum of 25,000 volts to jump the 3/4 inch gap. Therefore, never assume that the ignition system is okay because it fires a spark plug-always use a spark tester. *Remember that an intermittent spark across a spark tester should be interpreted as a no-spark condition.*

STEP 1 Set the meter to read kilohms (kO).

STEP 2 Measure the resistance between either the primary terminal and the secondary coil tower or between the secondary towers. The normal resistance of most coils ranges between 6,000 and 30,000 ohms. Check the manufacturer's specifications for the exact resistance values.

MAGNETIC SENSOR TESTING The pickup coil, located under the distributor cap on many electronic ignition engines, can cause a no-spark condition if defective. The pickup coil must generate an AC voltage pulse to the ignition module so that the module can pulse the ignition coil.

A pickup coil contains a coil of wire, and the resistance of this coil should be within the range specified by the manufacturer.

Some common tests for pickup coils and magnetic crankshaft position sensors include:

- **Resistance.** Usually between 150 and 1,500 ohms, but check service information for the exact specifications.
  ● **SEE FIGURE 18–25.**
- **Coil shorted to ground.** Check that the coil windings are insulated from ground by checking for continuity

FIGURE 18–25 Measuring the resistance of an HEI pickup coil using a digital multimeter set to the ohms position. The reading on the face of the meter is 0.796 kΩ or 796 ohms in the middle of the 500 to 1,500 ohm specifications.

using an ohmmeter. With one ohmmeter lead attached to ground, touch the other lead of the ohmmeter to the pickup coil terminal. The ohmmeter should read OL (over limit) with the ohmmeter set on the high scale. If the pickup coil resistance is not within the specified range or if it has continuity to ground, replace the pickup coil assembly.

- **AC voltage output.** The pickup coil also can be tested for proper voltage output. During cranking, most pickup coils should produce a minimum of 0.25 volt AC.

TESTING HALL-EFFECT SENSORS As with any other sensor, the output of the Hall-effect sensor should be tested first. Using a digital voltmeter, check for:

- Power and ground to the sensor
- Changing voltage (pulsed on and off or digital DC voltage) when the engine is being cranked
- Waveform, using an oscilloscope ● **SEE FIGURE 18–26.**

TESTING OPTICAL SENSORS Optical sensors will not operate if they are dirty or covered in oil. Perform a thorough visual inspection and look for an oil leak that could cause dirty oil to get on the LED or phototransistor. Also be sure that the light shield is securely fastened and that the seal is lightproof. An optical sensor also can be checked using an oscilloscope. ● **SEE FIGURE 18–27.**

Because of the speed of the engine and the number of slits in the optical sensor disk, a scope is one of the only tools that can capture useful information. For example, a Nissan has 360 slits and if it is running at 2000 RPM, a signal is generated 720,000 times per minute or 12,000 times per second.

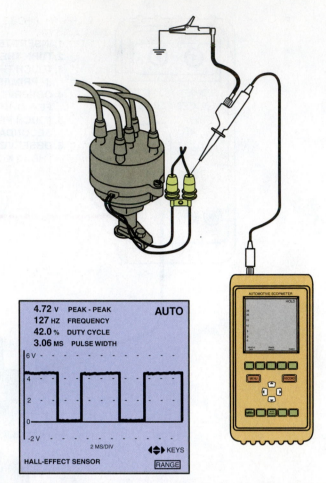

FIGURE 18–26 The connection required to test a Hall-effect sensor. A typical waveform from a Hall-effect sensor.

SPARK PLUG WIRE INSPECTION

Spark plug wires should be visually inspected for cuts or defective insulation. Faulty spark plug wire insulation can cause hard starting or no starting in rainy or damp weather conditions. When removing a spark plug wire, be sure to rotate the boot of the wire at the plug before pulling it off the spark plug. This will help prevent damaging the wire as many wires are stuck to the spark plug and are often difficult to remove.

VISUAL INSPECTION A thorough visual inspection should include a look at the following items.

- Check all spark plug wires for proper routing. All plug wires should be in the factory wiring separators and be clear of any metallic object that could damage the insulation and cause a short-to-ground fault.
- Check that all spark plug wires are securely attached to the spark plugs and to the distributor cap or ignition coil(s).

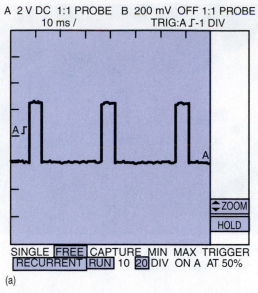

A 2 V DC 1:1 PROBE   B 200 mV OFF 1:1 PROBE
    10 ms /   TRIG:A ⌐-1 DIV

A ⌐

                                                    A

                                        ↕ZOOM
                                        HOLD

SINGLE FREE CAPTURE MIN MAX TRIGGER
RECURRENT RUN 10 20 DIV ON A AT 50%

(a)

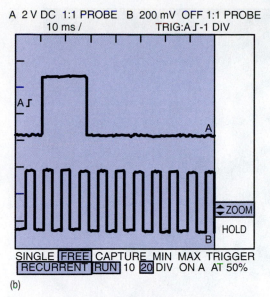

A 2 V DC 1:1 PROBE   B 200 mV OFF 1:1 PROBE
    10 ms /   TRIG:A ⌐-1 DIV

A ⌐

                                                    A

                                        ↕ZOOM
                                        HOLD
                                        B

SINGLE FREE CAPTURE MIN MAX TRIGGER
RECURRENT RUN 10 20 DIV ON A AT 50%

(b)

FIGURE 18–27 (a) The low-resolution signal has the same number of pulses as the engine has cylinders. (b) A dual-trace pattern showing both the low-resolution signal and the high-resolution signals that usually represent 1 degree of rotation.

 TECH TIP

Bad Wire? Replace the Coil!

When performing engine testing (such as a compression test), always ground the coil wire. Never allow the coil to discharge without a path to ground for the spark. High-energy ignition systems can produce 40,000 volts or more of electrical pressure. If the spark cannot spark to ground, the coil energy can (and usually does) arc inside the coil itself, creating a low-resistance path to the primary windings or the steel laminations of the coil. ● SEE FIGURE 18–28.

This low-resistance path is called a **track**, and could cause an engine misfire under load even though all of the remaining component parts of the ignition system are functioning correctly. Often these tracks do not show up on any coil test, including most scopes. Because the track is a lower resistance path to ground than normal, it requires that the ignition system be put under a load for it to be detected, and even then, the problem (engine missing) may be intermittent. If a misfire was the result of an open circuit in the secondary circuit, always replace the ignition coil.

When disabling an ignition system, perform one of the following procedures to prevent possible ignition coil damage.

1. Remove the power source wire from the ignition system to prevent any ignition operation.
2. On distributor-equipped engines, remove the secondary coil wire from the center of the distributor cap and connect a jumper wire between the disconnected coil wire and a good engine ground. This ensures that the secondary coil energy will be safely grounded and prevents high-voltage coil damage.

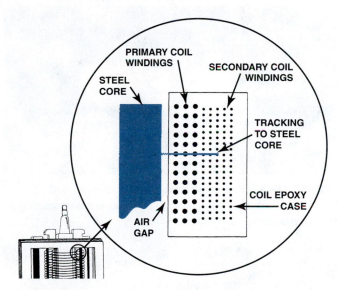

FIGURE 18–28 A track inside an ignition coil is not a short, but a low-resistance path or hole that has been burned through from the secondary wiring to the steel core.

- Check that all spark plug wires are clean and free from excessive dirt or oil. Check that all protective covers normally covering the coil and/or distributor cap are in place and not damaged.
- Carefully check the cap and distributor rotor for faults or coil secondary terminal on waste spark coils. ● SEE FIGURE 18–29.

Visually check the wires and boots for damage. ● SEE FIGURE 18–30.

Check all spark plug wires with an ohmmeter for proper resistance. Good spark plug wires should measure less than 10,000 ohms per foot of length. ● SEE FIGURE 18–31.

FIGURE 18–29 Corroded terminals on a waste-spark coil can cause misfire diagnostic trouble codes to be set.

FIGURE 18–30 This spark plug boot on an overhead camshaft engine has been arcing to the valve cover causing a misfire to occur.

FIGURE 18–31 Measuring the resistance of a spark plug wire with a multimeter set to the ohms position. The reading of 16.03 kΩ (16,030 ohms) is okay because the wire is about 2 ft long. Maximum allowable resistance for a spark plug wire this long would be 20 kΩ (20,000 ohms).

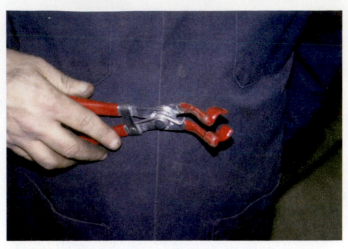

FIGURE 18–32 This spark plug wire boot pliers is a handy addition to any tool box.

TECH TIP

Spark Plug Wire Pliers Are a Good Investment

Spark plug wires are often difficult to remove. Using good-quality spark plug wire pliers, as shown in ● **FIGURE 18–32,** saves time and reduces the chance of harming the wire during removal.

TECH TIP

Route the Wires Right!

High voltage is present through spark plug wires when the engine is running. Surrounding the spark plug wires is a magnetic field that can affect other circuits or components of the vehicle. For example, if a spark plug wire is routed too closely to the signal wire from a mass airflow (MAF) sensor, the induced signal from the ignition wire could create a false MAF signal to the computer. The computer, not able to detect that the signal was false, would act on the MAF signal and command the appropriate amount of fuel based on the false MAF signal.

To prevent any problems associated with high-voltage spark plug wires, be sure to route them using all of the factory holding brackets and wiring combs. ● **SEE FIGURE 18–33.**

If the factory method is unknown, most factory service information shows the correct routing.

FIGURE 18–33 Always take the time to install spark plug wires back into the original holding brackets (wiring combs).

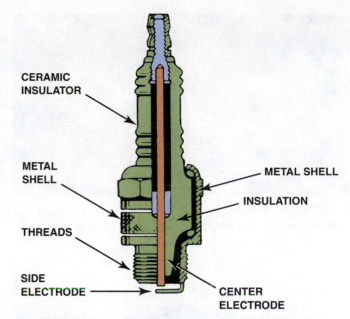

FIGURE 18–34 Parts of a spark plug.

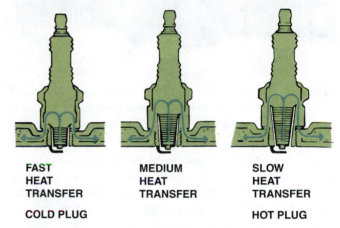

FAST HEAT TRANSFER COLD PLUG

MEDIUM HEAT TRANSFER

SLOW HEAT TRANSFER HOT PLUG

FIGURE 18–35 The heat range of a spark plug is determined by distance the heat flows from the tip to the cylinder head.

SPARK PLUGS

SPARK PLUG CONSTRUCTION Spark plugs are manufactured from ceramic insulators inside a steel shell. The threads of the shell are rolled and a seat is formed to create a gas-tight seal with the cylinder head. ● SEE FIGURE 18–34.

The physical differences in spark plugs include:

- **Reach.** This is the length of the threaded part of the plug.
- **Heat range.** This refers to how rapidly the heat created at the tip is transferred to the cylinder head. A spark plug with a long ceramic insulator path will run hotter at the tip than one that has a shorter path, because the heat must travel farther. ● SEE FIGURE 18–35.
- **Type of seat.** Some spark plugs use a gasket and others rely on a tapered seat to seal.

RESISTOR SPARK PLUGS Most spark plugs include a resistor in the center electrode, which helps to reduce electromagnetic noise or radiation from the ignition system. The closer the resistor is to the actual spark or arc, the more effective it becomes. The value of the resistor is usually between 2,500 and 7,500 ohms.

PLATINUM SPARK PLUGS Platinum spark plugs have a small amount of the precious metal platinum included on the end of the center electrode, as well as on the ground or side electrode. Platinum is a gray-white metal that does not react with oxygen and, therefore, will not erode away as can occur with conventional nickel alloy spark plug electrodes. Platinum is also used as a catalyst in catalytic converters where it is able to start a chemical reaction without itself being consumed.

IRIDIUM SPARK PLUGS Iridium is a white precious metal and is the most corrosion-resistant metal known. Most **iridium spark plugs** use a small amount of iridium welded onto the tip of a small center electrode, 0.0015 to 0.002 inch (0.4 to 0.6 mm)

in diameter. The small diameter reduces the voltage required to jump the gap between the center and the side electrode, thereby reducing possible misfires. The ground or side electrode is usually tipped with platinum to help reduce electrode gap wear.

Spark plugs should be inspected when an engine performance problem occurs and should be replaced at specified intervals to ensure proper ignition system performance.

- Nonplatinum spark plugs have a service life of over 20,000 miles (32,000 km).
- Platinum-tipped original equipment spark plugs have a typical service life of 60,000 to 100,000 miles (100,000 to 160,000 km) or longer.

Used spark plugs should *not* be cleaned and reused unless absolutely necessary. The labor required to remove and replace (R & R) spark plugs is the same whether the spark plugs are replaced or cleaned. Although cleaning spark plugs often restores proper engine operation, the service life of cleaned spark plugs is definitely shorter than that of new spark plugs.

FIGURE 18-36 When removing spark plugs, it is wise to arrange them so that they can be compared and any problem can be identified with a particular cylinder.

FIGURE 18-37 A spark plug thread chaser is a low-cost tool that hopefully will not be used often, but is necessary to use to clean the threads before new spark plugs are installed.

Platinum-tipped spark plugs should not be regapped! Using a gapping tool can break the platinum after it has been used in an engine. Check service information regarding the recommended type of spark plugs and the specified service procedures.

SPARK PLUG SERVICE When replacing spark plugs, perform the following steps.

STEP 1 Check service information. Check for the exact spark plug to use and the specified instructions and/or technical service bulletins that affect the number of plug to be used or a revised replacement procedure.

STEP 2 Allow the engine to cool before removing spark plugs. This is true especially on engines with aluminum cylinder heads.

STEP 3 Use compressed air or a brush to remove dirt from around the spark plug before removal. This step helps prevent dirt from getting into the cylinder of an engine while removing a spark.

STEP 4 Check the spark plug gap and correct as needed. Be careful not to damage the tip on the center electrode if adjusting a platinum or iridium type of spark plug.

STEP 5 Install the spark plugs by hand. After tightening by hand, use a torque wrench and tighten the spark plugs to factory specifications. ● **SEE FIGURES 18-36 AND 18-37.**

Spark plugs are the windows to the inside of the combustion chamber. A thorough visual inspection of the spark plugs often can lead to the root cause of an engine performance problem. Two indications on spark plugs and their possible root causes in engine performance include the following:

1. **Carbon fouling.** If the spark plug(s) has *dry black carbon* (soot), the usual causes include:
   - Excessive idling
   - Overly rich air-fuel mixture due to a fuel system fault
   - Weak ignition system output

2. **Oil fouling.** If the spark plug has *wet, oily* deposits with little electrode wear, oil may be getting into the combustion chamber from the following:
   - Worn or broken piston rings
   - Worn valve guides
   - Defective or missing valve stem seals

When removing spark plugs, place them in order so that they can be inspected to check for engine problems that might affect one or more cylinders. All spark plugs should be in the same condition, and the color of the center insulator should be light tan or gray. If all the spark plugs are black or dark, the engine should be checked for conditions that could cause an overly rich air-fuel mixture or possible oil burning. If only one or a few spark plugs are black, check those cylinders for proper firing (possible defective spark plug wire) or an engine condition affecting only those particular cylinders. ● **SEE FIGURES 18-38 THROUGH 18-41.**

If all spark plugs are white, check for possible overadvanced ignition timing or a vacuum leak causing a lean air-fuel mixture. If only one or a few spark plugs are white, check for a vacuum leak or injector fault affecting the air-fuel mixture only to those particular cylinders.

NOTE: The engine computer "senses" rich or lean air-fuel ratios by means of input from the oxygen sensor(s). If one cylinder is lean, the PCM may make all other cylinders richer to compensate.

Inspect all spark plugs for wear by first checking the condition of the center electrode. As a spark plug wears, the center electrode becomes rounded. If the center electrode is rounded, higher ignition system voltage is required to fire the spark plug.

When installing spark plugs, always use the correct tightening torque to ensure proper heat transfer from the spark plug shell to the cylinder head. ● **SEE CHART 18-1.**

NOTE: General Motors does not recommend the use of antiseize compound on the threads of spark plugs being installed in an aluminum cylinder head, because the spark plug will be overtightened. This excessive tightening torque places the threaded portion of the spark plug too far into the combustion chamber where carbon can accumulate and result in the spark plugs being difficult to remove. If antiseize compound is used on spark plug threads, reduce the tightening torque by 40%. Always follow the vehicle manufacturer's recommendations.

FIGURE 18–38 A normally worn spark plug that uses a tapered platinum-tipped center electrode.

FIGURE 18–40 A worn spark plug showing fuel and/or oil deposits.

FIGURE 18–39 A spark plug from an engine that had a blown head gasket. The white deposits could be from the additives in the coolant.

FIGURE 18–41 A platinum tipped spark plug that is fuel soaked indicating a fault with the fuel system or the ignition system causing the spark plug to not fire.

| SPARK PLUG TYPE | TORQUE WITH TORQUE WRENCH (LB-FT) | | TORQUE WITHOUT TORQUE WRENCH (TURNS AFTER SEATED) | |
	CAST-IRON HEAD	ALUMINUM HEAD	CAST-IRON HEAD	ALUMINUM HEAD
Gasket	26–30	18–22	1/4	1/4
14 mm	32–38	28–34	1/4	1/4
18 mm				
Tapered seat	7–15	7–15	1/16 (snug)	1/16 (snug)
14 mm	15–20	15–20	1/16 (snug)	1/16 (snug)
18 mm				

CHART 18–1

Typical spark plug installation torque.

 TECH TIP

Two-Finger Trick

To help prevent overtightening a spark plug when a torque wrench is not available, simply use two fingers on the ratchet handle. Even the strongest service technician cannot overtighten a spark plug by using two fingers.

IGNITION TIMING

PURPOSE **Ignition timing** refers to when the spark plug fires in relation to piston position. The time when the spark occurs depends on engine speed and, therefore, must be advanced (spark plugs fire sooner) as the engine rotates faster. The ignition in the cylinder takes a certain amount of time, usually 30 millisecond (30/1,000 of a second) and remains constant regardless of engine speed. Therefore, to maintain the most efficient combustion, the ignition sequence has to occur sooner as the engine speed increases. For maximum efficiency from the expanding gases inside the combustion chamber, the burning of the air-fuel mixture should end by about 10 degrees after top dead center (ATDC). If the burning of the mixture is still occurring after that point, the expanding gases do not exert much force on the piston because the gases are "chasing" the piston as it moves downward.

Therefore, to achieve the goal of having the air-fuel mixture be completely burned by the time the piston reaches 10 degrees after top dead center, the spark must be advanced (occur sooner) as the engine speed increases. This timing advance is determined and controlled by the PCM on most vehicles. ● **SEE FIGURES 18–42 AND 18–43.**

If the engine is equipped with a distributor, it may be possible to adjust the base or the initial timing. The initial timing is usually set to fire the spark plug between zero degrees (TDC)

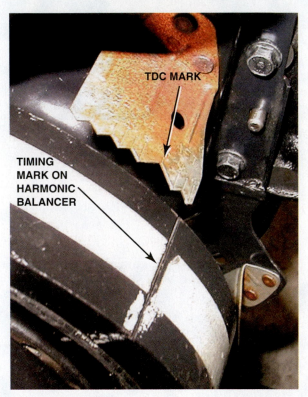

FIGURE 18–42 Ignition timing marks are found on the harmonic balancers on engines equipped with distributors that can be adjusted for timing.

or slightly before TDC (BTDC). Ignition timing changes as mechanical wear occurs to the following:

- Timing chain
- Distributor gear
- Camshaft drive gear

CHECKING IGNITION TIMING To be assured of the proper ignition timing, follow exactly the timing procedure indicated on the underhood vehicle emission control information (VECI) decal. ● **SEE FIGURE 18–44.**

NOTE: The ignition timing for waste-spark and coil-on-plug ignition systems cannot be adjusted.

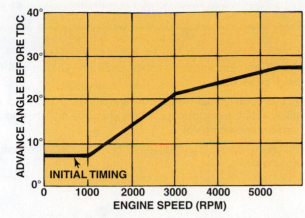

FIGURE 18-43 The initial (base) timing is where the spark plug fires at idle speed. The PCM then advances the timing based primarily on engine speed.

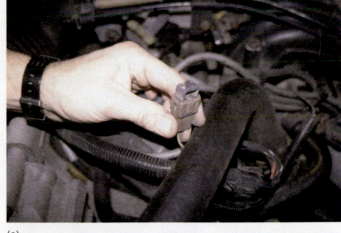

(a)

(b)

FIGURE 18-44 (a) Typical SPOUT connector as used on many Ford engines equipped with distributor ignition (DI). (b) The connector must be opened (disconnected) to check and/or adjust the ignition timing. On DIS/EDIS systems, the connector is called SPOUT/SAW (spark output/spark angle word).

 TECH TIP

Two Marks Are the Key to Success

When a distributor is removed from an engine, always mark where the rotor is pointing to ensure that the distributor is reinstalled in the correct position. Because of the helical cut on the distributor drive gear, the rotor rotates as the distributor is being removed from the engine. To help reinstall a distributor without any problems, simply make another mark where the rotor is pointing just as the distributor is lifted out of the engine. Then to reinstall, simply line up the rotor to the second mark and lower the distributor into the engine. The rotor should then line up with the original mark as a double check.

IGNITION SYSTEM SYMPTOM GUIDE

Problem	Possible Causes and/or Solutions
No spark out of the coil	• Open in the ignition switch circuit or theft deterrent system fault
	• Defective ignition control module
	• Defective triggering device (magnetic sensor, Hall-effect or optical sensor)
Weak spark out of the coil	• High-resistance coil wire or spark plug wire
	• Poor ground between the distributor or ignition control module and the engine block
Engine misfire	• Defective (open) spark plug wire
	• Worn or fouled spark plugs
	• Defective ignition control module (ICM)

1. All inductive ignition systems supply battery voltage to the positive side of the ignition coil and pulse the negative side of the coil on and off to ground to create a high-voltage spark.

2. If an ignition system uses a distributor, it is a distributor ignition (DI) system.

3. If an ignition system does not use a distributor, it is an electronic ignition (EI) system.

4. A waste-spark ignition system fires two spark plugs at the same time.

5. A coil-on-plug ignition system uses an ignition coil for each spark plug.

6. A thorough visual inspection should be performed on all ignition components when diagnosing an engine performance problem.

7. Platinum spark plugs should not be regapped after use in an engine.

REVIEW QUESTIONS

1. How can 12 volts from a battery be changed to 40,000 volts for ignition?

2. How does a magnetic sensor work?

3. How does a Hall-effect sensor work?

4. How does a waste-spark ignition system work?

5. Why should a spark tester be used to check for spark rather than a standard spark plug?

6. How do you test a pickup coil for resistance and AC voltage output?

7. What harm can occur if the engine is cranked or run with an open (defective) spark plug wire?

CHAPTER QUIZ

1. The primary (low-voltage) ignition system must be working correctly before any spark occurs from a coil. Which component is *not* in the primary ignition circuit?
   a. Spark plug wiring
   b. Ignition module (igniter)
   c. Pickup coil (pulse alternator)
   d. Ignition switch

2. The ignition module has direct control over the firing of the coil(s) of an ignition system. Which component(s) triggers (controls) the module?
   a. Pickup coil   c. Crankshaft sensor
   b. Computer   d. All of the above

3. Distributor ignition systems can be triggered by a _____.
   a. Hall-effect sensor   c. Spark sensor
   b. Magnetic sensor   d. Either a or b

4. Ignition coil primary resistance is usually _____ ohms.
   a. 6,000 to 30,000   c. Less than 1 to 3
   b. 150 to 1,500   d. Zero

5. Coil polarity is determined by the _____.
   a. Direction of rotation of the coil windings
   b. Turn ratio
   c. Direction of laminations
   d. Saturation direction

6. A compression-sensing ignition system uses a _____ type of ignition.
   a. Distributor   c. Waste spark
   b. Coil on plug   d. All of the above

7. The pulse generator _____.
   a. Fires the spark plug directly
   b. Signals the electronic control unit (module)
   c. Signals the computer that fires the spark plug directly
   d. Is used as a tachometer reference signal by the computer and has no other function

8. Two technicians are discussing coil-on-plug ignition systems. Technician A says that they can be called coil-near-plug or coil-by-plug ignition systems. Technician B says that some can use ion sensing. Which technician is correct?
   a. Technician A only
   b. Technician B only
   c. Both Technicians A and B
   d. Neither Technician A nor B

9. A waste-spark-type ignition system fires _____.
   a. Two spark plugs at the same time
   b. One spark plug with reverse polarity
   c. One spark plug with straight polarity
   d. All of the above

10. Technician A says that a defective crankshaft position sensor can cause a no-spark condition. Technician B says that a faulty ignition control module can cause a no-spark condition. Which technician is correct?
   a. Technician A only
   b. Technician B only
   c. Both Technicians A and B
   d. Neither Technician A nor B

chapter 19
EMISSION CONTROL DEVICES OPERATION AND DIAGNOSIS

LEARNING OBJECTIVES: **After studying this chapter, the reader should be able to:** • Explain exhaust gas recirculation systems. • Discuss OBD-II EGR monitoring strategies, diagnosing a defective EGR system, and EGR trouble codes. • Discuss crankcase ventilation, PCV system diagnosis, and PCV-related trouble codes. • Explain the secondary air-injection system and its diagnosis. • Explain the purpose and function of catalytic converters, their diagnosis, and guidelines to replace them. • Explain evaporative emission control system, and compare enhanced evaporative control systems and nonenhanced evaporative control systems. • Discuss the leak detection pump system and onboard refueling vapor recovery. • Discuss the diagnosis of the EVAP system and state inspection EVAP tests. • Describe evaporative system monitors and typical EVAP monitors.

KEY TERMS: Adsorption 270 • AIR 261 • Catalyst 264 • Catalytic converter 264 • Cerium 265 • Check valves 262 • Digital EGR 254 • DPFE sensor 255 • EGR 252 • EVP 254 • EVRV 256 • Fuel tank pressure (FTP) 275 • HO2S 265 • Inert 252 • Infrared thermometer (pyrometer) 267 • Leak detection pump (LDP) 273 • Light-off temperature 265 • Linear EGR 254 • LOC 265 • Mini converter 265 • Negative backpressure 253 • NOx 252 • OSC 265 • Palladium 265 • PCV 258 • PFE 254 • Platinum 265 • Positive backpressure 253 • Preconverter 265 • Pup converter 265 • Rhodium 265 • SAI 261 • Smog 251 • Smog pump 261 • Tap test 266 • Thermactor pump 261 • TWC 261 • Washcoat 264

INTRODUCTION

Most of the major advances in engines are a direct result of the need to improve fuel economy and reduce exhaust emissions. The engine changes needed to meet the latest emission standards include:

- More efficient combustion chambers
- Low friction engine components such as low tension piston rings, roller camshaft followers (rockers), and roller lifters
- More precise ignition timing with coil-on-plug ignition systems, which have the ability to change ignition timing on individual cylinders as needed to achieve the highest possible efficiency
- Closer engine tolerances to reduce unburned fuel emissions and to improve power output
- Variable valve timing systems used to increase engine power and reduce exhaust emissions

It has been said that engine changes are due to the need to reduce three things.

1. Emissions
2. Emissions
3. Emissions

SMOG

DEFINITION AND TERMINOLOGY The common term used to describe air pollution is **smog**, a word that combines two words: *smoke* and *fog*. Smog is formed in the atmosphere when sunlight combines with unburned fuel (hydrocarbon, or HC) and oxides of nitrogen (NOx) produced during the combustion process inside the cylinders of an engine. Carbon monoxide (CO) is a poisonous gas. Smog is ozone (O_3), a strong irritant to the lungs and eyes. Ozone is located two places.

1. Upper-atmospheric ozone is desirable because it blocks out harmful ultraviolet rays from the sun.
2. Ground-level ozone is considered to be unhealthy smog.

Emissions that are controlled include:

- **HC (unburned hydrocarbons).** Excessive HC emissions (unburned fuel) are controlled by the evaporative system (charcoal canister), the positive crankcase ventilation (PCV) system, the secondary air-injection (SAI) system, and the catalytic converter.
- **CO (carbon monoxide).** Excessive CO emissions are controlled by the positive crankcase ventilation (PCV) system, the secondary air-injection (SAI) system, and the catalytic converter.

FIGURE 19–1 Notice the red-brown haze which is often over many major cities. This haze is the result of oxides or nitrogen in the atmosphere.

- **NOx (oxides of nitrogen).** Excessive NOx emissions are controlled by the exhaust gas recirculation (EGR) system and the catalytic converter. An oxide of nitrogen (NO) is a colorless, tasteless, and odorless gas when it leaves the engine, but as soon as it reaches the atmosphere and mixes with more oxygen, nitrogen oxides (NO_2) are formed, which appear as red-brown emissions. ● **SEE FIGURE 19–1.**

EXHAUST GAS RECIRCULATION SYSTEMS

INTRODUCTION　　Exhaust gas recirculation (EGR) is an emission control system that lowers the amount of **nitrogen oxides (NOx)** formed during combustion. In the presence of sunlight, NOx reacts with hydrocarbons in the atmosphere to form ozone (O_3) or photochemical smog, an air pollutant.

NO$_X$ FORMATION　　Nitrogen (N_2) and oxygen (O_2) molecules are separated into individual atoms of nitrogen and oxygen during the combustion process. These molecules then bond to form NOx (NO, NO_2). When combustion flame front temperatures exceed 2,500°F (1,370°C), NOx is formed inside the cylinders which is then discharged into the atmosphere from the tailpipe.

CONTROLLING NO$_X$　　To handle the NOx generated above 2,500°F (1,370°C), the most efficient method to meet NOx emissions without significantly affecting engine performance, fuel economy, and other exhaust emissions is to use exhaust gas recirculation (EGR). The EGR system routes small quantities, usually between 6% and 10%, of exhaust gas into the intake manifold.

Here, the exhaust gas mixes with and takes the place of some of the intake charge. This leaves less room for the intake charge to enter the combustion chamber. The recirculated exhaust gas is **inert** (chemically inactive) and does not enter into the combustion process. The result is a lower peak combustion temperature. When the combustion temperature is lowered, the production of oxides of nitrogen is reduced.

The EGR system has some means of interconnecting the exhaust and intake manifolds. ● **SEE FIGURES 19–2 AND 19–3.**

The EGR valve controls the flow of exhaust gases through the interconnecting passages.

- On V-type engines, the intake manifold crossover is used as a source of exhaust gas for the EGR system. A cast passage connects the exhaust crossover to the EGR valve. The exhaust gas is sent from the EGR valve to openings in the manifold.
- On inline-type engines, an external tube is generally used to carry exhaust gas to the EGR valve. This tube is often designed to be long so that the exhaust gas is cooled before it enters the EGR valve.

EGR SYSTEM OPERATION　　Since small amounts of exhaust are all that is needed to lower peak combustion temperatures, the orifice that the exhaust passes through is small.

EGR is usually *not* required during the following conditions because the combustion temperatures are low.

- Idle speed
- When the engine is cold
- At wide-open throttle (WOT) (Not allowing EGR allows the engine to provide extra power when demanded. While the NOx formation is high during these times, the overall effect of not using EGR during wide-open throttle conditions is minor.)

The level of NOx emission changes according to engine speed, temperature, and load. EGR is not used at wide-open throttle (WOT) because it would reduce engine performance and the engine does not operate under these conditions for a long period of time.

EGR BENEFITS　　In addition to lowering NOx levels, the EGR system also helps control detonation. Detonation, also called spark knock or ping, occurs when high pressure and heat cause the air-fuel mixture to ignite. This uncontrolled combustion can severely damage the engine.

Using the EGR system allows for greater ignition timing advance and for the advance to occur sooner without detonation problems, which increases power and efficiency.

POSITIVE AND NEGATIVE BACKPRESSURE EGR VALVES　　Some vacuum-operated EGR valves used on older engines are designed with a small valve inside that

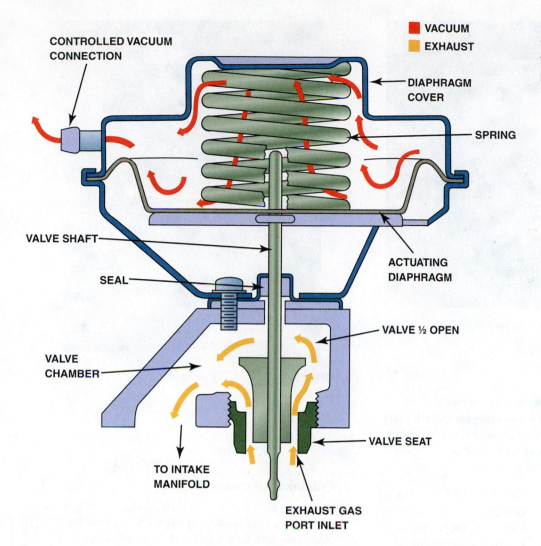

CONTROLLED VACUUM
CONNECTION

VACUUM

EXHAUST

FIGURE 19–2 When the EGR valve opens, the exhaust gases flow through the valve and into passages in the intake manifold.

DIAPHRAGM COVER

SPRING

VALVE SHAFT

ACTUATING DIAPHRAGM

SEAL

VALVE ½ OPEN

VALVE CHAMBER

VALVE SEAT

TO INTAKE MANIFOLD

EXHAUST GAS PORT INLET

EGR VALVE

EGR CONTROL SOLENOID

FIGURE 19–3 A vacuum-operated EGR valve. The vacuum to the EGR valve is computer controlled by the EGR valve control solenoid.

bleeds off any applied vacuum and prevents the valve from opening.

- **Positive backpressure.** These types of EGR valves require a positive backpressure in the exhaust system. At low engine speeds and light engine loads, the EGR system is not needed, and the backpressure in it is also low. Without sufficient backpressure, the EGR valve does not open even though vacuum may be present at the EGR valve.

- **Negative backpressure.** On each exhaust stroke, the engine emits an exhaust "pulse." Each pulse represents a positive pressure. Behind each pulse is a small area of low pressure. Some EGR valves react to this low-pressure area by closing a small internal valve, which allows the EGR valve to be opened by vacuum.

The following conditions must occur before a backpressure-type vacuum-controlled EGR will operate.

1. Vacuum must be applied to the EGR valve itself. The vacuum source can be ported vacuum (above the throttle plate) or manifold vacuum (below the throttle plate) and by the computer through a solenoid valve.

2. Exhaust backpressure must be present to close an internal valve inside the EGR to allow the vacuum to move the diaphragm.

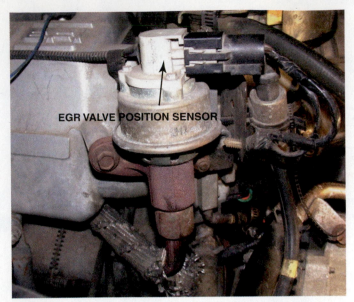

FIGURE 19–4 An EGR valve position sensor on top of an EGR valve.

THREE EGR SOLENOIDS

FIGURE 19–5 Digital EGR valve.

NOTE: **Installing a high-performance exhaust system could prevent a backpressure vacuum-operated EGR valve from opening. If this occurs, excessive combustion chamber temperature leads to severe spark knock, piston damage, or a blown head gasket.**

COMPUTER-CONTROLLED EGR SYSTEMS Many computer-controlled EGR systems have one or more solenoids controlling the EGR vacuum. The computer controls a solenoid to shut off vacuum to the EGR valve at cold engine temperatures, idle speed, and wide-open throttle operation. If two solenoids are used, one acts as an off-on control of supply vacuum, while the second solenoid vents vacuum when EGR flow is not desired or needs to be reduced. The second solenoid is used to control a vacuum air bleed, allowing atmospheric pressure in to modulate EGR flow according to vehicle operating conditions.

EGR VALVE POSITION SENSORS Most computer-controlled EGR systems use a sensor to indicate EGR operation. Onboard diagnostics generation-II (OBD-II) EGR system monitors require an EGR sensor to verify that the valve opened. A linear potentiometer on the top of the EGR valve stem indicates valve position for the computer. This is called an **EGR valve position (EVP)** sensor. Some later-model Ford EGR systems, however, use a feedback signal provided by an EGR exhaust backpressure sensor that converts the exhaust backpressure to a voltage signal. This sensor is called a **pressure feedback EGR (PFE)** sensor.

On some EGR systems, the top of the valve contains a vacuum regulator and EGR pintle-position sensor in one assembly sealed inside a nonremovable plastic cover. The pintle-position sensor provides a voltage output to the PCM, which increases as the duty cycle increases, allowing the PCM to monitor valve operation. ● SEE FIGURE 19–4.

DIGITAL EGR VALVES GM introduced a **digital EGR** valve design on some engines. Unlike vacuum-operated EGR valves, the digital EGR valve consists of three solenoids controlled by the powertrain control module (PCM). Each solenoid controls a different size orifice in the base—small, medium, and large. The PCM controls the ground circuit of each of the solenoids individually. It can produce any of seven different flow rates, using the solenoids to open the three valves in different combinations. The digital EGR valve offers precise control, and using a swivel pintle design helps prevent carbon deposit problems. ● SEE FIGURE 19–5.

LINEAR EGR Most General Motors and many other vehicles use a **linear EGR** that contains a pulse-width modulated solenoid to precisely regulate exhaust gas flow and a feedback potentiometer that signals the computer regarding the actual position of the valve. ● SEE FIGURES 19–6 AND 19–7.

FIGURE 19–6 A General Motors linear EGR valve.

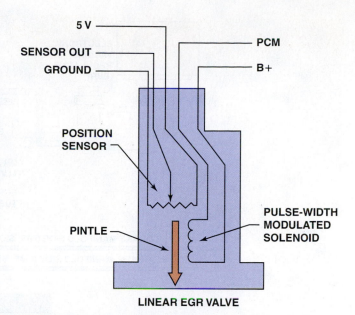

FIGURE 19–7 The EGR valve pintle is pulse-width modulated and a three-wire potentiometer provides pintle-position information back to the PCM.

OBD-II EGR MONITORING STRATEGIES

PURPOSE AND FUNCTION In 1996, the U.S. EPA began requiring OBD-II systems in all passenger cars and most light-duty trucks. These systems include emissions system monitors that alert the driver and the technician if an emissions system is malfunctioning. The OBD-II system performs this test by opening and closing the EGR valve. The PCM monitors an EGR function sensor for a change in signal voltage. If the EGR system fails, a diagnostic trouble code (DTC) is set. If the system fails two consecutive times, the malfunction indicator light (MIL) is lit.

MONITORING STRATEGIES EGR monitoring strategies include the following:

- Some vehicle manufacturers, such as Chrysler, monitor the difference in the exhaust oxygen sensor's voltage activity as the EGR valve opens and closes. Oxygen in the exhaust decreases when the EGR valve is open and increases when the EGR valve is closed. The PCM sets a DTC if the sensor signal does not change.

- Most Fords use an EGR monitor test sensor called a **delta pressure feedback EGR (DPFE) sensor**. This sensor measures the pressure differential between two sides of a metered orifice positioned just below the EGR valve's exhaust side. Pressure between the orifice and the EGR valve decreases when the EGR opens because it becomes exposed to the lower pressure in the intake. The DPFE sensor recognizes this pressure drop, compares it to the relatively higher pressure on the exhaust side of the orifice, and signals the value of the pressure difference to the PCM. ● **SEE FIGURE 19–8.**

- Many vehicle manufacturers use the manifold absolute pressure (MAP) sensor as the EGR monitor on some applications. After meeting the enable criteria (operating condition requirements), the EGR monitor is run. The PCM monitors the MAP sensor while it commands the EGR valve to open. The MAP sensor signal should change in response to the sudden change in manifold pressure or the fuel trim changes created by a change in the oxygen sensor voltage. If the signal value falls outside the acceptable value in the look-up table, a DTC sets. If the EGR fails on two consecutive trips, the PCM lights the MIL. ● **SEE FIGURE 19–9.**

DIAGNOSING A DEFECTIVE EGR SYSTEM

SYMPTOMS If the EGR valve is not opening or the flow of the exhaust gas is restricted, then the following symptoms are likely.

- Detonation (spark knock or ping) during acceleration or during cruise (steady-speed driving)
- Excessive oxides of nitrogen (NOx) exhaust emissions

If the EGR valve is stuck open or partially open, then the following symptoms are likely.

- Rough idle or frequent stalling
- Poor performance/low power, especially at low engine speed

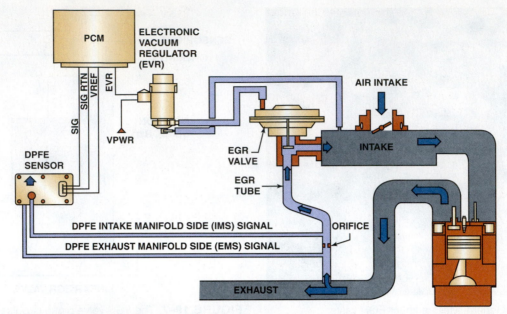

FIGURE 19–8 A DPFE sensor and related components.

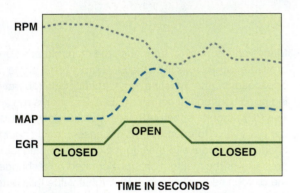

FIGURE 19–9 An OBD-II active test. The PCM opens the EGR valve and then monitors the MAP sensor and/or engine speed (RPM) to verify that it meets acceptable values.

 **TECH TIP**

Watch Out for Carbon Balls!

Exhaust gas recirculation (EGR) valves can get stuck partially open by a chunk of carbon. The EGR valve or solenoid will test as defective. When the valve (or solenoid) is removed, small chunks or balls of carbon often fall into the exhaust manifold passage. When the replacement valve is installed, the carbon balls can be drawn into the new valve again, causing the engine to idle roughly or stall.

To help prevent this problem, start the engine with the EGR valve or solenoid removed. Any balls or chunks of carbon will be blown out of the passage by the exhaust. Stop the engine and install the replacement EGR valve or solenoid.

 REAL WORLD FIX

The Blazer Story

The owner of a Chevrolet Blazer equipped with a 4.3 liter V-6 engine complained that the engine would stumble and hesitate at times. Everything seemed to be functioning correctly, except that the service technician discovered a weak vacuum going to the EGR valve at idle. This vehicle was equipped with an EGR valve-control solenoid, called an **electronic vacuum regulator valve (EVRV)** by General Motors Corporation. The computer pulses the solenoid to control the vacuum that regulates the operation of the EGR valve. The technician checked the service manual for details on how the system worked. The technician discovered that vacuum should be present at the EGR valve only when the gear selector indicates a drive gear (drive, low, reverse). Because the technician discovered the vacuum at the solenoid to be leaking, the solenoid was obviously defective and required replacement. After replacement of the solenoid (EVRV), the hesitation problem was solved.

NOTE: The technician also discovered in the service manual that blower-type exhaust hoses should not be connected to the tailpipe on any vehicle while performing an inspection of the EGR system. The vacuum created by the system could cause false EGR valve operation to occur.

EGR TESTING PROCEDURES

The first step in almost any diagnosis is to perform a thorough visual inspection. To check for proper operation of a vacuum-operated EGR valve, follow these steps.

STEP 1 **Check the vacuum diaphragm of the EGR valve to see if it can hold vacuum.** Because many EGR valves require exhaust backpressure to function correctly, the engine should be running at a fast idle during this test. Always follow the specified testing procedures.

STEP 2 **Apply vacuum from a hand-operated vacuum pump and check for proper operation.** The valve itself should move when vacuum is applied, and the engine operation should be affected. The EGR valve should be able to hold the vacuum that was applied. If the vacuum drops off, then the valve is likely to be defective.

STEP 3 **Monitor engine vacuum drop.** Connect a vacuum gauge to an intake manifold vacuum source and monitor the engine vacuum at idle (should be 17 to 21 inch Hg at sea level). Raise the speed of the engine to 2500 RPM and note the vacuum reading (should be 17 to 21 inch Hg or higher).

Activate the EGR valve using a scan tool or vacuum pump, if vacuum controlled, and observe the vacuum gauge. The results are as follows:

- The vacuum should drop 6 to 8 inch Hg.
- If the vacuum drops less than 6 to 8 inch Hg, the valve or the EGR passages are clogged.

Results

- If the EGR valve is able to hold vacuum, but the engine is not affected when the valve is opened, then the exhaust passage(s) must be checked for restriction.

TECH TIP

The Snake Trick

The EGR passages on many intake manifolds become clogged with carbon, which reduces the flow of exhaust and the amount of exhaust gases in the cylinders. This reduction can cause spark knock (detonation) and increased emissions of oxides of nitrogen (NOx) (especially important in areas with enhanced exhaust emissions testing).

To quickly and easily remove carbon from exhaust passages, cut an approximately 1 foot (30 cm) length from stranded wire, such as garage door guide wire or an old speedometer cable. Flare the end and place the end of the wire into the passage. Set your drill on reverse, turn it on, and the wire will pull its way through the passage, cleaning the carbon as it goes, just like a snake in a drain pipe. Some vehicles, such as Hondas, require that plugs be drilled out to gain access to the EGR passages, as shown in ● **FIGURE 19–10.**

FIGURE 19–10 Removing the EGR passage plugs from the intake manifold on a Honda.

See the Tech Tip, "The Snake Trick." If the EGR valve will not hold vacuum, the valve itself is likely to be defective and require replacement.

EGR-RELATED OBD-II DIAGNOSTIC TROUBLE CODES

Diagnostic Trouble Code	Description	Possible Causes
P0400	Exhaust gas recirculation flow problems	• EGR valve • EGR valve hose or electrical connection • Defective PCM
P0401	Exhaust gas recirculation flow insufficient	• EGR valve • Clogged EGR ports or passages
P0402	Exhaust gas recirculation flow excessive	• Stuck-open EGR valve • Vacuum hose(s) misrouted • Electrical wiring shorted

CRANKCASE VENTILATION

PURPOSE AND FUNCTION The problem of crankcase ventilation has existed since the beginning of the automobile, because no piston ring, new or old, can provide a perfect seal between the piston and the cylinder wall. When an engine is running, the pressure of combustion forces the piston downward. This same pressure also forces gases and unburned fuel

FIGURE 19–11 A PCV valve in a cutaway valve cover, showing the baffles that prevent liquid oil from being drawn into the intake manifold.

from the combustion chamber, past the piston rings, and into the crankcase. **Blowby** is the term used to describe when combustion gases are forced past the piston rings and into the crankcase.

These combustion by-products, particularly unburned hydrocarbons (HC) caused by blowby, must be ventilated from the crankcase. However, the crankcase cannot be vented directly to the atmosphere, because the hydrocarbon vapors add to air pollution. **Positive crankcase ventilation (PCV)** systems were developed to ventilate the crankcase and recirculate the vapors to the engine's induction system so they can be burned in the cylinders. PCV systems help reduce HC and CO emissions.

All systems use the following:

1. PCV valve, calibrated orifice, or orifice and separator
2. PCV inlet air filter plus all connecting hoses
   ● SEE FIGURE 19–11.

An oil/vapor or oil/water separator is used in some systems instead of a valve or orifice, particularly with turbocharged and fuel-injected engines. The oil/vapor separator lets oil condense and drain back into the crankcase. The oil/water separator accumulates moisture and prevents it from freezing during cold engine starts.

The air for the PCV system is drawn after the air cleaner filter, which acts as a PCV filter.

NOTE: Some older designs drew from the dirty side of the air cleaner, where a separate crankcase ventilation filter was used.

PCV VALVES The PCV valve in most systems is a one-way valve containing a spring-operated plunger that controls valve flow rate. ● SEE FIGURE 19–12.

Flow rate is established for each engine and a valve for a different engine should not be substituted. The flow rate is

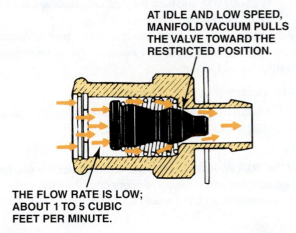

THIS END OF THE PCV VALVE IS SUBJECT TO CRANKCASE PRESSURE THAT TENDS TO CLOSE THE VALVE.

THIS END IS SUBJECT TO INTAKE MANIFOLD VACUUM THAT TENDS TO CLOSE THE VALVE.

THE SPRING FORCE OPERATES TO OPEN THE VALVE TO MANIFOLD VACUUM AND CRANKCASE PRESSURE.

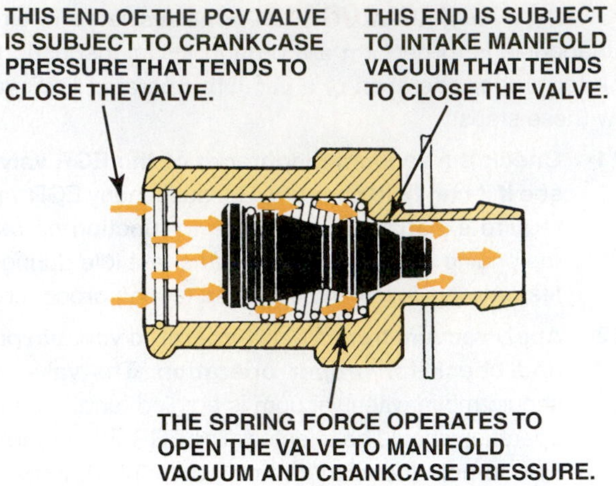

FIGURE 19–12 Spring force, crankcase pressure, and intake manifold vacuum work together to regulate the flow rate through the PCV valve.

AT IDLE AND LOW SPEED, MANIFOLD VACUUM PULLS THE VALVE TOWARD THE RESTRICTED POSITION.

THE FLOW RATE IS LOW; ABOUT 1 TO 5 CUBIC FEET PER MINUTE.

FIGURE 19–13 Air flows through the PCV valve during idle, cruising, and light-load conditions.

determined by the size of the plunger and the holes inside the valve. PCV valves usually are located in the valve cover or intake manifold.

The PCV valve regulates airflow through the crankcase under all driving conditions and speeds. When manifold vacuum is high (at idle, cruising, and light-load operation), the PCV valve restricts the airflow to maintain a balanced air-fuel ratio. ● SEE FIGURE 19–13.

It also prevents high intake manifold vacuum from pulling oil out of the crankcase and into the intake manifold. Under high speed or heavy loads, the valve opens and allows maximum airflow. ● SEE FIGURE 19–14.

If the engine backfires, the valve will close instantly to prevent a crankcase explosion. ● SEE FIGURE 19–15.

ORIFICE-CONTROLLED SYSTEMS The closed PCV system used on some 4-cylinder engines contains a calibrated orifice instead of a PCV valve. The orifice may be located in the

AT HIGHER SPEED OR IN A HEAVY LOAD CONDITION, MANIFOLD VACUUM DROPS. THE SPRING MOVES THE VALVE OPEN.

FLOW THROUGH THE VALVE INCREASES— FROM 3 TO 6 CUBIC FEET PER MINUTE.

FIGURE 19–14 Air flows through the PCV valve during acceleration and when the engine is under a heavy load.

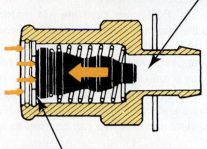

IF THE ENGINE BACKFIRES DURING CRANKING, IT CAUSES A HIGH PRESSURE IN THE INTAKE MANIFOLD.

PRESSURE CAUSES THE VALVE TO BACK-SEAT AND SEAL OFF THE INLET. THIS KEEPS THE BACKFIRE OUT OF THE CRANKCASE.

FIGURE 19–15 PCV valve operation in the event of a backfire.

valve cover or intake manifold, or in a hose connected between the valve cover, air cleaner, and intake manifold.

While most orifice flow control systems work the same as a PCV valve system, they may not use fresh air scavenging of the crankcase. Crankcase vapors are drawn into the intake manifold in calibrated amounts depending on manifold pressure and the orifice size. If vapor availability is low, as during idle, air is drawn in with the vapors. During off-idle operation, excess vapors are sent to the air cleaner.

At idle, PCV flow is controlled by a 0.05 inch (1.3 mm) orifice. As the engine moves off idle, ported vacuum pulls a spring-loaded valve off of its seat, allowing PCV flow to pass through a 0.09 inch (2.3 mm) orifice.

SEPARATOR SYSTEMS
Turbocharged and many fuel-injected engines use an oil/vapor or oil/water separator and a calibrated orifice instead of a PCV valve. In the most common applications, the air intake throttle body acts as the source for crankcase ventilation vacuum and a calibrated orifice acts as the metering device.

REAL WORLD FIX

The Whistling Engine

An older vehicle was being diagnosed for a whistling sound whenever the engine was running, especially at idle. It was finally discovered that the breather in the valve cover was plugged and caused high vacuum in the crankcase. The engine was sucking air from what was likely the rear main seal lip, making the "whistle" noise. After replacing the breather and PCV, the noise stopped.

🔧 **TECH TIP**

Check for Oil Leaks with the Engine Off

The owner of an older vehicle equipped with a V-6 engine complained to his technician that he smelled burning oil, but only *after* shutting off the engine. The technician found that the rocker cover gaskets were leaking. But why did the owner only notice the smell of hot oil when the engine was shut off? Because of the positive crankcase ventilation (PCV) system, engine vacuum tends to draw oil away from gasket surfaces. But when the engine stops, engine vacuum disappears and the oil remaining in the upper regions of the engine will tend to flow down and out through any opening. Therefore, a good technician should check an engine for oil leaks not only with the engine running but also shortly after shutdown.

PCV SYSTEM DIAGNOSIS

SYMPTOMS If the PCV valve or orifice is not clogged, intake air flows freely and the PCV system functions properly. Engine design includes the air and vapor flow as a calibrated part of the air-fuel mixture. In fact, some engines receive as much as 30% of the idle air through the PCV system. For this reason, a flow problem in the PCV system results in driveability problems.

A blocked or plugged PCV system can cause:

- Rough or unstable idle
- Excessive oil consumption
- Oil in the air filter housing
- Oil leaks due to excessive crankcase pressure

Before expensive engine repairs are attempted, check the condition of the PCV system.

PCV SYSTEM PERFORMANCE CHECK

A properly operating positive crankcase ventilation system should be able to draw vapors from the crankcase and into the intake manifold. If the pipes, hoses, and PCV valve itself are not restricted, vacuum is applied to the crankcase. A slight vacuum is created in the crankcase (usually less than 1 inch Hg if measured at the dipstick) and is also applied to other areas of the engine. Oil drainback holes provide a path for oil to drain back into the oil pan. These holes also allow crankcase vacuum to be applied under the rocker covers and in the valley area of most V-type engines. There are several methods that can be used to test a PCV system.

RATTLE TEST

The rattle test is performed by simply removing the PCV valve and shaking it in your hand.

- If the PCV valve does *not* rattle, it is definitely defective and must be replaced.
- If the PCV valve *does* rattle, it does not necessarily mean that the PCV valve is good. All PCV valves contain springs that can become weaker with age and with heating and cooling cycles. Replace any PCV valve with the *exact* replacement according to the vehicle manufacturer's recommended intervals, usually every three years or 36,000 miles (60,000 km).

REAL WORLD FIX

The Oil Burning Chevrolet Astro Van

An automotive instructor was driving a Chevrolet Astro van to Fairbanks, Alaska, in January. It was pretty cold out, somewhere around –32°F (–36°C). As he pulled into Fairbanks and stopped at a traffic light, he smelled burning oil. He thought it was the vehicle ahead of him as it was an older vehicle and did not look like it was in good condition. However, when he stopped at the hotel he still smelled burning oil. He looked under the van and discovered a large pool of oil. After checking the oil and finding very little left, he called a local shop and was told to bring it in. The technician looked over the situation and said, "You need to put some cardboard across the grill to stop the PCV valve from freezing up." Apparently the PCV valve froze, which then caused the normal blowby gases to force several quarts out the dipstick tube. After he installed the cardboard, he did not have any further problems.

CAUTION: Do not cover the radiator when driving unless under severe cold conditions and carefully watch the coolant temperature to avoid overheating the engine.

THE 3 × 5 CARD TEST

Remove the oil-fill cap (where oil is added to the engine) and start the engine.

NOTE: Use care on some overhead camshaft engines. With the engine running, oil may be sprayed from the open oil-fill opening.

Hold a 3 × 5 card over the opening (a dollar bill or any other piece of paper can be used for this test).

- If the PCV system, including the valve and hoses, is functioning correctly, the card should be held down on the oil-fill opening by the slight vacuum inside the crankcase.
- If the card will not stay, carefully inspect the PCV valve, hose(s), and manifold vacuum port for carbon buildup (restriction). Clean or replace as necessary.

NOTE: On some 4-cylinder engines, the 3 × 5 card may vibrate on the oil-fill opening when the engine is running at idle speed. This is normal because of the time intervals between intake strokes on a 4-cylinder engine.

SNAP-BACK TEST

The proper operation of the PCV valve can be checked by placing a finger over the inlet hole in the valve when the engine is running and removing the finger rapidly. Repeat several times. The valve should "snap back." If the valve does not snap back, replace the valve.

CRANKCASE VACUUM TEST

Sometimes the PCV system can be checked by testing for a weak vacuum at the oil dipstick tube using an inches-of-water manometer or gauge, as follows:

STEP 1 Remove the oil-fill cap or vent PCV opening and cover the opening.

STEP 2 Remove the oil dipstick (oil level indicator).

STEP 3 Connect a water manometer or gauge to the dipstick tube.

STEP 4 Start the engine and observe the gauge at idle and at 2500 RPM.

● **SEE FIGURE 19–16.**

The gauge should show some vacuum, especially at 2500 RPM. If not, carefully inspect the PCV system for blockages or other faults.

PCV MONITOR

Starting with 2004 and newer vehicles, all vehicle PCMs monitor the PCV system for proper operation as part of the OBD-II system. The PCV monitor will fail if the PCM detects an opening between the crankcase and the PCV valve or between the PCV valve and the intake manifold. ● **SEE FIGURE 19–17.**

FIGURE 19–16 Using a gauge that measures vacuum in units of inches of water to test the vacuum at the dipstick tube, being sure that the PCV system is capable of drawing a vacuum on the crankcase. Note that 28 inch of water equals 1 PSI, or about 2 inch of mercury (inch Hg) of vacuum.

FIGURE 19–17 Most PCV valves used on newer vehicles are secured with fasteners, which makes it more difficult to disconnect and therefore less likely to increase emissions.

RIVET HOLDING PCV VALVE RETAINER

PCV-RELATED DIAGNOSTIC TROUBLE CODE

Diagnostic Trouble Code	Description	Possible Causes
P0101	MAF or airflow circuit range problem	■ Defective PCV valve, hose/ connections, or MAF circuit fault
P0505	Idle control system problem	■ Defective PCV valve or hose/ connections

SECONDARY AIR-INJECTION SYSTEM

PURPOSE AND FUNCTION The **secondary air-injection (SAI)** system provides the air necessary for the oxidizing process either at the exhaust manifold or inside the catalytic converter.

NOTE: This system is commonly called AIR, meaning air-injection reaction. Therefore, an AIR pump does pump air.

PARTS AND OPERATION The SAI pump, also called an AIR pump, a **smog pump**, or a **thermactor pump**, is mounted at the front of the engine and can be driven by a belt from the crankshaft pulley. It pulls fresh air in through an external filter and pumps the air under slight pressure to each exhaust port through connecting hoses or a manifold. The typical SAI system includes the following components.

- A belt-driven pump with inlet air filter (older models) (● **SEE FIGURE 19–18.**)
- An electronic air pump (newer models)
- One or more air distribution manifolds and nozzles
- One or more exhaust check valves
- Connecting hoses for air distribution
- Air management valves and solenoids on all newer applications

With the introduction of NOx reduction converters (also called dual-bed, **three-way converters,** or **TWC**), the output of the SAI pump is sent to the center of the converter where the extra air can help oxidize unburned hydrocarbons (HC), carbon monoxide (CO) into water vapor (H_2O), and carbon dioxide (CO_2).

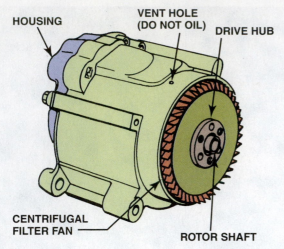

FIGURE 19–18 A typical belt-driven AIR pump. Air enters through the revolving fins behind the drive pulley. The fins act as an air filter because dirt is heavier than air and therefore the dirt is deflected off of the fins at the same time air is being drawn into the pump.

The computer controls the airflow from the pump by switching on and off various solenoid valves.

AIR DISTRIBUTION MANIFOLDS AND NOZZLES The secondary air-injection system sends air from the pump to a nozzle installed near each exhaust port in the cylinder head. This provides equal air injection for the exhaust from each cylinder and makes it available at a point in the system where exhaust gases are the hottest.

Air is delivered to the exhaust system in one of two ways.

1. An external air manifold, or manifolds, distributes the air through injection tubes with stainless steel nozzles. The nozzles are threaded into the cylinder heads or exhaust manifolds close to each exhaust valve. This method is used primarily with smaller engines.

2. An internal air manifold distributes the air to the exhaust ports near each exhaust valve through passages cast in the cylinder head or the exhaust manifold. This method is used mainly with larger engines.

EXHAUST CHECK VALVES All air-injection systems use one or more one-way check valves to protect the air pump and other components from reverse exhaust flow. A **check valve** contains a spring-type metallic disc or reed that closes under exhaust backpressure. Check valves are located between the air manifold and the switching valve(s). If exhaust pressure exceeds injection pressure, or if the air pump fails, the check valve spring closes the valve to prevent reverse exhaust flow. ● SEE FIGURE 19–19.

NOTE: These check valves commonly fail, resulting in excessive exhaust emissions (CO especially). When the check valve fails, hot exhaust can travel up to and destroy the switching valve(s) and air pump itself.

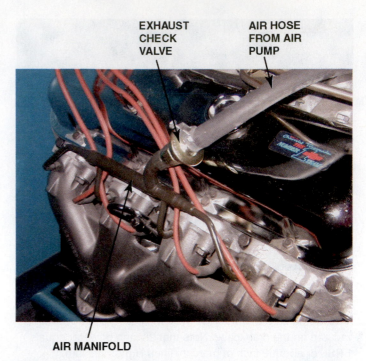

FIGURE 19–19 The external air manifold and exhaust check valve on a restored muscle car engine.

BELT-DRIVEN AIR PUMPS The belt-driven air pump uses a centrifugal filter just behind the drive pulley. As the pump rotates, underhood air is drawn into the pump and slightly compressed. The system uses either vacuum- or solenoid-controlled diverter valves to direct air to the following:

- Exhaust manifold when the engine is cold to help oxidize carbon monoxide (CO) and unburned hydrocarbons (HC) into carbon dioxide (CO_2) and water vapor (H_2O)
- Catalytic converter on many models to help provide the extra oxygen needed for the efficient conversion of CO and HC into CO_2 and H_2O
- Air cleaner during deceleration or wide-open throttle (WOT) engine operation
  ● SEE FIGURE 19–20.

ELECTRIC MOTOR-DRIVEN AIR PUMPS The electric motor-driven air pump is generally used only during cold engine operation and is computer controlled. The secondary air-injection (SAI) system helps reduce hydrocarbon (HC) and carbon monoxide (CO). It also helps to warm the three-way catalytic converters quickly on engine start-up so conversion of exhaust gases may occur sooner.

- The SAI pump solenoids are controlled by the PCM. The PCM turns on the SAI pump by providing the ground to complete the circuit which energizes the SAI pump solenoid relay. When air to the exhaust ports is desired, the PCM energizes the relay in order to turn on the solenoid and the SAI pump. ● SEE FIGURE 19–21.

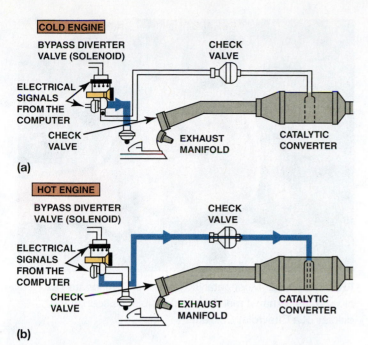

FIGURE 19–20 (a) When the engine is cold and before the oxygen sensor is hot enough to achieve closed loop, the airflow from the air pump is directed to the exhaust manifold(s) through the one-way check valves which keep the exhaust gases from entering the switching solenoids and the pump itself. (b) When the engine achieves closed loop, the air is directed to the catalytic converter.

- The PCM turns on the SAI pump during start-up any time the engine coolant temperature is above 32°F (0°C). A typical electric SAI pump operates for a maximum of four minutes, or until the system enters closed-loop operation.

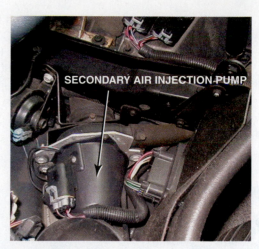

FIGURE 19–21 A typical electric motor-driven SAI pump. This unit is on a Chevrolet Corvette and only works when the engine is cold.

ENGINE OPERATION	NORMAL OPERATION OF A TYPICAL SAI SYSTEM
Cold engine (open-loop operation)	Air is diverted to the exhaust manifold(s) or cylinder head.
Warm engine (closed-loop operation)	Air is diverted to the catalytic converter.
Deceleration	Air is diverted to the air cleaner assembly.
Wide-open throttle	Air is diverted to the air cleaner assembly.

CHART 19–1

Typical SAI system operation showing the location of the airflow from the pump.

SECONDARY AIR-INJECTION SYSTEM DIAGNOSIS

SYMPTOMS The air pump system should be inspected if an exhaust emissions test failure occurs. In severe cases, the exhaust will enter the air cleaner assembly, resulting in a horribly running engine because the extra exhaust displaces the oxygen needed for proper combustion. With the engine running, check for normal operation. ● **SEE CHART 19–1.**

VISUAL INSPECTION Carefully inspect all secondary air-injection (SAI) systems, including:

- Any hoses or pipes that have holes and leak air or exhaust, which require replacement

- Check valve(s), when a pump has become inoperative
- Exhaust gases that may have gotten past the check valve and damaged the pump (Look for signs of overheated areas upstream from the check valves. In severe cases, the exhaust can enter the air cleaner assembly and destroy the air filter and greatly reduce engine power.)
- Drive belt on an engine-driven pump, for wear and proper tension (If the belt is worn or damaged, check that the AIR pump rotates.)

FOUR-GAS EXHAUST ANALYSIS An SAI system can be easily tested using an exhaust gas analyzer and the following steps.

STEP 1 Start the engine and allow it to run until normal operating temperature is achieved.

STEP 2 Connect the analyzer probe to the tailpipe and observe the exhaust readings for hydrocarbons (HC) and carbon monoxide (CO).

STEP 3 Using the appropriate pinch-off pliers, shut off the air-flow from the SAI system. Observe the HC and CO readings. If the SAI system is working correctly, the HC and CO should increase when the SAI system is shut off.

STEP 4 Record the O_2 reading with the SAI system still inoperative. Unclamp the pliers and watch the O_2 readings. If the system is functioning correctly, the O_2 level should increase by 1% to 4%.

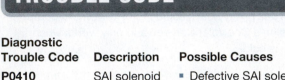

SAI-RELATED DIAGNOSTIC TROUBLE CODE

Diagnostic Trouble Code	Description	Possible Causes
P0410	SAI solenoid circuit fault	• Defective SAI solenoid • Loose or corroded electrical connections • Loose, missing, or defective rubber hose(s)

CATALYTIC CONVERTERS

PURPOSE AND FUNCTION A **catalytic converter** is an aftertreatment device used to reduce exhaust emissions outside of the engine. The catalytic converter uses a **catalyst**, which is a chemical that helps start a chemical reaction but does not enter into the chemical reaction.

- The catalyst materials on the surface of the material inside the converter help create a chemical reaction.
- The chemical reaction changes harmful exhaust emissions into nonharmful exhaust emissions.
- The converter, therefore, converts harmful exhaust gases into water vapor (H_2O) and carbon dioxide (CO_2).

This device is installed in the exhaust system between the exhaust manifold and the muffler, and usually is positioned beneath the passenger compartment. The location of the converter is important, since as much of the exhaust heat as possible must be retained for effective operation. The nearer it is to the engine, the better. ● **SEE FIGURE 19–22.**

CATALYTIC CONVERTER CONSTRUCTION Most catalytic converters are constructed of a ceramic material in a honeycomb shape with square openings for the exhaust gases.

- There are approximately 400 openings per square inch (62 openings per square centimeter) and the wall thickness is about 0.006 inch (1.5 mm).

FIGURE 19–22 Most catalytic converters are located as close to the exhaust manifold as possible, as seen in this display of a Chevrolet Corvette.

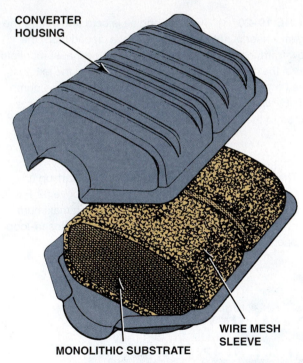

FIGURE 19–23 A typical catalytic converter with a monolithic substrate.

- The substrate is then coated with a porous aluminum material called the **washcoat**, which makes the surface rough.
- The catalytic materials are then applied on top of the washcoat. The substrate is contained within a round or oval shell made by welding together two stamped pieces of stainless steel. ● **SEE FIGURE 19–23.**

The ceramic substrate in monolithic converters is not restrictive; however, the converter can be physically broken if exposed to shock or severe jolts. Monolithic converters can be serviced only as a unit.

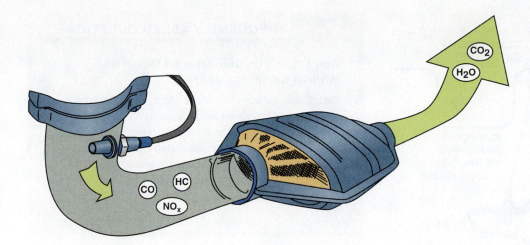

FIGURE 19–24 The three-way catalytic converter first separates the NOx into nitrogen and oxygen and then converts the HC and CO into harmless water (H_2O) and carbon dioxide (CO_2).

An exhaust pipe is connected to the manifold or header to carry gases through a catalytic converter and then to the muffler or silencer. V-type engines can use dual converters or route the exhaust into one catalytic converter by using a Y-exhaust pipe.

CATALYTIC CONVERTER OPERATION The converter substrate contains small amounts of **rhodium**, **palladium**, and **platinum**. These elements act as catalysts, which, as mentioned, start a chemical reaction without becoming part of, or being consumed in, the process. In a three-way catalytic converter (TWC), all three exhaust emissions (NOx, HC, and CO) are converted to carbon dioxide (CO_2) and water (H_2O). As the exhaust gas passes through the catalyst, oxides of nitrogen (NOx) are chemically reduced (i.e., nitrogen and oxygen are separated) in the first section of the catalytic converter. In the second section of the catalytic converter, most of the hydrocarbons and carbon monoxide remaining in the exhaust gas are oxidized to form harmless carbon dioxide (CO_2) and water vapor (H_2O). ● **SEE FIGURE 19–24.**

Since the early 1990s, many converters also contain **cerium**, an element that can store oxygen. The purpose of the cerium is to provide oxygen to the oxidation bed of the converter when the exhaust is rich and lacks enough oxygen for proper oxidation. When the exhaust is lean, the cerium absorbs the extra oxygen. For the most efficient operation, the converter should have a 14.7:1 air-fuel ratio but can use a mixture that varies slightly.

- A rich exhaust is required for reduction—stripping the oxygen (O_2) from the nitrogen in NOx.
- A lean exhaust is required to provide the oxygen necessary to oxidize HC and CO (combining oxygen with HC and CO to form H_2O and CO_2).

If the catalytic converter is not functioning correctly, check that the air-fuel mixture being supplied to the engine is correct and that the ignition system is free of defects.

CONVERTER LIGHT-OFF TEMPERATURE The catalytic converter does not work when cold, and it must be heated to its **light-off temperature** of close to 500°F

(260°C) before it starts working at 50% effectiveness. When fully effective, the converter reaches a temperature range of 900°F to 1,600°F (482°C to 871°C). In spite of the intense heat, however, catalytic reactions do not generate a flame associated with a simple burning reaction. Because of the extreme heat (almost as hot as combustion chamber temperatures), a converter remains hot long after the engine is shut off. Most vehicles use a series of heat shields to protect the passenger compartment and other parts of the chassis from excessive heat. Vehicles have been known to start fires because of the hot converter causing tall grass or dry leaves beneath the just-parked vehicle to ignite, especially if the engine is idling. This is most likely to occur if the heat shields have been removed from the converter.

CONVERTER USAGE A catalytic converter must be located as close as possible to the exhaust manifold to work effectively. The farther back the converter is positioned in the exhaust system, the more the exhaust gases cool before they reach the converter. Since positioning in the exhaust system affects the oxidation process, cars that use only an oxidation converter generally locate it underneath the front of the passenger compartment.

Some vehicles have used a small, quick heating oxidation converter called a **preconverter**, a **pup converter**, or a **mini converter** that connects directly to the exhaust manifold outlet. These have a small catalyst surface area close to the engine that heats up rapidly to start the oxidation process more quickly during cold engine warm-up. For this reason, they were often called **light-off converters (LOCs)**. The larger main converter, under the passenger compartment, completes the oxidation reaction started in the LOC.

OBD-II CATALYTIC CONVERTER PERFORMANCE With OBD-II equipped vehicles, catalytic converter performance is monitored by a **heated oxygen sensor (HO2S)**, both before and after the converter. The converters used on these vehicles have what is known as **oxygen storage capacity (OSC)**. This OSC is due mostly to the cerium coating in the catalyst rather than the precious metals used. When the three-way converter (TWC) is operating as it should, the postconverter HO2S is far less active than

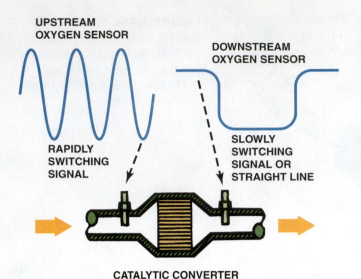

UPSTREAM
OXYGEN SENSOR

DOWNSTREAM
OXYGEN SENSOR

RAPIDLY
SWITCHING
SIGNAL

SLOWLY
SWITCHING
SIGNAL OR
STRAIGHT LINE

CATALYTIC CONVERTER

FIGURE 19–25 The OBD-II catalytic converter monitor compares the signals of the upstream and downstream HO2S to determine converter efficiency.

the preconverter sensor. The converter stores, then releases, the oxygen during normal reduction and oxidation of the exhaust gases, smoothing out the variations in O_2 being released.

Where a cycling sensor voltage output is expected before the converter, because of the converter action, the postconverter HO2S should read a steady signal without much fluctuation. ● **SEE FIGURE 19–25.**

CONVERTER-DAMAGING CONDITIONS
Since converters have no moving parts, they require no periodic service. Under federal law, catalyst effectiveness is warranted for 80,000 miles or eight years.

The three main causes of premature converter failure are as follows:

- **Contamination.** Substances that can destroy the converter include exhaust that contains excess engine oil, antifreeze, sulfur (from poor fuel), and various other chemical substances.

- **Excessive temperatures.** Although a converter operates at high temperature, it can be destroyed by excessive temperatures. This most often occurs either when too much unburned fuel enters the converter, or with excessively lean mixtures. Excessive temperatures may be caused by long idling periods on some vehicles, since more heat develops at those times than when driving at normal highway speeds. Severe high temperatures can cause the converter to melt down, leading to the internal parts breaking apart and either clogging the converter or moving downstream to plug the muffler. In either case, the restricted exhaust flow severely reduces engine power.

- **Improper air-fuel mixtures.** Rich mixtures or raw fuel in the exhaust can be caused by engine misfiring, or an excessively rich air-fuel mixture resulting from a defective coolant

? FREQUENTLY ASKED QUESTION

Can a Catalytic Converter Be Defective Without Being Clogged?

Yes. Catalytic converters can fail by being chemically damaged or poisoned without being mechanically clogged. Therefore, the catalytic converter should not only be tested for physical damage (clogging) by performing a backpressure or vacuum test and a rattle test, but also for temperature rise, usually with a pyrometer or propane test, to check the efficiency of the converter.

temp sensor or defective fuel injectors. Lean mixtures are commonly caused by intake manifold leaks. When either of these circumstances occurs, the converter can become a catalytic furnace, causing the previously described damage.

To avoid excessive catalyst temperatures and the possibility of fuel vapors reaching the converter, follow these rules.

1. Do not use fuel additives or cleaners that are not converter safe.

2. Do not crank an engine for more than 40 seconds when it is flooded or misfiring.

3. Do not turn off the ignition switch when the vehicle is in motion.

4. Do not disconnect a spark plug wire for more than 30 seconds.

5. Repair engine problems such as dieseling, misfiring, or stumbling as soon as possible.

DIAGNOSING CATALYTIC CONVERTERS

THE TAP TEST The simple **tap test** involves tapping (not pounding) on the catalytic converter using a rubber mallet. If the substrate inside the converter is broken, the converter will rattle when hit. If the converter rattles, a replacement converter is required.

TESTING BACKPRESSURE WITH A PRESSURE GAUGE Exhaust system backpressure can be measured directly by installing a pressure gauge in an exhaust opening. This can be accomplished in one of the following ways.

1. To test backpressure, remove the inside of an old, discarded oxygen sensor and thread in an adapter to convert it to a vacuum or pressure gauge.

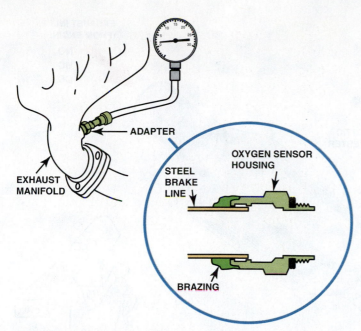

FIGURE 19–26 A back pressure tool can be made by using an oxygen sensor housing and epoxy or braze to hold the tube to the housing.

NOTE: An adapter can be easily made by inserting a metal tube or pipe into an old oxygen sensor housing. A short section of brake line works great. The pipe can be brazed to the oxygen sensor housing or it can be glued with epoxy. An 18 mm compression gauge adapter can also be adapted to fit into the oxygen sensor opening. ● SEE FIGURE 19–26.

2. To test the exhaust backpressure at the exhaust gas recirculation (EGR) valve, remove the EGR valve and fabricate a plate equipped with a fitting for a pressure gauge.

3. To test at the secondary air-injection (SAI) check valve, remove the check valve from the exhaust tubes leading to the exhaust manifold. Use a rubber cone with a tube inside to seal against the exhaust tube. Connect the tube to a pressure gauge.

At idle, the maximum backpressure should be less than 1.5 PSI (10 kPa), and it should be less than 2.5 PSI (15 kPa) at 2500 RPM. Pressure readings higher than these indicate that the exhaust system is restricted and further testing will be needed to determine the location of the restriction.

TESTING FOR BACKPRESSURE USING A VACUUM GAUGE
An exhaust restriction can be tested indirectly by checking the intake manifold vacuum with the engine operating at a fast idle speed (about 2500 RPM). If the exhaust is restricted, some exhaust can pass and the effect may not be noticeable when the engine is at idle speed. However, when the engine is operating at a higher speed, the exhaust gases can build up behind the restriction and eventually will be unable to leave the combustion chamber. When some of the exhaust is left behind at the end of the exhaust stroke, the resulting pressure in the combustion chamber reduces engine vacuum. To test for an exhaust restriction using a vacuum gauge, perform the following steps.

STEP 1   Attach a vacuum gauge to an intake manifold vacuum source.

STEP 2   Start the engine. Record the engine manifold vacuum reading. The engine vacuum should read 17 to 21 inch Hg when the engine is at idle speed.

STEP 3   Increase the engine speed to 2500 RPM and hold that speed for 60 seconds while looking at the vacuum gauge.

Results

- If the vacuum reading is equal to or higher than the vacuum reading when the engine was at idle speed, the exhaust system is *not* restricted.

- If the vacuum reading is lower than the vacuum reading when the engine was at idle speed, then the exhaust *is* restricted. Further testing will be needed to determine the location of the restriction.

TESTING A CATALYTIC CONVERTER FOR TEMPERATURE RISE
A properly working catalytic converter should be able to reduce NOx exhaust emissions into nitrogen (N) and oxygen (O_2) and oxidize unburned hydrocarbon (HC) and carbon monoxide (CO) into harmless carbon dioxide (CO_2) and water vapor (H_2O). During these chemical processes, the catalytic converter should increase in temperature at least 10% if the converter is working properly. To test the converter, operate the engine at 2500 RPM for at least two minutes to fully warm up the converter. Measure the inlet and the outlet temperatures using an **infrared thermometer (pyrometer)**, as shown in ● FIGURE 19–27.

NOTE: If the engine is extremely efficient, the converter may not have any excessive unburned hydrocarbons or carbon monoxide to convert! In this case, a spark plug wire could be grounded out using a vacuum hose and a test light to create some unburned hydrocarbon in the exhaust. Do not ground out a cylinder for longer than 10 seconds or the excessive amount of unburned hydrocarbon could overheat and damage the converter.

CATALYTIC CONVERTER EFFICIENCY TESTS
The efficiency of a catalytic converter can be determined using an exhaust gas analyzer.

- **Oxygen level test.** With the engine warm and in closed loop, check the oxygen (O_2) and carbon monoxide (CO) levels. A good converter should be able to oxidize the extra hydrocarbons caused by the rapid acceleration.
  - If O_2 is zero, go to the snap-throttle test.
  - If O_2 is greater than zero, check the CO level.
  - If CO is greater than zero, the converter is *not* functioning correctly.

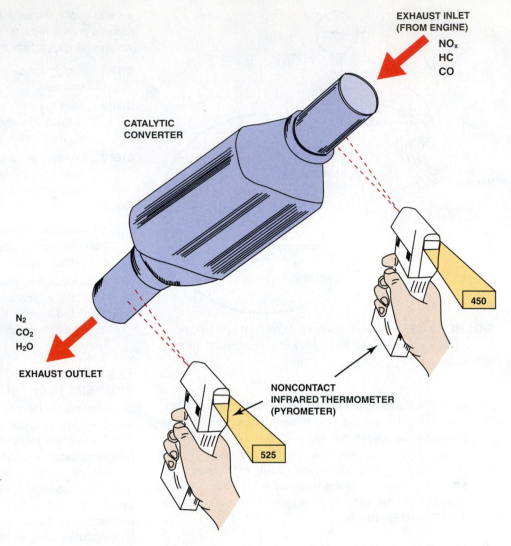

EXHAUST INLET
(FROM ENGINE)

NO_x
HC
CO

CATALYTIC
CONVERTER

N_2
CO_2
H_2O

EXHAUST OUTLET

NONCONTACT
INFRARED THERMOMETER
(PYROMETER)

FIGURE 19–27
The temperature of the outlet should be at least 10% hotter than the temperature of the inlet. If a converter is not working, the inlet temperature will be hotter than the outlet temperature.

■ **Snap-throttle test.** With the engine warm and in closed loop, snap the throttle to wide open (WOT) in park or neutral and observe the oxygen reading.

■ The O_2 reading should not exceed 1.2%; if it does, the converter is *not* working.

■ If the O_2 rises to 1.2%, the converter may have low efficiency.

■ If the O_2 remains below 1.2%, then the converter is okay.

TECH TIP

Aftermarket Catalytic Converters

Some replacement aftermarket (nonfactory) catalytic converters do not contain the same amount of cerium as the original part. Cerium is the element that is used in catalytic converters to store oxygen. As a result of the lack of cerium, the correlation between the oxygen storage and the conversion efficiency may be affected enough to set a false diagnostic trouble code (P0422).

NOTE: When an aftermarket converter is being installed, to be assured of proper operation, ensure that its distance from the rear of the catalyst block is the same as the distance between the rear oxygen sensor and the factory converter. Always follow the instructions that come with the replacement converter.
● **SEE FIGURE 19–28.**

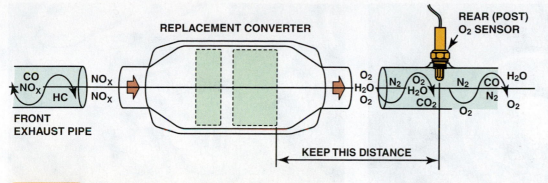

FRONT EXHAUST PIPE

REPLACEMENT CONVERTER

KEEP THIS DISTANCE

REAR (POST) O2 SENSOR

FIGURE 19–28 Whenever replacing a catalytic converter with a universal unit, first measure the distance between the rear brick and the center of the rear oxygen sensor. Be sure that the replacement unit is installed to the same dimension.

CATALYTIC CONVERTER-RELATED DIAGNOSTIC TROUBLE CODE

Diagnostic Trouble Code	Description	Possible Causes
P0420	Catalytic converter efficiency failure	1. Engine mechanical fault
		2. Exhaust leaks
		3. Fuel contaminants, such as engine oil, coolant, or sulfur

CATALYTIC CONVERTER REPLACEMENT GUIDELINES

Because a catalytic converter is a major exhaust gas emission control device, the Environmental Protection Agency (EPA) has strict guidelines for its replacement, including:

- If a converter is replaced on a vehicle with less than 80,000 miles or eight years, depending on the year of the vehicle, an original equipment catalytic converter *must* be used as a replacement.

- The replacement converter must be of the same design as the original. If the original had an air pump fitting, so must the replacement.

- The old converter must be kept for possible inspection by the authorities for 60 days.

- A form must be completed and signed by both the vehicle owner and a representative from the service facility. This form must state the cause of the converter failure and must remain on file for two years.

EVAPORATIVE EMISSION CONTROL SYSTEM

PURPOSE AND FUNCTION The purpose of the evaporative (EVAP) emission control system is to trap and hold gasoline vapors, also called volatile organic compounds, or VOCs. The evaporative control system includes the charcoal canister, hoses, and valves. These vapors are routed into a charcoal canister, then into the intake airflow where they are burned in the engine instead of being released into the atmosphere.

COMMON COMPONENTS The fuel tank filler caps used on vehicles with modern EVAP systems are a special design. Most EVAP fuel tank filler caps have pressure-vacuum relief built into them. When pressure or vacuum exceeds a calibrated value, the valve opens. Once the pressure or vacuum has been relieved, the valve closes. If a sealed cap is used on an EVAP system that requires a pressure-vacuum relief design, a vacuum lock may develop in the fuel system, or the fuel tank may be damaged by fuel expansion or contraction. ● SEE FIGURE 19–29.

FIGURE 19–29 A capless system from a Ford Flex does not use a replaceable cap; instead, it has a spring-loaded closure.

FIGURE 19–30 A charcoal canister can be located under the hood or underneath the vehicle.

? **FREQUENTLY ASKED QUESTION**

When Filling My Fuel Tank, Why Should I Stop When the Pump Clicks Off?

Every fuel tank has an upper volume chamber that allows for expansion of the fuel when hot. The volume of the chamber is between 10% and 20% of the volume of the tank. For example, if a fuel tank had a capacity of 20 gallons, the expansion chamber volume would be from 2 to 4 gallons. A hose is attached at the top of the chamber and vented to the charcoal canister. If extra fuel is forced into this expansion volume, liquid gasoline can be drawn into the charcoal canister. This liquid fuel can saturate the canister and create an overly rich air-fuel mixture when the canister purge valve is opened during normal vehicle operation. This extra-rich air-fuel mixture can cause the vehicle to fail an exhaust emissions test, reduce fuel economy, and possibly damage the catalytic converter. To avoid problems, simply add fuel to the next dime's worth after the nozzle clicks off. This will ensure that the tank is full, yet not overfilled.

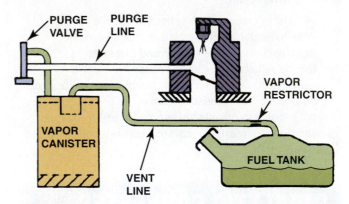

FIGURE 19–31 The evaporative emission control system includes all of the lines, hoses, and valves, plus the charcoal canister.

EVAPORATIVE CONTROL SYSTEM OPERATION

The canister is located under the hood or underneath the vehicle, and is filled with activated charcoal granules that can hold up to one-third of their own weight in fuel vapors. ● SEE FIGURE 19–30.

NOTE: Some vehicles with large or dual fuel tanks may have dual canisters.

Activated charcoal is an effective vapor trap because of its great surface area. Each gram of activated charcoal has a surface area of 1,100 m^2 (more than a quarter acre).

Typical canisters hold either 300 or 625 grams of charcoal *with a surface area equivalent to 80 or 165 football fields.* By a process called **adsorption**, the fuel vapor molecules adhere to the carbon surface. This attaching force is not strong, so the system purges the vapor molecules quite simply by sending a fresh airflow through the charcoal.

- **Vapor purging.** During engine operation, stored vapors are drawn from the canister into the engine through a hose connected to the throttle body or the air cleaner. This "purging" process mixes HC vapors from the canister with the existing air-fuel charge. ● SEE FIGURES 19–31 AND 19–32.
- **Computer-controlled purge.** The PCM controls when the canister purges on most engines. This is done by an electric vacuum solenoid, and one or more purge valves.

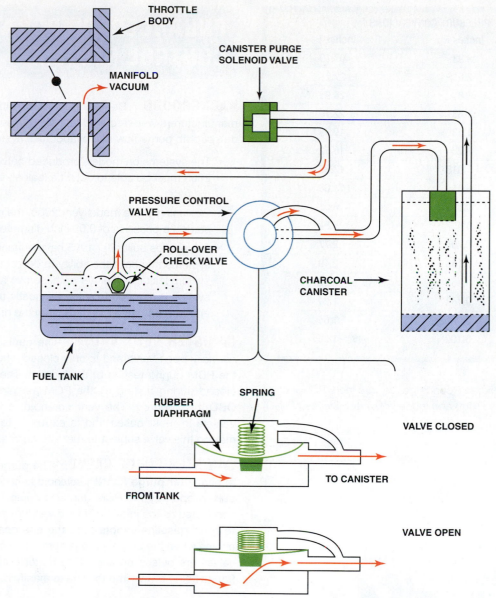

FIGURE 19–32 A typical evaporative emission control system. Note that when the computer turns on the canister purge solenoid valve, manifold vacuum draws any stored vapors from the canister into the engine. Manifold vacuum also is applied to the pressure control valve. When this valve opens, fumes from the fuel tank are drawn into the charcoal canister and eventually into the engine. When the solenoid valve is turned off (or the engine stops and there is no manifold vacuum), the pressure control valve is spring-loaded shut to keep vapors inside the fuel tank from escaping to the atmosphere.

Under normal conditions, most engine control systems permit purging only during closed-loop operation at cruising speeds. During other engine operation conditions, such as open-loop mode, idle, deceleration, or wide-open throttle, the PCM prevents canister purging.

Pressures can build inside the fuel system and are usually measured in units of inches of water (inch H_2O) (28 inch of water equals 1 PSI). Some scan tools display other units of measure for the EVAP system that make understanding the system difficult. ● **SEE CHART 19–2** for the conversion among PSI, inch Hg, and inch H_2O.

Pressure buildup in the EVAP system can be caused by:

- Fuel evaporation rates (volatility)
- Gas tank size (fuel surface area and volume)
- Fuel level (liquid versus vapor)
- Fuel slosh (driving conditions)
- Hot temperatures (ambient, in-tank, close to the tank)
- Returned fuel from the rail

PRESSURE CONVERSIONS		
PSI	Inches Hg	Inches H$_2$O
14.7	29.93	407.19
1.0	2.036	27.7
0.9	1.8	24.93
0.8	1.63	22.16
0.7	1.43	19.39
0.6	1.22	16.62
0.5	1.018	13.85
0.4	0.814	11.08
0.3	0.611	8.31
0.2	0.407	5.54
0.1	0.204	2.77
0.09	0.183	2.49
0.08	0.163	2.22
0.07	0.143	1.94
0.06	0.122	1.66
0.05	0.102	1.385

CHART 19–2

The conversion between Pounds per square inch (PSI) and inches of Mercury (in. Hg.) and inches of water (inches of H$_2$O)

NOTE: Pressure conversions.
1 PSI = 28 inch H$_2$O
1/4 PSI = 7 inch H$_2$O

NONENHANCED EVAPORATIVE CONTROL SYSTEMS

Prior to 1996, evaporative systems were referred to as nonenhanced evaporative (EVAP) control systems. This term refers to evaporative systems that had limited diagnostic capabilities. While they are often PCM controlled, their diagnostic capability is usually limited to their ability to detect if purge has occurred. Many systems have a diagnostic switch that could sense if purge is occurring and set a code if no purge is detected. This system does not check for leaks. On some vehicles, the PCM also has the capability of monitoring the integrity of the purge solenoid and circuit. These systems' limitations are their ability to check the integrity of the evaporative system on the vehicle. They could not detect leaks or missing or loose gas caps that could lead to excessive evaporative emissions from the vehicle. Nonenhanced evaporative systems use either a canister purge solenoid or a vapor management valve to control purge vapor.

ENHANCED EVAPORATIVE CONTROL SYSTEM

BACKGROUND Beginning in 1996, with OBD-II vehicles, manufacturers were required to install systems that are able to detect both purge flow and evaporative system leakage.

- The systems on models produced between 1996 and 2000 must be able to detect a leak as small as 0.04 inch diameter.
- Beginning in the model year 2000, the enhanced systems started a phase-in of 0.02 inch diameter leak detection.
- All vehicles built after 1995 have enhanced evaporative systems that have the ability to detect purge flow and system leakage. If either of these two functions fails, the system is required to set a diagnostic trouble code (DTC) and turn on the MIL light to warn the driver of the failure.

CANISTER VENT VALVE The canister vent valve is a *normally open* valve and is only closed when commanded by the PCM during testing of the system. The vent valve is only closed during testing by the PCM as part of the mandated OBD-II standards. The vent solenoid is located under the vehicle in most cases and is exposed to the environment, making this valve subject to rust and corrosion.

CANISTER PURGE VALVE The purge valve, also called the **canister purge (CANP)** solenoid is *normally closed* and is pulsed open by the PCM during purging. The purge valve is connected to the intake manifold vacuum and this line is used to draw gasoline vapors from the charcoal canister into the engine when the purge valve is commanded open. Most purge valves are pulsed on and off to better control the amount of fumes being drawn into the intake manifold.

 TECH TIP

Problems After Refueling? Check the Purge Valve.

The purge valve is normally closed and open only when the PCM is commanding the system to purge. If the purge solenoid were to become stuck in the open position, gasoline fumes would be allowed to flow directly from the gas tank to the intake manifold. When refueling, this would result in a lot of fumes being forced into the intake manifold; and as a result, would cause a hard-to-start condition after refueling. This would also result in a rich exhaust (likely black) when first starting the engine after refueling. Although the purge solenoid is usually located under the hood of most vehicles and less subject to rust and corrosion, as with the vent valve, it can still fail.

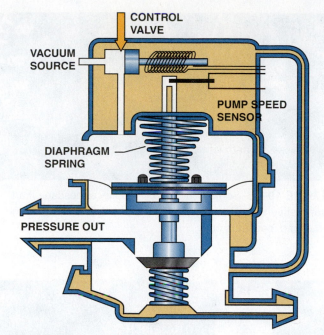

FIGURE 19–33 A leak detection pump (LDP) used on some Chrysler vehicles to pressurize (slightly) the fuel system to check for leaks.

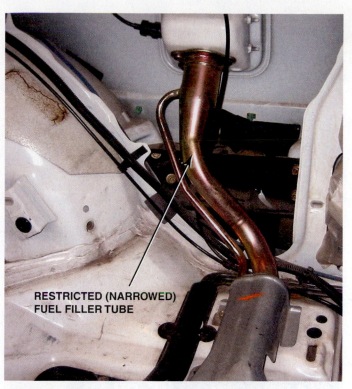

FIGURE 19–34 A restricted fuel fill pipe shown on a vehicle with the interior removed.

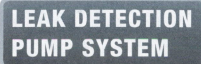

LEAK DETECTION PUMP SYSTEM

PURPOSE AND FUNCTION   Many vehicles use a **leak detection pump (LDP)** as part of the evaporative control system diagnosis equipment. ● **SEE FIGURE 19–33.**

OPERATION   The system works to test for leaks as follows:

- The purge solenoid is normally closed.
- The vent valve in the LDP is normally open. Filtered fresh air is drawn through the LDP to the canister.
- The LDP uses a spring attached to a diaphragm to apply pressure (7.5 inch H_2O) to the fuel tank.
- The PCM monitors the LDP switch that is triggered if the pressure drops in the fuel tank.
- The time between LDP solenoid off and LDP switch close is called the pump period. This time period is inversely proportional to the size of the leak. The shorter the pump period, the larger the leak. The longer the pump period, the smaller the leak.

  EVAP large leak (greater than 0.08 inch): less than 0.9 second

  EVAP medium leak (0.04 to 0.08 inch): 0.9 to 1.2 seconds

  EVAP small leak (0.02 to 0.04 inch): 1.2 to 6 seconds

ONBOARD REFUELING VAPOR RECOVERY

PURPOSE AND FUNCTION   The onboard refueling vapor recovery (ORVR) system was first introduced on some 1998 vehicles. Previously designed EVAP systems allowed fuel vapor to escape to the atmosphere during refueling.

OPERATION   The primary feature of most ORVR systems is the restricted tank filler tube, which is about 1 inch (25 mm) in diameter. This reduced size filler tube creates an aspiration effect, which tends to draw outside air into the filler tube. During refueling, the fuel tank is vented to the charcoal canister, which captures the gas fumes; and with air flowing into the filler tube, no vapors can escape to the atmosphere. ● **SEE FIGURE 19–34.**

STATE INSPECTION EVAP TESTS

In some states, a periodic inspection and test of the fuel system are mandated along with a dynamometer test. The emissions inspection includes tests on the vehicle before and during the dynamometer test. Before the running test, the fuel tank and cap, fuel lines, canister, and other fuel system components must be inspected and tested to ensure that they are not leaking gasoline vapors into the atmosphere.

- First, the fuel tank cap is tested to ensure that it is sealing properly and holds pressure within specs.
- Next, the cap is installed on the vehicle, and using a special adapter, the EVAP system is pressurized to approximately 0.5 PSI and monitored for two minutes.
- Pressure in the tank and lines should not drop below approximately 0.3 PSI.

If the cap or system leaks, hydrocarbon emissions are likely being released, and the vehicle fails the test. If the system leaks, an ultrasonic leak detector may be used to find the leak.

Finally, with the engine warmed up and running at a moderate speed, the canister purge line is tested for adequate flow using a special flow meter inserted into the system. In one example, if the flow from the canister to the intake system when the system is activated is at least 1 liter per minute, then the vehicle passes the canister purge test.

DIAGNOSING THE EVAP SYSTEM

SYMPTOMS Before vehicle emissions testing began in many parts of the country, little service work was done on the evaporative emission system. Common engine-performance problems that can be caused by a fault in this system include:

- **Poor fuel economy.** A leak in a vacuum-valve diaphragm can result in engine vacuum drawing in a constant flow of gasoline vapors from the fuel tank. This usually results in a drop in fuel economy of 2 to 4 miles per gallon (mpg). Use a hand-operated vacuum pump to check that the vacuum diaphragm can hold vacuum.
- **Poor performance.** A vacuum leak in the manifold or ported vacuum section of vacuum hose in the system can cause the engine to run rough. Age, heat, and time all contribute to the deterioration of rubber hoses.

Enhanced exhaust emissions (I/M-240) testing tests the evaporative emission system. A leak in the system is tested by pressurizing the entire fuel system to a level below 1 pound/inch^2 or 1 PSI (about 14 inch H_2O). The system is typically pressurized with nitrogen, a nonflammable gas that makes up 78% of our atmosphere. The pressure in the system is then shut off and monitored. If the pressure drops below a set standard, then the vehicle fails the test. This test determines if there is a leak in the system.

NOTE: To help pass the evaporative section of an enhanced emissions test, arrive at the test site with less than one-half tank of fuel. This means that the rest

FIGURE 19–35 Some vehicles will display a message if an evaporative control system leak is detected that could be the result of a loose gas cap.

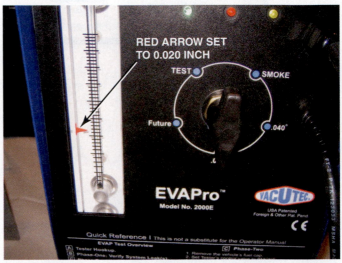

FIGURE 19–36 To test for a leak, this tester was set to the 0.02 inch hole and turned on. The ball rose in the scale on the left and the red arrow was moved to that location. When testing the system for leaks, if the ball rises higher than the arrow, then the leak is larger than 0.02 inch. If the ball does not rise to the level of the arrow, the leak is smaller than 0.02 inch.

of the volume of the fuel tank is filled with air. It takes longer for the pressure to drop from a small leak when the volume of the air is greater compared to when the tank is full and the volume of air remaining in the tank is small.

LOCATING LEAKS IN THE SYSTEM Leaks in the evaporative emission control system will cause the malfunction check gas cap indication lamp to light on some vehicles. ● **SEE FIGURE 19–35.**

A leak will also cause a gas smell, which would be most noticeable if the vehicle were parked in an enclosed garage. The first step is to determine if there is a leak in the system by setting the EVAP tester to rate the system, either a 0.04 inch or a 0.02 inch hole size leak. ● **SEE FIGURE 19–36.**

FIGURE 19–37 This unit is applying smoke to the fuel tank through an adapter and the leak was easily found to be the gas cap seal.

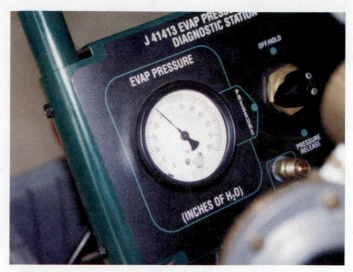

FIGURE 19–38 An emission tester that uses nitrogen to pressurize the fuel system.

After it has been determined that a leak exists and that it is larger than specified, then there are two methods that can be used to check for leaks in the evaporative system.

- **Smoke machine testing.** The most efficient method of leak detection is to introduce smoke under low pressure from a machine specifically designed for this purpose. ● **SEE FIGURE 19–37.**
- **Nitrogen gas pressurization.** This method uses nitrogen gas under a very low pressure (lower than 1 PSI) in the fuel system. The service technician then listens for the escaping air, using amplified headphones. ● **SEE FIGURE 19–38.**

EVAPORATIVE SYSTEM MONITOR

OBD-II REQUIREMENTS OBD-II computer programs not only detect faults, but also *periodically test various systems* and alert the driver before emissions-related components are harmed by system faults.

- Serious faults cause a blinking malfunction indicator lamp (MIL) or even an engine shutdown.
- Less serious faults may simply store a code but not illuminate the MIL.

The OBD-II requirements did not affect fuel system design. However, one new component, a fuel evaporative canister purge line pressure sensor, was added for monitoring purge line pressure during tests. The OBD-II requirements state that vehicle fuel systems are to be routinely tested *while underway* by the PCM.

All OBD-II vehicles perform a canister purge system pressure test, as commanded by the PCM. While the vehicle is

being driven, the vapor line between the canister and the purge valve is monitored for pressure changes.

- When the canister purge solenoid is open, the line should be under a vacuum since vapors must be drawn from the canister into the intake system. However, when the purge solenoid is closed, there should be no vacuum in the line. The pressure sensor detects if a vacuum is present, and the information is compared to the command given to the solenoid.
- If, during the canister purge cycle, no vacuum exists in the canister purge line, a code is set indicating a possible fault, which could be caused by an inoperative or clogged solenoid or a blocked or leaking canister purge fuel line. Likewise, if vacuum exists when no command for purge is given, a stuck solenoid is evident, and a code is set. The EVAP system monitor tests for purge volume and leaks.

A typical EVAP monitor first closes off the system to atmospheric pressure and opens the purge valve during cruise operation. A **fuel tank pressure (FTP)** sensor then monitors the rate with which vacuum increases in the system. The monitor uses this information to determine the purge volume flow rate. To test for leaks, the EVAP monitor closes the purge valve, creating a completely closed system. The fuel tank pressure sensor then monitors the leak-down rate. If the rate exceeds PCM-stored values, a leak greater than or equal to the OBD-II standard of 0.04 inch (1 mm) or 0.02 inch (0.5 mm) exists. After two consecutive failed trips testing either purge volume or the presence of a leak, the PCM lights the MIL and sets a DTC.

The fuel tank pressure sensor is similar to the MAP sensor, and instead of monitoring intake manifold absolute pressure, it is used to monitor fuel tank pressure. ● **SEE FIGURE 19–39.**

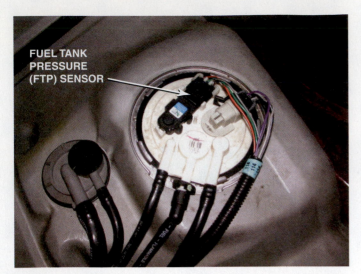

FIGURE 19–39 The fuel tank pressure sensor (black unit with three wires) looks like a MAP sensor and is usually located on top of the fuel pump module (white unit).

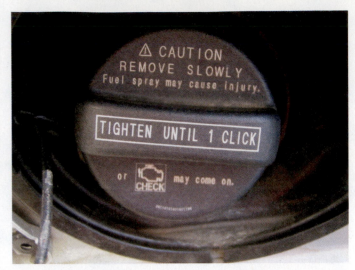

FIGURE 19–40 This Toyota cap has a warning. The check engine light will come on if not tightened until one click.

TECH TIP

Always Tighten the Cap Correctly

Many diagnostic trouble codes (DTCs) are set because the gas cap has not been properly installed. To be sure that a screw-type gas cap is properly sealed, it may need to be tightened until it clicks three times. The clicking is a ratchet device and the clicking does not harm the cap. Therefore, if a P0440 or similar DTC is set, check the cap. ● SEE FIGURE 19–40.

ENGINE-OFF NATURAL VACUUM System integrity (leakage) can also be checked after the engine is shut off. The premise is that a warm evaporative system will cool down after the engine is shut off and the vehicle is stable. A slight vacuum will be created in the gas tank during this cooling period. If a specific level of vacuum is reached and maintained, the system is said to have integrity (no leakage).

TYPICAL EVAP MONITOR

The PCM will run the EVAP monitor when the following enable criteria are met.

- Cold start
- Barometric pressure (BARO) greater than 70 kPa (20.7 inch Hg or 10.2 PSI)
- Intake air temperature (IAT) between 39°F and 86°F at engine start-up

- Engine coolant temperature (ECT) between 39°F and 86°F at engine start-up
- ECT and IAT within 39°F of each other at engine start-up
- Fuel level within 15% to 85%
- Throttle position (TP) sensor between 9% and 35%

RUNNING THE EVAP MONITOR There are three tests that are performed during a typical EVAP monitor. A DTC is assigned to each test.

1. **Weak vacuum test (P0440—large leak).** This test identifies gross leaks. During the monitor, the vent solenoid is closed and the purge solenoid is duty cycled. The fuel tank pressure (FTP) should indicate a vacuum of approximately 6 to 10 inch H_2O.

2. **Small leak test (P0442—small leak).** After the large leak test passes, the PCM checks for a small leak by keeping the vent solenoid closed and closing the purge solenoid. The system is now sealed. The PCM measures the change in FTP voltage over time.

3. **Excess vacuum test (P0446).** This test checks for vent path restrictions. With the vent solenoid open and purge commanded, the PCM should not see excessive vacuum in the EVAP system. Typical EVAP system vacuum with the vent solenoid open is about 5 to 6 inch H_2O.

TECH TIP

Keep the Fuel Tank Properly Filled

Most evaporative system monitors will not run unless the fuel level is between 15% and 85%. In other words, if a driver always runs with close to an empty tank or always tries to keep the tank full, the EVAP monitor may not run. ● SEE FIGURE 19–41.

FIGURE 19–41 The fuel level must be between 15% and 85% before the EVAP monitor will run on most vehicles.

EVAP SYSTEM-RELATED DIAGNOSTIC TROUBLE CODES

Diagnostic Trouble Code	Description	Possible Causes
P0440	Evaporative system fault	• Loose gas cap • Defective EVAP vent • Cracked charcoal canister • EVAP vent or purge vapor line problems
P0442	Small leak detected	• Loose gas cap • Defective EVAP vent or purge solenoid • EVAP vent or purge line problems
P0446	EVAP canister vent blocked	• EVAP vent or purge solenoid electrical problems • Restricted EVAP canister vent line

SUMMARY

1. Recirculating 6% to 10% inert exhaust gases back into the intake system by the EGR system reduces peak temperature inside the combustion chamber and reduces NOx exhaust emissions.

2. EGR is usually not needed at idle, at wide-open throttle, or when the engine is cold.

3. Many EGR systems use a feedback potentiometer to signal the PCM the position of the EGR valve pintle.

4. OBD-II requires that the flow rate be tested and then is achieved by opening the EGR valve and observing the reaction of the MAP sensor.

5. Positive crankcase ventilation (PCV) systems use a valve or a fixed orifice to control and direct the fumes from the crankcase back into the intake system.

6. A PCV valve regulates the flow of fumes depending on engine vacuum and seals the crankcase vent in the event of a backfire.

7. As much as 30% of the air needed by the engine at idle speed flows through the PCV system.

8. The secondary air-injection (SAI) system forces air at low pressure into the exhaust to reduce CO and HC exhaust emissions.

9. A catalytic converter is an aftertreatment device that reduces exhaust emissions outside of the engine. A catalyst is an element that starts a chemical reaction but is not consumed in the process.

10. The catalyst material used in a catalytic converter includes rhodium, palladium, and platinum.

11. The OBD-II system monitor compares the relative activity of a rear oxygen sensor to the precatalytic oxygen sensor to determine catalytic converter efficiency.

12. The purpose of the evaporative (EVAP) emission control system is to reduce the release of volatile organic compounds (VOCs) into the atmosphere.

13. A carbon (charcoal) canister is used to trap and hold gasoline vapors until they can be purged and run into the engine to be burned.

14. OBD-II regulation requires that the evaporative emission control system be checked for leakage and proper purge flow rates.

15. External leaks can best be located by pressurizing the fuel system with low-pressure smoke.

1. How does the use of exhaust gas recirculation reduce NOx exhaust emission?

2. How does the DPFE sensor work?

3. What exhaust emissions does the PCV valve and SAI system control?

4. How does a catalytic converter reduce NOx to nitrogen and oxygen?

5. How does the computer monitor catalytic converter performance?

CHAPTER QUIZ

1. Two technicians are discussing clogged EGR passages. Technician A says clogged EGR passages can cause excessive NOx exhaust emission. Technician B says that clogged EGR passages can cause the engine to ping (spark knock or detonation). Which technician is correct?
   a. Technician A only
   b. Technician B only
   c. Both Technicians A and B
   d. Neither Technician A nor B

2. An EGR valve that is partially stuck open would *most likely* cause what condition?
   a. Rough idle/stalling
   b. Excessive NOx exhaust emissions
   c. Ping (spark knock or detonation)
   d. Missing at highway speed

3. How much air flows through the PCV system when the engine is at idle speed?
   a. 1% to 3%
   b. 5% to 10%
   c. 10% to 20%
   d. Up to 30%

4. Technician A says that if a PCV valve rattles, then it is okay and does not need to be replaced. Technician B says that if a PCV valve does not rattle, it should be replaced. Which technician is correct?
   a. Technician A only
   b. Technician B only
   c. Both Technicians A and B
   d. Neither Technician A nor B

5. The switching valves on the AIR pump have failed several times. Technician A says that a defective exhaust check valve could be the cause. Technician B says that a leaking exhaust system at the muffler could be the cause. Which technician is correct?
   a. Technician A only
   b. Technician B only
   c. Both Technicians A and B
   d. Neither Technician A nor B

6. Two technicians are discussing testing a catalytic converter. Technician A says that a vacuum gauge can be used and observed to see if the vacuum drops with the engine at 2500 RPM for 60 seconds. Technician B says that a pressure gauge can be used to check for backpressure. Which technician is correct?
   a. Technician A only
   b. Technician B only
   c. Both Technicians A and B
   d. Neither Technician A nor B

7. At about what temperature does oxygen combine with the nitrogen in the air to form NOx?
   a. 500°F (260°C)
   b. 750°F (400°C)
   c. 1,500°F (815°C)
   d. 2,500°F (1,370°C)

8. A P0401 is being discussed. Technician A says that a stuck-closed EGR valve could be the cause. Technician B says that clogged EGR ports could be the cause. Which technician is correct?
   a. Technician A only
   b. Technician B only
   c. Both Technicians A and B
   d. Neither Technician A nor B

9. Which EVAP valve(s) is(are) normally closed?
   a. Canister purge valve
   b. Canister vent valve
   c. Both canister purge and canister vent valves
   d. Neither canister purge nor canister vent valve

10. Before an evaporative emission monitor will run, the fuel level must be where?
    a. At least 75% full
    b. Over 25%
    c. Between 15% and 85%
    d. The level of the fuel in the tank is not needed to run the monitor test

chapter 20

INTAKE AND EXHAUST SYSTEMS

LEARNING OBJECTIVES: After studying this chapter, the reader should be able to: • Explain air intake filtration. • Discuss the throttle-body injection intake manifolds and port fuel-injection intake manifolds. • Discuss exhaust gas recirculation passages and exhaust manifolds. • Describe the purpose and function of mufflers.

KEY TERMS: EGR 284 • Hangers 286 • Helmholtz resonator 281 • Micron 279 • Plenum 283

AIR INTAKE FILTRATION

NEED FOR AIR FILTERING Gasoline must be mixed with air to form a combustible mixture. Air movement into an engine occurs due to low pressure (vacuum) being created in the engine. ● SEE FIGURE 20–1.

Air contains dirt and other materials that cannot be allowed to reach the engine. Just as fuel filters are used to clean impurities from gasoline, an air cleaner and filter are used to remove contaminants from the air. The three main jobs of the air cleaner and filter include:

1. Clean the air before it is mixed with fuel

2. Silence intake noise

3. Act as a flame arrester in case of a backfire

The automotive engine uses about 9,000 gallons (34,000 liters) of air for every gallon of gasoline burned at an air-fuel ratio of 14.7:1 by weight. Without proper filtering of the air before it enters the engine, dust and dirt in the air can seriously damage engine parts and shorten engine life.

Abrasive particles can cause wear any place inside the engine where two surfaces move against each other, such as piston rings against the cylinder wall. The dirt particles then pass by the piston rings and into the crankcase. From the crankcase, the particles circulate throughout the engine in the oil. Large amounts of abrasive particles in the oil can damage other moving engine parts.

The filter that cleans the intake air is in a two-piece air cleaner housing made either of:

- Stamped steel or
- Composite (usually nylon reinforced plastic) materials.

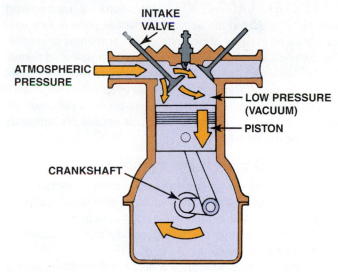

FIGURE 20–1 Downward movement of the piston lowers the air pressure inside the combustion chamber. The pressure differential between the atmosphere and the inside of the engine forces air into the engine.

AIR FILTER ELEMENTS The paper air filter element is the most common type of filter. It is made of a chemically treated paper stock that contains tiny passages in the fibers. These passages form an indirect path for the airflow to follow. The airflow passes through several fiber surfaces, each of which traps microscopic particles of dust, dirt, and carbon. Most air filters are capable of trapping dirt and other particles larger than 10 to 25 microns in size. One **micron** is equal to 0.000039 inch.

> NOTE: A person can only see objects that are 40 microns or larger in size. A human hair is about 50 microns in diameter.
> ● SEE FIGURE 20–2.

FIGURE 20–2 Dust and dirt in the air are trapped in the air filter so they do not enter the engine.

FIGURE 20–3 Most air filter housings are located on the side of the engine compartment and use flexible rubber hose to direct the airflow into the throttle body of the engine.

FILTER REPLACEMENT Manufacturers recommend cleaning or replacing the air filter element at periodic intervals, usually listed in terms of distance driven or months of service. The distance and time intervals are based on so-called normal driving. More frequent air filter replacement is necessary when the vehicle is driven under dusty, dirty, or other severe conditions.

It is best to replace a filter element before it becomes too dirty to be effective. A dirty air filter that passes contaminants can cause engine wear.

REMOTELY MOUNTED AIR FILTERS AND DUCTS Air cleaner and duct design depend on a number of factors such as the size, shape, and location of other engine compartment components, as well as the vehicle body structure.

Port fuel-injection systems generally use a horizontally mounted throttle body.

Some systems also have a mass airflow (MAF) sensor between the throttle body and the air cleaner. Because placing the air cleaner housing next to the throttle body would cause engine and vehicle design problems, it is more efficient to use this remote air cleaner placement. ● **SEE FIGURE 20–3.**

Turbocharged engines present a similar problem. The air cleaner connects to the air inlet elbow at the turbocharger. However, the tremendous heat generated by the turbocharger makes it impractical to place the air cleaner housing too close to the turbocharger. Remote air cleaners are connected to the turbocharger air inlet elbow or fuel-injection throttle body by composite ducting that is usually retained by clamps. The ducting used may be rigid or flexible, but all connections must be airtight.

AIR FILTER RESTRICTION INDICATOR Some vehicles, especially pickup trucks that are often driven in dusty conditions, are equipped with an air filter restriction indicator. The purpose of this device is to give a visual warning when the air filter is restricted and needs to be replaced. The device operates by detecting the slight drop in pressure that occurs

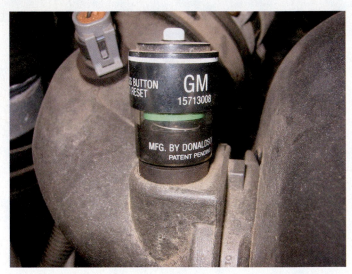

FIGURE 20–4 A typical air filter restriction indicator used on a General Motors truck engine. The indicator turns red when it detects enough restriction to require a filter replacement.

when an air filter is restricted. The calibration before the red warning bar or "replace air filter" message appears varies, but is usually:

- 15 to 20 inch of water (inch H_2O) for gasoline engines
- 20 to 30 inch of water (inch H_2O) for diesel engines

The unit of inches of water is used to measure the difference in air pressure before and after the air filter. The unit is very small, because 28 inch of water is equal to a pound per square inch (PSI).

Some air filter restriction indicators, especially on diesel engines, include an electrical switch used to light a dash-mounted warning lamp when the air filter needs to be replaced. ● **SEE FIGURE 20–4.**

(a)

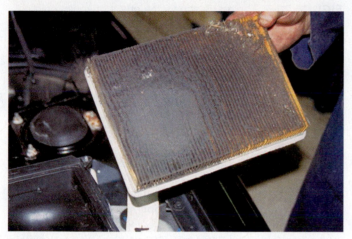

(b)

FIGURE 20–5 (a) Note the discovery as the air filter housing was opened during service on a Pontiac. The nuts were obviously deposited by squirrels (or some other animal). (b) Not only was the housing filled with nuts, but also this air filter was extremely dirty, indicating that this vehicle had not been serviced for a long time.

 TECH TIP

Always Check the Air Filter

Always inspect the air filter and the air intake system carefully during routine service. Debris or objects deposited by animals can cause a restriction to the airflow and can reduce engine performance. ● SEE FIGURE 20–5.

THROTTLE-BODY INJECTION INTAKE MANIFOLDS

TERMINOLOGY The *intake manifold* is also called an *inlet manifold.* Smooth engine operation can only occur when each combustion chamber produces the same pressure as

FIGURE 20–6 A resonance tube, called a Helmholtz resonator, is used on the intake duct between the air filter and the throttle body to reduce air intake noise during engine acceleration.

 FREQUENTLY ASKED QUESTION

What Does This Tube Do?

What is the purpose of the odd-shape tube attached to the inlet duct between the air filter and the throttle body, as seen in ● FIGURE 20–6?

The tube shape is designed to dampen out certain resonant frequencies that can occur at specific engine speeds. The length and shape of this tube are designed to absorb shock waves that are created in the air intake system and to provide a reservoir for the air that will then be released into the airstream during cycles of lower pressure. This resonance tube is often called a **Helmholtz resonator,** named for the discoverer of the relationship between shape and value of frequency, Herman L. F. von Helmholtz (1821–1894) of the University of Hönizsberg in East Prussia. The overall effect of these resonance tubes is to reduce the noise of the air entering the engine.

every other chamber in the engine. For this to be achieved, each cylinder must receive an intake charge exactly like the charge going into the other cylinders in quality and quantity. The charges must have the same physical properties and the same air-fuel mixture.

A throttle-body fuel injector forces finely divided droplets of liquid fuel into the incoming air to form a combustible air-fuel mixture. ● SEE FIGURE 20–7 for an example of a typical throttle-body injection (TBI) unit.

INTAKE AIR SPEEDS These droplets start to evaporate as soon as they leave the throttle-body injector nozzles. *The droplets stay in the charge as long as the charge flows at high velocities.* At maximum engine speed, these velocities may reach 300 ft per second. Separation of the droplets from the charge as it passes through the manifold occurs when the velocity drops below 50 ft per second. Intake charge velocities at idle

FIGURE 20–7 A throttle-body injection (TBI) unit used on a GM V-6 engine.

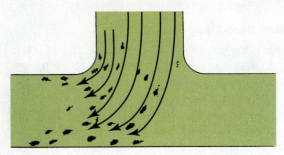

FIGURE 20–8 Heavy fuel droplets separate as they flow around an abrupt bend in an intake manifold.

speeds are often below this value. When separation occurs—at low engine speeds—extra fuel must be supplied to the charge in order to have a combustible mixture reach the combustion chamber.

Manifold sizes and shapes represent a compromise.

- They must have a cross section large enough to allow charge flow for maximum power.
- The cross section must be small enough that the flow velocities of the charge will be high enough to keep the fuel droplets in suspension. This is required so that equal mixtures reach each cylinder. Manifold cross-sectional size is one reason why engines designed especially for racing will not run at low engine speeds.
- Racing manifolds must be large enough to reach maximum horsepower. This size, however, allows the charge to move slowly, and the fuel will separate from the charge at low engine speeds. Fuel separation leads to poor accelerator response. ● **SEE FIGURE 20–8.**

Standard passenger vehicle engines are primarily designed for economy during light-load, partial-throttle operation. Their manifolds, therefore, have a much smaller cross-sectional area than do those of racing engines. This small size will help keep flow velocities of the charge high throughout the normal operating speed range of the engine.

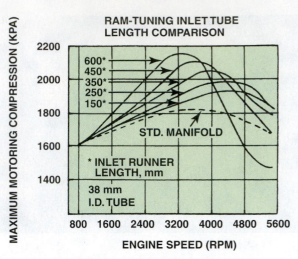

FIGURE 20–9 The graph shows the effect of sonic tuning of the intake manifold runners. The longer runners increase the torque peak and move it to a lower RPM. The 600 mm intake runner is about 24 inch long.

PORT FUEL-INJECTION INTAKE MANIFOLDS

TERMINOLOGY The size and shape of port fuel-injected engine intake manifolds can be optimized because the only thing in the manifold is air. The fuel injector is located in the intake manifold about 3 to 4 inch (70 to 100 mm) from the intake valve. Therefore, the runner length and shape are designed for tuning only. There is no need to keep an air-fuel mixture thoroughly mixed (homogenized) throughout its trip from the TBI unit to the intake valve. Intake manifold runners are tuned to improve engine performance.

- Long runners build low-RPM torque.
- Shorter runners provide maximum high-RPM power.
  ● **SEE FIGURES 20–9 AND 20–10.**

VARIABLE INTAKES Some engines with four valve heads utilize a dual or variable intake runner design. At lower engine speeds, long intake runners provide low-speed torque. At higher engine speeds, shorter intake runners are opened by means of a computer-controlled valve to increase high-speed power.

Many intake manifolds are designed to provide both short runners best for higher engine speed power and longer runners best for lower engine speed torque. The valve(s) that control the flow of air through the passages of the intake manifold are computer controlled. ● **SEE FIGURE 20–11.**

PLASTIC INTAKE MANIFOLDS Most intake manifolds are made from thermoplastic molded from fiberglass-reinforced nylon by either casting or by injection molding. Some manifolds are molded in two parts and bonded together. Plastic intake manifolds are lighter than aluminum manifolds and can better insulate engine heat from the fuel injectors.

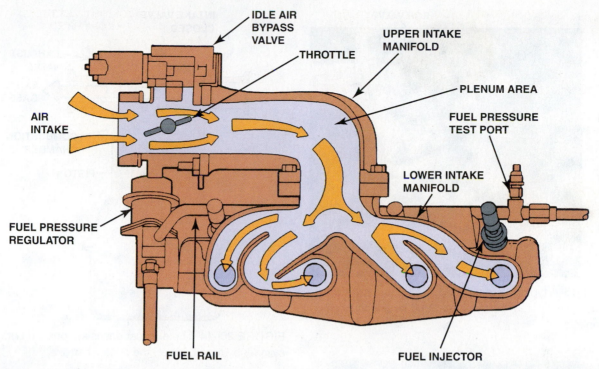

FIGURE 20–10 Airflow through the large diameter upper intake manifold is distributed to smaller diameter individual runners in the lower manifold in this two-piece manifold design.

FIGURE 20–11 The air flowing into the engine can be directed through long or short runners for best performance and fuel economy.

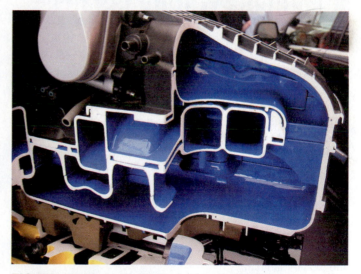

FIGURE 20–12 Many plastic intake manifolds are constructed using many parts glued together to form complex passages for airflow into the engine.

Plastic intake manifolds have smoother interior surfaces than do other types of manifolds, resulting in greater airflow. ● SEE FIGURE 20–12.

UPPER AND LOWER INTAKE MANIFOLDS Many intake manifolds are constructed in two parts.

- A lower section attaches to the cylinder heads and includes passages from the intake ports.
- An upper manifold, usually called the **plenum,** connects to the lower unit and includes the long passages needed to help provide the ram effect that helps the engine

deliver maximum torque at low engine speeds. The throttle body attaches to the upper intake.

The use of a two-part intake manifold allows for easier manufacturing as well as assembly, but can create additional locations for leaks.

If the lower intake manifold gasket leaks, not only could a vacuum leak occur affecting the operation of the engine, but a coolant leak or an oil leak can also occur if the manifold has coolant flowing through it. A leak at the gasket(s) of the upper intake manifold usually results in a vacuum (air) leak only.

FIGURE 20–13 A typical long exhaust gas line used to cool the exhaust gases before being recirculated back into the intake manifold.

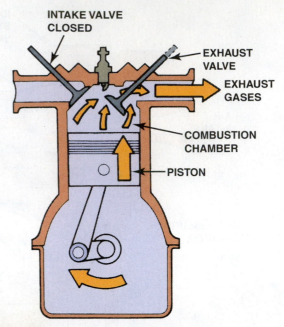

FIGURE 20–14 The exhaust gases are pushed out of the cylinder by the piston on the exhaust stroke.

EXHAUST GAS RECIRCULATION PASSAGES

PURPOSE AND FUNCTION To reduce the emission of oxides of nitrogen (NOx), engines have been equipped with **exhaust gas recirculation (EGR)** valves. From 1973 until recently, they were used on almost all vehicles. Most EGR valves are mounted on the intake manifold. Because of the efficiency of computer-controlled fuel injection, some newer engines do not require an EGR system to meet emission standards. These engines' variable valve timing to close the exhaust valve sooner than normal, trapping some exhaust in the cylinder, is an alternative to using an EGR valve.

On engines with EGR systems, the EGR valve opens at speeds above idle on a warm engine. When open, the valve allows a small portion of the exhaust gas (5% to 10%) to enter the intake manifold.

The EGR system has some means of interconnecting of the exhaust and intake manifolds. The EGR valve controls the gas flow through the passages.

- On V-type engines, the intake manifold crossover is used as a source of exhaust gas for the EGR system. A cast passage connects the exhaust crossover to the EGR valve.
- On inline-type engines, an external tube is generally used to carry exhaust gas to the EGR valve.

EXHAUST GAS COOLERS The exhaust gases are more effective in reducing oxide of nitrogen (NOx) emissions if the exhaust is cooled before being drawn into the cylinders. This tube is often designed to be long so that the exhaust gas is cooled before it enters the EGR valve. ● **SEE FIGURE 20–13.**

EXHAUST MANIFOLDS

PURPOSE AND FUNCTION The exhaust manifold is designed to collect high-temperature spent gases from the individual head exhaust ports and direct them into a single outlet connected to the exhaust system. ● **SEE FIGURE 20–14.**

The hot gases are sent to an exhaust pipe, then to a catalytic converter, to the muffler, to a resonator, and on to the tailpipe, where they are vented to the atmosphere. The exhaust system is designed to meet the following needs.

- Provide the least possible amount of restriction or backpressure
- Keep the exhaust noise at a minimum

Exhaust gas temperature will vary according to the power produced by the engine. The manifold must be designed to operate at both engine idle and continuous full power. Under full-power conditions, the exhaust manifold can become red-hot, causing a great deal of expansion.

The temperature of an exhaust manifold can exceed 1,500°F (815°C).

CONSTRUCTION Most exhaust manifolds are made from the following:

- Cast iron
- Steel tubing

During vehicle operation, manifold temperatures usually reach the high-temperature extremes. The manifold is bolted to the head in a way that will allow expansion and contraction. In some cases, hollow-headed bolts are used to maintain a

FIGURE 20–15 This exhaust manifold (red area) is equipped with a heat shield to help retain heat and reduce exhaust emissions.

FIGURE 20–16 Many exhaust manifolds are constructed of steel tubing and are free flowing to improve engine performance.

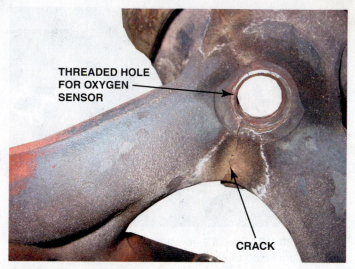

THREADED HOLE FOR OXYGEN SENSOR

CRACK

FIGURE 20–17 A crack in an exhaust manifold is often not visible because a heat shield usually covers the area. A crack in the exhaust manifold upstream of the oxygen sensor can fool the sensor and affect engine operation.

gas-tight seal while still allowing normal expansion and contraction.

Many exhaust manifolds have heat shields to help keep exhaust heat off the spark plug wires and to help keep the heat from escaping to improve exhaust emissions. ● SEE FIGURE 20–15.

Exhaust systems are especially designed for the engine–chassis combination. The exhaust system length, pipe size, and silencer are designed, where possible, to make use of the tuning effect within the exhaust system. Tuning occurs when the exhaust pulses from the cylinders are emptied into the manifold between the pulses of other cylinders. ● SEE FIGURE 20–16.

EXHAUST MANIFOLD GASKETS Exhaust heat will expand the manifold more than it will expand the head. The heat causes the exhaust manifold to slide on the sealing surface of the head. The heat also causes thermal stress. When the manifold is removed from the engine for service, the stress is relieved, which may cause the manifold to warp slightly. Exhaust manifold gaskets are included in gasket sets to seal slightly warped exhaust manifolds. These gaskets *should* be used, even if the engine did not originally use exhaust manifold gaskets. When an exhaust manifold gasket has facing on one side only, put the facing side against the head and put the manifold against the perforated metal core. The manifold can slide on the metal of the gasket just as it slid on the sealing surface of the head.

FIGURE 20–18 Typical exhaust manifold gaskets. Note how they are laminated to allow the exhaust manifold to expand and contract due to heating and cooling.

Gaskets are used on new engines with tubing- or header-type exhaust manifolds. They may have several layers of steel for high-temperature sealing. The layers are spot welded together. Some are embossed where special sealing is needed. ● SEE FIGURE 20–18.

Many new engines do not use gaskets with cast exhaust manifolds. The flat surface of the new cast-iron exhaust manifold fits tightly against the flat surface of the new head.

TECH TIP

Using the Correct Tool Saves Time

When cast-iron exhaust manifolds are removed, the stresses built up in the manifolds often cause the manifolds to twist or bend. This distortion even occurs when the exhaust manifolds have been allowed to cool before removal. Attempting to reinstall distorted exhaust manifolds is often a time-consuming and frustrating exercise.

However, special spreading jacks can be used to force the manifold back into position so that the fasteners can be lined up with the cylinder head. ● SEE FIGURE 20–19.

MUFFLERS

PURPOSE AND FUNCTION When the exhaust valve opens, it rapidly releases high-pressure gas. This sends a strong air pressure wave through the atmosphere inside the exhaust system, which produces a sound we call an explosion. It is the same sound produced when the high-pressure gases from burned gunpowder are released from a gun. In an engine, the pulses are released one after another. The explosions come so fast that they blend together in a steady roar.

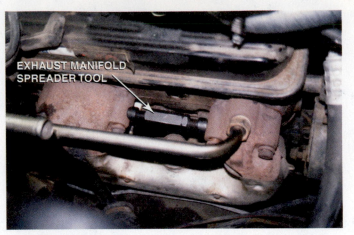

EXHAUST MANIFOLD SPREADER TOOL

FIGURE 20–19 An exhaust manifold spreader tool is absolutely necessary when reinstalling exhaust manifolds. When they are removed from the engine, the manifolds tend to warp slightly even though the engine is allowed to cool before being removed. The spreader tool allows the technician to line up the bolt holes without harming the manifold.

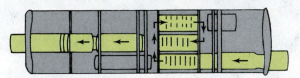

FIGURE 20–20 Exhaust gases expand and cool as they travel through passages in the muffler.

Sound is air vibration. When the vibrations are large, the sound is loud. The muffler catches the large bursts of high-pressure exhaust gas from the cylinder, smoothing out the pressure pulses and allowing them to be released at an even and constant rate. It does this through the use of perforated tubes within the muffler chamber. The smooth-flowing gases are released to the tailpipe. In this way, the muffler silences engine exhaust noise. ● SEE FIGURE 20–20.

CONSTRUCTION Most mufflers have a larger inlet diameter than outlet diameter. As the exhaust enters the muffler, it expands and cools. The cooler exhaust is denser and occupies less volume. The diameter of the outlet of the muffler and the diameter of the tailpipe can be reduced with no decrease in efficiency.

Sometimes resonators are used in the exhaust system and the catalytic converter also acts as a muffler. They provide additional expansion space at critical points in the exhaust system to smooth out the exhaust gas flow.

The tailpipe carries the exhaust gases from the muffler to the air, away from the vehicle. In most cases, the tailpipe exit is at the rear of the vehicle, below the rear bumper. In some cases, the exhaust is released at the side of the vehicle, just ahead of or just behind the rear wheel.

The muffler and tailpipe are supported with brackets, called **hangers,** which help to isolate the exhaust noise from

FIGURE 20–21 A hole in the muffler allows condensed water to escape.

FIGURE 20–22
A high-performance aftermarket air filter often can increase airflow into the engine for more power.

 FREQUENTLY ASKED QUESTION

Why Is There a Hole in My Muffler?

Many mufflers are equipped with a small hole in the lower rear part to drain accumulated water. About 1 gallon of water is produced in the form of steam for each gallon of gasoline burned. The water is formed when gasoline is burned in the cylinder. Water consists of two molecules of hydrogen and one of oxygen (H_2O). The hydrogen (H) comes from the fuel and the oxygen (O) comes from the air. During combustion, the hydrogen from the fuel combines with some of the oxygen in the air to form water vapor. The water vapor condenses on the cooler surfaces of the exhaust system, especially in the muffler, until the vehicle has been driven long enough to fully warm the exhaust above the boiling point of water (212°F [100°C]). ● **SEE FIGURE 20–21.**

HIGH-PERFORMANCE TIP

More Airflow = More Power

One of the most popular high-performance modifications is to replace the factory exhaust system with a low-restriction design and to replace the original air filter and air filter housing with a low-restriction unit, as shown in ● **FIGURE 20–22.**

The installation of an aftermarket air filter not only increases power, but also increases air induction noise, which many drivers prefer. The aftermarket filter housing, however, may not be able to effectively prevent water from being drawn into the engine if the vehicle is traveling through deep water.

Almost every modification that increases performance has a negative effect on some other part of the vehicle, or else the manufacturer would include the change at the factory.

the rest of the vehicle. The types of exhaust system hangers include:

- Rubberized fabric with metal ends that hold the muffler and tailpipe in position so that they do not touch any metal part, to isolate the exhaust noise from the rest of the vehicle

- Rubber material that looks like large rubber bands, which slip over the hooks on the exhaust system and the hooks attached to the body of the vehicle

SUMMARY

1. All air entering an engine must be filtered.

2. Engines that use throttle-body injection units are equipped with intake manifolds that keep the airflow speed through the manifold at 50 to 300 ft per second.

3. Most intake manifolds have an EGR valve that regulates the amount of recirculated exhaust that enters the engine to reduce NOx emissions.

4. Exhaust manifolds can be made from cast iron or steel tubing.

5. The exhaust system also contains a catalytic converter, exhaust pipes, and muffler. The entire exhaust system is supported by rubber hangers that isolate the noise and vibration of the exhaust from the rest of the vehicle.

1. Why is it necessary to have intake charge velocities of about 50 ft per second?

2. Why can port fuel-injected engines use larger (and longer) intake manifolds and still operate at low engine speed?

3. What is a tuned runner in an intake manifold?

4. How does a muffler quiet exhaust noise?

CHAPTER QUIZ

1. Intake charge velocity has to be _____ to prevent fuel droplet separation.
   a. 25 ft per second
   b. 50 ft per second
   c. 100 ft per second
   d. 300 ft per second

2. The air filter restriction indicator uses what to detect when it signals to replace the filter?
   a. Number of hours of engine operation
   b. Number of miles or vehicle travel
   c. The amount of light that can past through the filter
   d. The amount of restriction measured in inches of water

3. Why are the EGR gases cooled before entering the engine on some engines?
   a. Cool exhaust gas is more effective at controlling NOx emissions
   b. To help prevent the exhaust from slowing down
   c. To prevent damage to the intake valve
   d. To prevent heating the air-fuel mixture in the cylinder

4. The air-fuel mixture flows through the intake manifold on what type of system?
   a. Port fuel-injection systems
   b. Throttle-body fuel-injection systems
   c. Both a port-injected and throttle-body injected engine
   d. Any fuel-injected engine

5. Air filters can remove particles and dirt as small as _____.
   a. 5 to 10 microns
   b. 10 to 25 microns
   c. 30 to 40 microns
   d. 40 to 50 microns

6. Why do many port fuel-injected engines use long intake manifold runners?
   a. To reduce exhaust emissions
   b. To heat the incoming air
   c. To increase high-RPM power
   d. To increase low-RPM torque

7. Exhaust passages are included in some intake manifolds. Technician A says that the exhaust passages are used for exhaust gas recirculation (EGR) systems. Technician B says that the upper intake is often called the plenum. Which technician is correct?
   a. Technician A only
   b. Technician B only
   c. Both Technicians A and B
   d. Neither Technician A nor B

8. The upper portion of a two-part intake manifold is often called the _____.
   a. Housing
   b. Lower part
   c. Plenum
   d. Vacuum chamber

9. Technician A says that a cracked exhaust manifold can affect engine operation. Technician B says that a leaking lower intake manifold gasket could cause a vacuum leak. Which technician is correct?
   a. Technician A only
   b. Technician B only
   c. Both Technicians A and B
   d. Neither Technician A nor B

10. Technician A says that some intake manifolds are plastic. Technician B says that some intake manifolds are constructed in two parts or sections: upper and lower. Which technician is correct?
    a. Technician A only
    b. Technician B only
    c. Both Technicians A and B
    d. Neither Technician A nor B

chapter 21

TURBOCHARGING AND SUPERCHARGING

LEARNING OBJECTIVES: After studying this chapter, the reader should be able to: • Discuss airflow requirements and volumetric efficiency of engines. • Explain forced induction principles. • Discuss superchargers. • Discuss turbochargers and turbocharger failures. • Explain boost control. • Describe the purpose of a nitrous oxide system.

KEY TERMS: Boost 289 • BOV 296 • Bypass valve 292 • CBV 296 • Dry system 298 • Dump valve 296 • Forced induction systems 290 • Intercooler 295 • Naturally (normally) aspirated 289 • Nitrous oxide (N_2O) 298 • Positive displacement 292 • Power adder 298 • Roots supercharger 292 • Supercharger 291 • Turbocharger 293 • Turbo lag 294 • Vent valve 296 • Volumetric efficiency 289 • Wastegate 295 • Wet system 298

INTRODUCTION

AIRFLOW REQUIREMENTS Naturally aspirated engines with throttle plates use atmospheric pressure to push an air-fuel mixture into the combustion chamber vacuum created by the down stroke of a piston. The mixture is then compressed before ignition to increase the force of the burning, expanding gases. The greater the compression of the air-fuel mixture, the higher the engine power output resulting from combustion.

A four-stroke engine can take in only so much air, and how much fuel it needs for proper combustion depends on how much air it takes in. Engineers calculate engine airflow requirements using three factors.

1. Engine displacement
2. Engine revolutions per minute (RPM)
3. Volumetric efficiency

VOLUMETRIC EFFICIENCY **Volumetric efficiency** is a measure of how well an engine breathes. It is a comparison of the actual volume of air-fuel mixture drawn into an engine to the theoretical maximum volume that could be drawn in. Volumetric efficiency is expressed as a percentage. If the engine takes in the airflow volume slowly, a cylinder might fill to capacity. It takes a definite amount of time for the airflow to pass through all the curves of the intake manifold and valve port. Therefore, volumetric efficiency decreases as engine speed increases due to the shorter amount of time for the cylinders to be filled with air during the intake stroke. At high speed, it may drop to as low as 50%.

The average stock gasoline engine never reaches 100% volumetric efficiency. A new engine is about 85% efficient.

A race engine usually has 95% or better volumetric efficiency. These figures apply only to naturally aspirated engines. However, with either turbochargers or superchargers, engines can easily achieve more than 100% volumetric efficiency. Many vehicles are equipped with a supercharger or a turbocharger from the factory to increase power. ● **SEE FIGURES 21–1 AND 21–2.**

FORCED INDUCTION PRINCIPLES

PURPOSE AND FUNCTION The amount of force an air-fuel charge produces when it is ignited is largely a function of the charge density. Charge density is a term used to define the amount of the air-fuel charge introduced into the cylinders. Density is the mass of a substance in a given amount of space. ● **SEE FIGURE 21–3.**

The greater the density of an air-fuel charge forced into a cylinder, the greater the force it produces when ignited, and the greater the engine power.

An engine that uses atmospheric pressure for its intake charge is called a **naturally (normally) aspirated** engine. A better way to increase air density is to use some type of air pump such as a turbocharger or supercharger.

When air is pumped into the cylinder, the combustion chamber receives an increase of air pressure known as **boost,** and can be measured in:

- Pounds per square inch (PSI)
- Atmospheres (ATM) (1 atmosphere is 14.7 PSI)
- Bars (1 bar is 14.7 PSI)

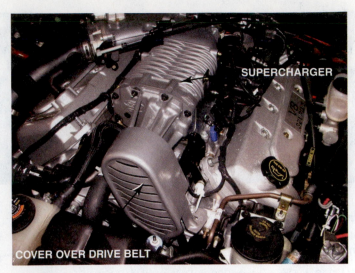

FIGURE 21–1 A supercharger on a Ford V-8.

FIGURE 21–2 A turbocharger on a Toyota engine.

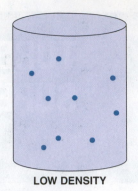 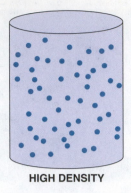

LOW DENSITY   HIGH DENSITY

FIGURE 21–3 The more air and fuel that can be packed in a cylinder, the greater the density of the air-fuel charge.

Pumping air into the intake system under pressure forces it through the bends and restrictions of the air intake system at a greater speed than it would travel under normal atmospheric pressure. This added pressure allows more air to enter the intake port before the intake valve closes. By increasing the airflow into the intake, more fuel can be mixed with the air while still maintaining the same air-fuel ratio. The denser the air-fuel charge entering the engine during its intake stroke, the greater the potential energy released during combustion. In addition to the increased power resulting from combustion, there are several other advantages of supercharging an engine, including:

- It increases the air-fuel charge density to provide high-compression pressure when power is required, but allows the engine to run on lower pressures when additional power is not required.

- The pumped air pushes the remaining exhaust from the combustion chamber during intake and exhaust valve overlap. (Overlap is when both the intake and exhaust valves are partially open when the piston is near the top at the end of the exhaust stroke and the beginning of the intake stroke.)

- The forced airflow and removal of hot exhaust gases lowers the temperature of the cylinder head, pistons, and valves, and helps extend the life of the engine.

A supercharger or turbocharger pressurizes air to greater than atmospheric pressure. The pressurization above atmospheric pressure, or boost, can be measured in the same way as atmospheric pressure. Atmospheric pressure drops as altitude increases, but boost pressure remains the same. If a supercharger develops 12 PSI (83 kPa) boost at sea level, it will develop the same amount at a 5,000 ft altitude because boost pressure is measured inside the intake manifold. ● SEE FIGURE 21–4.

BOOST AND COMPRESSION RATIOS Boost increases the amount of air drawn into the cylinder during the intake stroke. This extra air causes the effective compression ratio to be greater than the mechanical compression ratio designed into

While boost pressure increases air density, friction heats air in motion and causes an increase in temperature. This increase in temperature works in the opposite direction, decreasing air density. Because of these and other variables, an increase in pressure does not always result in greater air density.

FORCED INDUCTION PRINCIPLES Forced induction systems use an air pump to pack a denser air-fuel charge into the cylinders. Because the density of the air-fuel charge is greater, the following occurs.

- The weight of the air-fuel charge is higher.
- Power is increased because it is directly related to the weight of an air-fuel charge consumed within a given time period.

FIGURE 21–4 Atmospheric pressure decreases with increases in altitude.

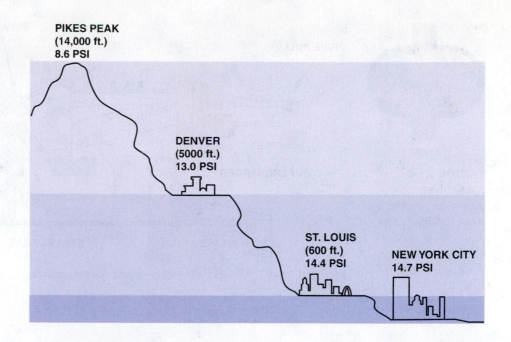

PIKES PEAK
(14,000 ft.)
8.6 PSI

DENVER
(5000 ft.)
13.0 PSI

ST. LOUIS
(600 ft.)
14.4 PSI

NEW YORK CITY
14.7 PSI

FINAL COMPRESSION RATIO CHART AT VARIOUS BOOST LEVELS										
Comp Ratio	Blower Boost (PSI)									
	2	4	6	8	10	12	14	16	18	20
6.5	7.4	8.3	9.2	10	10.9	11.8	12.7	13.6	14.5	15.3
7	8	8.9	9.9	10.8	11.8	12.7	13.6	14.5	15.3	16.2
7.5	8.5	9.5	10.6	11.6	12.6	13.6	14.6	15.7	16.7	17.8
8	9.1	10.2	11.3	12.4	13.4	14.5	15.6	16.7	17.8	18.9
8.5	9.7	10.8	12	13.1	14.3	15.4	16.6	17.8	18.9	19.8
9	10.2	11.4	12.7	13.9	15.1	16.3	17.6	18.8	20	21.2
9.5	10.8	12.1	13.4	14.7	16	17.3	18.5	19.8	21.1	22.4
10	11.4	12.7	14.1	15.4	16.8	18.2	19.5	20.9	22.2	23.6

CHART 21–1

The effective compression ratio compared to the boost pressure.

the engine. The higher the boost pressure, the greater the compression ratio. This means that any engine that uses a supercharger or turbocharger must use all of the following engine components.

- Forged pistons, to withstand the increased combustion pressures
- Stronger than normal connecting rods
- Piston oil squirters that direct a stream of oil to the underneath part of the piston, to keep piston temperatures under control
- Lower compression ratio compared to a naturally aspirated engine

  ●SEE CHART 21–1.

SUPERCHARGERS

INTRODUCTION A **supercharger** is an engine-driven air pump that supplies more than the normal amount of air into the intake manifold and boosts engine torque and power. A supercharger provides an instantaneous increase in power without any delay. However, a supercharger, because it is driven by the engine, requires horsepower to operate and is not as efficient as a turbocharger.

A supercharger is an air pump mechanically driven by the engine itself. Gears, shafts, chains, or belts from the crankshaft can all be used to turn the pump. This means that the air pump or supercharger pumps air in direct relation to engine speed.

FIGURE 21–5
A roots-type supercharger uses two lobes to force the air around the outside of the housing and into the intake manifold.

LOBE

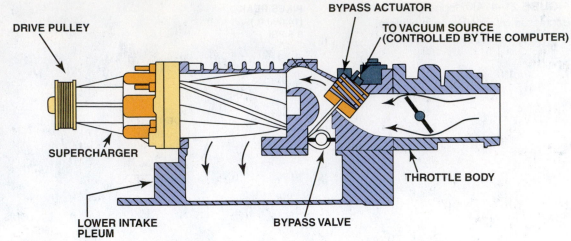

DRIVE PULLEY

BYPASS ACTUATOR

TO VACUUM SOURCE (CONTROLLED BY THE COMPUTER)

SUPERCHARGER

THROTTLE BODY

LOWER INTAKE PLEUM

BYPASS VALVE

FIGURE 21–6 The bypass actuator opens the bypass valve to control boost pressure.

TYPES OF SUPERCHARGERS

There are two general types of superchargers.

- **Roots type.** Named for Philander and Francis Roots, two brothers from Connersville, Indiana, the **roots supercharger** was patented in 1860 as a type of water pump to be used in mines. Later, it was used to move air and is used today on two-stroke-cycle Detroit diesel engines and other supercharged engines. The roots-type supercharger is called a **positive displacement** design, because all of the air that enters is forced through the unit. Examples of a roots-type supercharger include the GMC 6-71 (used originally on GMC diesel engines that had 6 cylinders each with 71 cubic inch). Eaton used the roots design for the supercharger on the 3800 V-6 GM engine. ● SEE FIGURE 21–5.

- **Centrifugal supercharger.** A centrifugal supercharger is similar to a turbocharger, but is mechanically driven by the engine instead of being powered by the hot exhaust gases. A centrifugal supercharger is not a positive displacement pump and all of the air that enters is not forced through the unit. Air enters a centrifugal supercharger housing in the center and exits at the outer edges of the compressor wheels at a much higher speed due to centrifugal force. The speed of the blades has to be higher than engine speed so a smaller pulley is used on the supercharger and the crankshaft overdrives the impeller through an internal gear box achieving about seven times the speed of the engine. Examples of centrifugal superchargers include Vortech and Paxton.

SUPERCHARGER BOOST CONTROL

Many factory installed superchargers are equipped with a **bypass valve** that allows intake air to flow directly into the intake manifold, bypassing the supercharger. The computer controls the bypass valve actuator. ● SEE FIGURE 21–6.

The airflow is directed around the supercharger whenever any of the following conditions occur.

- The boost pressure, as measured by the MAP sensor, indicates that the intake manifold pressure is reaching the predetermined boost level.

- During deceleration, to prevent excessive pressure buildup in the intake.

- Reverse gear is selected.

SUPERCHARGER SERVICE

Superchargers are usually lubricated with synthetic engine oil inside the unit. This oil level should be checked and replaced as specified by the vehicle or supercharger manufacturer. The drive belt should also be inspected and replaced as necessary. The air filter should be replaced regularly, and always use the filter specified for a supercharged engine. Many factory supercharger systems use a separate cooling system for the air charge cooler located under the supercharger. Check service information for the exact service procedures to follow. ● SEE FIGURE 21–7.

TECH TIP

Faster Moves More Air

One of the high-performance measures that can be used to increase horsepower on a supercharged engine is to install a smaller diameter pulley. The smaller the pulley diameter, the faster the supercharger will rotate and the higher the potential boost pressure will be. The change will require a shorter belt, and the extra boost could cause serious engine damage.

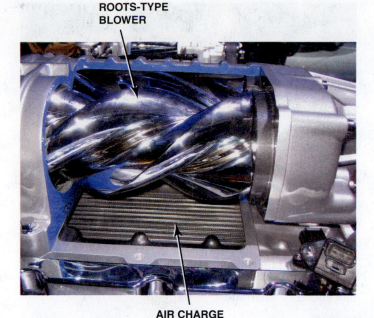

ROOTS-TYPE
BLOWER

AIR CHARGE
COOLER

FIGURE 21–7 A Ford supercharger cutaway display showing the roots-type blower and air charge cooler (intercooler). The air charge cooler is used to reduce the temperature of the compressed air before it enters the engine to increase the air charge density.

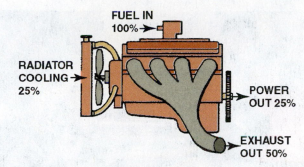

FUEL IN
100%

RADIATOR
COOLING
25%

POWER
OUT 25%

EXHAUST
OUT 50%

FIGURE 21–8 A turbocharger uses some of the heat energy that would normally be wasted.

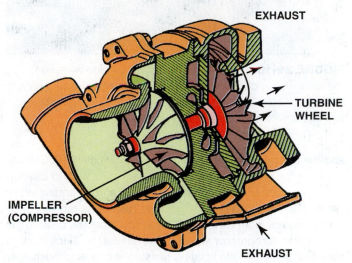

EXHAUST

TURBINE
WHEEL

IMPELLER
(COMPRESSOR)

EXHAUST

FIGURE 21–9 A turbine wheel is turned by the expanding exhaust gases.

TURBOCHARGERS

INTRODUCTION The major disadvantage of a supercharger is it takes some of the engine power to drive the unit. In some installations, as much as 20% of the engine power is used by a mechanical supercharger. A **turbocharger** uses the heat of the exhaust to power a turbine wheel and therefore does not directly reduce engine power. In a naturally aspirated engine, about half of the heat energy contained in the fuel goes out the exhaust system. However, some engine power is lost due to the exhaust restriction. This loss in power is regained, though, to perform other work and the combustion heat energy lost in the engine exhaust (as much as 40% to 50%) can be harnessed to do useful work. Another 25% is lost through radiator cooling. Only about 25% is actually converted to mechanical power. A mechanically driven pump uses some of this mechanical output, but a turbocharger gets its energy from the exhaust gases, converting more of the fuel's heat energy into useful mechanical energy. ● **SEE FIGURE 21–8.**

OPERATION A turbocharger turbine looks much like a typical centrifugal pump used for supercharging.

Hot exhaust gases flow from the combustion chamber to the *turbine wheel*. The gases are heated and expanded as they leave the engine. It is not the speed of force of the exhaust gases that forces the turbine wheel to turn, as is commonly thought, but the expansion of hot gases against the turbine wheel's blades.

A turbocharger consists of two chambers connected with a center housing. The two chambers contain a turbine wheel and an *impeller* (compressor) *wheel* connected by a shaft which passes through the center housing. ● **SEE FIGURE 21–9.**

To take full advantage of the exhaust heat which provides the rotating force, a turbocharger must be positioned as close as possible to the exhaust manifold. This allows the hot exhaust to pass directly into the unit with minimal heat loss. As exhaust gas enters the turbocharger, it rotates the turbine blades. The turbine wheel and compressor wheel are on the same shaft so that they turn at the same speed. Rotation of the compressor wheel draws air in through a central inlet and centrifugal force pumps it through an outlet at the edge of the housing. A pair of bearings in the center housing supports the turbine and compressor wheel shaft, and is lubricated by engine oil. ● **SEE FIGURE 21–10.**

Both the turbine and compressor wheels must operate with extremely close clearances to minimize possible leakage around their blades. Any leakage around the turbine blades causes a dissipation of the heat energy required for compressor rotation. Leakage around the compressor blades prevents the turbocharger from developing its full boost pressure.

TURBOCHARGER OPERATION When the engine is started and runs at low speed, both exhaust heat and pressure are low

FIGURE 21–10 The exhaust drives the turbine wheel on the left which is connected to the impeller wheel on the right through a shaft. The bushings that support the shaft are lubricated with engine oil under pressure.

FIGURE 21–11 Engine oil is fed to the center of the turbocharger to lubricate the bushings and returns to the oil pan through a return line.

and the turbine runs at a low speed (approximately 1000 RPM). Because the compressor does not turn fast enough to develop boost pressure, air simply passes through it and the engine works like any naturally aspirated engine. As the engine runs faster or load increases, both exhaust heat and flow increase, causing the turbine and compressor wheels to rotate faster. Since there is no brake and very little rotating resistance on the turbocharger shaft, the turbine and compressor wheels accelerate as the exhaust heat energy increases. When an engine is running at full power, the typical turbocharger rotates at speeds between 100,000 and 150,000 RPM. The turbocharger is lubricated by engine oil through an oil line to the center bearing assembly. ● SEE FIGURE 21–11.

Engine deceleration from full power to idle requires only a second or two because of its internal friction, pumping resistance, and drivetrain load. The turbocharger, however, has no such load on its shaft, and is already turning many times faster than the engine at top speed. As a result, it can take as much as a minute or more after the engine has returned to idle speed before the turbocharger also has returned to idle. If the engine is decelerated to idle and then shut off immediately, engine lubrication stops flowing to the center housing bearings while the turbocharger is still spinning at thousands of RPM. The oil in the center housing is then subjected to extreme heat and can gradually "coke" or oxidize. The coked oil can clog passages and will reduce the life of the turbocharger.

The high rotating speeds and extremely close clearances of the turbine and compressor wheels in their housings require equally critical bearing clearances. The bearings must keep radial clearances of 0.003 to 0.006 inch (0.08 to 0.15 mm). Axial clearance (endplay) must be maintained at 0.001 to 0.003 inch (0.025 to 0.08 mm). If properly maintained, the turbocharger also is a trouble-free device. However, to prevent problems, the following must be met.

- The turbocharger bearings must be constantly lubricated with clean engine oil. Turbocharged engines usually have specified oil changes at more frequent intervals than non-turbocharged engines. Always use the specified engine oil, which is likely to be vehicle specific and synthetic.
- Dirt particles and other contamination must be kept out of the intake and exhaust housings.
- Whenever a basic engine bearing (crankshaft or camshaft) has been damaged, the turbocharger must be flushed with clean engine oil after the bearing has been replaced.
- If the turbocharger is damaged, the engine oil must be drained and flushed and the oil filter replaced as part of the repair procedure.

Late-model turbochargers all have liquid-cooled center bearings to prevent heat damage. In a liquid-cooled turbocharger, engine coolant is circulated through passages cast in the center housing to draw off the excess heat. This allows the bearings to run cooler and minimize the probability of oil coking when the engine is shut down.

TURBOCHARGER SIZE AND RESPONSE TIME A time lag occurs between an increase in engine speed and the increase in the speed of the turbocharger. This delay between acceleration and turbo boost is called **turbo lag.** Like any material, moving exhaust gas has inertia. Inertia also is present in the turbine and compressor wheels, as well as the intake airflow. Unlike a supercharger, the turbocharger cannot supply an adequate amount of boost at low speed.

Turbocharger response time is directly related to the size of the turbine and compressor wheels. Small wheels accelerate rapidly; large wheels accelerate slowly. While small wheels would seem to have an advantage over larger ones, they may not have enough airflow capacity for an engine. To minimize turbo lag, the intake and exhaust breathing capacities of an engine must be matched to the exhaust and intake airflow capabilities of the turbocharger.

BOOST CONTROL

PURPOSE AND FUNCTION   Both supercharged and turbocharged systems are designed to provide a pressure greater than atmospheric pressure in the intake manifold. This increased pressure forces additional amounts of air into the combustion chamber over what would normally be forced in by atmospheric pressure. This increased charge increases engine power. The amount of "boost" (or pressure in the intake manifold) is measured in pounds per square inch (PSI), in inches of mercury (inch Hg), in bars, or in atmospheres. The following values will vary due to altitude and weather conditions (barometric pressure).

> 1 atmosphere = 14.7 PSI
>
> 1 atmosphere = 29.50 in. Hg
>
> 1 atmosphere = 1 bar
>
> 1 bar = 14.7 PSI

BOOST CONTROL FACTORS   The higher the level of boost (pressure), the greater the horsepower output potential. However, other factors must be considered when increasing boost pressure.

1. As boost pressure increases, the temperature of the air also increases.

2. As the temperature of the air increases, combustion temperatures also increase, as well as the possibility of detonation.

3. Power can be increased by cooling the compressed air after it leaves the turbocharger. *The power can be increased about 1% per 10°F by which the air is cooled.* A typical cooling device is called an **intercooler.** It is similar to a radiator, wherein outside air can pass through, cooling the pressurized heated air. An intercooler is located between the turbocharger and the intake manifold. ● **SEE FIGURE 21–12.** Some intercoolers use engine coolant to cool the hot compressed air that flows from the turbocharger to the intake.

4. As boost pressure increases, combustion temperature and pressures increase, which, if not limited, can do severe engine damage. The maximum exhaust gas temperature must be 1,550°F (840°C). Higher temperatures decrease the durability of the turbocharger *and* the engine.

WASTEGATE   Turbochargers use exhaust gases to increase boost, which causes the engine to make more exhaust gases, which in turn increases the boost from the turbocharger. To prevent overboost and severe engine damage, most turbocharger systems use a wastegate. A **wastegate** is a valve

FIGURE 21–12 The unit on top of this Subaru that looks like a radiator is the intercooler, which cools the air after it has been compressed by the turbocharger.

TECH TIP

Boost Is the Result of Restriction

The boost pressure of a turbocharger (or supercharger) is commonly measured in pounds per square inch. If a cylinder head is restricted because of small valves and ports, the turbocharger will quickly provide boost. Boost results when the air being forced into the cylinder heads cannot flow into the cylinders fast enough and "piles up" in the intake manifold, increasing boost pressure. If an engine had large valves and ports, the turbocharger could provide a much greater *amount* of air into the engine at the same boost pressure as an identical engine with smaller valves and ports. Therefore, by increasing the size of the valves, a turbocharged or supercharged engine will be capable of producing much greater power.

similar to a door that can open and close. It is a bypass valve at the exhaust inlet to the turbine, which allows all of the exhaust into the turbine, or it can route part of the exhaust past the turbine to the exhaust system. If the valve is closed, all of the exhaust travels to the turbocharger. When a predetermined amount of boost pressure develops in the intake manifold, the wastegate valve is opened. As the valve opens, most of the exhaust flows directly out the exhaust system, bypassing the turbocharger. With less exhaust flowing across the vanes of the turbocharger, the turbocharger decreases in speed, and boost pressure is reduced. When the boost pressure drops, the wastegate valve closes to direct the exhaust over the turbocharger vanes to again allow the boost pressure to rise. Wastegate operation is a continuous process to control boost pressure.

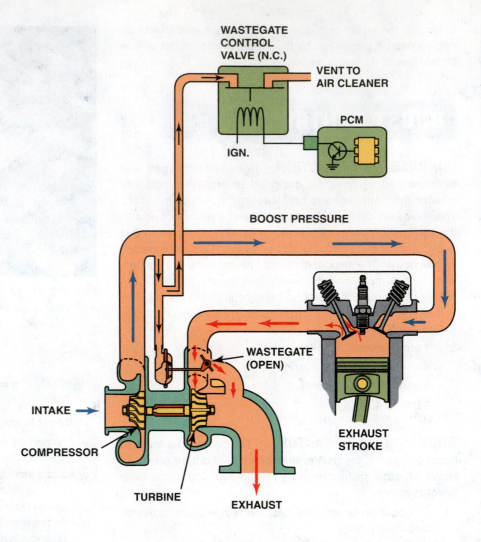

FIGURE 21–13 A wastegate is used on many turbocharged engines to control maximum boost pressure. The wastegate is controlled by a computer-controlled valve.

WASTEGATE CONTROL VALVE (N.C.)

VENT TO AIR CLEANER

PCM

IGN.

BOOST PRESSURE

WASTEGATE (OPEN)

INTAKE

COMPRESSOR

TURBINE

EXHAUST STROKE

EXHAUST

The wastegate is the pressure control valve of a turbocharger system. It is usually controlled by the engine control computer through a boost control solenoid, also called a wastegate control valve. ● SEE FIGURE 21–13.

RELIEF VALVES
A wastegate controls the exhaust side of the turbocharger. A relief valve controls the intake side. A relief valve vents pressurized air from the connecting pipe between the outlet of the turbocharger and the throttle whenever the throttle is closed during boost, such as during shifts. If the pressure is not released, the turbocharger turbine wheel will slow down, creating a lag when the throttle is opened again after a shift has been completed. There are two basic types of relief valves.

1. **Compressor bypass valve (CBV).** This type of relief valve routes the pressurized air to the inlet side of the turbocharger for reuse and is quiet during operation.
2. **Blow-off valve (BOV).** Also called a **dump valve** or **vent valve,** the BOV features an adjustable spring design that keeps the valve closed until a sudden release of the throttle. The resulting pressure increase opens the valve and vents the pressurized air directly into the atmosphere. This type of relief valve is noisy in operation and creates a whooshing sound when the valve opens. ● SEE FIGURE 21–14.

 **TECH TIP**

If One Is Good, Two Are Better

A turbocharger uses the exhaust from the engine to spin a turbine, which is connected to an impeller inside a turbocharger. This impeller then forces air into the engine under pressure, higher than is normally achieved without a turbocharger. The more air that can be forced into an engine, the greater the power potential. A V-type engine has two exhaust manifolds and so two small turbochargers can be used to help force greater quantities of air into an engine, as shown in ● FIGURE 21–15.

TURBOCHARGER FAILURES

SYMPTOMS OF FAILURE When turbochargers fail to function correctly, a noticeable drop in power occurs. To restore proper operation, the turbocharger must be rebuilt,

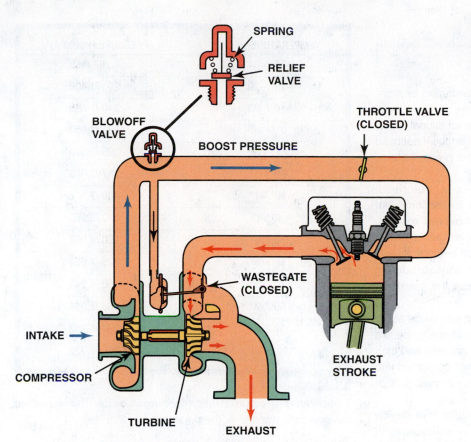

SPRING

RELIEF VALVE

BLOWOFF VALVE

BOOST PRESSURE

THROTTLE VALVE (CLOSED)

WASTEGATE (CLOSED)

INTAKE

COMPRESSOR

TURBINE

EXHAUST

EXHAUST STROKE

FIGURE 21–14 A blow-off valve is used in some turbocharged systems to relieve boost pressure during deceleration.

FIGURE 21–15 A dual turbocharger system installed on a small block Chevrolet V-8 engine.

repaired, or replaced. It is not possible to simply remove the turbocharger, seal any openings, and maintain decent driveability. Bearing failure is a common cause of turbocharger failure, and replacement bearings are usually only available to rebuilders. Another common turbocharger problem is excessive and continuous oil consumption resulting in blue exhaust smoke. Turbochargers use small rings similar to piston rings on the shaft to prevent exhaust (combustion

gases) from entering the central bearing. Because there are no seals to keep oil in, excessive oil consumption is usually caused by the following:

1. Plugged positive crankcase ventilation (PCV) system, resulting in excessive crankcase pressures forcing oil into the air inlet (This failure is not related to the turbocharger, but the turbocharger is often blamed.)

2. Clogged air filter, which causes a low-pressure area in the inlet, drawing oil past the turbo shaft rings and into the intake manifold.

3. Clogged oil return (drain) line from the turbocharger to the oil pan (sump), which can cause the engine oil pressure to force oil past the turbocharger's shaft rings and into the intake *and* exhaust manifolds (Obviously, oil being forced into both the intake and exhaust would create lots of smoke.)

PREVENTING TURBOCHARGER FAILURES To help prevent turbocharger failures, the wise vehicle owner should follow the vehicle manufacturer's recommended routine service procedures. The most critical of these services include:

- Regular oil changes (synthetic oil would be best)
- Regular air filter replacement intervals
- Performing any other inspections and services recommended such as cleaning the intercooler.

NITROUS OXIDE

INTRODUCTION Nitrous oxide is used for racing or high-performance only, and is not used from the factory on any vehicle. This system is a relatively inexpensive way to get additional power from an engine, but can cause serious engine damage if not used correctly or in excess amounts, or without proper precautions.

PRINCIPLES **Nitrous oxide (N_2O)** is a colorless, nonflammable gas. It was discovered by a British chemist, Joseph Priestly (1733–1804), who also discovered oxygen. Priestly found that if a person breathed in nitrous oxide, it caused light-headedness, and so the gas soon became known as *laughing gas*. Nitrous oxide was used in dentistry during tooth extractions to reduce the pain and cause the patient to forget the experience.

Nitrous oxide has two nitrogen atoms and one oxide atom. About 36% of the molecule weight is oxygen. Nitrous oxide is a manufactured gas because, even though both nitrogen and oxygen are present in our atmosphere, they are not combined into one molecule and require heat and a catalyst to be combined.

ENGINE POWER ADDER A **power adder** is a device or system added to an engine, such as a supercharger, turbocharger, or nitrous oxide, to increase power. When nitrous oxide is injected into an engine along with gasoline, engine power is increased. The addition of N_2O supplies the needed oxygen for the extra fuel. N_2O by itself does not burn, but provides the oxygen for additional fuel that is supplied along with the N_2O to produce more power.

NOTE: Nitrous oxide was used as a power adder in World War II on some fighter aircraft. Having several hundred more horsepower for a short time saved many lives.

PRESSURE AND TEMPERATURE It requires about 11 pound of pressure per degree Fahrenheit to condense nitrous oxide gas into liquid nitrous oxide. For example, at 70°F, it requires a pressure of about 770 PSI to condense N_2O into liquid. To change N_2O from liquid under pressure to gas, all that is needed is to lower its pressure below the pressure it takes to cause it to become liquid.

The temperature also affects the pressure of N_2O. ● **SEE CHART 21–2.**

Nitrous oxide is stored in a pressurized storage container and installed at an angle so the pickup tube is in the liquid. The front or discharge end of the storage bottle should be toward the front of the vehicle. ● **SEE FIGURE 21–16.**

WET AND DRY SYSTEM There are two different types of N_2O systems that depend on whether additional fuel (gasoline) is supplied at the same time as when the nitrous oxide is squirted.

- The **wet system** involves additional fuel being injected. It is identified as having both a red and a blue nozzle, with the red flowing gasoline and the blue flowing nitrous oxide.

TEMPERATURE (°F/°C)	PRESSURE (PSI/KPA)
−30°/−34°	67 /468
−20°/−29°	203 /1,400
−10°/−23°	240 /1,655
0°/−18°	283 /1,950
10°/−12°	335 /2,310
20°/−7°	387 /2,668
30°/−1°	460 /3,172
40°/4°	520 /3,585
50°/10°	590 /4,068
60°/16°	675 /4,654
70°/21°	760 /5,240
80°/27°	865 /5,964
90°/32°	985 /6,792
100°/38°	1,120 /7,722

CHART 21–2

Temperature/pressure relation for nitrous oxide: The higher the temperature, the higher the pressure.

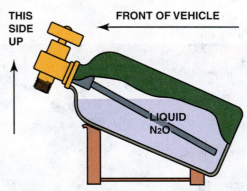

FIGURE 21–16 Nitrous bottles have to be mounted at an angle to ensure that the pickup tube is in the liquid N_2O.

- In a **dry system,** such as an engine using port fuel injection, only nitrous oxide needs to be injected because the PCM can be commanded to provide more fuel when the N_2O is being sprayed. As a result, the intake manifold contains only air and the injected gaseous N_2O.

TECH TIP

Increase Bottle Pressure

To increase the pressure of the nitrous oxide in a bottle, an electrical warming blanket can be used, as seen in ● **FIGURE 21–17.** The higher the temperature, the higher the pressure and the greater the amount of N_2O flow when energized.

FIGURE 21–17 An electrical heating mat is installed on the bottle of nitrous oxide to increase the pressure of the gas inside.

ENGINE CHANGES NEEDED FOR N₂O

If nitrous oxide is going to be used to increase horsepower more than 50 hp, the engine must be designed and built to withstand the greater heat and pressure that will occur in the combustion chambers. For example, the following items should be considered if adding a turbocharger, supercharger, or nitrous oxide system.

- Forged pistons are best able to withstand the pressure and temperature when using nitrous oxide or other power adder.

- Cylinder-to-wall clearance should be increased. Due to the greater amount of heat created by the extra fuel and N₂O injection, the piston temperature will be increased. Although using forged pistons will help, most experts recommend using increased cylinder-to-wall clearance.

- Using forged crankshaft and connecting rods.

Check the instructions from the nitrous oxide supplier for details and other suggested changes.

CAUTION: The use of a nitrous oxide injection system can cause catastrophic engine damage. Always follow the instructions that come with the kit and be sure that all of the internal engine parts meet the standard specified to help avoid severe engine damage.

SYSTEM INSTALLATION AND CALIBRATION

Nitrous oxide systems are usually purchased as a kit with all of the needed components included. The kit also includes one or more sizes of nozzle(s), which are calibrated to control the flow of nitrous oxide into the intake manifold.

The sizes of the nozzles are often calibrated in horsepower that can be gained by their use. Commonly sized nozzles include:

- 50 hp
- 100 hp
- 150 hp

Installation of a nitrous oxide kit also includes the installation of an on–off switch and a switch on or near the throttle, which is used to activate the system only when the throttle is fully opened (WOT).

SUMMARY

1. Volumetric efficiency is a comparison of the actual volume of air-fuel mixture drawn into the engine to the theoretical maximum volume that can be drawn into the cylinder.

2. A supercharger operates from the engine by a drive belt and, although it consumes some engine power, it forces a greater amount of air into the cylinders for even more power.

3. There are two types of superchargers: roots-type and centrifugal.

4. A turbocharger uses the normally wasted heat energy of the exhaust to turn an impeller at high speed. The impeller is linked to a turbine wheel on the same shaft and is used to force air into the engine.

5. A bypass valve is used to control the boost pressure on most factory installed superchargers.

6. An intercooler is used on many turbocharged and some supercharged engines to reduce the temperature of air entering the engine for increased power.

7. A wastegate is used on most turbocharger systems to limit and control boost pressures, as well as a relief valve, to keep the speed of the turbine wheel from slowing down during engine deceleration.

8. Nitrous oxide injection can be used as a power adder, but only with extreme caution.

1. What are the reasons why supercharging increases engine power?

2. How does the bypass valve work on a supercharged engine?

3. What are the advantages and disadvantages of supercharging?

4. What are the advantages and disadvantages of turbocharging?

5. What turbocharger control valves are needed for proper engine operation?

CHAPTER QUIZ

1. Boost pressure is generally measured in _____.
   a. inch Hg
   b. PSI
   c. inch H$_2$O
   d. inch pound

2. Two types of superchargers include _____.
   a. Rotary and reciprocating
   b. Roots-type and centrifugal
   c. Double and single acting
   d. Turbine and piston

3. Which valve is used on a factory supercharger to limit boost?
   a. Bypass valve
   b. Wastegate
   c. Blow-off valve
   d. Air valve

4. How are most superchargers lubricated?
   a. By engine oil under pressure through lines from the engine
   b. By an internal oil reservoir
   c. By greased bearings
   d. No lubrication is needed because the incoming air cools the supercharger

5. How are most turbochargers lubricated?
   a. By engine oil under pressure through lines from the engine
   b. By an internal oil reservoir
   c. By greased bearings
   d. No lubrication is needed because the incoming air cools the supercharger

6. Two technicians are discussing the term *turbo lag*. Technician A says that it refers to the delay between when the exhaust leaves the cylinder and when it contacts the turbine blades of the turbocharger. Technician B says that it refers to the delay in boost pressure that occurs when the throttle is first opened. Which technician is correct?
   a. Technician A only
   b. Technician B only
   c. Both Technicians A and B
   d. Neither Technician A nor B

7. What is the purpose of an intercooler?
   a. To reduce the temperature of the air entering the engine
   b. To cool the turbocharger
   c. To cool the engine oil on a turbocharged engine
   d. To cool the exhaust before it enters the turbocharger

8. Which type of relief valve used on a turbocharged engine is noisy?
   a. Bypass valve
   b. BOV
   c. Dump valve
   d. Both b and c

9. Technician A says that a stuck open wastegate can cause the engine to burn oil. Technician B says that a clogged PCV system can cause the engine to burn oil. Which technician is correct?
   a. Technician A only
   b. Technician B only
   c. Both Technicians A and B
   d. Neither Technician A nor B

10. What service operation is *most* important on engines equipped with a turbocharger?
   a. Replacing the air filter regularly
   b. Replacing the fuel filter regularly
   c. Regular oil changes
   d. Regular exhaust system maintenance

chapter 22

ENGINE CONDITION DIAGNOSIS

LEARNING OBJECTIVES: After studying this chapter, the reader should be able to: • Discuss typical engine-related complaints and engine smoke diagnosis. • Discuss the importance of visual checks. • Discuss engine noise diagnosis. • Explain oil pressure testing and the purpose of oil pressure warning lamps. • Explain compression test, and compare wet compression test and running compression test. • Describe cylinder leakage test and cylinder power balance test. • Explain the vacuum test and exhaust restriction test. • Explain how to test back pressure with a vacuum gauge and a pressure gauge, and how to diagnose head gasket failure. • Discuss the operation of warning lights.

KEY TERMS: Back pressure 313 • Compression test 306 • Cranking vacuum test 310 • Cylinder leakage test 309 • Dynamic compression test 308 • Idle vacuum test 310 • Inches of mercury (inch Hg) 310 • Paper test 307 • Power balance test 310 • Restricted exhaust 312 • Running compression test 308 • Vacuum test 310 • Wet compression test 308

If there is an engine operation problem, then the cause could be any one of many items, including the engine itself. The condition of the engine should be tested anytime the operation of the engine is not satisfactory.

TYPICAL ENGINE-RELATED COMPLAINTS

Many driveability problems are *not* caused by engine mechanical problems. A thorough inspection and testing of the ignition and fuel systems should be performed before testing for mechanical engine problems.

Typical engine mechanical-related complaints include the following:

- Excessive oil consumption
- Engine misfiring
- Loss of power
- Smoke from the engine or exhaust ● SEE FIGURE 22–1.
- Engine noise

ENGINE SMOKE DIAGNOSIS

The color of engine exhaust smoke can indicate what engine problem might exist.

Typical Exhaust Smoke Color	Possible Causes
Blue	Blue exhaust indicates that the engine is burning oil. Oil is getting into the combustion chamber either past the piston rings or past the valve stem seals. Blue smoke only after start-up is usually due to defective valve stem seals.
Black	Black exhaust smoke is due to excessive fuel being burned in the combustion chamber. Typical causes include a defective or misadjusted throttle body, leaking fuel injector, or excessive fuel-pump pressure.
White (steam)	White smoke or steam from the exhaust is normal during cold weather and represents condensed steam. Every engine creates about 1 gallon of water for each gallon of gasoline burned. If the steam from the exhaust is excessive, then water (coolant) is getting into the combustion chamber. Typical causes include a defective cylinder head gasket, a cracked cylinder head, or in severe cases a cracked block. ● SEE FIGURE 22–2.

Note: White smoke can also be created when automatic transmission fluid (ATF) is burned. A common source of ATF getting into the engine is through a defective vacuum modulator valve on older automatic transmissions.

FIGURE 22–1 Blowby gases coming out of the crankcase vent hose. Excessive amounts of combustion gases flow past the piston rings and into the crankcase.

FIGURE 22–2 White steam is usually an indication of a blown (defective) cylinder head gasket that allows engine coolant to flow into the combustion chamber where it is turned to steam.

THE DRIVER IS YOUR BEST RESOURCE

The driver of the vehicle knows a lot about the vehicle and how it is driven. *Before* diagnosis is started, always ask the folwing questions.

- When did the problem first occur?
- Under what conditions does it occur?

1. Cold or hot?
2. Acceleration, cruise, or deceleration?
3. How far was it driven?
4. What recent repairs have been performed?

After the nature and scope of the problem are determined, the complaint should be verified before further diagnostic tests are performed.

 TECH TIP

Your Nose Knows

Whenever diagnosing any vehicle try to use all senses including smell. Some smells and their cause include:

- **Gasoline.** If the exhaust smells like gasoline or unburned fuel, then a fault with the ignition system is a likely cause. Unburned fuel due to lean air-fuel mixture causing a lean misfire is also possible.
- **Sweet smell.** A coolant leak often gives off a sweet smell especially if the leaking coolant flows onto the hot exhaust.
- **Exhaust smell.** Check for an exhaust leak including a possible cracked exhaust manifold which can be difficult to find because it often does not make noise.

VISUAL CHECKS

The first and most important "test" that can be performed is a careful visual inspection.

OIL LEVEL AND CONDITION   The first area for visual inspection is oil level and condition.

1. Oil level—oil should be to the proper level
2. Oil condition
   a. Using a match or lighter, try to light the oil on the dipstick; if the oil flames up, gasoline is present in the engine oil.
   b. Drip some of the engine oil from the dipstick onto the hot exhaust manifold. If the oil bubbles or boils, there is coolant (water) in the oil.
   c. Check for grittiness by rubbing the oil between your fingers.

COOLANT LEVEL AND CONDITION   Most mechanical engine problems are caused by overheating. The proper operation of the cooling system is critical to the life of any engine.

NOTE: Check the coolant level in the radiator only if the radiator is cool. If the radiator is hot and the radiator cap is removed, the drop in pressure above the coolant will cause the coolant to boil immediately and can cause severe burns when the coolant explosively expands upward and outward from the radiator opening.

1. The coolant level in the coolant recovery container should be within the limits indicated on the overflow bottle. If this level is too low or the coolant recovery container is empty, then check the level of coolant in the radiator (only when cool) and also check the operation of the pressure cap.

FIGURE 22–3 What looks like an oil pan gasket leak can be a rocker cover gasket leak. Always look up and look for the highest place you see oil leaking; that should be repaired first.

 TECH TIP

What's Leaking?

The color of the leaks observed under a vehicle can help the technician determine and correct the cause. Some leaks, such as condensate (water) from the air-conditioning system, are normal, whereas a brake fluid leak is very dangerous. The folwing are colors of common leaks.

Sooty Black	Engine Oil
Yellow, green, blue, or orange	Antifreeze (coolant)
Red	Automatic transmission fluid
Murky brown	Brake or power steering fluid or very neglected antifreeze (coolant)
Clear	Air-conditioning condensate (water) (normal)

2. The coolant should be checked with a hydrometer for boiling and freezing temperature. This test indicates if the concentration of the antifreeze is sufficient for proper protection.

3. Pressure test the cooling system and look for leakage. Coolant leakage can often be seen around hoses or cooling system components because it will often cause:
   a. A grayish white stain
   b. A rusty cor stain
   c. Dye stains from antifreeze (greenish or yellowish depending on the type of coolant)

4. Check for cool areas of the radiator indicating clogged sections.

5. Check operation and condition of the fan clutch, fan, and coolant pump drive belt.

FIGURE 22–4 The transmission and flexplate (flywheel) were removed to check the exact location of this oil leak. The rear main seal and/or the oil pan gasket could be the cause of this leak.

OIL LEAKS Oil leaks can lead to severe engine damage if the resulting low oil level is not corrected. Besides causing an oily mess where the vehicle is parked, the oil leak can cause blue smoke to occur under the hood as leaking oil drips on the exhaust system. *Finding* the location of the oil leak can often be difficult. ● **SEE FIGURES 22–3 AND 22–4.** To help find the source of oil leaks follow these steps:

STEP 1 Clean the engine or area around the suspected oil leak. Use a high-powered hot-water spray to wash the engine. While the engine is running, spray the entire engine and the engine compartment. Avoid letting the water come into direct contact with the air inlet and ignition distributor or ignition coil(s).

Note: If the engine starts to run rough or stalls when the engine gets wet, then the secondary ignition wires (spark plug wires) or distributor cap may be defective or have weak insulation. Be certain to wipe all wires and the distributor cap dry with a soft, dry cloth if the engine stalls.

An alternative method is to spray a degreaser on the engine, then start and run the engine until warm. Engine heat helps the degreaser penetrate the grease and dirt. Use a water hose to rinse off the engine and engine compartment.

FIGURE 22–5 Using a black light to spot leaks after adding dye to the oil.

FIGURE 22–6 An accessory belt tensioner. Most tensioners have a mark that indicates normal operating location. If the belt has stretched, this indicator mark will be outside of the normal range. Anything wrong with the belt or tensioner can cause noise.

STEP 2 If the oil leak is not visible or oil seems to be coming from "everywhere," use a white talcum powder. The leaking oil will show as a dark area on the white powder. See the Tech Tip, "The Foot Powder Spray Trick."

STEP 3 Fluorescent dye can be added to the engine oil. Add about 1/2 oz (15 cc) of dye per 5 quarts of engine oil. Start the engine and allow it to run about 10 minutes to thoroughly mix the dye throughout the engine. A black light can then be shown around every suspected oil leak location. The black light will easily show all oil leak cations because the dye will show as a bright yellow/green area. ● **SEE FIGURE 22–5.**

NOTE: Fluorescent dye works best with clean oil.

 **TECH TIP**

The Foot Powder Spray Trick

The source of an oil or other fluid leak is often difficult to determine. A quick and easy method that works is the following. First, clean the entire area. This can best be done by using a commercially available degreaser to spray the entire area. Let it soak to loosen all accumulated oil and greasy dirt. Clean off the degreaser with a water hose. Let the area dry. Start the engine, and using spray foot powder or other aerosol powder product, spray the entire area. The leak will turn the white powder dark. The exact location of any leak can be quickly located.

NOTE: Most oil leaks appear at the bottom of the engine due to gravity. Look for the highest, most forward location for the source of the leak.

ENGINE NOISE DIAGNOSIS

An engine knocking noise is often difficult to diagnose. Several items that can cause a deep engine knock include:

- **Valves clicking.** This can happen because of lack of oil to the lifters. This noise is most noticeable at idle when the oil pressure is the lowest.

- **Torque converter.** The attaching bolts or nuts may be loose on the flex plate. This noise is most noticeable at idle or when there is no load on the engine.

- **Cracked flex plate.** The noise of a cracked flex plate is often mistaken for a rod- or main-bearing noise.

- **Loose or defective drive belts or tensioners.** If an accessory drive belt is loose or defective, the flopping noise often sounds similar to a bearing knock. ● **SEE FIGURE 22–6.**

- **Piston pin knock.** This knocking noise is usually not affected by load on the cylinder. If the clearance is too great, a double knock noise is heard when the engine idles. If all cylinders are grounded out one at a time and the noise does not change, a defective piston pin could be the cause.

- **Piston slap.** A piston slap is usually caused by an undersized or improperly shaped piston or oversized cylinder bore. A piston slap is most noticeable when the engine is cold and tends to decrease or stop making noise as the piston expands during engine operation.

- **Timing chain noise.** An excessively loose timing chain can cause a severe knocking noise when the chain hits

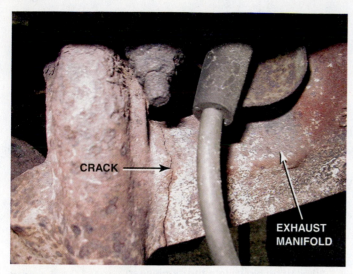

CRACK →

EXHAUST MANIFOLD

FIGURE 22–7 A cracked exhaust manifold on a Ford V-8.

Typical Noises	Possible Causes
Clicking noise—like the clicking of a ballpoint pen	1. Loose spark plug 2. Loose accessory mount (for air-conditioning compressor, alternator, power steering pump, etc.) 3. Loose rocker arm 4. Worn rocker arm pedestal 5. Fuel pump (broken mechanical fuel pump return spring) 6. Worn camshaft 7. Exhaust leak ● SEE FIGURE 22–7
Clacking noise—like tapping on metal	1. Worn piston pin 2. Broken piston 3. Excessive valve clearance 4. Timing chain hitting cover
Knock—like knocking on a door	1. Rod bearing(s) 2. Main bearing(s) 3. Thrust bearing(s) 4. Loose torque converter 5. Cracked flex plate (drive plate)
Rattle—like a baby rattle	1. Manifold heat control valve 2. Broken harmonic balancer 3. Loose accessory mounts 4. Loose accessory drive belt or tensioner
Clatter—like rolling marbles	1. Rod bearings 2. Piston pin 3. Loose timing chain
Whine—like an electric motor running	1. Alternator bearing 2. Drive belt 3. Power steering 4. Belt noise (accessory or timing)
Clunk—like a door closing	1. Engine mount 2. Drive axle shaft U-joint or constant vecity (CV) joint

the timing chain cover. This noise can often sound like a rod-bearing knock.

■ **Rod-bearing noise.** The noise from a defective rod bearing is usually ad sensitive and changes in intensity as the load on the engine increases and decreases. A rod-bearing failure can often be detected by grounding out the spark plugs one cylinder at a time. If the knocking noise decreases or is eliminated when a particular cylinder is grounded (disabled), then the grounded cylinder is the one from which the noise is originating.

■ **Main-bearing knock.** A main-bearing knock often cannot be isolated to a particular cylinder. The sound can vary in intensity and may disappear at times depending on engine ad.

Regardless of the type of loud knocking noise, after the external causes of the knocking noise have been eliminated, the engine should be disassembled and carefully inspected to determine the exact cause.

OIL PRESSURE TESTING

Proper oil pressure is very important for the operation of any engine. *Low oil pressure can cause engine wear, and engine wear can cause low oil pressure.*

If main thrust or rod bearings are worn, oil pressure is reduced because of leakage of the oil around the bearings. Oil pressure testing is usually performed with the following steps.

STEP 1 Operate the engine until normal operating temperature is achieved.

STEP 2 With the engine off, remove the oil pressure sending unit or sender, usually located near the oil filter. Thread an oil pressure gauge into the threaded hole. ● **SEE FIGURE 22–8.**

NOTE: An oil pressure gauge can be made from another gauge, such as an old air-conditioning gauge and a flexible brake hose. The threads are often the same as those used for the oil pressure sending unit.

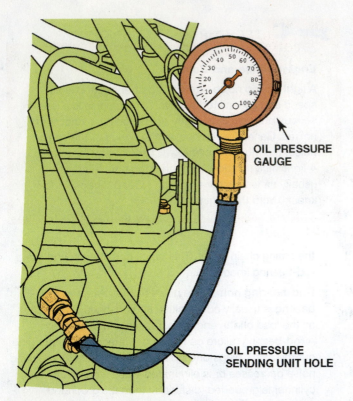

FIGURE 22–8 To measure engine oil pressure, remove the oil pressure sending (sender) unit usually located near the oil filter. Screw the pressure gauge into the oil pressure sending unit hole.

OIL PRESSURE GAUGE

OIL PRESSURE SENDING UNIT HOLE

STEP 3 Start the engine and observe the gauge. Record the oil pressure at idle and at 2500 RPM. Most vehicle manufacturers recommend a minimum oil pressure of 10 PSI per 1000 RPM. Therefore, at 2500 RPM, the oil pressure should be at least 25 PSI. Always compare your test results with the manufacturer's recommended oil pressure.

Besides engine bearing wear, other possible causes for low oil pressure include:

- Low oil level
- Diluted oil
- Stuck oil pressure relief valve

OIL PRESSURE WARNING LAMP

The red oil pressure warning lamp in the dash usually lights when the oil pressure is less than 4 to 7 PSI, depending on vehicle and engine. The oil light should not be on during driving. If the oil warning lamp is on, stop the engine immediately. Always confirm oil pressure with a reliable mechanical gauge before performing engine repairs. The sending unit or circuit may be defective.

 **TECH TIP**

Use the KISS Test Method

Engine testing is done to find the cause of an engine problem. All the simple things should be tested first. Just remember KISS—"keep it simple, stupid." A loose alternator belt or loose bolts on a torque converter can sound just like a lifter or rod bearing. A loose spark plug can make the engine perform as if it had a burned valve. Some simple items that can cause serious problems include the following:

Oil Burning

- Low oil level
- Clogged PCV valve or system, causing blowby and oil to be blown into the air cleaner
- Clogged drainback passages in the cylinder head
- Dirty oil that has not been changed for a long time (Change the oil and drive for about 1,000 miles, or 1,600 km, and change the oil and filter again.)

Noises

- Carbon on top of the piston(s) can sound like a bad rod bearing (often called a carbon knock)
- Loose torque-to-flex plate bolts (or nuts), causing a loud knocking noise

NOTE: Often this problem will cause noise only at idle; the noise tends to disappear during driving or when the engine is under load.

- A loose and/or defective drive belt, which may cause a rod- or main-bearing knocking noise (A loose or broken mount for the generator [alternator], power steering pump, or air-conditioning compressor can also cause a knocking noise.)

COMPRESSION TEST

An engine **compression test** is one of the fundamental engine diagnostic tests that can be performed. For smooth engine operation, all cylinders must have equal compression. An engine can se compression by leakage of air through one or more of only three routes.

- Intake or exhaust valve
- Piston rings (or piston, if there is a hole)
- Cylinder head gasket

For best results, the engine should be warmed to normal operating temperature before testing. An accurate compression test should be performed as follows:

STEP 1 Remove all spark plugs. This allows the engine to be cranked to an even speed. Be sure to label all spark plug wires.

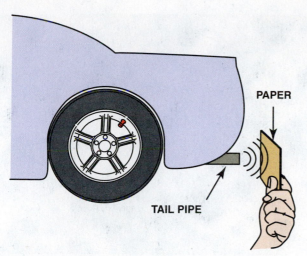

FIGURE 22–9 The paper test involves holding a piece of paper near the tailpipe of an idling engine. A good engine should produce even, outward puffs of exhaust. If the paper is sucked in toward the tailpipe, a burned valve is a possibility.

CAUTION: Disable the ignition system by disconnecting the primary leads from the ignition coil or module or by grounding the coil wire after removing it from the center of the distributor cap. Also disable the fuel-injection system to prevent the squirting of fuel into the cylinder.

 TECH TIP

The Paper Test

A soundly running engine should produce even and steady exhaust at the tailpipe. You can test this with the **paper test**. Hold a piece of paper or a 3″ × 5″ index card (even a dollar bill works) within 1 inch (25 mm) of the tailpipe with the engine running at idle. ● SEE FIGURE 22–9.

The paper should blow out evenly without "puffing." If the paper is drawn *toward* the tailpipe at times, the exhaust valves in one or more cylinders could be burned. Other reasons why the paper might be sucked toward the tailpipe include the following:

1. The engine could be misfiring because of a lean condition that could occur normally when the engine is cold.
2. Pulsing of the paper toward the tailpipe could also be caused by a hole in the exhaust system. If exhaust escapes through a hole in the exhaust system, air could be drawn in during the intervals between the exhaust puffs from the tailpipe to the hole in the exhaust, causing the paper to be drawn toward the tailpipe.
3. Ignition fault causing misfire.

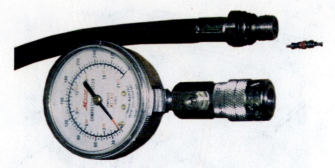

FIGURE 22–10 A two-piece compression gauge set. The threaded hose is screwed into the spark plug hole after removing the spark plug. The gauge part is then snapped onto the end of the hose.

STEP 2 Block open the throttle. This permits the maximum amount of air to be drawn into the engine. This step also ensures consistent compression test results.

STEP 3 Thread a compression gauge into one spark plug hole and crank the engine. ● SEE FIGURE 22–10.

Continue cranking the engine through *four* compression strokes. Each compression stroke makes a puffing sound.

NOTE: Note the reading on the compression gauge after the first puff. This reading should be at least one-half the final reading. For example, if the final, highest reading is 150 PSI, then the reading after the first puff should be higher than 75 PSI. A low first-puff reading indicates possible weak piston rings. Release the pressure on the gauge and repeat for the other cylinders.

STEP 4 Record the highest readings and compare the results. Most vehicle manufacturers specify the minimum compression reading and the maximum allowable variation among cylinders. Most manufacturers specify a maximum difference of 20% between the highest reading and the lowest reading. For example:

If the high reading is	150 PSI
Subtract 20%	−30 PSI
Lowest allowable compression is	120 PSI

NOTE: To make the math quick and easy, think of 10% of 150, which is 15 (move the decimal point to the left one place). Now double it: 15 × 2 = 30. This represents 20%.

NOTE: During cranking, the oil pump cannot maintain normal oil pressure. Extended engine cranking, such as that which occurs during a compression test, can cause hydraulic lifters to collapse. When the engine starts, loud valve clicking noises may be heard. This should be considered normal after performing a compression test, and the noise should stop after the vehicle has been driven a short distance.

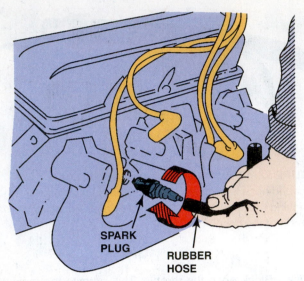

FIGURE 22–11 Use a vacuum or fuel line hose over the spark plug to install it without danger of cross-threading the cylinder head.

SPARK PLUG

RUBBER HOSE

 TECH TIP

The Hose Trick

Installing spark plugs can be made easier by using a rubber hose on the end of the spark plug. The hose can be a vacuum hose, fuel line, or even an old spark plug wire end. ● SEE FIGURE 22–11.

   The hose makes it easy to start the threads of the spark plug into the cylinder head. After starting the threads, continue to thread the spark plug for several turns. Using the hose eliminates the chance of cross-threading the plug. This is especially important when installing spark plugs in aluminum cylinder heads.

WET COMPRESSION TEST

If the compression test reading indicates low compression on one or more cylinders, add three squirts of oil to the cylinder and retest. This is called a **wet compression test**, when oil is used to help seal around the piston rings.

CAUTION: Do not use more oil than three squirts from a hand-operated oil squirt can. Too much oil can cause a hydrostatic lock, which can damage or break pistons or connecting rods or even crack a cylinder head.

   Perform the compression test again and observe the results. If the first-puff readings greatly improve and the readings are much higher than without the oil, the cause of the low compression is worn or defective piston rings. If the

FIGURE 22–12 Badly burned exhaust valve. A compression test could have detected a problem, and a cylinder leakage test (leak-down test) could have been used to determine the exact problem.

compression readings increase only slightly (or not at all), then the cause of the low compression is usually defective valves. ● SEE FIGURE 22–12.

NOTE: During both the dry and wet compression tests, be sure that the battery and starting system are capable of cranking the engine at normal cranking speed.

RUNNING (DYNAMIC) COMPRESSION TEST

A compression test is commonly used to help determine engine condition and is usually performed with the engine cranking.

   What is the RPM of a cranking engine? An engine idles at about 600 to 900 RPM, and the starter motor obviously cannot crank the engine as fast as the engine idles. Most manufacturers' specifications require the engine to crank at 80 to 250 cranking RPM. Therefore, a check of the engine's compression at cranking speed determines the condition of an engine that does not run at such low speeds.

   But what should be the compression of a running engine? Some would think that the compression would be substantially higher, because the valve overlap of the cam is more effective at higher engine speeds, which would tend to increase the compression.

   A **running compression test**, also called a **dynamic compression test**, is done with the engine running rather than during engine cranking as is done in a regular compression test.

   Actually, the compression pressure of a running engine is much *lower* than cranking compression pressure. This results from the volumetric efficiency. The engine is revolving faster, and therefore, there is less *time* for air to enter the combustion chamber. With less air to compress, the compression pressure is

FIGURE 22–13 A typical handheld cylinder leakage tester.

FIGURE 22–14 A whistle stop used to find top dead center. Remove the spark plug and install the whistle stop, then rotate the engine by hand. When the whistle stops making a sound, the piston is at the top.

lower. Typically, the higher the engine RPM, the lower the running compression. For most engines, the value ranges are as follows:

- Compression during cranking: 125 to 160 PSI
- Compression at idle: 60 to 90 PSI
- Compression at 2000 RPM: 30 to 60 PSI

As with cranking compression, the running compression of all cylinders should be equal. Therefore, a problem is not likely to be detected by single compression values, but by *variations* in running compression values among the cylinders. Broken valve springs, worn valve guides, bent pushrods, and worn cam lobes are some items that would be indicated by a low running compression test reading on one or more cylinders.

PERFORMING A RUNNING COMPRESSION TEST To perform a running compression test, remove just one spark plug at a time. With one spark plug removed from the engine, use a jumper wire to *ground* the spark plug wire to a good engine ground. This prevents possible ignition coil damage. Start the engine, push the pressure release on the gauge, and read the compression. Increase the engine speed to about 2000 RPM and push the pressure release on the gauge again. Read the gauge. Stop the engine, reinstall the spark plug, reattach the spark plug wire, and repeat the test for each of the remaining cylinders. Just like the cranking compression test, the running compression test can inform a technician of the *relative* compression of all the cylinders.

CYLINDER LEAKAGE TEST

One of the best tests that can be used to determine engine condition is the **cylinder leakage test**. This test involves injecting air under pressure into the cylinders one at a time. The amount and location of any escaping air helps the technician determine the condition of the engine. The air is injected into the cylinder through a cylinder leakage gauge into the spark plug hole. ● **SEE FIGURE 22–13.** To perform the cylinder leakage test, take the folwing steps:

STEP 1 For best results, the engine should be at normal operating temperature (upper radiator hose hot and pressurized).

STEP 2 The cylinder being tested must be at top dead center (TDC) of the compression stroke. ● **SEE FIGURE 22–14.**

NOTE: **The greatest amount of wear occurs at the top of the cylinder because of the heat generated near the top of the cylinders. The piston ring flex also adds to the wear at the top of the cylinder.**

STEP 3 Calibrate the cylinder leakage unit as per manufacturer's instructions.

STEP 4 Inject air into the cylinders one at a time, rotating the engine as necessitated by firing order to test each cylinder at TDC on the compression stroke.

STEP 5 Evaluate the results:

Less than 10% leakage: good
Less than 20% leakage: acceptable
Less than 30% leakage: poor
More than 30% leakage: definite problem

NOTE: **If leakage seems unacceptably high, repeat the test, being certain that it is being performed correctly and that the cylinder being tested is at TDC on the compression stroke.**

STEP 6 Check the source of air leakage.

a. If air is heard escaping from the oil filler cap, the *piston rings* are worn or broken.

b. If air is observed bubbling out of the radiator, there is a possible blown *head gasket* or cracked *cylinder head*.

c. If air is heard coming from the throttle body or air inlet on fuel-injection-equipped engines, there is a defective *intake valve(s)*.

d. If air is heard coming from the tailpipe, there is a defective *exhaust valve(s)*.

CYLINDER POWER BALANCE TEST

Most large engine analyzers and scan tools have a cylinder power balance feature. The purpose of a cylinder **power balance test** is to determine if all cylinders are contributing power equally. It determines this by shorting out one cylinder at a time. If the engine speed (RPM) does not drop as much for one cylinder as for other cylinders of the same engine, then the shorted cylinder must be weaker than the other cylinders. For example:

Cylinder Number	RPM Drop When Ignition Is Shorted
1	75
2	70
3	15
4	65
5	75
6	70

Cylinder 3 is the weak cylinder.

NOTE: Most automotive test equipment uses automatic means for testing cylinder balance. Be certain to correctly identify the offending cylinder. Cylinder 3 as identified by the equipment may be the third cylinder in the firing order instead of the actual cylinder 3.

POWER BALANCE TEST PROCEDURE

When point-type ignition was used on all vehicles, the common method for determining which, if any, cylinder was weak was to remove a spark plug wire from one spark plug at a time while watching a tachometer and a vacuum gauge. This method is not recommended on any vehicle with any type of electronic ignition. If any of the spark plug wires are removed from a spark plug with the engine running, the ignition coil tries to supply increasing levels of voltage attempting to jump the increasing gap as the plug wires are removed. This high voltage could easily track the ignition coil, damage the ignition module, or both.

The acceptable method of canceling cylinders, which will work on all types of ignition systems, including distributorless, is to *ground* the secondary current for each cylinder. ● SEE FIGURE 22–15. The cylinder with the least RPM drop is the cylinder not producing its share of power.

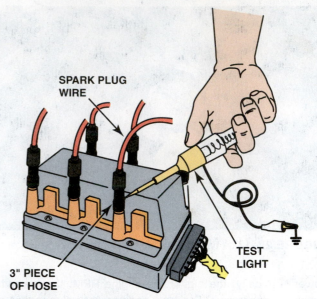

FIGURE 22–15 Using a vacuum hose and a test light to ground one cylinder at a time on a distributorless ignition system. This works on all types of ignition systems and provides a method for grounding out one cylinder at a time without fear of damaging any component. To avoid possible damage to the catalytic converter, do not short out a cylinder for longer than five seconds.

VACUUM TESTS

Vacuum is pressure below atmospheric pressure and is measured in **inches** (or millimeters) **of mercury (Hg).** An engine in good mechanical condition will run with high manifold vacuum. Manifold vacuum is deveped by the pistons as they move down on the intake stroke to draw the charge from the throttle body and intake manifold. Air to refill the manifold comes past the throttle plate into the manifold. Vacuum will increase anytime the engine turns faster or has better cylinder sealing while the throttle plate remains in a fixed position. Manifold vacuum will decrease when the engine turns more slowly or when the cylinders no longer do an efficient job of pumping. **Vacuum tests** include testing the engine for **cranking vacuum**, **idle vacuum**, and vacuum at 2500 RPM.

CRANKING VACUUM TEST   Measuring the amount of manifold vacuum during cranking is a quick and easy test to determine if the piston rings and valves are properly sealing. (For accurate results, the engine should be warm and the throttle closed.) To perform the **cranking vacuum test**, take the following steps.

STEP 1   Disable the ignition or fuel injection.

STEP 2   Connect the vacuum gauge to a manifold vacuum source.

STEP 3   Crank the engine while observing the vacuum gauge.

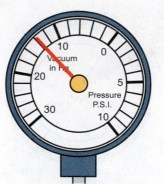

FIGURE 22–17 A steady but low reading could indicate retarded valve or ignition timing.

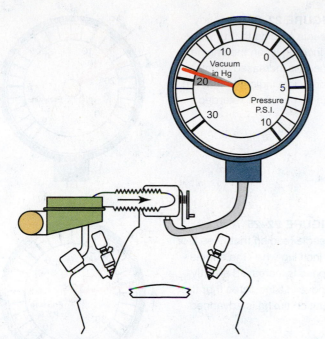

FIGURE 22–16 An engine in good mechanical condition should produce 17 to 21 inch Hg of vacuum at idle at sea level.

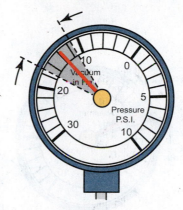

FIGURE 22–18 A gauge reading with the needle fluctuating 3 to 9 inch Hg below normal often indicates a vacuum leak in the intake system.

Cranking vacuum should be higher than 2.5 inch Hg. (Normal cranking vacuum is 3 to 6 inch Hg.) If it is lower than 2.5 inch Hg, then the folwing could be the cause.

- Too slow a cranking speed
- Worn piston rings
- Leaking valves
- Excessive amounts of air bypassing the throttle plate (This could give a false low vacuum reading. Common sources include a throttle plate partially open or a high-performance camshaft with excessive overlap.)

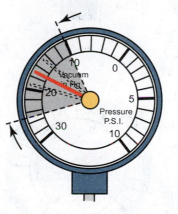

FIGURE 22–19 A leaking head gasket can cause the needle to vibrate as it moves through a range from below to above normal.

IDLE VACUUM TEST
An engine in proper condition should idle with a steady vacuum between 17 and 21 inch Hg. ● SEE FIGURE 22–16.

NOTE: Engine vacuum readings vary with altitude. A reduction of 1 inch Hg per 1,000 feet (300 m) of altitude should be subtracted from the expected values if testing a vehicle above 1,000 feet (300 m).

LOW AND STEADY VACUUM
If the vacuum is lower than normal, yet the gauge reading is steady, the most common causes include:

- Retarded ignition timing
- Retarded cam timing (check timing chain for excessive slack or timing belt for proper installation) ● SEE FIGURE 22–17.

FLUCTUATING VACUUM
If the needle drops, then returns to a normal reading, then drops again, and again returns, this indicates a sticking valve. A common cause of sticking valves is lack of lubrication of the valve stems. ● SEE FIGURES 22–18 THROUGH 22–26. If the vacuum gauge fluctuates above and below a center point, burned valves or weak valve springs may be indicated. If the fluctuation is slow and steady, unequal fuel mixture could be the cause.

NOTE: A common trick that some technicians use is to squirt some automatic transmission fluid (ATF) down the throttle body or into the air inlet of a warm engine. Often the idle quality improves and normal vacuum gauge readings are restored. The use of ATF does create excessive exhaust smoke for a short time, but it should not harm oxygen sensors or catalytic converters.

FIGURE 22–20 An oscillating needle 1 or 2 inch Hg below normal could indicate an incorrect air-fuel mixture (either too rich or too lean).

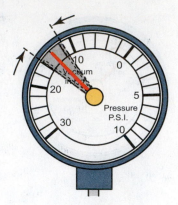

FIGURE 22–21 A rapidly vibrating needle at idle that becomes steady as engine speed is increased indicates worn valve guides.

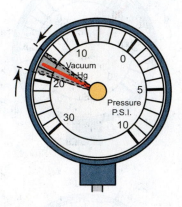

FIGURE 22–22 If the needle drops 1 or 2 inch Hg from the normal reading, one of the engine valves is burned or not seating properly.

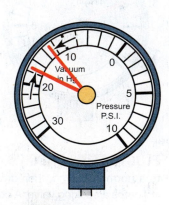

FIGURE 22–23 Weak valve springs will produce a normal reading at idle, but as engine speed increases, the needle will fluctuate rapidly between 12 and 24 inch Hg.

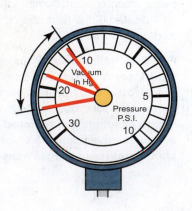

FIGURE 22–24 A steady needle reading that drops 2 or 3 inch Hg when the engine speed is increased slightly above idle indicates that the ignition timing is retarded.

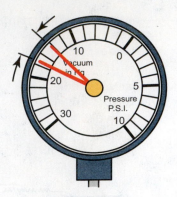

FIGURE 22–25 A steady needle reading that rises 2 or 3 inch Hg when the engine speed is increased slightly above idle indicates that the ignition timing is advanced.

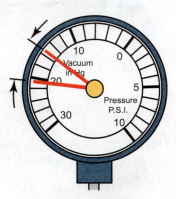

FIGURE 22–26 A needle that drops to near zero when the engine is accelerated rapidly and then rises slightly to a reading below normal indicates an exhaust restriction.

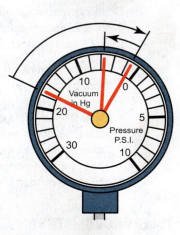

EXHAUST RESTRICTION TEST

If the exhaust system is restricted, the engine will be low on power, yet smooth. Common causes of **restricted exhaust** include the following:

- **Clogged catalytic converter.** Always check the ignition and fuel-injection systems for faults that could cause excessive amounts of unburned fuel to be exhausted. Excessive unburned fuel can overheat the catalytic converter and cause the beads or structure of the converter to fuse together, creating the restriction. A defective fuel delivery system could also cause excessive unburned fuel to be dumped into the converter.

- **Clogged or restricted muffler.** This can cause low power. Often a defective catalytic converter will shed particles that can clog a muffler. Broken internal baffles can also restrict exhaust flow.
- **Damaged or defective piping.** This can reduce the power of any engine. Some exhaust pipe is constructed with double walls, and the inside pipe can collapse and form a restriction that is not visible on the outside of the exhaust pipe.

TESTING BACK PRESSURE WITH A VACUUM GAUGE

A vacuum gauge can be used to measure manifold vacuum at a high idle (2000 to 2500 RPM). If the exhaust system is restricted, pressure increases in the exhaust system. This pressure is called **back pressure**. Manifold vacuum will drop gradually if the engine is kept at a constant speed if the exhaust is restricted.

The reason the vacuum will drop is that all exhaust leaving the engine at the higher engine speed cannot get through the restriction. After a short time (within one minute), the exhaust tends to "pile up" above the restriction and eventually remains in the cylinder of the engine at the end of the exhaust stroke. Therefore, at the beginning of the intake stroke, when the piston traveling downward should be lowering the pressure (raising the vacuum) in the intake manifold, the extra exhaust in the cylinder *lowers* the normal vacuum. If the exhaust restriction is severe enough, the vehicle can become undriveable because cylinder filling cannot occur except at idle.

TESTING BACK PRESSURE WITH A PRESSURE GAUGE

Exhaust system back pressure can be measured directly by installing a pressure gauge into an exhaust opening. This can be accomplished in one of the following ways.

- **With an oxygen sensor.** Use a back pressure gauge and adapter or remove the inside of an old, discarded oxygen sensor and thread in an adapter to convert to a vacuum or pressure gauge.

   NOTE: An adapter can be easily made by inserting a metal tube or pipe. A short section of brake line works great. The pipe can be brazed to the oxygen sensor housing or it can be glued in with epoxy. An 18 mm compression gauge adapter can also be adapted to fit into the oxygen sensor opening. ● SEE FIGURE 22–27.

FIGURE 22–27 A technician-made adapter used to test exhaust system back pressure.

- **With the exhaust gas recirculation (EGR) valve.** Remove the EGR valve and fabricate a plate to connect to a pressure gauge.
- **With the air-injection reaction (AIR) check valve.** Remove the check valve from the exhaust tubes leading down to the exhaust manifold. Use a rubber cone with a tube inside to seal against the exhaust tube. Connect the tube to a pressure gauge.

At idle, the maximum back pressure should be less than 1.5 PSI (10 kPa), and it should be less than 2.5 PSI (15 kPa) at 2500 RPM.

DIAGNOSING HEAD GASKET FAILURE

Several items can be used to help diagnose a head gasket failure.

- **Exhaust gas analyzer.** With the radiator cap removed, place the probe from the exhaust analyzer above the radiator filler neck. If the HC reading increases, the exhaust (unburned hydrocarbons) is getting into the coolant from the combustion chamber.
- **Chemical test.** A chemical tester using blue liquid is also available. The liquid turns yellow if combustion gases are present in the coolant. ● SEE FIGURE 22–28.
- **Bubbles in the coolant.** Remove the coolant pump belt to prevent pump operation. Remove the radiator cap and start the engine. If bubbles appear in the coolant before it begins to boil, a defective head gasket or cracked cylinder head is indicated.
- **Excessive exhaust steam.** If excessive water or steam is observed coming from the tailpipe, this means that coolant is getting into the combustion chamber from a defective head gasket or a cracked head. If there is leakage between cylinders, the engine usually misfires and a power balancer test and/or compression test can be used to confirm the problem.

FIGURE 22–28 A tester that uses a blue liquid to check for exhaust gases in the exhaust, which would indicate a head gasket leak problem.

If any of the preceding indicators of head gasket failure occur, remove the cylinder head(s) and check all of the following:

1. Head gasket
2. Sealing surfaces—for warpage
3. Castings—for cracks

NOTE: A leaking thermal vacuum valve can cause symptoms similar to those of a defective head gasket. Most thermal vacuum valves thread into a coolant passage, and they often leak only after they get hot.

DASH WARNING LIGHTS

Most vehicles are equipped with several dash warning lights often called "telltale" or "idiot" lights. These lights are often the only warning a driver receives that there may be engine problems. A summary of typical dash warning lights and their meanings follows.

OIL (ENGINE) LIGHT The red oil light indicates that the engine oil pressure is too low (usually lights when oil pressure is 4 to 7 PSI [20 to 50 kPa]). Normal oil pressure should be 10 to 60 PSI (70 to 400 kPa) or 10 PSI per 1000 engine RPM.

When this light comes on, the driver should shut off the engine immediately and check the oil level and condition for possible dilution with gasoline caused by a fuel system fault. If the oil level is okay, then there is a possible serious engine problem or a possible defective oil pressure sending (sender) unit. The automotive technician should always check the oil pressure using a reliable mechanical oil pressure gauge if low oil pressure is suspected.

NOTE: Some automobile manufacturers combine the dash warning lights for oil pressure and coolant temperature into one light, usually labeled "engine." Therefore, when the engine light comes on, the technician should check for possible coolant temperature and/or oil pressure problems.

COOLANT TEMPERATURE LIGHT Most vehicles are equipped with a coolant temperature gauge or dash warning light. The warning light may be labeled "coolant," "hot," or "temperature." If the coolant temperature warning light comes on during driving, this usually indicates that the coolant temperature is above a safe level, or above about 250°F (120°C). Normal coolant temperature should be about 200°F to 220°F (90°C to 105°C).

If the coolant temperature light comes on during driving, the folwing steps should be followed to prevent possible engine damage.

1. Turn off the air conditioning and turn on the heater. The heater will help get rid of some of the heat in the cooling system.
2. Raise the engine speed in neutral or park to increase the circulation of coolant through the radiator.
3. If possible, turn the engine off and allow it to cool (this may take over an hour).
4. Do not continue driving with the coolant temperature light on (or the gauge reading in the red warning section or above 260°F) or serious engine damage may result.

NOTE: If the engine does not feel or smell hot, it is possible that the problem is a faulty coolant temperature sensor or gauge.

TECH TIP

Misfire Diagnosis
If a misfire goes away with propane added to the air inlet, suspect a lean injector.

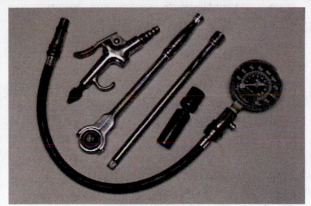

1 The tools and equipment needed to perform a compression test include a compression gauge, an air nozzle, and the socket ratchets and extensions that may be necessary to remove the spark plugs from the engine.

2 To prevent ignition and fuel-injection operation while the engine is being cranked, remove both the fuel-injection fuse and the ignition fuse. If the fuses cannot be removed, disconnect the wiring connectors for the injectors and the ignition system.

3 Block open the throttle (and choke, if the engine is equipped with a carburetor). Here a screwdriver is being used to wedge the throttle linkage open. Keeping the throttle open ensures that enough air will be drawn into the engine so that the compression test results will be accurate.

4 Before removing the spark plugs, use an air nozzle to blow away any dirt that may be around the spark plug. This step helps prevent debris from getting into the engine when the spark plugs are removed.

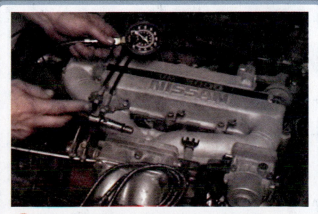

5 Remove all of the spark plugs. Be sure to mark the spark plug wires so that they can be reinstalled onto the correct spark plugs after the compression test has been performed.

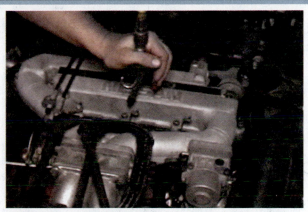

6 Select the proper adapter for the compression gauge. The threads on the adapter should match those on the spark plug.

CONTINUED ▶

7 If necessary, connect a battery charger to the battery before starting the compression test. It is important that consistent cranking speed be available for each cylinder being tested.

8 Make a note of the reading on the gauge after the first "puff," which indicates the first compression stroke that occurred on that cylinder as the engine was being rotated. If the first puff reading is low and the reading gradually increases with each puff, weak or worn piston rings may be indicated.

9 After the engine has been cranked for four "puffs," stop cranking the engine and observe the compression gauge.

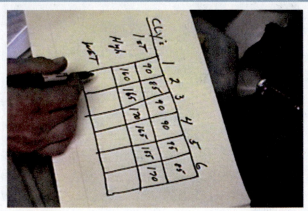

10 Record the first puff and this final reading for each cylinder. The final readings should all be within 20% of each other.

11 If a cylinder(s) is lower than most of the others, use an oil can and squirt two squirts of engine oil into the cylinder and repeat the compression test. This is called performing a wet compression test.

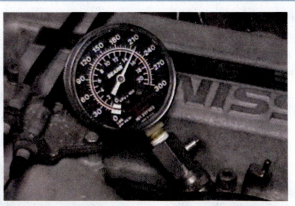

12 If the gauge reading is now much higher than the first test results, then the cause of the low compression is due to worn or defective piston rings. The oil in the cylinder temporarily seals the rings which causes the higher reading.

SUMMARY

1. The first step in diagnosing engine condition is to perform a thorough visual inspection, including a check of oil and coolant levels and condition.

2. Oil leaks can be found by using a white powder or a fluorescent dye and a black light.

3. Many engine-related problems make a characteristic noise.

4. Oil analysis by an engineering laboratory can reveal engine problems by measuring the amount of dissolved metals in the oil.

5. A compression test can be used to test the condition of valves and piston rings.

6. A cylinder leakage test fills the cylinder with compressed air, and the gauge indicates the percentage of leakage.

7. A cylinder balance test indicates whether all cylinders are working okay.

8. Testing engine vacuum is another procedure that can help the service technician determine engine condition.

REVIEW QUESTIONS

1. Describe the visual checks that should be performed on an engine if a mechanical malfunction is suspected.

2. List three simple items that could cause excessive oil consumption.

3. List three simple items that could cause engine noises.

4. Describe how to perform a compression test and how to determine what is wrong with an engine based on a compression test result.

5. Describe the cylinder leakage test.

6. Describe how a vacuum gauge would indicate if the valves were sticking in their guides.

7. Describe the test procedure for determining if the exhaust system is restricted (clogged) using a vacuum gauge.

CHAPTER QUIZ

1. Technician A says that the paper test could detect a burned valve. Technician B says that a grayish white stain on the engine could be a coolant leak. Which technician is correct?
   a. Technician A only
   b. Technician B only
   c. Both Technicians A and B
   d. Neither Technician A nor B

2. Two technicians are discussing oil leaks. Technician A says that an oil leak can be found using a fluorescent dye in the oil with a black light to check for leaks. Technician B says that a white spray powder can be used to locate oil leaks. Which technician is correct?
   a. Technician A only
   b. Technician B only
   c. Both Technicians A and B
   d. Neither Technician A nor B

3. Which of the following is the *least likely* to cause an engine noise?
   a. Carbon on the pistons
   b. Cracked exhaust manifold
   c. Loose accessory drive belt
   d. Vacuum leak

4. A good engine should produce how much compression during a running (dynamic) compression test at idle?
   a. 150 to 200 PSI
   b. 100 to 150 PSI
   c. 60 to 90 PSI
   d. 30 to 60 PSI

5. A smoothly operating engine depends on _____.
   a. High compression on most cylinders
   b. Equal compression between cylinders
   c. Cylinder compression levels above 100 PSI (700 kPa) and within 70 PSI (500 kPa) of each other
   d. Compression levels below 100 PSI (700 kPa) on most cylinders

6. A good reading for a cylinder leakage test would be _____.
   a. Within 20% between cylinders
   b. All cylinders below 20% leakage
   c. All cylinders above 20% leakage
   d. All cylinders above 70% leakage and within 7% of each other

7. Technician A says that during a power balance test, the cylinder that causes the biggest RPM drop is the weak cylinder. Technician B says that if one spark plug wire is grounded out and the engine speed does not drop, a weak or dead cylinder is indicated. Which technician is correct?
   a. Technician A only
   b. Technician B only
   c. Both Technicians A and B
   d. Neither Technician A nor B

8. *Cranking* vacuum should be _____.
   a. 2.5 inch Hg or higher
   b. Over 25 inch Hg
   c. 17 to 21 inch Hg
   d. 6 to 16 inch Hg

9. Technician A says that a leaking head gasket can be tested for using a chemical tester. Technician B says that leaking head gasket can be found using an exhaust gas analyzer.
   a. Technician A only
   b. Technician B only
   c. Both Technicians A and B
   d. Neither Technician A nor B

10. The low oil pressure warning light usually comes on _____.
   a. Whenever an oil change is required
   b. Whenever oil pressure drops dangerously low (4 to 7 PSI)
   c. Whenever the oil filter bypass valve opens
   d. Whenever the oil filter antidrainback valve opens

chapter 23

IN-VEHICLE ENGINE SERVICE

LEARNING OBJECTIVES: After studying this chapter, the reader should be able to: • Explain thermostat replacement and water pump replacement in engines. • Discuss intake manifold gasket inspection and replacement. • Describe the steps involved in timing belt replacement. • Discuss hybrid engine precautions.

KEY TERMS: EREV 322 • Fretting 320 • HEV 322 • Idle stop 322 • Skewed 319

THERMOSTAT REPLACEMENT

FAILURE PATTERNS All thermostat valves move during operation to maintain the desired coolant temperature. Thermostats can fail in the following ways.

- **Stuck open.** If a thermostat fails open or partially open, the operating temperature of the engine will be less than normal. ● SEE FIGURE 23–1.
- **Stuck closed.** If the thermostat fails closed or almost closed, the engine will likely overheat.
- **Stuck partially open.** This will cause the engine to warm up slowly if at all. This condition can cause the powertrain control module (PCM) to set a P0128 diagnostic trouble code (DTC) which means that the engine coolant temperature does not reach the specified temperature.
- **Skewed.** A **skewed** thermostat works, but not within the correct temperature range. Therefore, the engine could overheat or operate cooler than normal or even do both.

REPLACEMENT PROCEDURE Before replacing the thermostat, double-check that the cooling system problem is not due to another fault, such as being low on coolant or an inoperative cooling fan. Check service information for the specified procedure to follow to replace the thermostat. Most recommended procedures include the following steps.

STEP 1 Allow the engine to cool for several hours so the engine and the coolant should be at room temperature.

STEP 2 Drain the coolant into a suitable container. Most vehicle manufacturers recommend that new coolant be used and the old coolant disposed of properly or recycled.

FIGURE 23–1 If the thermostat has a jiggle valve, it should be placed toward the top to allow air to escape. If a thermostat were to become stuck open or open too soon, this can set a diagnostic trouble code P0128 (coolant temperature below thermostat regulating temperature).

STEP 3 Remove any necessary components to get access to the thermostat.

STEP 4 Remove the thermostat housing and thermostat.

STEP 5 Replace the thermostat housing gasket and thermostat. Torque all fasteners to specifications.

STEP 6 Refill the cooling system with the specified coolant and bleed any trapped air from the system.

STEP 7 Pressurize the cooling system to verify that there are no leaks around the thermostat housing.

STEP 8 Run the engine until it reaches normal operating temperature and check for leaks.

STEP 9 Verify that the engine is reaching correct operating temperature.

FIGURE 23–2 Use caution if using a steel scraper to remove a gasket from aluminum parts. It is best to use a wood or plastic scraper.

FIGURE 23–3 An intake manifold gasket that failed and allowed coolant to be drawn into the cylinder(s).

WATER PUMP REPLACEMENT

NEED FOR REPLACEMENT A water pump will require replacement if any of the following conditions are present.

- Leaking coolant from the weep hole
- Bearing noisy or loose
- Lack of proper coolant flow caused by worn or slipping impeller blades

REPLACEMENT GUIDELINES After diagnosis has been confirmed that the water pump requires replacement, check service information for the exact procedure to follow. The steps usually include the following:

STEP 1 Allow the engine to cool to room temperature.

STEP 2 Drain the coolant and dispose of properly or recycle.

STEP 3 Remove engine components to gain access to the water pump as specified in service information.

STEP 4 Remove the water pump assembly.

STEP 5 Clean the gasket surfaces and install the new water pump using a new gasket or seal as needed. ● SEE FIGURE 23–2. Torque all fasteners to factory specifications.

STEP 6 Install removed engine components.

STEP 7 Fill the cooling system with the specified coolant.

STEP 8 Run the engine, check for leaks, and verify proper operation.

INTAKE MANIFOLD GASKET INSPECTION

CAUSES OF FAILURE Many V-type engines leak oil, coolant, or experience an air (vacuum) leak caused by a leaking intake manifold gasket. This failure can be contributed to one or more of the following:

1. Expansion/contraction rate difference between the cast-iron head and the aluminum intake manifold can cause the intake manifold gasket to be damaged by the relative motion of the head and intake manifold. This type of failure is called **fretting**.

2. Plastic (Nylon 6.6) gasket deterioration caused by the coolant. ● SEE FIGURE 23–3.

DIAGNOSIS OF LEAKING INTAKE MANIFOLD GASKET Because intake manifold gaskets are used to seal oil, air, and coolant in most causes, determining that the intake manifold gasket is the root cause can be a challenge. To diagnose a possible leaking intake manifold gasket, perform the following tests.

Visual inspection. Check for evidence of oil or coolant between the intake manifold and the cylinder heads.

Coolant level. Check the coolant level and determine if the level has been dropping. A leaking intake manifold gasket can cause coolant to leak and then evaporate, leaving no evidence of the leak.

Air (vacuum) leak. If there is a stored diagnostic trouble code (DTC) for a lean exhaust (P0171, P0172, or P0174), a leaking intake manifold gasket could be the cause. Use propane to check if the engine changes when dispensed around the intake manifold gasket. If the engine changes in speed or sound, then this test verifies that an air leak is present.

FIGURE 23–4 The lower intake manifold attaches to the cylinder heads.

FIGURE 23–5 The upper intake manifold, often called a plenum, attaches to the lower intake manifold.

INTAKE MANIFOLD GASKET REPLACEMENT

When replacing the intake manifold gasket, always check service information for the exact procedure to follow. The steps usually include the following:

STEP 1 Be sure the engine has been off for about an hour and then drain the coolant into a suitable container.

STEP 2 Remove covers and other specified parts needed to get access to the retaining bolts.

STEP 3 To help ensure that the manifold does not warp when removed, loosen all fasteners in the reverse order of the tightening sequence. This means that the bolts should be loosened starting at the ends and working toward the center.

STEP 4 Remove the upper intake manifold (plenum), if equipped, and inspect for faults. ● **SEE FIGURES 23–4 AND 23–5.**

STEP 5 Remove the lower intake manifold, using the same bolt removal procedure of starting at the ends and working toward the center.

STEP 6 Thoroughly clean the area and replace the intake manifold if needed. Check that the correct replacement manifold is being used, and even the current part could look different from the original. ● **SEE FIGURE 23–6.**

STEP 7 Install the intake manifold using new gaskets as specified. Some designs use gaskets that are reusable. Replace as needed.

STEP 8 Torque all fasteners to factory specifications and in the proper sequences. The tightening sequences usually start at the center and work outward to the ends.

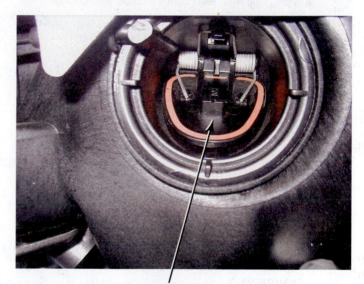

SPRING-LOAD PRESSURE RELIEF VALUE

FIGURE 23–6 Some plastic intake manifold are equipped with a pressure relief valve that would open in the event of a backfire condition to prevent the higher internal pressures from causing damage to the manifold.

CAUTION: Double-check the torque specifications and be sure to use the correct values. Many intake manifolds use fasteners that are torqued to values expressed in pound-inches and not pound-feet.

STEP 9 Reinstall all parts needed to allow the engine to start and run, including refilling the coolant if needed.

STEP 10 Start the engine and check for leaks and proper engine operation.

STEP 11 Reset or relearn the idle if specified, using a scan tool.

STEP 12 Install all of the remaining parts and perform a test drive to verify proper operation and no leaks.

STEP 13 Check and replace the air filter if needed.

STEP 14 Change the engine oil if the intake manifold leak could have caused coolant to leak into the engine, which would contaminate the oil.

TIMING BELT REPLACEMENT

NEED FOR REPLACEMENT Timing belts have a limited service and a specified replacement interval ranging from 60,000 miles (97,000 km) to about 100,000 miles (161,000 km). Timing belts are required to be replaced if any of the following conditions occur.

- Meets or exceeds the vehicle manufacturer's recommended timing belt replacement interval.

- The timing belt has been contaminated with coolant or engine oil.

- The timing belt has failed (missing belt teeth or broken).

TIMING BELT REPLACEMENT GUIDELINES Before replacing the timing belt, check service information for the recommended procedure to follow. Most timing belt replacement procedures include the following steps.

STEP 1 Allow the engine to cool before starting to remove components to help eliminate the possibility of personal injury or warpage of the parts.

STEP 2 Remove all necessary components to gain access to the timing belt and timing marks.

STEP 3 If the timing belt is not broken, rotate the engine until the camshaft and crankshaft timing marks are aligned according to the specified marks. ● SEE FIGURE 23–7.

STEP 4 Loosen or remove the tensioner as needed to remove the timing belt.

STEP 5 Replace the timing belt and any other recommended items. Components that some vehicle manufacturers recommend replacing in addition to the timing belt include:

- Tensioner assembly
- Water pump
- Camshaft oil seal(s)
- Front crankshaft seal

STEP 6 Check (verify) that the camshaft timing is correct by rotating the engine several revolutions.

STEP 7 Install enough components to allow the engine to start to verify proper operation. Check for any leaks, especially if seals have been replaced.

STEP 8 Complete the reassembly of the engine and perform a test drive before returning the vehicle to the customer.

FIGURE 23–7 A single overhead camshaft engine with a timing belt that also rotates the water pump.

HYBRID ENGINE PRECAUTIONS

HYBRID VEHICLE ENGINE OPERATION Gasoline engines used in **hybrid electric vehicles (HEVs)** and in **extended range electric vehicles (EREVs)** can be a hazard to be around under some conditions. These vehicles are designed to stop the gasoline engines unless needed. This feature is called **idle stop**. This means that the engine is not running, but could start at any time if the computer detects the need to charge the hybrid batteries or other issue that requires the gasoline engine to start and run.

PRECAUTIONS Always check service information for the exact procedures to follow when working around or under the hood of a hybrid electric vehicle. These precautions could include the following:

- Before working under the hood or around the engine, be sure that the ignition is off and the key is out of the ignition.

- Check that the "Ready" light is off. ● SEE FIGURE 23–8.

- Do not touch any circuits that have orange electrical wires or conduit. The orange color indicates dangerous high-voltage wires, which could cause serious injury or death if touched.

- Always use high-voltage linesman's gloves whenever depowering the high-voltage system.

FIGURE 23–8 A Toyota/Lexus hybrid electric vehicle has a ready light. If the ready light is on, the engine can start at anytime without warning.

HYBRID ENGINE SERVICE The gasoline engine in most hybrid electric vehicles specifies low viscosity engine oil as a way to achieve maximum fuel economy. ● SEE FIGURE 23–9. The viscosity required is often:

- SAE 0W-20
- SAE 5W-20

Many shops do not keep this viscosity in stock so preparations need to be made to get and use the specified engine oil.

In addition to engine oil, some hybrid electric vehicles such as the Honda Insight (1999–2004) require special spark plugs. Check service information for the specified service procedures and parts needed if a hybrid electric vehicle is being serviced.

GASOLINE DIRECT INJECTION SERVICE

NOISE ISSUES Gasoline direct-injection systems operate at high pressure and the injectors can often be heard with the engine running and the hood open. This noise can be a customer concern because the clicking sound is similar to noisy valves. If a noise issue is the customer concern, check the following:

- Check a similar vehicle to determine if the sound is louder or more noticeable than normal.
- Check that nothing under the hood is touching the fuel rail. If another line or hose is in contact with the fuel rail, the sound of the injectors clicking can be transmitted

FIGURE 23–9 Always use the viscosity of oil as specified on the oil fill cap.

FIGURE 23–10 There may become a driveability issue because the gasoline direct-injection injector is exposed to combustion carbon and fuel residue.

throughout the engine, making the sound more noticeable.

- Check for any technical service bulletins (TSBs) that may include new clips or sound insulators to help reduce the noise.

CARBON ISSUES Carbon is often an issue in engines equipped with gasoline direct-injection systems.

Check service information for the specified procedures to follow.

Specified process and procedures will likely restore power if the intake valves are coated.

VALVE ADJUSTMENT

1 Before starting the process of adjusting the valves, look up the specifications and exact procedures. The technician is checking this information from a computer CD-ROM-based information system.

2 The tools necessary to adjust the valves on an engine with adjustable rocker arms include basic hand tools, feeler gauge, and a torque wrench.

3 An overall view of the 4-cylinder engine that is due for a scheduled valve adjustment according to the vehicle manufacturer's recommendations.

4 Start the valve adjustment procedure by first disconnecting and labeling, if necessary, all vacuum lines that need to be removed to gain access to the valve cover.

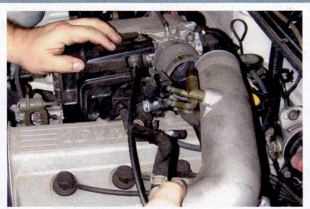

5 The air intake tube is being removed from the throttle body.

6 With all vacuum lines and the intake tube removed, the valve cover can be removed after removing all retaining bolts.

7 Notice how clean the engine appears. This is a testament of proper maintenance and regular oil changes by the owner.

8 To help locate how far the engine is being rotated, the technician is removing the distributor cap to be able to observe the position of the rotor.

TIMING PLATE WITH DEGREES

9 The engine is rotated until the timing marks on the front of the crankshaft line up with zero degrees—top dead center (TDC)—with both valves closed on #1 cylinder.

10 With the rocker arms contacting the base circle of the cam, insert a feeler gauge of the specified thickness between the camshaft and the rocker arm. There should be a slight drag on the feeler gauge.

11 If the valve clearance (lash) is not correct, loosen the retaining nut and turn the valve adjusting screw with a screwdriver to achieve the proper clearance.

12 After adjusting the valves that are closed, rotate the engine one full rotation until the engine timing marks again align.

CONTINUED ▶

13 The engine is rotated until the timing marks again align indicating that the companion cylinder will now be in position for valve clearance measurement.

14 On some engines, it is necessary to watch the direction the rotor is pointing to help determine how far to rotate the engine. Always follow the vehicle manufacturer's recommended procedure.

15 The technician is using a feeler gauge that is one-thousandth of an inch thinner and another one thousandth of an inch thicker than the specified clearance as a double-check that the clearance is correct.

16 Adjusting a valve takes both hands—one to hold the wrench to loosen and tighten the lock nut and one to turn the adjusting screw. Always double check the clearance after an adjustment is made.

17 After all valves have been properly measured and adjusted as necessary, start the reassembly process by replacing all gaskets and seals as specified by the vehicle manufacturer.

18 Reinstall the valve cover being careful to not pinch a wire or vacuum hose between the cover and the cylinder head.

19 Use a torque wrench and torque the valve cover retaining bolts to factory specifications.

20 Reinstall the distributor cap.

21 Reinstall the spark plug wires and all brackets that were removed to gain access to the valve cover.

22 Reconnect all vacuum and air hoses and tubes. Replace any vacuum hoses that are brittle or swollen with new ones.

23 Be sure that the clips are properly installed. Start the engine and check for proper operation.

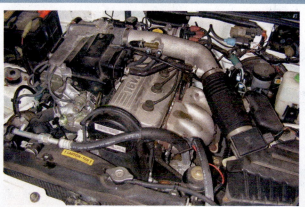

24 Double-check for any oil or vacuum leaks after starting the engine.

SUMMARY

1. Thermostats can fail in the following ways.
   - Stuck open
   - Stuck closed
   - Stuck partially open
   - Skewed
2. A water pump should be replaced if any of the following conditions are present.
   - Leaking from the weep hole
   - Noisy bearing
   - Loose bearing
   - Lack of normal circulation due to worn impeller blades
3. A leaking intake manifold gasket can cause coolant to get into the oil or oil into the coolant, as well as other faults, such as a poor running engine.
4. When a timing belt is replaced, most vehicle manufacturers also recommend that the following items be replaced.
   - Tensioner assembly
   - Water pump
   - Camshaft seal(s)
   - Front crankshaft seal
5. When working on a Toyota/Lexus hybrid electric vehicle (HEV), be sure that the key is off and out of the ignition and the READY light is off.

REVIEW QUESTIONS

1. How can a thermostat fail?
2. How can a water pump fail requiring replacement?
3. What will happen to the engine if the intake manifold gasket fails?
4. Why must timing belts be replaced?
5. Why is it important that the READY light be out on the dash before working under the hood of a hybrid electric vehicle?

CHAPTER QUIZ

1. A thermostat can fail in which way?
   - a. Stuck open
   - b. Stuck closed
   - c. Stuck partially open
   - d. Any of the above
2. A skewed thermostat means it is _____.
   - a. Working, but not at the correct temperature
   - b. Not working
   - c. Missing the thermo wax in the heat sensor
   - d. Contaminated with coolant
3. Coolant drained from the cooling system when replacing a thermostat or water pump should be _____.
   - a. Reused
   - b. Disposed of properly or recycled
   - c. Filtered and reinstalled after the repair
   - d. Poured down a toilet
4. A water pump can fail to provide the proper amount of flow of coolant through the cooling system if what has happened?
   - a. The coolant is leaking from the weep hole.
   - b. The bearing is noisy.
   - c. The impeller blades are worn or slipping on the shaft.
   - d. A bearing failure has caused the shaft to become loose.
5. Intake manifold gaskets on a V-type engine can fail due to what factor?
   - a. Fretting
   - b. Coolant damage
   - c. Relative movement between the intake manifold and the cylinder head
   - d. All of the above
6. A defective thermostat can cause the powertrain control module to set what diagnostic trouble code (DTC)?
   - a. P0171
   - b. P0172
   - c. P0128
   - d. P0300
7. A replacement plastic intake manifold may have a different design or appearance from the original factory-installed part.
   - a. True
   - b. False
8. The torque specifications for many plastic intake manifolds are in what unit?
   - a. Pound-inches
   - b. Pound-feet
   - c. Ft-lb per minute
   - d. Lb-ft per second
9. When replacing a timing belt, many experts and vehicle manufacturers recommend that what other part(s) should be replaced?
   - a. Tensioner assembly
   - b. Water pump
   - c. Camshaft oil seal(s)
   - d. All of the above
10. Hybrid electric vehicles usually require special engine oil of what viscosity?
    - a. SAE 5W-30
    - b. SAE 10W-30
    - c. SAE 0W-20
    - d. SAE 5W-40

chapter 24

ENGINE REMOVAL AND DISASSEMBLY

LEARNING OBJECTIVES: **After studying this chapter, the reader should be able to:** • Discuss the different engine repair options. • Explain the engine removal procedure. • Explain the engine disassembly procedure. • Explain disassembly of the short block, rotating engine assemblies removal, and cylinder head disassembly.

KEY TERMS: Freshening 330 • Long block 330 • Rebuilding 330 • Short block 330 • Vibration damper 335

ENGINE REPAIR OPTIONS

TECHNICIAN AND OWNER DECISION   The decision to repair an engine should be based on all the information about the engine that is available to the service technician and the vehicle owner.

- In some cases, the engine might not be worth repairing. It is the responsibility of the technician to discuss the advantages and disadvantages of the different repair options with the customer.
- The customer, who is paying for the repair, must make the final decision on the reconditioning procedure to be used. The repair might involve replacing a worn component instead of reconditioning. The decision will be based on the recommendation of the service technician.

REPAIR OPTIONS   Most customers want to spend the least amount of money possible, so they have only the faulty component repaired. This is the correct procedure in many cases. Examples of component repairs include:

- **Component replacement.** Timing chain replacement is an example of a component repair due to wear that can cause a loss of engine performance. If testing indicates that the timing chain has excessive slack, the front of the engine can be disassembled and the actual slack measured. Usually a slack of 0.5 inch (13 mm) or more indicates that the timing chain and gears need to be replaced. ● **SEE FIGURE 24–1.**
- **Valve job.** Valve leakage is corrected by doing a valve job. This does not necessarily correct the

FIGURE 24–1 A worn timing sprocket that resulted in a retarded valve timing and reduced engine performance.

customer's concerns, however. Stopping valve leakage improves manifold vacuum. After completing a valve job, the greater manifold vacuum may draw the oil past worn piston rings and into the combustion chamber during the intake stroke, causing oil consumption to increase.

- **Minor overhaul.** A minor overhaul can usually be done without removing the engine from the chassis. It requires removal of both the head and the oil pan. The overhaul is usually done when the engine lacks power, has poor fuel economy, uses an excessive amount of oil, produces visible tailpipe emissions, runs rough, or is hard to start. It is still only a repair procedure. Parts normally replaced include the piston rings, rod bearings and gaskets, as well as a valve job. Other engine problems may be noticed after the oil pan is removed and the piston and rod assemblies are taken out. The customer should be informed about any other engine problem, in order to authorize the service that the engine requires. In the high-performance industry, this procedure is called **freshening** the engine.

- **Major overhaul.** A complete engine reconditioning job is called **rebuilding.** Sometimes, this type of reconditioning is called a major overhaul. To rebuild the engine, the engine must be removed from the chassis and be completely disassembled. All serviceable parts are reconditioned to either new or service standards. All bearings, gaskets, and seals are replaced. When the reconditioning is done properly, a rebuilt engine should operate like a new engine.

- **Short block.** The quickest way to get a vehicle back in service is to exchange the faulty engine for a different one. In an older vehicle, the engine may be replaced with a used engine from a salvage yard. In some cases, only a reconditioned block, including the crankshaft, rods, and pistons, is used. This replacement assembly is called a **short block.** The original heads, valve train, oil pump, and all external components are reconditioned and used on the short block.

- **Long block.** The replacement assembly is called a **long block** when the reconditioned assembly includes the heads and valve train. Many automotive machine shops maintain a stock of short and long blocks of popular engines. Usually, the original engine parts, called the core, are exchanged for the reconditioned assembly. The core parts are reconditioned by the automotive machine shop and put back in stock for the next customer.

- **Crate engines.** Crate engines are new engines built by the engine manufacturer and sold through vehicle dealers. ● **SEE FIGURE 24–2.**

- **Remanufactured engines.** Some engines are remanufactured and can be replaced in a day or two, greatly reducing the amount of time the customer is without a vehicle. The engine cores are completely disassembled, and each serviceable part is reconditioned with specialized machinery. Engines are then assembled on an engine assembly line similar to the original manufacturer's assembly line. The parts that are assembled together as an engine have not come out of the same engine. The remanufactured engine usually has new pistons, valves, and lifters, together with other parts that are normally replaced in a rebuilt engine. All clearances and fits in the remanufactured engine are the same as in a new engine. A remanufactured engine should give service as good as that of a new engine, and it will cost about half as much. Remanufactured engines usually carry a warranty. This means that they will be replaced if they fail during the period of the warranty. They may even cost less than a rebuilt engine, because much of the reconditioning is done by specialized machines rather than by expensive skilled labor.

FIGURE 24–2 A crate engine from Chrysler to be used in a restored muscle car. Using a complete new engine costs more than rebuilding an existing engine, but it has a warranty and uses all new parts.

ENGINE REMOVAL

CHECK SERVICE INFORMATION Whenever any engine-related work is being performed, always print out the specified procedure as published in service information to avoid doing any harm to the vehicle or the engine.

USUAL ENGINE REMOVAL PROCEDURES The procedures that are usually specified include:

- **Remove the hood.** Removing the hood allows easier access to all of the components around the engine. Store the hood in a place where it will not be damaged. Some technicians place a fender cover on the roof of the vehicle and then place the hood upside down on top of the fender cover.

- **Clean the engine area.** The engine exterior and the engine compartment should be cleaned before work is begun. Using a power washer is the most commonly used way to clean the engine compartment area. A clean engine is easier to work on, and the cleaning not only helps to keep dirt out of the engine, but also minimizes accidental damage from slipping tools.

- **Disconnect the negative (–) battery cable,** and remove the battery from the vehicle if it could interfere with the removal of the engine.

- **Remove the air cleaner assembly.** Remove the hoses and other components of the air intake system. Mark or bag and tag all fasteners.

- **Remove all accessories.** Those that usually need to be removed include the alternator, engine driven fan, and AIR pump, if equipped.

- **Drain the coolant.** Draining coolant from the radiator and the engine block help reduce the chance of coolant getting into the cylinders when the cylinder head is removed. Dispose of the used coolant properly.

- **Remove the radiator.** Disconnect the transmission oil cooler lines and radiator hoses from the radiator. Removing the radiator helps provide room for moving the engine during removal and helps prevent the possibility of damage.

- **Disconnect the exhaust system.** On some engines, it may be easier to remove the exhaust manifold(s) from the cylinder head(s), whereas on others, it may be easier to disconnect the exhaust pipe from the manifold(s).

- **Recover the air-conditioning refrigerant.** Set the air-conditioning compressor aside and do not open the system unless absolutely necessary. If the air-conditioning system has to be opened to remove components, then the system must be evacuated. Tape or cover all open refrigerant fittings and hoses to prevent contaminates from entering the A/C system. Check service information for the exact procedures to follow.

- **Remove the power steering pump.** Remove the fasteners to the power steering pump and set aside the pump and hoses.

- **Drain the engine oil.** Draining the engine oil and removing the oil filter also helps prevent fluid loss during the removal process.

- **Disconnect fuel lines.** Disconnect and plug all fuel supply and return lines.

- **Disconnect wiring and vacuum hoses.** Mark and remove all vacuum hoses and electrical wiring attached to the engine.

PROCEDURE FOR ENGINE REMOVAL

There are two ways to remove the engine.

1. The engine can be lifted out of the chassis with the transmission/transaxle attached.

2. The transmission/transaxle can be separated from the engine and left in the chassis.

The method to be used must be determined before the engine is removed from the vehicle.

- **Rear-wheel-drive vehicle.** The removal procedure for most rear-wheel-drive vehicles includes the following steps.

  STEP 1 Under the vehicle, remove the driveshaft (propeller shaft) and disconnect the exhaust pipes. Also remove the engine (motor) mounts. In some installations, it may be necessary to loosen the steering linkage idler arm to give clearance. The transmission controls and wiring need to be disconnected at the connectors, and clutch linkages disconnected and labeled.

  STEP 2 Attach a sling, either a chain or lift cable, to one of the following:

  - Factory-installed lifting hooks
  - Intake manifold
  - Cylinder head bolts, on top of the engine

  An engine lift hoist chain or cable is attached and snugged to take most of the weight. This leaves the engine resting on the mounts.

  NOTE: For the best results, use the factory-installed lifting hooks that are attached to the engine. These hooks are used in the assembly plant to install the engine and are usually in the best location to remove the engine.

  STEP 3 Remove the rear cross-member, and lower the transmission. Cover the extension housing with a plug or a plastic bag to help prevent the automatic transmission fluid from leaking during the removal process. If the engine alone is being removed, the transmission retaining bolts and torque converter fasteners will need to be removed. Check service information for exact procedures to follow when removing an automatic transmission.

  STEP 4 The front of the engine must come almost straight up as the transmission slides from under the floor pan. The engine and transmission are hoisted free of the automobile, swung clear, and lowered on an open floor area. ● **SEE FIGURE 24–3.**

- **Front-wheel-drive vehicle.** Check service information for the exact procedure to follow to remove the engine from a front-wheel-drive vehicle. Depending on the vehicle, the engine could be removed from the top or

FIGURE 24–3 An engine must be tipped as it is pulled from the chassis.

FIGURE 24–4 When removing just the engine from a front-wheel-drive vehicle, the transaxle must be supported. Shown here is a typical fixture that can be used to hold the engine if the transaxle is removed or to hold the transaxle if the engine is removed.

lowered and removed from underneath on many front-wheel-drive vehicles. Typical steps include:

STEP 1   Disconnect units that might interfere with engine removal, including the steering unit, engine electrical harness, and radiator.

STEP 2   If removing the engine from underneath, the upper strut and lower engine cradle fasteners will have to be removed.

STEP 3   Disconnect the torque converter and bell housing bolts and clutch linkage if required.

STEP 4   Often special holding fixtures are required to help hold the transaxle in place while removing the engine. ● **SEE FIGURES 24–4 AND 24–5.**

ENGINE DISASSEMBLY

MOUNTING THE ENGINE ON A STAND   Engines should be installed to a sturdy engine stand. For safety, always check the following:

- Always use at least four grade 8 bolts when mounting an engine to an engine stand. Using low-quality nongraded

FIGURE 24–5 The entire cradle, which included the engine, transaxle, and steering gear, was removed and placed onto a stand. The rear cylinder head has been removed to check for the root cause of a coolant leak.

RACK AND PINION STEERING GEAR

CRADLE

FIGURE 24–6 Always use graded bolts—either grade 5 or 8 bolts—whenever mounting an engine to a stand.

bolts or fewer than four bolts can cause the engine to fall. Also check to ensure that the proper threads of bolts are being used. Some engines use fractional threads, whereas others use metric threads.

- Install the bolts so that at least $1/2$ inch (13 mm) of thread is engaged in the back of the engine to ensure that the fasteners are securely attached the engine block.
- Check that the engine is properly balanced on the engine stand before work is started on the engine. ● **SEE FIGURE 24–6.**

DISASSEMBLING A CAM-IN-BLOCK (OHV) ENGINE
Check service information for the specified engine disassembly procedure. Read, understand, and follow all safety instructions. Following are the usual steps involved.

FIGURE 24-7 Keeping the pushrods and the lifters sorted by cylinder, including the spark plugs, is a wise way to proceed when disassembling the cylinder heads.

FIGURE 24-8 Sometimes after the cylinder head has been removed, the engine condition is discovered to be so major that the entire engine may need to be replaced rather than overhauled.

STEP 1 Engines should be cold before disassembly to minimize the chance of warpage of the components that are being removed.

STEP 2 Removal of the rocker arm covers gives the first opportunity to see inside a part of the engine. Examine the rocker arms, valve springs, and valve tips for obvious defects. Remove the rocker arms and pushrods and, if they are to be reused, place them in a location so that the rockers and the pushrods can be installed back to their original location. ● SEE FIGURE 24-7.

STEP 3 Remove the intake manifold bolts and lift off the manifold. Use care to avoid damaging the parting surface as the gasket is loosened. When the intake manifold and lifter valley cover (if equipped) are off of V-type engines, the technician has another opportunity to examine the interior of the engine. On some V-type engines, it is possible to see the condition of the cam at the bottom of the lifter valley.

STEP 4 The lifters can be removed at this time if they are causing the problem or if the engine valve train is to be serviced.

STEP 5 Remove the cylinder head bolts (also called cap screws) following the reverse of the installation procedure. Loosening the fasteners at the ends of the cylinder head first, then working toward the center, helps reduce the chance of warpage to the cylinder head. Be sure to notice and mark the head bolt locations as they are often different lengths depending on their location in the head. Carefully lift the head from the block deck. If the head gasket is stuck, carefully pry the head to loosen the gasket. Use care not to scratch the block or head machined surfaces. The combustion chamber in the head and the top of the piston should be given a thorough visual examination. ● SEE FIGURE 24-8.

TECH TIP

Disassembly Is the Reverse Order of Assembly

Cylinder heads often warp upward in the center. Loosening the center head bolts first will tend to increase the warpage, especially if the head is being removed to replace a head gasket because of overheating. Always follow the torque table backwards, starting with the highest-number bolt and working toward the lowest number. In other words, always loosen fasteners starting at the end or outside of the component and work toward the inside or center of the component.

- Check the cylinder head and head gasket for signs of leakage.
- A normal combustion chamber is coated with a layer of hard, light-colored deposits.
- If the combustion chamber has been running too hot, the deposits will be very thin and white.

OVERHEAD CAMSHAFT (OHC) ENGINE DISASSEMBLY

Disassembling an overhead camshaft engine differs from a cam-in-block (OHV) engine. Check service information for the specified disassembly procedure for the engine being serviced. Read, understand, and follow all safety notices and warnings included in the instructions to help avoid causing damage to parts or components during the disassembly process. The usual steps include:

STEP 1 Remove the intake and exhaust manifolds if they have not already been removed and bag and tag all fasteners.

STEP 2 Remove the crankshaft harmonic balancer pulley that will allow access to the timing chain or belt cover.

STEP 3 Remove the timing belt/chain cover(s) and then the timing belt(s) or chain(s).

STEP 4 With most overhead camshaft engines, the camshaft(s) must be removed before removing the cylinder head due to location of the head bolts.

STEP 5 Remove the cylinder head by removing the cylinder head bolts in the opposite order of assembly. This means to loosen the outermost fasteners first, then work toward the center of the cylinder head.

STEP 6 Carefully lift the cylinder head from the block.

FIGURE 24–9 These connecting rods were numbered from the factory. If they are not, then they should be marked.

DISASSEMBLY OF THE SHORT BLOCK

REMOVING THE OIL PAN   To remove the oil pan, turn the engine upside down.

NOTE: Some engine builders prefer to remove the oil pan before turning it upside down so the technician can see the oil pan deposits first.

Deposits are a good indication of the condition and care taken of the engine. Heavy sludge indicates infrequent oil changes; hard carbon indicates overheating. The oil pump pickup screen should be checked to see how much plugging exists.

MARKING CONNECTING RODS AND CAPS   The connecting rod caps should be marked (numbered) so that they can be reassembled in exactly the same position. If the connecting rods are not marked from the factory, then they should be marked using a number stamp, electric pencil, or permanent marker. ● **SEE FIGURE 24–9.**

CAUTION: Some vehicle manufacturers warn *not* to use a punch or an electric pencil on powdered metal connection rods. Use only a permanent marker to label powdered metal rods. If in doubt as to the type of rod that is in the engine, use a marker to be safe.

REMOVING THE CYLINDER RIDGE   Before the pistons can be removed from the block, the ridge must be removed. Piston wear against the cylinder wall leaves an upper ridge, because the top ring does not travel all the way to the top of the cylinder. Ridge removal is necessary to avoid catching a ring on the ridge and breaking the piston. ● **SEE FIGURE 24–10.**

The ridge is removed with a cutting tool that has a guide to help prevent accidental cutting below the ridge. ● **SEE FIGURE 24–11.**

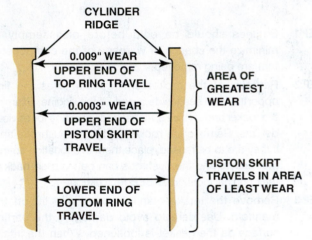

FIGURE 24–10 Most of the cylinder wear is on the top inch just below the cylinder ridge. This wear is due to the heat and combustion pressures that occur when the piston is near the top of the cylinder.

 **TECH TIP**

Measure the Cylinder Bore Before Further Disassembly

As soon as the cylinder head has been removed from the engine, take a measurement of the cylinder bore. This is done for the following reasons.

- To verify that the engine size is the same as specified by the vehicle identification number (VIN)
- To measure the bore and compare it to factory specifications, to help the technician determine if the cylinder(s) are too worn to use or cannot be restored

FIGURE 24–11 This ridge is being removed with one type of ridge reamer before the piston assemblies are removed from the engine.

FIGURE 24–12 Puller being used to pull the vibration damper from the crankshaft.

PISTON REMOVAL Removing the piston and rod assembly includes the following steps.

STEP 1 Rotate the engine until the piston that is to be removed is at bottom dead center (BDC).

STEP 2 Remove connecting rod nuts from the rod so that the rod cap with its bearing half can be removed.

STEP 3 Fit the rod bolts with protectors to keep the bolt threads from damaging the crankshaft journals, and then carefully remove the piston and rod assemblies.

STEP 4 After removal of each piston, replace the rod cap and nuts to avoid losing or mismatching them.

ROTATING ENGINE ASSEMBLIES REMOVAL

HARMONIC BALANCER REMOVAL The next step after the water pump has been removed is to remove the crankshaft **vibration damper** (also called a *harmonic balancer*). The bolt and washer that hold the damper are removed. The damper should be removed only with a threaded puller. ● **SEE FIGURE 24–12.**

If a hook-type puller is used around the edge of the damper, it may pull the damper ring from the hub. If this happens, the damper assembly will have to be replaced with a new assembly. With the damper assembly off, the timing cover can be removed, exposing the timing gear or timing chain. Examine these parts for excessive wear and looseness. ● **SEE FIGURE 24–13.**

Bolted cam sprockets can be removed to free the timing chain. On some engines this will require removal of the crankshaft gear at the same time. Pressed-on gears and sprockets are removed from the shaft *only* if they are faulty. They are removed after the camshaft is removed from the block. It is

FIGURE 24–13 When the timing chain cover was removed, the broken timing gear explained why this GM 4.3 liter V-6 engine stopped running.

necessary to remove the camshaft thrust plate retaining screws when they are used.

CAMSHAFT REMOVAL The camshaft and balance shafts, if equipped, can be removed at this time, or they can be removed after the crankshaft is out. For best results, insert a

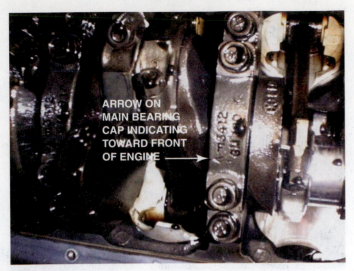

FIGURE 24–14 Most engines such as this Chevrolet V-8 with four-bolt main bearing caps have arrows marked on the bearing caps which should point to the front of the engine.

long bolt into one of the camshaft threaded holes to serve as handles for removing (or installing) a camshaft. It must be carefully eased from the engine to avoid damaging the cam bearings or cam lobes. This is done most easily with the front of the engine pointing up. Bearing surfaces are soft and scratch easily, and the cam lobes are hard and can chip easily.

CRANKSHAFT AND MAIN BEARING REMOVAL The main bearing caps should be checked for position markings before they are removed. If they are not marked, use steel number stamps to mark them and also be sure to indicate which side of each main cap faces to the front of the engine. ● **SEE FIGURE 24–14**.

They have been machined in place and will not fit perfectly in any other location. After marking, they can be removed to free the crankshaft. When the crankshaft is removed, the main bearing caps and bearings are reinstalled on the block to reduce the chance of damage to the caps.

BLOCK INSPECTION After the pistons and crankshaft have been removed, remove all cups and plugs and carefully inspect the block for faults that could affect whether the engine can be rebuilt. ● **SEE FIGURE 24–15**.

Further detailed inspection should be completed after the components have been cleaned.

CYLINDER HEAD DISASSEMBLY

OHV ENGINE CYLINDER HEADS After the heads are removed and placed on the bench, the valves can be removed.

FIGURE 24–15 This small block Chevrolet V-8 had water standing in the cylinders, causing a lot of rust, which was discovered as soon as the head was removed.

 TECH TIP

The Wax Trick

Before the engine block can be thoroughly cleaned, all oil gallery plugs must be removed. A popular trick of the trade for plug removal involves heating the plug (not the surrounding metal) with an oxyacetylene torch. The heat tends to expand the plug and make it tighter in the block. Do not overheat.

As the plug is cooling, touch the plug with paraffin wax (beeswax or candle wax may be used). ● **SEE FIGURE 24–16**.

The wax will be drawn down around the threads of the plug by capillary attraction as the plug cools and contracts. After being allowed to cool, the plug is easily removed.

CAUTION: Always wear safety glasses when working on a cylinder head. Valve springs can release quickly, causing valve parts to fly.

To disassemble a cylinder head, perform the following steps.

STEP 1 Tap the valve spring retainer with a brass hammer, hitting the retainer on an angle to "break the taper" of the valve keepers (locks).

STEP 2 Using a valve spring compressor, compress the valve spring far enough to expose the keepers. ● **SEE FIGURE 24–17**.

STEP 3 Remove the two keepers using a magnet.

STEP 4 After the valve keepers have been removed, slowly release the compressor to remove and to free the valve retainer and spring.

STEP 5 The valve tip edge and keeper (lock) area should be lightly filed or stoned to remove any burrs *before*

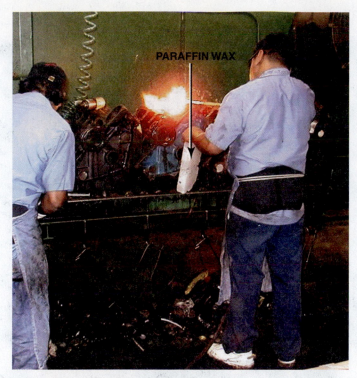

FIGURE 24–16 A torch is used to heat gallery plugs. Paraffin wax is then applied and allowed to flow around the threads. This procedure results in easier removal of the plugs and other threaded fasteners that cannot otherwise be loosened.

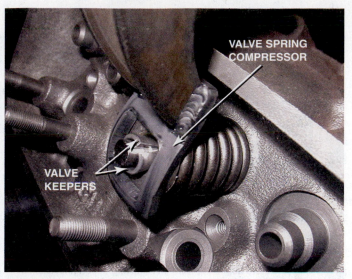

FIGURE 24–17 A valve spring compressor is used to compress the valve spring before removing the keepers (locks).

sliding the valve from the head. Burrs will scratch the valve guide.

STEP 6 Remove all valve stem seals and the metal spring seats that are used on aluminum heads.

STEP 7 When all valves are removed following the same procedure, carefully inspect the valve springs, retainers, keepers (locks), guides, and seats.

OHC ENGINE CYLINDER HEADS After the heads are removed and placed on the bench, the valves can be removed after the camshaft is removed. Often a special valve spring compressor is required to reach the valve retainers. Always read, understand, and follow all vehicle manufacturer's instructions.

TECH TIP

Mark It to Be Safe

Whenever you disassemble anything, it is always wise to mark the location of parts, bolts, hoses, and other items that could be incorrectly assembled. Remember, the first part removed will be the last part that is assembled. If you think you will remember where everything goes—forget it! It just does not happen in the real world.

One popular trick is to use correction fluid to mark the location of parts before they are removed. Most of these products are alcohol or water based, dry quickly, and usually contain a brush in the cap for easy use.

1 Before beginning work on removing the engine, mark and remove the hood and place it in a safe location.

2 For safety, remove the negative battery cable to avoid any possible electrical problems from occurring.

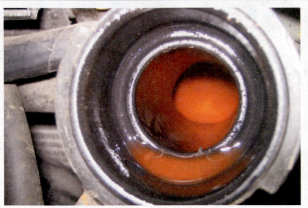

3 Drain the coolant and dispose of properly.

4 Disconnect all cooling system and heater hoses and remove the radiator.

5 Remove the accessory drive belt(s) and set the alternator, power steering pump, and air-conditioning compressor aside.

6 Remove the air intake system including the air filter housing as needed.

7 Remove the electrical connector from all sensors and label.

8 Disconnect the engine wiring harness connector at the bulkhead.

9 Safely hoist the vehicle and disconnect the exhaust system from the exhaust manifolds.

10 Mark and then remove the fasteners connecting the flex plate to the torque converter.

11 Lower the vehicle and remove the engine mount bolts and transaxle bell housing fasteners.

12 Secure the lifting chain to the engine hooks and carefully remove the engine from the vehicle.

SUMMARY

1. A repair, valve job, overhaul, and entire engine replacement are some of the solution options for an engine failure.

2. A short block is the block assembly with pistons and crankshaft. A long block also includes the cylinder head(s).

3. Factory lifting hooks should be used when hoisting an engine.

4. Cylinder heads should only be removed when the engine is cold. Also, always follow the torque table backwards, starting with the highest-number head bolt and working toward the lowest number. This procedure helps prevent cylinder head warpage.

5. The ridge at the top of the cylinder should be removed before removing the piston(s) from the cylinder.

6. The connecting rod and main bearing caps should be marked before being removed to ensure that they can be reinstalled in the exact same location when the engine is reassembled.

7. The tip of the valve stem should be filed before removing valves from the cylinder head to help prevent damage to the valve guide.

REVIEW QUESTIONS

1. What are the differences between a minor and a major overhaul?

2. When should the factory-installed lifting hooks be used?

3. Why should the cylinder bore be measured before continuing with an engine disassembly?

4. State two reasons for the removal of the ridge at the top of the cylinder.

5. Explain why the burrs must be removed from valves before removing the valves from the cylinder head.

CHAPTER QUIZ

1. A short block includes the _____.
   a. Block
   b. Crankshaft and main bearings
   c. Pistons, rods, and rod bearings
   d. All of the above

2. When removing cylinder heads, the fasteners should be removed in which order?
   a. The reverse order of tightening
   b. The same order as the specified tightening sequence
   c. Any order
   d. Loosened slightly in the same order as the tightening sequence and then removed in any order

3. A long block can be made from a short block with the addition of _____.
   a. Cylinder heads and valve train
   b. Intake and exhaust manifolds
   c. Oil pump, oil pan, and timing chain cover
   d. Fuel pump, carburetor, and air cleaner assembly

4. What needs to be removed before the valves can be removed from the cylinder head?
   a. The valve keepers
   b. The camshaft if OHV engine
   c. The cylinder head from the block
   d. Both a and c

5. With the rocker cover (valve cover) removed, the technician can inspect all items *except* _____.
   a. Combustion chamber deposits
   b. Rocker arms and valve spring
   c. Camshaft (overhead camshaft engine only)
   d. Valve stems and pushrods (overhead valve engines only)

6. After the oil pan (sump) is removed, the technician should inspect _____.
   a. The oil pump and pickup screen
   b. To make certain that all rod and main bearings are numbered or marked
   c. The valve lifters (tappets) for wear
   d. Both a and b

7. The ridge at the top of the cylinder _____.
   a. Is caused by the rings that do not travel all the way to top of the cylinder
   b. Represents a failure of the top piston ring to correctly seal against the cylinder wall
   c. Should not be removed before removing pistons except when reboring the cylinders
   d. Means that a crankshaft with an incorrect stroke was installed in the engine

8. Before the timing chain can be inspected and removed, the _____ must be removed.
   a. Valve cover
   b. Vibration damper
   c. Cylinder head(s)
   d. Intake manifold (V-type engines only)

9. Before the valves are removed from the cylinder head, what operations need to be completed?
   a. Remove valve keepers (locks)
   b. Remove cylinder head(s) from the engine
   c. Remove burrs from the stem of the valve(s)
   d. All of the above

10. Technician A says that a minor overhaul can often be done with the engine remaining in the vehicle. Technician B says that a core is required for most remanufactured engines. Which technician is correct?
    a. Technician A only
    b. Technician B only
    c. Both Technicians A and B
    d. Neither Technician A nor B

chapter 25

ENGINE CLEANING AND CRACK DETECTION

LEARNING OBJECTIVES: **After studying this chapter, the reader should be able to:** • Explain the mechanical cleaning procedure of engines. • Discuss chemical cleaners. • Compare spray and steam washing, thermal cleaning, tank and vapor cleaning, and ultrasonic and vibratory cleaning. • Explain crack detection and crack repair.

KEY TERMS: Acid materials 344 • Agitation 346 • Aqueous-based solutions 344 • Caustic materials 343 • Fusible link 346 • Hydroseal 346 • pH 343 • Putty knife 342 • Pyrolytic 345 • Ultrasonic cleaning 346 • Zyglo 347

INTRODUCTION

After an engine has been disassembled and before it can be overhauled or repaired, the engine and engine parts should go through two important operations.

1. All parts, including fasteners, must be thoroughly cleaned.

2. All components and parts must be inspected to ensure that they are serviceable and free from faults such as cracks.

MECHANICAL CLEANING

PRINCIPLES Heavy deposits should be removed by mechanical cleaning before using other cleaning methods. Mechanical cleaning involves:

- Scraping
- Abrasive brushing
- Abrasive blasting

SCRAPING The scraper most frequently used is a **putty knife,** or a plastic card. The broad blade of the putty knife helps avoid scratching the surface as it is used to clean the parts. A plastic card such as an old gift, credit, or other similar card can be used to clean aluminum parts such as cylinder head gasket surfaces without causing any damage.

ABRASIVE PADS OR DISCS An abrasive pad or disc can be used on *disassembled* parts only. After an abrasive pad or disc has been used, the part *must* be thoroughly cleaned to remove the particles from the plastic bristles or pad. The

abrasive aluminum oxide particles from the bristles can get into the engine and cause major damage.

There are three colors of rotary discs, and each is made from a different grit size of abrasive. The three colors of bristle discs and their applications include:

- **White.** Has the finest grit size, and is to used for cleaning aluminum parts
- **Yellow.** Has a coarse grit, and can be used on aluminum
- **Green.** For use on cast-iron components only

● **SEE FIGURES 25–1 AND 25–2.**

CAUTION: Do not use steel wire brushes on aluminum parts! Steel is harder than aluminum and will remove some of the aluminum from the surface during cleaning.

MEDIA BLASTING Media blasting with baking soda is the cleaning method of choice for most shops. Baking soda (bicarbonate of soda) works well because it is:

- Nontoxic
- Nonflammable
- Nonhazardous
- Environmentally safe

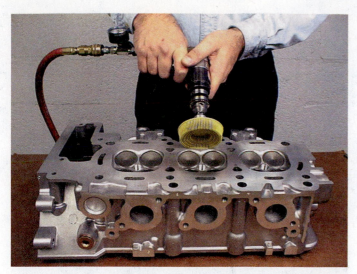

FIGURE 25-1 An air-powered grinder attached to a bristle pad being used to clean the gasket surface of a cylinder head. This type of cleaning pad should not be used on the engine block where the grit could get into the engine oil and cause harm when the engine is started and run after the repair.

FIGURE 25-2 An abrasive disc commonly called by its trade name, Scotch Brite™ pad.

A soda blasting machine uses compressed air to deliver the baking soda media onto the part being cleaned. ● SEE FIGURE 25-3.

Cleaning cast-iron or aluminum engine parts with solvents or heat usually requires another operation to achieve a uniform surface finish. Blasting the parts with steel, cast-iron, aluminum, or stainless steel shot, baking soda, or glass beads is a simple way to achieve a matte or satin surface finish on the engine parts. To keep the shot or beads from sticking to the parts, they must be dry, without a trace of oil or grease, prior to blasting. This means that blasting is the second cleaning method after the part has been precleaned in a tank, spray washer, or oven. Some blasting is done automatically in an airless shot-blasting machine. Another method is to hard-blast parts in a sealed cabinet. ● SEE FIGURE 25-4.

FIGURE 25-3 Using baking soda is the recommended way to clean engine parts because any soda that is left on or in the part is dissolved in oil or water, unlike either sand or glass beads, which can be engine damaging.

FIGURE 25-4 Small engine parts can be blasted clean in a sealed cabinet.

CAUTION: Glass beads often remain in internal passages of engine parts, where they can come loose and travel through the cylinders when the engine is started. Among other places, these small but destructive beads can easily be trapped under the oil baffles of rocker covers and in oil pans and piston ring grooves. To help prevent the glass beads from sticking, be sure the parts being cleaned are free of grease and dirt, and completely *dry*.

CHEMICAL CLEANERS

pH Most chemical cleaners used for cleaning carbon-type deposits are strong soaps called **caustic materials. pH** value, measured on a scale from 1 to 14, indicates the amount of chemical activity in the soap. The term *pH* is from the French *pouvoir hydrogine,* meaning "hydrogen power." Pure water is neutral; on the pH scale, water is pH 7. Caustic materials have pH numbers from 8 through 14. The higher the number, the stronger the caustic action will be. **Acid materials** have pH numbers from 1 through 6. The lower the number, the stronger the acid action will be. Caustic materials and acid materials neutralize each other. This is what happens when baking soda (a caustic) is used to clean the outside of the battery (an acid surface). The caustic baking soda neutralizes any sulfuric acid that has been spilled or splashed on the outside of the battery.

CAUTION: Whenever working with chemicals, you must use eye protection.

SOLVENT-BASED CLEANING Cleaning chemicals applied to engine parts will mix with and dissolve deposits. The chemicals loosen the deposits so that they can be brushed or rinsed from the surface. A deposit is said to be *soluble* when it can be dissolved with a chemical or solvent. Chemical cleaning can involve a spray washer or a soak in a cold or hot tank. The cleaning solution is usually solvent based, with a medium pH rating of between 10 and 12. Most chemical solutions also contain silicates to protect the metal (aluminum) against corrosion.

Strong caustics do an excellent job on cast-iron items but are often too corrosive for aluminum parts. Aluminum cleaners include mineral spirit solvents as well as alkaline detergents.

CAUTION: When cleaning aluminum cylinder heads, blocks, or other engine components, make sure that the chemicals used are "aluminum safe." Many chemicals that are not aluminum safe may turn the aluminum metal black. Try to explain that to a customer!

WATER-BASED CHEMICAL CLEANING Because of environmental concerns, most chemical cleaning is now performed using water-based solutions (also called **aqueous-based solutions**). Most aqueous-type chemicals are silicate based and are mixed with water. Aqueous-based solutions can be used in one of two ways.

- Sprayed on
- Used in a tank for soaking parts

Aluminum heads and blocks usually require overnight soaking in a solution kept at about 190°F (90°C). For best results, the cleaning solution should be agitated.

FIGURE 25–5 A pressure jet washer is similar to a large industrial-sized dishwasher. Each part is then rinsed with water to remove chemicals or debris that may remain there while it is still in the tank.

hitting the surface, combined with the chemical action of the cleaning solution, produces a clean surface. Spray washing is typically performed in an enclosed washer (like a dishwasher), where parts are rotated on a washer turntable.
● **SEE FIGURE 25–5**.

Spray washing is faster than soaking. A typical washer cycle is less than 30 minutes per load, compared to eight or more hours for soaking. Most spray washers use an aqueous-based cleaning solution heated to 160°F to 180°F (70°C to 80°C) with foam suppressants. High-volume remanufacturers use industrial dishwashing machines to clean the disassembled engine component parts.

STEAM CLEANING Steam vapor is mixed with high-pressure water and sprayed on the parts. The heat of the steam plus the force of the high-pressure water perform the actual cleaning. Steam cleaning must be used with extreme care. Usually, a caustic cleaner is added to the steam and water to aid in the cleaning. This mixture is so active that it will damage and even remove paint, so painted surfaces must be protected from the spray. Engines are often steam cleaned before they are removed from the vehicle.

SPRAY WASHING A spray washer directs streams of liquid through numerous high-pressure nozzles to dislodge dirt and grime on an engine surface. The force of the liquid

TEMPERATURES INVOLVED Thermal cleaning uses heat to vaporize and change dirt, oil, and grease into a dry, powdery ash. Thermal cleaning is best suited for cleaning cast iron, where temperatures as high as 800°F (425°C) are used, whereas aluminum should not be heated to over 600°F (315°C).

FIGURE 25–6 A microbial cleaning tank uses microbes to clean grease and oil from parts.

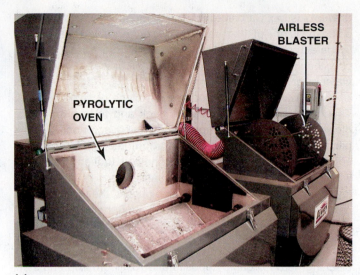

(a)

(b)

FIGURE 25–7 (a) A pyrolytic (high-temperature) oven cleans by baking the engine parts. After the parts have been cleaned, they are then placed into an airless blaster. This unit uses a paddle to scoop stainless steel shot from a reservoir and forces it against the engine part. The parts must be free of grease and oil to function correctly. (b) This cleaned engine block has been baked and shot blasted.

ADVANTAGES The major advantages of thermal cleaning include the following:

1. This process cleans the inside as well as the outside of the casting or part.

2. The waste generated is nonhazardous and is easy to dispose of. However, the heat in the oven usually discolors the metal, leaving it looking dull.

MICROBIAL CLEANING Microbial cleaning uses microbes that are living organisms (single-celled bacteria) that literally "eat" the hydrocarbons (grease and oils) off of the parts being cleaned. The typical microbial cleaning system includes three parts.

- A liquid assists the microbes by breaking the hydrocarbons to a smaller (molecular) size.

- The microbes, stored in a dormant phase until ready for use, give an indefinite shelf life to the product. Once the microbes come into contact with the liquid, they wake up from the dormant state and begin to feed.

- A third part is a blend of nutrients to ensure that the microbes start to multiply in the shortest amount of time to help speed the cleaning time needed.

Microbial cleaning is environment friendly, but is slower to clean parts. ● **SEE FIGURE 25–6**.

PYROLYTIC OVEN A **pyrolytic** (high-temperature) oven cleans engine parts by decomposing dirt, grease, and gaskets with heat in a manner similar to that of a self-cleaning oven. This method of engine parts cleaning is the least hazardous method and is becoming the most popular because there is no hazardous waste associated with it. Labor costs are also reduced because the operator does not need to be present during the actual cleaning operation. ● **SEE FIGURE 25–7**.

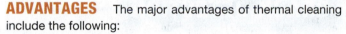

TANK AND VAPOR CLEANING

COLD TANK CLEANING The cold soak tank is used to remove grease and carbon. The disassembled parts are placed in the tank so that they are *completely* covered with the chemical cleaning solution. After a soaking period, the parts are removed and rinsed until the milky appearance of the emulsion is gone. The parts are then dried with compressed air. The clean, dry parts are then usually given a very light coating of clean oil to prevent rusting. Carburetor cleaner, purchased with a basket in a bucket, is one of the most common types of cold soak agents in the automotive shop. Usually, there will be a layer of water over the chemical to prevent evaporation of the chemical. This water layer is called a **hydroseal.**

Parts washers are often used in place of soaking tanks. This equipment can move parts back and forth through the cleaning solution or pumps the cleaning solution over the parts. This movement, called **agitation,** keeps fresh cleaning solution moving past the soil to help it loosen. The parts washer is usually equipped with a safety cover held open by a low-temperature **fusible link.** If a fire occurs, the fusible link will melt and the cover will drop closed to snuff the fire out.

HOT TANK CLEANING
The hot soak tank is used for cleaning heavy organic deposits and rust from iron and steel parts. The caustic cleaning solution used in the hot soak tank is heated to near 200°F (93°C) for rapid cleaning action. The solution must be inhibited when aluminum is to be cleaned. After the deposits have been loosened, the parts are removed from the tank and rinsed with hot water or steam cleaned, which dries them rapidly. They must then be given a light coating of oil to prevent rusting.

HINT: Fogging oil from a spray can does an excellent job of coating metal parts to keep them from rusting.

VAPOR CLEANING
Vapor cleaning is popular in some automotive service shops. The parts to be cleaned are suspended in hot vapors above a perchloroethylene solution. The vapors of the solution loosen the soil from the metal so that it can be blown, wiped, or rinsed from the surface.

ULTRASONIC AND VIBRATORY CLEANING

ULTRASONIC CLEANING
Ultrasonic cleaning is used to clean small parts that must be absolutely clean, such as hydraulic lifters and diesel injectors. The disassembled parts are placed in a tank of cleaning solution that is then vibrated at ultrasonic speeds to loosen all the soil from the parts. The soil goes into the solution or falls to the bottom of the tank. ● **SEE FIGURE 25–8.**

VIBRATORY CLEANING
The vibratory method of cleaning is best suited for small parts. Parts are loaded into a vibrating bin with small odd-shaped ceramic or steel pieces, called media, with a cleaning solution of mineral spirits or water-based detergents that usually contain a lubricant additive to help the media pieces slide around more freely. The movement of the vibrating solution and the scrubbing action of the media do an excellent job of cleaning metal.

FIGURE 25–8 An ultrasonic cleaner is used to clean fuel injectors.

CRACK DETECTION

VISUAL INSPECTION
After the parts have been thoroughly cleaned, they should be reexamined for defects. A magnifying glass is helpful in finding defects. Internal parts such as pistons, connecting rods, and crankshafts that have cracks should be replaced. Cracks in the block and heads, however, can often be repaired.

MAGNETIC CRACK DETECTION
The process of detecting cracks using a magnetic field is commonly referred to by the brand name Magnafluxing. Cracks in engine blocks, cylinder heads, crankshafts, and other engine components are sometimes difficult to find during a normal visual inspection, which is why all remanufacturers and most engine builders use a crack detection procedure on critical engine parts.

Magnetic flux testing is the method most often used on steel and iron components. A metal engine part (such as a cast-iron cylinder head) is connected to a large electromagnet. Magnetic lines of force are easily conducted through the iron part and concentrate on the edges of a crack. A fine iron powder is then applied to the part being tested, and the powder will be attracted to the strong magnetic concentration around the crack. ● **SEE FIGURES 25–9 THROUGH 25–11.**

DYE-PENETRANT TESTING
Dye-penetrant testing is often used on pistons and other parts constructed of aluminum or other nonmagnetic material. A dark red penetrating chemical is first sprayed on the component being tested. After cleaning, a white powder is sprayed over the test area. If a crack is present, the red dye will stain the white powder. Even though this method will also work on iron and steel (magnetic) parts, it is often used only on nonmagnetic parts because magnetic methods do not work on these parts.

FIGURE 25–9 The top deck surface of a block is being tested using magnetic crack inspection equipment.

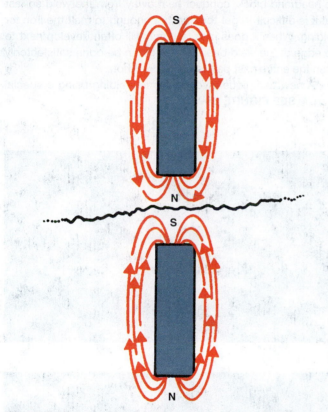

FIGURE 25–10 If the lines of force are interrupted by a break (crack) in the casting, then two magnetic fields are created and the powder will lodge in the crack.

FLUORESCENT-PENETRANT TESTING To be seen, fluorescent penetrant requires a black light. It can be used on iron, steel, or aluminum parts. Cracks show up as bright lines when viewed with a black light. The method is commonly called **Zyglo,** a trademark of the Magnaflux Corporation.

PRESSURE TESTING Cylinder heads and blocks are often pressure tested with air and checked for leaks. All coolant passages are blocked with rubber plugs or gaskets, and compressed air is applied to the water jacket(s). The head or

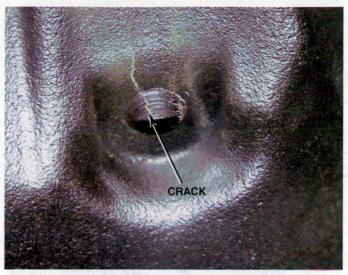

FIGURE 25–11 This crack in a vintage Ford 289, V-8 block was likely caused by the technician using excessive force trying to remove the plug from the block. The technician should have used heat and wax, not only to make the job easier, but also to prevent damaging the block.

FIGURE 25–12 To make sure that the mark observed in the cylinder wall was a crack, compressed air was forced into the water jacket while soapy water was sprayed on the cylinder wall. Bubbles confirmed that the mark was indeed a crack.

block is then lowered into water, where air bubbles indicate a leak. For more accurate results, the water should be heated because the hot water expands the casting by about the same amount as an operating engine would. An alternative method involves running heated water with a dye through the cylinder or block. Any leaks revealed by the dyed water indicate a crack.
● SEE FIGURES 25–12 AND 25–13.

CRACK REPAIR

CRACK CONCERNS Cracks in the engine block can cause coolant to flow into the oil or oil into the coolant. A cracked block can also cause coolant to leak externally from a crack that

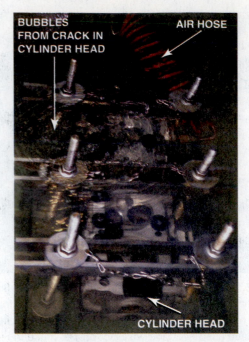

FIGURE 25–13 A cylinder head is under water and being pressure tested using compressed air. Note that the air bubbles indicate a crack.

goes through to a coolant passage. Cracks in the head will allow coolant to leak into the engine, or they will allow combustion gases to leak into the coolant. Cracks across the valve seat cause hot spots on the valve, which will burn the valve face. A head with a crack will either have to be replaced or the crack will have to be repaired.

STOP DRILLING   A hole can be drilled at each end of the crack to keep it from extending further, a step sometimes called *stop drilling*. Cracks that do not cross oil passages, bolt holes, or seal surfaces can sometimes be left alone if stopped.

CRACK-WELDING CAST IRON   It takes a great deal of skill to weld cast iron. The cast iron does not puddle or flow as steel does when it is heated. Heavy cast parts, such as the head and block, conduct heat away from the weld so fast that it is difficult to get the part hot enough to melt the iron for welding. When it does melt, a crack will often develop next to the edge of the weld bead. Welding can be done satisfactorily when the entire cast part is heated red-hot.

A new technique involves flame welding using a special torch. ● **SEE FIGURE 25–14.**

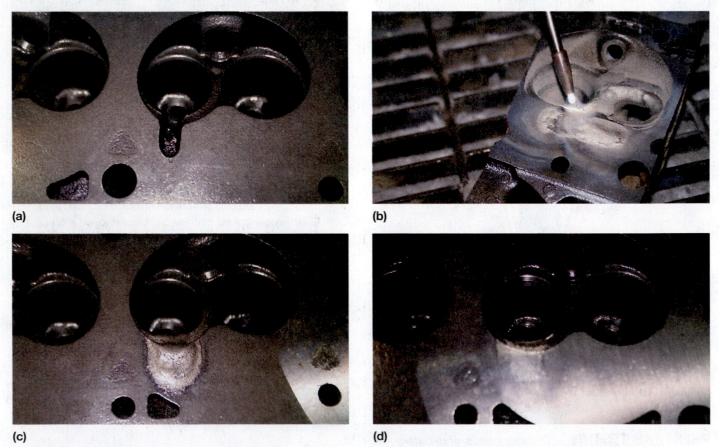

FIGURE 25–14 (a) Before welding, the crack is ground out using a carbide grinder. (b) Here the technician is practicing using the special cast-iron welding torch before welding the cracked cylinder head. (c) This is the finished welded crack before final machining. (d) Note the finished cylinder head after the crack has been repaired using welding.

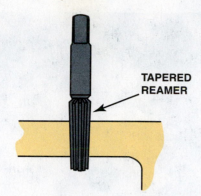

FIGURE 25-15 Reaming a hole for a tapered plug.

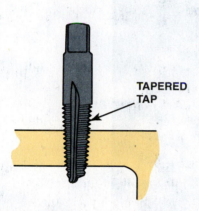

FIGURE 25-16 Tapping a tapered hole for a plug.

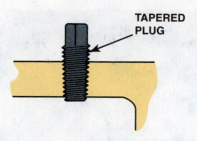

FIGURE 25-17 Screwing a tapered plug in the hole.

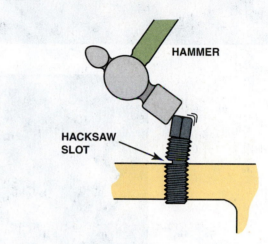

FIGURE 25-18 Cutting the plug with a hacksaw.

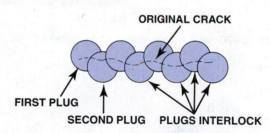

FIGURE 25-19 Interlocking plugs.

CRACK-WELDING ALUMINUM Cracks in aluminum can be welded using a Heli-arc® or similar welder that is specially designed to weld aluminum. The crack should be cut or burned out before welding begins. The old valve-seat insert should be removed if the crack is in or near the combustion chamber.

CRACK PLUGGING In the process of crack plugging, a crack is closed using interlocking tapered plugs. This procedure can be performed to repair cracks in both aluminum and cast-iron engine components. The ends of the crack are center punched and drilled with the proper size of tap drill for the plugs. The hole is reamed with a tapered reamer (● FIGURE 25–15) and is then tapped with a special tap to give full threads (● FIGURE 25–16).

The plug is coated with sealer; then it is tightened into the hole (● FIGURE 25–17), sawed about one-fourth of the way through, and broken off.

The saw slot controls the breaking point (● FIGURE 25–18).

If the plug should break below the surface, it will have to be drilled out and a new plug installed. The plug should go to the full depth or thickness of the cast metal. After the first plug is installed on each end, a new hole is drilled with the tap drill so that it cuts into the edge of the first plug. This new hole is reamed and tapped, and a plug is inserted as before. The plug should fit about one-fourth of the way into the first plug to lock it into place (● FIGURE 25–19).

Interlocking plugs are placed along the entire crack, alternating slightly from side to side. The exposed ends of the plugs are peened over with a hammer to help secure them in place. The surface of the plugs is then ground or filed down nearly to the gasket surface. In the combustion chamber and at the ports, the plugs are ground down to the original surface using a hand grinder. The gasket surface of the head must be resurfaced after the crack has been repaired. ● **SEE FIGURE 25–20** for an example of a cylinder head repair using plugs.

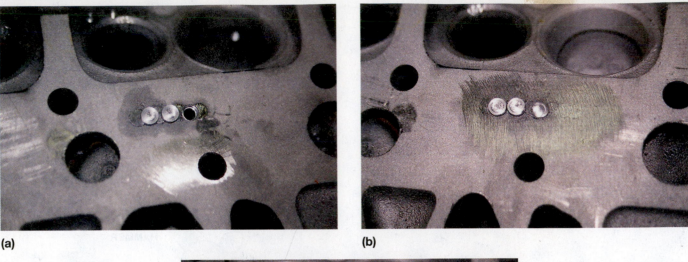

(a)

(b)

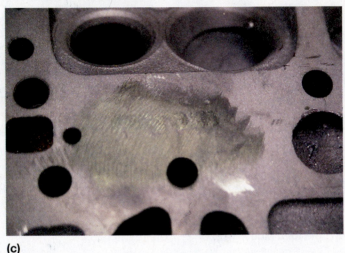

(c)

FIGURE 25–20 (a) A hole is drilled and tapped for the plugs. (b) The plugs are installed. (c) After final machining, the cylinder head can be returned to useful service.

SUMMARY

1. Mechanical cleaning with scrapers or wire brushes is used to remove deposits.

2. Steel wire brushes should never be used to clean aluminum parts.

3. Most chemical cleaners are strong soaps called caustic materials.

4. Always use aluminum-safe chemicals when cleaning aluminum parts or components.

5. Thermal cleaning is done in a pyrolytic oven in temperatures as high as 800°F (425°C) to turn grease and dirt into harmless ash deposits.

6. Blasters use metal shot or glass beads to clean parts. All of the metal shot or glass beads must be thoroughly cleaned from the part so as not to cause engine problems.

7. All parts should be checked for cracks using magnetic, dye-penetrant, fluorescent-penetrant, or pressure testing methods.

8. Cracks can be repaired by welding or by plugging.

1. Describe five methods that could be used to clean engines or engine parts.

2. Explain magnetic crack inspection, dye-penetrant testing, and fluorescent-penetrant testing methods and where each can be used.

3. How can engine block and cylinder heads be repaired if cracked?

CHAPTER QUIZ

1. Abrasive pads or discs should be used _____.
   a. On disassembled engine parts only
   b. According to the specified grit size for the material being cleaned
   c. But clean the part thoroughly to wash away the abrasive material
   d. All of the above

2. What actually does the cleaning when using steam?
   a. Heat from the steam
   b. Pressure behind the steam
   c. Abrasives used
   d. Both a and b

3. Aqueous-based cleaning means _____.
   a. Water based
   b. Abrasive based
   c. Strong chemical based
   d. All of the above

4. A pyrolytic oven is used to clean parts; however, caution should be used to limit the temperature, to prevent damaging engine parts. What are the maximum recommended temperatures?
   a. 300°F (150°C) for all engine parts
   b. 600°F (315°C) for aluminum parts
   c. 800°F (425°C) for cast iron
   d. Both b and c

5. Which media is best to use for cleaning parts as it does not need to be thoroughly cleaned after using?
   a. Baking soda
   b. Stainless steel shot
   c. Glass beads
   d. Aluminum shot

6. Cleaning chemicals are usually either a caustic material or an acid material. Which of the following statements is true?
   a. Both caustics and acids have a pH of 7 if rated according to distilled water.
   b. An acid is lower than 7 and a caustic is higher than 7 on the pH scale.
   c. An acid is higher than 7 and a caustic is lower than 7 on the pH scale.
   d. Pure water is a 1 and a strong acid is a 14 on the pH scale.

7. Many cleaning methods involve chemicals that are hazardous to use. The least hazardous method is generally considered to be the _____.
   a. Pyrolytic oven
   b. Hot vapor tank
   c. Hot soak tank
   d. Cold soak tank

8. Magnetic crack inspection _____.
   a. Uses a red dye to detect cracks in aluminum
   b. Uses a black light to detect cracks in iron parts
   c. Uses a fine iron powder to detect cracks in iron parts
   d. Uses a magnet to remove cracks from iron parts

9. Technician A says that engine parts should be cleaned before a thorough test can be done to detect cracks. Technician B says that pressure testing can be used to find cracks in blocks or cylinder heads. Which technician is correct?
   a. Technician A only
   b. Technician B only
   c. Both Technicians A and B
   d. Neither Technician A nor B

10. Plugging can be used to repair cracks _____.
    a. In cast-iron cylinder heads
    b. In aluminum cylinder heads
    c. In both cast-iron and aluminum cylinder heads
    d. Only in cast-iron blocks

CYLINDER HEAD AND VALVE GUIDE SERVICE

LEARNING OBJECTIVES: After studying this chapter, the reader should be able to: • Explain the design and construction of cylinder heads. • Discuss intake and exhaust ports. • Discuss cylinder head passages and cylinder head servicing. • Explain aluminum cylinder head straightening, cylinder head resurfacing, and intake manifold alignment. • Explain valve guides and the procedure for valve guide replacement.

KEY TERMS: Arithmetic average roughness height (RA) 360 • Bend 359 • Bronze guide liners 365 • Bronze guides 364 • Cam tunnel 359 • Cast-iron guides 364 • Concentric 362 • Crossflow head 354 • Distortion 359 • Fire deck 359 • Milling 360 • Oversize (OS) stems 363 • Port 355 • Porting (relieving) 356 • Quench area 353 • Root-mean-square (RMS) 360 • Siamese port 356 • Spiral bronze alloy bushing 365 • Squish area 352 • Surface grinder 360 • Surface-to-volume ratio 353 • Thin-walled bronze alloy sleeve bushing 365 • Twist 359 • Unshrouding 356 • Valve duration 354 • Valve guide knurling 364 • Valve guides 362 • Valve seat inserts 362 • Valve shrouding 354 • Warpage 359

INTRODUCTION

The repair and reconditioning of cylinder heads represents the most frequent engine repair operation of any engine component. The highest temperatures and pressures in the entire engine are located in the combustion chamber of the cylinder head. Its valves must open and close thousands of times when the engine is operated.

CYLINDER HEADS

CONSTRUCTION Cylinder heads support the valves and valve train, and contain passages for the flow of intake, exhaust gases, coolant, and sometimes engine oil. In an overhead camshaft design engine, the cylinder head also supports all of the valve train components including the camshaft, rocker arms, or followers, as well as the intake and exhaust valves and valve guides. ● SEE FIGURE 26–1.

DESIGN FEATURES Most cylinder head designs incorporate the following design factors to achieve fast burning of the air-fuel mixture and to reduce exhaust emissions. These factors include:

- **Squish area.** This is an area of the combustion chamber where the piston nearly contacts the cylinder head. When

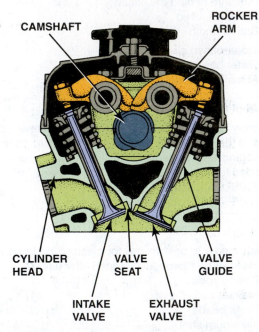

FIGURE 26–1 The seats and guides for the valves are in the cylinder head as well as the camshaft and the entire valve train if it is an overhead camshaft design.

the piston is moving upward toward the cylinder head, the air-fuel mixture is rapidly pushed out of the squish area, causing turbulence. Turbulence helps mix the air and fuel, thereby ensuring a more uniform and complete combustion. ● SEE FIGURE 26–2.

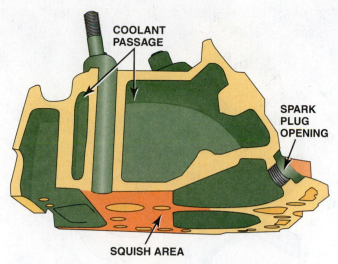

FIGURE 26–2 A wedge-shaped combustion chamber showing the squish area where the air-fuel mixture is squeezed, causing turbulence that pushes the mixture toward the spark plug.

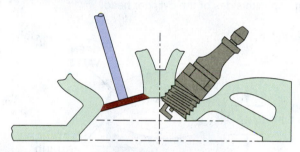

FIGURE 26–3 Locating the spark plug in the center of the combustion chamber reduces the distance the flame front must travel.

- **Quench area.** The squish area can also be the quench area where the air-fuel mixture is cooled by the cylinder head. The quench area is the flat area of the combustion chamber that is above the flat area of the piston. As the piston moves upward on the compression stroke, the air-fuel mixture is forced from this area as the piston gets near the top. The quench area operates at lower temperatures than the rest of the combustion chamber and can cause the gasoline vapors to condense on these cooler surfaces, thereby helping to reduce detonation caused by the autoignition of the end gases in the combustion chamber.

- **Spark plug placement.** The best spark plug placement is at the center of the combustion chamber. ● **SEE FIGURE 26–3.**

    The closer to the center, the shorter the flames travel to all edges of the combustion chamber, which also reduces abnormal combustion (ping or spark knock). While it is best to have the spark plug in the center, some combustion chamber designs do not allow this, due to valve size, combustion chamber design, and valve placement. Some engines use two spark plugs per cylinder to achieve rapid combustion needed to meet exhaust emissions standards. ● **SEE FIGURE 26–4** for an

FIGURE 26–4 The combustion chamber of the 5.7 liter Chrysler Hemi cylinder head shows the two spark plugs used to ensure rapid burn for best power and economy with the lowest possible exhaust emissions.

? FREQUENTLY ASKED QUESTION

What Is Carbon Knock?

Carbon knock was a common occurrence in older engines that were equipped with carburetors and high compression ratios. As carburetors aged, the mixture would tend to be richer than normal, due to a leaking needle and seat, as well as a fuel-saturated float. This richer mixture would often cause carbon deposits to form in the combustion chamber. During light load conditions when the spark advance was greatest, a spark knock would occur, caused by a higher compression ratio due to the carbon deposits. This knocking was often very loud, sounding like a rod bearing noise, because in some cases the carbon deposits actually caused physical contact between the piston and the carbon. Many engines were disassembled in the belief that the cause of the knocking sound was a bearing, only to discover that the bearings were okay.

Carbon knock can still occur in newer engines, especially if there is a fault in the fuel system that would allow a much richer-than-normal air-fuel mixture, causing excessive carbon deposits to form in the combustion chamber. Often a decarbonization using chemicals will correct the knocking.

example of a two–spark plug combustion chamber used in a hemispherical (Hemi) cylinder head design.

- **Surface-to-volume ratio.** This ratio is an important design consideration for combustion chambers. A typical surface-to-volume ratio is 7.5:1, which means the surface area of the combustion chamber divided by the volume is 7.5. If the ratio is too high, there is a lot of surface area

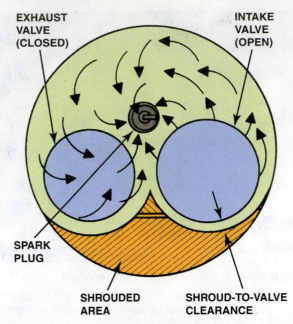

FIGURE 26–5 The shrouded area around the intake valve causes the intake mixture to swirl as it enters the combustion chamber.

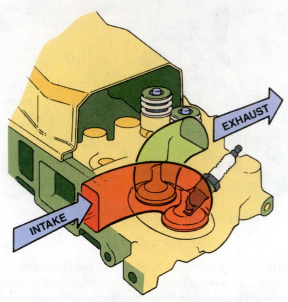

FIGURE 26–6 A typical cross flow cylinder head design, where the flow into and out of the combustion chamber is from opposite sides of the cylinder head.

where fuel can adhere, causing an increase in unburned hydrocarbon (HC) emissions. The cool cylinder head causes some of the air-fuel mixture to condense, resulting in a layer of liquid fuel on the surfaces of the combustion chamber. This layer of condensed fuel will not burn because it is not surrounded by oxygen needed for combustion. As a result, this unburned fuel is pushed out of the cylinder by the piston on the exhaust stroke.

- **Valve shrouding.** Shrouding means that the valve is kept close to the walls of the combustion chamber to help increase mixture turbulence. Although shrouding the intake valve can help swirl and increase turbulence, it also reduces the flow into the engine at higher engine speeds. ● SEE FIGURE 26–5.

- **Crossflow valve placement.** Valve placement in the cylinder head is an important factor in breather efficiency. By placing the intake and the exhaust valves on the opposite sides of the combustion chamber, an easy path from the intake port through the combustion chamber to the exhaust port is provided. This is called a **crossflow head** design. ● SEE FIGURE 26–6.

COMBUSTION CHAMBER DESIGNS Combustion chamber shape has an effect on engine power and efficiency. The combustion chamber is created as two parts.

- The upper part consists of the cylinder head and cylinder walls.

- The lower part is the top of the piston.

The most commonly used combustion chamber shapes include:

- **Wedge.** Commonly found on many two-valve pushrod engines (cam-in-block) designs

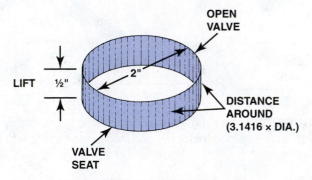

OPENING AREA = DISTANCE × LIFT

FIGURE 26–7 Method for measuring the valve opening space.

- **Pentroof.** Commonly found on many four-valve overhead camshaft design engines

- **Hemi.** Found on both cam-in-block and overhead camshaft design engines

FOUR-VALVE CYLINDER HEADS Adding more than two valves per cylinder permits more gas to flow into and out of the engine with greater velocity without excessive valve duration. **Valve duration** is the number of degrees by which the crankshaft rotates when the valve is off the valve seat. Increased valve duration increases valve overlap. The valve overlap occurs when both valves are open at the same time at the end of the exhaust stroke and at the beginning of the intake stroke. At lower engine speeds, the gases can move back and forth between the open valves. Therefore, the greater valve duration hurts low engine speed performance and driveability, but it allows for more air-fuel mixture to enter the engine for better high-speed power.

The maximum amount of gas moving through the opening area of a valve depends on the distance around the valve and the degree to which it lifts open. ● SEE FIGURE 26–7.

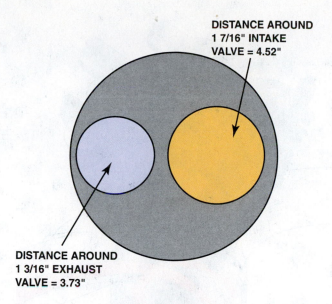

DISTANCE AROUND
1 7/16" INTAKE
VALVE = 4.52"

DISTANCE AROUND
1 3/16" EXHAUST
VALVE = 3.73"

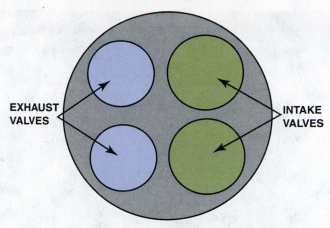

EXHAUST
VALVES

INTAKE
VALVES

FIGURE 26–9 Typical four-valve head. The total area of opening of two small intake valves and two smaller exhaust valves is greater than the area of a two-valve head using much larger valves. The smaller valves also permit the use of smaller intake runners for better low-speed engine response.

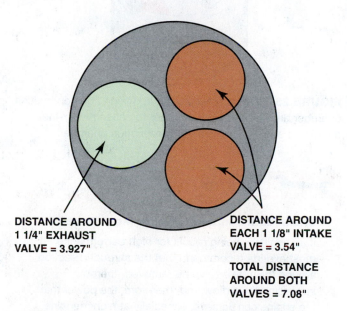

DISTANCE AROUND
1 1/4" EXHAUST
VALVE = 3.927"

DISTANCE AROUND
EACH 1 1/8" INTAKE
VALVE = 3.54"

TOTAL DISTANCE
AROUND BOTH
VALVES = 7.08"

FIGURE 26–8 Comparing the valve opening areas between a two- and three-valve combustion chamber when the valves are open.

Using normal opening lift of about 25% of the valve head diameter as an example, if the intake valve is 2 inch diameter, the normal amount of lift off the seat (not cam lobe height) is 25% of 2 inch, or 1/2 (0.5) inch. However, the amount of air-fuel mixture that can enter a cylinder depends on the total area around the valve, not just the amount of lift. The distance around a valve is calculated by the equation:

$$pi \times D \text{ or}$$
$$3.1416 \times \text{Valve diameter}$$

● SEE FIGURE 26–8.

More total area under the valve is possible when two smaller valves are used rather than one larger valve at the same valve lift. The smaller valves allow smooth low-speed operation

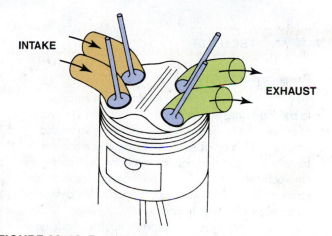

INTAKE

EXHAUST

FIGURE 26–10 Four valves in a pentroof combustion chamber.

(because of increased velocity of the mixture as it enters the cylinder as a result of smaller intake ports). Good high-speed performance is also possible because of the increased valve area and lighter weight valves. ● **SEE FIGURE 26–9.**

When four valves are used, either the combustion chamber has a pentroof design, with each pair of valves in line, or it is hemispherical, with each valve on its own axis. ● **SEE FIGURE 26–10.**

Four valves on the pentroof design will be operated with dual overhead camshafts or with single overhead camshafts and rocker arms. When four valves are used, it is possible to place the spark plug at the center of the combustion chamber.

INTAKE AND EXHAUST PORTS

PURPOSE AND FUNCTION The part of the intake or exhaust system passage that is cast in the cylinder head is called a **port**. Ports lead from the manifolds to the valves. The most

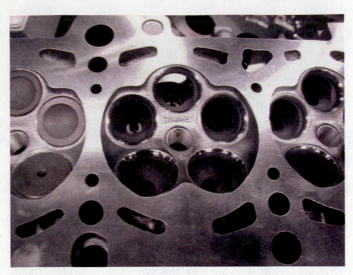

FIGURE 26–11 An Audi five-valve cylinder head, which uses three intake valves and two exhaust valves.

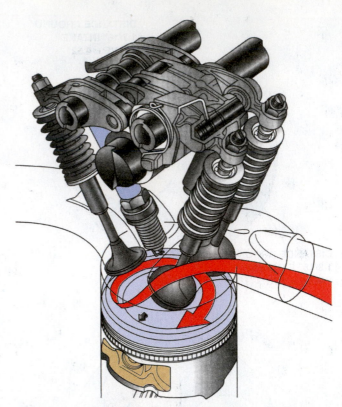

FIGURE 26–12 The intake manifold design and combustion chamber design both work together to cause the air-fuel mixture to swirl as it enters the combustion chamber.

TECH TIP

Horsepower Is Airflow

To get more power from an engine, more air needs to be drawn into the combustion chamber. One way to achieve more airflow is to increase the valve and port size of the cylinder heads along with a change in camshaft lift and duration to match the cylinder heads. One popular, but expensive, method is to replace the stock cylinder heads with high-performance cast-iron or aluminum cylinder heads.

Some vehicle manufacturers, such as Audi, go to great expense to design high-flow rate cylinder heads by installing five-valve cylinder heads on some of their high-performance engines. ● **SEE FIGURE 26–11.**

TECH TIP

Unshroud the Intake Valve for More Power

If an engine is being rebuilt for high performance, most experts recommend that the shrouded section around the intake valve be removed, thereby increasing the airflow and, therefore, the power that the engine can achieve, especially at higher engine speeds. This process is often called **unshrouding**.

desirable port shape is not always possible because of space requirements in the head. Space is required for the head bolt bosses, valve guides, cooling passages, and pushrod openings. Inline engines may have both intake and exhaust ports located on the same side of the engine. On some older engines two cylinders share the same port because of the restricted space available. Shared ports are called **Siamese ports**.

INTAKE PORTS Larger ports and better breathing are possible in engines that have the intake port on one side of the head and the exhaust port on the opposite side. Sometimes a restricting hump within a port may actually increase the airflow capacity of the port.

It does this by redirecting the flow to an area of the port that is large enough to handle the flow. Modifications in the

field, such as **porting or relieving**, would result in restricting the flow of such a carefully designed port.

The intake port in a cylinder head designed for use with a carburetor or throttle-body-type fuel injection is relatively long, whereas the exhaust port is short. On engines designed for use with port fuel injection, the cylinder head ports are designed to help promote swirl in the combustion chamber, as shown in ● **FIGURE 26–12.**

EXHAUST PORTS Like the intake ports, exhaust ports are designed to allow the free flow of exhaust gases from the engine. The length of the exhaust ports is shorter than the intake ports to help reduce the amount of heat transferred to the coolant. ● **SEE FIGURE 26–13.**

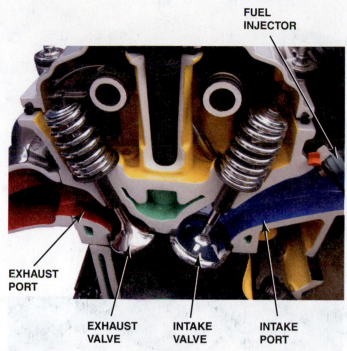

FIGURE 26–13 A port-injected engine showing the straight free-flowing intake and exhaust ports.

FIGURE 26–14 A cutaway head showing the coolant passages in green.

FIGURE 26–15 Coolant flows through the cylinder head, and the passages are sealed by the head gasket.

CYLINDER HEAD PASSAGES

COOLANT FLOW PASSAGES The engine is designed so that coolant will flow from the coolest portion of the engine to the warmest portion. The water pump takes the coolant from the radiator. The coolant is circulated through the block, where it is directed all around the cylinders. The coolant then flows upward through the gasket to the cooling passages cast into the cylinder head. The heated coolant is collected at a common point and returned to the radiator to be cooled and recycled.

NOTE: Reversed-flow cooling systems, such as that used on the Chevrolet LT1 V-8, send the coolant from the radiator to the cylinder heads first. This results in a cooler cylinder head and allows for more spark advance without engine-damaging detonation.

Typical coolant passages in a head are shown in ● **FIGURE 26–14.**

HEAD GASKET HOLES There are relatively large holes in the gasket surface of the head leading to the head cooling passages. The openings between the head and the block are usually too large for the correct coolant flow. When the openings are too large, the head gasket performs an important coolant flow function. Special-size and smaller holes are made in the gasket. These holes correct the coolant flow

rate at each opening. Therefore, it is important that the head gasket be installed correctly for proper engine cooling. ● **SEE FIGURE 26–15.**

LUBRICATING OIL PASSAGES Lubricating oil is delivered to the overhead valve mechanism, either through the valve pushrods or through drilled passages in the head and block casting. There are special openings in the head gasket to allow the oil to pass between the block and head without leaking. After the oil passes through the valve mechanisms, it returns to the oil pan through oil return passages. Some engines have drilled oil return holes, but most engines have large cast holes that allow the oil to return freely to the engine oil pan. The cast holes are large and do not easily become plugged.

NOTE: Many aluminum cylinder heads have smaller-than-normal drainback holes. If an engine has excessive oil consumption, check the drain holes before removing the engine.

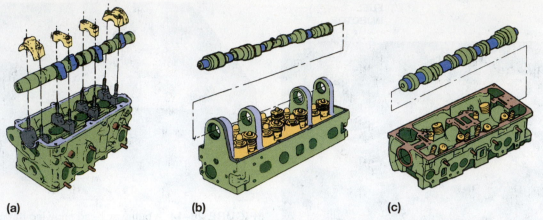

(a)   **(b)**   **(c)**

FIGURE 26–16 Overhead camshafts may be (a) held in place with bearing caps, (b) supported by towers, or (c) fitted into bearing bores machined directly into the head.

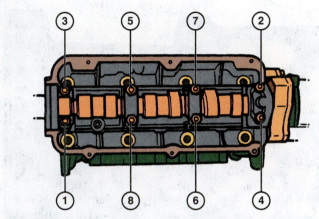

FIGURE 26–17 Always follow the specified loosening sequence to prevent valve spring tension from bending the camshaft.

FIGURE 26–18 Pushrods can be kept labeled if stuck through a cardboard box. Individual parts become worn together. Using cardboard is a crude but effective material to keep all valve train parts together and labeled exactly as they came from the engine.

CYLINDER HEAD SERVICING

CYLINDER HEAD SERVICING SEQUENCE Although not all cylinder heads require all service operations, cylinder heads should be reconditioned using the following sequence.

1. Disassemble and thoroughly clean the heads. (See Chapter 25.)
2. Check for cracks and repair as necessary. (See Chapter 25.)
3. Check the surface that contacts the engine block and machine, if necessary. (See discussion later in this chapter.)
4. Check valve guides and replace or service, as necessary. (See discussion later in this chapter.)
5. Grind valves and reinstall them in the cylinder head with new valve stem seals. (See Chapter 27.)

DISASSEMBLING OVERHEAD CAMSHAFT HEAD The overhead camshaft will have either one-piece bearings in a solid bearing support or split bearings and a bearing cap. When one-piece bearings are used, the valve springs will have to be

compressed with a fixture or the finger follower will have to be removed before the camshaft can be pulled out endwise. When bearing caps are used, they should be loosened alternately so that bending loads are not placed on either the cam or bearing caps. ● **SEE FIGURES 26–16 AND 26–17.**

VALVE TRAIN DISASSEMBLY Disassemble the cylinder head as discussed in Chapter 24. All valve train components that are to be reused must be kept together. As wear occurs, parts are worn together.

- Be sure to keep the top part of the pushrod at the top.
- Keep the rocker arms with the same pushrods as they wear together.
- Intake and exhaust valve springs can be different and must be kept with the correct valve.
  ● **SEE FIGURE 26–18.**

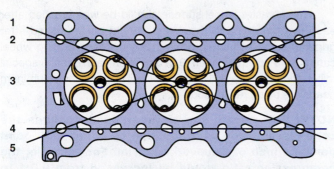

FIGURE 26–19 Cylinder heads should be checked in five planes for warpage, distortion, bend, and twist.

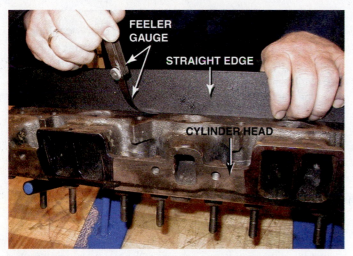

FIGURE 26–20 A precision ground straightedge and a feeler gauge are used to check the cylinder head for flatness.

CYLINDER HEAD INSPECTION The surface must be thoroughly cleaned and inspected as follows:

STEP 1 After removing the old gasket material, use a file and draw it across the surface of the head to remove any small burrs.

STEP 2 The head should be checked in five planes. Checking the cylinder head gasket surface in five planes checks the head for **warpage**, **distortion**, **bend**, and **twist**. ● SEE FIGURE 26–19.

These defects are determined by trying to slide a 0.004 inch (0.1 mm) feeler gauge under a precision straightedge held against the head surface. The clearance between the cylinder head and the straightedge should not vary by over 0.002 inch (0.05 mm) in any 6 inch (15 cm) length, or by more than 0.004 inch overall. Always check the manufacturer's recommended specifications. ● SEE FIGURE 26–20.

NOTE: The cylinder head surface that mates with the top deck of the block is often called the fire deck.

NOTE: Always check the cylinder head thickness and specifications to be sure that material can be safely removed from the surface. Some manufacturers do not recommend *any* machining, but rather require cylinder head replacement if cylinder head surface flatness is not within specifications.

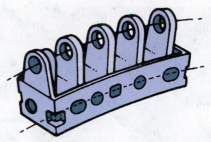

FIGURE 26–21 Warped overhead camshaft cylinder head. If the gasket surface is machined to be flat, the camshaft bearings will still not be in proper alignment. The solution is to straighten the cylinder head or to align bore the cam tunnel.

ALUMINUM CYLINDER HEAD STRAIGHTENING

PURPOSE AND FUNCTION Aluminum expands at about twice the rate of cast iron when heated. Aluminum cylinder heads used on cast-iron blocks can warp and/or crack if they are overheated. The expanding cylinder head first hits the head bolts. Further expansion of the head causes the head to expand upward and bow in the center. If a warped (bowed) cylinder head is resurfaced, the stresses of expansion are still present, and if the cylinder head uses an overhead camshaft, further problems exist. If the cylinder head is distorted into a D shape, the camshaft centerline bearing supports must also be restored. ● SEE FIGURE 26–21.

To restore the straightness of the cam bearing bore (sometimes called the **cam tunnel**), align boring and/or honing may be necessary.

The best approach to restore a warped aluminum cylinder head (especially an overhead camshaft head) is to relieve the stress that has caused the warpage *and* to straighten the head before machining.

STEP 1 Determine the amount of warpage with a straightedge and thickness (feeler) gauge. Cut shim stock (thin strips of metal) to one-half of the amount of the warpage. Place shims of this thickness under each end of the head.

STEP 2 Tighten the center of the cylinder head down on a strong, flat base. A 2 inch thick piece of steel that is 8 inch wide by 20 inch long makes a good support for the gasket surface of the cylinder head (use antiseize compound on the bolt threads to help in bolt removal).

STEP 3 Place the head and base in an oven for 5 hours at 500°F (260°C). Turn the oven off and leave the assembly in the oven.

NOTE: If the temperature is too high, the valve seat inserts may fall out of the head! At 500°F, a typical valve seat will still be held into the aluminum head with a 0.002 inch interference fit based on calculations of thermal expansion of the aluminum head and steel insert.

FIGURE 26–22 A cast-iron cylinder head being resurfaced using a surface grinder.

Allow the head to cool in the oven for four to five hours to relieve any stress in the aluminum from the heating process. For best results, the cooling process should be allowed to occur overnight. Several cylinder heads can be "cooked" together.

If the cylinder head is still warped, the heating and cooling process can be repeated. After the head is straightened and the stress relieved, the gasket surface (fire deck) can be machined in the usual manner. To prevent possible camshaft bore misalignment problems, do not machine more than 0.01 to 0.015 inch (0.25 to 0.38 mm) from the head gasket surface.

CYLINDER HEAD RESURFACING

REFINISHING METHODS Two common resurfacing methods are:

- Milling or broaching
- Grinding

A **milling** type of resurfacer uses metal-cutting tool bits fastened in a disc. This type is also called a *broach*. The disc is the rotating workhead of the mill.

The **surface grinder** type uses a large-diameter abrasive wheel. Both types of resurfacing can be done with table-type and with precision-type surfacers. With a table-type surfacer, the head or block is passed over the cutting head that extends slightly above a worktable. The abrasive wheel is dressed before grinding begins. The wheel head is adjusted to just touch the surface. At this point, the feed is calibrated to zero. This is necessary so that the operator knows exactly the size of the cut being made. Light cuts are taken. The abrasive wheel cuts are limited to 0.005 inch (0.015 mm). ● **SEE FIGURE 26–22.**

The abrasive wheel surface should be wire brushed after each five passes, and the wheel should be redressed after grinding each 0.1 inch (2.5 mm). The mill-type cutting wheel can remove up to 0.03 inch (0.075 mm) on each pass. A special mill-cutting tool or a dull grinding wheel is used when aluminum heads are being resurfaced.

NOTE: Resurfacing the cylinder head changes the compression ratio of the engine by about 1/10 point per 0.01 inch of removed material. For example, the compression ratio would be increased from 9.0:1 to 9.2:1 if 0.02 inch were removed from a typical cylinder head.

SURFACE FINISH The surface finish of a reconditioned part is as important as the size of the part. Surface finish is measured in units called microinches (abbreviated "μ in."). The symbol in front of the inch abbreviation is the Greek letter *mu*. One microinch equals 0.000001 inch, or 0.025 micrometer (μ m). The finish classification in microinches gives the distance between the highest peak and the deepest valley. The usual method of expressing surface finish is by the **arithmetic average roughness height** (RA), that is, the average of the distances of all peaks and valleys from the mean (average) line. Surface finish is measured using a machine with a diamond stylus. ● **SEE FIGURE 26–23.**

Another classification of surface finish, which is becoming obsolete, is called the **root-mean-square (RMS)**. The RMS is a slightly higher number and can be obtained by multiplying RA × 1.11.

Typical surface finish roughness recommendations for cast-iron and aluminum cylinder heads and blocks include the following:

Cast Iron

Maximum: 110 RA (125 RMS) (Rough surfaces can limit gasket movement and conformity.)

Minimum: 30 RA (33 RMS) (Smoother surfaces increase the tendency of the gasket to flow and *reduce* gasket sealing ability.)

Recommended range: 60 to 100 RA (65 to 110 RMS)

Aluminum

Maximum: 60 RA (65 RMS)

Minimum: 30 RA (33 RMS)

Recommended range: 50 to 60 RA (55 to 65 RMS)

The rougher the surface is, the higher the microinch finish measurement will be.

Typical preferred microinch finish standards for other engine components include the following:

Crank and rod journal:	10 to 14 RA (12 to 15 RMS)
Honed cylinder:	18 to 32 RA (20 to 35 RMS)
Connecting rod big end:	45 to 72 RA (50 to 80 RMS)

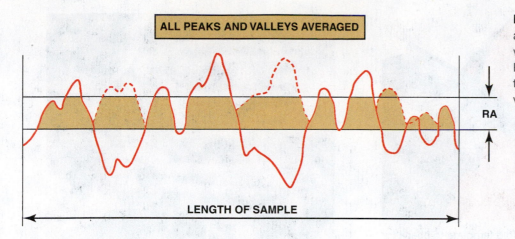

ALL PEAKS AND VALLEYS AVERAGED

RA

LENGTH OF SAMPLE

FIGURE 26–23 A graph showing a typical rough surface as would be viewed through a magnifying glass. RA is an abbreviation indicating the average height of all peaks and valleys.

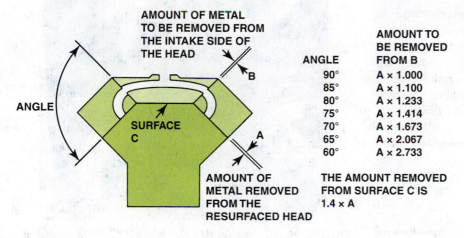

AMOUNT OF METAL TO BE REMOVED FROM THE INTAKE SIDE OF THE HEAD

B

ANGLE

SURFACE C

A

AMOUNT OF METAL REMOVED FROM THE RESURFACED HEAD

ANGLE	AMOUNT TO BE REMOVED FROM B
90°	A × 1.000
85°	A × 1.100
80°	A × 1.233
75°	A × 1.414
70°	A × 1.673
65°	A × 2.067
60°	A × 2.733

THE AMOUNT REMOVED FROM SURFACE C IS

1.4 × A

FIGURE 26–24 The material that must be removed for a good manifold fit.

TECH TIP

The Potato Chip Problem

Most cylinder heads are warped or twisted in the shape of a typical potato chip (high at the ends and dipped in the center). After a cylinder head is ground, the surface *should* be perfectly flat. A common problem involves grinding the cylinder head in both directions while it is being held on the table that moves to the left and right. Most grinders are angled by about 4 degrees. The lower part of the stone should be the cutting edge. If grinding occurs along the angled part of the stone, then too much heat is generated. This heat warps the head (or block) upward in the middle. The stone then removes this material, and the end result is a slight (about 0.0015 inch) depression in the center of the finished surface. To help prevent this from happening, always feed the grinder in the forward direction only (especially during removal of the last 0.003 inch of material).

INTAKE MANIFOLD ALIGNMENT

PURPOSE The intake manifold of a V-type engine may no longer fit correctly after the gasket surfaces of the heads are ground. The ports and the assembly bolt holes may no longer match. The intake manifold surface must be resurfaced to remove enough metal to rematch the ports and bolt holes. The amount of metal that must be removed depends on the angle between the head gasket surface and the intake manifold gasket surface. ● SEE FIGURE 26–24.

PROCEDURE Automotive machine shops that perform head resurfacing have tables that specify the exact amount of metal to be removed. It is usually necessary to also remove some metal from both the front and the back gasket surfaces of closed-type intake manifolds used on V-type engines. This is necessary to provide a good gasket seal that will prevent oil leakage from the lifter valley. ● SEE FIGURE 26–25.

FIGURE 26–25 Using an intake manifold template to check for the proper angles after the cylinder heads have been machined.

CAUTION: Do not remove any more material than is necessary to restore a flat cylinder head-to-block surface. Some manufacturers limit *total* material that can be removed from the block deck and cylinder head to 0.008 inch (0.2 mm). Removal of material from the cylinder head of an overhead camshaft engine shortens the distance between the camshaft and the crankshaft. This causes the valve timing to be *retarded* unless a special copper spacer shim is placed between the block deck and the gasket to restore proper crankshaft-to-camshaft centerline dimension.

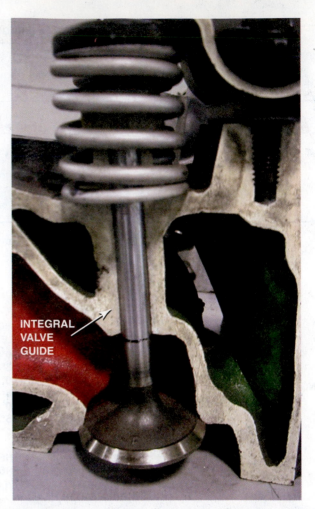

FIGURE 26–26 An integral valve guide is simply a guide that has been drilled into the cast-iron cylinder head.

VALVE GUIDES

TYPES The valve guide supports the valve stem so that the valve face will remain perfectly centered, or **concentric**, with the valve seat. The valve guide is generally integral with the head casting in cast-iron heads for better heat transfer and for lower manufacturing costs. ● **SEE FIGURE 26–26.**

Removable or pressed-in **valve guides** and **valve seat inserts** are always used in aluminum heads. ● **SEE FIGURE 26–27.**

No matter how good the valves or seats are, they cannot operate properly if the valve guide is not accurate. In use, the valve opening mechanism pushes the valve tip sideways. This is the major cause of valve stem and guide wear. The movement of the valve causes both the top and bottom ends of the guide to wear until the guide has bell-mouth shapes at both ends. ● **SEE FIGURE 26–28.**

VALVE STEM-TO-GUIDE CLEARANCE Engine manufacturers usually recommend the following valve stem-to-guide clearances.

- Intake valve: 0.001 to 0.003 inch (0.025 to 0.076 mm)
- Exhaust valve: 0.002 to 0.004 inch (0.05 to 0.1 mm)

Be sure to check the exact specifications for the engine being serviced. The exhaust valve clearance is greater than the

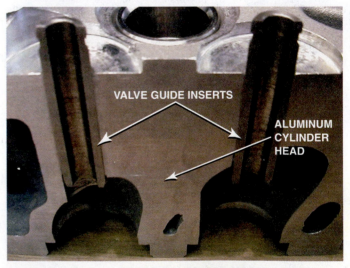

FIGURE 26–27 All aluminum cylinder heads use valve guide inserts.

intake valve clearance because the exhaust valve runs hotter and therefore expands more than the intake valve.

Excessive valve stem-to-guide clearance can cause excessive oil consumption. The intake valve guide is exposed to

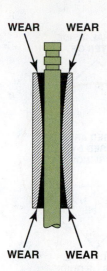

WEAR WEAR

WEAR WEAR

FIGURE 26–28 Valve guides often wear to a bell-mouth shape to both ends due to the forces exerted on the valve by the valve train components.

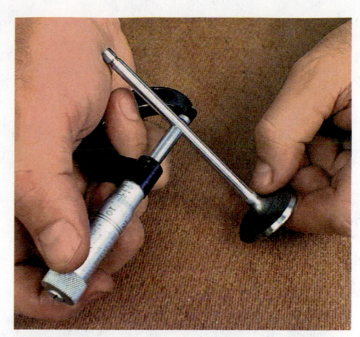

FIGURE 26–30 The diameter of the valve stem is being measured using a micrometer. The difference between the inside diameter of the valve guide and the diameter of the valve stem is the valve guide-to-stem clearance.

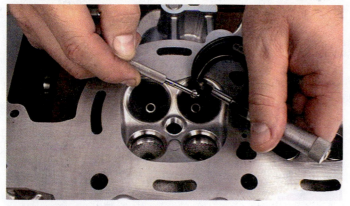

FIGURE 26–29 A small-hole gauge and a micrometer are being used to measure the valve guide. The guide should be measured in three places: at the top, middle, and bottom.

manifold vacuum that can draw oil from the top of the cylinder head down into the combustion chamber. In this situation, valves can also run hotter than usual because much of the heat in the valve is transferred to the cylinder head through the valve guide.

NOTE: A human hair is about 0.002 inch (0.05 mm) in diameter. Therefore, the typical clearance between a valve stem and the valve guide is only the thickness of a human hair.

MEASURING VALVE GUIDES Valves should be measured for stem wear before valve guides are measured. The valve guide is measured in the middle with a small-hole gauge. The gauge size is checked with a micrometer. The guide is then checked at each end.

The expanded part of the ball should be placed crosswise to the engine where the greatest amount of valve guide wear exists. The dimension of the valve stem diameter is subtracted from the dimension of the valve guide diameter. If the clearance exceeds the specified clearance, then the valve guide will have to be reconditioned. ● **SEE FIGURES 26–29 AND 26–30.**

Valve stem-to-guide clearance can also be checked using a dial indicator (gauge) to measure the amount of movement of the valve when lifted off the valve seat. ● **SEE FIGURE 26–31.**

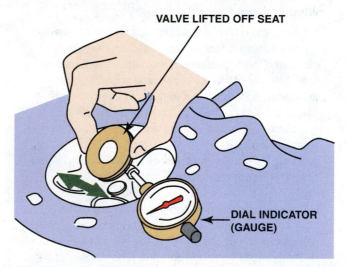

VALVE LIFTED OFF SEAT

DIAL INDICATOR (GAUGE)

FIGURE 26–31 Measuring valve guide-to-stem clearance with a dial indicator while rocking the stem in the direction of normal thrust. The reading on the dial indicator should be compared to specifications because it does not give the guide-to-stem clearance directly. The valve is usually held open to its maximum operating lift.

OVERSIZE STEM VALVES Some domestic vehicle manufacturers that have integral valve guides in their engines recommend reaming worn valve guides and installing new valves with **oversize (OS) stems**. When a valve guide is worn, the valve stem is also likely to be worn. In this case, new valves are required. If new valves are used, they can just as well have oversize stems as standard stems. Typically, available sizes

TECH TIP

Tight Is Not Always Right

Many engine manufacturers specify a valve stem-to-guide clearance of 0.001 to 0.003 inch (0.025 to 0.076 mm). However, some vehicles, especially those equipped with aluminum cylinder heads, may specify a much greater clearance. For example, many Chrysler 2.2 and 2.5 liter engines have a specified valve stem-to-guide clearance of 0.003 to 0.005 inch (0.076 to 0.127 mm). This amount of clearance feels loose to those technicians accustomed to normal valve stem clearance specifications. Although this large amount of clearance may seem excessive, remember that the valve stem increases in diameter as the engine warms up. Therefore, the *operating* clearance is smaller than the clearance measured at room temperature. Always double-check factory specifications before replacing a valve guide for excessive wear.

 FREQUENTLY ASKED QUESTION

What Is Valve Guide Knurling?

In an old and now outdated process known as **valve guide knurling**, a tool is rotated as it is driven into the guide. The tool *displaces* the metal to reduce the hole diameter of the guide. Knurling is ideally suited to engines with integral valve guides (guides that are part of the cylinder head and are nonremovable). It is recommended that knurling not be used to correct wear exceeding 0.006 inch (0.15 mm). In the displacing process, the knurling tool pushes a small tapered wheel or dull threading tool into the wall of the guide hole. This makes a groove in the wall of the guide, similar to a threading operation without removing any metal.

The metal piles up along the edge of the groove just as dirt would pile up along the edge of a tire track as the tire rolled through soft dirt. (The dirt would be displaced from under the wheel to form a small ridge alongside the tire track.) ● SEE FIGURE 26–32.

The knurling tool is driven by an electric drill and an attached speed reducer that slows the rotating speed of the knurling tool. The reamers that accompany the knurling set will ream just enough to provide the correct valve stem clearance for commercial reconditioning standards. The valve guides are honed to size in the precision shop when precise fits are desired. Clearances of knurled valve guides are usually one-half of the new valve guide clearances. Such small clearance can be used because knurling leaves so many small oil rings down the length of the guide for lubrication.

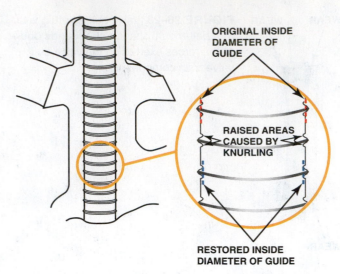

FIGURE 26–32 Sectional view of a knurled valve guide.

include 0.003, 0.005, 0.015, and 0.03 inch OS. The valve guide is reamed or honed to the correct size to fit the oversize stem of the new valve.

The resulting clearance of the valve stem in the guide is the same as the original clearance. The oil clearance and the heat transfer properties of the original valve and guide are not changed when new valves with oversize stems are installed.

NOTE: Many remanufacturers of cylinder heads use oversize valve stems to simplify production.

VALVE GUIDE REPLACEMENT

PURPOSE When an engine is designed with replaceable valve guides, their replacement is always recommended when the valve assembly is being reconditioned. The original valve guide height should be measured before the guide is removed so that the new guide can be properly positioned.

After the valve guide height is measured, the worn guide is pressed from the head with a proper fitting *driver*. ● SEE FIGURE 26–33.

The driver has a stem to fit the guide opening and a shoulder that pushes on the end of the guide. If the guide has a flange, care should be taken to ensure that the guide is pushed out from the correct end, usually from the port side and toward the rocker arm side. The new guide is pressed into the guide bore using the same driver. Make sure that the guide is pressed to the correct depth. After the guides are replaced, they are reamed or honed to the proper inside diameter.

Replacement valve guides can also be installed to repair worn integral guides. Both **cast-iron** and **bronze guides** are available.

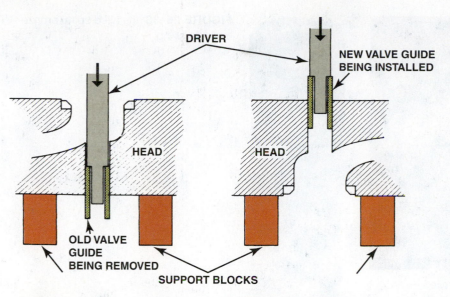

FIGURE 26–33
Valve guide replacement procedure.

DRIVER

NEW VALVE GUIDE BEING INSTALLED

HEAD

HEAD

OLD VALVE GUIDE BEING REMOVED

SUPPORT BLOCKS

 **TECH TIP**

Right Side Up

When replacing valve guides, it is important that the recommended procedures be followed. Most manufacturers specify that replaceable guides be driven from the combustion chamber side toward the rocker arm side. For example, big block Chevrolet V-8 heads (396, 402, 427, and 454 cu.^{3}) have a 0.004 inch (0.05 mm) taper (small end toward the combustion chamber).

Other manufacturers, however, may recommend driving the old guide from the rocker arm side to prevent any carbon buildup on the guide from damaging the guide bore. Always check the manufacturer's recommended procedures before attempting to replace a valve guide.

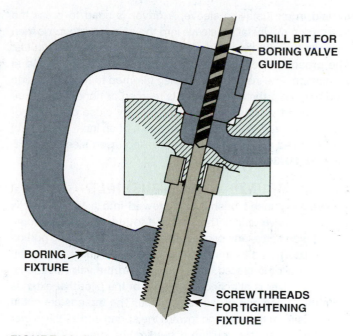

DRILL BIT FOR BORING VALVE GUIDE

BORING FIXTURE

SCREW THREADS FOR TIGHTENING FIXTURE

FIGURE 26–34 A type of fixture required to bore the valve guide to accept a thin-walled insert sleeve.

VALVE GUIDE SIZES

Three common valve guide sizes are as follows:

- 5/16 or 0.313 inch
- 11/32 or 0.343 inch
- 3/8 or 0.375 inch

VALVE GUIDE INSERTS

When the integral valve guide is badly worn, it can be reconditioned using an insert. This repair method is usually preferred in heavy-duty and high-speed engines. Two types of guide inserts are commonly used for guide repair.

- **Thin-walled bronze alloy sleeve bushing**
- **Spiral bronze alloy bushing**

The thin-walled bronze sleeve bushings are also called **bronze guide liners.** The valve guide rebuilding kit used to install each of these bushings includes all of the reamers,

installing sleeves, broaches, burnishing tools, and cutoff tools that are needed to install and properly size the bushings.

The valve guide must be bored to a large enough size to accept the thin-walled insert sleeve. The boring tool is held in alignment by a rugged fixture. One type is shown in ● **FIGURE 26–34.**

Depending on the make of the equipment, the boring fixture is aligned with the valve guide hole, the valve seat, or the head gasket surface. First, the boring fixture is properly aligned. The guide is then bored, making a hole somewhat smaller than the insert sleeve that will be used. The bored hole is reamed to make a precise smooth hole that is still slightly smaller than the insert sleeve. The insert sleeve is installed with a press fit that holds it in the guide. The press fit also helps to maintain normal heat transfer from the valve to the head. The thin-walled insert sleeve

FIGURE 26–35 Trimming the top of the thin-walled insert.

FIGURE 26–36 Installed spiral bronze insert bushing.

is held in an installing sleeve. A driver is used to press the insert from the installing sleeve into the guide. A broach is then pressed through the insert sleeve to firmly seat it in the guide. The broach is designed to put a knurl in the guide to aid in lubrication. The insert sleeve is then trimmed to the valve guide length. Finally, the insert sleeve is reamed or honed to provide the required valve stem clearance. A very close clearance of 0.0005 inch (one-half of one-thousandth of an inch) (0.013 mm) is often used with the bronze thin-walled insert sleeve. ● SEE FIGURE 26–35.

SPIRAL BRONZE INSERT BUSHINGS The spiral bronze alloy insert bushing is screwed into a thread that is put in the valve guide. The tap used to put cut threads in the valve guide has a long pilot ahead of the thread-cutting portion of the tap. This aids in restoring the original guide alignment. The long pilot is placed in the guide from the valve seat end. A power driver is attached to the end of the pilot that extends from the spring end of the valve guide. The threads are cut in the guide from the seat end toward the spring end as the power driver turns the tap, pulling it toward the driver. The tap is stopped before it comes out of the guide, and the power driver is removed. The thread is carefully completed by hand to avoid breaking either the end of the guide or the tap. An installed spiral bronze insert bushing can be seen in ● FIGURE 26–36.

The spiral bronze bushing is tightened on an inserting tool. This holds it securely in the wound-up position so that it can be screwed into the spring end of the guide. It is screwed in until the bottom of the bushing is flush with the seat end of the guide. The holding tool is removed, and the bushing material is trimmed to one coil *above* the spring end of the guide. The end of the bushing is temporarily secured with a plastic serrated bushing retainer and a worm gear clamp. This holds the bushing in place as a broach is driven through the bushing to firmly seat it in the threads. The bushing is reamed or honed to size before the temporary bushing retainer is removed. The final step is to trim the end of the bushing with a special cutoff tool that is included in the bushing installation tool set. This type of spiral bronze bushing can be removed by using a pick to free the end of the bushing. It can then be stripped out and a new bushing inserted in the original threads in the guide hole. New threads do not have to be put in the guide. The spiral bushing design has natural spiral grooves to hold oil for lubrication. The valve stem clearances are the same as those used for knurling and for the thin-walled insert (about one-half of the standard recommended clearance).

SUMMARY

1. The most commonly used combustion chamber types include hemispherical, wedge, and pentroof.

2. Coolant and lubricating openings and passages are located throughout most cylinder heads.

3. Cylinder head resurfacing machines include grinders and milling machines.

4. Valve guides should be checked for wear using a ball gauge or a dial indicator. Typical valve stem-to-guide clearance is 0.001 to 0.003 inch for intake valves and 0.002 to 0.004 inch for exhaust valves.

5. Valve guide repair options include use of oversize stem valves, replacement valve guides, valve guide inserts, and knurling of the original valve guide.

1. What is meant by the term *crossflow head*?
2. What is a Siamese port?
3. What is the recommended cylinder head reconditioning sequence?
4. What are the advantages of using four valves per cylinder?

CHAPTER QUIZ

1. Cylinder heads with four valves flow more air than those with two valves because they _____.
   a. Have a greater open area
   b. Use a higher lift camshaft
   c. Increase the velocity of the air
   d. Both a and c

2. Two technicians are discussing a Hemi engine. Technician A says that a Hemi is an engine with a hemispherical-shaped combustion chamber. Technician B says that all Hemi engines are cam-in-block designs. Which technician is correct?
   a. Technician A only
   b. Technician B only
   c. Both Technicians A and B
   d. Neither Technician A nor B

3. Technician A says that an Audi five-valve engine uses three intake valves and two exhaust valves. Technician B says that it uses three exhaust valves and two intake valves. Which technician is correct?
   a. Technician A only
   b. Technician B only
   c. Both Technicians A and B
   d. Neither Technician A nor B

4. The gasket surface of a cylinder head, as measured with a precision straightedge, should have a maximum variation of _____.
   a. 0.002 inch in any 6 inch length, or 0.004 inch overall
   b. 0.001 inch in any 6 inch length, or 0.004 inch overall
   c. 0.020 inch in any 10 inch length, or 0.02 inch overall
   d. 0.004 inch in any 10 inch length, or 0.008 inch overall

5. A warped aluminum cylinder head can be restored to useful service by _____.
   a. Grinding the gasket surface and then align honing the camshaft bore
   b. Heating it in an oven at 500°F with shims under each end, allowing it to cool, and then machining it
   c. Heating it to 500°F for five hours and cooling it rapidly before final machining
   d. Machining the gasket surface to one-half of the warped amount and then heating the head in an oven and allowing it to cool slowly

6. Some vehicle manufacturers recommend repairing integral guides with _____.
   a. OS stem valves
   b. Knurling
   c. Replacement valve guides
   d. Valve guide inserts

7. Typical valve stem-to-guide clearance is _____.
   a. 0.03 to 0.045 inch (0.8 to 1 mm)
   b. 0.015 to 0.02 inch (0.4 to 0.5 mm)
   c. 0.005 to 0.01 inch (0.13 to 0.25 mm)
   d. 0.001 to 0.004 inch (0.03 to 0.05 mm)

8. What other engine component may have to be machined if the cylinder heads are machined on a V-type engine?
   a. Exhaust manifold
   b. Intake manifold
   c. Block deck
   d. Distributor mount (if the vehicle is so equipped)

9. Which type of valve guide is most used in a cast-iron head?
   a. Integral
   b. Bronze
   c. Powdered metal (PM)
   d. Thin-walled sleeve type

10. Which statement is true about surface finish?
    a. Cast-iron surfaces should be smoother than aluminum surfaces.
    b. The rougher the surface, the higher the microinch finish measurement.
    c. The smoother the surface, the higher the microinch finish measurement.
    d. A cylinder head should be much smoother than a crankshaft journal.

chapter 27

VALVE AND SEAT SERVICE

LEARNING OBJECTIVES: **After studying this chapter, the reader should be able to:** • Discuss intake and exhaust valves. • Describe valve seats and the valve fault diagnosis procedure. • Explain valve springs, and valve keepers and rotators. • Discuss the procedure for valve reconditioning, valve face grinding, and valve seat reconditioning. • Discuss valve guide pilots, valve seat grinding stones, and valve seat cutters. • Explain valve seat testing and valve seat replacement. • Discuss valve stem height and installed height. • Describe the procedure of installing the valves and explain valve stem seals.

KEY TERMS: Expandable pilots 380 • Finishing stone 380 • Free rotators 375 • Hard seat stones 380 • Inertia friction welding 370 • Insert seats 370 • Installed height 384 • Integral seat 370 • Locks 368 • Poppet valve 368 • Positive rotators 375 • Retainer 368 • Roughing stone 380 • Stellite® 369 • Tapered pilots 379 • Thermal shock 372 • Three-angle valve job 379 • Throating angle 379 • Topping angle 379 • Total indicator runout (TIR) 381 • Truing 376 • Valve face 368 • Valve face angle 376 • Valve float 374 • Valve guide 368 • Valve seat 368 • Valve spring 368 • Valve spring inserts (VSI) 384 • Valve spring surge 374 • Valve stem height 384 • Variable rate springs 374

INTAKE AND EXHAUST VALVES

TERMINOLOGY Automotive engine valves are of a **poppet valve** design. The term *poppet* refers to the shape of the valve and their operation in automotive engines. The valve is opened by means of a valve train that is operated by a cam. The cam is timed to the piston position and crankshaft cycle. The valve is closed by one or more springs.

A typical valve is shown in ● **FIGURE 27–1.**

Intake valves control the inlet of cool, low-pressure induction charges. Exhaust valves handle hot, high-pressure exhaust gases. This means that exhaust valves are exposed to more severe operating conditions. They are, therefore, made from much higher quality materials than the intake valves, which makes them more expensive.

The valve is held in place and is positioned in the head by the **valve guide.** The portion of the valve that seals against the **valve seat** in the cylinder head is called the **valve face.** The face and seat will have an angle of either 30 or 45 degrees, which are the nominal angles; actual service angles may vary. Most engines use a nominal 45 degree valve and seat angle.

PARTS INVOLVED

- A **valve spring** holds the valve against the seat.
- The valve *keepers* (also called **locks**) secure the spring **retainer** to the stem of the valve.

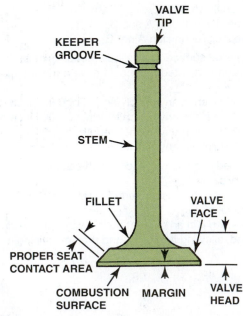

FIGURE 27–1 Identification of the parts of a valve.

For valve removal, it is necessary to compress the spring and remove the valve keepers. Then the spring, valve seals, and valve can be removed from the head. A typical valve assembly is shown in ● **FIGURE 27–2.**

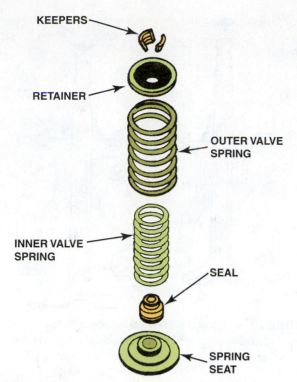

FIGURE 27–2 Typical valve spring and related components. Dual valve springs are used to reduce valve train vibrations and a spring seat is used to protect aluminum heads.

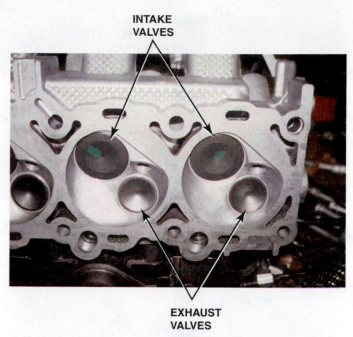

FIGURE 27–3 The intake valve is larger than the exhaust valve because the intake charge is being drawn into the combustion chamber at a low speed due to differences in pressure between atmospheric pressure and the pressure (vacuum) inside the cylinder. The exhaust is actually pushed out by the piston and, therefore, the size of the valve does not need to be as large, leaving more room in the cylinder head for the larger intake valve.

VALVE SIZE RELATIONSHIPS
Extensive testing has shown that a normal relationship exists between the different dimensions of valves.

- **Intake valves.** Engines with cylinder bores that measure from 3 to 8 inch (80 to 200 mm) will have intake valve head diameters that measure approximately 45% of the bore size. The intake valve must be larger than the exhaust valve to handle the same mass of gas. The larger intake valve controls low-velocity, low-density gases. The distance the valve opens is close to 25% of the valve head diameter.

- **Exhaust valves.** The exhaust valve head diameter is approximately 38% of the cylinder bore size. Exhaust valve heads are, therefore, approximately 85% of the size of intake valve heads. The exhaust valve, however, controls high-velocity, high-pressure, denser gases. These gases can be handled by a smaller valve. ● SEE FIGURE 27–3.

VALVE MATERIALS
- **Alloy steel.** Alloys used in exhaust valve materials are largely of chromium for oxidation resistance, with small amounts of nickel, manganese, and nitrogen added. Heat-treating is used whenever it is necessary to produce special valve properties.

- **Stellite®.** An alloy of nickel, chromium, and tungsten, **Stellite®** is nonmagnetic. Some valves use this product just only on the tip of the valve to help reduce wear in

TECH TIP

Hot Engine + Cold Weather = Trouble

Serious valve damage can occur if cold air reaches hot exhaust valves soon after the engine is turned off. An engine equipped with exhaust headers and/or straight-through mufflers can allow cold air a direct path to the hot exhaust valve. The exhaust valve can warp and/or crack as a result of rapid cooling. This can easily occur during cold windy waeather when the wind can blow cold outside air directly up the exhaust system. Using reverse-flow mufflers with tailpipes and a catalytic converter reduces the possibilities of this occurring.

places where the rocker arm contacts the valve stem on engines that do not use a roller rocker arm. Stellite® is also used on some valve faces.

- **Inconal®.** A type of alloy containing nickel, chrome, and iron and is used mostly in racing engines.

- **Titanium.** About half the weight of conventional valves, titanium reduces the tension on valve springs resulting in higher RPM engine operation. The valve stems are often moly coated to help prevent sticking in the valve guide.

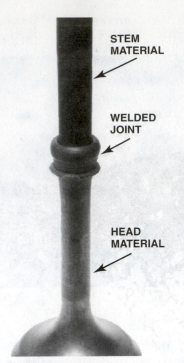

FIGURE 27-4 Inertia welded valve stem and head before machining.

STEM MATERIAL

WELDED JOINT

HEAD MATERIAL

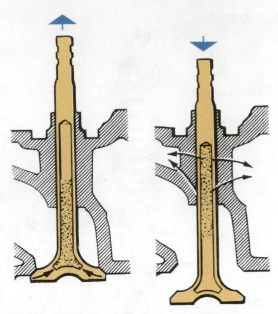

FIGURE 27-5 A sodium-filled valve uses a hollow stem, which is partially filled with metallic sodium (a liquid when hot) to conduct heat away from the head of the valve.

- **Stainless steel.** Used in many heavy-duty applications, stainless steel often uses chrome-plated valve stems and Stellite tips to improve long-term durability.
- **Aluminized.** The valve is aluminized where corrosion may be a problem. Aluminized valve facing reduces valve recession when unleaded gasoline is used. Aluminum oxide forms to separate the valve steel from the cast-iron seat to keep the face metal from sticking.

TWO-MATERIAL VALVES Some exhaust valves are manufactured from two different materials when a one-piece design cannot meet the desired hardness and corrosion resistance specifications. The joint cannot be seen after valves have been used. The valve heads are made from special alloys that can operate at high temperatures, have physical strength, resist lead oxide corrosion, and have indentation resistance. These heads are welded to stems that have good wear resistance properties. These types of valves are usually welded together using a process called **inertia friction welding.** Inertia friction welding is performed by spinning one end and then forcing the two pieces together until the materials reach their melting temperature. Then the parts are held together until they fuse, resulting in a uniform weld between two different materials. ● **FIGURE 27-4** shows an inertia welded valve before final machining.

SODIUM-FILLED VALVES Some heavy-duty applications use hollow stem exhaust valves that are partially filled with metallic sodium. The sodium in the valve becomes a liquid at

operating temperatures. As it splashes back and forth in the valve stem, the sodium transfers heat from the valve head to the valve stem. The heat goes through the valve guide into the coolant. In general, a one-piece valve design using properly selected materials will provide satisfactory service for automotive engines. ● **SEE FIGURE 27-5.**

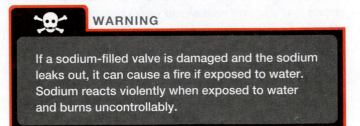

☠ **WARNING**

If a sodium-filled valve is damaged and the sodium leaks out, it can cause a fire if exposed to water. Sodium reacts violently when exposed to water and burns uncontrollably.

VALVE SEATS

INTEGRAL SEATS The valve face closes against a valve seat to seal the combustion chamber. The seat is generally formed as part of the cast-iron head of automotive engines, called an **integral seat.** ● **SEE FIGURE 27-6.**

The seats are usually induction hardened so that unleaded gasoline can be used. This minimizes valve recession as the engine operates. Valve recession is the wearing away of the seat, so that the valve sits further into the head.

INSERT SEATS An **insert seat** fits into a machined recess in the steel or aluminum cylinder head. Insert seats are used in *all* aluminum head engines and in applications for which

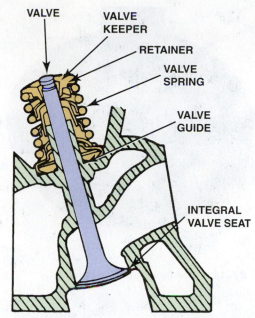

FIGURE 27–6 Integral valve seats are machined directly into the cast-iron cylinder head and are induction hardened to prevent wear.

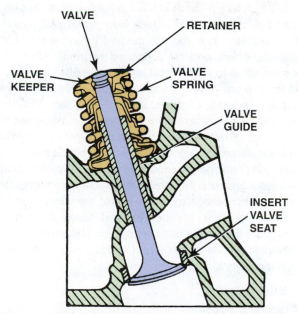

FIGURE 27–7 Insert valve seats are a separate part that is interference fitted to a counterbore in the cylinder head.

corrosion and wear resistance are critical. Aluminum heads also include insert valve guides.

The exhaust valve seat runs as much as 180°F (100°C) *cooler* in aluminum heads than in cast-iron heads, because aluminum conducts heat faster than cast iron. Insert seats are also used to recondition integral valve seats that have been badly damaged. ● SEE FIGURE 27–7.

FIGURE 27–8 Typical intake valve seat wear.

FIGURE 27–9 Carbon deposits on the intake valve are often caused by oil getting past the valve stems or fuel deposits.

VALVE FAULT DIAGNOSIS

Careful inspection of the cylinder head and valves can often reveal the root cause of failure.

POOR VALVE SEATING   Poor seating results from too small a valve lash, hard carbon deposits, valve stem deposits, excessive valve stem-to-guide clearances, or out-of-square valve guide and seat. A valve seat recession can result from improper valve lash adjustments on solid lifter engines. It can also result from misadjustments on a valve train using hydraulic lifters. The valve clearance will also be reduced as a result of valve head cupping or valve face and seat wear. ● FIGURE 27–8 shows typical intake valve and seat wear.

CARBON DEPOSITS   If there is a large clearance between the valve stem and guide or faulty valve stem seals, too much oil will go down the stem. This will increase deposits, as shown on the intake valve in ● FIGURE 27–9.

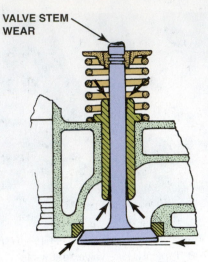

FIGURE 27–10 Excessive wear of the valve stem or guide can cause the valve to seat in a cocked position.

FIGURE 27–11 Valve face guttering caused by thermal shock.

In addition, a large valve guide clearance will allow the valve to cock or lean sideways, especially with the effect of the rocker arm action. Continued cocking keeps the valve from seating properly and causes it to leak, burning the valve face. ● **SEE FIGURE 27–10.**

Sometimes, the cylinder head will warp slightly as the head is tightened to the block deck during assembly. In other cases, heating and cooling will cause warpage. When head warpage causes valve guide and seat misalignment, the valve cannot seat properly and it will leak, burning the valve face.

EXCESSIVE TEMPERATURES High valve temperatures occur when the valve does not seat properly. Root causes include the following:

1. Cooling system passages in the head may be partially blocked by faulty casting or by deposits built up from the coolant. A corroded head gasket will change the coolant flow. This can cause overheating when the coolant is allowed to flow to the wrong places.

2. Extremely high temperatures are also produced by preignition and by detonation. These conditions are the result of abnormal combustion. Both of these produce a very rapid increase in temperature that can cause uneven heating. The rapid increase in temperature will give a **thermal shock** to the valve. (A thermal shock is a sudden change in temperature.) The shock will often cause radial cracks in the valve. The cracks will allow the combustion gases to escape and gutter the valve face. ● **SEE FIGURE 27–11.**

VALVE SEAT EROSION Valve seats can wear especially in those engines that were designed for use with leaded gasoline (prior to 1975). Without lead, the valve movement against the seat tears away tiny iron oxide particles during engine operation. The valve movement causes these particles of iron oxide to act like valve grinding compound, cutting into the valve seat

surface. As the valve seat is eroded, the valve recedes further into the cylinder head. When the valve seat erodes, the valve lash decreases. This can lead to valve burning because the valve may not close all the way.

HIGH-VELOCITY SEATING High-velocity seating is indicated by excessive valve face wear, valve seat recession, and impact failure. It can be caused by excessive lash in mechanical lifters and by collapsed hydraulic lifters. Lash allows the valve to hit the seat without the effects of the cam ramp to ease the valve onto its seat. Excessive lash may also be caused by wear of parts, such as the cam, lifter base, pushrod ends, rocker arm pivot, and valve tip. Weak or broken valve springs allow the valves to float away from the cam lobes so that the valves are uncontrolled as they hit the seat.

Impact breakage may occur under the valve head or at the valve keeper grooves. The break lines radiate from the starting point. Impact breakage may also cause the valve head to fall into the combustion chamber. In most cases, it will ruin the piston before the engine can be stopped. This situation causes catastrophic engine damage and is described in the field by several terms, including:

- Sucking a valve
- Dropping a valve
- Swallowing a valve

● **SEE FIGURE 27–12.**

VALVE SPRINGS

PURPOSE AND FUNCTION A valve spring holds the valve against the seat when the valve is not being opened. One end of the valve spring is seated against the head. The other

Valve Seat Recession and Engine Performance

If unleaded fuel is used in an engine without hardened valve seats, valve seat recession is likely to occur over time. Without removing the cylinder heads, how can a technician identify valve seat recession?

As the valve seat wears up into the cylinder head, the valve itself also is located further up in the head. As this wear occurs, the valve clearance (lash) *decreases.* If hydraulic lifters are used on the engine, this wear will go undetected until the reduction in valve clearance finally removes all clearance (bottoms out) in the lifter. When this occurs, the valve does not seat fully, and compression, power, and fuel economy are drastically reduced. With the valve not closing completely, the valve cannot release its heat and will burn or begin to melt. If the valve burns, the engine will miss and not idle smoothly.

If solid lifters are used on the engine, the decrease in valve clearance will first show up as a rough idle only when the engine is hot. As the valve seat recedes farther into the head, low power, rough idle, poor performance, and lower fuel economy will be noticed sooner than if the engine were equipped with hydraulic lifters.

To summarize, refer to the following symptoms as valve seat recession occurs.

1. Valve lash (clearance) decreases (valves are *not* noisy).
2. The engine idles roughly when hot as a result of reduced valve clearance.
3. Missing occurs, and the engine exhibits low power and poor fuel economy, along with a rough idle, as the valve seat recedes farther into the head.
4. As valves burn, the engine continues to run poorly; the symptoms include difficulty in starting (hot and cold engine), backfiring, and low engine power.

NOTE: If valve lash is adjustable, valve burning can be prevented by adjusting the valve lash regularly. Remember, as the seat recedes, the valve itself recedes, which decreases the valve clearance. Many technicians do not think to adjust valves unless they are noisy. If, during the valve adjustment procedure, a *decrease* in valve lash is noticed, then valve seat recession could be occurring.

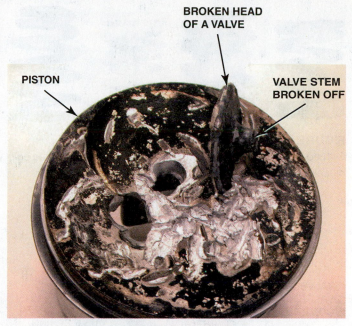

FIGURE 27–12 Note the broken piston caused by a valve breaking from the stem.

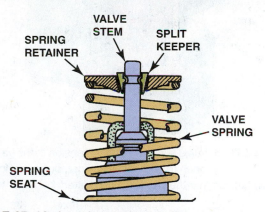

FIGURE 27–13 A retainer and two split keepers hold the spring in place on the valve. A spring seat is used on aluminum heads. Otherwise, the spring seat is a machined area in the head.

end of the spring is attached under compression to the valve stem through a valve spring retainer and a valve spring keeper (lock). ● SEE FIGURE 27–13.

SPRING MATERIALS AND DESIGN Valves usually have a single inexpensive valve spring. The springs are generally made of chromium vanadium alloy steel. When one spring cannot control the valve, another spring or damper is added. Some valve springs use a flat coiled damper inside the spring. The damper helps to reduce valve seat wear. This eliminates spring surge and adds some valve spring tension. The normal valve spring winds up as it is compressed. This causes a small but important turning motion as the valve closes on the seat. The turning motion helps to keep the wear even around the valve face. ● SEE FIGURE 27–14.

FIGURE 27–14 Valve spring types (*left to right*): coil spring with equally spaced coils; spring with damper inside spring coil; closely spaced spring with a damper; taper wound coil spring.

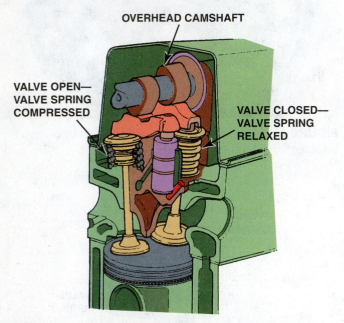

OVERHEAD CAMSHAFT

VALVE OPEN— VALVE SPRING COMPRESSED

VALVE CLOSED— VALVE SPRING RELAXED

FIGURE 27–15 Valve springs maintain tension in the valve train when the valve is open to prevent valve float, but must not exert so much tension that the cam lobes and lifters begin to wear.

FREQUENTLY ASKED QUESTION

What Is Valve Float?

Valve float occurs when the valve continues to stay open after the camshaft lobe has moved from under the lifter. This happens when the inertia of the valve train overcomes the valve spring tension at high engine speeds. ●SEE FIGURE 27–15.

Multiple valve springs are used where large camshaft lobe lifts are required and a single spring does not have enough strength to control the valve.

- If dual coil springs are wrapped in same direction, they are used for extra tension.
- If the inner spring or flat damper is wrapped in the opposite direction, it is used as a damper to control

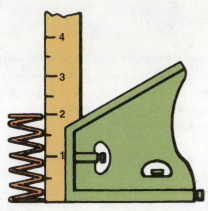

FIGURE 27–16 All valve springs should be checked for squareness by using a square on a flat surface and rotating the spring while checking. The spring should be replaced if more than 1/16 inch (1.6 mm) is measured between the top of the spring and the square.

spring oscillations. This is done to control valve spring surge and to prevent excessive valve rotation. These are sometimes called *surge dampers.*

Valve spring surge is the tendency of a valve spring to vibrate.

VARIABLE RATE SPRINGS   **Variable rate springs,** also called *progressive rate* or *variable pitch springs,* have uneven spacing between the coils. Where nonprogressive rate (linear) valve springs provide the same rate through all heights, a variable rate valve spring has a different spring rate depending on how much it is compressed. One advantage of using a variable rate spring is that it provides a low seat pressure and still provides the rate needed for high lift camshaft designs. This type of spring is used to help control valve surge.

VALVE SPRING INSPECTION   Valve springs close the valves after they have been opened by the cam. They must close squarely to form a tight seal and to prevent valve stem and guide wear. It is necessary, therefore, that the springs be square and have the proper amount of closing force. The valve springs are checked for squareness by rotating them on a flat surface with a square held against the side. They should be within 1/16 in. (1.6 mm) of being square. Out-of-square springs will have to be replaced. ●SEE FIGURE 27–16.

Only the springs that are square should be checked to determine their compressed force. The surge damper is often specified to be *removed* from the valve spring when the spring force is being checked. Check service information for the exact procedure to follow for the engine being checked. A valve spring scale is used to measure the valve spring force at a specific height measurement. ●SEE FIGURE 27–17.

Another type uses a torque wrench on a lever system to measure the valve spring force. Valve springs are checked for the following:

1. Free height (or length) without being compressed, should be within 1/16 (0.06) inch of specifications.

FIGURE 27–17 One popular type of valve spring tester used to measure the compressed force of valve springs. Specifications usually include (1) free height (height without being compressed), (2) pressure at installed height with the valve closed, and (3) pressure with the valve open to the height specified.

2. Pressure with valve closed and height as per specifications
3. Pressure with valve open and height as per specifications

Most specifications allow for variations of plus or minus 10% from the published figures.

VALVE KEEPERS AND ROTATORS

VALVE KEEPERS Valve keepers (locks) are used on the end of the valve stem to retain the spring. The inside surfaces of the keeper use a variety of grooves or beads. The design depends on the holding requirements. The outside of the keeper fits into a cone-shaped seat in the center of the valve spring retainer. ● SEE FIGURE 27–18.

VALVE ROTATORS Some valve spring retainers have built-in devices called valve rotators. They cause the valve to rotate in a controlled manner as it is opened. The purposes and functions of valve rotators include the following:

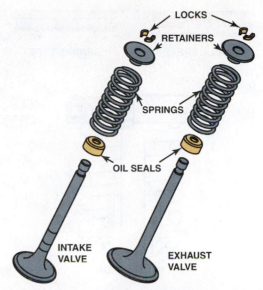

FIGURE 27–18 Valve keepers (also called locks) are tapered so they wedge into a tapered hole in the retainer.

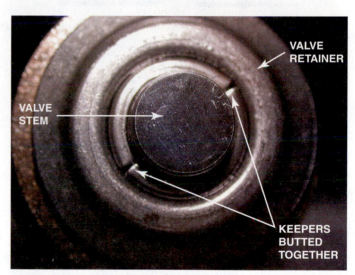

FIGURE 27–19 Notice that there is no gap between the two keepers (ends butted together). As a result, the valve is free to rotate because the retainer applies a force, holding the keepers in place but not tight against the stem of the valve. Most engines, however, do not use free rotators and, therefore, have a gap between the keepers.

- Help prevent carbon buildup from forming by providing a "wiping" action of the valve face
- Reduce hot spots on the valves by constantly turning them
- Help to even out the wear on the valve face and seat
- Improve valve guide lubrication
  The two types of valve rotators are free and positive.
- **Free rotators** simply take the pressure off the valve to allow engine vibration to rotate the valve. ● SEE FIGURE 27–19.
- The opening of the valve forces the valve to rotate. One type of **positive rotator** uses small steel balls and slight

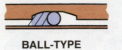
BALL-TYPE

SPRING-TYPE

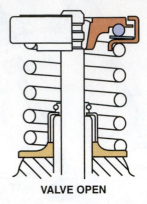
VALVE OPEN

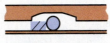
BALL-TYPE

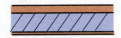
SPRING-TYPE

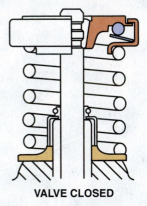
VALVE CLOSED

FIGURE 27–20 Type of valve rotator operation. Ball-type operation is on the left and spring-type operation is on the right.

ramps. Each ball moves down its ramp to turn the rotator sections as the valve opens. A second type uses a coil spring. The spring lies down as the valve opens. This action turns the rotator body in relation to the collar. Valve rotators are only used when it is desirable to increase the valve service life, because rotors cost more than plain retainers. ● SEE FIGURE 27–20.

VALVE RECONDITIONING PROCEDURE

After proper cleaning, inspection, and measurement procedures have been completed, valve reconditioning, usually called a "valve job," can be performed using the following sequence.

STEP 1 The valve stem is lightly ground and chamfered. This step helps to ensure that the valve will rest in the collet (holder of the valve stem during valve grinding) of the valve grinder correctly. This process is often called **truing** the valve tip.

STEP 2 The face of the valve is ground to the proper angle using a valve grinder.

STEP 3 The valve seat is ground in the head. (The seat must be matched to the valve that will be used in that position.)

STEP 4 Valve spring installed height and valve stem height are checked and corrected as necessary.

STEP 5 After a thorough cleaning, the cylinder head should be assembled with new valve stem seals installed.

The rest of the chapter discusses valve face and seat reconditioning, and cylinder head reassembly.

VALVE FACE GRINDING

PURPOSE AND FUNCTION   Each valve grinder operates somewhat differently. The operation manual that comes with the grinder should be followed for lubrication, adjustment, and specific operating procedures. The general procedures given in the following paragraphs apply to all valve resurfacer equipment. Set the grinder head at the **valve face angle** as specified by the vehicle manufacturer.

CAUTION: Safety glasses should *always* be worn for valve and seat reconditioning work. During grinding operations, fine hot chips fly from the grinding stones.

NOTE: Some valve grinders use the end of the valve to center the valve while grinding. If the tip of the valve is not square with the stem, the face of the valve may be ground improperly.

The valve stem is clamped in the work head as close to the fillet under the valve head as possible to prevent vibrations. The work head motor is turned on to rotate the valve. The wheel head motor is turned on to rotate the grinding wheel. The coolant flow is adjusted to flush the material away, but not so much that it splashes.

For best results perform the following:

- The rotating grinding wheel is fed slowly to the rotating valve face.
- Light grinding is done as the valve is moved back and forth across the grinding wheel face.
- Do not feed the valve into the grinding stone more than 0.001 to 0.002 inch at one time.
- The valve is never moved off the edge of the grinding wheel. It is ground only enough to clean the face. ● SEE FIGURE 27–21.

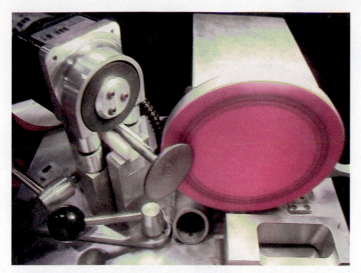

FIGURE 27–21 Resurfacing the face of a valve. Both the valve and the grinder stone or disc are turned to ensure a smooth surface finish on the face of the valve.

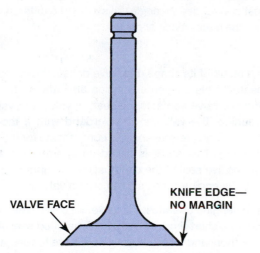

VALVE FACE

KNIFE EDGE— NO MARGIN

FIGURE 27–22 Never use a valve that has been ground to a sharp edge. This weakens the valve and increases the chance of valve face burning.

MARGIN The margin is the distance between the head of the valve and the seat of the value. This distance should be 0.03 inch (0.8 mm). Some vehicle manufacturers specify a minimum margin of less than 0.03 inch for some engines, especially for intake valves. Always check service information for the exact specifications for the engine being serviced. ● SEE FIGURE 27–22.

NOTE: To help visualize a 0.03 inch margin, note that this dimension is equal to about 1/32 inch or the thickness of a U.S. dime.

Intake valves can usually perform satisfactorily with a margin less than 0.03 inch. Always check the engine manufacturer's

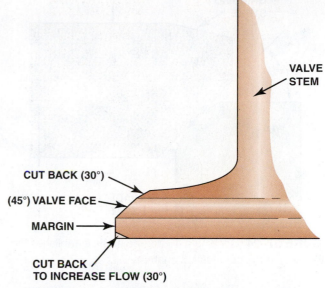

VALVE STEM

CUT BACK (30°)

(45°) VALVE FACE

MARGIN

CUT BACK TO INCREASE FLOW (30°)

FIGURE 27–23 After grinding the 45 degree face angle, additional airflow into the engine can be accomplished by grinding a transition between the face angle and the stem, and by angling or rounding the transition between the margin and the top of the valve.

TECH TIP

Grinding the Valves for More Power

A normal "valve job" includes grinding the face of the valve to clean up any pits and grinding the valve stems to restore the proper stem height. However, a little more airflow in and out of the cylinder head can be accomplished by performing two more simple grinding operations.

- Use the valve grinder and adjust to 30 degrees (for a 45 degree valve) and grind a transition between the valve face and the valve stem area of the valve. While this step may reduce some desirable swirling of the air-fuel mixture at lower engine speeds, it also helps increase cylinder filling, especially at times when the valve is not fully open.

- Chamfer or round the head of the valve between the top of the valve and the margin on the side. By rounding this surface, additional airflow into the cylinder is achieved. ● SEE FIGURE 27–23.

specifications for the cylinder being serviced. Aluminized valves will lose their corrosion resistance properties when ground. For satisfactory service, aluminized valves must be replaced if they require refacing.

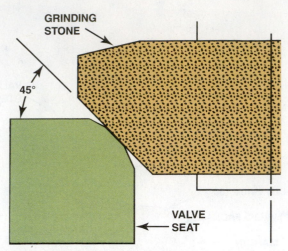

FIGURE 27–24 Grinding a 45 degree angle establishes the valve seat in the combustion chamber.

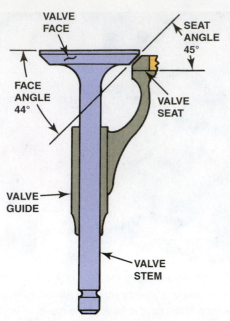

FIGURE 27–25 Some vehicle manufacturers recommend that the valve face be resurfaced at a 44 degree angle and the valve seat at a 45 degree angle. This 1 degree difference is known as the interference angle.

VALVE SEAT RECONDITIONING

PURPOSE AND FUNCTION The valve seats are reconditioned at the following times:

- After the cylinder head has been properly cleaned, resurfaced, and the valve guides have been resized or reconditioned
- When the valve guides have been replaced

The final valve seat width and position are checked with the valve that is to be used on the seat being reconditioned.

VALVE SEAT ANGLES Valve seats will have a normal seat angle of either 45 or 30 degrees.

- **45 degrees.** This is the most commonly used, and the narrow 45 degree valve seats will crush carbon deposits to prevent buildup of deposits on the seat and the valve heat will transfer to the seat and cylinder head.
- **30 degrees.** Usually used on intake valves only. The 30 degree valve seat is more likely to burn than a 45 degree seat because some deposits can build up to keep the valve from seating properly. The 30 degree valve seat will, however, allow more gas flow than a 45 degree valve seat when both are opened to the same amount of lift. ● **SEE FIGURE 27–24.**

INTERFERENCE ANGLE Ideally, the valve face and valve seat should have exactly the same angle. This is impossible, especially on exhaust valves, because the valve head becomes much hotter than the seat and so the valve expands more than the seat. This expansion causes the hot valve to contact the seat in a different place on the valve than it did when it was cold.

As a result of its shape, the valve does not expand evenly when heated. This uneven expansion also affects the way in which the hot valve contacts the seat. In valve and valve seat reconditioning, the valve is often ground with a face angle 1 degree less than the seat angle to compensate for the change in hot seating. This angle is called an *interference angle.* It makes a positive seal at the combustion chamber edge of the seat when the engine is first started after a valve job.

- As the engine operates, the valve will peen itself on the seat. In a short time, it will make a matched seal. After a few thousand miles, the valve will have formed its own seat.
- The interference angle has another benefit. The valve and seat are reconditioned with different machines. Each machine must have its angle set before it is used for reconditioning.
- It is nearly impossible to set the exact same angles on both valve and seat reconditioning machines. Making an interference angle will ensure that any slight angle difference favors a tight seal at the combustion chamber edge of the valve seat when the valve servicing has been completed. ● **SEE FIGURE 27–25.**

VALVE SEAT WIDTH As the valve seats are resurfaced, their widths increase. The resurfaced seats must be narrowed to make the seat width correct and to position the seat properly on the valve face. The normal automotive engine cylinder head valve seat is from 1/16 to 3/32 inch (1.5 to 2.5 mm) wide. There should be at least 1/32 inch (0.8 mm) of the ground valve face extending above the seat, called *overhang.*

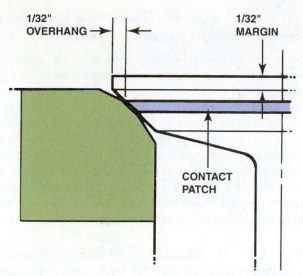

FIGURE 27–26 The seat must contact evenly around the valve face. For good service life, both margin and overhang should be at least 1/32 inch (0.8 mm).

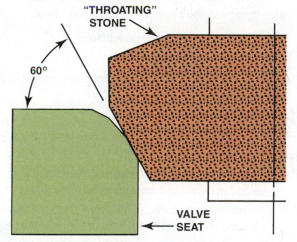

FIGURE 27–27 Grinding a 60 degree angle removes metal from the bottom to raise and narrow the seat.

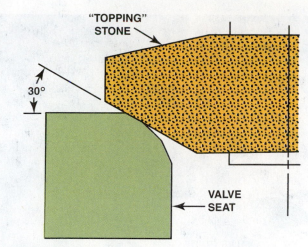

FIGURE 27–28 Grinding a 30 degree angle removes metal from the top to lower and narrow the seat.

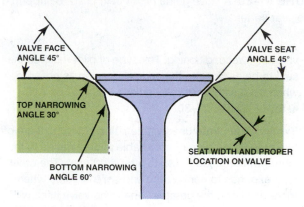

FIGURE 27–29 A typical three-angle valve job using 30-, 45-, and 60-degree stones or cutters.

Some manufacturers recommend having the valve seat contact the middle of the valve face. In all cases, the valve seat width and the contact with the valve face match the manufacturer's specifications. ● SEE FIGURE 27–26.

THREE-ANGLE VALVE JOB
A **three-angle valve job** means that the valve seats are ground three times.

- The first angle is the angle of the valve seat specified by the vehicle manufacturer, usually 45 degrees.
- The second angle uses a 60 degree stone or cutter to remove material right below the valve seat to increase flow in or out of the combustion chamber. This angle is called the **throating angle.** ● SEE FIGURE 27–27.
- The third angle uses a 30 degree stone or cutter to smooth the transition between the valve seat and the

cylinder head, again to increase flow in or out of the combustion chamber. This angle is called the **topping angle.** ● SEE FIGURE 27–28.

The three stones or cutters can be used in combination to create the desired seat width and where it contacts the face of the valve. The 60 degree throating stone will rise and narrow the seat. The 45 degree stone will widen the seat, and the 30 degree stone will lower and narrow the seat. ● SEE FIGURE 27–29.

VALVE GUIDE PILOTS

TYPES OF PILOTS
Valve seat reconditioning equipment uses a pilot in the valve guide to align the stone holder or cutter in the exact same location as the valve stem. This ensures accurate valve seat-to-valve face sealing. Two types of pilots used include:

- **Tapered pilots** locate themselves in the least worn section of the guide. They are made in standard sizes and in oversize increments of 0.001 inch, usually up to 0.004 inch OS. The largest pilot that will fit into the guide is used for

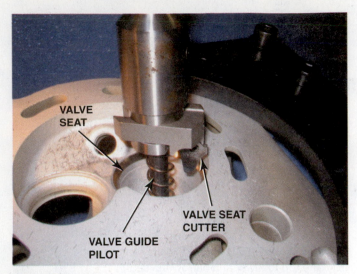

FIGURE 27–30 A valve guide pilot being used to support a valve seat cutter.

valve seat reconditioning. This type of pilot restores the seat to be as close to the original position as possible when used with worn valve guides.

● **SEE FIGURE 27–30.**

- **Expandable pilots** used with seating equipment are of two types. One type of adjustable pilot expands in the center of the guide to fit like a tapered pilot. The other type expands to contact the ends of the guide where there has been the greatest wear. The valve itself will align in the same way as the pilot.

NOTE: If the guide is not reconditioned, the valve will match the seat when an expandable pilot is used.

The pilot and guide should be thoroughly cleaned.

VALVE SEAT GRINDING STONES

TYPES OF STONES   Three basic types of grinding stones are used. All are used dry.

- A **roughing stone** is used to rapidly remove large amounts of seat metal. This would be necessary on a badly pitted seat or when installing new valve seat inserts. The roughing stone is sometimes called a seat *forming stone.*

- After the seat forming stone, a **finishing stone** is used to put the proper finish on the seat. The finishing stone is also used to recondition cast-iron seats that are only slightly worn.

- **Hard seat stones** are used on hard Stellite® exhaust seat inserts.

NOTE: Stellite® is a nonmagnetic hard alloy used for valve seats in heavy-duty applications.

The stone diameter and face angle must be correct. The diameter of the stone must be larger than the valve head, but it must be small enough that it does not contact the edge of the combustion chamber. The angle of the grinding surface of the stone must be correct for the seat. When an interference angle is used with reground valves, it is common practice to use a seat with the standard seat angle. The interference angle is ground on the valve face. In some cases, such as with an aluminized valve, the valve has the standard angle and the seat is ground to give the interference angle. The required seat angle must be determined *before* the seat grinding stone is dressed.

DRESSING THE GRINDING STONE   The selected grinding stone is installed on the stone holder. The holder and grinding stone assembly is rotated with the driver. The diamond is adjusted so that it just touches the stone face. The diamond dressing tool is moved slowly across the face of the spinning stone, taking a very light cut. Dressing the stone in this way will give it a clean, sharp cutting surface. It is necessary to redress the stone at the following times.

- Each time a stone is placed on a holder
- At the beginning of each valve job
- Any time the stone is not cutting smoothly and cleanly while grinding valve seats

GRINDING THE VALVE SEAT   The typical procedure includes the following steps.

STEP 1   The valve seat should be cleaned before grinding. This keeps the grinding dust from filling the grinding stone.

STEP 2   The pilot is then placed in the valve guide. A drop of oil is placed on the end of the pilot to lubricate the holder.

STEP 3   The holder, with the dressed grinding stone, is placed over the pilot. The driver should be supported so that no driver weight is on the holder. This allows the stone abrasive and the metal chips to fly out from between the stone and seat to give fast, smooth grinding.

STEP 4   Grinding is done in short bursts, such as two to three seconds each burst. Check to see if the seat is properly ground at the end of each burst. This procedure helps prevent the seat from being ground too deep.

STEP 5   The holder and stone should be lifted from the seat between each grinding burst to check the condition of the seat. The finished seat should be bright and smooth across the entire surface, with no pits or roughness remaining. Some of the induction hardness from the exhaust valve seat may extend over into the intake seat. It may be necessary to apply a slight pressure on the driver toward the hardened spot to form a concentric seat.

STEP 6   Check the seat with a dial indicator gauge to make sure that it is concentric within 0.002 inch (0.05 mm)

FIGURE 27–31 Checking valve seat concentricity using a dial indicator.

FIGURE 27–32 Typical dial indicator type of micrometer for measuring valve seat concentricity.

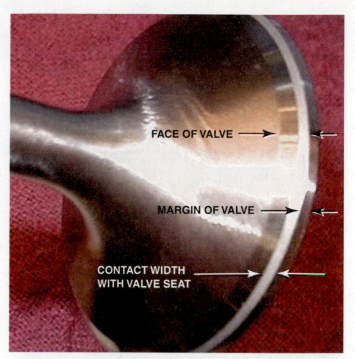

FIGURE 27–33 After the valve face and the valve seat are ground (reconditioned), lapping compound is used to smooth the contact area between the two mating surfaces. Notice that the contact is toward the top of the face. For maximum life, the contact should be in the middle of the face.

before the seat is finished. The dial gauge measurement of the valve seat is very important. The maximum acceptable variation is 0.002 inch, called the **total indicator runout (TIR)** of the valve seat. ● **SEE FIGURES 27–31 AND 27–32.**

NARROWING THE VALVE SEAT The valve seat becomes wider as it is ground. It is therefore necessary to narrow the seat so that it will contact the valve properly. The seat is *topped* with a grinding stone dressed to 15 degrees less than the seat angle. Therefore, use:

- A 30 degree stone to narrow a 45 degree seat angle
- A 15 degree stone for a 30 degree seat angle

Topping lowers the top edge of the seat. The amount of topping required can best be checked by measuring the maximum valve face diameter using dividers. The dividers are then adjusted to a setting 1/16 inch smaller to give the minimum valve face overhang. The seat is measured and then topped with short grinding bursts, as required, to equal the diameter set on the dividers. The seat width is then measured. If it is too wide, the seat must be *throated* with a stone with a 60 degree angle. This removes metal from the port side of the seat, raising the lower edge of the seat. Generally accepted seat widths are as follows:

- For intake valves: 1/16 inch or 0.0625 inch (about the thickness of a nickel) (1.5 mm)
- For exhaust valves: 3/32 inch or 0.0938 inch (about the thickness of a dime and a nickel together) (2.4 mm)

The completed seat must be checked with the valve that is to be used on the seat. This can be done using lapping compound or by marking across the valve face at four or five places with a felt-tip marker. The valve is then inserted in the guide so that the valve face contacts the seat. The valve is rotated 20 to 30 degrees and then removed. The location of the seat contact on the valve is observed where the felt-tip marking has been rubbed off from the valve. Valve seating can be seen in ● **FIGURE 27–33.**

Valve seat grinding is complete when each of the valve seats has been properly ground, topped, and throated.

To summarize:

- Using a 30 degree topping stone (for a 45 degree seat) *lowers* the upper outer edge and narrows the seat.

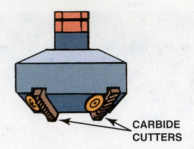

FIGURE 27–34 A cutter is used to remove metal and form the valve seat angles.

- Using a 60 degree throating stone *raises* the lower inner edge and narrows the seat.
- Using a 45 degree stone *widens* the seat.

VALVE SEAT CUTTERS

Some vehicle manufacturers and automotive service technicians recommend the use of valve seat cutters rather than valve seat grinders. ● **SEE FIGURE 27–34.**

The valve seats can be reconditioned to commercial standards in much less time when using the cutters rather than the grinders. The advantages of using a seat cutter compared to a grinding stone include:

- A number of cutting blades are secured at the correct seat angle in the cutting head of this valve seat reconditioning tool.
- The cutter angle usually includes the interference angle so that new valves with standard valve face angles can be used without grinding the new valve face.
- The cutters do not require dressing as stones do.
- The cutter is rotated by hand or by using a special speed reduction motor. Only metal chips are produced.
- The finished seat is checked for concentricity and fit against the valve face.

CAUTION: A cutter should only be rotated clockwise. If a cutter is rotated counterclockwise, damage to the cutting surfaces ruins the cutter.

VALVE SEAT TESTING

PURPOSE After the valves have been refaced and the guides and valve seats have been resurfaced, the valves should be inspected for proper sealing and to ensure that the valve seat is concentric with the valve face.

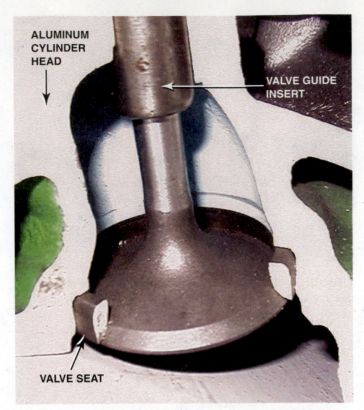

FIGURE 27–35 All aluminum cylinder heads use valve seat inserts. If an integral valve seat (cast-iron head) is worn, it can be replaced with a replacement valve seat by machining a pocket (counterbore) to make a place for the new insert seat.

METHODS Following are methods often used to check valve face-to-seat concentricity and valve seating.

1. Vacuum testing can be done by applying vacuum to the intake and/or exhaust port using a tight rubber seal and a vacuum pump. A good valve face-to-seat seal is indicated by maintaining at least 28 inch Hg of vacuum. This method also tests for leakage around the valve guides. Put some engine oil around the guides; if vacuum increases, valve guides may have excessive clearance.

2. The ports or chamber can be filled with mineral spirits or some other suitable fluid. A good seal should not leak fluid for at least 45 seconds.

3. Valve seating can be checked by applying air pressure to the combustion chamber and checking for air leakage past the valve seat.

4. The valves can be lapped using valve grinding compound and looking at the "parting line" between the valve face on the valve and the valve seat in the cylinder head.

VALVE SEAT REPLACEMENT

PURPOSE Valve seats need to be replaced if they are cracked or if they are burned or eroded too much to be reground. ● **SEE FIGURE 27–35.**

The MIG Welder Seat Removal Trick

A quick and easy method to remove insert valve seats is to use a *metal inert gas (MIG)* welder, also called a *gas metal arc welder (GMAW)*. After the valve has been removed, use the MIG welder and lay a welding bead around the seat area of the insert. As the welder cools, it shrinks and allows the insert to be easily removed from the cylinder head. The weld bead also provides a surface that can be used to pry the seat from the cylinder head.

It may not be possible to determine whether a valve seat needs to be replaced before an attempt is made to recondition the valve seat. Valve seat replacement is accomplished by using a pilot in the valve guide. This means that the valve guide must be reconditioned *before* the seat can be replaced.

- Damaged insert valve seats are removed and the seat counterbore is cleaned to accept a new oversize seat insert.
- Damaged integral valve seats must be counterbored to make a place for the new insert seat.

INSERT SEAT REMOVAL METHODS

The old insert seat is removed by one of several methods.

- A small pry bar can be used to snap the seat from the counterbore.
- It is sometimes easier to do this if the old seat is drilled to weaken it. Be careful not to drill into the head material.
- Sometimes, an expandable hook-type puller is used to remove the seat insert. See the Tech Tip, "The MIG Welder Seat Removal Trick." The seat counterbore must be cleaned before the new, oversize seat is installed. The replacement inserts have a 0.002 to 0.003 inch (0.05 to 0.07 mm) interference fit in the counterbore. The counterbores are cleaned and properly sized, using the same equipment described in the following paragraph for installing replacement seats in place of faulty integral valve seats.

TYPES OF VALVE SEATS

If an insert is being replaced, the new insert must be of the same type of material as the original insert or better. Insert exhaust valve seats operate at temperatures that are 100°F to 150°F (56°C to 83°C) hotter than those of integral seats up to 900°F (480°C). Upgraded valve and valve seat materials are required to give the same service life as that of the original seats. Removable valve seats are available in different materials, including:

- Cast iron
- Stainless steel

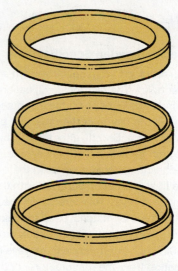

FIGURE 27–36 Insert valve seats are rings of metal driven into the head.

- Nickel cobalt
- Powdered metal (PM)

● SEE FIGURE 27–36.

REPLACING AN INTEGRAL VALVE SEAT

A counterbore cutting tool is selected that will cut the correct diameter for the outside of the insert. The diameter of the bore is smaller than the outside diameter of the seat insert. The procedure usually includes the following steps.

STEP 1 The cutting tool is positioned securely in the tool holder so that it will cut the counterbore at the correct diameter.

STEP 2 The tool holder is attached to the size of pilot that fits the valve guide. The tool holder feed mechanism is screwed together so that it has enough threads to properly feed the cutter into the head. This assembly is placed in the valve guide so that the cutting tool rests on the seat that is to be removed.

STEP 3 The new insert is placed between the support fixture and the stop ring. The stop ring is adjusted against the new insert so that cutting will stop when the counterbore reaches the depth of the new insert.

STEP 4 The boring tool is turned by hand or with a reduction gear motor drive. It cuts until the stop ring reaches the fixture.

STEP 5 The support fixture and the tool holder are removed. The pilot and the correct size of adapter are placed on the driving tool.

STEP 6 The seats should be cooled with dry ice to cause them to shrink. Each insert should be left in the dry ice until it is to be installed. This will allow it to be installed with little chance of metal being sheared from the counterbore. Sheared chips could become jammed under the insert, keeping it from seating properly. The chilled seat is placed on the counterbore.

Use the Recommended Specifications

A technician replaced valve seat inserts in an aluminum cylinder head. The *factory* specification called for a 0.002 inch interference fit (the insert should be 0.002 inch larger in diameter than the seat pocket in the cylinder head). Shortly after the engine was started, the seat fell out, ruining the engine.

The technician should have used the interference fit specification supplied with the replacement seat insert. Interference fit specifications depend on the type of material used to make the insert. Some inserts for aluminum heads require as much as 0.007 inch interference fit. Always refer to the specification from the manufacturer of the valve inserts when replacing valve seats in aluminum cylinder heads.

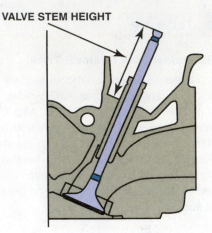

VALVE STEM HEIGHT

FIGURE 27–37 Valve stem height is measured from the spring seat to the tip of the valve after the valve seat and valve face have been refinished. If the valve stem height is too high, up to 0.02 inch can be ground from the tips of most valves.

STEP 7 The driver with a pilot is then quickly placed in the valve guide so that the seat will be driven squarely into the counterbore. The driver is hit with a heavy hammer to seat the insert.

STEP 8 Heavy blows are used to start the insert, and lighter blows are used as the seat reaches the bottom of the counterbore.

STEP 9 The installed valve seat insert is peened in place by running a peening tool around the metal on the outside of the seat. The peened metal is slightly displaced over the edge of the insert to help hold it in place.

VALVE STEM HEIGHT

DEFINITION   **Valve stem height** is the distance the valve stem is above the spring seat. Valve stem height is a different measurement from installed height. ● SEE FIGURE 27–37.

- Valve stem height is important to maintain for all engines, but especially for overhead camshaft engines.

- When the valve seat and the valve face are ground, the valve stem extends deeper into the combustion chamber and extends higher or farther into the cylinder head.

- The valve is put in the head, and the length from the tip to the valve spring seat is measured.

- The tip is ground to shorten the valve stem length to compensate for the valve face and seat grinding.

- The valve will not close if the valve tip extends too far from the valve guide on engines that have hydraulic lifters and nonadjustable rocker arms.

- If the valve is too long, the tip may be ground by as much as 0.02 inch (0.5 mm) to reduce its length. If more grinding

is required, the valve must be replaced. If it is too short, the valve face or seat may be reground, within limits, to allow the valve to seat deeper.

- Where excessive valve face and seat grinding has been done, shims can be placed under the rocker shaft on some engines as a repair to provide correct hydraulic lifter plunger centering. These shims must have the required lubrication holes to allow oil to enter the shaft.

INSTALLED HEIGHT

DEFINITION   **Installed height** is the distance between the valve spring seat and the underside of the valve spring retainer. When the valves and/or valve seats have been machined, the valve projects farther than before on the rocker arm side of the head. The valve face is slightly recessed into the combustion chamber side of the head. The valve spring tension is, therefore, reduced because the spring is not as compressed as it was originally.

CORRECTING INSTALLED HEIGHT   To restore original valve spring tension, special valve spring spacers, inserts, or shims are installed under the valve springs. These shims are usually called **valve spring inserts (VSI).** Valve spring inserts are generally available in three different thicknesses.

- **0.015 inch (0.38 mm).** Used for balancing valve spring pressure

- **0.03 inch (0.75 mm).** Generally used for new springs on cylinder heads that have had the valve seats ground and valves refaced

- **0.06 inch (1.5 mm).** Necessary to bring assembled height to specifications (These thicker inserts may be required if the seats have been resurfaced more than once.)

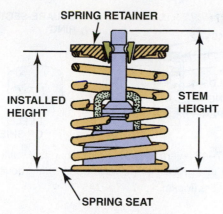

FIGURE 27–38 Installed height is determined by measuring the distance from the spring seat to the bottom of the valve spring retainer.

FIGURE 27–39 Valve spring inserts are used to restore proper installed height.

STEP 1 To determine the exact thickness of insert to install, measure the valve spring installed height. ● **SEE FIGURE 27–38.**

STEP 2 If the installed height is greater than specifications, select the valve spring insert (shim) that brings the installed height to within specifications. Be sure to install the valve spring inserts with the grooves facing toward the cylinder head. These are used to allow air to flow between the cylinder and the insert to help insulate the valve springs. Most inserts are labeled with the message, "This Side Up," which means toward the valve spring. ● **SEE FIGURE 27–39.**

CAUTION: Do not use more than one valve spring insert. If the correct installed height cannot be achieved using one insert, replace the valve seat to restore the proper installed height.

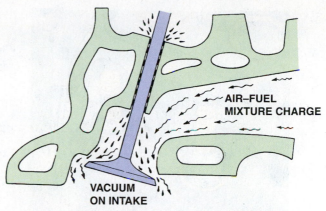

FIGURE 27–40 Engine vacuum can draw oil past the valve guides and into the combustion chamber. The use of valve stem seals limits the amount of oil that is drawn into the engine. If the seals are defective, excessive blue (oil) smoke is most often observed during engine start-up.

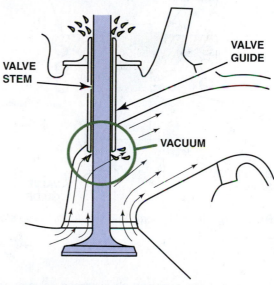

FIGURE 27–41 Engine oil can also be drawn past the exhaust valve guide because of a small vacuum created by the flow of exhaust gases. Any oil drawn past the guide would simply be forced out through the exhaust system and not enter the engine. Some engine manufacturers do not use valve stem seals on the exhaust valves.

VALVE STEM SEALS

PURPOSE AND FUNCTION Leakage past the valve guides is a major oil consumption problem in any overhead valve or overhead cam engine. A high vacuum exists in the intake port, as shown in ● **FIGURE 27–40.**

Most engine manufacturers use valve stem seals on the exhaust valve, because a weak vacuum in the exhaust port area can draw oil into the exhaust stream, as illustrated in ● **FIGURE 27–41.**

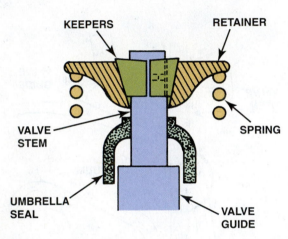

UMBRELLA
SEALS

FIGURE 27–42 Umbrella seals install over the valve stems and cover the guide.

Valve stem seals are used on overhead valve engines to control the amount of oil used to lubricate the valve stem as it moves in the guide. The stem and guide will scuff if they do not have enough oil. Too much oil will cause excessive oil consumption and will cause heavy carbon deposits to build up on the spark plug nose and on the valves.

TYPES OF VALVE STEM SEALS
The types of valve stem seals include the following:

- The *umbrella valve stem seal* holds tightly on the valve stem and moves up and down with the valve. Any oil that spills off the rocker arms is deflected out over the valve guide, much as water is deflected over an umbrella. As a result, umbrella valve stem seals are often called *deflector valve stem seals*. ● **SEE FIGURE 27–42.**

- The *O-ring valve stem seal* used on Chevrolet engines keeps oil from leaking between the valve stem and valve spring retainer. The oil is deflected over the retainer and shield. The assembly controls oil like an umbrella-type oil seal. Both types of valve stem seals allow only the

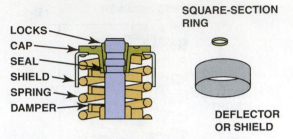

FIGURE 27–43 A small square cut O-ring is installed under the retainer in a groove in the valve under the groove(s) used for the keepers (locks).

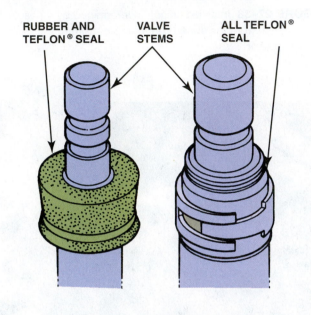

FIGURE 27–44 Positive valve stem seals are the most effective type because they remain stationary on the valve guide and wipe the oil from the stem as the valve moves up and down.

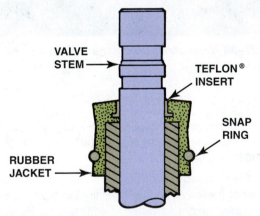

correct amount of oil to reach the valve guide to lubricate the valve stem. The rest of the oil flows back to the oil pan. ● **SEE FIGURE 27–43.**

- *Positive valve stem seals* hold tightly around the valve guide, and the valve stem moves through the seal. The Teflon® wiping ring wipes the excess oil from the valve stem. ● **SEE FIGURES 27–44 AND 27–45.**

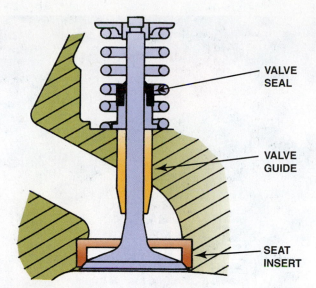

FIGURE 27–45 The positive valve stem seal is installed on the valve guide.

FIGURE 27–46 An assortment of shapes, colors, and materials of positive valve stem seals.

VALVE SEAL MATERIALS Valve stem seals are made from many different types of materials. They may be made from nylon or Teflon, but most valve stem seals are made from synthetic rubber. Three types of synthetic rubbers are in common use.

- Nitrile (Nitril)
- Polyacrylate
- Viton

Nitrile is the oldest valve stem seal material. It has a low cost and a low useful temperature. Engine temperatures have increased with increased emission controls and improved efficiencies, which made it necessary to use premium polyacrylate, even with its higher cost. In many cases, it is being retrofit to the older engines because it will last much longer than Nitrile. Diesel engines and engines used for racing, heavy trucks, and trailer towing, along with turbocharging, operate at still higher temperatures. These engines may require expensive Viton valve stem seals that operate at higher temperatures.
● **SEE FIGURE 27–46.**

TECH TIP

Purchase Engine Parts from a Known Manufacturer

It is interesting to note that an automotive service technician cannot tell the difference between these synthetic rubber valve stem seals if they have come out of the same mold for the same engine. Often suppliers that package gasket sets for sale at a low price will include low-temperature Nitrile, even when the engine needs higher-temperature polyacrylate. The best chances of getting the correct valve stem seal material for an engine is to purchase gaskets and seals packaged by a major brand gasket company.

TECH TIP

Check Before Bolting It On

Using new assembled cylinder heads, whether aluminum or cast iron, is a popular engine buildup option. However, experience has shown that metal shavings and casting sand are often found inside the passages.

Before bolting on these "ready to install" heads, disassemble them and clean all passages. Often machine shavings are found under the valves. If this debris were to get into the engine, the results would be extreme wear or damage to the pistons, rings, block, and bearings. This cleaning may take several hours, but how much is your engine worth?

INSTALLING THE VALVES

PROCEDURE Assembling a cylinder head includes the following steps.

STEP 1 Clean the reconditioned cylinder head thoroughly with soap and water to wash away any remaining grit and metal shavings from the valve grinding operation.

STEP 2 Valves are assembled in the head, one at a time. The valve guide and stem are given a liberal coating of engine oil, and the valve is installed in its guide.

STEP 3 Umbrella and positive valve stem seals are installed. Push umbrella seals down until they touch the valve guide. Use a plastic sleeve over the tip of the valve when installing positive seals to prevent damage to the seal lip. Make sure that the positive seal is fully seated on the valve guide and that it is square.

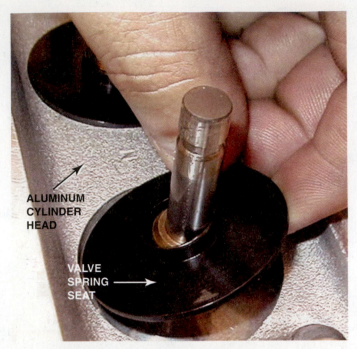

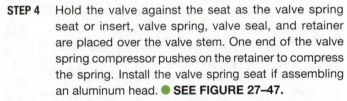

FIGURE 27–47 A metal valve spring seat must be used between the valve spring and the aluminum cylinder head. Many Chrysler aluminum cylinder heads use a combination valve spring seat and valve stem seal.

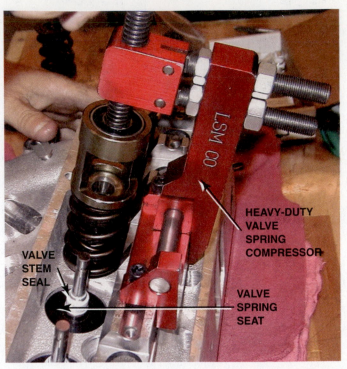

FIGURE 27–48 Assembling a race engine using a heavy-duty valve spring compressor.

STEP 4 Hold the valve against the seat as the valve spring seat or insert, valve spring, valve seal, and retainer are placed over the valve stem. One end of the valve spring compressor pushes on the retainer to compress the spring. Install the valve spring seat if assembling an aluminum head. ● **SEE FIGURE 27–47.**

STEP 5 The O-ring type of valve stem seal, if used, is installed in the lower groove. The valve keepers are installed while

the valve spring is compressed. Using grease helps to keep them attached to the valve stem as the valve spring compressor is released.

STEP 6 Release the valve spring compressor slowly and carefully while making sure that the valve keepers seat properly between the valve stem grooves and the retainer. ● **SEE FIGURE 27–48.**

1 After the valve guide has been replaced or checked for being within specification, insert a pilot into the valve guide.

2 Level the bubble on the pilot by moving the cylinder head, which is clamped to a seat/guide machine.

3 Select the proper guide for the application. Consult guide manufacturer's literature for recommendations.

4 Select the correct cutter and check that the cutting bits are sharp.

5 Carefully measure the exact outside diameter (O.D.) of the valve seat.

6 Adjust the depth of the cutter bit to achieve the specified interference fit for the valve seat.

CONTINUED ▶

7 Install the pilot into the valve guide to support the seat cutter.

8 Install the seat cutter onto the pilot.

9 Adjust the depth of cut, using the new valve seat to set it to the same depth as the thickness of the seat.

10 With the cylinder head still firmly attached to the seat and guide machine, start the cutter motor and cut the head until it reaches the stop.

11 The finish cut valve seat pocket. Be sure to use a vacuum to remove all of the metal shavings from the cutting operation.

12 Place the chilled valve seat over the pilot being sure that the chamfer is facing toward the head as shown.

13 Install the correct size driver onto the valve seat.

14 Using the air hammer or press, press the valve seat into the valve pocket.

15 A new valve seat is now ready to be machined or cut.

SUMMARY

1. The exhaust valve is about 85% of the size of the intake valve.

2. Valve springs should be tested for squareness and proper spring force.

3. Two designs of valve rotators are free and positive.

4. Valve grinding should start with truing the valve tip; then the face should be refinished. A pilot is placed into the valve guide to position the stone or cutter correctly for resurfacing the valve seat.

5. The installed height should be checked and corrected with valve spring inserts, if needed.

6. Valve stem height should be checked and the top of the valve ground, if necessary.

7. After a thorough cleaning, the cylinder head should be assembled using new valve stem seals.

1. What is the procedure for grinding valves?

2. When is the valve tip ground? How do you know how much to remove from the tip?

3. What is an interference angle between the valve and the seat?

4. Describe the difference between cutting and grinding valve seats.

5. How is a valve seat insert installed?

6. How are the correct valve spring inserts (shims) selected and why are they used?

CHAPTER QUIZ

1. In a normally operating engine, intake and exhaust valves are opened by a cam and closed by the _____.
   a. Rocker arms or cam follower
   b. Valve spring
   c. Lifters (tappets)
   d. Valve guide and/or pushrod

2. If an interference angle is machined on a valve or seat, this angle is usually _____.
   a. 1 degree
   b. 0.005 degree
   c. 1 to 3 degrees
   d. 0.5 to 0.75 degree

3. Never remove more material from the tip of a valve than _____.
   a. 0.001 inch
   b. 0.002 inch
   c. 0.02 inch
   d. 0.05 inch

4. A valve should be discarded if the margin is less than _____ after refacing.
   a. 0.001 inch
   b. 0.006 inch
   c. 0.03 inch
   d. 0.06 inch

5. A valve seat should be concentric to the valve guide to a maximum TIR of _____.
   a. 0.006 inch
   b. 0.004 inch
   c. 0.002 inch
   d. 0.00015 inch

6. To lower and narrow a valve seat that has been cut at a 45-degree angle, use a cutter or stone of what angle?
   a. 60 degrees
   b. 45 degrees
   c. 30 degrees
   d. 15 degrees

7. Valve spring inserts (shims) are designed to _____.
   a. Increase installed height of the valve
   b. Decrease installed height of the valve
   c. Adjust the correct valve spring installed height
   d. Decrease valve spring pressure to compensate for decreased installed height

8. The proper relationship between intake and exhaust valve diameter is _____.
   a. Intake valve size is 85% of exhaust valve size
   b. Exhaust valve size is 85% of intake valve size
   c. Exhaust valve size is 38% of intake valve size
   d. Intake valve size is 45% of exhaust valve size

9. Dampers (damper springs) are used inside some valve springs to _____.
   a. Prevent valve spring surge
   b. Keep the valve spring attached to the valve
   c. Decrease valve spring pressure
   d. Retain valve stem seals

10. Umbrella-type valve stem seals _____.
   a. Fit tightly onto the valve guide
   b. Fit on the valve face to prevent combustion leaks
   c. Fit tightly onto the valve stem
   d. Lock under the valve retainer

chapter
28

CAMSHAFTS AND VALVE TRAINS

LEARNING OBJECTIVES: After studying this chapter, the reader should be able to: • Describe the purpose and function of camshaft and camshaft design. • Discuss camshaft drives and camshaft movement. • Discuss rocker arms, pushrods, and lifters or tappets. • Explain overhead camshaft valve trains, valve train lubrication, and valve train problem diagnosis. • Explain camshaft specifications. • Explain the procedure for camshaft removal, measuring camshafts, and selecting a camshaft. • Explain variable valve timing, and variable lift and cylinder deactivation systems.

KEY TERMS: Aerated 409 • Asymmetrical 398 • Bucket 402 • Cam chucking 398 • Cam follower 402 • Cam-in-block 394 • Camshaft bearings 394 • Camshaft duration 403 • Composite camshaft 394 • Double roller chain 397 • Dual overhead camshaft (DOHC) 394 • Finger follower 402 • Flat-link type 396 • Freewheeling engine 397 • Hydraulic lash adjusters (HLA) 403 • Hydraulic valve lifter 407 • Interference engine 398 • Lobe 393 • Lobe centers 404 • Lobe displacement angle (LDA) 404 • Lobe lift 398 • Lobe separation 404 • Lobe spread 404 • Morse type 396 • Oil control valve (OCV) 412 • Overhead camshaft (OHC) 394 • Overhead valve (OHV) 394 • Pump-up 408 • Ramp 407 • Roller chain type 397 • Scavenging 406 • Seat duration 411 • Silent chain type 396 • Single overhead camshaft (SOHC) 394 • Solid valve lifter 407 • Symmetrical 398 • Thrust plate 398 • Total indicator runout (TIR) 410 • Valve cam phaser (VCP) 412 • Valve (camshaft) overlap 404 • Valve float 408 • Valve lash 407 • Variable valve timing (VVT) 412 • Variable valve timing and lift electronic control (VTEC) 416

CAMSHAFT

PURPOSE AND FUNCTION The major function of a camshaft is to open the valves. Camshafts have eccentric shapes called **lobes** that open the valve against the force of the valve springs. The valve spring closes the valve when the camshaft rotates off of the lobe. The camshaft lobe changes rotary motion (camshaft) to linear motion (valves). Cam shape or contour is the major factor in determining the operating characteristics of the engine.

OPERATION The camshaft is driven by:

- Timing gears
- Timing chains
- Timing belts

The gear or sprocket on the camshaft has twice as many teeth, or notches, as the one on the crankshaft. This results in two crankshaft revolutions for each revolution of the camshaft. *The camshaft turns at one-half the crankshaft speed in all four-stroke cycle engines.*

Cam lobe shape has more control over engine performance characteristics than any other single engine part. Engines identical in every way except cam lobe shape may have

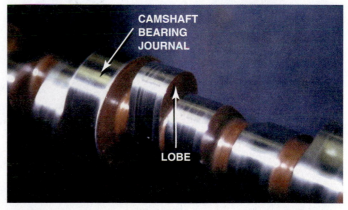

FIGURE 28–1 This high-performance camshaft has a lobe that opens the valve quickly and keeps it open for a long time.

completely different operating characteristics and performance.
● **SEE FIGURE 28–1.**

The camshaft may also operate the following:

- Mechanical fuel pump (carburetor-equipped engines)
- Oil pump
- Distributor (if equipped)

● **SEE FIGURE 28–2.**

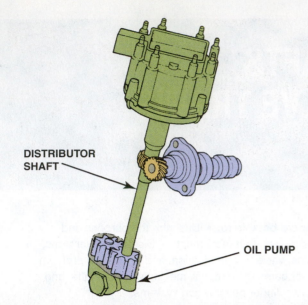

DISTRIBUTOR
SHAFT

OIL PUMP

FIGURE 28–2 In many engines, the camshaft drives the distributor and the oil pump through a shaft from the end of the distributor.

FIGURE 28–3 The camshaft rides on bearings inside the engine block above the crankshaft on a typical cam-in-block engine.

CAMSHAFT LOCATION   There are two basic areas where the camshaft can be located in an engine.

- **In the engine block.** This design is called the **cam-in-block** design. The camshaft is supported in the block by **camshaft bearings** and driven by the crankshaft with a gear or sprocket and chain drive. Engines with the cam located in the block are called pushrod or **overhead valve (OHV)** engines. ● **SEE FIGURE 28–3.**

- **Overhead.** Overhead camshafts are either belt or chain driven from the crankshaft and are located in the cylinder head(s). This arrangement is called **overhead camshaft (OHC)** design. If there is a single overhead camshaft for *each bank* of cylinders, the engine is classified as a **single overhead camshaft (SOHC)** engine design. If an engine uses two overhead camshafts per bank of cylinders, this type of engine design is called a **dual overhead camshaft (DOHC).**

CAMSHAFT DESIGN

CONSTRUCTION   The camshaft is usually a one-piece casting from chilled cast iron for many production engines that includes:

- Lobes
- Bearing journals
- Accessory drive gear

  ● **SEE FIGURE 28–4.**

Other types of camshaft construction include:

- Forged steel (often used in diesel engines)
- Steel machined from a solid billet
- **Composite camshafts,** which use a lightweight tubular shaft with hardened steel lobes press-fitted over the shaft. (The actual production of these camshafts involves placing the lobes over the tube shaft in the correct position. A steel ball is then

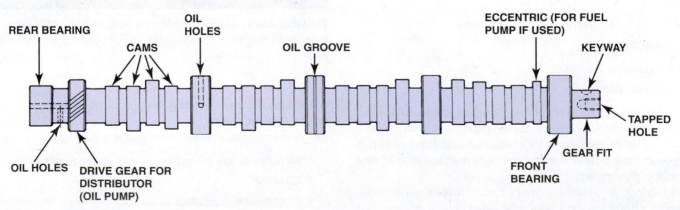

REAR BEARING

CAMS

OIL HOLES

OIL GROOVE

ECCENTRIC (FOR FUEL PUMP IF USED)

KEYWAY

TAPPED HOLE

OIL HOLES

DRIVE GEAR FOR DISTRIBUTOR (OIL PUMP)

FRONT BEARING

GEAR FIT

FIGURE 28–4 Parts of a cam and camshaft terms (nomenclature).

CAM LOBES

HOLLOW STEEL TUBE

FIGURE 28–5 A composite camshaft is lightweight and yet flexible, because the hollow tube can absorb twisting forces and the lobes are hard enough to withstand the forces involved in opening valves.

drawn through the hollow steel tube, expanding the tube and securely locking the cam lobes in position. ● **SEE FIGURE 28–5.)**

CAMSHAFT BEARING JOURNALS
On pushrod engines, camshaft-bearing journals must be larger than the cam lobe so that the camshaft can be installed in the engine through the cam bearings. Some overhead cam engines have bearing caps on the cam bearings. These cams can have large cam lobes with small bearing journals. Cam bearings on some engines are progressively smaller from the front journal to the rear. Other engines use the same size of camshaft bearing on all the journals.

HARDNESS
Older automotive camshafts were used with flat or convex-faced lifters and made from hardened alloy cast iron. It resists wear and provides the required strength. The very hardness of the camshaft causes it to be susceptible to chipping as the result of edge loading or careless handling.

Cast-iron camshafts have about the same hardness throughout. If reground, they should be recoated with a phosphate coating.

Steel camshafts are usually constructed from SAE 4160 or 4180 steel and are usually induction hardened. Induction hardening involves heating the camshaft to cherry red in an electric field (heating occurs by electrical induction). The heated camshaft is then dropped into oil. The rapid cooling hardens the surface. Camshafts can also be hardened by using the following methods.

- Liquid nitriding, which hardens to 0.001 to 0.0015 inch thick
- Gas nitriding, which hardens to 0.004 to 0.006 inch thick

Typical camshaft hardness should be 42 to 60 on the Rockwell "c" scale.

FIGURE 28–6 Worn camshaft with two lobes worn to the point of being almost round.

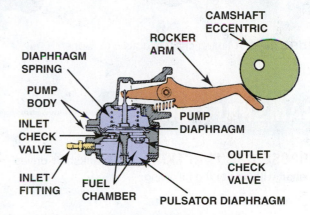

DIAPHRAGM SPRING
PUMP BODY
INLET CHECK VALVE
INLET FITTING
FUEL CHAMBER
ROCKER ARM
CAMSHAFT ECCENTRIC
PUMP DIAPHRAGM
OUTLET CHECK VALVE
PULSATOR DIAPHRAGM

FIGURE 28–7 The fuel pump rocker arm rides on the camshaft eccentric.

NOTE: Rockwell is a type of hardness test, and the c represents the scale used. The higher the number, the harder the surface. The abbreviation *Rc60*, therefore, indicates Rockwell hardness of 60 as measured on the "c" scale.

If this outer hardness wears off, the lobes of the camshaft are easily worn until they are almost completely rounded. ● **SEE FIGURE 28–6.**

CAMSHAFT LUBRICATION
Some engines transfer lubricating oil from the main oil gallery to the crankshaft around the camshaft journal or around the outside of the camshaft bearing. Cam bearing clearance is critical in these engines. If the clearance is too great, oil will leak out and the crankshaft bearings will not get enough oil. Other engines use drilled holes in the camshaft bearing journals to meter lubricating oil to the overhead rocker arm. Oil goes to the rocker arm each time the holes line up between the bearing oil gallery passage and the outlet passage to the rocker arm.

FUEL PUMP ECCENTRICS
An eccentric cam lobe for the mechanical fuel pump is often cast as part of the camshaft used in older engines before fuel injection. ● **SEE FIGURE 28–7.**

Some engines use a steel cup type of eccentric that is bolted to the front of the cam drive gear. This allows a damaged fuel pump eccentric to be replaced without replacing an entire camshaft.

FIGURE 28–8 A timing chain hydraulic tensioner.

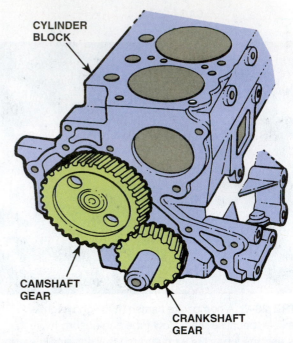

FIGURE 28–9 The larger camshaft gear is usually made from fiber and given a helical cut to help reduce noise. By making the camshaft gear twice as large as the crankshaft gear, the camshaft rotates one revolution for every two of the crankshaft.

FIGURE 28–10 A replacement silent chain and sprockets. The original camshaft sprocket was aluminum with nylon teeth to help control noise. This replacement set will not be noticeably louder than the original and should give the owner many thousands of miles of useful service.

CAMSHAFT DRIVES

PURPOSE AND FUNCTION The crankshaft drives the camshaft with one of the following:

- Timing gears
- Sprockets and chains
- Sprockets and timing belts

Timing chains often have tensioners (dampers) pressing on the unloaded side of the chain. The tensioner pad is a Nylatron molding that is filled with molybdenum disulfide to give it low friction. The tensioner is held against the chain by either a spring or hydraulic oil pressure. ● SEE FIGURE 28–8.

The gears or sprockets are keyed to their shafts so that they can be installed in only one position. The gears and sprockets are then indexed together by marks on the gear teeth or chain links. However, some engines use a tolerance ring that locks the drive sprocket to the camshaft such as the Ford modular V-8s. In these engines, the drive sprocket should *not* be removed from the camshaft unless the specified procedures are followed. When the crankshaft and camshaft timing marks are properly lined up, the cam lobes are indexed to the crankshaft throws of each cylinder so that the valves will open and close correctly in relation to the piston position.

CAMSHAFT CHAIN DRIVES The crankshaft gear or sprocket that drives the camshaft is usually made of sintered iron. When gears are used on the camshaft, the teeth must be made from a soft material to help reduce noise. Usually, the whole gear is made of aluminum or fiber, especially in older engines. ● SEE FIGURE 28–9.

When a chain and sprocket are used, the camshaft sprocket may be made of iron or it may have an aluminum hub with nylon teeth for noise reduction.

Two types of timing chains are used.

1. The **silent chain type** (also known as a **flat-link type,** or **Morse type** for its original manufacturer) operates quietly but tends to stretch with use. The metal links themselves do not "stretch" but, instead, the pin bushings at each joint wear, which causes the chain to become longer. ● SEE FIGURES 28–10 AND 28–11.

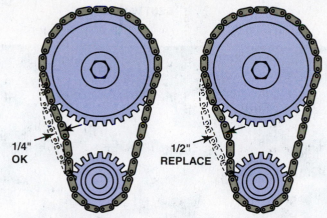

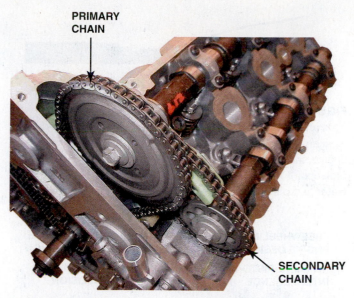

FIGURE 28–11 The industry standard for when to replace a timing chain and gears is when 1/2 inch (13 mm) or more of slack is measured in the chain. However, it is best to replace the timing chain and gear anytime the camshaft is replaced or the engine is disassembled for repair or overhaul.

FIGURE 28–13 This dual overhead camshaft (DOHC) engine uses one chain from the crankshaft to the intake cam and a secondary chain to rotate the exhaust camshaft.

FIGURE 28–12 A replacement high-performance double roller chain. Even though a bit noisier than a flat-link chain, a roller chain does not stretch as much and will therefore be able to maintain accurate valve timing for a long time.

NOTE: When the timing chain stretches, the valve timing will be retarded and the engine will lack low-speed power. In some instances, the chain can wear through the timing chain cover and create an oil leak.

2. The **roller chain type** is noisier but operates with less friction and stretches less than the silent type of chain. If two chains are used side by side, this type of chain is called a **double roller chain.** ● SEE FIGURE 28–12.

    Some four-cam engines use a two-stage camshaft drive system:

    ▪ Primary, from crankshaft to camshaft
    ▪ Secondary, from one camshaft to another

    ● SEE FIGURE 28–13.

FIGURE 28–14 A timing belt failed when the teeth were sheared off. This belt failed at 88,000 miles because the owner failed to replace it at the recommended interval of 60,000 miles.

CAMSHAFT BELT DRIVES Many overhead camshaft engines use a timing belt rather than a chain. Cam drive belts are made from rubber and fabric and are often reinforced with fiberglass or Kevlar. The belt sprocket teeth are square-cut or cogged. Drive belts and sprockets reduce weight compared to a chain drive and require no lubrication with reduced noise. However, the belt requires periodic replacement, usually every 60,000 miles (100,000 km) or longer in some vehicles. ● SEE FIGURES 28–14 AND 28–15.

Unless the engine is freewheeling, the piston can hit the valves if the belt breaks. A **freewheeling engine** is one that causes no internal damage if the camshaft drive belt breaks

FIGURE 28–15 This timing belt broke because an oil leak from one of the camshaft seals caused oil to get into and weaken the belt. Most experts recommend replacing all engine seals in the front of the engine anytime a timing belt is replaced. If the timing belt travels over the water pump, the water pump should also be replaced as a precaution.

FREEWHEELING
ENGINE DESIGN

NO VALVE/PISTON
INTERFERENCE

INTERFERENCE
ENGINE DESIGN

VALVE/PISTON
COLLISION

 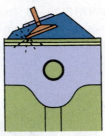

FIGURE 28–16 Many engines are of the interference design. If the timing belt (or chain) breaks, the piston still moves up and down in the cylinder while the valves remain stationary. With a freewheeling design, nothing is damaged, but in an interference engine, the valves are often bent.

when the engine is running. An **interference engine,** however, will cause some of the valves that are open to hit the pistons, causing major engine damage. ● **SEE FIGURES 28–16 AND 28–17.**

CAMSHAFT MOVEMENT

REASONS CAMSHAFTS MOVE   On engines equipped with flat bottom lifters, as the camshaft lobe pushes the lifter upward against the valve spring force, a backward twisting force is developed on the camshaft. After the lobe goes past its high point, the lifter moves down the backside of the lobe. This makes a forward twisting force. This action produces an alternating torsion force forward, then backward, at each cam lobe. The number of cam lobes on the shaft multiplies this alternating torsion force.

Cam chucking is the movement of the camshaft *lengthwise in the engine during operation.* Each camshaft must have some means to control the shaft end thrust. One method is to use a **thrust plate** between the camshaft drive gear or sprocket and a flange on the camshaft.

BENT VALVES

FIGURE 28–17 A head from a Mercedes showing bent valves when the timing chain stretched and skipped over the crankshaft sprocket. When this happened, the piston kept moving and bent the valves.

A thrust plate is attached to the engine block with cap screws. In a few camshafts, a button, spring, or retainer that contacts the timing cover limits forward motion of the camshaft.

WHY FLAT-BOTTOM LIFTERS ROTATE   Valve trains that use flat bottom lifters use a spherical (curved) lifter face that slides against the cam lobe. This produces a surface on the lifter face that is slightly convex, by about 0.002 inch The lifter also contacts the lobe at a point that is slightly off center. This produces a small turning force on the lifter to cause some lifter rotation for even wear. In operation, there is a wide line of contact between the lifter and the high point of the cam lobe. ● **SEE FIGURE 28–18.**

These are the highest loads that are produced in an engine. This surface is the most critical lubrication point in an engine.

CAMSHAFT LOBE LIFT   The **lobe lift** of the cam is usually expressed in decimal inches and represents the distance that the valve lifter or follower is moved. The amount that the valve is lifted is determined by the lobe lift times the ratio of the rocker arm. ● **SEE FIGURES 28–19 AND 28–20.**

The higher the lift of the camshaft lobe, the greater the amount of air and fuel that can enter the engine. The more air and fuel burned in an engine, the greater the power potential of the engine. The amount of lift of a camshaft is often different for the intake and exhaust valves.

- If the specifications vary, the camshaft is called **asymmetrical.**
- If the lift is the same, the cam is called **symmetrical.**

However, when the amount of lift increases, so do the forces on the camshaft and the rest of the valve train. Generally, a camshaft with a lift of over 0.5 inch (1.3 cm) is unsuitable for

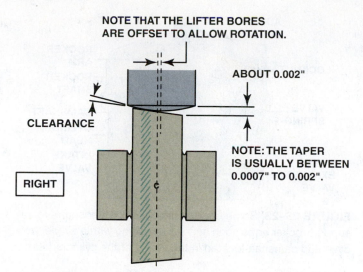

FIGURE 28–18 The slight angle and the curve on the bottom of a flat bottom lifter cause the lifter and the pushrod to rotate during normal operation.

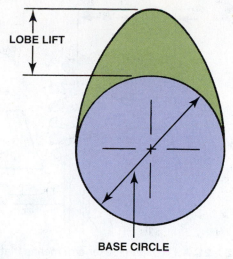

FIGURE 28–19 The lobe lift is the amount the cam lobe lifts the lifter. The blue circle is called the base circle. Because the rocker arm adds to this amount, the entire valve train has to be considered when selecting a camshaft that has the desired lift and duration.

 TECH TIP

Best to Warn the Customer

A technician replaced a timing chain and gears on a high mileage Chevrolet V-8. The repair was accomplished correctly, yet after starting, the engine burned an excessive amount of oil. Before the timing chain replacement, oil consumption was minimal. The replacement timing chain restored proper operation of the engine by restoring the proper cam and valve timing which increased engine vacuum. Increased vacuum can draw oil from the crankcase past worn piston rings and through worn valve guides during the intake stroke. Similar increased oil consumption problems occur if a valve job is performed on a high-mileage engine with worn piston rings and/or cylinders.

To satisfy the owner of the vehicle, the technicians had to disassemble and refinish the cylinders and replace the piston rings. Therefore, all technicians should warn customers that increased oil usage might result from almost any engine repair to a high-mileage engine.

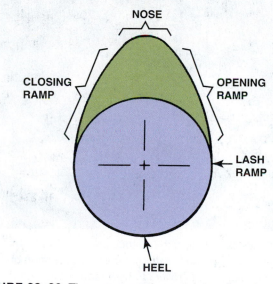

FIGURE 28–20 The ramps on the cam lobe allow the valves to be opened and closed quickly yet under control to avoid damaging valve train components, especially at high engine speeds.

ROCKER ARMS

PURPOSE AND FUNCTION A rocker arm reverses the upward movement of the pushrod to produce a downward movement on the tip of the valve. Engine designers make good use of the rocker arm. It is designed to reduce the travel of the cam follower or lifter and pushrod while maintaining the required valve lift. This is done by using a rocker arm ratio usually of 1.5:1.

street operation except for use in engines that are over 400 inch^3 (6 liters).

The lift specifications at the valve face assume the use of the stock rocker arm ratio. If nonstock rocker arms with a higher ratio are installed (for example, 1.6:1 rockers replacing the stock 1.5:1 rocker arms), the lift at the valve is increased. Also, because the rocker arm rotation covers a greater distance at the pivot of the rocker arm, the rocker arm can hit the edge of the valve retainer.

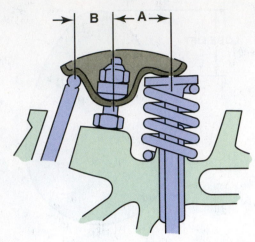

FIGURE 28–21 A 1.5:1 ratio rocker arm means that dimension A is 1.5 times the length of dimension B. Therefore, if the pushrod is moved up 0.4 inch by the camshaft lobe, the valve will be pushed down (opened) 0.4 inch × 1.5, or 0.6 inch

FIGURE 28–22 A high-performance aluminum roller rocker arm. Both the pivot and the tip that contacts the stem of the valve are equipped with rollers to help reduce friction for more power and better fuel economy.

For a given amount of lift on the pushrod, the valve will open to 1.5 times the cam lobe lift. This ratio allows the camshaft to be smaller, so the engine can be smaller. ● **SEE FIGURE 28–21.**

CAUTION: Using rocker arms with a higher ratio than stock can also cause the valve spring to compress too much and actually bind. Valve spring bind (coil bind) occurs when the valve spring is compressed to the point where there is no clearance in the spring. (It is completely compressed.) When coil bind occurs in a running engine, bent pushrods, broken rocker arms, or other valve train damage can result. ● SEE FIGURE 28–22.

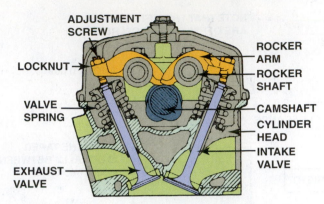

FIGURE 28–23 Some engines today use rocker shafts to support rocker arms such as the V-6 engine with a single overhead camshaft located in the center of the cylinder head.

Rocker arms may be:
- Cast
- Forged
- Stamped steel

Forged rocker arms are the strongest, but they require expensive manufacturing operations. Rocker arms may have bushings or bearings installed to reduce friction and increase durability. Cast rocker arms cost less to make and do not usually use bushings, but they do require several machining operations. They are not as strong as forged rocker arms but are satisfactory for passenger vehicle service. Stamped steel rocker arms are lightweight and cost effective.

SHAFT-MOUNTED ROCKER ARMS
On some overhead valve and most single overhead camshaft engines, the rocker arms are mounted on a shaft that runs the full length of the cylinder head. ● **SEE FIGURE 28–23.**

Because the shaft provides a strong and stable platform for the rocker arms, shaft-mounted rocker arms work well, especially at high engine speeds. While most overhead camshaft engines that use rocker arm shafts do use an adjustable rocker arm, most OHV engines using rocker arm shafts have no provision for adjustment. Shaft-mounted rocker arms are lubricated through oil passages that travel from the block through the head and into the shaft, and then to the rocker arms.

STUD-MOUNTED ROCKER ARMS
Stud-mounted rockers are only found on overhead valve (OHV) engines and each rocker arm is attached to a stud that is pressed or threaded into the cylinder head. A ball on top of the rocker arm provides the bearing surface as the rocker arm pivots and is held in place and adjusted for valve clearance by a nut. While this design looks less stable than a shaft-mounted rocker, this design has proved to be reliable and is inexpensive to manufacture. The rocker arms receive lubricating oil under pressure through hollow pushrods. ● **SEE FIGURE 28–24.**

Some engines use pushrod guide plates fastened to the head. ● **SEE FIGURE 28–25.**

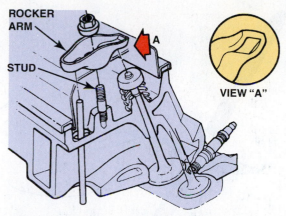

FIGURE 28–24 A typical stud-mounted rocker arm.

PUSH ROD GUIDE PLATE

FIGURE 28–25 Pushrod guide plates are bolted to the head and help stabilize the valve train, especially at high engine speeds.

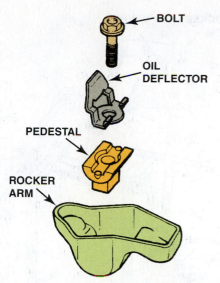

FIGURE 28–26 A pedestal-type rocker arm design that used one bolt for each rocker arm and is nonadjustable. If valve lash needs to be adjusted, different length pushrod(s) must be used.

 FREQUENTLY ASKED QUESTION

Are the Valves Adjustable?

If the stud has the same diameter for its whole length, the rockers *are adjustable* and the nut will be the "interference" type (lock-type nut). If the stud has a shoulder of a different diameter, the rockers are *nonadjustable* and the nut will not have interference threads.

PEDESTAL-MOUNTED ROCKER ARMS Pedestal-mounted rocker arms are similar to stud-mounted rocker arms but do not use a stud and are used only in overhead valve engines. Two rocker arms are attached to and pivot on a pedestal attached to the cylinder head with one or two bolts. The pedestal is usually made from aluminum and the rocker arms are usually stamped steel, which is lightweight and nonadjustable. ● SEE FIGURE 28–26.

 **TECH TIP**

Rocker Arm Shafts Can Cause Sticking Valves

As oil oxidizes, it forms a varnish. Varnish buildup is particularly common on hot upper portions of the engine, such as rocker arm shafts. The varnish restricts clean oil from getting into and lubricating the rocker arms. The cam lobe can easily *force* the valves open, but the valve springs often do not exert enough force to fully close the valves. The result is an engine miss, which may be intermittent. Worn valve guides and/or weak valve springs can also cause occasional rough idle, uneven running, or an engine misfire.

PUSHRODS

PURPOSE AND FUNCTION Pushrods transfer the lifting motion of the valve train from the cam lobe and lifters to the rocker arms. ● SEE FIGURE 28–27.

TYPES OF PUSHRODS Pushrods are designed to be as light as possible and still maintain their strength. They may be either solid or hollow. If they are to be used as passages for oil to lubricate rocker arms, they *must* be hollow. Pushrods use a convex ball on the lower end that seats in the lifter. The rocker arm end is also a convex ball, unless there is an adjustment screw in the pushrod end of the rocker arm. In this case, the rocker arm end of the pushrod has a concave socket. It mates with the convex ball on the adjustment screw in the rocker arm.

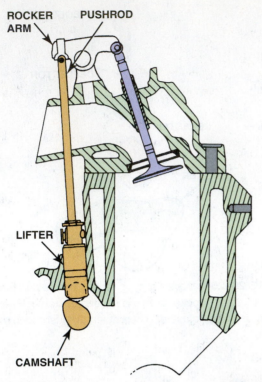

ROCKER ARM   PUSHROD

LIFTER

CAMSHAFT

FIGURE 28–27 Overhead valve engines are also known as pushrod engines because of the long pushrod that extends from the lifter to the rocker arm.

FIGURE 28–28 When the timing chain broke, the valves stopped moving up and down but the pistons kept moving and hit the valves causing the pushrods to bend.

 TECH TIP

Hollow Pushrod Dirt

Many engine rebuilders and remanufacturers do not reuse old hollow pushrods. Dirt, carbon, and other debris are difficult to thoroughly clean from inside a hollow pushrod. When an engine is run with used pushrods, the trapped particles can be dislodged and ruin new bearings and other new engine parts. Therefore, for best results, consider purchasing new hollow pushrods instead of trying to clean and reuse the originals.

All pushrods should be rolled on a flat surface to check for straightness. ● **SEE FIGURE 28–28**.

The tolerance in the valve train allows for some machining of engine parts without the need to change pushrod length.

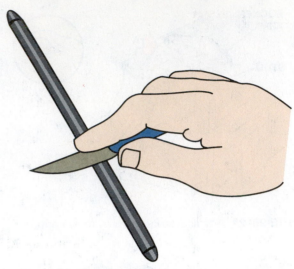

FIGURE 28–29 Hardened pushrods should be used in any engine that uses pushrod guides (plates). To determine if the pushrod is hardened, simply try to scratch the side of the pushrod with a pocketknife.

 **TECH TIP**

The Scratch Test

All pushrods used with guide plates *must* be hardened on the sides and on the tips. To easily determine if a pushrod is hardened, simply use a sharp pocketknife to scrape the wall of the pushrod. A heat-treated pushrod will not scratch. ● **SEE FIGURE 28–29**.

However, if one or more of the following changes have been made to an engine, a different pushrod length may be necessary.

- Block deck height machined
- Cylinder head deck height machined
- Camshaft base circle size reduced
- Valve length increased
- Lifter design changed

OVERHEAD CAMSHAFT VALVE TRAINS

TERMINOLOGY   Overhead camshaft engines use several different types of valve opening designs.

1. One type opens the valves directly with a **bucket**. ● **SEE FIGURE 28–30**.
2. The second type uses a **cam follower,** also called a **finger follower,** that provides an opening ratio similar to

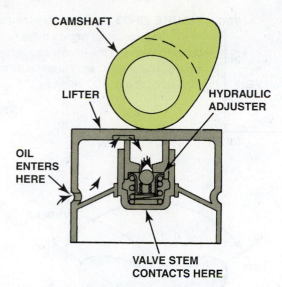

FIGURE 28–30 Hydraulic lifters may be built into bucket-type lifters on some overhead camshaft engines.

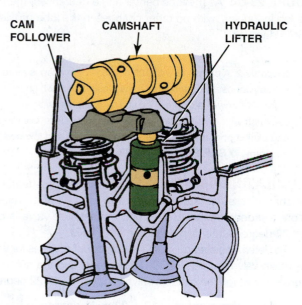

FIGURE 28–31 The use of cam followers allows the use of hydraulic lifters with an overhead camshaft design.

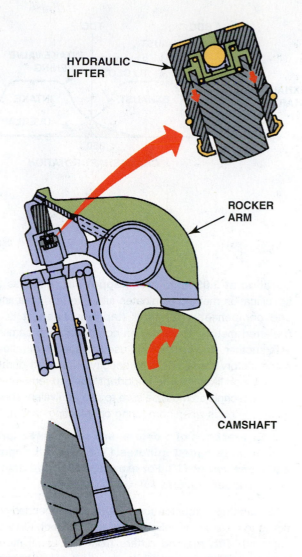

FIGURE 28–32 Hydraulic lash adjusters (HLA) are built into the rocker arm on some OHC engines. Sometimes hydraulic lash adjusters may not bleed down properly if the wrong viscosity (SAE rating) oil is used.

that of a rocker arm. Finger followers open the valves by approximately 1 1/2 times the cam lift. The pivot point of the finger follower may have a mechanical adjustment or it may have an automatic hydraulic adjustment. ● **SEE FIGURE 28–31.**

3. A third type moves the rocker arm directly through a hydraulic lifter.

4. In the fourth design, some newer engines have the hydraulic adjustment in the rocker arm and are commonly called **hydraulic lash adjusters (HLA).** ● **SEE FIGURE 28–32.**

CAMSHAFT SPECIFICATIONS

DURATION **Camshaft duration** is the number of degrees of *crankshaft* (not camshaft) rotation for which a valve is lifted off the seat.

The specification for duration can be expressed by several different methods, which must be considered when comparing one cam with another. The three most commonly used methods include:

1. **Duration of valve opening at zero lash (clearance).** If a hydraulic lifter is used, the lash is zero. If a solid lifter is used, this method of expression refers to the duration of the opening of the valve after the specified clearance (lash) between the rocker arm and the valve stem tip has been closed.

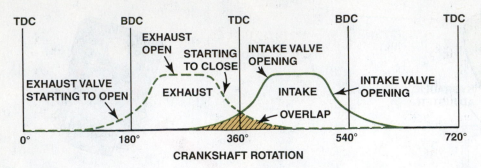

FIGURE 28–33 Graphic representation of a typical camshaft showing the relationship between the intake and exhaust valves. The shaded area represents the overlap period of 100 degrees.

2. **Duration at 0.05 inch lifter (tappet) lift.** Because this specification method eliminates all valve lash clearances and compensates for lifter (tappet) styles, it is the preferred method to use when comparing one camshaft with another. Another method used to specify duration of some factory camshafts is to specify crankshaft duration at 0.01 inch lifter lift. The important point to remember is that the technician must be sure to use equivalent specification methods when comparing or selecting camshafts.

   NOTE: Fractions of a degree are commonly expressed in units called minutes ('). Sixty (60) minutes equal one degree (1°). For example, 45' = 3/4 degree, 30' = 1/2 degree, and 15' = 1/4 degree.

3. **SAE camshaft specifications.** SAE's recommended practice is to measure all valve events at 0.006 inch (0.15 mm) valve lift. This method differs from the usual method used by vehicle or camshaft manufacturers. Whenever comparing valve timing events, be certain that the exact same methods are used on all camshafts being compared.

VALVE OVERLAP
Another camshaft specification is the number of degrees of overlap. **Valve (camshaft) overlap** is the number of degrees of crankshaft rotation during which both intake and exhaust valves are open. In other words, overlap occurs at the beginning of the intake stroke and at the end of the exhaust stoke. All camshafts provide for some overlap to improve engine performance and efficiency, especially at higher engine speeds.

- A lower amount of overlap results in smoother idle and low-engine speed operation, but it also means that a lower amount of power is available at higher engine speeds.
- A greater valve overlap causes rougher engine idle, with decreased power at low speeds, but it also means that high-speed power is improved.

   Example 1: A camshaft with 50 degrees (or less) of overlap may be used in an engine in which low-speed torque and smooth idle qualities are desired. Engines used with overdrive automatic transmissions benefit from the low-speed torque and fuel economy benefits of a small-overlap cam.

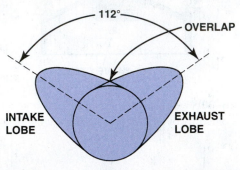

FIGURE 28–34 As the lobe center angle decreases, the overlap increases, with no other changes in the lobe profile lift and duration.

   Example 2: A camshaft with 100 degrees of overlap is more suitable for use with a manual transmission, with which high-RPM power is desired. An engine equipped with a camshaft with over 100 degrees of overlap tends to idle roughly and exhibit poorer low-engine speed response and lowered fuel economy. ● SEE FIGURE 28–33.

CALCULATING VALVE OVERLAP
An engine features a camshaft where the intake valve starts to open at 19 degrees before top dead center (BTDC) and the exhaust valve is open until 22 degrees after top dead center (ATDC).

To determine overlap, total the number of degrees for which the intake valve is open BTDC (19 degrees) and the number of degrees for which the exhaust valve is open ATDC (22 degrees):

Valve overlap = 19 + 22 = 41 degree

LOBE CENTERS
Another camshaft specification that creates some confusion is the angle of the centerlines of the intake and exhaust lobes. This separation between the centerlines of the intake and exhaust lobes is called:

- **Lobe center**
- **Lobe separation**
- **Lobe displacement angle (LDA)**
- **Lobe spread**

   The lob center's measurement is measured in degrees. ● SEE FIGURE 28–34.

   Two camshafts with identical lift and duration can vary greatly in operation because of variation in the angle between the lobe centerlines.

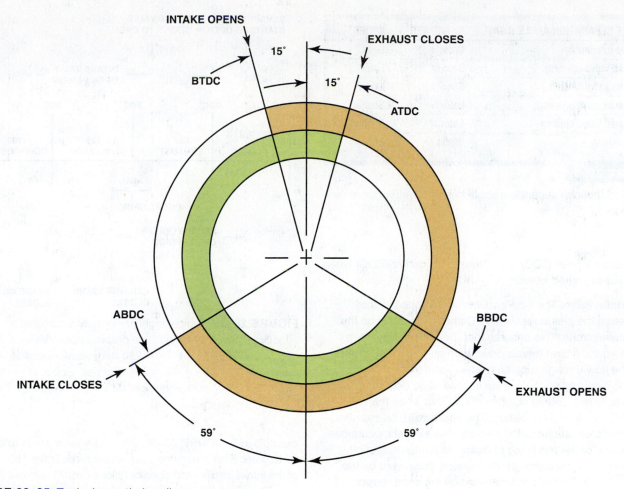

FIGURE 28–35 Typical cam timing diagram.

1. The smaller the angle between the lobe centerlines, the greater the amount of overlap. For example, 108 degrees is a narrower lobe center angle.

2. The larger the angle between the lobe centerlines, the less the amount of overlap. For example, 114 degrees is a wider lobe center angle.

NOTE: Some engines that are equipped with dual overhead camshafts and four valves per cylinder use a different camshaft profile for each of the intake and exhaust valves. For example, one intake valve for each cylinder could have a cam profile designed for maximum low-speed torque. The other intake valve for each cylinder could be designed for higher engine speed power. This results in an engine that is able to produce a high torque over a broad engine speed range.

To find the degree of separation between intake and exhaust lobes of a cam, use the following formula:

$$\frac{(\text{Intake duration} + \text{Exhaust duration})}{4} - \frac{\text{Overlap}}{2}$$

= **Number of degrees of separation**

● **SEE FIGURE 28–35.**

The lobe separation angle can be determined by transferring the intake and exhaust duration and overlap into the formula, as follows:

Intake duration = 15 degrees + 180 degrees + 59 degrees = 254 degrees

Exhaust duration = 59 degrees + 180 degrees + 15 degrees = 254 degrees

Overlap = 15 degrees + 15 degrees = 30 degrees

The lobe separation angle can be calculated by taking the center of the intake lobe use: Intake valve duration plus exhaust valve duration divided by 4 minus the overlap divided by 2.

$$\frac{(254 + 254)}{4} - \frac{30}{2} = \frac{508}{4} - \frac{30}{2}$$

= 127 − 15 = 112 degrees (lobe separation angle)

EFFECTS OF LOBE SEPARATION ON VALVE OPERATION
● **SEE CHART 28–1** for what effect a change in lobe separation angle (LSA) has on engine operation.

CAM TIMING SPECIFICATIONS
Cam timing specifications are stated in terms of the angle of the crankshaft in relation

LOBE SEPARATION ANGLE (LSA)	NARROWER	WIDER
Valve overlap	Greater	Less
Intake valve opening	Sooner	Later
Intake valve closing	Sooner	Later
Exhaust valve opening	Later	Sooner
Exhaust valve closing	Later	Sooner
Idle quality	Worst	Better

CHART 28–1

Changing the lobe separation angle has major effect on engine operation.

to top dead center (TDC) or bottom dead center (BDC) when the valves open and close.

- **Intake valve.** The intake valves should open slightly before the piston reaches TDC and starts down on the intake stroke. This ensures that the valve is fully open when the piston travels downward on the intake stroke. The flow through a partially open valve (especially a valve ground at 45 degrees instead of 30 degrees) is greatly reduced as compared with that when the valve is in its fully open position. The intake valve closes after the piston reaches BDC because the air-fuel mixture has inertia, or the tendency of matter to remain in motion. Even after the piston stops traveling downward on the intake stroke and starts upward on the compression stroke, the inertia of the air-fuel mixture can still be used to draw in additional charge. Typical intake valve specifications are to open at 19 degrees before top dead center (BTDC) and close at 46 degrees after bottom dead center (ABDC).

- **Exhaust valve.** The exhaust valve opens while the piston is traveling down on the power stroke, before the piston starts up on the exhaust stroke. Opening the exhaust valve before the piston starts up on the exhaust stroke ensures that the combustion pressure is released and the exhaust valve is mostly open when the piston starts up. The exhaust valve does not close until after the piston has traveled past TDC and is starting down on the intake stroke. Because of inertia of the exhaust, some of the burned gases continue to flow out the exhaust valve after the piston is past TDC. This can leave a partial vacuum in the combustion chamber to start pulling in the fresh charge. This partial vacuum is called **scavenging** and helps bring in a fresh air-fuel charge into the cylinders. Typical exhaust valve specifications are to open at 49 degrees before bottom dead center (BBDC) and close at 22 degrees after top dead center (ATDC).

CAM TIMING CHART

During the four strokes of a four-stroke cycle gasoline engine, the crankshaft revolves 720 degrees (it makes two complete revolutions [2 × 360 = 720 degrees]). Camshaft specifications are given in crankshaft degrees. In the

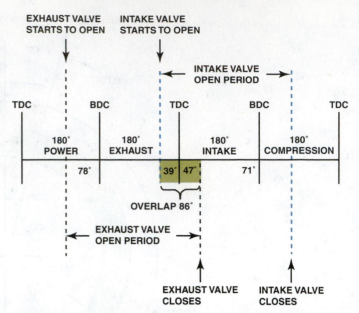

FIGURE 28–36 Typical high-performance camshaft specifications on a straight-line graph. Intake valve duration = 39 + 180 + 71 = 290 degrees. Exhaust valve duration = 7 + 180 + 47 = 234 degrees. Because intake and exhaust valve specifications are different, the camshaft grind is called asymmetrical.

example in ● **FIGURE 28–36,** the intake valve starts to open at 39 degrees BTDC, remains open through the entire 180 degrees of the intake stroke, and does not close until 71 degrees ATDC.

Therefore, the duration of the intake valve is 39 degrees + 180 degrees + 71 degrees, or 290 degrees.

The exhaust valve of the example camshaft opens at 78 degrees BBDC and closes at 47 degrees ATDC. When the exhaust valve specifications are added to the intake valve specifications in the diagram, the overlap period is easily observed. The overlap in the example is 39 degrees + 47 degrees, or 86 degrees. The duration of the exhaust valve opening is 78 degrees + 180 degrees + 47 degrees, or 305 degrees. Because the specifications of this camshaft indicate close to and over 300 degrees of duration, this camshaft should only be used where power is more important than fuel economy.

The usual method of drawing a camshaft timing diagram is in a circle illustrating two revolutions (720 degrees) of the crankshaft. ● **SEE FIGURE 28–37** for an example of a typical camshaft timing diagram for a camshaft with the same specifications as the one illustrated in Figure 28–36.

LIFTERS OR TAPPETS

PURPOSE AND FUNCTION   Valve lifters or tappets follow the contour or shape of the camshaft lobe. This arrangement changes the rotary cam motion to a reciprocating motion in the valve train. Older-style lifters have a relatively flat surface that slides on the cam.

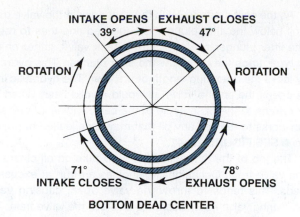

THIS VALVE TIMING DIAGRAM SHOWS TWO
REVOLUTIONS (720°) OF THE CRANKSHAFT

FIGURE 28–37 Typical camshaft valve timing diagram with the same specifications as those shown in Figure 28–36.

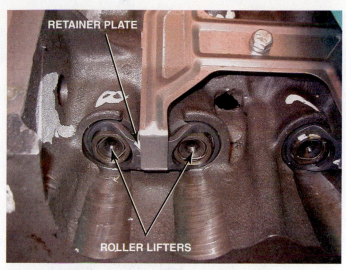

FIGURE 28–39 All roller lifters must use some method to keep the lifter straight and not rotating.

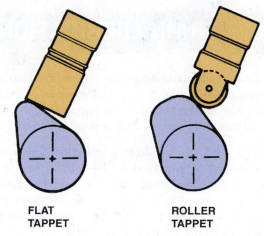

FIGURE 28–38 Older engines used flat-bottom lifters, whereas all engines since the 1990s use roller lifters.

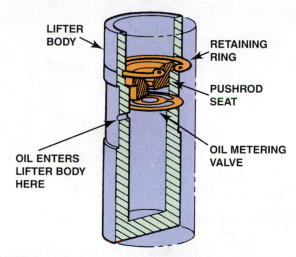

FIGURE 28–40 A cutaway of a flat-bottom solid lifter. Because this type of lifter contains a retaining ring and oil holes, it is sometimes confused with a hydraulic lifter that also contains additional parts. The holes in this lifter are designed to supply oil to the rocker arms through a hollow pushrod.

Most lifters, however, are designed with a roller to follow the cam contour. Roller lifters are used primarily in production engines to reduce valve train friction (by up to 8%). This friction reduction can increase fuel economy and help to offset the greater manufacturing cost. ● **SEE FIGURE 28–38.**

All roller lifters must use a retainer or a guide plate to prevent lifter rotation. The retainer ensures that the roller is kept in line with the cam. ● **SEE FIGURE 28–39.**

VALVE LASH   Valve train clearance is also called **valve lash**, which is needed to help compensate for thermal expansion and wear. Valve train clearance must not be excessive, or it will cause noise or result in premature failure. Two methods are commonly used to make the necessary valve clearance adjustments.

- One involves a **solid valve lifter**, which can be adjusted mechanically at the rocker arm or by changing shims on certain overhead camshaft engines.
- The other involves a lifter with an automatic hydraulic adjustment built into the lifter body, called a **hydraulic valve lifter**.

SOLID LIFTERS   Overhead valve engines with mechanical lifters have an adjustment screw at the pushrod end of the rocker arm or an adjustment nut at the ball pivot. Adjustable pushrods are available for specific applications.

Valve trains using solid lifters must run with some clearance to ensure positive valve closure, regardless of the engine temperature. This clearance is matched by a gradual rise in the cam contour, called a **ramp**. (Hydraulic lifter camshafts do not have this ramp.) The ramp will take up the clearance before the valve begins to open. The camshaft lobe also has a closing ramp to ensure quiet operation.

A lifter is solid in the sense that it transfers motion directly from the cam to the pushrod or valve. Its physical construction is that of a lightweight cylinder, either hollow or with a small-diameter center section and full-diameter ends. In some types that transfer oil through the pushrod, the external appearance is the same as for hydraulic lifters. ● **SEE FIGURE 28–40.**

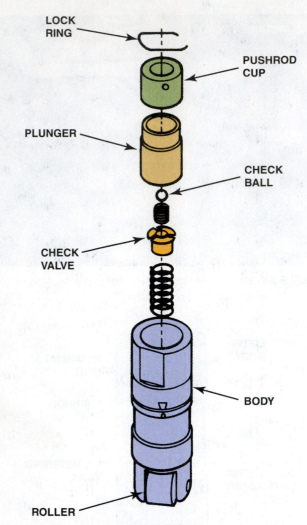

LOCK RING

PUSHROD CUP

PLUNGER

CHECK BALL

CHECK VALVE

BODY

ROLLER

FIGURE 28–41 An exploded view of a hydraulic roller lifter.

HYDRAULIC LIFTERS

A hydraulic lifter consists primarily of a hollow cylinder body enclosing a closely fit hollow plunger, a check valve, and a pushrod cup. Lifters that feed oil up through the pushrod have a metering disc or restrictor valve located under the pushrod cup. Engine oil under pressure is fed through an engine passage to the exterior lifter body. An undercut portion allows the oil under pressure to surround the lifter body. Oil under pressure goes through holes in the undercut section into the center of the plunger. From there, it goes down through the check valve to a clearance space between the bottom of the plunger and the interior bottom of the lifter body. It fills this space with oil at engine pressure. Slight leakage allowance is designed into the lifter so that the air can bleed out and the lifter can leak down if it should become overfilled.

The pushrod fits into a cup in the top, open end of the lifter plunger. Holes in the pushrod cup, pushrod end, and hollow pushrod allow oil to transfer from the lifter piston center, past a metering disc or restrictor valve, and up through the pushrod to the rocker arm. Oil leaving the rocker arm lubricates the rocker arm assembly.

As the cam starts to push the lifter against the valve train, the oil below the lifter plunger is squeezed and tries to return to the lifter plunger center. A lifter check valve, either ball or disc type, traps the oil below the lifter plunger. This hydraulically locks the operating length of the lifter. The hydraulic lifter then opens the engine valve as would a solid lifter. When the lifter returns to the base circle of the cam, engine oil pressure again works to replace any oil that may have leaked out of the lifter. ●**SEE FIGURE 28–41**.

The job of the hydraulic lifter is to take up all clearance in the valve train. Occasionally, engines are run at excessive speeds. This tends to throw the valve open, causing **valve float**. During valve float, clearance exists in the valve train. The hydraulic lifter will take up this clearance as it is designed to do. When this occurs, it will keep the valve from closing on the seat, a process called **pump-up**. Pump-up will not occur when the engine is operated in the speed range for which it is designed.

VALVE TRAIN LUBRICATION

The lifters in an overhead valve (OHV) engine are lubricated through oil passages drilled through the block. The engine oil then flows through the lifter, and up through the hollow pushrod where the oil flows to lubricate and cool the rocker arm, valve and valve spring.

NOTE: The Chrysler 5.7 liter Hemi engine is opposite because the oil is first sent to the rocker arm through passages in the block and head and then *down* through the hollow pushrod to the lifters. In all other engine designs, the oil flows through the lifter and *up* to the rocker arm through the hollow pushrod.

CAMSHAFT LUBRICATION

The camshaft in overhead valve (OHV) engines is lubricated by splash oil thrown up by the movement of the crankshaft counterweights and connecting rods. At low engine speed there is less splash lubrication than occurs at higher engine speeds. This is the major reason why an engine equipped with flat-bottom lifters should be operated at a fast idle of about 2500 RPM during the first 10 minutes of engine operation. The high idle speed helps ensure that there is enough splash oil to properly lubricate and break in a new camshaft and lifters.

VALVE TRAIN PROBLEM DIAGNOSIS

SYMPTOMS

A camshaft with a partially worn lobe is often difficult to diagnose. Sometimes a valve "tick, tick, tick" noise is heard if the cam lobe is worn. The ticking noise can

FIGURE 28–42 The cause of a misfire diagnostic trouble code was discovered to be a pushrod that had worn through the rocker arm on a General Motors 3.1 liter V-6 engine.

PUSHROD PUNCHED THROUGH ROCKER ARM

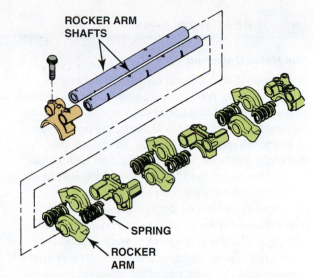

ROCKER ARM SHAFTS

SPRING

ROCKER ARM

FIGURE 28–43 Shaft-mounted rocker arms are held in position by an assortment of springs, spacers, and washers, which should be removed so that the entire shaft can be inspected for wear.

be intermittent, which makes it harder to determine the cause. If the engine has an overhead camshaft (OHC), it is usually relatively easy to remove the cam cover and make a visual inspection of all cam lobes and the rest of the valve train. In an overhead valve (OHV) engine, the camshaft is in the block, where easy visual inspection is not possible. However, it always pays to perform a visual inspection. ● SEE FIGURE 28–42.

VALVE NOISE DIAGNOSIS Valve lifters are often noisy, especially at engine start-up. When the engine is off, some valves are open. The valve spring pressure forces the inner plunger to leak down (oil is forced out of the lifter). Therefore, many vehicle manufacturers consider valve ticking at one-half engine speed after start-up to be normal, especially if the engine is quiet after 10 to 30 seconds. Be sure that the engine is equipped with the correct oil filter, and that the filter has an internal check valve. If in doubt, use an original equipment oil filter. If all of the valves are noisy, check the oil level. If low, the oil may have been **aerated** (air mixed with the oil), which would prevent proper operation of the hydraulic lifter. Aeration can be caused by:

- Low oil pressure, which can also cause all valves to be noisy
- The oil level being too high, which can also cause noisy valve lifters (The crankshaft counterweights create foam as they rotate through the oil. This foam can travel through the oiling systems to the lifters. The foam in the lifters prevents normal operation and allows the valves to make noise.)

If the valves are abnormally noisy, remove the valve cover and use a stethoscope to listen or apply pressure to the rocker

arms to determine which valves or valve train parts may be causing the noise. Check for all of the following items.

- Valve lash too loose
- Worn camshaft lobe
- Dirty, stuck, or worn lifters
- Worn rocker arm (if the vehicle is so equipped)
- Worn rocker arm shaft (● SEE FIGURE 28–43.)
- Worn or bent pushrods (if the vehicle is so equipped)
- Broken or weak valve springs
- Sticking or warped valves

Any of the above can cause the engine to idle roughly, misfire, or even backfire during acceleration.

TECH TIP

The Rotating Pushrod Test

To quickly and easily test whether the camshaft is okay, observe if the pushrods are rotating when the engine is running. This test will work on any overhead valve pushrod engine that uses flat-bottom lifters. Due to the slight angle on the cam lobe and lifter offset, the lifter (and pushrod) should rotate whenever the engine is running. To check, simply remove the rocker arm cover and observe the pushrods when the engine is running. If one or more pushrods are *not* rotating, this camshaft and/or the lifter for that particular valve is worn and needs to be replaced.

The Noisy Camshaft

The owner of an overhead cam 4-cylinder engine complained of a noisy engine. After taking the vehicle to several technicians and getting high estimates to replace the camshaft and followers, the owner tried to find a less expensive solution. Finally, another technician replaced the serpentine drive belt on the front of the engine and "cured" the "camshaft" noise for a fraction of the previous estimates.

Remember, accessory drive belts can often make noises similar to valve or bad bearing types of noises. Many engines have been disassembled and/or overhauled because of a noise that was later determined to be from one of the following:

• Loose or defective accessory drive belt(s)
• Loose torque converter-to-flex plate (drive plate) bolts (nuts)
• Defective mechanical fuel pump (if equipped)

Hot Lifter in 10 Minutes?

A technician working at a shop discovered a noisy (defective) valve lifter on an older Chevrolet small block V-8. Another technician questioned how long it would take to replace the lifter and was told, "Less than an hour"! (The factory flat rate was much longer than one hour.) Ten minutes later the repair technician handed the questioning technician a hot lifter that had been removed from the engine. The lifter was removed using the following steps.

1. The valve cover was removed.
2. The rocker arm and pushrod for the affected valve were removed.
3. The distributor was removed.
4. A strong magnet was fed through the distributor opening into the valley area of the engine. (If the valve lifter is not mushroomed or does not have varnish deposits, the defective lifter can be lifted up and out of the engine; remember, the technician was working on a new vehicle.)
5. A replacement lifter was attached to the magnet and fed down the distributor hole and over the lifter bore.
6. The pushrod was used to help guide the lifter into the lifter bore.

After the lifter preload was adjusted and the valve cover was replaced, the vehicle was returned to the customer in less than one hour.

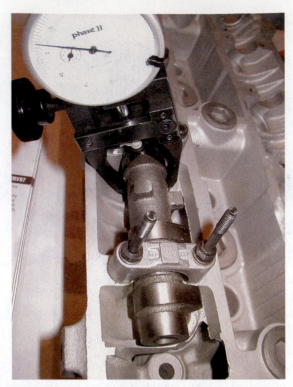

FIGURE 28–44 A dial indicator being used to measure cam lobe height.

CAMSHAFT REMOVAL

CAM-IN-BLOCK ENGINES If the engine is of an overhead valve (OHV) design, the camshaft is usually located in the block above the crankshaft. The timing chain and gears (if the vehicle is so equipped) should be removed after the timing chain (gear) cover is removed. Loosen the rocker arms (or rocker arm shaft) and remove the pushrods. Then remove the valve lifters before removing the camshaft from the block.

NOTE: Be sure to keep the pushrods and rocker arms together if they are to be reused.

MEASURING CAMSHAFTS

TOTAL INDICATOR RUNOUT All camshafts should be checked for straightness by placing them on V-blocks and measuring the cam bearings for runout by using a dial indicator. The maximum **total indicator runout (TIR)** (also called total indicated runout) should be less than 0.002 inch (0.05 mm).

CAM LOBE HEIGHT Sometimes the camshaft lobe height needs to be measured to verify the exact camshaft that is installed in the engine. This can be done by attaching a dial indicator and then slowly rotating the engine while observing the indicator and comparing the measurement to factory specifications. ● **SEE FIGURE 28–44.**

COMMON USAGE	SEAT DURATION (IN DEGREES)	LIFT (IN INCHES)	DURATION @ 0.05 INCH (IN DEGREES)	CHARACTERISTICS
Street	246–254	0.400	192–199	Smooth idle; power = idle to 4500 RPM
Street	262	0.432	207	Broad power range, smooth idle; power = idle to 4800 RPM
Street	266	0.441	211	Good idle for 350 cu. in. engines; power = idle to 5200 RPM
Street/drag strip	272	0.454	217	Lope idle; power = idle to 5500 RPM
Street/race track	290	0.500	239	Shaky idle; power = idle to 5500–6500 RPM

CHART 28–2

A comparison showing the effects of valve timing and lift on engine performance.

SELECTING A CAMSHAFT

DETERMINING ENGINE USAGE For stock rebuilds, use a replacement camshaft with the same specifications as the engine had from the factory for like-new performance. However, if more power is desired, then many engine builders will want to select a different camshaft than the stock version.

A common mistake of beginning engine builders is to install a camshaft with too much duration for the size of the engine. This extended duration of valve opening results in a rough idle and low manifold vacuum, which causes lack of low-speed power.

For example, a hydraulic cam with duration of greater than 225 degrees at 0.05 inch lift for a 350 cu. inch engine will usually not be suitable for street driving. **Seat duration** is the number of degrees of crankshaft rotation that the valve is off the seat. ● SEE CHART 28–2.

Check with the camshaft manufacturer for their recommendation for the best camshaft to use. Be prepared to furnish them with the following information.

- Engine make and size
- Weight of the vehicle
- Type of transmission
- Final drive gear ratio
- Intended use of the vehicle

VARIABLE VALVE TIMING

PURPOSE AND FUNCTION Conventional camshafts are permanently synchronized to the crankshaft so that they operate the valves at a specific point in each combustion cycle. In an engine, the intake valve opens slightly before the piston reaches the top of the cylinder and closes about 60 degrees after the piston reaches the bottom of the stroke on every cycle, regardless of the engine speed or load.

On newer engines, the camshaft can have the capability of a variable valve-timing feature that changes the camshaft specifications during different operating modes. For example, many vehicle manufacturers use three basic types of variable valve timing.

1. Exhaust camshaft variable action only on overhead camshaft engines, such as on many inline 4- and 6-cylinder engines
2. Intake and exhaust camshaft variable action on both camshafts used in many engines
3. Changing the relationship of the camshaft to the crankshaft, in overhead valve cam-in-block engines

Variable-cam timing allows the valves to be operated at different points in the combustion cycle, to improve performance. ● SEE CHART 28–3.

Variable camshaft timing is used on engines from the following vehicle manufacturers.

- General Motors 4-, 5-, 6-, and 8-cylinder engines
- BMW
- Chrysler
- Ford
- Nissan/Infinity
- Toyota/Lexus

On a system that controls the intake camshaft only, the camshaft timing is advanced at low engine speed, closing the intake valves earlier to improve low RPM torque. At high engine speeds, the camshaft is retarded by using engine oil pressure against a helical gear to rotate the camshaft. When the camshaft is retarded, the intake valve closing is delayed, improving cylinder filling at higher engine speeds. Variable cam timing can be used to control exhaust cam timing only. Engines that use this system, such as the 4.2 liter GM inline 6-cylinder engines, can eliminate the exhaust gas recirculation (EGR) valve because the computer can close the exhaust valve sooner than normal, trapping some exhaust gases in the combustion chamber and therefore eliminating the need for an EGR valve. Some engines use variable camshaft timing on both intake and exhaust cylinder cams.

DRIVING CONDITION	CHANGE IN CAMSHAFT POSITION	OBJECTIVE	RESULT
Idle	No change	Minimize valve overlap	Stabilize idle speed
Light engine load	Retard valve timing	Decrease valve overlap	Stable engine output
Medium engine load	Advance valve timing	Increase valve overlap	Better fuel economy with lower emissions
Low to medium RPM with heavy load	Advance valve timing	Advance intake valve closing	Improve low to midrange torque
High RPM with heavy load	Retard valve timing	Retard intake valve closing	Improve engine output

CHART 28–3

The purpose for varying the cam timing includes providing for more engine torque and power over a wide engine speed and load range.

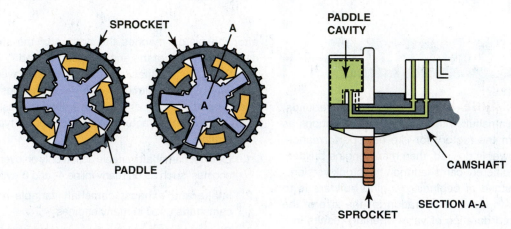

FIGURE 28–45 Camshaft rotation during advance and retard.

OPERATION The camshaft position actuator **oil control valve (OCV)** directs oil from the oil feed in the head to the appropriate camshaft position actuator oil passages. There is one OCV for each camshaft position actuator. The OCV is sealed and mounted to the front cover. The ported end of the OCV is inserted into the cylinder head with a sliding fit. A filter screen protects each OCV oil port from any contamination in the oil supply.

The camshaft position actuator is mounted to the front end of the camshaft, and the timing notch in the nose of the camshaft aligns with the dowel pin in the camshaft position actuator to ensure proper cam timing and camshaft position actuator oil hole alignment. ● **SEE FIGURE 28–45.**

OHV VARIABLE TIMING The variable valve timing system uses an electronically controlled, hydraulic gear-driven cam phaser that can alter the relationship of the camshaft from 15 degrees retard to 25 degrees advance (40 degrees overall) relative to the crankshaft. By using **variable valve timing (VVT)**, engineers were able to eliminate the EGR valve. The VVT also works in conjunction with an active intake manifold that gives the engine a broader torque curve.

A valve in the intake manifold creates a longer path for intake air at low speeds, improving combustion efficiency and torque output. At higher speed, the valve opens and creates a shorter air path for maximum power production. ● **SEE FIGURE 28–46.**

Varying the exhaust and/or the intake camshaft position allows for reduced exhaust emissions and improved performance. ● **SEE CHART 28–4.**

By varying the exhaust cam phasing, vehicle manufacturers are able to meet newer NOx reduction standards and eliminate the exhaust gas recirculation (EGR) valve. Also, by using exhaust cam phasing, the powertrain control module (PCM) can close the exhaust valves sooner than usual, thereby trapping some exhaust gases in the combustion chamber. Manufacturers use one or two actuators that allow the camshaft piston to change by up to 50 degrees in relation to the crankshaft position.

The two types of cam phasing devices commonly used are:

- **Spline phaser.** Used on overhead camshaft (OHC) engines
- **Vane phaser.** Used on overhead camshaft (OHC) and overhead valve (OHV) cam-in-block engines

SPLINE PHASER SYSTEM The spline phaser system is also called the **valve cam phaser (VCP)** and consists of the following components.

- Engine control module (ECM)
- Four-way pulse-width-modulated (PWM) control valve

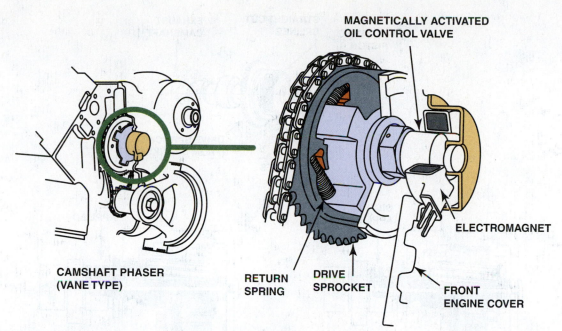

CAMSHAFT PHASER
(VANE TYPE)

RETURN
SPRING

DRIVE
SPROCKET

FRONT
ENGINE COVER

ELECTROMAGNET

MAGNETICALLY ACTIVATED
OIL CONTROL VALVE

FIGURE 28–46 The camshaft is rotated in relation to the crankshaft by the PCM to provide changes in valve timing.

CAMSHAFT PHASING CHANGED	IMPROVES
Exhaust cam phasing	Reduces exhaust emissions
Exhaust cam phasing	Increases fuel economy (reduced pumping losses)
Intake cam phasing	Increases low-speed torque
Intake cam phasing	Increases high-speed power

CHART 28–4

Changing the exhaust cam timing mainly helps reduce exhaust emissions, whereas changing the intake cam timing mainly helps the engine produce increased power and torque.

- Cam phaser assembly
- Camshaft position (CMP) sensor

●SEE FIGURE 28–47.

SPLINE PHASER SYSTEM OPERATION
On most engines, the pulse-width-modulated (PWM) control valve is located on the front of the cylinder head. Oil pressure is regulated by the control valve and then directed to the ports in the cylinder head leading to the camshaft and cam phaser position. The cam phaser is located on the exhaust cams and is part of the exhaust cam sprocket. When the PCM commands an increase in oil pressure, the piston is moved inside the cam phaser and rides along the helical splines, which compresses the coil spring. This movement causes the cam phaser gear and the camshaft to move in an opposite direction, thereby retarding the cam timing. ●SEE FIGURE 28–48.

 TECH TIP

Check the Screen on the Control Valve If There are Problems

If a NOx emission failure at a state inspection occurs or a diagnostic trouble code is set related to the cam timing, remove the control valve and check for a clogged oil screen. A lack of regular oil changes can cause the screen to become clogged, thereby preventing proper operation. A rough idle is a common complaint because the spring may not be able to return the camshaft to the idle position after a long highway trip. ●SEE FIGURE 28–49.

NOTE: **A unique cam-within-a-cam is used on 2008 and newer Dodge Viper V-10 OHV engines. This design allows the exhaust lobes to be moved by up to 36 degrees to improve idle quality and reduction of exhaust emissions.**

VANE PHASER SYSTEM ON AN OVERHEAD CAMSHAFT ENGINE
The vane phaser system used on overhead camshaft (OHC) engines uses a camshaft piston (CMP) sensor on each camshaft. Each camshaft has its own actuator and its own *oil control valve* (OCV). Instead of using a piston along a helical spline, the vane phaser uses a rotor with four vanes, which is connected to the end of the camshaft. The rotor is located inside the stator, which is bolted to the cam sprocket. The stator and rotor are not connected. Oil pressure is

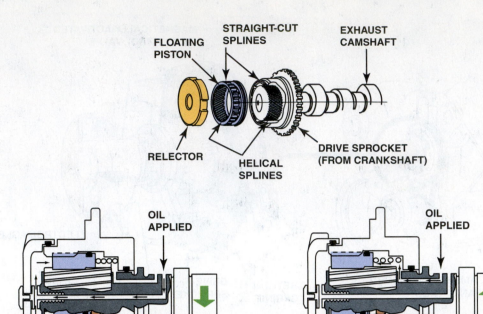

FIGURE 28–47 Spline cam phaser assembly.

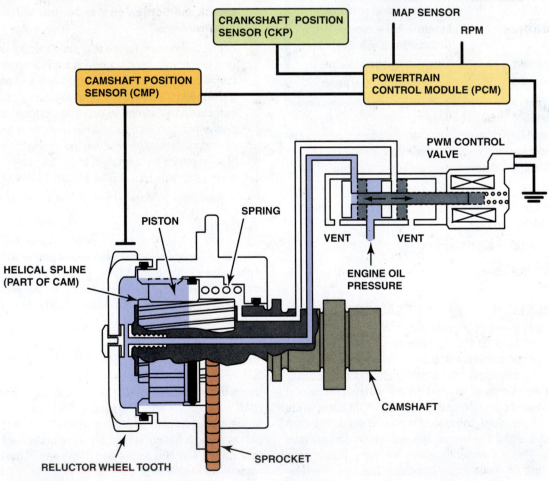

FIGURE 28–48 A spline phaser.

FIGURE 28–49 The screen(s) protect the solenoid valve from dirt and debris that can cause the valve to stick. This fault can set a P0017 diagnostic trouble code (crankshaft position/camshaft position correlation error).

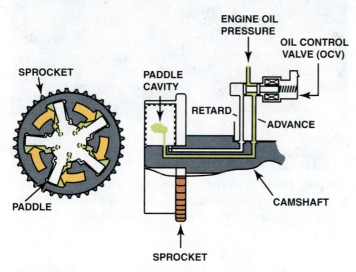

FIGURE 28–50 A vane phaser is used to move the camshaft, using changes in oil pressure from the oil control valve.

controlled on both sides of the vanes of the rotor, which creates a hydraulic link between the two parts. The oil control valve varies the balance of pressure on either side of the vanes and thereby controls the position of the camshaft. A return spring is used under the reluctor of the phaser to help return it to the home or zero degrees position. ● **SEE FIGURE 28–50.**

MAGNETICALLY CONTROLLED VANE PHASER On this type, the PCM controls a magnetically controlled vane phaser by using a 12 volt pulse-width-modulated (PWM) signal

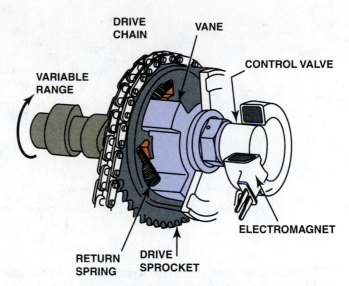

FIGURE 28–51 A magnetically controlled vane phaser.

to an electromagnet, which operates the oil control valve (OCV). A magnetically controlled vane phaser is used on many double overhead camshaft engines on both the intake and exhaust camshafts. The OCV directs pressurized engine oil to either advance or retard chambers of the camshaft actuator to change the camshaft position in relation to the crankshaft position. ● **SEE FIGURE 28–51.**

The following occurs when the pulse width is changed.

- **0% pulse width.** The oil is directed to the advance chamber of the exhaust camshaft actuator and the retard chamber of the intake camshaft activator.
- **50% pulse width.** The computer is holding the camshaft steady in the desired position.
- **100% pulse width.** The oil is directed to the retard chamber of the exhaust camshaft actuator and the advance chamber of the intake camshaft actuator.

The cam phasing is continuously variable with a range from 40 degrees for the intake camshaft and 50 degrees for the exhaust camshaft. The ECM uses the following sensors to determine the best position of the camshaft for maximum power and lowest possible exhaust emissions.

- Engine speed (RPM)
- MAP sensor
- Crankshaft position (CKP)
- Camshaft position (CMP)
- Barometric pressure (BARO)

CAM-IN-BLOCK ENGINE CAM PHASER Overhead valve engines that use a cam-in-block design use a magnetically controlled cam phaser to vary the camshaft in relation to the crankshaft. This type of phaser is not capable of changing the duration of valve opening or valve lift.

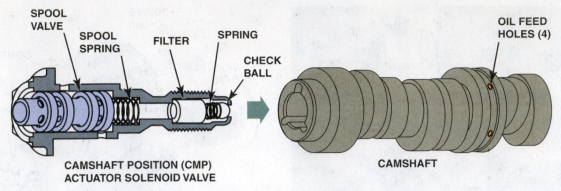

FIGURE 28–52 A camshaft position actuator used in a cam-in-block engine.

Inside the camshaft actuator is a rotor with vanes that are attached to the camshaft. Oil pressure is supplied to the vanes, which causes the camshaft to rotate in relation to the crankshaft. The camshaft actuator solenoid valve directs the flow of oil to either the advance or retard side vanes of the actuator. ● SEE FIGURE 28–52.

The ECM sends a pulse-width-modulated (PWM) signal to the camshaft actuator magnet. The movement of the pintle is used to direct oil flow to the actuator. The higher the duty cycle, the greater the movement in the valve position and change in camshaft timing.

NOTE: When oil pressure drops to zero when the engine stops, a spring-loaded locking pin is used to keep the camshaft locked to prevent noise at engine start. When the engine starts, oil pressure releases the locking pin.

VARIABLE LIFT AND CYLINDER DEACTIVATION SYSTEMS

VARIABLE VALVE LIFT SYSTEMS Variable camshafts include the system used by Honda/Acura, called **variable valve timing and lift electronic control (VTEC).** This system uses two different camshafts for low and high RPM. When the engine is operating at idle and speeds below about 4000 RPM, the valves are opened by camshafts that are optimized by maximum torque and fuel economy. When engine speed reaches a predetermined speed, depending on the exact make and model, the computer turns on a solenoid, which opens a spool valve. When the spool valve opens, engine oil pressure pushes against pins that lock the three intake rocker arms together. With the rocker arms lashed, the valves must follow the profile of the high RPM cam lobe in the center. This process of switching from the low-speed camshaft profile to the high-speed profile takes about 100 milliseconds (0.1 sec). ● SEE FIGURES 28–53 AND 28–54.

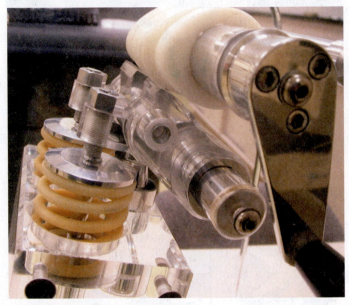

FIGURE 28–53 A plastic mockup of a Honda VTEC system that uses two different camshaft profiles—one for low-speed engine operation and the other for high speed.

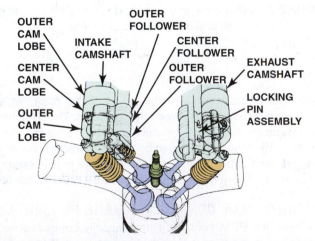

FIGURE 28–54 Engine oil pressure is used to switch cam lobes on a VTEC system.

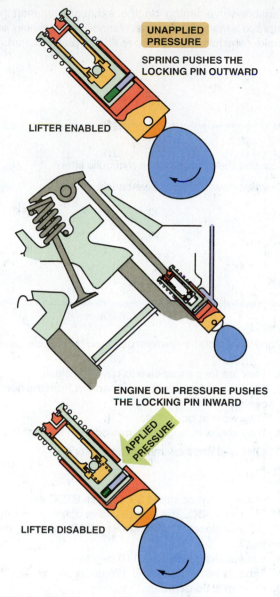

UNAPPLIED PRESSURE

SPRING PUSHES THE LOCKING PIN OUTWARD

LIFTER ENABLED

ENGINE OIL PRESSURE PUSHES THE LOCKING PIN INWARD

APPLIED PRESSURE

LIFTER DISABLED

FIGURE 28–55 Oil pressure applied to the locking pin causes the inside of the lifter to freely move inside the outer shell of the lifter, thereby keeping the valve closed.

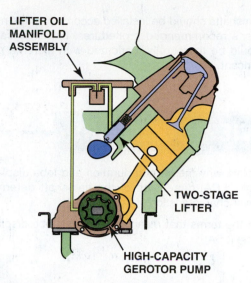

LIFTER OIL MANIFOLD ASSEMBLY

TWO-STAGE LIFTER

HIGH-CAPACITY GEROTOR PUMP

FIGURE 28–56 Active fuel management includes many different components and changes to the oiling system, which makes routine oil changes even more important on engines equipped with this system.

CYLINDER DEACTIVATION SYSTEMS

Some engines are designed to operate on four of eight cylinders, or three of six cylinders, during low load conditions to improve fuel economy.

The powertrain control module (PCM) monitors engine speed, coolant temperature, throttle position, and load, and determines when to deactivate cylinders. The key to this process is the use of two-stage hydraulic valve lifters. In normal operation, the inner and outer lifter sleeves are held together by a pin and operate as an assembly. When the computer determines that the cylinder can be deactivated, oil pressure is delivered to a passage, which depresses the pin and allows the outer portion of the lifter to follow the contour of the cam while the inner portion remains stationary, keeping the valve closed. The electronic operation is achieved through the use of the lifter oil manifold containing solenoids to control the oil flow, which is used to activate or deactivate the cylinders. General Motors once called this system "displacement on demand (DOD)," but now calls it "active fuel management." Chrysler calls this a "multiple displacement system (MDS)." ● **SEE FIGURES 28–55 AND 28–56.**

SUMMARY

1. The camshaft rotates at one-half the crankshaft speed.

2. The pushrods should be rotating while the engine is running if the camshaft and lifters are okay.

3. On overhead valve engines, the camshaft is usually placed in the block above the crankshaft. The lobes of the camshaft are usually lubricated by splash lubrication.

4. Silent chains are quieter than roller chains but tend to stretch with use.

5. Valve lift is usually expressed in decimal inches and represents the distance that the valve is lifted off the valve seat.

6. In many engines, camshaft lobe lift is transferred to the tip of the valve stem to open the valve by the use of a rocker arm or follower.

7. Pushrods transfer camshaft lobe movement upward from the camshaft to the rocker arm.

8. Camshaft duration is the number of degrees of crankshaft rotation for which the valve is lifted off the seat.

9. Valve overlap is the number of crankshaft degrees for which both intake and exhaust valves are open at the same time.

10. Camshafts should be installed according to the manufacturer's recommended procedures. Flat lifter camshafts should be thoroughly lubricated with extreme pressure lubricant.

11. Variable valve timing on the exhaust camshaft helps improve exhaust emissions. Variable valve timing of the intake camshaft helps improve engine power output.

REVIEW QUESTIONS

1. Explain why the lift and duration and lobe displacement angle (LDA) dimension of the camshaft determine the power characteristics of the engine.

2. List the terms that mean the same as lobe displacement angle (LDA).

3. Describe the operation of a hydraulic lifter.

4. Describe how variable valve timing works.

CHAPTER QUIZ

1. The camshaft makes _____ for every revolution of the crankshaft.
   a. One-quarter revolution
   b. One-half revolution
   c. One revolution
   d. Two revolutions

2. Flat-bottom valve lifters rotate during operation because of the _____ of the camshaft.
   a. Taper of the lobe
   b. Thrust plate
   c. Chain tensioner
   d. Bearings

3. If lift and duration remain constant and the lobe center angle decreases, then _____.
   a. The valve overlap decreases
   b. The effective lift increases
   c. The effective duration increases
   d. The valve overlap increases

4. Which timing chain type is also called a "silent chain"?
   a. Roller
   b. Morse
   c. Flat link
   d. Both b and c

5. Two technicians are discussing variable valve timing. Technician A says that changing the exhaust valve timing helps reduce exhaust emissions. Technician B says that changing the intake valve timing helps increase low-speed torque. Which technician is correct?
   a. Technician A only
   b. Technician B only
   c. Both Technicians A and B
   d. Neither Technician A nor B

6. Many technicians always use new pushrods because _____.
   a. They are less expensive to buy than clean
   b. All of the dirt cannot be cleaned out from the hollow center
   c. They wear at both ends
   d. They shrink in length if removed from an engine

7. A DOHC V-6 has how many camshafts?
   a. 4
   b. 3
   c. 2
   d. 1

8. The intake valve opens at 39 degrees BTDC and closes at 71 degrees ABDC. The exhaust valve opens at 78 degrees BBDC and closes at 47 degrees ATDC. Which answer is correct?
   a. Intake valve duration is 110 degrees.
   b. Exhaust valve duration is 125 degrees.
   c. Overlap is 86 degrees.
   d. Both a and b

9. Hydraulic valve lifters can make a ticking noise when the engine is running if _____.
   a. The valve lash is too close
   b. The valve lash is too loose
   c. The lobe centerline is over 110 degrees
   d. Both a and c

10. Hydraulic lifters or hydraulic lash adjusters (HLA) may not bleed down properly and cause an engine miss if _____.
    a. The engine oil is 1 quart low
    b. The wrong API-rated engine oil is used
    c. The wrong SAE-rated engine oil is used
    d. Both a and b

chapter 29

PISTONS, RINGS, AND CONNECTING RODS

LEARNING OBJECTIVES: After studying this chapter, the reader should be able to: • Explain the purpose and function of pistons and piston construction. • Discuss piston pins and piston pin retaining methods. • Explain piston rings and construction of piston rings. • Discuss connecting rods and connecting rod service. • Explain piston and rod assembly and piston ring service.

KEY TERMS: • Back clearance 426 • Balancing bosses (pads) 429 • Barrel face ring 428 • Bleed hole 431 • Blowby 427 • Cam ground 422 • Compression rings 426 • Connecting rod bearing journal 420 • Crankpin 420 • Crank throw 420 • Double knock 424 • Ductile iron 428 • Freewheeling 422 • Full floating 424 • Grooves 420 • Heat dams 423 • Hypereutectic 421 • Interference fit 425 • Lands 420 • Lock ring 424 • Major thrust surface 423 • Oil control ring 426 • Piston 419 • Piston pin 419 • Piston ring expander 435 • Piston rings 420 • Positive twist ring 427 • Reverse twist ring 428 • Ring gap 427 • Scraper ring 428 • Side clearance 426 • Skirt 420 • Slipper skirt 422 • Spit hole 430 • Struts 423 • Taper face ring 427 • Wrist pin 419

PISTONS

PURPOSE AND FUNCTION All engine power is developed by burning fuel mixed with air in the combustion chamber. Heat from the combustion causes the burned gas to increase in pressure. The force of this pressure is converted into useful work through the piston, connecting rod, and crankshaft. Therefore, the piston serves three purposes.

1. **Transfers force.** The piston transfers the force of combustion to the crankshaft through the connecting rod.

2. **Seals the combustion chamber.** The piston and piston rings seal the compressed air during the compression stroke and the combustion gases on the power stroke.

3. **Conducts heat.** The piston transfers heat from the combustion chamber to the cylinder walls through the piston rings and to the engine oil through the piston.

PARTS INVOLVED The **piston** forms a movable bottom to the combustion chamber. ●**SEE FIGURE 29–1.**

The piston is attached to the connecting rod with a **piston pin,** also called a **wrist pin.** The piston pin is allowed to have a rocking movement because of a swivel joint at the piston end of the connecting rod. The crankshaft changes the up-and-down (reciprocating) motion of the pistons into rotary motion.

FIGURE 29–1 The piston seals the bottom of the combustion chamber and is attached to a connecting rod.

The connecting rod is connected to a part of the crankshaft called a **crank throw, crankpin,** or **connecting rod bearing journal.**

Piston rings seal the small space between the piston and cylinder wall, keeping the pressure above the piston. When the pressure builds up in the combustion chamber, it pushes on the piston. The piston, in turn, pushes on the piston pin and upper end of the connecting rod. The lower end of the connecting rod pushes on the crank throw. This provides the force to turn the crankshaft. As the crankshaft turns, it develops inertia. *Inertia is the force that causes the crankshaft to continue rotating.* This action will bring the piston back to its original position, where it will be ready for the next power stroke. While the engine is running, the combustion cycle keeps repeating as the piston reciprocates (moves up and down) and the crankshaft rotates.

PISTON OPERATION When the engine is running, the piston starts at the top of the cylinder. As it moves downward, it accelerates until it reaches a maximum velocity slightly before it is halfway down. The piston comes to a stop at the bottom of the cylinder at 180 degrees of crankshaft rotation. During the next 180 degrees of crankshaft rotation, the piston moves upward. It accelerates to reach a maximum velocity slightly above the halfway point and then comes to a stop at the top of the stroke. Thus, the piston starts, accelerates, and stops twice in each crankshaft revolution.

NOTE: A typical piston in an engine operating at 4000 RPM accelerates from 0 to 60 mph (97 km/h) in about 0.004 second (4 ms) as it travels about halfway down the cylinder.

This reciprocating action of the piston produces large *inertia forces*. Inertia is the force that causes a part that is stopped to stay stopped or a part that is in motion to stay in motion. The lighter the piston can be made, the less inertia force that is developed. Less inertia will allow higher engine operating speeds. For this reason, pistons are made to be as light as possible while still having the strength that is needed.

The piston operates with its top or head exposed to the hot combustion gases, whereas the skirt contacts the relatively cool cylinder wall. This results in a temperature difference of about 275°F (147°C) between the top and bottom of the piston.

PISTON CONSTRUCTION

PISTON RING GROOVES Piston ring **grooves** are located between the piston head and skirt. The width of the grooves, the width of the **lands** between the ring grooves, and the number of rings are major factors in determining minimum piston height. The outside diameter of the lands is about 0.02 to 0.04 inch (0.5 to 1 mm) smaller than the **skirt** diameter.
● **SEE FIGURE 29–2.**

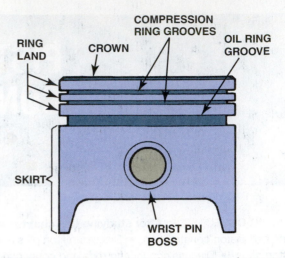

FIGURE 29–2 All pistons share the same parts in common.

TECH TIP

Piston Weight Is Important!

All pistons in an engine should weigh the same to help ensure a balanced engine. Piston weight becomes a factor when changing pistons. Most aluminum pistons range in weight from 10 to 30 ounces (280 to 850 grams) (1 oz = 28.35 g). *A typical paper clip weighs 1 g.* If the cylinder has been bored, larger replacement pistons are obviously required. If the replacement pistons weigh more, this puts additional inertia loads on the rod bearings. Therefore, to help prevent rod bearing failure on an overhauled engine, the replacement pistons should not weigh more than the original pistons.

CAUTION: Some less expensive replacement cast pistons or high-performance forged pistons are much heavier than the stock pistons, even in the stock bore size. This means that the crankshaft may need heavy metal added to the counterweights of the crankshaft for the engine to be balanced.

For the same reason, if one piston is being replaced, all pistons should be replaced or at least checked and corrected to ensure the same weight.

● **SEE FIGURE 29–3** for an example of how to measure the diameter of a piston.

CAST PISTONS Cast aluminum pistons usually are made using *gravity die casting*. In this process, molten aluminum alloy and about 10% silicon are poured into a mold. The silicon is used to increase the strength and help control the expansion of the piston when it gets hot. Other metals used in the aluminum

FIGURE 29–3 A piston diameter is measured across the thrust surfaces.

FIGURE 29–4 A cast piston showing the sprues which were used to fill the mold with molten aluminum alloy.

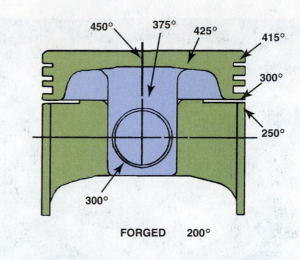

FORGED   200°

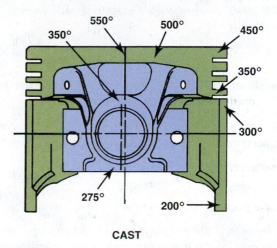

CAST

FIGURE 29–5 The top of the piston temperature can be 100°F (38°C) lower on a forged piston compared to a cast piston.

alloy include copper, nickel, manganese, and magnesium. ● SEE FIGURE 29–4.

HYPEREUTECTIC PISTONS
A standard cast aluminum piston contains about 9% to 12% silicon and is called a *eutectic* piston. To add strength, the silicon content is increased to about 16%, and the resulting piston is called a **hypereutectic** piston. Other advantages of a hypereutectic piston are its 25% weight reduction and lower expansion rate. The disadvantage of hypereutectic pistons is their higher cost, because they are more difficult to cast and machine.

Hypereutectic pistons are commonly used in the after-market and as original equipment in many turbocharged and supercharged engines.

FORGED PISTONS
High-performance engines need pistons with added strength. Forged pistons have a dense grain structure and are very strong. Forged pistons are often used in turbocharged or supercharged engines. Because forged pistons are less porous than cast pistons, they conduct heat more quickly. Forged pistons generally run about 20% cooler than cast pistons. ● SEE FIGURE 29–5.

PISTON HEAD DESIGNS
Because the piston head forms a portion of the combustion chamber, its shape is vital to the combustion process. Many newer engines have *flat-top* pistons. Some of these flat-top pistons come so close to the cylinder head that *recesses* are cut in the piston top for valve clearance. Pistons used in high-powered engines may have raised domes or *pop-ups* on the piston heads. These are used to increase the compression ratio. Pistons used in other engines may be provided with a depression or a *dish*. The varying depths of the dish provide different compression ratios required by different engine models.

NOTE: Newer engines do not use valve reliefs because this requires that the thickness of the top of the piston be increased to provide the necessary strength. The thicker the top of the piston, the lower down from the top the top piston ring sits. To reduce unburned hydrocarbon (HC) exhaust emissions, engineers attempt to place the top piston ring as close to the top of the piston as possible to prevent the unburned fuel from being

FIGURE 29–6 Valve reliefs are used to provide valve clearance.

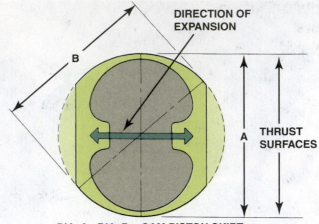

DIA. A - DIA. B = CAM PISTON SKIRT

FIGURE 29–7 Piston cam shape. The largest diameter is across the thrust surfaces and perpendicular to the piston pin (labeled A).

trapped (and not burned) between the top of the piston and the top of the top piston ring.

Recesses machined or cast into the tops of the pistons for valve clearance are commonly called:

- Eyebrows
- Valve reliefs
- Valve pockets

The depth of the eyebrows has a major effect on the compression ratio and is necessary to provide clearance for the valves if the timing belt or chain of an overhead camshaft engine should break. Without the eyebrows, the pistons could hit the valves near TDC if the valves are not operating (closing) because of nonrotation of the camshaft. If an engine is designed not to have the pistons hitting the valves, if the timing belt or chain breaks, the engine is called **freewheeling.** ●**SEE FIGURE 29–6.**

SLIPPER SKIRT PISTONS   A **slipper skirt** design piston is shorter on the two sides that are not thrust surfaces. Advantages of using a slipper skirt design include:

- Lighter weight
- Allows for a shorter overall engine height, because the crankshaft counterweights can be closer to the piston when they are at the bottom of the stroke

Most engines today use a slipper skirt piston design.

CAM GROUND PISTONS   Aluminum pistons expand when they get hot. A method of expansion control was devised using a **cam ground** piston skirt. With this design, the piston thrust surfaces closely fit the cylinder, and the piston pin boss diameter is fitted loosely. As the cam ground piston is heated, it expands along the piston pin so that it becomes nearly round at its normal operating temperatures. A cam ground piston skirt is illustrated in ●**FIGURE 29–7.**

FIGURE 29–8 A moly graphite coating on this piston from a General Motors 3800 V-6 engine helps to prevent piston scuffing.

PISTON FINISH   The finish on piston skirts varies with the manufacturer, but all are designed to help reduce scuffing. Scuffing is a condition where the metal of the piston actually contacts the cylinder wall. When the piston stops at the top of the cylinder, welds or transfer of metal from one part to the other can take place. Scuffing can be reduced by coating the piston skirts with tin 0.0005 inch (0.0125 mm) thick or a moly graphite coating. ●**SEE FIGURE 29–8.**

PISTON HEAD SIZE   The top or head of the piston is smaller in diameter than the rest of the piston. The top of the piston is exposed to the most heat and therefore tends to expand more than the rest of the piston. ●**SEE FIGURE 29–9.**

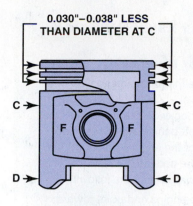

0.030"–0.038" LESS THAN DIAMETER AT C

DIAMETERS AT (C) AND (D) CAN BE EQUAL OR DIAMETER AT (D) CAN BE 0.0015" GREATER THAN (C).

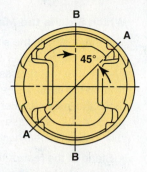

THE ELLIPTICAL SHAPE OF THE PISTON SKIRT SHOULD BE 0.010"–0.012" LESS AT DIAMETER (A) THAN ACROSS THE THRUST FACES AT DIAMETER (B). MEASUREMENT IS MADE 1/8" BELOW LOWER RING GROOVE.

FIGURE 29–9 The head of the piston is smaller in diameter than the skirt of the piston to allow it to expand when the engine is running.

Most pistons have horizontal separation slots that act as **heat dams.** These slots reduce heat transfer from the hot piston head to the lower skirt. This, in turn, keeps the skirt temperature lower to reduce skirt expansion. Because the slot is placed in the oil ring groove, it can be used for oil drainback and expansion control.

PISTON STRUT INSERTS
A major development in expansion control occurred when the piston aluminum was cast around two stiff steel **struts.**

- The struts add strength to the piston in the piston pin area where additional strength is needed.
- The struts help control thermal expansion.
- Pistons with steel strut inserts allow good piston-to-cylinder wall clearance at normal temperatures. At the same time, they allow the cold operating clearance to be as small as 0.0005 inch (one-half thousandth of an inch) (0.0127 mm). This small clearance will prevent cold piston slap and noise. A typical piston expansion control strut is visible in ● **FIGURE 29–10.**

PISTON PINS

TERMINOLOGY
Piston pins are used to attach the piston to the connecting rod. Piston pins are also known as *wrist pins* or *gudgeon pins*, a British term. The piston pin transfers the force produced by combustion chamber pressures and piston inertia to the connecting rod. The piston pin is made

STEEL STRUT

FIGURE 29–10 Steel struts cast inside the piston help control expansion and add strength to the piston pin area.

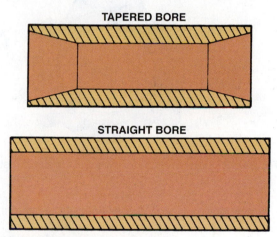

TAPERED BORE

STRAIGHT BORE

FIGURE 29–11 Most piston pins are hollow to reduce weight and have a straight bore. Some pins have a tapered bore to reinforce the pin.

from high-quality steel in the shape of a tube to make it both strong and light. Sometimes, the interior hole of the piston pin is tapered, so it is large at the ends and small in the middle of the pin. This gives the pin strength that is proportional to the location of the load placed on it. A double-taper hole such as this is more expensive to manufacture, so it is used only where its weight advantage merits the extra cost. ● **SEE FIGURE 29–11.**

PISTON PIN OFFSET
Some piston pin holes are not centered in the piston. They are located toward the **major thrust surface,** approximately 0.062 inch (1.57 mm) from the piston centerline, as shown in ● **FIGURE 29–12.**

Pin offset is designed to reduce piston slap and the noise that can result as the large end of the connecting rod crosses over top dead center.

- **Minor thrust.** The minor thrust side of the piston head has a greater area than the major side. This is caused by the pin offset. As the piston moves up in the cylinder on

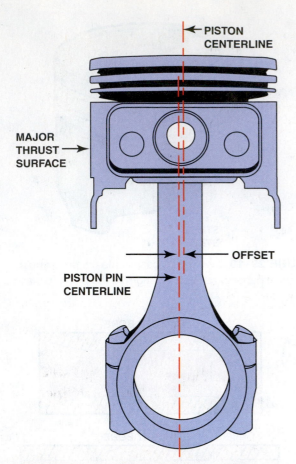

PISTON CENTERLINE

MAJOR THRUST SURFACE

OFFSET

PISTON PIN CENTERLINE

FIGURE 29–12 Piston pin offset toward the major thrust surface.

? **FREQUENTLY ASKED QUESTION**

Which Side Is the Major Thrust Side?

The thrust side is the side the rod points to when the piston is on the power stroke. Any V-block engine (V-6 or V-8) that rotates clockwise is viewed from the front of the engine. The left bank piston thrust side faces the inside (center) of the engine. The right bank piston thrust side faces the outside of the block. This rule, called the *left-hand rule*, states the following:

- Stand at the rear of the engine and point toward the front of the engine.
- Raise your thumb straight up, indicating the top of the engine.
- Point your other fingers toward the right. This represents the major thrust side of the piston.

Always assemble the connecting rods onto the rods so that the notch or "F" on the piston is pointing toward the front of the engine and the oil squirt hole on the connecting rod is pointing toward the major thrust side with your left hand.

the compression stroke, it rides against the minor thrust surface. When compression pressure becomes high enough, the greater head area on the minor side causes the piston to cock slightly in the cylinder. This keeps the *top* of the minor thrust surface on the cylinder. It forces the *bottom* of the major thrust surface to contact the cylinder wall. As the piston approaches top center, both thrust surfaces are in contact with the cylinder wall.

- **Major thrust.** When the crankshaft crosses over top center, the force on the connecting rod moves the entire piston toward the major thrust surface. The lower portion of the major thrust surface has already been in contact with the cylinder wall. The rest of the piston skirt slips into full contact just after the crossover point, thereby controlling piston slap. This action is illustrated in
● **FIGURE 29–13.**

Off-setting the piston toward the minor thrust surface would provide a better mechanical advantage. It would also cause less piston-to-cylinder friction, and increase piston noise. For these reasons, the offset is often placed toward the minor thrust surface in racing engines. Noise and durability are not as important in racing engines as maximum performance.

NOTE: Not all piston pins are offset. In fact, many engines operate without the offset to help reduce friction and improve power and fuel economy.

PISTON PIN FIT   The finish and size of piston pins are closely controlled. Piston pins have a smooth, mirrorlike finish. Their size is held to tens of thousandths of an inch so that exact fits can be maintained. If the piston pin is loose in the piston or in the connecting rod, it will make a sound while the engine is running. This is often described as a **double knock.** The noise is created when the piston stops at top dead center and occurs again as it starts to move downward, creating a doubleknock or rattling sound. If the piston pin is too tight in the piston, it will restrict piston expansion along the pin diameter and lead to piston scuffing. Normal piston pin clearances range from 0.0005 to 0.0007 inch (0.0126 to 0.018 mm).

PISTON PIN RETAINING METHODS

FULL FLOATING   **Full-floating** piston pins are free to "float" in the connecting rod and the piston. Often, a bronze bushing is installed in the small end of the connecting rod to support the piston pin. Full-floating pins require a retaining device to keep the piston pin from moving endwise and scrape against the cylinder wall. Most full-floating piston pins use some type of **lock ring** to retain the piston pin. There are two common types of lock rings.

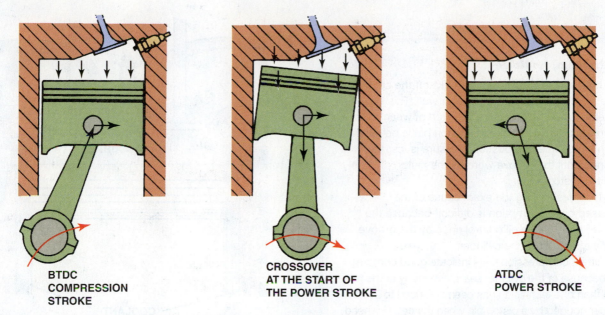

BTDC
COMPRESSION
STROKE

CROSSOVER
AT THE START OF
THE POWER STROKE

ATDC
POWER STROKE

FIGURE 29–13 Engine rotation and rod angle during the power stroke cause the piston to press harder against one side of the cylinder, called the major thrust surface.

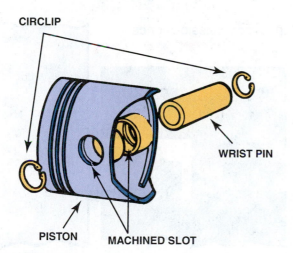

CIRCLIP

WRIST PIN

PISTON   MACHINED SLOT

FIGURE 29–14 Circlips hold full-floating piston pins in place.

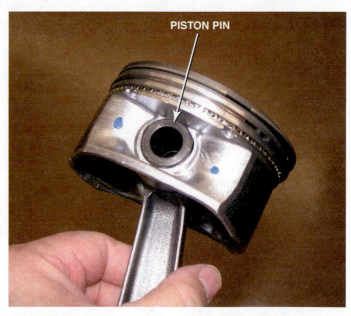

PISTON PIN

FIGURE 29–15 A typical interference fit piston pin.

- One is an internal snap ring that fits into a groove in the piston pin bore. These internal snap rings or "circle clips" are commonly called "circlips."
- The other is a "spiral lock" ring, which is a wound flat ring with two or three layers made from hardened steel. The spiral lock is inserted into a groove cut into the piston pin bore by starting with the bottom layer and twisting the spiral ring into place until all layers are in the groove.

Full-floating piston pins are most often used in high-performance modified engines and in diesel engines. ● SEE FIGURE 29–14.

Some engines use aluminum or plastic plugs in both ends of the piston pin. These plugs touch the cylinder wall without scoring, to hold the piston pin centered in the piston.

INTERFERENCE FIT   Another method of retaining the piston pin in the connecting rod is to make the connecting rod hole slightly smaller than the piston pin. The pin is installed by heating the rod to expand the hole or by pressing the pin into the rod. This retaining method will securely hold the pin. ● SEE FIGURE 29–15.

This press or shrink fit is called an **interference fit.** Care must be taken to have the correct hole sizes, and the pin must be centered in the connecting rod. Because the interference fit method is the least expensive to use, it is found in the majority of engines.

Big Problem, No Noise

Sometimes the piston pin can "walk" off the center of the piston and score the cylinder wall. This scoring is often not noticed because this type of wear does not create noise. Because the piston pin is below the piston rings, little combustion pressure is lost past the rings until the groove worn by the piston pin has worn the piston rings.

Troubleshooting the exact cause of the increased oil consumption is difficult because the damage done to the oil control rings by the groove usually affects only one cylinder.

Often, compression tests indicate good compression because of the cylinder seals, especially at the top. More than one technician has been surprised to see the cylinder gouged by a piston pin when the cylinder head has been removed for service. In such a case, the cost of the engine repair immediately increases far beyond that of normal cylinder head service.

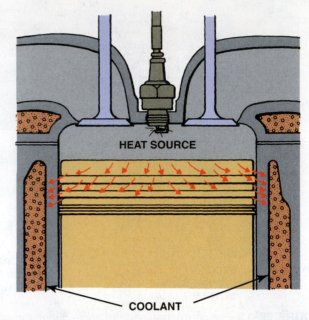

FIGURE 29–16 The rings conduct heat from the piston to the cylinder wall.

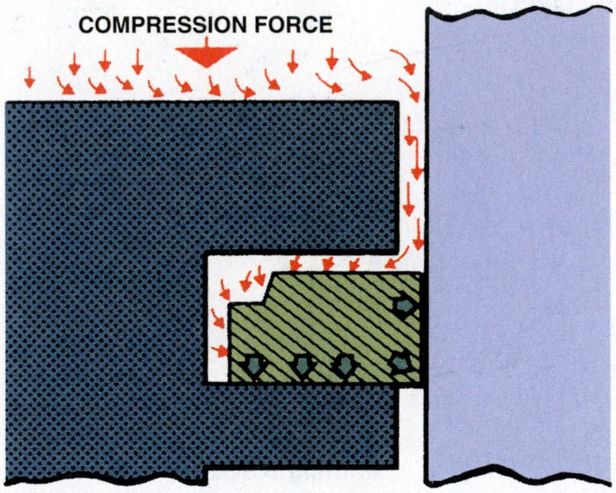

PISTON RINGS

PURPOSE AND FUNCTION Piston rings serve several major functions in engines.

- They form a sliding combustion chamber seal that prevents the high-pressure combustion gases from leaking past the piston.
- They keep engine oil from getting into the combustion chamber.
- The rings transfer some of the piston heat to the cylinder wall, where it is removed from the engine through the cooling system. ● **SEE FIGURE 29–16.**

CLASSIFICATIONS Piston rings are classified into two types.

1. Two **compression rings,** located toward the top of the piston
2. One **oil control ring,** located below the compression rings

NOTE: Some engines, such as Honda high-fuel economy engines, use pistons with only two rings: one compression ring and one oil control ring.

COMPRESSION RINGS A compression ring is designed to form a seal between the moving piston and the cylinder wall. This is necessary to get maximum power from the combustion

FIGURE 29–17 Combustion chamber pressure forces the ring against the cylinder wall and the bottom of the ring groove to effectively seal the cylinder.

pressure. At the same time, the compression ring must keep friction at a minimum. This is made possible by providing only enough static or built-in mechanical tension to hold the ring in contact with the cylinder wall during the intake stroke. Combustion chamber pressure during the compression, power, and exhaust strokes is applied to the top and back of the ring. This pressure will add extra force on the ring that is required to seal the combustion chamber during these strokes. ● **FIGURE 29–17** illustrates how the combustion chamber pressure adds force to the ring.

The space in the ring groove above the ring is called the **side clearance** and the space behind the ring is called the **back clearance.** ● **SEE FIGURE 29–18.**

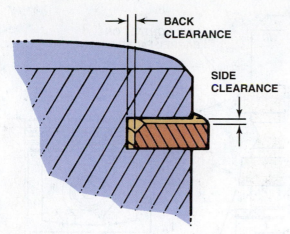

FIGURE 29-18 The side and back clearances must be correct for the compression rings to seal properly.

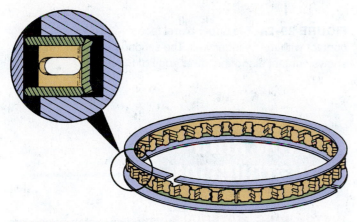

FIGURE 29-19 This typical three-piece oil control ring uses a hump-type stainless steel spacer-expander. The expander separates the two steel rails and presses them against the cylinder wall.

OIL CONTROL RINGS
The scraping action of the oil control ring allows oil to return through the expander and openings in the piston.

Steel spring expanders were placed in the ring groove behind the ring to improve static radial tension. They forced the ring to conform to the cylinder wall. Many expander designs are used. On the three-piece ring, a spacer expander lies between the top and bottom rails. The spacer expander keeps the rails separated and pushes them out against the cylinder wall. ● SEE FIGURE 29-19.

RING GAP
The piston **ring gap** will allow some leakage past the top compression ring. This leakage is useful in providing pressure on the second ring to develop a dynamic sealing force. The amount of piston ring gap is critical.

- **Too much gap.** A ring gap that is too great will allow excessive **blowby**. Blowby is the leakage of combustion gases past the rings. Blowby will blow oil from the cylinder wall. This oil loss is followed by piston ring scuffing.

- **Too little gap.** A ring gap that is too little will allow the piston ring ends to touch together when the engine is

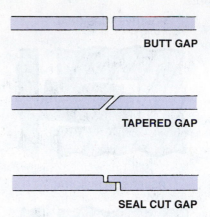

FIGURE 29-20 Typical piston ring gaps.

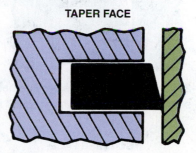

FIGURE 29-21 The taper face ring provides oil control by scraping the cylinder wall. This style of ring must be installed right side up or the ring will not seal and oil will be drawn into the combustion chamber.

hot. Ring end touching increases the mechanical force against the cylinder wall, causing excessive wear and possible engine failure.

A butt-type piston ring gap is the most common type used in automotive engines. Some low-speed industrial engines and some diesel engines use a more expensive tapered or seal-cut ring gap. These gaps are necessary to reduce losses of the high-pressure combustion gases. At low speeds, the gases have more time to leak through the gap. Typical ring gaps are illustrated in ● FIGURE 29-20.

PISTON RING SHAPES
As engine speeds have increased, inertia forces on the piston rings have also increased. As a result, engine manufacturers have found it desirable to reduce inertia forces on the rings by reducing their weight. This has been done by reducing the thickness of the piston ring from 1/4 inch (6 mm) to as little as 1/16 inch (1.6 mm). There are several types of piston rings.

- **Taper face ring** will contact the cylinder wall at the lower edge of the piston ring. ● SEE FIGURE 29-21.

When either a chamfer or counterbore relief is made on the *upper inside* corner of the piston ring, the ring cross section is unbalanced, causing the ring to twist in the groove in a positive direction.

- **Positive twist ring** will give the same wall contact as the taper face ring. It will also provide a line contact seal on

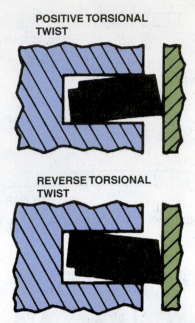

FIGURE 29–22 Torsional twist rings provide better compression sealing and oil control than regular taper rings.

FIGURE 29–23 Scraper-type rings provide improved oil control.

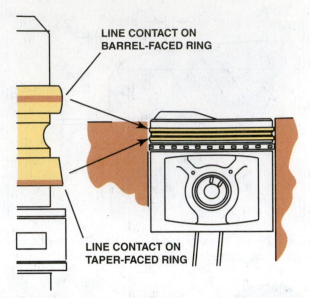

FIGURE 29–24 The upper barrel face ring has a line showing contact with the cylinder wall. The second taper face ring shows contact along the lower edge of the ring.

the bottom side of the groove. Sometimes, twist and a taper face are used on the same compression ring.

Some second rings are notched on the *outer lower* corner. This, too, provides a positive ring twist. The sharp, lower outer corner becomes a scraper that helps in oil control, but this type of ring has less compression control than the preceding types.

- **Reverse twist ring** is produced by chamfering the ring's *lower inner* corner. This seals the lower outer section of the ring and piston ring groove, thus improving oil control. Reverse twist rings require a greater taper face or barrel face to maintain the desired ring face-to-cylinder wall contact. ● **SEE FIGURE 29–22.**

    Another style of positive twist ring has a counterbore at the lower outside edge. ● **SEE FIGURE 29–23.**

- **Scraper ring** does a good job of oil control and is usually recommended for use at the second compression ring.

- **Barrel face ring** can replace the outer ring taper on some rings. The barrel is 0.0003 inch per 0.1 inch (0.0076 mm per 0.254 mm) of piston ring width. Barrel faces are found on rectangular rings and on torsionally twisted rings. ● **SEE FIGURE 29–24.**

PISTON RING CONSTRUCTION

PISTON RING MATERIALS The first piston rings were made with a simple rectangular cross section, modified with tapers, chamfers, counterbores, slots, rails, and expanders. Piston ring materials can include:

- Plain cast iron
- Pearlitic cast iron
- Nodular cast iron
- Steel
- **Ductile iron** (This is also used as a piston ring material in some automotive engines, which is very flexible and can be twisted without breaking.)

CHROMIUM PISTON RINGS A chromium facing on cast iron rings greatly increases piston ring life, especially where abrasive materials are present in the air. During manufacture, the chromium-plated ring is slightly chamfered at the outer corners. About 0.004 inch (0.01 mm) of chrome is then plated on the ring face. Chromium-faced rings are then prelapped or honed before they are packaged and shipped to the customer. The finished chromium facing is shown in a sectional view in ● **FIGURE 29–25.**

MOLYBDENUM PISTON RINGS Early in the 1960s, molybdenum piston ring faces were introduced. These rings proved to have good service life, especially under scuffing conditions. The plasma method is a spray method used to deposit

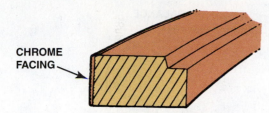

FIGURE 29–25 The chrome facing on this compression ring is about 0.004 inch (0.10 mm) thick.

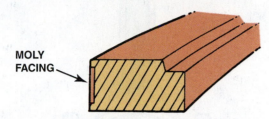

FIGURE 29–26 The moly facing on this compression ring is about 0.005 inch (0.13 mm) thick.

molybdenum on cast iron to produce a long-wearing and low-friction piston ring. The plasma method involves an electric arc plasma (ionized gas) that generates an extremely high temperature to melt the molybdenum and spray-deposit a molten powder of it onto a piston ring. Therefore, plasma rings are molybdenum (moly) rings that have the moly coating applied by the plasma method. Most molybdenum face piston rings have a groove that is 0.004 to 0.008 inch (0.1 to 0.2 mm) deep cut into the ring face. This groove is filled with molybdenum, using a metallic (or plasma) spray method, so that there is a cast iron edge above and below the molybdenum. This edge may be chamfered in some applications. A sectional view of a molybdenum face ring is shown in ● **FIGURE 29–26.**

Molybdenum face piston rings will survive under high-temperature and scuffing conditions better than chromium face rings. Under abrasive wear conditions, chromium face rings will have a better service life. There is little measurable difference between these two facing materials with respect to blowby, oil control, break-in, and horsepower. Piston rings with either of these two types of facings are far better than plain cast iron rings with phosphorus coatings. A molybdenum face ring, when used, will be found in the top groove, and a plain cast iron or chromium face ring will be found in the second groove.

MOLY-CHROME-CARBIDE RINGS Rings with moly-chrome-carbide coating are also used in some original equipment (OE) and replacement applications. The coating has properties that include the hardness of the chrome and carbide combined with the heat resistance of molybdenum.

CERAMIC-COATED RINGS The ceramic-coated ring surface is created by applying a ceramic coating to the ring using a process called *physical vapor deposition (PVD).* Ceramic-coated rings are also being used where additional heat resistance is needed, such as in some heavy-duty, turbocharged, or supercharged engines. For example, the General Motors Duramax 6.6 liter diesel engine uses ceramic-coated rings.

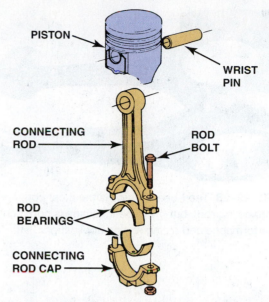

FIGURE 29–27 The connecting rod is the most highly stressed part of any engine because combustion pressure tries to compress it and piston inertia tries to pull it apart.

CONNECTING RODS

PURPOSE AND FUNCTION The connecting rod transfers the force and reciprocating motion of the piston to the crankshaft. The small end of the connecting rod reciprocates with the piston. The large end rotates with the crankpin. ● **SEE FIGURE 29–27.**

These dynamic motions make it desirable to keep the connecting rod as light as possible while still having a rigid beam section. ● **SEE FIGURE 29–28.**

Connecting rods are manufactured by casting, forging, and powdered (sintered) metal processes.

CONNECTING ROD DESIGN The big end of the connecting rod must be a perfect circle. Once a rod and cap are initially machined, they must remain a "matched set," due to the precise machining required to obtain a perfect circle. Therefore, the rod caps must not be interchanged. Assembly bolt holes are closely reamed in both the cap and connecting rod to ensure alignment. The connecting rod bolts have *piloting surfaces* that closely fit these reamed holes. The fit of the connecting rod bolts is so tight that a press must be used to remove the bolts when they are to be replaced, as shown in ● **FIGURE 29–29.**

In some engines, offset connecting rods provide the most economical distribution of main bearing space and crankshaft cheek clearance.

Many connecting rods are made with **balancing bosses (pads)** so that their weight can be adjusted to specifications. Some have balancing bosses only on the rod cap. Others also have a balancing boss at the small end. Some manufacturers put balancing bosses on the side of the rod, near the center of

FIGURE 29–28 The I-beam shape is the most common (top connecting rod), but the H-beam shape is common in high-performance and racing engine applications.

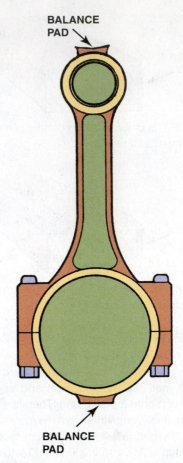

FIGURE 29–30 Some rods have balancing pads on each end of the connecting rod.

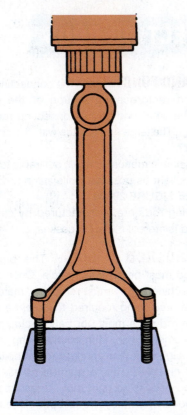

FIGURE 29–29 Rod bolts are quickly removed using a press.

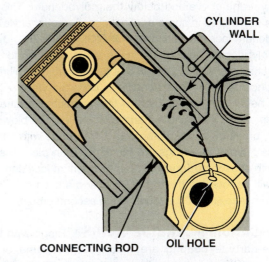

FIGURE 29–31 Some connecting rods have spit holes to help lubricate the cylinder wall or piston pin.

gravity of the connecting rod. Typical balancing bosses can be seen in ● FIGURE 29–30.

Balancing is done on automatic balancing machines as the final machining operation before the rod is installed in an engine.

Some connecting rods have a **spit hole** that bleeds some of the oil from the connecting rod journal. ● SEE FIGURES 29–31 AND 29–32.

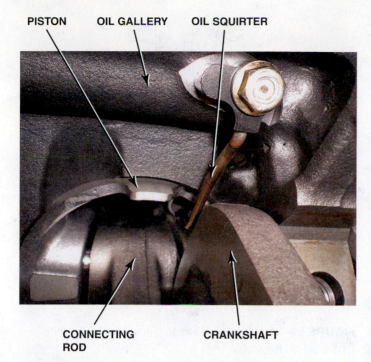

PISTON   OIL GALLERY   OIL SQUIRTER

CONNECTING ROD   CRANKSHAFT

FIGURE 29–32 Some engines, such as this Ford diesel, are equipped with oil squirters that spray or stream oil toward the underneath side of the piston head to cool the piston.

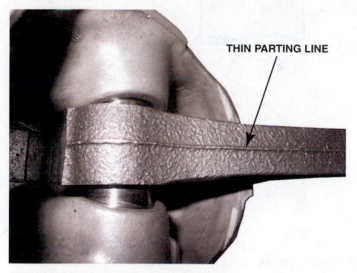

THIN PARTING LINE

FIGURE 29–33 A cast connecting rod is found on many stock engines and can be identified by the thin parting line.

On inline engines, oil is thrown up from the spit hole into the cylinder in which the rod is located. On V-type engines, it is often thrown into a cylinder in the opposite bank. The oil that is spit from the rod is aimed so that it will splash into the interior of the piston to help lubricate the piston pin. A hole similar to the spit holes may be used, called a **bleed hole,** to control the oil flow through the bearing.

CAST CONNECTING RODS
Casting materials and processes have been improved so that they are used in most vehicle engines with high production standards. Cast connecting rods can be identified by their *narrow parting line*. A typical rough connecting rod casting is shown in ● **FIGURE 29–33.**

OIL HOLE

BRONZE BUSHING

FIGURE 29–34 This high-performance connecting rod uses a bronze bushing in the small end of the rod and oil hole to allow oil to reach the full-floating piston pin.

FORGED CONNECTING RODS
Forged connecting rods have been used for years. They are generally used in heavy-duty and high-performance engines. Generally, the forging method produces lighter weight and stronger but more expensive connecting rods. Forged connecting rods can be identified by their *wide parting line.* Many high-performance connecting rods use a bronze bushing in the small end as shown in ● **FIGURE 29–34.**

POWDERED METAL CONNECTING RODS
Most new production engines, including the General Motors Northstar, the Ford 4.6, 5.0, and 6.6 liter OHC V-8s, and the Chrysler Hemi, use powdered metal (PM) connecting rods.

Powdered metal connecting rods have many advantages over convention cast or forged rods including precise weight control. Each rod is created using a measured amount of material so that rod balancing, and therefore engine balancing, is now achieved without extra weighting and machining operations.

- Powdered metal connecting rods start as powdered metal, which includes iron, copper, carbon, and other alloying agents.
- This powder is then placed in a die and compacted (forged) under a pressure of 30 to 50 tons per square inch.

FIGURE 29–35 Powdered metal connecting rods feature a fractured parting line at the big end of the rod.

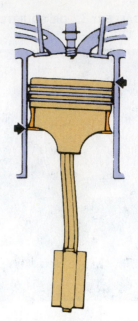

FIGURE 29–37 If the rod is twisted, it will cause diagonal-type wear on the piston skirt.

FIGURE 29–36 A press used to remove the connecting rod from the piston.

- After the part is shaped in the die, it is taken through a sintering operation where the part is heated, without melting, to about 2,000°F. During the sintering process, the ingredients are transformed into metallurgical bonds, giving the part strength.

- Machining is very limited and includes boring the small and big end and drilling the holes for the rod bearing cap retaining bolts.

- The big end is then fractured using a large press. The uneven parting line helps ensure a perfect match when the pieces are assembled. ● SEE FIGURE 29–35.

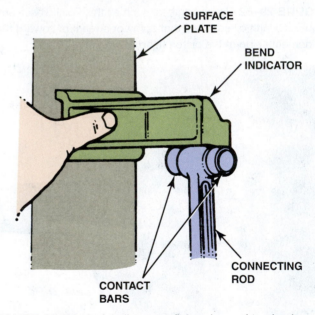

FIGURE 29–38 A rod alignment fixture is used to check a connecting rod for bends or twists.

CONNECTING ROD SERVICE

REMOVING PISTONS FROM RODS The pistons are removed from the rods using a special fixture shown in ● FIGURE 29–36.

INSPECTION Before connecting rod reconditioning, the rod should be checked for twist. ● SEE FIGURE 29–37.

In other words, the hole at the small end and the hole at the big end of the connecting rod should be parallel. No more than a 0.002 inch (0.05 mm) twist is acceptable. ● SEE FIGURE 29–38 for the fixture used to check connecting rods for twist.

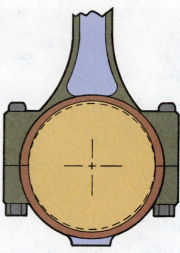

FIGURE 29–39 Rod bearing bores normally stretch from top to bottom, with most wear concentrated on the rod cap.

FIGURE 29–40 To help ensure that the big ends are honed straight, many experts recommend placing two rods together when performing the honing operation.

If measured rod twist is excessive, some specialty shops can remove the twist by bending the rod cold. Both cast and forged rods can be straightened. However, many engine builders replace the connecting rod if it is twisted.

RECONDITIONING PROCEDURE As an engine operates, the forces go through the large end of the connecting rod. This causes the crankshaft end opening of the rod (eye) to gradually deform. ● **SEE FIGURE 29–39.**

The large eye of the connecting rod is resized during precision engine service.

STEP 1 The parting surfaces of the rod and cap are smoothed to remove all high spots before resizing. A couple of thousandths of an inch of metal is removed from the rod cap parting surface. This is done using the same grinder that is used to remove a slight amount of metal from the parting surface of main bearing caps. The amount removed from the rod and rod cap only reduces the bore size 0.003 to 0.006 inch (0.08 to 0.15 mm).

NOTE: Powdered metal connecting rods cannot be reconditioned using this method. Most manufacturers recommend replacing worn powdered metal connecting rods.

STEP 2 The cap is installed on the rod, and the nuts or cap screws are properly torqued. The hole is then bored or honed to be perfectly round and of the size and finish required to give the correct connecting rod bearing crush. ● **FIGURE 29–40** shows the setup for resizing the rod on a typical hone used in engine reconditioning.

Even though material is being removed at the big end of the rod, the compression ratio is changed very little. The inside of the bore at the big end should have a 60 to 90 microinch finish for proper bearing contact and heat transfer.

PISTON AND ROD ASSEMBLY

INTERFERENCE FIT RODS To assemble the piston and rod, the piston pin is put in one side of the piston. The small end of the connecting rod should be checked for proper size.

The small eye of the connecting rod is heated before the pin is installed. ● **SEE FIGURE 29–41.**

This causes the rod eye to expand so that the pin can be pushed into place with little force. The pin must be rapidly pushed into the correct center position. There is only one chance to get it in the right place because the rod will quickly seize on the pin as the rod eye is cooled by the pin.

FULL-FLOATING RODS Full-floating piston pins operate in a bushing in the small eye of the connecting rod. The bushing can be replaced. The bushing and the piston are honed to the same diameter. This allows the piston pin to slide freely through both. The full-floating piston pin is held in place with a lock ring at each end of the piston pin. The lock ring expands into a small groove in the pin hole of the piston.

NOTE: The original lock rings should always be replaced with new rings.

PISTON RING SERVICE

STEPS Each piston ring, one at a time, should be placed backward in the groove in which it is to be run.

STEP 1 **Check side clearance.** As the piston goes rapidly up and down in the cylinder, it tosses the rings to the top and to the bottom of the ring grooves.

FIGURE 29–41 The small end of the rod is being heated in an electric heater and the piston is positioned properly so the piston pin can be installed as soon as the rod is removed from the heater.

The pounding of each ring in its groove gradually increases the piston ring side clearance. Material is worn from both the ring and the groove. Replace the piston if the ring groove is larger than factory specifications. The side clearance in the groove should be checked with a feeler gauge, as shown in ● FIGURE 29–42.

STEP 2 **Check ring gap.** After the block and cylinder bores have been reconditioned, invert the piston and push each ring into the lower quarter of the cylinder; then measure the ring gap. ● SEE FIGURE 29–43.

The usual ring gap should be approximately 0.004 inch for each inch of bore diameter (0.004 mm for each centimeter of bore diameter). The second ring also needs to have a similar or even larger end gap.

- If excessive ring gap is present, the blowby gases can enter the crankcase. Replace the ring(s) if the gap is too large.
- If the gap is too narrow, use a file or hand-operated piston ring grinder to achieve the necessary ring gap. ● SEE FIGURE 29–44.

STEP 3 **Installing the oil control ring.** The oil rings are installed first. The expander-spacer of the oil ring is

FIGURE 29–42 The side clearance of the piston ring is checked with a feeler gauge.

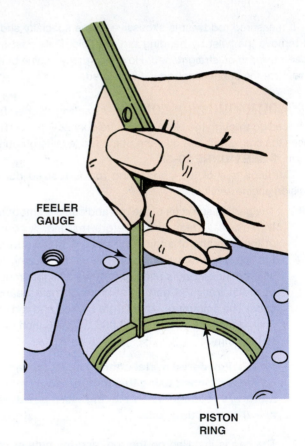

FEELER GAUGE

PISTON RING

FIGURE 29–43 The ring gap is measured using a feeler gauge.

placed in the lower ring groove. One oil ring rail is carefully placed above the expander-spacer by winding it into the groove. The other rail is placed below the expander-spacer. The ring should be rotated in the groove to ensure that the expander-spacer ends have not overlapped. If they have, the ring must be removed and reassembled correctly.

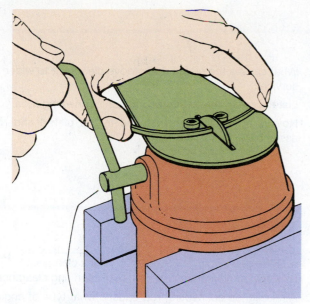

FIGURE 29–44 A hand-operated piston ring end gap grinder being used to increase the end gap of a piston ring so that it is within factory specifications.

FIGURE 29–45 A typical ring expander being used to install a piston ring on a piston.

STEP 4 **Installing the compression rings**. Installing the compression rings requires the use of a **piston ring expander** tool that will only open the ring gap enough to slip the ring on the piston. ● **SEE FIGURE 29–45.**

Be careful to install the ring with the correct side up. The top of the compression ring is marked with one of the following:
- One dot
- The letter *T*
- The word *top*
● **SEE FIGURE 29–46.**

STEP 5 **Double-check everything**. After the rings are installed they should be rotated in the groove to ensure that they move freely, and checked to ensure that they will go fully into the groove so that the ring face is flush with the surface of the piston ring lands. Usually, the rings are placed on all pistons before any pistons are installed in the cylinders.

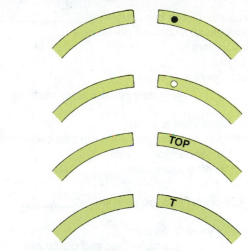

FIGURE 29–46 Identification marks used to indicate the side of the piston ring to be placed toward the head of the piston.

SUMMARY

1. Pistons are cam ground so that when operating temperature is reached, the piston will have expanded enough across the piston pin area to become round.
2. Replacement pistons should weigh the same as the original pistons to maintain proper engine balance.
3. Some engines use an offset piston pin to help reduce piston slap when the engine is cold.
4. Piston rings usually include two compression rings at the top of the piston and an oil control ring below the compression rings.

5. If the ring end gap is excessive, blowby gases can travel past the rings and into the crankcase.
6. Many piston rings are made of coated cast iron to provide proper sealing.
7. If the connecting rod is twisted, diagonal wear will be noticed on the piston skirt.
8. Powdered metal connecting rods are usually broken at the big end parting line. Because of this rough junction, powdered metal connecting rods cannot be reconditioned, but replaced if damaged or worn.

1. List the methods used to control piston heat expansion.
2. Why are some piston skirts tin plated?
3. How does piston pin offset control piston slap?
4. Why are forged pistons recommended for use in high-performance engines?
5. What causes the piston ring groove clearance to widen in service?
6. List the steps needed to recondition connecting rods.
7. How is the piston pin installed in the piston and rod assembly?

CHAPTER QUIZ

1. A hypereutectic piston _____.
   a. Uses about 16% silicon
   b. Is a cast piston
   c. Is a forged piston
   d. Both a and b

2. Many aluminum piston skirts are plated with _____.
   a. Tin or moly graphite
   b. Lead
   c. Antimony
   d. Terneplate

3. A hypereutectic piston has a higher _____.
   a. Weight than an aluminum piston
   b. Silicon content
   c. Tin content
   d. Nickel content

4. The purpose of casting steel struts into an aluminum piston is to _____.
   a. Provide increased strength
   b. Provide increased weight at the top part of the piston where it is needed for stability
   c. Control thermal expansion
   d. Both a and c

5. Full-floating piston pins are retained by _____.
   a. Lock rings
   b. A drilled hole with roll pin
   c. An interference fit between rod and piston pin
   d. An interference fit between piston and piston pin

6. The space behind the ring is called _____.
   a. Side clearance
   b. Forward clearance
   c. Back clearance
   d. Piston ring clearance

7. A misaligned connecting rod causes what type of engine wear?
   a. Cylinder taper
   b. Barrel shape cylinders
   c. Ridge wear
   d. Diagonal wear on the piston skirt

8. Side clearance is a measure taken between the _____ and the _____.
   a. Piston (side skirt); cylinder wall
   b. Piston pin; piston pin retainer (clip)
   c. Piston ring; piston ring groove
   d. Compression ring; oil control ring

9. Piston ring gap should only be measured after _____.
   a. All cylinder work has been performed
   b. Installing the piston in the cylinder
   c. Installing the rings on the piston
   d. Both a and c

10. Which type of connecting rod needs to be heated to install the piston pin
    a. Forged
    b. Interference fit
    c. Floating
    d. PM rods

chapter 30

ENGINE BLOCKS

LEARNING OBJECTIVES: After studying this chapter, the reader should be able to: • Explain the construction of engine blocks. • Explain the procedure for engine block service. • Explain block preparation for assembly.

KEY TERMS: Bedplate 439 • Block deck 440 • Bores 437 • Compacted graphite Iron (CGI) 438 • Cooling jacket 440 • Core plugs 438 • Crosshatch finish 447 • Decking the block 444 • Dry cylinder sleeve 439 • Fiber-reinforced matrix (FRM) 439 • Freeze plugs 438 • Frost plugs 438 • Girdle 441 • Grit size 448 • Monoblock 437 • Oil gallery 440 • Oil gallery plugs 441 • Plateau honing 447 • Saddles 443 • Siamese cylinder bores 440 • Sleeving 446 • Wet cylinder sleeve 439

ENGINE BLOCKS

CONSTRUCTION The engine block, which is the supporting structure for the entire engine, is made from one of the following:

- Gray cast iron
- Cast aluminum
- Die-cast aluminum alloy

Cast iron contains about 3% carbon (graphite), which makes it gray in color. Steel is iron with most of the carbon removed. The carbon in cast iron makes it hard but brittle. Cast iron is used to make engine blocks and cylinder heads for the following reasons.

- The carbon in the cast iron allows for easy machining, often without coolant.
- The graphite in the cast iron also has lubricating properties.
- Cast iron is strong for its weight and usually is magnetic.

The liquid cast iron is poured into a mold made from either sand or Styrofoam. All other engine parts are mounted on or in the block. This large casting supports the crankshaft and camshaft (on OHV engines) and holds all the parts in alignment. Newer blocks use thinner walls to reduce weight. Blocks are often of the **monoblock** design, which means that the cylinder, water jacket, main bearing supports (saddles), and oil passages are all cast as one structure for strength and quietness. Large-diameter holes in the block casting form the cylinders to guide the pistons. The cylinder holes are called **bores** because they are made by a machining process called boring. ● **SEE FIGURE 30–1.**

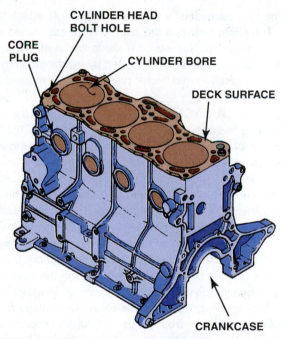

FIGURE 30–1 The cylinder block usually extends from the oil pan rails at the bottom to the deck surface at the top.

Combustion pressure loads are carried from the head to the crankshaft bearings through the block structure. The block has webs, walls, and drilled passages to contain the coolant and lubricating oil and to keep them separated from each other.

Mounting pads or lugs on the block transfer the engine torque reaction to the vehicle frame through attached engine mounts. A large mounting surface at the rear of the engine block is used for fastening a bell housing or transmission.

FIGURE 30–2 An expansion (core) plug is used to block the opening in the cylinder head or block the holes where the core sand was removed after the part was cast.

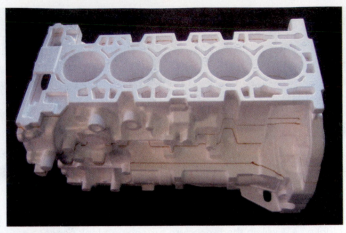

FIGURE 30–3 A Styrofoam casting mold used to make the five cylinder engine blocks for the Chevrolet Colorado and the Hummer H3. The brown lines are glue used to hold the various parts together. Sand is packed around the mold and molten aluminum is poured into the sand which instantly vaporizes the Styrofoam. The aluminum then flows and fills the area of the mold.

The cylinder head(s) and other components attach to the block. The joints between the components are sealed using gaskets or sealants. Gaskets or sealants are used in the joints to take up differences that are created by machining irregularities and that result from different pressures and temperatures.

BLOCK MANUFACTURING Cast-iron cylinder block sand casting technology continues to be improved. The trend is to make blocks with larger cores, using fewer individual pieces. Oil-sand cores are forms that shape the internal openings and passages in the engine block. Before casting, the cores are supported within a core box. The core box also has a liner to shape the outside of the block. Special alloy cast iron is poured into the box. It flows between the cores and the core box liner. As the cast iron cools, the core breaks up. When the cast iron has hardened, it is removed from the core box, and the pieces of sand core are removed through the openings in the block by vigorously shaking the casting. These openings in the block are plugged with **core plugs**. Core plugs are also called **freeze plugs** or **frost plugs**. Although the name seems to mean that the plugs would be pushed outward if the coolant in the passages were to freeze, they seldom work this way.
● **SEE FIGURE 30–2.**

One way to keep the engine weight as low as possible is to make the block with minimum wall thickness. The cast iron used with thin-wall casting techniques has higher nickel content and is harder than the cast iron previously used. Engine designers have used foundry techniques to make engines lightweight by making the cast-iron block walls and bulkheads only as heavy as necessary to support their required loads.

ALUMINUM BLOCKS Aluminum is used for some cylinder blocks and is nonmagnetic and lightweight. Styrofoam is often used as a core when casting an aluminum block. The

? **FREQUENTLY ASKED QUESTION**

What Is Compacted Graphite Iron?
Compacted graphite iron (CGI) has increased strength, ductility, toughness, and stiffness compared to gray iron. If no magnesium is added, the iron will form gray iron when cooled, with the graphite present in flake form. If a very small amount of magnesium is added, more and more of the sulfur and oxygen form in the molten solution, and the shape of the graphite begins to change to compacted graphite forms. Compacted graphite iron is used for bedplates and many diesel engine blocks. It has higher strength, stiffness, and toughness than gray iron. The enhanced strength has been shown to permit reduced weight while still reducing noise vibration and harshness. Compacted graphite iron is commonly used in the blocks of diesel and some high-performance engines.

Styrofoam vaporizes as soon as the molten aluminum comes in contact with the foam leaving behind a cavity where the aluminum flows. ● **SEE FIGURE 30–3.**

Aluminum block engines usually require cast-iron cylinder walls for proper wear and longevity. Aluminum blocks may have one of several different types of cylinder walls.

- Most cast-aluminum blocks have cast-iron cylinder sleeves (liners) such as Saturn, Northstar, and Ford modular V-8s and V-6s. The cast-iron cylinder sleeves are either cast into the aluminum block during manufacturing or pressed into the aluminum block. These sleeves are

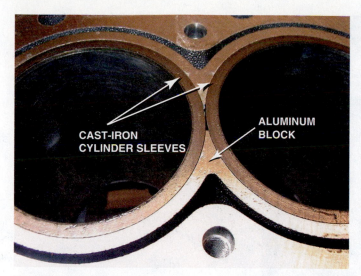

FIGURE 30–4 Cast-iron dry sleeves are used in aluminum blocks to provide a hard surface for the rings.

CAST-IRON CYLINDER SLEEVES

ALUMINUM BLOCK

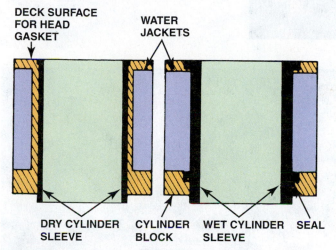

DECK SURFACE FOR HEAD GASKET

WATER JACKETS

DRY CYLINDER SLEEVE

CYLINDER BLOCK

WET CYLINDER SLEEVE

SEAL

FIGURE 30–5 A dry sleeve is supported by the surrounding cylinder block. A wet sleeve must be thicker to be able to withstand combustion pressures without total support from the block.

not in contact with the coolant passages and are called **dry cylinder sleeves.** ● SEE FIGURE 30–4.

- Another aluminum block design has the block die cast from silicon-aluminum alloy with no cylinder liners. Pistons with zinc-copper-hard iron coatings are used in these aluminum bores (in some Porsche engines).
- Some engines have die-cast aluminum blocks with replaceable cast-iron cylinder sleeves. The sleeves are sealed at the block deck and at their base. Coolant flows around the cylinder sleeve, so this type of sleeve is called a **wet cylinder sleeve** (in Cadillac 4.1, 4.5, and 4.9 liter V-8 engines). ● SEE FIGURE 30–5.

Cast-iron main bearing caps are used with aluminum blocks to give the required strength.

BEDPLATE DESIGN BLOCKS
A **bedplate** is a structural member that attaches to the bottom of the block and supports

FIGURE 30–6 A bedplate is a structural part of the engine which is attached between the block and the oil pan and supports the crankshaft.

? **FREQUENTLY ASKED QUESTION**

What Are FRM-Lined Cylinders?
Fiber-reinforced matrix (FRM) is used to strengthen cylinder walls in some Honda/Acura engines. FRM is a ceramic material similar to that used to construct the insulators of spark plugs. The lightweight material has excellent wear resistance and good heat transfer properties, making it ideal for use as a cylinder material. FRM inserts are placed in the mold and the engine block is cast over them. The inserts are rough and can easily adhere to the engine block. The inserts are then bored and honed to form the finished cylinders. FRM blocks were first used in a production engine on the Honda S2000 and are also used on the turbocharged Acura RDX sport utility vehicle.

the crankshaft. The oil pan is mounted under the bedplate which in most cases is also part of the structure and support for the block assembly. ● SEE FIGURE 30–6.

CASTING NUMBERS
Whenever an engine part such as a block is cast, a number is put into the mold to identify the casting. These casting numbers can be used to check dimensions, such as the cubic inch displacement, and other information, such as year of manufacture. Sometimes changes are made to the mold, yet the casting number is not changed. Most often the casting number is the best piece of identifying information that the service technician can use. ● SEE FIGURE 30–7.

FIGURE 30–7 Casting numbers identify the block.

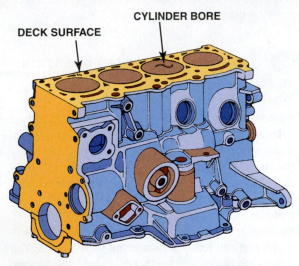

FIGURE 30–8 The deck is the machined top surface of the block.

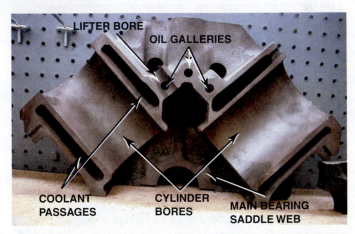

FIGURE 30–9 Cutaway of a Chevrolet V-8 block showing all of the internal passages.

BLOCK DECK The cylinder head is fastened to the top surface of the block. This surface is called the **block deck.** The deck has a smooth surface to seal *against* the head gasket. Bolt holes are positioned around the cylinders to form an even holding pattern. Four, five, or six head bolts are used around each cylinder in automobile engines. These bolt holes go into reinforced areas within the block that carry the combustion pressure load to the main bearing bulkheads. Additional holes in the block are used to transfer coolant and oil, as seen in ● FIGURE 30–8.

COOLING PASSAGES Cylinders are surrounded by cooling passages. These coolant passages around the cylinders are often called the **cooling jacket.** In most cylinder designs, the cooling passages extend nearly to the bottom of the cylinder. In some engine blocks where the block ends at the centerline of the crankshaft, the cooling passages are limited to the upper portion of the cylinder.

Some engines are built with **Siamese cylinder bores** where the cylinder walls are cast together without a water jacket (passage) between the cylinders. While this design improves the strength of the block and adds stability to the cylinder bores, it can reduce the cooling around the cylinders. ● FIGURE 30–9 is a typical V-8 engine cutaway that shows the coolant jackets and some of the lubrication holes.

LUBRICATING PASSAGES An engine block has many oil holes that carry lubricating oil to the required locations. During manufacture, all oil holes, called the **oil gallery,** are drilled from outside the block. When a curved passage is needed, intersecting straight drilled holes are used. In some engines, plugs are placed in the oil holes to direct oil to another point before it comes

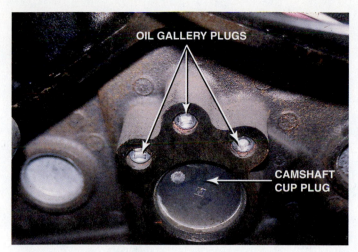

FIGURE 30–10 Typical oil gallery plugs on the rear of a Chevrolet small block V-8 engine.

back to the original hole, on the opposite side of the plug. After oil holes are drilled, the unneeded open ends may be capped by pipe plugs, steel balls, or cup-type soft plugs, often called **oil gallery plugs.** These end plugs in the oil passages can be a source of oil leakage in operating engines. ● SEE FIGURE 30–10.

MAIN BEARING CAPS The main bearing caps are cast or manufactured from sintered or billeted materials, separately from the block.

 TECH TIP

What Does LHD Mean?

The abbreviation LHD means *left-hand dipstick,* which is commonly used by rebuilders and remanufacturers in their literature in describing Chevrolet small block V-8 engines. Before about 1980, most small block Chevrolet V-8s used an oil dipstick pad on the left side (driver's side) of the engine block. Starting in about 1980, when oxygen sensors were first used on this engine, the dipstick was relocated to the right side of the block.

Therefore, to be assured of ordering or delivering the correct engine, knowing the dipstick location is critical. An LHD block cannot be used with the exhaust manifold setup that includes the oxygen sensor without major refitting or the installing of a different style of oil pan that includes a provision for an oil dipstick. Engine blocks with the dipstick pad cast on the right side are, therefore, coded as right-hand dipstick (RHD) engines.

NOTE: Some blocks cast around the year 1980 are cast with both right- and left-hand oil dipstick pads, but only one is drilled for the dipstick tube. ● SEE FIGURE 30–11.

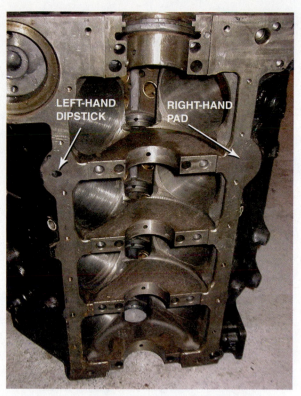

FIGURE 30–11 Small block Chevrolet block. Note the left-hand dipstick hole and a pad cast for a right-hand dipstick.

- They are machined and then installed on the block for a final bore finishing operation.
- With caps installed, the main bearing bores and cam bearing bores (on OHV engines) are machined to the correct size and alignment. On some engines, these bores are honed to a very fine finish and exact size.
- Main bearing caps are not interchangeable or reversible, because they are individually finished in place.
- Main bearing caps may have cast numbers indicating their position on the block. If not, they should be marked with numbers and arrows pointing toward the front of the engine.

Standard production engines usually use two bolts to hold the main bearing cap in place. ● SEE FIGURE 30–12.

Heavy-duty and high-performance engines often use additional main bearing support bolts. A four-bolt, and even six-bolt, main cap can be of a cross-bolted design in a deep skirt block or of a parallel design in a shallow skirt block. ● SEE FIGURES 30–13 AND 30–14.

Expansion force of the combustion chamber gases will try to push the head off the top and the crankshaft off the bottom of the block. The engine is held together with the head bolts and main bearing cap bolts screwed into bolt bosses and ribs in the block. The extra bolts on the main bearing cap help to support the crankshaft when there are high combustion pressures and mechanical loads, especially during high engine speed operation. Many engines use a **girdle** which ties all of the main bearing caps together to add strength to the lower part of the block. ● SEE FIGURE 30–15.

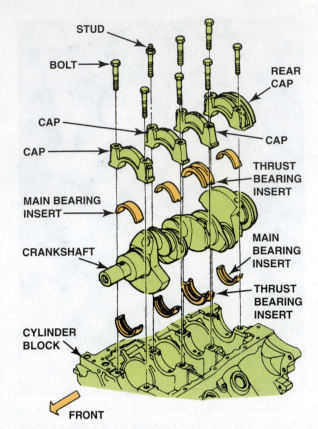

FIGURE 30–12 Two-bolt main bearing caps provide adequate bottom end strength for most engines.

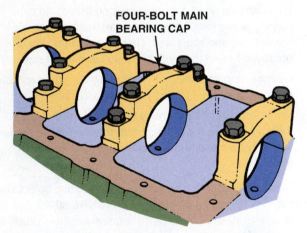

FIGURE 30–13 High-performance and truck engines often use four-bolt main bearing caps for greater durability.

ENGINE BLOCK SERVICE

PROCEDURES The engine block is the foundation of the engine. All parts of the block must be of the correct size and they must be aligned. The parts must also have the proper finishes if the engine is to function dependably for a normal service life. Engine blueprinting is the reconditioning of all the critical surfaces and dimensions so that the block is actually like new.

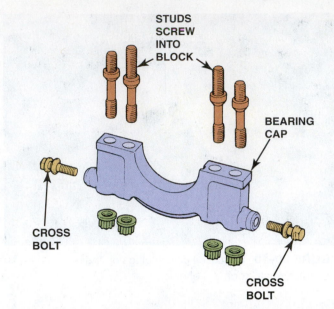

FIGURE 30–14 Some engines add to the strength of a four-bolt main bearing cap by also using cross bolts through the bolt on the sides of the main bearing caps.

FIGURE 30–15 A girdle is used to tie all of the main bearing caps together.

After a thorough cleaning, the block should be inspected for cracks or other flaws before machine work begins. After the block has been cleaned and cracked checked, the block should be prepared in the following sequence.

OPERATION 1 Main bearing housing bore alignment, often called "align boring" (or honing)

OPERATION 2 Machining of the block deck surface parallel to the crankshaft

OPERATION 3 Cylinder boring and honing

MAIN BEARING HOUSING BORE ALIGNMENT The main bearing journals of a straight crankshaft are in alignment. If the main bearing housing bores in the block are not in alignment,

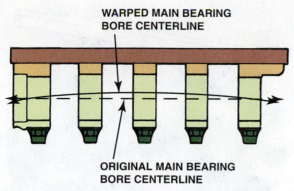

FIGURE 30–16 The main bearing bores of a warped block usually bend into a bowed shape. The greatest distortion is in the center bores.

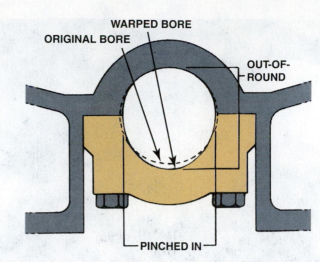

FIGURE 30–17 When the main bearing caps bow downward, they also pinch in at the parting line.

FREQUENTLY ASKED QUESTION

What Is a Seasoned Engine?

A new engine is machined and assembled within a few hours after the heads and block are cast from melted iron. Newly cast parts have internal stresses within the metal. The stress results from the different thickness of the metal sections in the head. Forces from combustion in the engine, plus continued heating and cooling, gradually relieve these stresses. By the time the engine has accumulated 20,000 to 30,000 miles (32,000 to 48,000 km), the stresses have been completely relieved. This is why some engine rebuilders prefer to work with used heads and blocks that are stress relieved. Used engines are often called "seasoned" because of the reduced stress and movement these components have as compared with new parts.

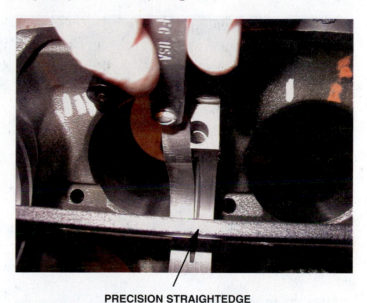

PRECISION STRAIGHTEDGE

FIGURE 30–18 The main bearing bore alignment can be checked using a precision straightedge and a feeler gauge.

the crankshaft will bend as it rotates. This condition increases rotational friction of the crankshaft and will lead to premature bearing failure or a broken crankshaft. The original stress in the block casting is gradually relieved as the block is used. Some slight warpage may occur as the stress is relieved. In addition, the continued pounding caused by combustion will usually cause some stretch in the main bearing caps. ● **SEE FIGURE 30–16.**

The main bearing bores gradually bow upward and elongate vertically. This means that the bearing bore becomes smaller at the centerline as the block distorts, pinching the bore inward at the sides. ● **SEE FIGURE 30–17.**

The procedure includes the following steps.

STEP 1 The first step in determining the condition of the main bearing bores is to determine if the bore alignment in the block is straight. These bores are called the **saddles.** A precision ground straightedge and a feeler gauge are used to determine the amount of warpage.

The amount of variation along the entire length of the block should not exceed 0.0015 inch (0.038 mm).

CAUTION: When performing this measurement, be sure that the block is resting on a flat surface. If the engine is mounted to an engine stand, the weight of the block on the unsupported end can cause an error in the measurement of the main bearing bores and saddle alignment.

STEP 2 If the block saddles exceed one-and-a-half thousandth of an inch distortion, then align honing is required to restore the block. If the block saddles are straight, the bores should be measured to be sure that the bearing caps are not distorted. ● **SEE FIGURE 30–18.**

STEP 3 The bearing caps should be installed and the retaining bolts tightened to the specified torque before measuring the main bearing bores. Using a telescoping

(a)

(b)

FIGURE 30–19 (a) A precision arbor can be used to check the main bearing bore alignment. (b) If the sleeve can be inserted into all of the main bearing bores, then they are aligned.

gauge, measure each bore in at least two directions. Check the service information for the specified main bearing bore diameter. The bearing bore should not vary by more than one-half of a thousandth of an inch or 0.0005 inch (0.0127 mm). A dial bore gauge is often used to measure the main bearing bore. Set up the dial bore gauge in the fixture with the necessary extensions to achieve the nominal main bearing bore diameter.

Check the service information for the specified main bearing bore diameter and determine the exact middle of the range.

ARBOR CHECK METHOD
The arbor is installed, then all main caps are tightened to specifications. After tightening, the arbor is checked to make sure it rotates freely, indicating a true centerline. However, because of all the different diameters required, it is an expensive method. ● SEE FIGURE 30–19.

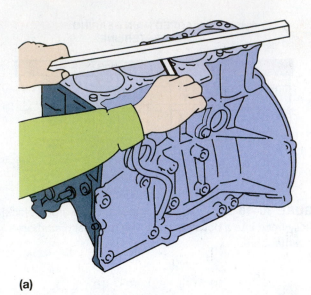

(a)

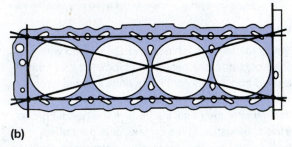

(b)

FIGURE 30–20 (a) Checking the flatness of the block deck surface using a straightedge and a feeler gauge. (b) To be sure that the top of the block is flat, check the block in six locations as shown.

MACHINING THE DECK SURFACE OF THE BLOCK
An engine should have the same combustion chamber size in each cylinder. For this to occur, each piston must come up an equal distance from the block deck. The connecting rods are attached to the rod bearing journals of the crankshaft. Pistons are attached to the connecting rods. As the crankshaft rotates, the pistons come to the top of the stroke. When all parts are sized equally, all the pistons will come up to the same level. This can only happen if the block deck is parallel to the main bearing bores. Therefore, the flatness of the block deck should be checked. ● SEE FIGURE 30–20.

The block deck must be resurfaced in a surfacing machine that can control the amount of metal removed when it is necessary to match the size of the combustion chambers. This procedure is called **decking the block.** The block is set up on a bar located in the main bearing saddles, or set up on the oil pan rails of the block. The bar is parallel to the direction of cutting head movement. The block is leveled sideways, and then the deck is resurfaced in the same manner as the head is resurfaced. ● FIGURE 30–21 shows a block deck being resurfaced by grinding.

FIGURE 30–21 Grinding the deck surface of the block.

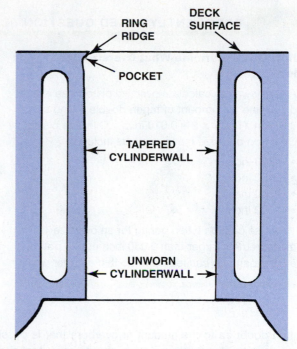

FIGURE 30–22 Cylinders wear in a taper, with most of the wear occurring at the top of the cylinder where the greatest amount of heat and pressure are created. The ridge is formed because the very top part of the cylinder is not contacted by the rings.

DECK SURFACE FINISH
The surface finish of the block deck should be:

- 60 to 100 Ra (65 to 110 RMS) for cast iron
- 50 to 60 Ra (55 to 65 RMS) for aluminum block decks to be assured of a proper head gasket surface

The surface finish is determined by the type of grinding stone used, as well as the speed and coolant used in the finishing operation. The higher the surface finish number the rougher the surface.

CYLINDER BORING
Cylinders should be measured across the engine (perpendicular to the crankshaft), where the greatest wear occurs. In other words, measure the bores at 90 degrees to the piston pin. Most wear will be found just below the ridge, and the least amount of wear will occur below the lowest ring travel. ● **SEE FIGURE 30–22.**

The cylinder should be checked for out-of-round and taper. ● **SEE FIGURE 30–23.**

Most cylinders are serviceable if they:

- Are a maximum of 0.003 inch (0.076 mm) out-of-round
- Have no more than a 0.005 inch (0.127 mm) taper
- Have no deep scratches in the cylinder wall

NOTE: Always check the specifications for the engine being serviced. For example, the General Motors 4.8, 5.3, 5.7, 6, and 6.2 liter LS series V-8s have a maximum out-of-round of only 0.0003 inch (3/10 of one-thousandths of an inch). This specification is about one-third of the normal dimension of about 0.001 inch.

The most effective way to correct excessive cylinder out-of-round, taper, or scoring is to rebore the cylinder. The rebored cylinder requires the use of a new, oversize piston.

The maximum bore oversize is determined by two factors.

1. Cylinder wall thickness—at least 0.17 inch for street engines and 0.2 inch for high-performance or racing applications
2. Size of the available oversize pistons

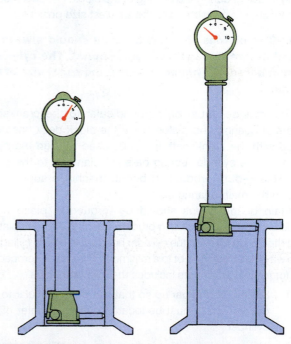

FIGURE 30–23 Using a dial bore gauge to measure the bore diameter at the top just below the ridge (maximum wear section) and at the bottom below the ring travel (minimum wear section). The difference between these two measurements is the amount of cylinder taper. Take the measurements in line with the crankshaft and then repeat the measurements at right angles to the centerline of the block in each cylinder to determine out-of-round.

How Do I Determine What Oversize Bore Is Needed?

An easy way to calculate oversize piston size is to determine the amount of taper, double it, and add 0.010 in. (Taper × 2 + 0.010 inch = Oversize piston). Common oversize measurements include:

- 0.020 inch
- 0.030 inch
- 0.040 inch
- 0.060 inch

Use caution when boring for an oversize measurement larger than 0.030 inch due to potential engine damage caused from too thin cylinder walls.

FIGURE 30–24 A cylinder boring machine is used to enlarge cylinder bore diameter so a replacement oversize piston can be used to restore a worn engine to useful service or to increase the displacement of the engine in an attempt to increase power output.

If in doubt as to the amount of overbore that is possible without causing structural weakness, an ultrasonic test should be performed on the block to determine the thickness of the cylinder walls. An ultrasonic tester can measure the thickness of the cylinder walls and is used to determine if a cylinder can be bored oversize and, if so, by how much. All cylinders should be tested. Variation in cylinder wall thickness occurs because of core shifting (moving) during the casting of the block. For best results, cylinders should be rebored to the smallest size possible.

NOTE: The pistons that will be used should always be in hand before the cylinders are rebored. The cylinders are then bored and honed to match the exact size of the pistons.

The cylinder must be perpendicular to the crankshaft for normal bearing and piston life. If the block deck has been aligned with the crankshaft, it can be used to align the cylinders. Portable cylinder boring bars are clamped to the block deck. Heavy-duty production boring machines support the block on the main bearing bores.

Main bearing caps should be torqued in place when cylinders are being rebored. In precision boring, a torque plate is also bolted on in place of the cylinder head while boring cylinders. In this way, distortion is kept to a minimum. The general procedure used for reboring cylinders includes the following steps.

STEP 1 Set the boring bar up so that it is perpendicular to the crankshaft. It must be located over the center of the cylinder.

STEP 2 The cylinder center is found by installing centering pins in the bar.

STEP 3 The bar is lowered so that the centering pins are located near the bottom of the cylinder, where the least wear has occurred. This locates the boring bar over the original cylinder center. Once the boring bar is centered, the boring machine is clamped in place to hold it securely. This will allow the cylinder to be rebored on

What Is a Boring Hone?

Many shops now use "boring" hones instead of boring bars. Boring hones have the advantages of being able to resize and finish hone with only one machine setup. Often a diamond hone is used and rough honed to within about 0.003 inch of the finished bore size. Then a finish hone is used to provide the proper surface finish.

the original centerline, regardless of the amount of cylinder wear.

STEP 4 A sharp, properly ground cutting tool is installed and adjusted to the desired dimension. Rough cuts remove a great deal of metal on each pass of the cutting tool. The rough cut is followed by a fine cut that produces a much smoother and more accurate finish. Different-shaped tool bits are used for rough and finish boring.

STEP 5 The last cut is made to produce a diameter that is at least 0.002 inch (0.05 mm) smaller than the required diameter. ● **SEE FIGURE 30–24.**

SLEEVING THE CYLINDER Sometimes cylinders have a gouge so deep that it will not clean up when the cylinder is rebored to the maximum size. This could happen if the piston pin moved endways and rubbed on the cylinder wall. Cylinder blocks with deep gouges may be able to be salvaged by **sleeving** the cylinder. The cylinder wall thickness has to be checked to see if sleeving is possible. Sleeving a cylinder is done by boring the cylinder to a dimension that is greatly oversize to almost match the outside diameter of the cylinder sleeve. The sleeve is pressed into the rebored block and then the center

FIGURE 30–25 A dry cylinder sleeve can also be installed in a cast-iron block to repair a worn or cracked cylinder.

FIGURE 30–26 An assortment of ball-type deglazing hones. This type of hone does not straighten wavy cylinder walls.

of the sleeve is bored to the diameter required by the piston. The cylinder can be sized to use a standard-size piston when it is sleeved. ● **SEE FIGURE 30–25.**

CYLINDER HONING It is important to have the proper surface finish on the cylinder wall for the rings to seat against. Honing includes two basic operations depending on the application.

1. When installing new piston rings on a cylinder that is not being bored, some ring manufacturers recommend breaking the hard surface glaze on the cylinder wall with a hone before installing new piston rings. This process is often called "deglazing" the cylinder walls.

2. The cylinder wall should be honed to straighten the cylinder when the wall is wavy or scuffed. If honing is being done with the crankshaft remaining in the block, the crankshaft should be protected to keep honing chips from getting on the shaft.

Two types of hones are used for cylinder service.

- A *deglazing hone* removes the hard surface glaze remaining in the cylinder. It is a flexible hone that follows the shape of the cylinder wall, even when the wall is wavy. It cannot be used to straighten the cylinder. A brush-type (ball-type) deglazing hone is shown in ● **FIGURE 30–26.**

- A *sizing hone* can be used to straighten the cylinder and to provide a suitable surface for the piston rings. Honing the cylinder removes the fractured metal that is created by boring. The cylinders must be honed a minimum of 0.002 inch (0.05 mm) after boring to cut below the rough surface and provide an adequate finish. Honing leaves a plateau surface that can support the oil film for the rings and piston skirt. This plateau surface is achieved by first using a coarse stone followed by a smooth stone to achieve the desired surface. The process of using a course and fine stone is called **plateau honing.** ● **SEE FIGURE 30–27.**

Its honing stones are held in a rigid fixture with an expanding mechanism to control the size of the hone. The sizing hone can be used to straighten the cylinder taper by honing the lower

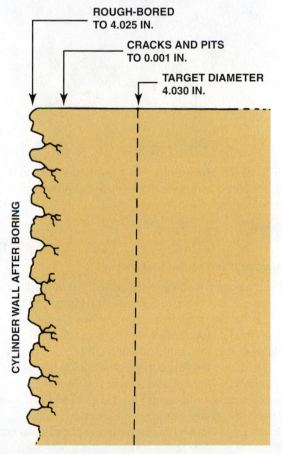

FIGURE 30–27 After boring, the cylinder surface is rough, pitted, and fractured to a depth of about 0.001 inch.

cylinder diameter more than the upper diameter. As it rotates, the sizing hone only cuts the high spots so that cylinder out-of-round is also reduced. The cylinder wall surface finish is about the same when the cylinder is refinished with either type of hone. ● **SEE FIGURE 30–28.**

The hone is stroked up and down in the cylinder as it rotates to produce a **crosshatch finish** on the cylinder wall which

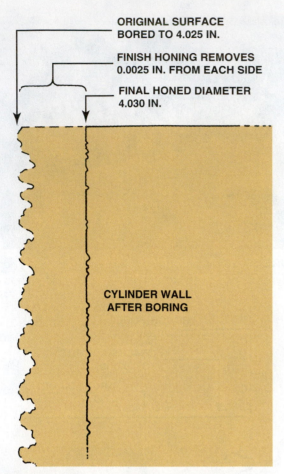

ORIGINAL SURFACE
BORED TO 4.025 IN.

FINISH HONING REMOVES
0.0025 IN. FROM EACH SIDE

FINAL HONED DIAMETER
4.030 IN.

CYLINDER WALL
AFTER BORING

FIGURE 30–28 Honing enlarges the cylinder bore to the final size and leaves a plateau surface finish that retains oil.

TECH TIP

Always Use Torque Plates

Torque plates are thick metal plates that are bolted to the cylinder block to duplicate the forces on the block that occur when the cylinder head is installed. Even though not all machine shops use torque plates during the boring operation, the use of torque plates during the final dimensional honing operation is beneficial. Without torque plates, cylinders can become out-of-round (up to 0.003 inch) and distorted when the cylinder heads are installed and torqued down. Even though the use of torque plates does not eliminate all distortion, their use helps to ensure a truer cylinder dimension. ● **SEE FIGURE 30–29.**

aides in proper ring break-in. The speed that the operator moves the hone up and down controls the angle. Always check service information for the specified crosshatch angle.

The angle of the crosshatch should be between 20 and 60 degrees. Higher angles are produced when the hone is stroked more rapidly in the cylinder. A typical honed cylinder is pictured in ● **FIGURE 30–30.**

FIGURE 30–29 A torque plate being used during a cylinder honing operation. The thick piece of metal is bolted to the block and simulates the forces exerted on the block by the head bolts when the cylinder head is attached.

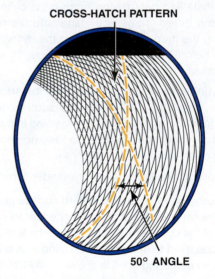

CROSS-HATCH PATTERN

50° ANGLE

FIGURE 30–30 The crosshatched pattern holds oil to keep the rings from wearing excessively, and also keeps the rings against the cylinder wall for a gas-tight fit.

CYLINDER SURFACE FINISH The size of the abrasive particles in the grinding and honing stones controls the surface finish. The size of the abrasive is called the **grit size.** The abrasive is sifted through a screen mesh to sort out the grit size. A coarse-mesh screen has few wires in each square inch, so large pieces can fall through the screen. A fine-mesh screen has many wires in each square inch so that only small pieces can fall through. The screen is used to separate the different grit sizes. The grit size is the number of wires in each square inch of the mesh. A low-numbered grit has large pieces of abrasive material;

Bore to Size, Hone for Clearance

Many engine rebuilders and remanufacturers bore the cylinders to the exact size of the oversize pistons that are to be used. After the block is bored to a standard oversize measurement, the cylinder is honed.

The rigid hone stones, along with an experienced operator, can increase the bore size by 0.001 to 0.003 inch (one to three thousandths of an inch) for the typical clearance needed between the piston and the cylinder walls.

For example:

Actual piston diameter = 4.028 inch
Bore diameter = 4.028 inch
Diameter after honing = 4.03 inch
Amount removed by honing = 0.002 inch

NOTE: The minimum amount recommended to be removed by honing is 0.002 inch, to remove the fractured metal in the cylinder wall caused by boring.

GRIT SIZING CHART		
GRIT/SIEVE SIZE	INCHES	MILLIMETERS
12	0.063	1.600
16	0.043	1.092
20	0.037	0.939
24	0.027	0.685
30	0.022	0.558
36	0.019	0.482
46	0.014	0.355
54	0.012	0.304
60	0.010	0.254
70	0.008	0.203
80	0.0065	0.165
90	0.0057	0.144
100	0.0048	0.121
120	0.0040	0.101
150	0.0035	0.088
180	0.0030	0.076
220	0.0025	0.063
240	0.0020	0.050

CHART 30–1

Grit size numbers and their dimensions in inches and millimeters.

a high-numbered grit has small pieces of abrasive material. The higher the grit number is, the smoother the surface finish will be. ●SEE CHART 30–1.

A given grit size will produce the same finish as long as the cutting pressure is constant. With the same grit size, light cutting pressure produces fine finishes, and heavy cutting pressure produces rough finishes.

The surface finish should match the surface required for the type of piston rings to be used. Typical grit and surface finish standards include the following:

- Chrome rings: 180 grit (25 to 35 microinches)
- Cast-iron rings: 200 grit (20 to 30 microinches)
- Moly rings: 220 grit (18 to 25 microinches)

NOTE: The correct honing oil and coolant are critical to proper operation of the honing equipment and to the quality of the finished cylinders.

CYLINDER HONING PROCEDURE The procedure includes the following steps.

STEP 1 The hone is placed in the cylinder. Before the drive motor is turned on, the hone is moved up and down in the cylinder to get the feel of the stroke length needed. The end of the hone should just break out of the cylinder bore on each end. The hone must *not* be pulled from the top of the cylinder while it is rotating. Also, it must not be pushed so low in the cylinder that it hits the main bearing web or crankshaft.

STEP 2 The sizing hone is adjusted to give a solid drag at the lower end of the stroke.

STEP 3 The hone drive motor is turned on and stroking begins immediately. Stroking continues until the sound of the drag is reduced.

STEP 4 The hone drive motor is turned off while it is still stroking. Stroking is stopped as the rotation of the hone stops. After rotation stops, the hone is collapsed and removed from the cylinder.

STEP 5 The cylinder is examined to check the bore size and finish of the wall. If more honing is needed, the cylinder is again coated with honing oil and is honed once again. The finished cylinder should be within 0.0005 inch (0.013 mm) on both out-of-round and taper measurements. ●SEE FIGURE 30–31 for an example of cylinder surface finish reading.

CHAMFERING THE CYLINDER BORES Whenever machining is performed on the block such as boring and decking, the top edge of the cylinder bores have sharp edges. These sharp edges must be removed to allow the piston with rings to be installed. The slight chamfer allows the rings to enter the cylinder easily when the pistons are installed. A tapered rubber cone covered in sanding cloth is used to remove the sharp edges. ●SEE FIGURE 30–32.

(a)

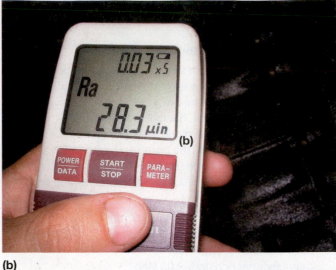

(b)

FIGURE 30–31 (a) The surface finish tool is being held against the cylinder wall. (b) The reading indicates the Ra roughness of the cylinder. More work is needed if moly piston rings are to be used.

FIGURE 30–32 Using a tapered sanding cone to remove the sharp edges at the top of the cylinders created when the block was machined.

BLOCK PREPARATION FOR ASSEMBLY

BLOCK CLEANING After the cylinders have been honed and before the block is cleaned, use a sandpaper cone to chamfer the top edge of the cylinder. Cleaning the honed cylinder wall is an important part of the honing process. If any grit remains on the cylinder wall, it will rapidly wear the piston rings. This wear will

FIGURE 30–33 High-performance engine builders will often install bronze sleeves in the lifter bores.

🔧 **TECH TIP**

Install Lifter Bore Bushings

Lifter bores in a block can be out-of-square with the camshaft, resulting in premature camshaft wear and variations in the valve timing from cylinder to cylinder. To correct for this variation, the lifter bores are bored and reamed oversize using a fixture fastened to the block deck to ensure proper alignment. Bronze lifter bushings are then installed and finish honed to achieve the correct lifter-to-bore clearance. ● **SEE FIGURE 30–33.**

The lifter bores should be "honed" with a ball-type hone. This should be done even if they are "in-line" and do not need bushings. This is often overlooked by technicians and can lead to lifter problems later on, causing lifters to stick on the bores.

FIGURE 30–34 Notice on this cutaway engine block that some of the head bolt holes do not extend too far into the block and dead end. Debris can accumulate at the bottom of these holes and it must be cleaned out before final assembly.

FIGURE 30–35 A tread chaser or bottoming tap should be used in all threaded holes before assembling the engine.

cause premature failure of the reconditioning job. Degreasing and decarbonizing procedures will only remove the honing oil but will *not* remove the abrasive. The *best* way to clean the honed cylinders is to scrub the cylinder wall with a brush using a mixture of *soap* or *detergent* and *water*. The block is scrubbed until it is absolutely clean. This can be determined by wiping the cylinder wall with a clean lint free cloth. The cloth will pick up no soil when the cylinder wall is clean. Be sure that the cylinders are dried as soon as possible to avoid rust from forming.

BLOCK DETAILING Before the engine block can be assembled, a final detailed cleaning should be performed.

1. All oil passages (galleries) should be cleaned by running a long bottle-type brush through all holes in the block.
2. All tapped holes should have the sharp edges at the top of the holes removed chamfered) and cleaned with the correct size of thread chaser to remove any dirt and burrs. ● **SEE FIGURES 30–34 AND 30–35.**
3. Coat the newly cleaned block with fogging oil to prevent rust. Cover the block with a large plastic bag to keep out dirt until it is time to assemble the engine.

SUMMARY

1. Engine blocks are either cast iron or aluminum.
2. Cores are used inside a mold to form water jackets and cylinder bores. After the cast iron has cooled, the block is shaken, which breaks up the cores so that they fall out of openings in the side of the block. Core plugs are used to fill the holes.
3. The block deck is the surface to which the cylinder head attaches. This surface must be flat, true, and parallel with the centerline of the main bearing journals for proper engine operation.
4. The cylinder should be bored and/or honed to match the size of the pistons to be used.
5. All bolt holes should be chamfered and cleaned with a thread chaser before assembly.

REVIEW QUESTIONS

1. How is Styrofoam used to cast an engine block?
2. What does "decking the block" mean?
3. What is the difference between deglazing and honing a cylinder?
4. What is the best method to use to clean an engine block after honing?

1. The block deck is the _____.
   a. Bottom (pan rail) of the block
   b. Top surface of the block
   c. Valley surface of a V-type engine
   d. Area where the engine mounts are attached to the block

2. The surface finish for the cylinder walls usually depends on _____.
   a. The type of piston rings to be used
   b. The type of engine oil that is going to be used in the engine
   c. The cylinder wall-to-piston clearance
   d. Both b and c

3. What should be installed and torqued to factory specification before machining a block?
   a. Front timing chain cover
   b. Main bearing caps
   c. Oil pan
   d. All of the above

4. Cast iron has about how much carbon content?
   a. Less than 1%   c. 3%
   b. 2%   d. 4% or higher

5. Engine blocks can be manufactured using which method(s)?
   a. Sand cast
   b. Sand cast or die cast
   c. Extruded cylinder
   d. Machined from a solid piece of metal (either cast iron or aluminum)

6. A bedplate is located between the _____ and the _____.
   a. Cylinder bores; water jacket
   b. Cylinder head; block deck
   c. Bottom of the block; oil pan
   d. Block deck; cylinder bore

7. Siamese cylinder bores are _____.
   a. Cylinders that do not have a coolant passage between them
   b. Aluminum cylinders
   c. Another name for cylinder liners
   d. Cast-iron cylinders

8. Ultrasonic testing is used to test _____.
   a. For cracks in the block
   b. Surface finish of the cylinder bores
   c. Cylinder wall thickness
   d. Both b and c

9. An engine block should be machined in which order?
   a. Align honing, cylinder boring, block deck machining
   b. Block decking, align honing, cylinder boring
   c. Cylinder boring, align honing, block decking
   d. Align honing, block decking, cylinder boring

10. After the engine block has been machined, it should be cleaned using _____.
    a. Soap and water
    b. SAE 10W-30 oil and a shop cloth
    c. Sprayed-on brake cleaner to remove the cutting oil
    d. Sprayed-on WD-40

chapter 31

CRANKSHAFTS, BALANCE SHAFTS, AND BEARINGS

LEARNING OBJECTIVES: After studying this chapter, the reader should be able to: • Explain the purpose of crankshaft, crankshaft construction, and crankshaft oiling holes. • Discuss the different engine crankshaft types. • Explain the purpose and function of counterweights. • Discuss engine balance, and explain externally and internally balanced engines. • Explain the purpose of balance shafts. • Discuss crankshaft service. • Describe engine bearings and discuss the importance of bearing clearance. • Discuss camshaft bearings.

KEY TERMS: Aluminum 465 • Amplitude 459 • Babbitt 465 • Bank 456 • Bearing crown 465 • Bearing shell 465 • Billet 456 • Case hardening 454 • Conformability 468 • Copper-lead alloy 465 • Corrosion resistance 468 • Counterweights 458 • Crankpins 454 • Crankshaft centerline 453 • Crush 468 • Elastomer 459 • Electroplating 465 • Embedability 468 • Fatigue life 467 • Flying web 458 • Frequency 459 • Full round bearing 470 • Fully counterweighted 458 • Half-shell bearing 465 • Hub 459 • Inertia ring 459 • Nitriding 454 • Overlay 465 • Plain bearing 465 • Precision insert-type bearing shells 465 • Primary vibration 460 • Resonate 459 • Score resistance 468 • Secondary vibration 461 • Sleeve bearing 465 • Splay angle 458 • Split-type (half-shell) bearing 470 • Spread 468 • Spun bearing 469 • Surface finish 454 • Thrust bearing 454 • Tuftriding 455 • Work hardened 467

CRANKSHAFT

PURPOSE AND FUNCTION
Power from expanding gases in the combustion chamber is delivered to the crankshaft through the piston, piston pin, and connecting rod. The connecting rods and their bearings are attached to a bearing journal on the crank throw. The crank throw is offset from the **crankshaft centerline**. The distance between the centerline of the connecting rod bearing journal and the centerline of the crankshaft main bearing journal determines the stroke of the engine. The engine stroke is calculated by multiplying the distance between the two centerlines by 2. The combustion force is applied to the crank throw after the crankshaft has moved past top center. This produces the turning

effort or torque, which rotates the crankshaft. The crankshaft rotates on the main bearings. These bearings are split in half so that they can be assembled around the crankshaft main bearing journals. The crankshaft includes the following parts.

- Main bearing journals
- Rod bearing journals
- Crankshaft throws
- Counterweights
- Front snout
- Flywheel flange
- Keyways
- Oil passages

● **SEE FIGURE 31–1.**

FIGURE 31–1 Typical crankshaft with main journals that are supported by main bearings in the block. Rod journals are offset from the crankshaft centerline.

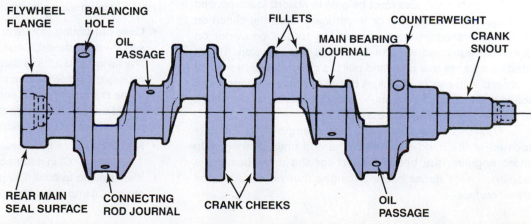

FLYWHEEL FLANGE • BALANCING HOLE • OIL PASSAGE • FILLETS • MAIN BEARING JOURNAL • COUNTERWEIGHT • CRANK SNOUT

REAR MAIN SEAL SURFACE • CONNECTING ROD JOURNAL • CRANK CHEEKS • OIL PASSAGE

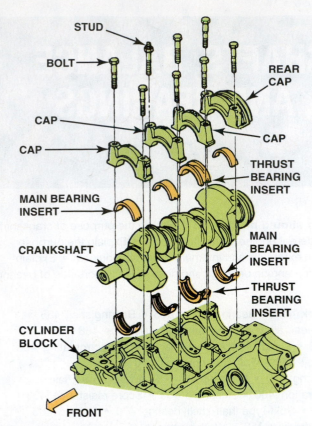

FIGURE 31–2 The crankshaft rotates on main bearings. Longitudinal (end-to-end) movement is controlled by the thrust bearing.

FIGURE 31–3 A ground surface on one of the crankshaft cheeks next to a main bearing supports thrust loads on the crank.

MAIN BEARING JOURNALS The crankshaft rotates in the cylinder block supported on main bearings. ● SEE FIGURE 31–2.

The main bearings support the crankshaft and allow it to rotate easily without excessive wear. The number of cylinders usually determines the number of main bearings.

- Four-cylinder engines and V-8 engines usually have five main bearings.
- Inline 6-cylinder engines usually have seven main bearings.
- V-6 engines normally have only four main bearings.

The crankshaft also must be able to absorb loads applied longitudinally (end to end) or thrust loads from the clutch on a manual transmission vehicle or the torque converter on a vehicle equipped with an automatic transmission. Thrust loads are forces that push and pull the crankshaft forward and rearward in the engine block. A **thrust bearing** supports these loads and maintains the front-to-rear position of the crankshaft in the block. ● SEE FIGURE 31–3.

The thrust surface on many engines is usually located at the middle or one of the end main bearings. On most engines, the bearing insert for the main bearing is equipped with thrust bearing flanges that ride against the thrust surface.

ROD BEARING JOURNALS The rod bearing journals, also called **crankpins**, are offset from the centerline of the crank. Insert-type bearings fit between the big end of the connecting rod and the crankpin of the crankshaft. The crankshaft throw distance that measures one-half of the stroke has a direct relationship to the displacement of the engine.

Engine stroke is equal to *twice* the leverage distance or two times the length of the crankshaft throw. ● SEE FIGURE 31–4.

SURFACE FINISH All crankshaft journals are ground to a very smooth finish. **Surface finish** is measured in microinches; and the smaller the number, the smoother the surface. The typical specification for main and rod crankshaft journals is between 10 and 20 roughness average (Ra). This very smooth surface finish is achieved by polishing the crank journals after the grinding operation.

JOURNAL HARDNESS To improve wear resistance, some manufacturers harden the crankshaft journals. Methods used to harden the crankshaft journals include:

- **Case hardening**, where only the outer portion of the surface is hardened. Case hardening involves heating the crankshaft and adding carbon to the journals where it causes the outer surface to become harder than the rest of the crankshaft. If the entire crankshaft was hardened, it would become too brittle to absorb the torsional stresses of normal engine operation.
- **Nitriding**, where the crankshaft is heated to about 1,000°F (540°C) in a furnace filled with ammonia gas, and then allowed to cool. The process adds nitrogen (from the ammonia) into the surface of the metal, thus forming hard

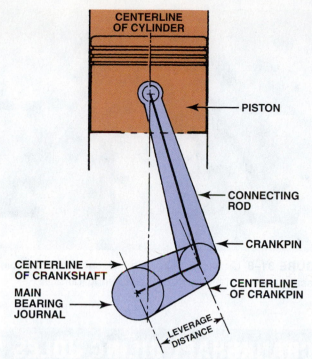

FIGURE 31–4 The distance from the crankpin centerline to the centerline of the crankshaft determines the stroke, which is the leverage available to turn the crankshaft.

nitrides in the surface of the crankshaft to a depth of about 0.007 inch (0.8 mm).

- **Tuftriding**, another variation of this process, involves heating the crankshaft in a molten cyanide salt bath. Tuftriding is a trade name of General Motors.

CRANKSHAFT CONSTRUCTION

FORGED Crankshafts used in high-production automotive engines may be either forged or cast. Forged crankshafts are stronger than the cast crankshaft, but they are more expensive. Forged crankshafts may have a wide separation line. The wide separation line is the result of a grinding process to remove the metal that was extruded from the forging die during the forging process. ● **SEE FIGURE 31–5.**

Most high-performance forged crankshafts are made from SAE 4340 or a similar type of steel. The crankshaft is formed from a hot steel billet through the use of a series of forging dies. Each die changes the shape of the billet slightly. The crankshaft blank is finally formed with the last die. The blanks are then machined to finish the crankshaft. Forging makes a very dense, tough crankshaft with the metal's grain structure running parallel to the principal direction of stress.

FIGURE 31–5 Wide separation lines of a forged crankshaft.

Two methods are used to forge crankshafts.

- One method is to forge the crankshaft *in place.* This is followed by straightening. The forging in place method is primarily used with forged 4- and 6-cylinder crankshafts.
- A second method is to forge the crankshaft in a *single plane.* It is then twisted in the main bearing journal to index the throws at the desired angles. Most newer crankshafts are not twisted.

CAST CRANKSHAFTS Casting materials and techniques have improved cast crankshaft quality so that cast crankshafts are used in most production automotive engines. Automotive crankshafts may be cast in steel, nodular iron, or malleable iron. Advantages of a cast crankshaft are as follows:

- Crankshaft material and machining costs are less than they are with forging. The reason is that the crankshaft can be made close to the required shape and size, including all complicated counterweights. The only machining required on a carefully designed cast crankshaft is the grinding of bearing journal surfaces and the finishing of front and rear drive ends.
- Metal grain structure in the cast crankshaft is uniform and random throughout; therefore, the shaft is able to handle loads from all directions.
- Counterweights on cast crankshafts are slightly larger than counterweights on a forged crankshaft, because the cast shaft metal is less dense and therefore somewhat lighter.

The narrow mold parting surface lines can be seen on the cast crankshaft in ● **FIGURE 31–6.**

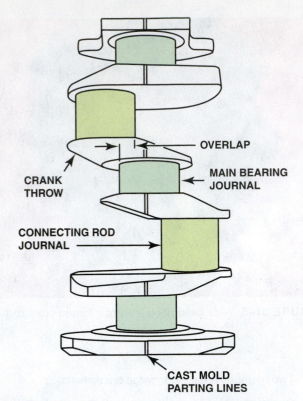

FIGURE 31–6 Cast crankshaft showing the bearing journal overlap and a straight, narrow cast mold parting line. The amount of overlap determines the strength of the crankshaft.

FIGURE 31–7 A billet crankshaft showing how it is machined from a solid chuck of steel, usually 4340 steel, at the right and the finished crankshaft on the left.

BILLET CRANKSHAFTS A billet crankshaft is machined from a solid piece of forged steel called a **billet**. This solid piece of steel, usually SAE 4340, is then machined through several operations to create a finished crankshaft.

The advantages of a billet crankshaft include:

- Uniform grain structure created by the forging process
- Stiff, strong, and very durable

The disadvantage is the high cost. Billet crankshafts tend to be very expensive because of the large amount of material removal during the machining process and the high material cost and the additional heat treatment required. ● **SEE FIGURE 31–7.**

FIGURE 31–8 Crankshaft sawed in half, showing drilled oil passages between the main and rod bearing journals.

CRANKSHAFT OILING HOLES

PURPOSE AND FUNCTION The crankshaft is drilled to allow oil from the main bearing oil groove to be directed to the connecting rod bearings. ● **SEE FIGURE 31–8.**

The oil on the bearings forms a hydrodynamic oil film to support bearing loads. Some of the oil may be sprayed out through a spit or bleed hole in the connecting rod. The rest of the oil leaks from the edges of the bearing. It is thrown from the bearing against the inside surfaces of the engine. Some of the oil that is thrown from the crankshaft bearings will land on the camshaft to lubricate the lobes. A part of the throw-off, oil splashes on the cylinder wall to lubricate the piston and rings.

Stress tends to concentrate at oil holes drilled through the crankshaft journals. These holes are usually located where the crankshaft loads and stresses are the lowest. The edges of the oil holes are carefully chamfered to relieve as much stress concentration as possible. Chamfered oil holes are shown in ● **FIGURE 31–9.**

ENGINE CRANKSHAFT TYPES

V-8 ENGINE ARRANGEMENT The V-8 engine has four inline cylinders in each of the two blocks that are placed at a 90 degree angle to each other. Each group of four inline cylinders is called a **bank**. The crankshaft for the V-8 engine has four throws. The connecting rods from two cylinders are connected to each throw, one from each bank. This arrangement results in a condition of being only minimally unbalanced.

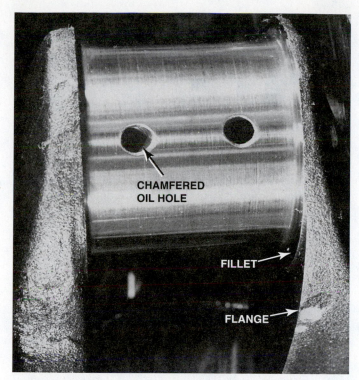

FIGURE 31-9 Typical chamfered hole in a crankshaft bearing journal.

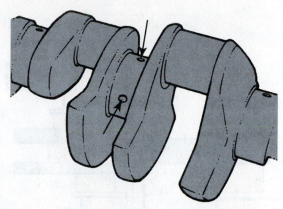

FIGURE 31-10 A cross-drilled crankshaft is used on some production engines and is a common racing modification.

The V-8 engine crankshaft has two planes, so there is one throw every 90 degrees. A plane is a flat surface that cuts through the part. These planes could be seen if the crankshaft were cut lengthwise through the center of the main bearing and crankpin journals. Looking at the front of the crankshaft:

- The first throw is at 360 degrees (up).
- The second throw is at 90 degrees (to the right).
- The third throw is at 270 degrees (to the left).
- The fourth throw is at 180 degrees (down).

In operation with this arrangement, one piston reaches top center at each 90 degrees of crankshaft rotation so that the engine operates smoothly with even firing at each 90 degrees of crankshaft rotation.

FOUR-CYLINDER ENGINE CRANKSHAFTS
The crankshaft used on 4-cylinder inline engines has four throws on a single plane. There is usually a main bearing journal between each throw, making it a five main bearing crankshaft. Pistons also move as pairs in this engine.

- Pistons in cylinders 1 and 4 move together, and pistons 2 and 3 move together.
- Each piston in a pair is 360 degrees out-of-phase with the other piston in the 720 degree four-stroke cycle. With this arrangement, the 4-cylinder inline engine fires one cylinder at each 180 degrees of crankshaft rotation.

A 4-cylinder opposed (flat) engine and a 90 degree V-4 engine have crankshafts that look like that of the 4-cylinder inline engine.

FIGURE 31–12 A fully counterweighted 4-cylinder crankshaft.

This angle between the crankpins on the crankshaft throws is called a **splay angle**. A flange was left between the split crankpin journals. This provides a continuous fillet or edge for machining and grinding operations. It also provides a normal flange for the rod and bearing. This flange between the splayed crankpin journals is sometimes called a **flying web**.

60-DEGREE V-6 ENGINE CRANKSHAFTS The 60-degree V-6 engine is similar to the even-firing 90 degree V-6 engine. The adjacent pairs of crankpins on the crankshaft used in the 60 degree V-6 engine have a splay angle of 60 degrees.

The crankshaft of the 60 degree V-6 engine also uses four main bearings.

COUNTERWEIGHTS

PURPOSE AND FUNCTION Crankshafts are balanced by **counterweights**, which are cast, forged, or machined as part of the crankshaft. A crankshaft that has counterweights on both sides of each connecting rod journal is called **fully counterweighted**. ● SEE FIGURE 31–12.

A fully counterweighted crankshaft is the smoothest running and most durable design, but it is also the heaviest and most expensive to manufacture. Most vehicle manufacturers do not use fully counterweighted crankshafts in an effort to lighten the rotating mass of the engine. An engine with a light crankshaft allows the engine to accelerate quicker. Even crankshafts that are not fully counterweighted are still balanced.

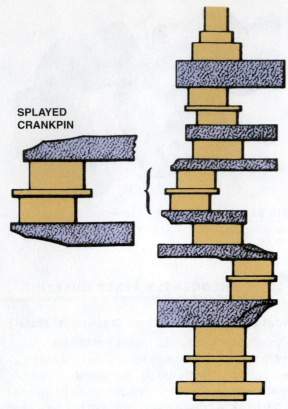

SPLAYED CRANKPIN

FIGURE 31–11 A splayed crankshaft design is used to create an even-firing 90 degree V-6.

FIVE-CYLINDER ENGINE CRANKSHAFTS The inline 5-cylinder engine has a five-throw crankshaft with one throw at each 72 degrees. Six main bearings are used on this crankshaft. The piston in one cylinder reaches top center at each 144 degrees of crankshaft rotation. Dynamic balancing has been one of the major problems with this engine design, yet the vibration was satisfactorily dampened and isolated on both the Audi and Acura 5-cylinder engines.

THREE-CYLINDER ENGINE CRANKSHAFTS A 3-cylinder engine uses a 120 degree three-throw crankshaft with four main bearings. This engine requires a balancing shaft that turns at crankshaft speed, but in the opposite direction, to reduce the vibration to an acceptable level.

INLINE SIX-CYLINDER ENGINE CRANKSHAFT Inline six-cylinder engine crankshafts ride on four or seven main bearings and use six crank throws in three planes 120 degrees apart. An inline six cylinder is in perfect primary and secondary balance.

90-DEGREE V-6 ENGINE CRANKSHAFTS The crank throws for an even-firing V-6 engine are split, making separate crankpins for each cylinder. The split throw can be seen in ● FIGURE 31–11.

> **? FREQUENTLY ASKED QUESTION**
>
> **What Is an Offset Crankshaft?**
>
> To reduce side loads, some vehicle manufacturers offset the crankshaft from center. For example, if an engine rotates clockwise as viewed from the front, the crankshaft may be offset to the left to reduce the angle of the connecting rod during the power stroke. ● SEE FIGURE 31–13.
>
> The offset usually varies from 1/16 to 1/2 inch, depending on make and model. Many inline 4-cylinder engines used in hybrid electric vehicles use an offset crankshaft.

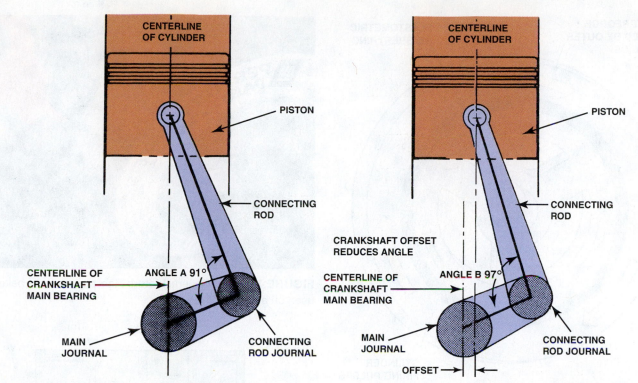

FIGURE 31-13 The crank throw is halfway down on the power stroke. The piston on the left without an offset crankshaft has a sharper angle than the engine on the right with an offset crankshaft.

VIBRATION DAMAGE Each time combustion occurs, the force deflects the crankshaft as it transfers torque to the output shaft. This deflection occurs in two ways, to bend the shaft sideways and to twist the shaft in torsion. The crankshaft must be rigid enough to keep the deflection forces to a minimum.

Crankshaft deflections are directly related to the operating roughness of an engine. When back-and-forth deflections occur at the same vibration **frequency** (number of vibrations per second) as that of another engine part, the parts will vibrate together. When this happens, the parts are said to **resonate**. These vibrations may become great enough to reach the audible level, producing a thumping sound. If this type of vibration continues, the crankshaft may fail.
● SEE FIGURE 31-14.

Harmful crankshaft twisting vibrations are dampened with a torsional vibration damper. It is also called a harmonic balancer. This damper or balancer usually consists of a cast-iron **inertia ring** mounted to a cast-iron **hub** with an **elastomer** sleeve.

NOTE: Push on the rubber (elastomer sleeve) of the vibration damper with your fingers or a pencil. *If the rubber does not spring back, replace the damper.*

Elastomers are actually synthetic, rubberlike materials. The inertia ring size is selected to control the **amplitude** of the crankshaft vibrations for each specific engine model.
● SEE FIGURE 31-15.

FIGURE 31-14 A crankshaft broken as a result of using the wrong torsional vibration damper.

 **TECH TIP**

High Engine Speeds Require High-Performance Parts

Do not go racing with stock parts. A stock harmonic balancer can come apart and the resulting vibration can break the crankshaft if the engine is used for racing. Check the Internet or race part suppliers for the recommended balancer to use.
● SEE FIGURE 31-16.

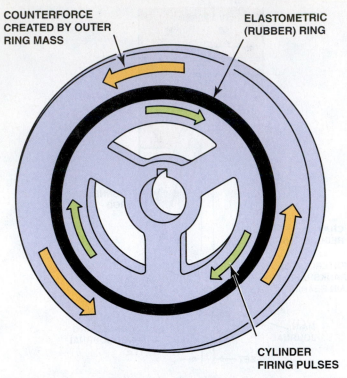

FIGURE 31-15 The hub of the harmonic balancer is attached to the front of the crankshaft. The elastomer (rubber) between the inertia ring and the center hub allows the absorption of crankshaft firing impulses.

COUNTERFORCE CREATED BY OUTER RING MASS

ELASTOMETRIC (RUBBER) RING

CYLINDER FIRING PULSES

FIGURE 31-16 A General Motors high-performance balancer used on a race engine.

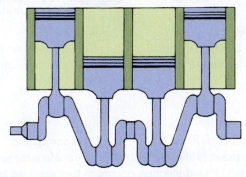

FIGURE 31-17 In a 4-cylinder engine, the two outside pistons move upward at the same time as the inner pistons move downward, which reduces primary unbalance.

EXTERNALLY AND INTERNALLY BALANCED ENGINES

DEFINITION Most crankshaft balancing is done during manufacture. Holes are drilled in the counterweight to lighten and improve balance. Sometimes these holes are drilled after the crankshaft is installed in the engine. Some manufacturers are able to control casting quality so closely that counterweight machining for balancing is not necessary.

Engine manufacturers balance an engine in one of two ways.

- **Externally balanced.** Weight is added to the harmonic balancer (vibration damper) and flywheel or the flexplate.
- **Internally balanced.** All rotating parts of the engine are individually balanced, including the harmonic balancer and flywheel (flexplate).

For example, the 350 cu. inch Chevrolet V-8 is internally balanced, whereas the 400 cu. inch Chevrolet V-8 uses an externally balanced crankshaft. The harmonic balancer used on an externally balanced engine has additional weight.

ENGINE BALANCE

PRIMARY AND SECONDARY BALANCE Anything that rotates will vibrate. This means that an engine will vibrate during operation, although engine designers attempt to reduce the vibration as much as possible.

- **Primary balance.** When pistons move up and down in the cylinders, they create a **primary vibration**, which is a strong low-frequency vibration.

A counterweight on the crankshaft opposite the piston/rod assembly helps reduce this vibration. An inline 4-cylinder engine has very little primary vibration, because as two pistons are traveling upward in the cylinders, two are moving downward at the same time, effectively canceling out primary unbalances. ● SEE FIGURE 31-17.

- **Secondary balance.** Four-cylinder engines, however, suffer from a vibration at twice engine speed. This is

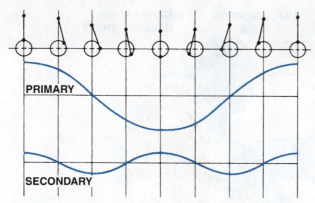

FIGURE 31–18 Primary and secondary vibrations in relation to piston position.

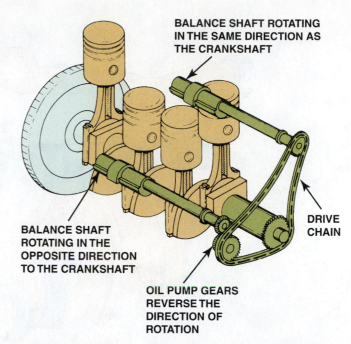

FIGURE 31–19 Two counterrotating balance shafts used to counterbalance the vibrations of a 4-cylinder engine.

called a **secondary vibration**, which is a weak high-frequency vibration caused by a slight difference in the inertia of the pistons at top dead center compared to bottom dead center. This vibration is most noticeable at high engine speeds, especially if the engine size is greater than 2 liters. The larger the displacement of the engine, the larger the bore and the heavier the pistons contribute to the buzzing-type secondary vibration. ● SEE FIGURE 31–18.

BALANCE SHAFTS

PURPOSE AND FUNCTION Some engines use balance shafts to dampen normal engine vibrations. *Dampening* is reducing the vibration to an acceptable level. A balance shaft that is turning at crankshaft speed, but in the opposite direction, is used on a 3-cylinder inline engine. Weights on the ends of the balance shaft move in a direction opposite to the direction of the end piston. When the piston goes up, the weight goes down, and when the piston goes down, the weight goes up. This reduces the end-to-end rocking action on the 3-cylinder inline engine.

Another type of balance shaft system is designed to counterbalance vibrations on a four-stroke, 4-cylinder engine. Two shafts are used, and they turn at *twice* the engine speed. In most applications, both shafts rotate in the same direction and are driven by a chain or gear off the crankshaft. Counterweights on the balance shafts are positioned to oppose the natural rolling action of the engine, as well as the secondary vibrations caused by the piston and rod movements. ● SEE FIGURE 31–19.

BALANCE SHAFT APPLICATIONS Balance shafts are commonly found on the larger displacement (over 2 liter) 4-cylinder automotive engines.

- Most 4-cylinder engines larger than 2.2 liters use balance shafts. These are often located underneath the crankshaft. ● SEE FIGURE 31–20.

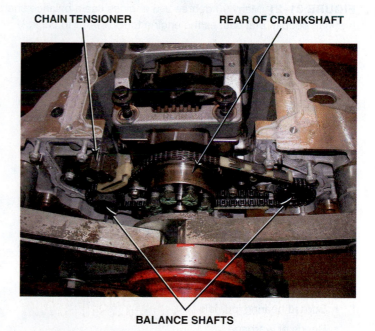

FIGURE 31–20 This General Motors 4-cylinder engine uses two balance shafts driven by a chain at the rear of the crankshaft.

- Since the late 1980s, both Ford and General Motors added a balance shaft to many of their V-6 engines. These 90-degree V-6 engines use a split crank journal to create an even-firing arrangement, but these engines suffer from forces that cause the engine to rock back and forth. This motion is called a *rocking couple* and is dampened by the use of a balance shaft. ● SEE FIGURE 31–21.

The addition of balance shafts makes a big improvement in the smoothness of the engine. In V-6 engines, the improvement

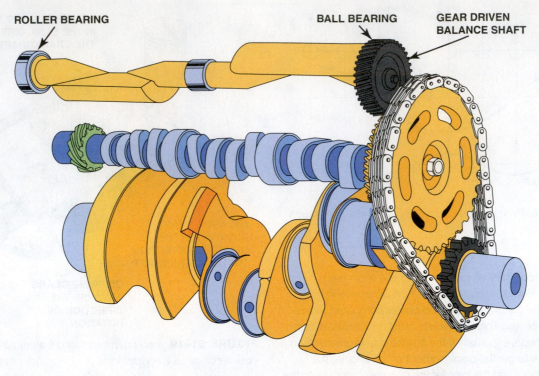

ROLLER BEARING   BALL BEARING   GEAR DRIVEN BALANCE SHAFT

FIGURE 31-21 Many 90 degree V-6 engines use a balance shaft to reduce vibrations and effectively cancel a rocking motion (rocking couple) that causes the engine to rock front to back.

is most evident during idling and low-speed operation, whereas in the 4-cylinder engines, balance shafts are especially helpful at higher engine speeds. The V-6 engines that use a 60 degree design do not create a rocking couple and, therefore, do not need a balance shaft.

CRANKSHAFT SERVICE

CRANKSHAFT VISUAL INSPECTION Crankshaft damage includes:

- Worn journals
- Scored bearing journals
- Bends or warpage
- Cracks
- Thread damage (flywheel flange or front snout)
- Worn front or rear seal surfaces

Damaged shafts must be reconditioned or replaced. The crankshaft is one of the most highly stressed engine parts. *The stress on the crankshaft increases by four times every time the engine speed doubles.* Any sign of a crack is a cause to reject the crankshaft. Most cracks can be seen during a close visual inspection. Crankshafts should also be checked with Magnaflux, which will highlight tiny cracks that would lead to failure.

Bearing journal scoring is a common crankshaft defect. Scoring appears as scratches around the bearing journal surface.

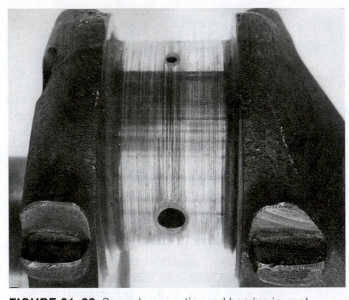

FIGURE 31-22 Scored connecting rod bearing journal.

Generally, there is more scoring near the center of the bearing journal, as shown in ● **FIGURE 31-22.**

Crankshaft journals should be inspected for nicks, pits, or corrosion. Roughness and slight bends in journals can be corrected by grinding the journals.

NOTE: If your fingernail catches on a groove when rubbed across a bearing journal, the journal is too rough to reuse and must be reground. Another test is to rub a copper penny across the journal. If any copper remains on the crankshaft, it must be reground.

FIGURE 31–23 All crankshaft journals should be measured for diameter as well as taper and out-of-round.

CHECK FOR OUT-OF-ROUNDNESS
AT EACH END OF JOURNAL

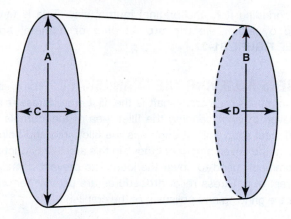

A VS. B = VERTICAL TAPER
C VS. D = HORIZONTAL TAPER
A VS. C = OUT OF ROUND
B VS. D = OUT OF ROUND

FIGURE 31–24 Check each journal for taper and out-of-round.

MEASURING THE CRANKSHAFT Crankshafts should be carefully measured to determine the following:

- Size of main and rod bearing journals compared to factory specifications
- Each journal checked for out-of-round condition
- Each journal checked for taper
- ● SEE FIGURES 31–23 AND 31–24.

CRANKSHAFT GRINDING Crankshaft journals that have excessive scoring, out-of-round, or taper should be reground.

FIGURE 31–25 The rounded fillet area of the crankshaft is formed by the corners of the grinding stone.

The typical procedure includes the following steps.

STEP 1   Crankshafts may require straightening before grinding.

STEP 2   Both crankshaft ends are placed in rotating heads on one style of crankshaft grinder.

STEP 3   The main bearing journals are ground on the centerline of the crankshaft.

STEP 4   The crankshaft is then offset in the two rotating heads just enough to make the crankshaft main bearing journal centerline rotate around the centerline of the crankpin. The crankshaft will then be rotating around the crankpin centerline. The journal on the crankpin is reground in this position.

STEP 5   The crankshaft must be repositioned for each different crankpin center.

In another type of crankshaft grinder, the crankshaft always turns on the main bearing centerline. The grinding head is programmed to move in and out as the crankshaft turns to grind the crankpin bearing journals.

Crankshafts are usually ground to the following undersize.

- 0.010 inch
- 0.020 inch
- 0.030 inch

The finished journal should be accurately ground to size with a smooth surface finish. The radius of the fillet area on the sides of the journal should also be the same as the original. ● SEE FIGURE 31–25.

CRANKSHAFT POLISHING The journal is polished after grinding using a 320-grit polishing cloth and oil to remove

FIGURE 31–26 An excessively worn crankshaft can be restored to useful service by welding the journals, and then machining them back to the original size.

FIGURE 31–27 All crankshafts should be polished after grinding. Both the crankshaft and the polishing cloth are being revolved.

the fine metal "fuzz" remaining on the journal. This fuzz feels smooth when the shaft turns in its direction. As the shaft turns in the opposite direction, the fuzz feels like a fine milling cutter. Polishing removes this fuzz. The crankshaft is rotated in its normal direction of rotation so that the polishing cloth can remove the fuzz. This leaves a smooth shaft with the proper surface finish. *Most crankshaft grinders grind in the direction opposite of rotation and then polish in the same direction as rotation.* ● SEE FIGURE 31–26.

The crankshaft oil passages should be cleaned and the journals tagged with the undersize dimensions.

WELDING A CRANKSHAFT Sometimes it is desirable to salvage a crankshaft by building up a bearing journal and

FIGURE 31–28 Crankshafts should be stored vertically to prevent possible damage or warpage. This clever bench-mounted tray for crankshafts not only provides a safe place to store crankshafts but is also out of the way and cannot be accidentally tipped.

then grinding it to the original journal size. This is usually done by either electric arc welding or a metal spray. ● SEE FIGURE 31–27.

STRESS RELIEVING THE CRANKSHAFT The greatest area of stress on a crankshaft is the fillet area. Stress relief is achieved by *shot peening* the fillet area of the journals with #320 steel shot. This strengthens the fillet area and helps to prevent the development of cracks in this area. Gray duct tape is commonly used to cover the journal to prevent damage to the rest of it. Stress relief procedures are usually performed after the grinding and polishing of the crankshaft.

STORING CRANKSHAFTS All crankshafts should be coated with oil to keep them from rusting, and stored vertically until time for engine assembly. All crankshafts should be placed on the floor vertically to help prevent warping due to gravity. ● SEE FIGURE 31–28.

ENGINE BEARINGS

INTRODUCTION Engine bearings are the main supports for the major moving parts of any engine. Engine bearings are important for the following reasons.

1. The clearance between the bearings and the crankshaft is a major factor in maintaining the proper oil pressure throughout the engine. Most engines are designed to provide the maximum protection and lubrication to the engine bearings above all else.

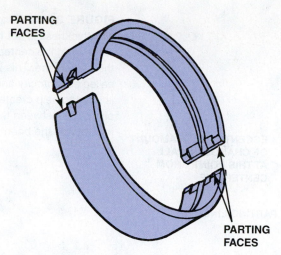

PARTING FACES

PARTING FACES

FIGURE 31–29 The two halves of a plain bearing meet at the parting faces.

2. Engine durability relies on bearing life. Bearing failure usually results in immediate engine failure.

3. Engine bearings are designed to support the operating loads of the engine and, with the lubricant, provide minimum friction. This must be achieved at all designed engine speeds. The bearings must be able to operate for long periods of time, even when small foreign particles are in the lubricant.

TYPES OF BEARINGS
Most engine bearings are one of two types.

- **Plain bearing**
- **Sleeve bearing**
  - ● **SEE FIGURE 31–29.**

Most bearing halves, or shells, do not have uniform thickness. The wall thickness of most bearings is largest in the center, called the **bearing crown**. The bearing thickness then tapers to a thinner measurement at each parting line. ● **SEE FIGURE 31–30.**

The tapered wall keeps bearing clearances close at the top and bottom of the bearing, which are the more loaded areas and allow more oil flow at the sides of the bearing. Both need a constant flow of lubricating oil. In automotive engines, the lubricating system supplies oil to each bearing continuously when the engine runs. Bearings and journals *only* wear when the parts come in contact with each other or when foreign particles are present.

Oil enters the bearing through the oil holes and grooves. It spreads into a smooth wedge-shaped oil film that supports the bearing load.

BEARING MATERIALS
Three materials are used for automobile engine bearings.

- **Babbitt**
- **Copper-lead alloy**
- **Aluminum**

A layer of the bearing materials that is 0.01 to 0.02 inch (0.25 to 0.5 mm) thick is applied over a low carbon steel backing. An engine bearing is called a **bearing shell**, which is a steel backing with a surface coating of bearing material. The steel provides support needed for the shaft load. The bearing material meets the rest of the bearing operating requirements.

- **Babbitt.** Babbitt is the oldest automotive bearing material. Isaac Babbitt (1799–1862) first formulated this material in 1839. An excellent bearing material, it was originally made from a combination of lead, tin, and antimony. Lead and tin are alloyed with small quantities of copper and antimony to give it the required strength. Babbitt is still used in applications in which material is required for soft shafts running under moderate loads and speeds. It will work with occasional borderline lubrication and oil starvation without failure.

- **Trimetal.** Copper-lead alloy is a stronger and more expensive bearing material than babbitt. It is used for intermediate- and high-speed applications. Tin, in small quantities, is often alloyed with the copper-lead bearings. This bearing material is most easily damaged by corrosion from acid accumulation in the engine oil. Corrosion results in bearing journal wear as the bearing is eroded by the acids. Many of the copper-lead bearings have an **overlay**, or third layer, of metal. This overlay is usually of babbitt. Babbitt-overlayed bearings have high fatigue strength, good conformity, good embedability, and good corrosion resistance. The overplated bearing is a premium bearing. It is also the most expensive because the overplating layer, from 0.0005 to 0.001 inch (0.0125 to 0.025 mm) thick, is put on the bearing with an **electroplating** process. The layers of bearing material on a bearing shell are illustrated in ● **FIGURE 31–31.**

- **Aluminum.** Aluminum was the last of the three materials to be used for automotive bearings. Automotive bearing aluminum has small quantities of tin and silicone alloyed with it. This makes a stronger but more expensive bearing than either babbitt or copper-lead alloy. Most of its bearing characteristics are equal to or better than those of babbitt and copper lead. Aluminum bearings are well suited to high-speed, high-load conditions and do not contain lead, which is a benefit to the environment both at the manufacturing plant and for the technician who may be exposed to the bearings.

BEARING MANUFACTURING
Modern automotive engines use **precision insert-type bearing shells**, sometimes called **half-shell bearings**. The bearing is manufactured to very close tolerance so that it will fit correctly in each application. The bearing, therefore, must be made from precisely the correct materials under closely controlled manufacturing conditions. ● **FIGURE 31–32** shows the typical bearing types found in most engines.

BEARING SIZES
Bearings are usually available in standard (std.) size, and in measurements 0.010, 0.020, and 0.030 inch *undersize*. ● **SEE FIGURE 31–33.**

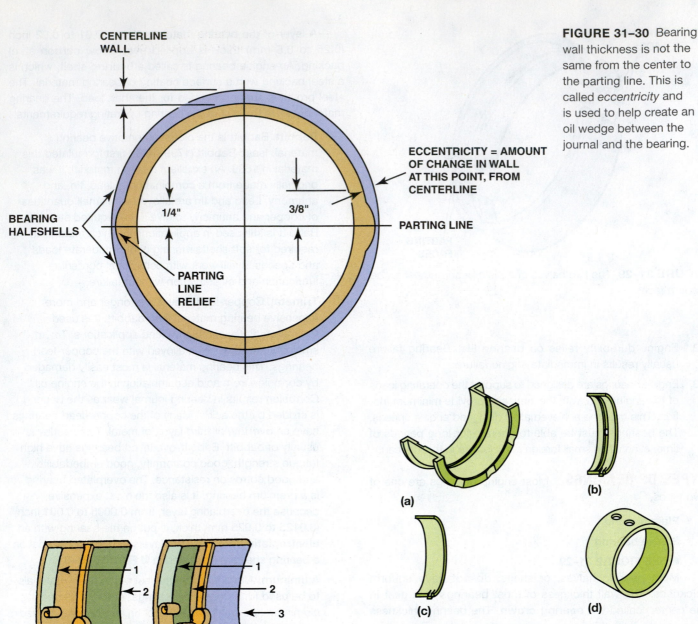

FIGURE 31–30 Bearing wall thickness is not the same from the center to the parting line. This is called *eccentricity* and is used to help create an oil wedge between the journal and the bearing.

CENTERLINE WALL

ECCENTRICITY = AMOUNT OF CHANGE IN WALL AT THIS POINT, FROM CENTERLINE

BEARING HALFSHELLS

1/4"   3/8"

PARTING LINE

PARTING LINE RELIEF

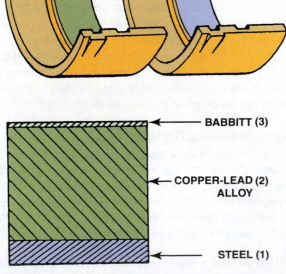

BABBITT (3)

COPPER-LEAD (2) ALLOY

STEEL (1)

FIGURE 31–31 Typical two- and three-layer engine bearing inserts showing the relative thickness of the various materials.

FIGURE 31–32 Typical bearing shell types found in modern engines: (a) half-shell thrust bearing, (b) upper main bearing insert, (c) lower main bearing insert, (d) full round-type camshaft bearing.

(a)
(b)
(c)
(d)

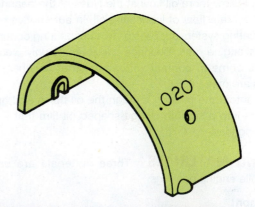

.020

FIGURE 31–33 Bearings are often marked with an undersize dimension. This bearing is used on a crankshaft with a ground journal that is 0.020 inch smaller in diameter than the stock size.

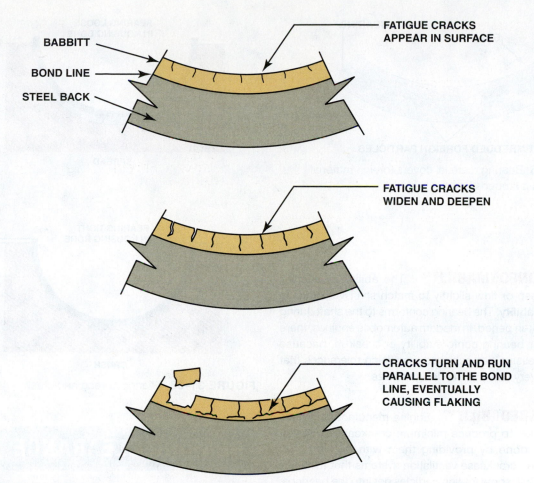

BABBITT

BOND LINE

STEEL BACK

FATIGUE CRACKS APPEAR IN SURFACE

FATIGUE CRACKS WIDEN AND DEEPEN

CRACKS TURN AND RUN PARALLEL TO THE BOND LINE, EVENTUALLY CAUSING FLAKING

FIGURE 31–34 Work hardened bearing material becomes brittle and cracks, leading to bearing failure.

Even though the bearing itself is thicker for use on a machined crankshaft, the bearing is referred to as undersize because the crankshaft journals are undersize. Factory bearings may be available in 0.0005 or 0.001 inch undersize for precision fitting of a production crankshaft.

Before purchasing bearings, be sure to use a micrometer to measure *all* main and connecting rod journals. Replacement bearings are also available in 0.001, 0.002, and 0.003 inch, to allow the technician to achieve the proper bearing clearance without needing to machine the crankshaft.

BEARING LOADS The forces on the engine bearings vary with engine speed and load. On the intake stroke, the inertia force is opposed by the force of drawing in the air-fuel mixture. On the compression and power strokes, there is also an opposing force on the rod bearings. On the exhaust stroke, however, there is no opposing force to counteract the inertia force of the piston coming to a stop at TDC. The result is a higher force load on the *bottom* rod bearing due to inertia at TDC of the exhaust stroke. These forces tend to stretch the big end of the rod in the direction of rod movement.

1. As engine speed (RPM) increases, rod bearing loads decrease because of the balancing of inertia and opposing loads.

2. As engine speed (RPM) increases, the main bearing loads increase.

   NOTE: This helps explain why engine blocks with four-bolt main bearing supports are only needed for high-engine speed stability.

3. Because the loads on bearings vary and affect both rod and main bearings, it is generally recommended that *all* engine bearings be replaced at one time.

BEARING FATIGUE Bearings tend to flex or bend slightly under changing loads. This is especially noticeable in reciprocating engine bearings. Bearing metals, like other metals, tend to fatigue and break after being flexed or bent a number of times. Flexing starts fatigue, which shows up as fine cracks in the bearing surface because the bearing material became **work hardened**. These cracks gradually deepen almost to the bond between the bearing metal and the backing metal. The cracks then cross over and intersect with each other. In time, this will allow a piece of bearing material to fall out. The length of time before fatigue will cause failure is called the **fatigue life** of the bearing. ● SEE FIGURE 31–34.

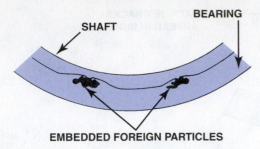

FIGURE 31–35 Bearing material covers foreign material (such as dirt) as it embeds into the bearing.

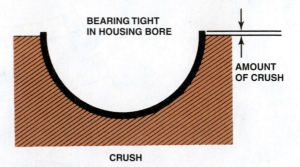

FIGURE 31–36 Bearing spread and crush.

BEARING CONFORMABILITY The ability of bearing materials to creep or flow slightly to match shaft variations is called **conformability**. The bearing conforms to the shaft during the engine break-in period. In modern automobile engines, there is little need for bearing conformability or break-in, because automatic processing has achieved machining tolerances that keep the shaft very close to the designed size.

BEARING EMBEDABILITY Engine manufacturers have designed engines to produce minimum crankcase deposits. This has been done by providing them with oil filters, air filters, and closed crankcase ventilation systems that minimize contaminants. Still, some foreign particles get into the bearings. The bearings must be capable of embedding these particles into the bearing surface so that they will not score the shaft. To fully embed the particle, the bearing material gradually works across the particle, completely covering it. The bearing property that allows it to do this is called **embedability**. ● SEE FIGURE 31–35.

BEARING DAMAGE RESISTANCE Under some operating conditions, the bearing will be temporarily overloaded. This will cause the oil film to break down and allow the shaft metal to come in contact with the bearing metal. As the rotating crankshaft contacts the bearing high spots, the spots become hot from friction. The friction causes localized hot spots in the bearing material that seize or weld to the crankshaft. The crankshaft then breaks off particles of the bearing material and pulls the particles around with it, scratching or scoring the bearing surface.

Bearings have a characteristic called **score resistance**. It prevents the bearing materials from seizing to the shaft during oil film breakdown.

By-products of combustion form acids in the oil. The bearings' ability to resist attack from these acids is called **corrosion resistance**. Corrosion can occur over the entire surface of the bearing. This will remove material and increase the oil clearance. It can also leach or eat into the bearing material, dissolving some of the bearing material alloys. Either type of corrosion will reduce bearing life.

BEARING CLEARANCE

IMPORTANCE OF PROPER CLEARANCE The bearing-to-journal clearance may be from 0.0005 to 0.0025 inch (0.025 to 0.06 mm), depending on the engine. Doubling the journal clearance will allow more than *four* times more oil to flow from the edges of the bearing. The oil clearance must be large enough to allow an oil film to build up, but small enough to prevent excess oil leakage, which would cause loss of oil pressure. A large amount of oil leakage at one of the bearings would starve other bearings farther along in the oil system. This would result in the failure of the oil-starved bearings.

CHECKING BEARING CLEARANCE Bearing oil clearance can be checked in the following ways.

1. Using Plastigage® between the crankshaft journal and the bearing. The thin plasticlike strip material will deform depending on the clearance.

2. Measuring the crankshaft journal diameter and the inside diameter of the bearing as it is installed and subtracting the two measurements. The difference is the bearing clearance.

BEARING SPREAD AND CRUSH The bearing design also includes bearing **spread** and **crush**. ● SEE FIGURE 31–36.

▪ **Bearing spread.** The bearing shell has a slightly larger arc than the bearing housing. This difference, called bearing spread, makes the shell 0.005 to 0.02 inch (0.125 to 0.5 mm)

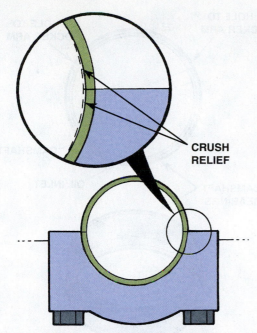

FIGURE 31–37 Bearings are thinner at the parting line faces to provide crush relief.

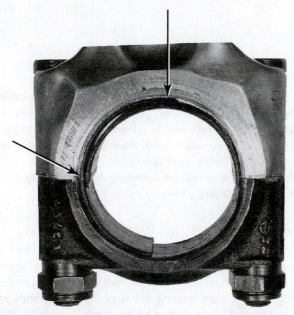

FIGURE 31–38 Spun bearing. The lower cap bearing has rotated under the upper rod bearing.

wider than the housing bore. Spread holds the bearing shell in the housing while the engine is being assembled.

- **Bearing crush.** When the bearing is installed, each end of the bearing shell is slightly above the parting surface. When the bearing cap is tightened, the ends of the two bearing shells touch and are forced together. This force is called bearing crush. Crush holds the bearing in place and keeps the bearing from turning when the engine runs. Crush must exert a force of at least 12,000 PSI (82,740 kPa) at 250°F (121°C) to hold the bearing securely in place. A stress of 40,000 PSI (275,790 kPa) is

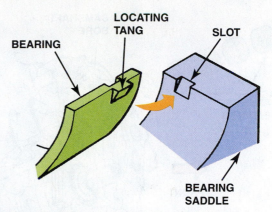

FIGURE 31–39 The tang and slot help index the bearing in the bore.

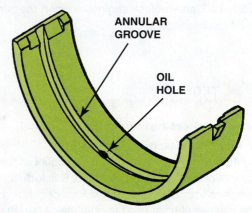

FIGURE 31–40 Many bearings are manufactured with a groove down the middle to improve the oil flow around the main journal.

considered maximum to avoid damaging the bearing or housing. ● SEE FIGURE 31–37.

Bearing shells that do not have enough crush may rotate with the shaft. The result is called a **spun bearing**. ● SEE FIGURE 31–38.

- **Bearing tang.** A *tang* or lip helps locate the bearing shell in the housing. When the bearing clearance and "crush" have been worn or destroyed, the bearing can "spin," thus creating catastrophic failure. The tang often helps prevent this from occurring. ● SEE FIGURE 31–39.

Many newer engines do *not* use a tang on the bearing. Always check service information for the exact bearings and procedures to use for the engine being serviced.

Replacement bearings should be of a quality as good as or better than that of the original bearings. The replacement bearings must also have the same oil holes and grooves.

CAUTION: Some bearings may have oil holes in the top shell only. If these are installed incorrectly, no oil will flow to the connecting or main rods, resulting in instant engine failure. To help the oil spread across the entire bearing, some bearings use an oil groove. ● SEE FIGURE 31–40.

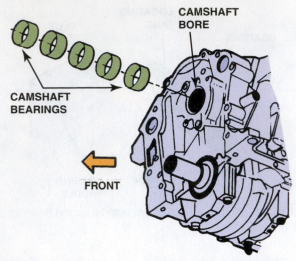

FIGURE 31–41 Cam-in-block engines support the camshaft with sleeve-type bearings.

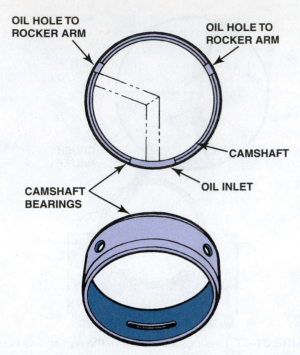

FIGURE 31–42 Camshaft bearings must be installed correctly so that oil passages are not blocked.

Modified engines have more demanding bearing requirements and therefore usually require a higher quality bearing to provide satisfactory service.

CAMSHAFT BEARINGS

TYPES OF CAMSHAFT BEARINGS The camshaft in pushrod engines rotates in sleeve bearings that are pressed into bearing bores within the engine block. Overhead camshaft bearings may be one of two sleeve-type bushings, depending on the design of the bearing supports.

- **Full round bearings**
- **Split-type (half-shell) bearings**

The split-type bearing has direct contact with aluminum saddles integral with the head depending on the design of the bearing supports. The integral aluminum head bearing design often requires the replacement of the entire cylinder head in the event of bearing failure from lack of lubrication.

In pushrod engines, the cam bearings are installed in the block. ● **SEE FIGURE 31–41.**

CAMSHAFT BEARING INSTALLATION The best rule of thumb to follow is to replace the cam bearings whenever the main bearings are replaced. The replacement cam bearings must have the correct outside diameter to fit snugly in the cam bearing bores of the block. They must have the correct oil holes and be positioned correctly. ● **SEE FIGURE 31–42.**

Cam bearings must also have the proper inside diameter to fit the camshaft bearing journals. Details regarding cam bearings include the following:

- In many engines, each cam bearing is a different size. The largest is in the front and the smallest is in the rear.

- The cam bearing journal size must be checked and each bearing identified before assembly is begun.

- The location of each new cam bearing can be marked on the outside of the bearing with a felt-tip marker to help avoid mixing up bearings. Marking in this way will not affect the bearing size or damage the bearing in any way.

- Many vehicle manufacturers specify that the cam bearings should be installed "dry" (not oiled) to prevent the cam bearing from moving (spinning) after installation. If the cam bearing were oiled, the rotation of the camshaft could cause the cam bearing to rotate and block oil holes that lubricate the camshaft.

- Many aluminum cylinder heads have "integral" cam bearings that are not replaceable. The entire cylinder head may need to be replaced if a lubrication problem occurs to the cam bearings, because the entire cylinder head may need to be replaced.

- Camshaft bearings used on overhead camshaft engines may be either full round or split depending on the engine design. ● SEE FIGURE 31–43.

Always follow the installation tool instructions when installing cam bearings.

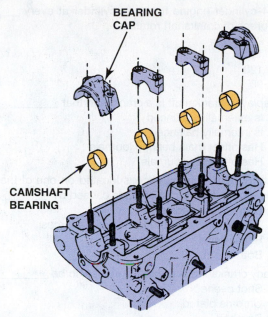

FIGURE 31–43 Some overhead camshaft engines use split bearing inserts.

SUMMARY

1. Cast crankshafts have a narrow mold parting line, and forged crankshafts have a wide parting line.

2. Even-fire 90 degree V-6 engines require that the crankshaft be splayed to allow for even firing.

3. Oil for the rod bearings comes from holes in the crankshaft drilled between the main journal and the rod journal.

4. A vibration damper, also known as a harmonic balancer, is used to dampen harmful twisting vibrations of the crankshaft.

5. Most engines are internally balanced. This means that the crankshaft and vibration damper are both balanced.

Other engines use an offset weight in the vibration damper to balance the crankshaft, called externally balanced engines.

6. Most crankshafts can be reground to be 0.01, 0.02, or 0.03 inch undersize.

7. Most engine bearings are constructed with a steel shell for strength and are covered with a copper-lead alloy. Many bearings also have a thin overlay of babbitt.

8. Bearings should have spread and crush to keep them from spinning when the crankshaft rotates.

REVIEW QUESTIONS

1. How many degrees of crankshaft rotation are there between cylinder firings on an inline 4- cylinder engine, an inline 6-cylinder engine, and a V-8 engine?

2. List the types of engine bearing materials.

3. Describe bearing crush and bearing spread.

CHAPTER QUIZ

1. A forged crankshaft has a _____.
   a. Wide parting line
   b. Thin parting line
   c. Parting line in one plane
   d. Both b and c

2. A typical V-8 engine crankshaft has _____ main bearings.
   a. Three
   b. Four
   c. Five
   d. Seven

3. A 4-cylinder engine fires one cylinder at every _____ degrees of crankshaft rotation.
   a. 27
   b. 180
   c. 120
   d. 90

4. A splayed crankshaft is a crankshaft that _____.
   a. Is externally balanced
   b. Is internally balanced
   c. Has offset main bearing journals
   d. Has offset rod journals

5. The thrust bearing surface is located on one of the main bearings to control thrust loads caused by _____.
   a. Lugging the engine
   b. Torque converter or clutch release forces
   c. Rapid deceleration forces
   d. Both a and c

6. If any crankshaft is ground, it must also be _____.
   a. Shot peened
   b. Chrome plated
   c. Polished
   d. Externally balanced

7. If bearing-to-journal clearance is doubled, how much oil will flow?
   a. One-half as much
   b. The same amount if the pressure is kept constant
   c. Double the amount
   d. Four times the amount

8. Typical journal-to-bearing clearance is _____.
   a. 0.00015 to 0.00018 inch
   b. 0.0005 to 0.0025 inch
   c. 0.15 to 0.25 inch
   d. 0.02 to 0.035 inch

9. A bearing shell has a slightly larger arc than the bearing housing. This difference is called _____.
   a. Bearing crush
   b. Bearing tang
   c. Bearing spread
   d. Bearing saddle

10. Bearing _____ occurs when a bearing shell is slightly above the parting surface of the bearing cap.
    a. Overlap
    b. Crush
    c. Cap lock
    d. Interference fit

chapter 32

GASKETS AND SEALANTS

LEARNING OBJECTIVES: **After studying this chapter, the reader should be able to:** • Discuss the need for gaskets and sealants. • Describe head gaskets and the types of head gaskets. • Discuss cover gasket materials and gasket failures. • Discuss the purpose and function of oil seals. • Discuss the purpose and function of assembly sealants.

KEY TERMS: Anaerobic sealers 479 • Armor 475 • Fire ring 475 • Formed in place gaskets (FIPG) 476 • Fretting 477 • Multilayered steel (MLS) gaskets 475 • No-retorque-type gaskets 474 • Room-temperature vulcanization (RTV) 478 • Rubber-coated metal (RCM) gaskets 476

INTRODUCTION

NEED FOR GASKETS AND SEALANTS Gaskets and sealants are used in engines to seal gaps and potential gaps between two or more parts. Gaskets and sealants must be able to withstand:

- Temperatures to which the engine part may be exposed during normal operation
- Vibrations produced in the engine and the accessories that are attached to the engine
- Acids and other chemicals that are found in and throughout an engine
- Expanding and contracting at different rates (They must be able to seal even though the two parts are expanding and contracting at different rates as the engine is started at low temperature all the way to normal operating temperature and repeating this cycle every time the engine is operated.)
  ● SEE FIGURE 32–1.

HEAD GASKETS

REQUIREMENTS NEEDED The head gasket is under the highest clamping loads. It must seal passages that carry coolant and often is required to seal a passage that carries hot engine oil. The most demanding job of the head gasket is to

seal the combustion chamber. As a rule of thumb, about 75% of the head bolt clamping force is used to seal the combustion chamber. The remaining 25% seals the coolant and oil passages. ● SEE FIGURE 32–2.

The gasket must seal when the temperature is as low as −40°F (−40°C) and as high as 400°F (204°C). The combustion pressures can get up to 1,000 PSI (6,900 kPa) on gasoline engines.

Cylinder head bolts are tightened to a specified torque, which stretches the bolt. The following forces are applied to a head gasket.

- The combustion pressure tries to push the head upward and the piston downward on the power stroke. This puts additional stress on the head bolts and it reduces the clamping load on the head gasket just when the greatest seal is needed.
- A partial vacuum during the intake stroke tries to pull the head down against the gasket.
- As the crankshaft rotates, the force on the head changes from pressure on the combustion stroke to vacuum on the intake stroke, then back to pressure.

Newer engines have lightweight thin-wall castings. The castings are quite flexible, so that they move as the pressure in the combustion chamber changes from high pressure to vacuum. The gasket must be able to compress and recover fast enough to maintain a seal as the pressure in the combustion chamber changes back and forth between pressure and vacuum. As a result, head gaskets are made of several different materials that are assembled in numerous ways, depending on the engine.

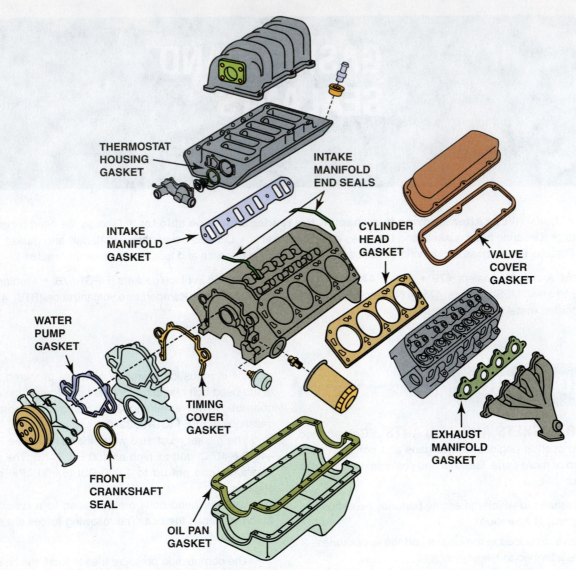

THERMOSTAT HOUSING GASKET

INTAKE MANIFOLD END SEALS

INTAKE MANIFOLD GASKET

CYLINDER HEAD GASKET

VALVE COVER GASKET

WATER PUMP GASKET

TIMING COVER GASKET

EXHAUST MANIFOLD GASKET

FRONT CRANKSHAFT SEAL

OIL PAN GASKET

FIGURE 32–1 Gaskets are used in many locations in the engine.

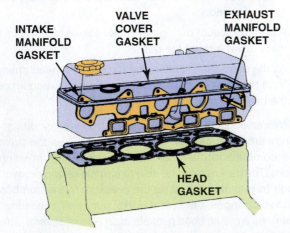

INTAKE MANIFOLD GASKET

VALVE COVER GASKET

EXHAUST MANIFOLD GASKET

HEAD GASKET

FIGURE 32–2 Gaskets help prevent leaks between two surfaces.

NOTE: Older head gasket designs often contained asbestos and required that the head bolts be retorqued after the engine had been run to operating temperature. Head gaskets today are dense and do not compress like those older-style gaskets. Therefore, most head gaskets are called no-retorque-type gaskets, meaning the cylinder head bolts do not have to be retorqued after the engine has run. New gaskets do not contain asbestos.

TYPES OF HEAD GASKETS

- **Perforated steel core gaskets.** A perforated steel core gasket uses a wire mesh core with fiber facings. Another design has rubber-fiber facings cemented to a solid steel core with an adhesive. ● **SEE FIGURES 32–3 AND 32–4.**

   The thickness of the gasket is controlled by the thickness of the metal core. The facing is thick enough to compensate for minor warpage and surface defects. The fiber facing is protected around the combustion chamber

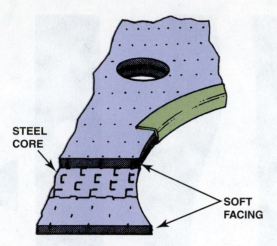

FIGURE 32–3 A typical perforated steel core head gasket with a graphite or composite facing material.

STEEL CORE

SOFT FACING

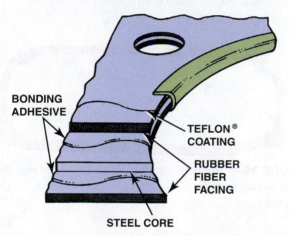

BONDING ADHESIVE

TEFLON® COATING

RUBBER FIBER FACING

STEEL CORE

FIGURE 32–4 A solid steel core head gasket with a nonstick coating, which allows some movement between the block and the head, and is especially important on engines that use cast-iron blocks with aluminum cylinder heads.

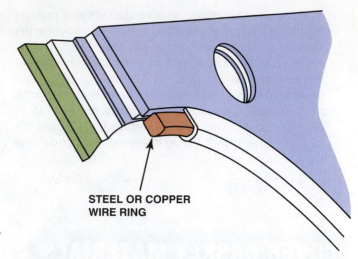

STEEL OR COPPER WIRE RING

FIGURE 32–5 The armor ring can be made from steel or copper.

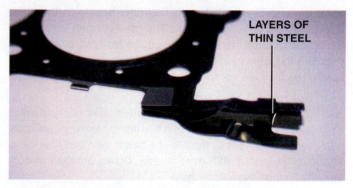

LAYERS OF THIN STEEL

FIGURE 32–6 Multilayer steel (MLS) gaskets are used on many newer all-aluminum engines as well as on engines that use a cast block with aluminum cylinder heads. This type of gasket allows the aluminum to expand without losing the sealing ability of the gasket.

TECH TIP

Wow! I Can't Believe a Cylinder Can Deform That Much!

An automotive instructor used a dial bore gauge in a 4-cylinder, cast-iron engine block to show students how much a block can deform. Using just one hand, the instructor was able to grasp both sides of the block and then squeeze it. The dial bore gauge showed that the cylinder deflected about 0.0003 inch (3/10,000 of an inch) just by squeezing the block with one hand—and that was with a cast-iron block!

After this demonstration, the students were more careful during engine assembly and always used a torque wrench on each and every fastener that was installed in or on the engine block.

with a metal **armor** (also called a **fire ring**). ● SEE FIGURE 32–5.

The metal also increases the gasket thickness around the cylinder so that it uses up to 75% of the clamping force and forms a tight combustion seal.

■ **Multilayered steel gaskets.** The **multilayered steel (MLS) gaskets** are constructed in the following manner.

■ Three to five layers of stainless steel sheet are separated by elastomer (rubber) material.

■ The elastomer material is between the layers of the sheet metal and on both surfaces.

■ The multiple layers of metal provide a springlike effect to the gasket, which allows it to keep the combustion chamber sealed.

The many layers of thin steel reduce bore and overhead camshaft distortion with less clamping force loss than previous designs. ● SEE FIGURE 32–6.

The use of multilayered steel gaskets also reduces the torque requirement and, therefore, reduces the stresses on the fastener and engine block. MLS gaskets are used in most engines that use aluminum cylinder heads and cast-iron blocks. The use of MLS head gaskets requires that both the head and the block deck surface have a smooth surface finish of 15 to 30 microinches. This smooth surface finish allows the head to move slightly during operation and not damage the gasket.

COVER GASKET MATERIALS

COVER GASKET REQUIREMENTS Cover gaskets are used to seal valve covers, oil pans, timing chain, and other covers. The gasket must be *impermeable* to the fluids it is designed to seal in or out. The gasket must *conform* to the shape of the surface, and it must be *resilient,* or elastic, to maintain the sealing force as it is compressed. Gaskets work best when they are compressed about 30%.

CORK GASKETS Older engines often used gaskets made from cork. Cork is the bark from a Mediterranean cork oak tree. It is made of very small, flexible, 14-sided, air-filled fiber cells, about 0.001 inch (0.025 mm) in size. Disadvantages of cork gaskets include the following:

- Because cork is mostly wood, it expands when it gets wet and shrinks when it dries. This causes cork gaskets to change in size when they are in storage and while installed in the engine.
- Oil gradually wicks through the organic binder of the cork, so a cork gasket often looks like it is leaking.
- Problems with cork gaskets led the gasket industry to develop cork cover gaskets using synthetic rubber as a binder for the cork. This type of gasket is called a *cork-rubber gasket.* These cork-rubber gaskets are easy to use, and they outlast the old cork gaskets.

FIBER GASKETS Some oil pans use fiber gaskets. Covers with higher clamping forces use gaskets with fibers that have greater density. For example, timing covers may have either fiber or paper gaskets.

SYNTHETIC RUBBER GASKETS Molded, oil-resistant synthetic rubber is being used in more applications to seal covers. When it is compounded correctly, it forms a superior cover gasket. It operates at high temperatures for a longer period of time than does a cork-rubber cover gasket. ● **SEE FIGURE 32–7.**

FIGURE 32–7 Left to right: Cork-rubber, paper, composite, and synthetic rubber (elastomer) gaskets.

FIGURE 32–8 Rubber-coated steel gaskets have replaced many oil pan gaskets that once had separate side rail gaskets and end seals.

RUBBER-COATED METAL GASKETS The **rubber-coated metal (RCM) gasket** uses a metal core to give strength to the gasket. The metal is coated with a layer on both sides with silicone rubber and molded in sealing beads. RCM gaskets are used in many places, including:

- Water pump gaskets
- Valve cover gaskets
- Oil pan gaskets

  ● **SEE FIGURE 32–8.**

FORMED IN PLACE GASKETS **Formed in place gaskets (FIPG)** are commonly used because they can be applied at the engine plant using a robot. The sealing material is extruded and placed onto the sealing surface and then the two parts being sealed are placed together and the fasteners tightened. When FIPG are being replaced during an engine repair or overhaul, check service information for the exact gasket material to use. ● **SEE FIGURE 32–9.**

PLASTIC/RUBBER GASKETS Most intake manifold gaskets use a nylon (usually nylon 6.6) reinforced body with silicone rubber sealing surfaces.

FIGURE 32–9 Formed in place gaskets often use silicone rubber and are applied at the factory using a robot. Check gasket manufacturers for the correct gasket replacement.

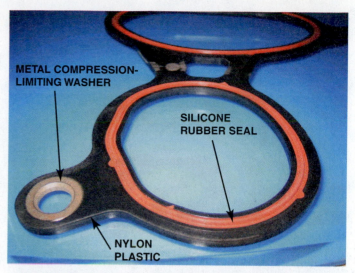

FIGURE 32–10 A typical intake manifold gasket showing the metal washer at each fastener location which keeps the gasket from being compressed too much.

 **TECH TIP**

Rubber and Contact Cement

One of the reasons why gaskets fail is due to their movement during installation. Some gaskets, such as cork or rubber valve cover gaskets or oil pan gaskets, can be held onto the cover using a rubber or contact cement.

To use a rubber or contact cement, use the following steps.

STEP 1 Apply a thin layer to one side of the gasket and to the cover where the gasket will be placed.

STEP 2 Allow the surfaces to air dry until touch free.

STEP 3 Carefully place the gaskets onto the cover being sure to align all of the holes.

CAUTION: Do not attempt to remove the gasket and reposition it. The glue is strong and the gasket will be damaged if removed. If the gasket has been incorrectly installed, remove the entire gasket, clean the gasket surface, and repeat the installation using a new gasket.

The nylon is used for two reasons.

1. It provides a thermal barrier to help stop the heat from the cylinder heads to flow to the intake manifold. This helps keep the intake air cooler, resulting in increased engine power.

2. The nylon plastic is strong and provides a stable foundation for the silicone rubber seal.
● **SEE FIGURE 32–10.**

GASKET FAILURES

CAUSES OF GASKET FAILURE Gaskets can fail to seal properly, but the root cause is often a severe condition. A head gasket can fail for the following reasons.

- Detonation (spark knock or ping) may cause extreme pressure to be exerted on the armor of the head gasket, causing it to deform.

- A plugged PCV system can increase crankcase pressure resulting in engine gasket failures such as oil pan, valve cover, timing cover, and main oil seals.

- Improper installation such as incorrect torquing sequence can cause gasket failure.

FRETTING Fretting is a condition that can destroy intake manifold gaskets, caused by the unequal expansion and contraction of two different engine materials. For example, if the intake manifold is constructed of aluminum and the cylinder heads are cast iron, the intake manifold will expand more than the cylinder heads. This causes a shearing effect, which can destroy the gasket. Therefore, before assembling an engine, check for the latest design gaskets that are often different from the type originally used in the engine. ● **SEE FIGURE 32–11.**

OIL SEALS

PURPOSE AND FUNCTION Oil seals allow the shaft to rotate and seal the area around the shaft to prevent oil or coolant from leaking. Seals come in varied sizes and styles.

FIGURE 32–11 This intake manifold gasket was damaged due to fretting. Newer designs allow for more movement between the intake manifold and the cylinder head.

OIL PAN   REAR   CRANKSHAFT
               MAIN SEAL

FIGURE 32–12 A rear main seal has to be designed to seal oil from leaking around the crankshaft under all temperature conditions.

🔧 **TECH TIP**

Hints for Gasket Usage

1. **Never reuse an old gasket.** A used gasket or seal has already been compressed, has lost some of its resilience, and has taken a set. If a used gasket does reseal, it will not seal as well as a new gasket or seal.

2. **A gasket should be checked to make sure it is the correct gasket.** Also check the list on the outside of the gasket set to make sure that the set has all the gaskets that may be needed *before* the package is opened.

3. **Read the instruction sheet.** An instruction sheet is included with most gaskets. It includes a review of the things the technician should do to prepare and install the gaskets, to give the best chance of a good seal. The instruction sheet also includes special tips on how to seal spots that are difficult to seal or that require special care to seal on a particular engine.

🔧 **TECH TIP**

Always Check the VIN

There are so many variations in engines that it is important that the correct gasket or seal be used. For example, a similar engine may be used in a front-wheel-drive or a rear-wheel-drive application and this could affect the type or style of gasket or seal used. For best results, the wise technician should know the vehicle identification number (VIN) when ordering any engine part.

ASSEMBLY SEALANTS

RTV SILICONE   RTV silicone is used by most technicians in sealing engines. **RTV**, or **room-temperature vulcanization,** means that the silicone rubber material will cure at room temperature. It is not really the temperature that causes RTV silicone to cure, but the moisture in the air. RTV silicone cures to a tack-free state in about 45 minutes. It takes 24 hours to fully cure.

RTV silicone is available in several different colors. The color identifies the special blend within a manufacturer's product line. Equal grades of silicone made by different manufacturers may have different colors. RTV silicone can be used in two ways in engine sealing.

1. It can be used as a gasket substitute between a stamped cover and a cast surface.

2. It is used to fill gaps or potential gaps. A joint between gaskets or between a gasket and a seal is a potential gap.

SEAL MATERIALS   Most seals use a steel backing for strength and a variety of sealing materials, including:

- Buna-N
- Viton® (fluorocarbon)
- Teflon® (polytetrafluorethylene, also called PTFE)
  - ● **SEE FIGURE 32–12.**

CAUTION: Do not use oil on a Teflon® seal because this type of seal requires that some of the material be transferred to the rotating shaft to seal properly. If oil is used on the seal, the seal will leak.

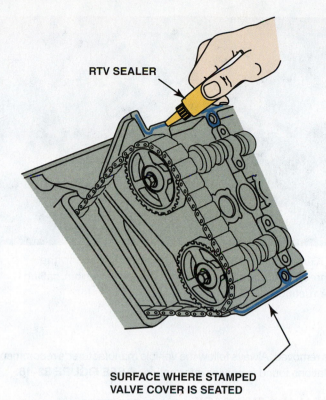

RTV SEALER

SURFACE WHERE STAMPED VALVE COVER IS SEATED

FIGURE 32–13 Room-temperature vulcanization (RTV) is designed to be a gasket substitute on nonmachined surfaces. Be sure to follow the instructions as printed on the tube for best results.

RTV precautions include:

1. Some RTV silicone sealers use *acetic acid,* and the fumes from this type can be drawn through the engine through the PCV system and cause damage to oxygen sensors. Always use an *amine-type* RTV silicone or one that states on the package that it is safe for oxygen sensors.

2. RTV should not be used with a gasket as a sealer because it is slippery and could easily cause the gasket to move out of proper location.

3. RTV silicone should *never* be used around fuel because the fuel will cut through it. Silicone should not be used as a sealer on gaskets. It will squeeze out to leave a bead inside and a bead outside the flange. The inside bead might fall into the engine, plugging passages and causing engine damage. The thin film still remaining on the gasket stays uncured, just as it would be in the original tube. The uncured silicone is likely to let the gasket or seal slip out of place. ● **SEE FIGURE 32–13.**

ANAEROBIC SEALERS
Anaerobic sealers cure in the absence of air. They are used as thread lockers (such as Loctite®), and they are used to seal rigid machined joints between cast parts. Anaerobic sealers lose their sealing ability at temperatures above 300°F (149°C). On production lines, the curing process is speeded up by using ultraviolet light.

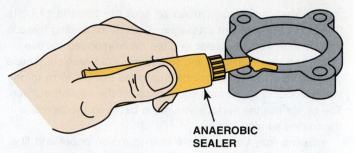

ANAEROBIC SEALER

FIGURE 32–14 Anaerobic sealer is used to seal machined surfaces. Always follow the instructions on the tube for best results.

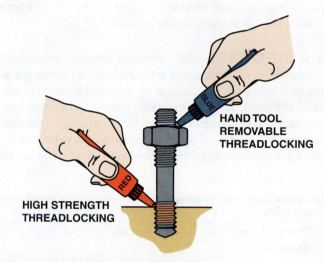

HAND TOOL REMOVABLE THREADLOCKING

HIGH STRENGTH THREADLOCKING

FIGURE 32–15 The strength of the thread locker depends on whether the fastener is to be removed by hand (blue). High-strength thread locker (red) can only be removed if heated.

When the anaerobic sealer is used on threads, air does not get to it so it hardens to form a seal to prevent the fastener from loosening. Anaerobic sealers can be used to seal machined surfaces without a gasket. The surfaces *must* be thoroughly clean to get a good seal. Special primers are recommended for use on the sealing surface to get a better bond with anaerobic sealers. ● **SEE FIGURES 32–14 AND 32–15.**

NONHARDENING SEALERS
Sealers are nonhardening materials. Examples of sealer trade names include:

- Form-A-Gasket 2
- Pli-A-Seal
- Tight Seal 2
- Aviation Form-A-Gasket
- Brush Tack
- Copper Coat
- Spray Tack
- High Tack

Sealers are always used to seal the threads of bolts that break into coolant passages. Sealers for sealing threads may include Teflon. Sealer is often recommended for use on shim-type head gaskets and intake manifold gaskets. These gaskets have a metal surface that does not conform to any small amounts of surface roughness on the sealing surface. The sealer fills the surface variations between the gasket and the sealing surface.

Sealer may be used as a sealing aid on paper and fiber gaskets if the gasket needs help with sealing on a scratched, corroded, or rough surface finish. The sealer may be used on one side or on both sides of the gasket.

CAUTION: Sealer should *never* be used on rubber or cork-rubber gaskets. Instead of holding the rubber gasket or seal, it will help the rubber to slip out of place because the sealer will never harden.

ANTISEIZE COMPOUNDS
Antiseize compounds are used on fasteners in the engine that are subjected to high temperatures to prevent seizing caused by galvanic action between dissimilar metals. These compounds minimize corrosion from moisture. Exhaust manifold bolts or nuts, and oxygen sensors, keep them from seizing. The antiseize compound minimizes the chance of threads being pulled or breaking as the oxygen sensor

FIGURE 32–16 Applying antiseize compound to the threads of a bolt helps prevent the threads from galling or rusting.

is removed. Always follow the vehicle manufacturer's recommendations found in service information. ● **SEE FIGURE 32–16.**

SEALANT SUMMARY   ● SEE CHART 32–1.

PRODUCTS	COMMON TRADE NAMES	USES	EXAMPLES
RTV (room-temperature vulcanization)	Silicone	As a gasket substitute or fill gaps	Valve covers, oil pans, intake manifold end seals, timing covers, transmission pans
Anaerobic sealer (thread-locker) medium strength	Loctite® Blue	Keeps fasteners from vibrating loose	For nut and bolt applications 1/4 to 3/4 inch (6 to 20 mm)
Anaerobic sealer (thread-locker) high temperature, high strength	Loctite® Red	Heavy-duty applications	For larger fasteners 3/8 to 1 inch (9.5 to 25 mm)
Antiseize (general purpose)	Neverseez™ Kopr Kote™ E-Z Break™	For preventing corrosion seizing	Oxygen sensors, spring bolts, exhaust manifold bolts/nuts
Antiseize (nickel)	Neverseez™ Thred-Gard™	For stainless steel and other metal applications	Harsh chemical environments
Hardening gasket sealant	Permatex® #1	Holds gaskets in place during assembly; also seals paper and cork gaskets	Transmission and engine oil pan gaskets, timing cover (paper gaskets) valve cover gaskets, and intake manifold gaskets
Nonhardening sealant	Permatex® #2	Allows repeated disassembly and reassembly	Thermostat housings, differential coverings, intake manifolds, fuel injectors and fuel pumps, transmission and torque converter seals
Aviation cement/ contact cement	Aviation Form-A-Gasket#3™	Holds gaskets in place for assembly	All types of hoses and gaskets

CHART 32–1

Summary chart showing where sealants are used and their common trade names.

SUMMARY

1. Gaskets are used to fill a space or gap between two objects to prevent leakage from occurring.
2. There are many types of gaskets including cylinder head gaskets, valve cover gaskets, and timing cover gaskets.
3. Rubber or contact cement is used to hold a gasket in place.
4. RTV and anaerobic sealers are commonly used to seal engines.
5. Sealers are used to help gaskets seal.

REVIEW QUESTIONS

1. What is the purpose of a gasket?
2. What are the types of cover gaskets?
3. Why is armor used in head gaskets?
4. What is the difference between RTV and anaerobic sealers?

CHAPTER QUIZ

1. What force causes a head gasket to be drawn downward during engine operation?
   a. Intake stroke vacuum
   b. Gravity
   c. Head bolt torque
   d. Exhaust gas pressure

2. Where is a multilayered steel (MLS) gasket most often used in an engine?
   a. Valve cover gasket
   b. Oil pan gasket
   c. Head gasket
   d. Intake manifold gasket

3. A steel or copper wire used in a head gasket around the cylinder is called _____.
   a. Armor
   b. Fire ring
   c. Ridge block
   d. Either a or b

4. A one-piece oil pan gasket often uses _____ in the middle to add strength.
   a. Plastic (nylon)
   b. Steel
   c. Hard rubber
   d. Carbon fiber

5. Some gaskets use a steel washer around each bolt hole. The purpose of this washer is to _____.
   a. Improve the strength of the gasket
   b. Help seal around the bolt hole
   c. Help prevent the gasket from shrinking
   d. Prevent the gasket from being overly compressed

6. A gasket failure caused by the movement of dissimilar materials is called _____.
   a. Fretting
   b. Corrosion
   c. Collapsing
   d. Tearing

7. Which type of oil seal must *not* have oil applied for it to work correctly?
   a. Silicone rubber
   b. Buna-N
   c. Teflon®
   d. Viton®

8. Which type of *sealer* is to be used on nonmachined surfaces?
   a. RTV
   b. Anaerobic sealer
   c. Either a or b
   d. Neither a nor b

9. Which product requires heat to remove?
   a. Red thread locker
   b. Blue thread locker
   c. RTV
   d. Antiseize

10. What precautions should be followed when using gaskets?
    a. Never reuse an old gasket.
    b. A gasket should be checked to make sure it is the correct gasket.
    c. Read the instruction sheet.
    d. All of the above.

chapter 33
BALANCING AND BLUEPRINTING

LEARNING OBJECTIVES: **After studying this chapter, the reader should be able to:** • Explain the purpose of balancing an engine. • Describe the blueprinting process. • Discuss the importance of combustion chamber volume. • Discuss the purpose of flow testing cylinder heads. • Discuss the purpose of degreeing the camshaft. • Explain the procedure of determining proper push rod length. • Discuss short block blueprinting.

KEY TERMS: Blueprinting 484 • Bob weight 483 • Inertial weight 482 • Intake lobe centerline method 487 • Reciprocating weight 482 • Rotating weight 482

BALANCING AN ENGINE

PURPOSE For any engine to operate with a minimum amount of vibration, all of the reciprocating parts must be close to the same weight. Production engines use parts that are usually within 3 grams of each other and result in a relatively smooth operating engine.

NOTE: A gram is 1/28 of an ounce or the weight of a typical small paper clip.

Custom engine builders attempt to get all reciprocating parts to weigh within 1 gram or less of each other. The reason for such accuracy is that any unbalance is increased greatly by centrifugal force as the engine operates. The force of the unbalance increases by the square of the speed. In other words, if the engine RPM doubles, the force of any unbalance quadruples. An unbalance of 1 ounce that is 1 inch from the center of rotation becomes a force of 7 ounces at 500 RPM. At 5000 RPM, this same 1 ounce of unbalance would be increased to 44 lb. This small amount of imbalance can cause serious vibrations and potential internal engine damage especially at high engine RPM.

ENGINE BALANCING PROCEDURE Whenever all rotating and reciprocating parts of an engine are to be balanced, the following components are needed to balance inline engines.

- Crankshaft
- Vibration damper (harmonic balancer)
- Flywheel or flexplate
- Pressure plate

- All bolts, lock washers, keys, and spacers needed to assemble the above parts on the crankshaft
- Connecting rods
- Pistons
- Wrist pins

To balance a V-type engine, the following additional parts are needed.

- Rod bearings
- Piston rings
- Wrist pin locks (if full-floating piston pins)

The typical procedure includes the following steps.

STEP 1 The first step is to equalize the **reciprocating weight**, which includes the pistons and rods. Reciprocating weight is also called **inertial weight**. The pistons should be weighed, including the piston pin and rings, to determine the lightest weight piston. Material should be ground from the heavier pistons until they match the weight of the lightest piston. Material should be removed from the weight balancing pads.

CAUTION: Do not grind or attempt to remove weight from the piston pin. This could weaken a highly stressed part and lead to engine failure.

STEP 2 Connecting rods have a big end and a small end. The big end of the rod is considered to be part of the **rotating weight** and the small end part of the reciprocating weight after the rod has been reconditioned. The two ends should be weighed and matched separately. ● **SEE FIGURE 33–1.**

FIGURE 33–1 Weighing the big end of a connecting rod on a scale that keeps it perfectly horizontal so that each end can be weighed separately.

FIGURE 33–2 Removing material from the balancing pad on the small end of the rod to match it to the weight of the small end of the lightest rod being used in the engine.

After both the large and small ends of all the rods have been weighed, material should be removed from the balancing pads of both the heavier and lighter ends of the rods until they match the lightest rods. ● **SEE FIGURE 33–2.**

BOB WEIGHTS

Bob weights are attached to the rod journals on V-type engines to simulate the weight of the rods and pistons. ● **SEE FIGURE 33–3.**

The bob weight must equal the total of the following for each journal.

- Rotating weight
- A percentage of the reciprocating weight
- An amount for the weight of the oil trapped between the journal and the bearing

FIGURE 33–3 A crankshaft with bob weights attached as well as the flexplate and the harmonic balancer.

The rotating weight includes the big end of the connecting rod and the connecting rod bearings.

NOTE: On V-8 engines, two rods share a crank pin so that the calculations for bob weight, including the weight of both big ends of the connecting rods and bearings, should be taken into consideration.

The reciprocating weight includes the small end of the rod(s) and the piston assemblies, which include the rings, pin, and locks, if equipped.

BALANCING FACTOR

A balancing factor is a formula used to determine what percentage (usually 50%) of the reciprocating weight needs to be included in the bob weight. A bob weight is a special fixture that attaches to the rod journal of the V-type crankshaft, where different values of weights are added to usually equal one-half of the total weight of two pistons, two connecting rods, two sets of rings, wrist pins, bearings, and the equivalent amount of oil coating on the parts. When properly assembled, the bob weights allow V-type crankshafts to be rotated at balancing speeds for engine balance adjustments.

BALANCING MACHINES

Some machines operate from a stroboscopic light that picks up vibrations in the assembly and a meter indicates the exact location of heaviness to be removed. Other balancing machines use electronics with meter readouts that define the exact amount and location of the metal to be removed. This process usually involves removing metal from the counterweight area of the crankshaft, by drilling a specific sized hole to a calculated depth. Most balancing machines calculate the bob weight automatically after inputting all of the weight information and then display where and how much material needs to be removed to achieve proper balance. ● **SEE FIGURE 33–4.**

A drill is commonly used to remove weight from the counterweight of the crankshaft to achieve proper balance. ● **SEE FIGURE 33–5.**

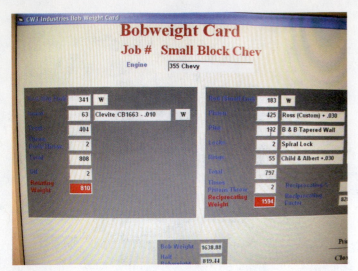

FIGURE 33–4 The display of a crankshaft balancer showing where weight needs to be removed to achieve a balanced assembly.

FIGURE 33–5 A drill is often used to remove weight from the crankshaft to achieve proper balance.

FREQUENTLY ASKED QUESTION

What Is "Heavy Metal"?

Heavy metal, also called mallory metal, is an alloy of tungsten that is 1.5 times heavier than lead. It is used to add weight to a crankshaft if needed, usually on engines that have been stroked using a stroker crankshaft. The heavy metal must be installed parallel to the centerline axis of the crankshaft. ● **SEE FIGURE 33–6.**

After the specified material has been removed, the counterweight is checked again by the balance machine. When the procedure has been completed, the rotating assembly is then in balance.

FIGURE 33–6 Heavy metal installed and welded in place.

Sometimes weight has to be added to a crankshaft to achieve proper balance. In this case, a hole is drilled parallel to the crankshaft in a counterweight and extra heavy metal is added.

BLUEPRINTING PROCESS

GENERAL USE QUESTIONS   **Blueprinting** is the process used to custom fit and select variables to best match a predetermined level of performance. Unless the engine is going to be a stock rebuild or used as intended from the factory, certain decisions have to be made before an engine is built. ● **SEE CHART 33–1** for questions and reasons.

SPECIFIC REQUIREMENT NEEDS   After the overall decisions about general use of the engine have been determined, the individual parts of the engine need to be selected, including:

- **Block.** The higher the cubic inch displacement, the higher the potential torque and horsepower.
- **Rotating assembly.** For a stock rebuild, using the stock parts is all that is needed. Depending on the power level and RPM needed, parts have to be selected to withstand the forces involved, such as using forged crankshafts, pistons, and connecting rods instead of cast pieces.
- **Breathing system.** The amount of horsepower that any engine produces is directly related to the amount of air-fuel mixture that can enter and exit the engine. This means that the camshaft, cylinder head, and intake manifolds must be correctly sized and matched for optimum performance.

SIZE MATTERS   Almost every part is selected according to the needs of the engine's size. The entire breathing system, such as the heads, camshaft, intake manifold, exhaust system, and fuel delivery system, is selected based on the cubic inch displacement of the engine. Therefore, the first consideration is to determine the size of the engine. Due to engine machining

QUESTION	REASON
General Use • Street (almost stock?) • High-performance street • Street/strip (daily driver who wants to drag race on weekends) • Drag race (which class, etc.?) • Racing (oval, dirt, 1/2 mile?)	The real use of the engine helps determine the following: • Compression ratio • Knowing the rules of the racing organization regarding parts that can be used • Anticipated maximum engine RPM, which has a huge effect on the short block components needed
Power Adder?	Using nitrous or an add-on turbocharger or supercharger requires great piston-to-cylinder wall clearances, plus the use of forged pistons and connecting rods in most cases.
Type of Fuel	This will affect many factors including the compression ratio and fuel system needs, especially if designed to operate on E85.

CHART 33–1

Knowing exactly how the engine will be used is a necessary first step in the engine building process.

ENGINE	STOCK (CUBIC INCHES)	STOCK BORE (INCHES)	STOCK STROKE (INCHES)	0.030"BORE OVERSIZE (CUBIC INCHES)	AMOUNT OF STROKE CHANGE (INCHES)	NEW STROKE (INCHES)	DISP W/ 0.03 inch BORE & NEW STROKE (CUBIC INCHES)
CHEVROLET 5.7 L	350	4.000	3.480	354.90 (+ 4.90)	0.270	3.750	382.44 (+ 32.44)
CHEVROLET 7.4 L	454	4.250	4.000	460 (+ 6)	0.250	4.250	489.00 (+ 35)
FORD 5.0 L	302	4.000	3.000	305.95 (+ 2.95)	0.400	3.400	347.33 (+ 45.33)
FORD 4.6 L	281	3.550	3.540	284.93 (+ 3.93)	0.300	3.840	305.78 (+ 24.78)
MOPAR 5.2 L	340	4.040	3.310	344.24 (+ 4.24)	0.690	4.000	416 (+ 76)
HONDA 1.8 L Non-VTEC & VTEC	112 (1834 cc)	3.189 (81 mm)	3.500 (89 mm)	113.95 (+ 1.95)	0.250	3.750	122 (+ 10)

CHART 33–2

Boring an engine increases the engine displacement slightly, whereas stroking an engine has a greater effect on engine displacement.

and selection of the crankshaft, the displacement will be changed.

- **Boring the block.** Boring for oversize pistons has a limited effect on the displacement of the engine.
- **Stroking the engine.** Replacing the crankshaft and installing all new pistons and connecting rods makes a big difference in the displacement of the engine. ● SEE CHART 33–2.

PARTS MANUFACTURER HELP Now that the basic parameters for the engine have been determined, parts selection and the recommendation of the parts manufacturer should be

followed. Most manufacturers of high-performance parts, such as camshafts, have available specific guidelines for the selection of the best part number to select for the anticipated use of the engine. Before selecting a camshaft or another high-performance part or calling for advice, have the following information determined and available.

- Vehicle weight
- Type of transmission (automatic or manual)
- Final drive ratio (helps determine engine RPM needs)
- Type of use (drag racing, street performance, etc.)

FIGURE 33–7 Setup needed to measure the combustion chamber volume in cubic centimeters (cc).

FIGURE 33–8 Cylinder head setup for flow testing. Note the weak valve springs that are strong enough to keep the valves shut, yet weak enough to permit the flow bench operator to vary the intake valve opening amount.

FOLLOW PARTS MANUFACTURER'S RECOMMENDATIONS If the above items have been achieved, the parts selected should produce the desired engine performance. For best results, perform the following steps.

STEP 1 Read, understand, and follow all instructions that accompany the parts.

STEP 2 Perform all of the suggested steps including the specified clearances (piston-to-wall, bearings, and end play specifications) that often differs from factory specifications.

STEP 3 Use the specified lubricant on parts such as fasteners and the torque specification which often differs from factory specifications.

COMBUSTION CHAMBER VOLUME

PURPOSE AND FUNCTION For best engine performance and smooth operation, make the following a priority.

- All cylinders should have the same compression. This means that all cylinders should have the same combustion chamber volume.

- The technician or engine builder needs to know the combustion chamber volume to accurately calculate the compression ratio.

- To accurately measure the volume of the combustion chamber, a graduated burette is used with mineral spirits (or automatic transmission fluid) to measure the exact volume of the chamber in cubic centimeters (cc). ● **SEE FIGURE 33–7.**

FLOW TESTING CYLINDER HEADS

PURPOSE Many specialty engines are tested for the amount of air that can flow through the ports and valves of the engine. A flow bench is used to measure the amount of air in cubic feet per minute (cfm) that can flow through the valves at various valve openings.

After completion of the valve job and any port or combustion chamber work, weak valve springs are installed temporarily. ● **SEE FIGURE 33–8.**

Modeling clay is then temporarily applied around the port areas to improve flow characteristics where the intake manifold would normally direct the flow into the port. ● **SEE FIGURE 33–9.**

Various thicknesses of metal spacers are placed between the cylinder head holding fixture and the valve stem. Typical thicknesses used are 0.1 inch through 0.7 inch, using 0.1 inch increments. The results are recorded on a worksheet.

FLOW RATE AND HORSEPOWER Most comprehensive engine machine shops have the equipment to measure the airflow through cylinder head ports and valves. ● **SEE FIGURE 33–10.**

After the airflow through the open intake valve has been determined, a formula can be used to estimate horsepower. The following formula has proven to be a fairly accurate estimate of horsepower when compared with dynamometer testing after the engine is built.

NOTE: The first part of the formula is used to convert airflow measurement from a basis of being tested at 28 inch H_2O to that of being tested at 20 inch H_2O.

FIGURE 33–9 Modeling clay is installed around the port to duplicate the flow improvement characteristics of an intake manifold.

FIGURE 33–10 A flow bench that can measure and record the airflow through the intake and exhaust ports of each cylinder.

$$\text{Horsepower per cylinder} = \text{Airflow}$$
$$\text{at 28 inch } H_2O = 0.598 \times 0.43$$

For example, for a V-8 that measures 231 cfm of airflow at 28 inch H_2O:

$$\text{Horsepower} = 231 \times 0.598 = 138 \text{ cfm at}$$
$$20 \text{ inch } H_2O \times 0.43 = 59.4 \text{ hp per cylinder} \times 8 = 475 \text{ hp}$$

FIGURE 33–11 A piston stop is used to help determine top dead center.

CAUTION: Even though this formula has proven to be fairly accurate, there are too many variables in the design of any engine besides the airflow through the head for this formula to be accurate under all conditions.

DEGREEING THE CAMSHAFT

PURPOSE The purpose of degreeing the camshaft in the engine is to locate the valve action exactly as the camshaft manufacturers intended. The reason this should be checked is due to possible variations on the following parts that could affect the designed valve opening and closing events.

- Cam gear locating pin position
- Camshaft grinding variations
- Timing chain or gear variations

PROCEDURE The method most often recommended by camshaft manufacturers is the **intake lobe centerline method**. This method determines the exact centerline of the intake lobe and compares it to the specifications supplied with the replacement camshaft. On an overhead valve engine, the camshaft is usually degreed after the crankshaft, piston, and camshaft are installed and before the cylinder heads are installed.

To determine the centerline of the intake lobe, follow these steps using a degree wheel mounted on the crankshaft.

STEP 1 Locate the exact top dead center. Install a degree wheel and bring the cylinder 1 piston close to TDC. Install a piston stop. (A piston stop is any object attached to the block that can act as a solid mechanical stop to prevent the piston from reaching the top of the cylinder.) By hand, slowly rotate the crankshaft clockwise until the piston *gently* hits the stop. ● SEE FIGURE 33–11.

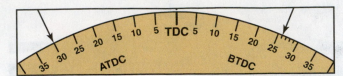

FIGURE 33–12 The degree wheel indicates where the piston stopped near top dead center. By splitting the difference between the two readings, the true TDC (28 degrees) can be located on the degree wheel.

CAUTION: Do not use the starter motor to rotate the engine. Use a special wrench on the flywheel or the front of the crankshaft.

Record the reading on the degree wheel, and then turn the engine in the opposite direction until it stops again and record that number. ● **FIGURE 33–12** indicates a reading of 30 degrees ATDC and 26 degrees BTDC. Add the two readings together and divide by two (30 + 26 = 56 ÷ 2 = 28 degrees). Move the degree wheel until it is 28 degrees and the engine has stopped rotating in either direction. Now TDC on the degree wheel is exactly at top dead center.

STEP 2   After finding exact TDC (28 degrees in this case), remove the piston stop, then rotate the engine until the degree wheel indicates 28 degrees. Now adjust the degree wheel to read exactly TDC. Place a dial indicator on an intake valve lifter. To accurately locate the point of maximum lift (intake lobe centerline), rotate the engine until the lifter drops 0.05 inch on each side of the maximum lift point. Mark the degree wheel at these points on either side of the maximum lift point. Now count the degrees between these two points and mark the halfway point. This halfway point represents the intake centerline. This point is often located between 100 and 110 degrees. ● **SEE FIGURE 33–13.**

STEP 3   Now that both TDC and intake centerline have been marked, compare the actual intake centerline with the specification. For example, if the actual intake centerline is 106 degrees and the camshaft specification indicates 106 degrees, then the camshaft is installed *straight up.* ● **SEE FIGURE 33–14.** If the actual reading is 104 degrees, the camshaft is advanced by 2 degrees. If the actual reading is 108 degrees, the camshaft is retarded by 2 degrees.

ADVANCED CAM TIMING   If the camshaft is slightly ahead of the crankshaft, the camshaft is called *advanced.* An advanced camshaft (maximum of 4 degrees) results in more low-speed torque with a slight decrease in high-speed power. Some aftermarket camshaft manufacturers design about a 4-degree advance into their timing gears or camshaft. This permits the use of a camshaft with more lift and duration, yet still provides the smooth idle and low-speed responses of a milder camshaft.

FIGURE 33–13 Note the setup required to degree a camshaft. The pointer, the degree wheel, and the piston stop are used to find exact top dead center.

RETARDED CAM TIMING   If the camshaft is slightly behind the crankshaft, the camshaft is called *retarded.* A retarded camshaft (maximum of 4 degrees) results in more high-speed power at the expense of low-speed torque.

If the measured values are different from specifications, special offset pins (bushings) or keys are available to relocate the cam gear by the proper amount. Some manufacturers can provide adjustable cam timing sprockets for overhead cam engines.

DETERMINING PROPER PUSHROD LENGTH

PURPOSE   The length of the pushrod is determined by the geometry of the engine when it was originally built. Unless machining was performed, using the stock length pushrods is fine and there is no need to replace the pushrods that are longer or

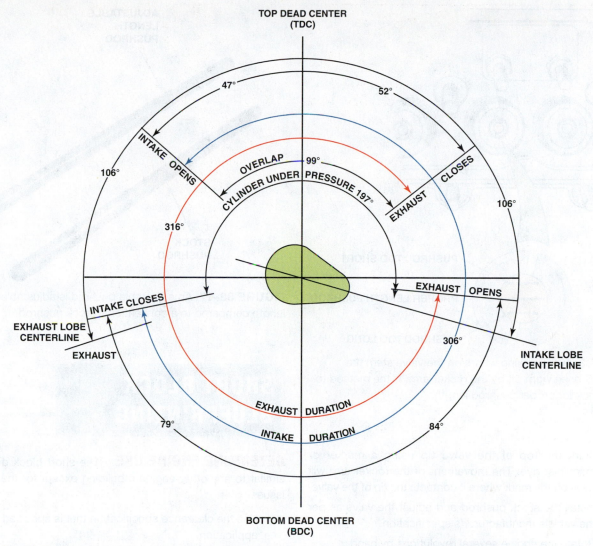

FIGURE 33–14 Typical valve timing diagram showing the intake lobe centerline at 106 degrees ATDC.

shorter. If, however, machining of the head (OHV engines) or the block deck, then a different length pushrod may be needed to restore the proper valve train geometry. If the pushrod length is correct, then the rocker arm will be contacting the center of the valve stem. ● **SEE FIGURE 33–15.**

WHEN NEEDED If any of the following operations have been performed, the proper pushrod length *must* be determined.

- Regrinding the camshaft (reduces base circle dimensions)
- Milling or resurfacing cylinder heads
- Milling or resurfacing block deck
- Grinding valves and/or facing valve stems
- Changing to a head gasket thinner or thicker than the original

PROCEDURE To determine the pushrod length, assemble the engine and select one cylinder to find out if the pushrod length is okay. Perform the following steps.

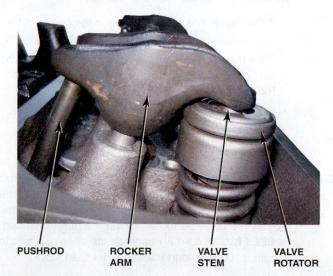

PUSHROD   ROCKER ARM   VALVE STEM   VALVE ROTATOR

FIGURE 33–15 A side view of a small block Chevrolet engine showing that the rocker arm is contacting the top of the valve stem. A roller-tipped rocker arm will show a more definite line of contact than a stamped steel rocker.

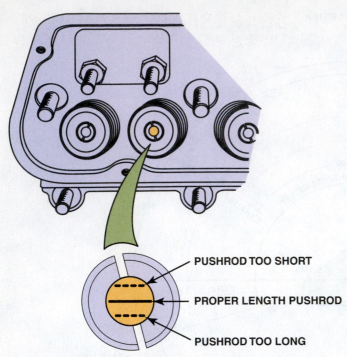

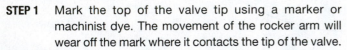

FIGURE 33–16 Checking where on the valve stem the marker has been worn off by the rocker arm, is the method to use to check for proper pushrod length.

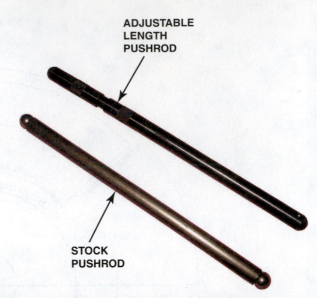

FIGURE 33–17 An adjustable pushrod is adjustable for length compared to a conventional stock pushrod.

STEP 1 Mark the top of the valve tip using a marker or machinist dye. The movement of the rocker arm will wear off the mark where it contacts the tip of the valve.

STEP 2 Install the stock pushrod and adjust the valve as per the vehicle manufacturer's specification.

STEP 3 Rotate the engine several revolutions by hand.

STEP 4 Remove the rocker arm and check where the marker has been worn from the tip of the valve.

- If the marker has been worn off in the center of the valve tip, the pushrod length is correct.

- If the marker has been worn off toward the exhaust outside (exhaust side of the head), the pushrod is too long.

- If the marker has been worn off toward the upper part of the valve stem (toward the intake side of the head), the pushrod is too short. ● **SEE FIGURE 33–16.**

STEP 5 Use an adjustable pushrod and adjust the pushrod length a little at a time until testing results in the correct wear at the center of the valve tip. Measure the adjustable pushrod to determine the length needed. ● **SEE FIGURE 33–17.** Pushrods are often available in length 0.100 inch longer and shorter than stock.

SHORT BLOCK BLUEPRINTING

DETERMINE ENGINE USE The short block detailing is similar to any other engine rebuilding except for the following issues.

- Use the clearance specification that is specified for the application.

- Use the torque specification that is recommended by the manufacturer of the crankshaft.

- Always use the specified thread lubricant and/or sealer on fasteners as recommended by the fastener manufacturer.

TRIAL ASSEMBLY Before the engine is assembled it should be partially assembled to double check all clearances. This is also a good time to verify that the following are correct.

- Cam timing
- Side clearances
- Crankshaft end play
- Piston-to-wall clearance
- Valve-to-piston clearance
- Crankshaft to block clearance
- Camshaft to connecting rod clearance

1 The crankshaft should always be balanced with the flywheel (or flexplate) and harmonic balancer installed.

2 Use a worksheet so that all weights can be measured and recorded.

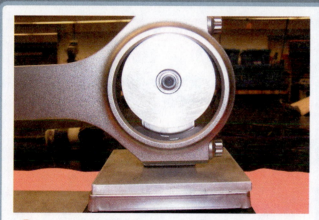

3 Using a fixture to hold the connecting rod horizontally, measure and record the weight of the big end of the rod.

4 Using a fixture to hold the connecting rod horizontally, measure and record the weight of the small end of the rod.

5 Weigh each piston. Remove some metal from the heaviest pistons to match their weight with the lightest.

6 Weigh and record the weight of each piston pin.

CONTINUED ▶

7 Weigh and record the weight of each piston pin locks if used.

8 Weigh and record the weight of the piston rings for each piston.

9 Weigh and record the weight of the rod bearings for each connecting rod.

10 Using the worksheet and plugging the measured values into the balancer, adjust the BOB weight to the desired weight.

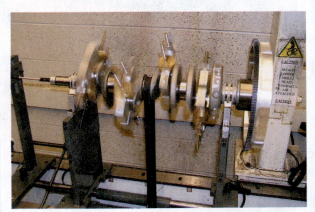

11 Install the BOB weights and operate the balancer according to the instructions for the balancer being used.

12 Use a drill and drill the counterweight in the designated location as indicated on the balancer.

1. Proper balancing of the engine is important for smooth operation.
2. Both rotating weight and reciprocating weight are considered during the balancing procedure.
3. Blueprinting means following the exact procedures and specifications for the parts used.
4. Checking combustion chamber volume is used to ensure that all cylinders have the exact same compression ratio.
5. Degreeing a camshaft is done to ensure that the valve events occur at the correct time.
6. Checking for proper pushrod length is important after the machining operations have changed the height of the cylinder head(s).

REVIEW QUESTIONS

1. What parts are considered to be rotating weight?
2. What parts must be measured when measuring reciprocating weight?
3. What is done to the crankshaft to achieve a balanced rotating engine assembly?
4. What questions should be answered before starting the blueprint process?
5. List the parts and supplies needed to check combustion chamber volume.
6. List the steps needed to degree a camshaft.

CHAPTER QUIZ

1. A gram weighs about the same as a _____.
   a. Paper clip
   b. Chicken feather
   c. Penny
   d. Dime

2. Reciprocating weight is also called _____.
   a. Balance weight
   b. Bob weight
   c. Rotating weight
   d. Inertial weight

3. Connecting rods should be weighed and balanced _____.
   a. Before reconditioning
   b. After reconditioning

4. Pistons and connecting rods can be ground from what area when removing weight?
   a. Balancing pad
   b. Weight bore
   c. Sides
   d. Thrust surface(s)

5. Which of the following is not reciprocating weight?
   a. Piston
   b. Big end of a connecting rod
   c. Small end of a connecting rod
   d. Piston ring

6. How is the crankshaft *usually* balanced?
   a. Material is welded onto the counterweight.
   b. Pistons are replaced until a matched set is achieved.
   c. Material is drilled out of the counterweight.
   d. Heavy metal is used to increase the weight of the counterweight.

7. Blueprinting is a process that _____.
   a. Uses factory-only specification
   b. Uses the parts manufacturer's recommended specification for many of the critical clearances
   c. Includes identifying the use of the engine and the vehicle it is going to be used in
   d. Both b and c

8. Combustion chamber volume is measured using a fluid and what unit of measure?
   a. Cubic inches (inch^3)
   b. Cubic centimeters (cc)
   c. Liters (L)
   d. Ounces (oz.)

9. Why is it recommended that a new camshaft be "degreed"?
   a. Cam gear locating pin position could be different
   b. Because of camshaft grinding variations
   c. Due to timing chain or gear variations
   d. All of the above

10. During flow bench testing cylinders, what is used to hold the valves closed?
    a. Weaker than normal test springs
    b. Normal valve springs
    c. The same valve springs that will be used in the engine
    d. Double counter-wound special high-tension valve springs

FIGURE 34–2 Deburring all sharp edges is an important step to achieve proper engine assembly.

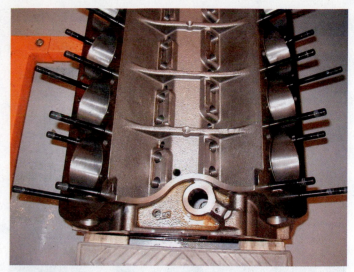

FIGURE 34–3 Studs installed in the block, replacing head bolts.

ENGINE PART MATERIAL	GASKET MATERIAL	ACCEPTABLE SURFACE FINISH (RA)
Cast iron/cast iron	Composite	60 to 80 μinch
Aluminum/cast iron	Composite	20 to 30 μinch
Aluminum/cast iron	Rubber-coated multilayered steel (MLS)	15 to 30 μinch

CHART 34–1

The surface finish of the block and cylinder head depends on the type of gasket being used.

- All cups and plugs should be installed.
- The final bore dimension is correct for the piston.
- The surface finish of the cylinder bore matches with the specified finish required for the piston rings that are going to be used.
- All sharp edges and burrs have been removed.
  ● SEE FIGURE 34–2.
- The main bearing bores (saddles) are straight and inline.
- The lifter bores have been honed and checked for proper dimension.

SURFACE FINISH
The surface finish is important for the proper sealing of any gasket.

- **Surface too rough.** If the surface finish is too rough, the gasket will not be able to seal the deep grooves in the surface.
- **Surface too smooth.** If the surface finish is too smooth, the gasket can move out of proper location, causing leakage.

Surface finish is measured in microinches, usually abbreviated by using the Greek letter mu (μ) and the abbreviation for inches together (μinch).

- The higher the microinch finish, the rougher the surface.
- The lower the microinch finish, the smoother the surface. The specification for surface finish is usually specified in roughness average, or Ra.

● SEE CHART 34–1 for the acceptable roughness for the head gasket surface.

Check the instruction sheet that comes with the gasket for the specified surface finish.

CHECKING SURFACES BEFORE ASSEMBLY
All surfaces of an engine should be clean and straight and have the specified surface finish and flatness. Flatness is a measure of how much the surface varies in any 6 inch span. An industry standard maximum limit for flatness is usually 0.002 inch. If the surface is not flat, the gaskets will not be able to seal properly.

PREPARING THE BLOCK FOR STUDS
Using studs instead of head bolts for cylinder heads is recommended for all high-performance applications. However, studs should not be used on a street-driven vehicle engine, because the studs would prevent the cylinder heads from being removed unless the engine is first removed from the vehicle. Most vehicles do not have enough room under the hood to allow the cylinder heads to be moved upward far enough for removal.

Studs provide for more accurate and consistent torque loading and clamping force. For example, when a bolt is used to attach a cylinder head, it is being twisted and pulled at the same time. In comparison, a stud is only being stretched. Also, a stud uses a fine thread for the retaining nut, which allows for more precise torque readings.

● SEE FIGURE 34–3.

FIGURE 34–4 Main bearing studs installed on a V-8 block.

FIGURE 34–6 A thread chaser (top) is the preferred tool to clean threaded holes because it cleans without removing metal compared to a tap (bottom).

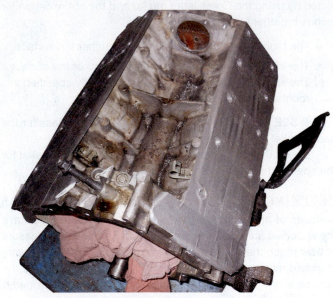

FIGURE 34–5 A Cadillac Northstar engine being rebuilt. The shop doing the work is installing Heli-coils® in all threaded cylinder head bolt holes as a precaution. Using duct tape to cover the engine helps prevent aluminum chips from getting into passages.

The use of studs for the main bearing saddles helps main cap alignment, because the torque applied is more consistent and there is less chance of the bearing cap moving during the tightening operation. ● SEE FIGURE 34–4.

Screw the studs into the block but finger tighten only. Do not tighten a stud more than finger tight. A nut should not be used to double nut a stud to keep it in position.

NOTE: The tightening torque in the installation instructions is for the *nut* and not the stud itself.

TECH TIP

Be Aware of BMW Engine Procedures

If rebuilding a BMW engine, check service information carefully because most BMW engines require that threaded inserts be installed in all head bolt threads. Performing this operation can increase the cost and time needed. Always follow all recommended service procedures on the engine being serviced. ● SEE FIGURE 34–5.

In most cases, a thread locker such as Loctite® 242 can be used on the threads of the stud being inserted into the block to make the installation of the stud more permanent.

CAUTION: If a thread locker is used, be sure to immediately install the main bearing caps before the compound cures to help avoid misalignment.

PREPARING THREADED HOLES

STEP 1 All threads in the block should be thoroughly cleaned. Many experts recommend using a thread chaser, because a tap could cut and remove metal. A chaser will restore the threads without removing metal. ● SEE FIGURE 34–6.

STEP 2 Check that all liquid has been removed from the bolt holes in the block. If liquid is in the bottom of a blind hole, the block can be cracked when the bolt is installed.

FIGURE 34–7 Using a plastic trash bag is an excellent way to keep the engine clean during all stages of assembly.

FIGURE 34–8 A trial assembly showed that some grinding of the block will be needed to provide clearance for the counterweight of the crankshaft. Also, notice that the engine has been equipped with studs for the four-bolt main bearing caps.

CYLINDER HEAD PREPARATION

ITEMS TO CHECK Check the following details on the cylinder head(s).

- The surface finish of the fire deck is as specified for the head gasket type to be used.
- All valves should be checked for leakage by pouring mineral spirits into the intake and exhaust parts and look for leakage past the valves.
- All valve springs should be checked for even spring pressure and installed height.
- Check for proper pushrod length. If the cylinder head(s) has been machined and/or the block deck machined, the pushrods may be too long. If the pushrods are too long, the rocker arm geometry will not be correct. One problem that can occur with incorrect rocker arm geometry is spring bind, which can cause severe engine damage.
- If replacement rocker arms are used, be sure that the geometry and total lift will be okay.

TRIAL ASSEMBLY

SHORT BLOCK Before performing final engine assembly, the wise technician checks that all parts will fit and work. This is especially important if using a different crankshaft that changes the stroke. ● **SEE FIGURE 34–8** for an example of a 400 cu. inch Chevrolet crankshaft being fitted to a 350 cu. inch Chevrolet engine.

VALVE TRAIN Another place where a trial fit is needed is in the valve train. Some timing chain mechanisms require more space than the stock component so some machining may be needed.

If the rocker arms have been upgraded to roller rockers, these should be installed and checked that the tip of the roller rests at the center of the valve stem. ● **SEE FIGURE 34–9.**

If there is a problem, further investigation will be needed because the pushrods may be too long due to machining of the

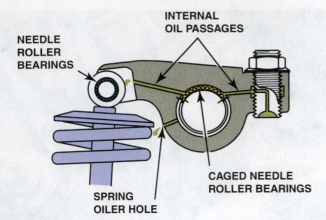

NEEDLE
ROLLER
BEARINGS

INTERNAL
OIL PASSAGES

CAGED NEEDLE
ROLLER BEARINGS

SPRING
OILER HOLE

FIGURE 34–9 A typical high-performance aftermarket rocker arm which is equipped with needle roller bearings at the valve stem end and caged needle bearing at the pivot shaft end to reduce friction, which increases engine horsepower and improves fuel economy.

 TECH TIP

Fogging Oil and Assembly Lube

When assembling an engine, the parts should be coated with a light oil film to keep them from rusting. This type of oil is commonly referred to as **fogging oil** and is available in spray cans. ● **SEE FIGURE 34–10.**

During engine assembly, the internal parts should be lubricated. While engine oil or grease could be used, most experts recommend the use of a specific lubricant designed for engine assembly. This lubricant, designed to remain on the parts and not drip or run, is called **assembly lube**. ● **SEE FIGURE 34–11.**

block deck and/or cylinder head. Rotate the engine and check for proper clearance throughout the entire opening and closing of the valves. Use a feeler gauge between the coils of the valve spring to check for coil bind. If coil bind occurs, a different camshaft or valve spring should be used.

CHECK THE ANGLE BETWEEN HEADS During the trial assembly, use a gauge to check that the heads are at the correct angle to ensure proper intake manifold gasket sealing. If the angle is not correct, then remachining of the head or block will be needed. ● **SEE FIGURE 34–12.**

FINAL SHORT BLOCK ASSEMBLY

BLOCK PREPARATION All surfaces should be checked for damage resulting from the machining processes. Items that should be done before assembly begins include the following:

FIGURE 34–10 Fogging oil is used to cover bare metal parts when the engine is being stored to prevent corrosion.

FIGURE 34–11 Engine assembly lube is recommended to be used on engine parts during assembly.

1. The block, including the oil gallery passages, should be thoroughly cleaned. ● **SEE FIGURES 34–13 AND 34–14.**
2. All threaded bolt holes should be chamfered.
3. All threaded holes should be cleaned with a thread chaser before final assembly.

INSTALLING CUPS AND PLUGS Oil gallery plugs should be installed using sealant on the threads.

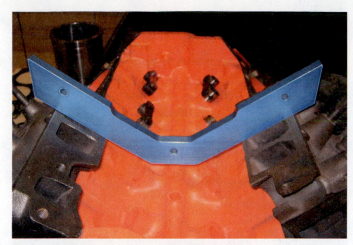

FIGURE 34–12 An angle gauge being used to check the angle between the cylinder heads on this small block Chevrolet V-8 engine.

FIGURE 34–13 The best way to thoroughly clean cylinders is to use soap (detergent), water, and a large washing brush. This method floats the machining particles out of the block and washes them away.

CAUTION: Avoid using Teflon tape on the threads of oil gallery plugs or coolant drain plugs. The tape is often cut by the threads, and thin strips of the tape are then free to flow through the oil galleries where the tape can cause a clog, thereby limiting lubricating engine oil to important parts of the engine.

Core holes left in the external block wall are machined and sealed with **soft core plugs** or **expansion plugs** (also called **freeze plugs** or **Welsh plugs**).

Soft plugs are of two designs.

- **Convex type.** The core hole is counterbored with a shoulder. The convex soft plug is placed in the counterbore, convex side out. It is driven in with a fitted seating tool. This causes the edge of the soft plug to enlarge to hold it in place. A convex plug should be driven in until it reaches the counterbore of the core plug hole.

FIGURE 34–14 All oil galleries should be cleaned using soap (detergent), water, and a long oil gallery cleaning brush.

CUP PLUGS

FIGURE 34–15 This engine uses many cup plugs to block off coolant and oil passages as well as a large plug over the end of the camshaft bore.

- **Cup type.** This most common type fits into a smooth, straight hole. The outer edge of the cup is slightly bell mouthed. The bell mouth causes it to tighten when it is driven into the hole to the correct depth with a seating tool. An installed cup-type soft plug is shown in ● **FIGURE 34–15.**

A cup plug is installed about 0.02 to 0.05 inch (0.5 to 1.3 mm) below the surface of the block, using sealant to prevent leaks. ● **SEE FIGURE 34–16.**

FIGURE 34–16 Sealer should be applied to the cup plug before being driven into the block.

? FREQUENTLY ASKED QUESTION

What Causes Premature Bearing Failure?

According to a major manufacturer of engine bearings, the major causes of premature (shortly after installation) bearing failure include the following:

Dirt (45%)

Misassembly (13%)

Misalignment (13%)

Lack of lubrication (11%)

Overloading or lugging (10%)

Corrosion (4%)

Other (4%)

Many cases of premature bearing failure may result from a combination of several of these items. Therefore, to help prevent bearing failure, *keep everything as clean as possible*.

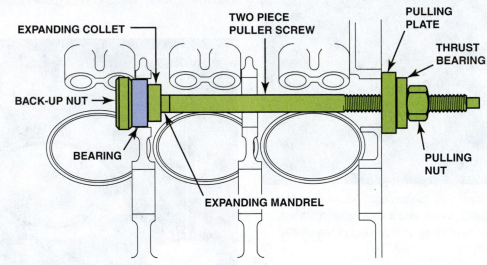

FIGURE 34–17 Screw-type puller being used to install a new cam bearing. Most cam bearings are crush fit. The full round bearing is forced into the cam bearing bore. Most vehicle manufacturers specify that the cam bearings be installed "dry" without lubrication to help prevent them from spinning, which would cause the bearing to block the oil feed hole.

CAM BEARINGS A cam bearing installing tool is required to insert the new cam bearing without damaging the bearing. A number of tool manufacturers design and sell cam bearing installation tools. Their common feature is a shoulder on a bushing that fits inside the cam bearing, with a means of keeping the bearing aligned as it is installed.

The bearing is placed on the bushing of the tool and rotated to properly align the oil hole. The bearing is then forced into the bearing bore of the block by either a pulling screw or a slide hammer. A pulling screw type of tool is illustrated in
● **FIGURE 34–17.**

The installed bearing must be checked to ensure that it has the correct depth and that the oil hole is indexed with the oil passage in the block. No additional service is required on cam bearings that have been properly installed. The opening at the back of the camshaft is closed with a cup plug.

MEASURING MAIN BEARING CLEARANCE The main bearings are properly fit *before* the crankshaft is lubricated or turned. The oil clearance of both main and connecting rod bearings is set by selectively fitting the bearings. In this way, the oil clearance can be adjusted to within 0.0005 inch of the desired clearance.

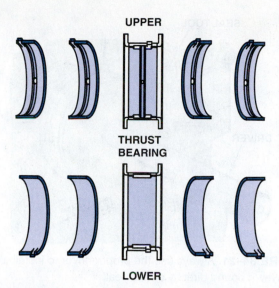

FIGURE 34–18 Typical main bearing set. Note that the upper halves are grooved for better oil flow and the lower halves are plain for better load support. This bearing set uses the center main bearing for thrust control. Notice that the upper bearing set has the holes for oil, whereas the lower set does not.

CAUTION: Avoid touching bearings with bare hands. The oils on your fingers can start corrosion of the bearing materials. Always wear protective cloth or rubber gloves to avoid the possibility of damage to the bearing surface.

Bearings are usually made in 0.010, 0–.020, and 0.030 inch *undersize* for use on reground journals. ● SEE FIGURE 34–18 for a typical main bearing set.

The crankshaft bearing journals should be measured with a micrometer to select the required bearing size.

- Each of the main bearing caps will only fit one location and the caps must be positioned correctly.

- The correct-size bearings should be placed in the block and cap, making sure that the bearing tang locks into its slot.

- The upper main bearing has an oil feed hole. The lower bearing does not have an oil hole.

- Lower the crankshaft squarely so that it does not damage the thrust bearing. Carefully rest the clean crankshaft in the block on the upper main bearings.

- After making sure that there is no oil on the crank journal of the bearing, place a strip of Plastigage® (gauging plastic) on each main bearing journal. Install the main bearing caps and tighten the bolts to specifications.

- Remove each cap and check the width of the Plastigage® with the markings on the gauge envelope, as shown in ● FIGURE 34–19.

- The width of the plastic strip indicates the oil clearance.

FIGURE 34–19 The width of the plastic gauging strip determines the oil clearance of the main bearing. An alternate method of determining oil clearance includes careful measurement of the crankshaft journal and bearings after they are installed and the main housing bore caps are torqued to specifications.

CORRECTING BEARING CLEARANCE Oil clearances normally run from 0.0005 to 0.002 inch (half a thousandth to two thousandths).

- The oil clearance can be reduced by 0.001 inch by replacing both bearing shells with bearing shells that are 0.001 inch undersize.

- The clearance can be reduced by 0.0005 inch by replacing only one of the bearing shells with a bearing shell that is 0.001 inch smaller.

- This smaller bearing shell should be placed in the engine block side of the bearing (the upper shell). Oil clearance can be adjusted accurately using this procedure. Try to avoid mismatching the bearing shells by more than a 0.001 inch difference in size.

LIP SEAL INSTALLATION Seals are always used at the front and rear of the crankshaft. Overhead cam engines may also have a seal at the front end of the camshaft and at the front end of an auxiliary accessory shaft. Either a lip seal or a rope seal is used in these locations. ● SEE FIGURE 34–20.

The rear crankshaft oil seal is installed after the main bearings have been properly fit. The lip seal may be molded in a steel case or it may be molded around a steel stiffener. The counterbore or guide that supports the seal must be thoroughly

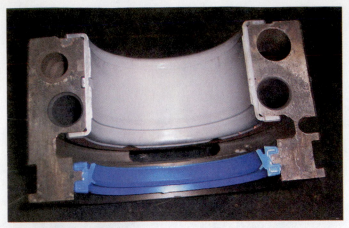

FIGURE 34–20 Lip-type rear main bearing seal in place in the rear main bearing cap. The lip should always be pointing toward the inside of the engine.

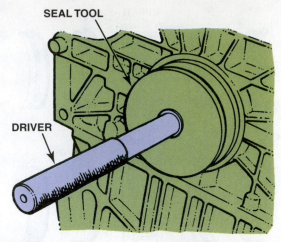

FIGURE 34–21 Always use the proper driver to install a main seal. Never pound directly on the seal.

FIGURE 34–22 The rear seal for this engine mounts to a retainer plate. The retainer is then bolted to the engine block.

clean. In most cases, the back of the lip seal is dry when it is installed. Occasionally, a manufacturer will recommend the use of sealants behind the seal. Check service information for the specified sealing instructions. The lip of the seal should be well lubricated before the shaft and cap are installed. ● SEE FIGURES 34–21 AND 34–22.

CAUTION: Teflon seals should *not* be lubricated. This type of seal should be installed dry. When the engine is first started, some of the Teflon transfers to the crankshaft, to create a Teflon-to-Teflon surface. Even touching the seal with your hands could remove some of the outer coating on the seal and cause a leak. Carefully read, understand, and follow the installation instructions that come with the seal.

ROPE SEAL INSTALLATION Some older engines use rope-type seals at both the front and rear of the crankshaft. Rope-type seals, usually called *braided fabric seals,* are sometimes used as rear crankshaft oil seals. Rope-type oil seals must be compressed tightly into the groove so that no oil can leak behind them. With the crankshaft removed, the upper half of the rope seal is put in a clean groove and compressed by rolling a round object against it to force it tightly into the groove. A piece of pipe, a large socket, or even a hammer handle can be used for this.

When the seal is fully seated in the groove, the ends that extend above the parting surface are cut to be flush with the surface using a sharp single-edge razor blade or a sharp tool specially designed to cut the seal. Some technicians find that leaving a little of the seal higher than the bearing cap creates a better seal, because when the bearing cap is installed and tightened, the extra seal length forces the rope seal further into the groove. ● SEE FIGURE 34–23.

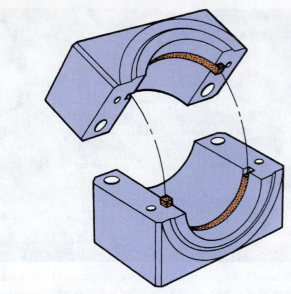

FIGURE 34–23 Many engine builders prefer to stagger the parting lines of a rope-type seal.

FIGURE 34–24 A dial indicator is being used to check the crankshaft end play, known as thrust bearing clearance. Always follow the manufacturer's recommended testing procedures.

CRANKSHAFT INSTALLATION

The main bearing caps and crankshaft should be removed after checking for proper bearing clearance. The surface of the bearings should then be given a thin coating of oil or assembly lubricant to provide initial lubrication for engine start-up. Install the crankshaft using the following steps.

STEP 1 The crankshaft should be carefully placed in the bearings to avoid damage to the thrust bearing surfaces.

STEP 2 The bearing caps are installed with their identification numbers correctly positioned. The caps were originally machined in place, so they can only fit correctly in their original position.

STEP 3 The main bearing cap bolts are tightened finger tight, and the crankshaft is rotated. It should rotate freely.

THRUST BEARING CLEARANCE

Tighten all main bearing cap bolts to factory specification except for the bearing cap that is used for thrust (usually the center or the rear cap). Pry the crankshaft forward and rearward to align the cap half of the thrust bearing with the block saddle half. Most engine specifications for thrust bearing clearance (also called *crankshaft end play*) can range from 0.002 to 0.012 inch (0.02 to 0.3 mm). This clearance or play can be measured with a:

- Feeler gauge
- Dial indicator ● SEE FIGURE 34–24.

If the clearance is too great, oversize main thrust bearings may be available for the engine. Semifinished bearings may have to be purchased and machined to size to restore proper tolerance.

NOTE: Some engines use a separate replaceable thrust bearing. ● SEE FIGURE 34–25.

MAIN BEARING TIGHTENING PROCEDURE

Tighten the main bearing caps to the specified assembly torque, and in the specified sequence. The procedure specified

FIGURE 34–25 A thrust bearing insert being installed before the crankshaft is installed.

usually includes tightening the main bearing cap bolts in three stages.

- Torque to one-third of the specified torque.
- Then tighten to two-thirds of the specified torque.
- Finally tighten the bolts to the factory specified torque.

Many manufacturers require that the crankshaft be pried forward or rearward during the main bearing tightening process. The crankshaft should turn freely after all main bearing cap bolts are fully torqued.

CRANKSHAFT ROTATING TORQUE

It should never require over 5 pound-feet (lb-ft) (6.75 newton-meters, or N-m) of torque to rotate the crankshaft. An increase in the torque needed to rotate the crankshaft is often caused by a foreign particle that was not removed during cleanup. It may be on the bearing surface, on the crankshaft journal, or between the bearing and saddle.

FIGURE 34–26 Installing a camshaft is easier if the engine is vertical so gravity can help, and this method reduces the possibility of damaging the cam bearings.

FIGURE 34–27 A commercial additive designed to protect a flat-bottom lifter camshaft used in older vehicles when using newer oils that do not have enough ZDDP to protect the camshaft and lifters.

 TECH TIP

Use a Long Bolt to Hold the Camshaft

To help install a camshaft without harming the cam bearings, install a long bolt into one of the end threaded holes in the camshaft. Then tilt the engine vertically so that gravity will cause the camshaft to fall straight down while holding onto the camshaft using the long bolt. ● **SEE FIGURE 34–26.**

INSTALLING THE CAMSHAFT

PRELUBRICATION When the camshaft is installed, the lobes must be coated with a special lubricant that contains molydisulfide. This special lube helps to ensure proper initial lubrication to the critical cam lobe sections of the camshaft. Many manufacturers recommend multiviscosity engine oil such as SAE 5W-30 or SAE 10W-30. Some camshaft manufacturers recommend using straight SAE 30 or SAE 40 engine oil and not a multiviscosity oil for the first oil fill. Some manufacturers also recommend the use of an antiwear additive such as zinc dithiophosphate (ZDP).

CAMSHAFT PRECAUTIONS Whenever repairing an engine, follow these rules regarding the camshaft and lifters.

1. When installing a new camshaft, always install new valve lifters (tappets).

2. When installing new lifters, if the original cam is not excessively worn and if the pushrods all rotate with the original camshaft, the camshaft may be reused.

 **TECH TIP**

Two Choices If Using Flat-Bottom Lifters

An old or rebuilt engine that uses flat-bottom lifters must use one of two lubricants.

1. Oils that contain at least 0.15% or 1,500 parts per million (ppm) of zinc in the form of ZDDP. Oils that contain this much zinc are designed for off-road use only and in a vehicle that does not have a catalytic converter, such as racing oils. If the vehicle is equipped with a catalytic converter, replace the camshaft and lifters to roller type, so that newer oils with lower levels of zinc can be used.

2. Use a newer oil and an additive such as:
   a. GM engine oil supplement (EOS) (Part #1052367 or #88862586)
   b. Comp Cams® camshaft break-in oil additive (Part #159)
   c. Crane Cams® Moly Paste (Part #99002-1)
   d. Crane Cams® Super Lube oil additive (Part #99003-1)
   e. Lumati Assembly lube (Part #99010)
   f. Mell-Lube camshaft tube oil additive (Part # M-10012)
   g. Other available additives designed to protect the camshaft (● **SEE FIGURE 34–27.**)

NOTE: Some manufacturers recommend that a new camshaft always be installed when replacing valve lifters.

3. *Never* use a hydraulic lifter camshaft with solid lifters or hydraulic lifters with a solid lifter camshaft.

FIGURE 34–28 A feeler gauge is used to check piston ring gap.

FIGURE 34–29 The notch on a piston should always face toward the front of the engine.

PISTON DIAMETER (INCHES)	RING GAP (INCHES)
2 to 3	0.007 to 0.018
3 to 4	0.01 to 0.02
4 to 5	0.013 to 0.023

CHART 34–2

The approximate ring gap based on the size of the bore in inches. Always check service information for the exact specifications for the engine being assembled.

PISTON/ROD INSTALLATION

FIGURE 34–30 On V-type engines that use paired rod journals, the side of the rod with the large chamfer should face toward the crank throw (outward).

CHECKING PISTON RINGS Before installing the piston assemblies, all piston rings should be checked for proper side clearance and ring gap. ● **SEE FIGURE 34–28.**

Typical ring gap clearances are about 0.004 inch per inch of cylinder bore. ● **SEE CHART 34–2.**

NOTE: If the gap is greater than recommended, some engine performance is lost. However, too small a gap will result in scuffing, because ring ends can be forced together during operation, which forces the rings to scrape the cylinders.

- If the ring gap is too large, the ring should be replaced with one having the next oversize diameter.
- If the ring gap is too small, the ring should be removed and filed to make the gap larger.

PISTON MARKINGS Care must be taken to ensure that the pistons and rods are in the correct cylinder. They must face in the correct direction. There is usually a *notch* on the piston head indicating the *front*. Using this will correctly position the

piston pin offset toward the right side of the engine. ● **SEE FIGURE 34–29.**

- The connecting rod *identification marks* on pushrod 4- and 6-cylinder inline engines are normally placed on the camshaft side.
- On V-type engines, the connecting rod cylinder identification marks are on the side of the rods that can be seen from the bottom of the engine when the piston and rod assemblies are installed in the engine. Make sure the connecting rod has been installed on the piston correctly— the chamfer on the side of the big end should face outward (toward the crank throw). ● **SEE FIGURE 34–30.**
- Check service information for any special piston and rod assembly instructions.

CONNECTING ROD BEARING CLEARANCE The rod cap, with the bearing in place, is put on the rod. There are two

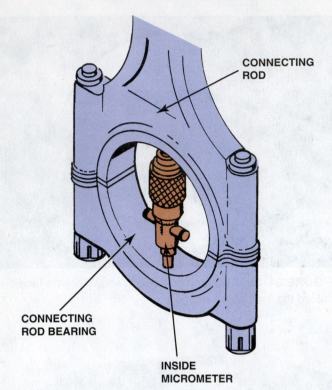

FIGURE 34–31 An inside micrometer can be used to measure the inside diameter of the big end of the connecting rod with the bearings installed. This dimension subtracted from the rod journal diameter is equal to the bearing clearance.

methods that can be used to check for proper connecting rod bearing clearance.

- Use Plastigage® following the same procedure discussed for main bearing clearance.

- Measure the assembled connecting rod big end devices with the bearing installed and the caps torqued to specification. Subtract the diameter of the rod journal to determine the bearing clearance. ● SEE FIGURE 34–31.

NOTE: Be certain to check for piston-to-crankshaft counterweight clearance. Most manufacturers specify a minimum 0.06 inch (1.5 mm).

PISTON INSTALLATION
To install a piston, perform the following steps.

STEP 1 Apply a coating of clean engine oil to the cylinder walls. This oil should be spread over the entire cylinder wall surface by hand.

STEP 2 Apply oil or assembly lube to the rod bearings.

STEP 3 Align the piston ring gaps (ring gap stagger) to the locations specified in service information. ● SEE FIGURE 34–32.

STEP 4 Using a squirt-type oil can, squirt oil over the rings and the skirt of the piston.

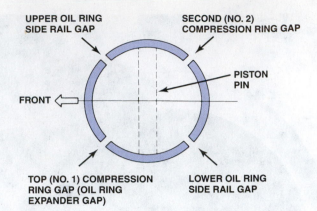

FIGURE 34–32 One method of piston ring installation showing the location of ring gaps. Always follow the manufacturer's recommended method for the location of ring gaps and for ring gap spacing.

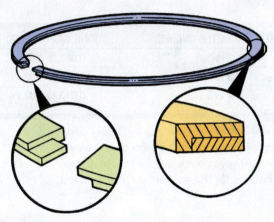

FIGURE 34–33 A gapless ring is made in two pieces that overlap.

NOTE: Special types of piston rings (overlapping or gapless) are installed dry, without oil. ● SEE FIGURE 34–33. Some manufacturers recommend oiling only the oil control ring. Always check the piston ring instruction sheet for the exact procedure.

STEP 5 The **piston ring compressor** is then put on the piston to hold the rings in their grooves. ● SEE FIGURES 34–34 AND 34–35.

STEP 6 Rotate the crankshaft so the crankshaft journal is at the bottom (BDC) to help prevent the rod from touching the crankshaft when the piston is installed.

STEP 7 Remove the bearing cap from the rod, and install the bearings.

STEP 8 Install protectors over the rod bolts. These help prevent damage to the crankshaft journal when the piston/rod assembly is installed. ● SEE FIGURE 34–36.

STEP 9 The upper rod bearing should be in the rod and the piston should be turned so that the notch on the piston head is facing the front of the engine.

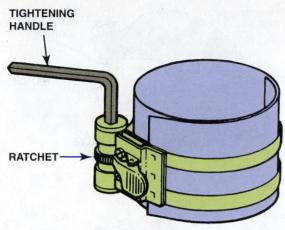

FIGURE 34–34 This style of ring compressor uses a ratchet to contract the spring band and compress the rings into their grooves.

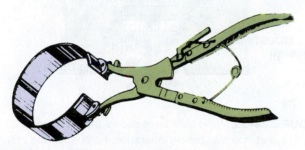

FIGURE 34–35 This pliers-like tool is used to close the metal band around the piston to compress the rings. An assortment of bands is available to service different size pistons.

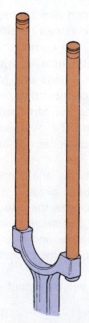

FIGURE 34–36 When threaded onto the rod bolts, these guides not only help align the rod but also protect the threads and holds the bearing shell in place. The soft ends also will not damage the crankshaft journals.

FIGURE 34–37 Installing a piston using a ring compressor to hold the rings into the ring grooves of the piston and then using a hammer handle to drive the piston into the bore. Connecting rod bolt protectors have been installed to help prevent possible damage to the crankshaft during piston installation.

STEP 10 The piston and rod assembly is placed in the cylinder through the block deck. The ring compressor must be kept tightly against the block deck as the piston is pushed into the cylinder.

The ring compressor holds the rings in their grooves so that they will enter the cylinder. ● **SEE FIGURE 34–37.**

STEP 11 The piston is pushed into the cylinder until the rod bearing is fully seated on the journal.

CONNECTING ROD SIDE CLEARANCE The connecting rods should be checked to ensure that they still have the correct side clearance. This is measured by fitting the correct thickness of feeler gauge between the connecting rod and the crankshaft cheek of the bearing journal. ● **SEE FIGURE 34–38.**

- *If the side clearance is too great,* excessive amounts of oil may escape that can cause lower-than-normal oil pressure. To correct excessive clearance:
  1. Weld and regrind or replace the crankshaft.
  2. Carefully measure all connecting rods and replace those that are too thin or mismatched.

- *If the side clearance is too small,* there may not be enough room for heat expansion. To correct a side clearance that is too small:
  1. Regrind the crankshaft.
  2. Replace the rods.

FIGURE 34–38 The connecting rod side clearance is measured with a feeler gauge.

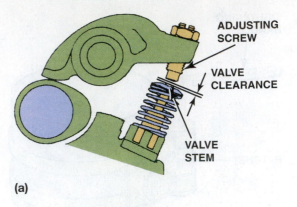

(a)

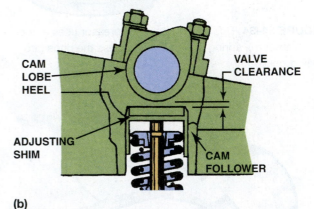

(b)

FIGURE 34–39 Valve clearance allows the metal parts to expand and maintain proper operation, both when the engine is cold and at normal operating temperature. (a) Adjustment is achieved by turning the adjusting screw. (b) Adjustment is achieved by changing the thickness of the adjusting shim.

TECH TIP

Tightening Tip for Rod Bearings

Even though the bearing clearances are checked, it is still a good idea to check and record the torque required to rotate the crankshaft with all piston rings dragging on the cylinder walls. The retaining nuts on one bearing should be torqued, and then the torque that is required to rotate the crankshaft should be rechecked and recorded. Follow the same procedure on all rod bearings. If tightening any one of the rod bearing caps causes a large increase in the torque required to rotate the crankshaft, immediately stop the tightening process. Determine the cause of the increased rotating torque using the same method as used on the main bearings. Rotate the crankshaft for several revolutions to ensure that the assembly is turning freely and that there are no tight spots.

The rotating torque of the crankshaft with all connecting rod cap bolts fully torqued should be as follows:

- 4-cylinder engine: 20 lb-ft maximum (88 N-m)
- 6-cylinder engine: 25 lb-ft maximum (110 N-m)
- 8-cylinder engine: 30 lb-ft maximum (132 N-m)

CYLINDER HEAD INSTALLATION

INSTALLING THE CAMSHAFT FOR OHC ENGINES On some overhead camshaft engines, the camshaft is installed before the head is fastened to the block deck. Some engines have the camshaft located directly over the valves. The cam bearings on these engines can be either one piece or split. In other engine types, the camshaft bearings are split to allow the camshaft to be installed without the valves being depressed. The cam bearings and journals are lubricated before assembly. The cam bearing caps must be tightened evenly to avoid bending the camshaft. The valve clearance or lash is checked with the overhead camshaft in place. Some engines use shims under a follower disk, as shown in
● **FIGURE 34–39.**

On these engine types, the camshaft is turned so that the follower is on the base circle of the cam. The clearance of each bucket follower can then be checked with a feeler gauge. The amount of clearance is recorded and compared with the specified clearance, and then a shim of the required thickness is put in the top of the bucket followers, as shown in
● **FIGURE 34–40.**

Always follow the vehicle manufacturer's recommended procedures.

HEAD BOLT TORQUE SEQUENCE The torque put on the bolts is used to control the clamping force that is applied to the gasket. The clamping force is correct only when the threads are clean and properly lubricated.

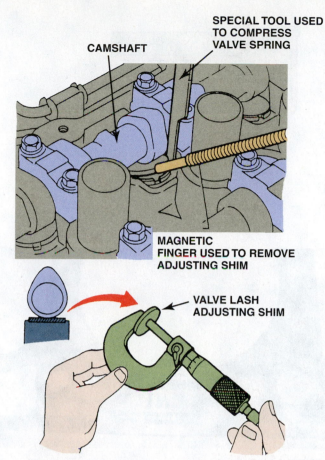

CAMSHAFT

SPECIAL TOOL USED TO COMPRESS VALVE SPRING

MAGNETIC FINGER USED TO REMOVE ADJUSTING SHIM

VALVE LASH ADJUSTING SHIM

FIGURE 34–40 Some overhead camshaft engines use valve lash adjusting shims to adjust the valve lash. A special tool is usually required to compress the valve spring so that a magnet can remove the shim.

 **TECH TIP**

Watch Out for Wet and Dry Holes

Many engines, such as the small block Chevrolet V-8, use head bolts that extend through the top deck of the block and end in a coolant passage. These bolt holes are called *wet holes*. When installing head bolts into holes that end up in the coolant passage, always use sealer on the threads of the head bolt. Some engines have head bolts that are "wet," whereas others are "dry" because they end in solid cast-iron material. Dry hole bolts do not require sealant, but they still require some oil on the threads of the bolts for lubrication. Do not put oil into a dry hole because the bolt may bottom out in the oil. The liquid oil cannot compress, so the force of the bolt being tightened is transferred to the block by hydraulic force, which can crack the block.

NOTE: Apply oil to a shop cloth and rotate the bolt in the cloth to lubricate the threads. This procedure lubricates the threads without applying too much oil.

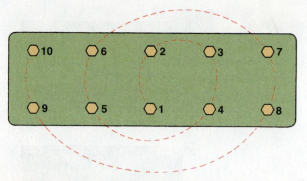

FIGURE 34–41 Typical cylinder head tightening sequence.

TECH TIP

The Piece of Paper Demonstration

Some students and beginning technicians forget the correct order to tighten head bolts or other fasteners of a component. Try the following demonstration:

- Place a single sheet of paper on a table.
- Place both hands on the paper in the center and then move your hands outward.
- Nothing should have happened and the paper should have not moved.
- Now place your hands on the paper at the ends and move them toward the center.
- The paper will wrinkle as the hands move toward the center.

This demonstration shows that the forces are moved away toward the ends of the cylinder head if the fasteners are tightened from the inside toward the outside. However, if the cylinder head bolts were tightened incorrectly, the head would likely crack due to the forces exerted during the tightening.

CAUTION: Always use the specified lubricant on the threads. If SAE 30 engine oil is specified, do not use SAE 10W-30 or any other viscosity, because using the incorrect viscosity oil can affect the clamping force exerted on the head gaskets.

In general, the head bolts are tightened in a specified torque sequence in three steps. The procedure starts with the head bolts in the center and then moves to those farther and farther from the center. This procedure helps spread the forces toward the ends of the cylinder.

By tightening the head bolts in three steps, the head gasket has time to compress and conform to the block deck and cylinder head gasket surfaces. Follow that sequence and tighten the bolts in the following manner.

1. Tighten to *one-third* the specified torque.
2. Tighten them a second time following the torque sequence to *two-thirds* the specified torque.
3. Follow the sequence with a final tightening to the specified torque. ● **SEE FIGURES 34–41 AND 34–42.**

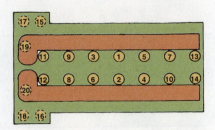
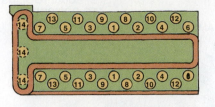

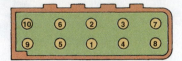

FIGURE 34–42 Examples of cylinder head bolt torquing sequences.

TECH TIP

Always "Exercise" New Bolts

New bolts and studs are manufactured by rolling the threads and heat treating. Due to this operation, the threads usually have some rough areas, which affect the clamping force on the gasket. Many engine building experts recommend that all new bolts be installed in the engine using a new or used gasket and torqued to specifications at least five times, except for torque-to-yield bolts. This process burnishes the ramps of the threads and makes the fastener provide a more even clamping force. Using the recommended lubricant, the bolts should be torqued and removed and then torqued again.

FIGURE 34–43 Typical head gasket markings. The front means that the gasket should be at the accessory drive belt end of the block.

CLAMPING FORCE   **Clamping force** is the amount of force exerted on a gasket. The clamping force is not the same as the torque applied to the fastener. When tightening a bolt or nut, about 80% of the applied torque is used to overcome friction between the threads. Therefore, it is very important that the threads be clean and lubricated with the proper (specified) lubricant.

FASTENER CONSIDERATION   Because most of the torque applied to a fastener is absorbed by friction, it is extremely important that the following steps be performed.

STEP 1   Clean the threads of all fasteners before using.

STEP 2   Check service information for the specified thread lubricant.

THREAD LUBRICANT   If using aftermarket bolts or studs, such as ARP (American Racing Products®), use the lubricant and torque that the company specifies. Do not use ARP lubricant and the factory torque specifications or the fasteners will be greatly overtightened. The same applies if using thread sealant to the threads of fasteners being installed in wet holes (holes that extend into the cooling passages). Many vehicle manufacturers recommend the use of 30 weight engine oil (SAE 30).

? FREQUENTLY ASKED QUESTION

Why Do Both Head Gaskets Have "Front" Marked?

A common question asked by beginning technicians or students include how to install head gaskets on a V-6 engine that is mounted transversely (sideways) in the vehicle. The technician usually notices that "front" is marked on one gasket and therefore installs that gasket on the block, on top of the forward-facing cylinder bank. Then, the technician notices that the other gasket is also marked with "front." How could both be marked "front"? There must be some mistake. The mistake is in the terminology used. In the case of head gaskets, the "front" means toward the accessory drive belt end of the engine and not on the cylinder bank toward the front of the vehicle. ● **SEE FIGURE 34–43.**

CAUTION: SAE 5W-30 or SAE 10W-30 is not the same as SAE 30 engine oil. Multiviscosity oil such as SAE 5W-30 is actually SAE 5W oil with additives to provide the protection of SAE 30 oil when it gets hot. Always use the exact oil specified by the vehicle manufacturer.

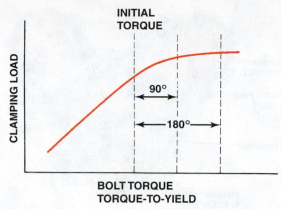

FIGURE 34–44 Due to variations in clamping force with turning force (torque) of head bolts, some engines are specifying the torque-to-yield procedure. The first step is to torque the bolts by an even amount called the initial torque. Final clamping load is achieved by turning the bolt a specified number of degrees. Bolt stretch provides the proper clamping force.

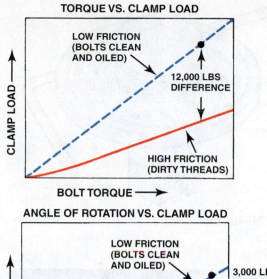

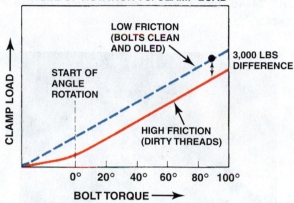

FIGURE 34–45 To ensure consistent clamp force (load), many manufacturers are recommending the torque-angle or torque-to-yield method of tightening head bolts. The torque-angle method specifies tightening fasteners to a low-torque setting and then giving an additional angle of rotation. Notice that the difference in clamping force is much smaller than it would be if just a torque wrench with dirty threads were used.

TECH TIP

Creep Up on the Torque Value

Do not jerk or rapidly rotate a torque wrench. For best results and more even torque, slowly apply force to the torque wrench until it reaches the preset value or the designated torque. Jerky or rapidly moving the torque wrench will often cause the torque to be uneven and not accurate.

TORQUE-TO-YIELD HEAD BOLTS

DEFINITION AND TERMINOLOGY Many engines use a tightening procedure called the **torque-to-yield (TTY)** method. The purpose of the TTY procedure is to have a more constant clamping load from bolt to bolt. This aids in head gasket sealing performance and eliminates the need for retorquing.

BOLT CONSTRUCTION Many torque-to-yield head bolts are made with a narrow section between the head and threads. As the bolts are tightened past their elastic limit, they yield and begin to stretch in this narrow section.

Torque-to-yield head bolts will not become any tighter once they reach this elastic limit, as seen on the graph in ● FIGURE 34–44.

The torque angle method also decreases the differences in clamping force that can occur depending on the condition or lubrication of the threads. ● SEE FIGURE 34–45.

As a result, many engine manufacturers specify *new* head bolts each time the head is installed. If these bolts are reused, they are likely to break during assembly or fail prematurely as the engine runs. If there is any doubt about the head bolts, replace them.

TORQUE-TO-YIELD PROCEDURE Torque-to-yield bolts are tightened to a specific initial torque, from 18 to 50 pound-feet (25 to 68 N-m). The bolts are then tightened an additional specified number of degrees, following the tightening sequence. In some cases they are turned a specified number of degrees two or three times. Some specifications limit the maximum torque that can be applied to the bolt while the degree turn is being made. Torque tables in a service manual will show how much initial torque should be applied to the bolt and how many degrees the bolt should be rotated after torquing. Torque-to-yield head bolts should be tightened as per specified in service information.

FIGURE 34-46 Torque angle can be measured using a special adaptor.

FIGURE 34-47 An electronic torque wrench showing the number of degrees of rotation. These very accurate and expensive torque wrenches can be programmed to display torque or number of degrees of rotation.

The procedure includes the following steps.

STEP 1 Tighten the fasteners to an initial torque in the specified sequence.

STEP 2 Turn the fasteners a specific number of degrees using an angle gauge again following the same sequence.

STEP 3 Turn the fasteners another specific number of degrees again following the designated sequence.

For example, a specified head bolt tightening specification may include:

- Initial torque, such as 44 lb-ft
- Rotate 90 degrees
- Rotate head bolts an additional 90 degrees ● **SEE FIGURES 34-46 AND 34-47.**

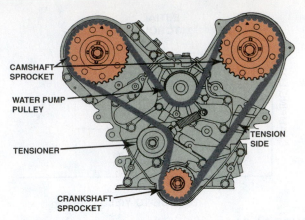

FIGURE 34-48 Both camshafts have to be timed on this engine and the timing belt also drives the water pump.

TORQUE ANGLE METHOD The *torque angle method,* also called the *torque-turn method,* does not necessarily mean torque-to-yield. Some engine specifications call for a beginning torque and then a specified angle, but the fastener is not designed to yield. These head bolts can often be reused. Always follow the manufacturer's recommended procedures.

VALVE TRAIN ASSEMBLY

TIMING DRIVES FOR OHC ENGINES After the head bolts have been torqued, the cam drive can be installed on overhead cam (OHC) engines. This is done by aligning the timing marks of the crankshaft and camshaft drive sprockets with their respective timing marks. The location of these marks differs between engines, but the marks can be identified by looking carefully at the sprockets. ● **SEE FIGURES 34-48 AND 34-49.**

The tensioner may be on either or both sides of the timing belt or chain. After the camshaft drive is engaged, rotate the crankshaft through two full revolutions. On the first full revolution, the exhaust valve will be almost closed and the intake valve will just be starting to open when the *crankshaft* timing mark aligns. At the end of the second revolution, both valves should be closed, and all the timing marks should align on most engines. This is the position the crankshaft should have when cylinder 1 is to fire.

NOTE: Always check the manufacturer's recommended timing chain installation procedure. Engines that use primary and secondary timing chains often require an exact detailed procedure for proper installation.

HYDRAULIC VALVE LIFTER INSTALLATION Most vehicle manufacturers recommend installing lifters *without* filling or pumping the lifter full of oil. If the lifter is filled with oil during engine start-up, the lifter may not be able to bleed down quickly enough and the valves may be kept open. Not only will the engine not operate correctly with the valves held open, but the

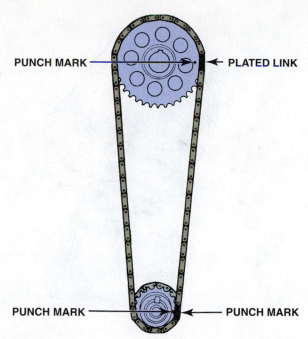

PUNCH MARK — PLATED LINK

PUNCH MARK — PUNCH MARK

FIGURE 34–49 Some timing chains have plated links that are used to correctly position the chain on the sprockets.

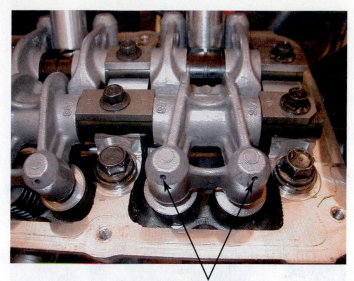

BLEED HOLES FROM
HYDRAULIC LASH
ADJUSTERS (HLA)

FIGURE 34–50 A special tool may be needed to bleed air from the hydraulic lash adjusters (HLA) through the bleed hole. These lash adjusters are part of the valve end of the rocker arms in this example.

 TECH TIP

Soak the Timing Chain

Many experts recommend that a new timing chain be soaked in engine oil prior to engine assembly to help ensure full lubrication at engine start-up. The timing chain is one of the last places in the engine to get lubrication when the engine first starts. This procedure may even extend the life of the chain.

 TECH TIP

Watch Out for Different Length Pushrods

The very popular General Motors family of engines, including 2.8 liter, 3.1 liter, 3.4 liter, and 3.5 liter, each use different pushrod lengths for intake and exhaust valves. If the wrong pushrods are used, two things can occur.
1. The pushrod(s) can be bent.
2. The engine will run rough because the longer pushrod prevents the valve from closing all the way.
   Always check service information for the exact location of the pushrods.

piston also could hit the open valves, causing serious engine damage. Most manufacturers usually specify that the lifter be lubricated. Roller hydraulic lifters can be lubricated with engine oil, whereas flat lifters require that engine assembly lube or extreme pressure (EP) grease be applied to the base.

BLEEDING HYDRAULIC LIFTERS Air trapped inside a hydraulic valve lifter can be easily bled by simply operating the engine at a fast idle (2500 RPM). Normal oil flow through the lifters will allow all of the air inside the lifter to be bled out.

NOTE: Some engines, such as many Nissan overhead camshaft engines, *must* have the air removed from the lifter before installation. This is accomplished by submerging the lifter in a container of engine oil and using a straightened paper clip to depress the oil passage check ball.

Check service information if in doubt about the bleeding procedure for the vehicle being serviced. ● **SEE FIGURE 34–50.**

TIMING CHAINS AND GEARS INSTALLATION On cam-in-block (OHV) engines, the timing gears or chain and sprocket can be installed after the crankshaft and camshaft. The timing marks should be aligned according to the factory specified marks. ● **SEE FIGURE 34–51.**

When used, the replaceable fuel pump eccentric is installed as the cam sprocket is fastened to the cam. The crankshaft should be rotated several times to see that the camshaft and timing gears or chain rotate freely. The timing mark alignment should be rechecked at this time. If the engine is equipped with a slinger ring, it should also be installed on the crankshaft, in front of the crankshaft gear.

OHV ENGINE LIFTER AND PUSHROD INSTALLATION
The outside of the lifters and the lifter bores in the block should be cleaned and coated with assembly lubricant. The lifters are

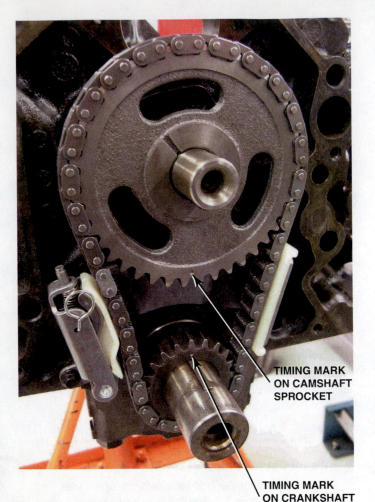

TIMING MARK ON CAMSHAFT SPROCKET

TIMING MARK ON CRANKSHAFT SPROCKET

FIGURE 34–51 Timing chain and gears can be installed after the crankshaft and camshaft have been installed and the timing marks are aligned with cylinder 1 at top dead center (TDC).

installed in the lifter bores and the pushrods put in place. There are different length pushrods on some engines. Make sure that the pushrods are installed in the proper location. The rocker arms are then put in place, aligning with the valves and pushrods. Rocker arm shafts should have their retaining bolts tightened a little at a time, alternating between the retaining bolts. This keeps the shaft from bending as the rocker arm pushes some of the valves open.

HYDRAULIC LIFTER ADJUSTMENT

The retaining nut on some rocker arms mounted on studs can be tightened to a specified torque. The rocker arm stud will have a shoulder on this type of rocker assembly. The rocker arm will be adjusted correctly at this torque when the valve tip has the correct height. Other types of rocker arms require tightening the nut to a position that will center the hydraulic lifter. The general procedure includes the following steps.

STEP 1 Rotate the engine until cylinder 1 is at TDC on the compression stroke to be assured that both the intake and exhaust valves are on the base circle of the cam lobes.

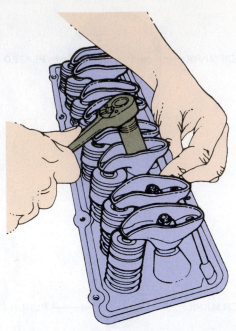

FIGURE 34–52 With the lifter resting on the base circle of the cam, zero lash is achieved by tightening the rocker arm lock nut until the pushrod no longer rotates freely.

STEP 2 Tighten the retaining nut to the point that all free lash is gone and the pushrod cannot be easily rotated. ● **SEE FIGURE 34–52.**

STEP 3 From this point, the retaining nut is tightened by a specified amount, such as three-fourths of a turn or one and one-half turns.

NOTE: This method usually results in about three threads showing above the adjusting nut on a *stock* small block Chevrolet V-8 equipped with flat-bottom hydraulic lifters.

STEP 4 Rotate the engine until the next cylinder in the firing order is at top dead center on the compression stroke. The valves on this next cylinder are adjusted in the same manner as those on cylinder 1. This procedure is repeated on each cylinder *following the engine firing order* until all the valves have been adjusted. Always follow the specified procedure found in service information.

SOLID LIFTER ADJUSTMENT

The valve clearance or **lash** must be set on a solid lifter engine, so that the valves can positively seat. Check service information for the specified adjustment sequence to follow to set the lash. If this is not available, then the following procedure can be used on all engines requiring valve lash adjustment. The valve lash is adjusted with the valves completely closed. ● **SEE FIGURE 34–53.**

The procedure is similar to that used to adjust hydraulic lifters that are adjustable except that a feeler gauge is used to check the lash. The same valve lash adjustment sequence is used on overhead cam engines. Those engines with rocker arms or with adjustable finger follower pivots are adjusted in the same way as pushrod engines with rocker arms.

chapter 34

ENGINE ASSEMBLY AND DYNAMOMETER TESTING

LEARNING OBJECTIVES: After studying this chapter, the reader should be able to: • Explain short block preparation and cylinder head preparation. • Discuss trial assembly and final short block assembly. • Describe camshaft installation and piston/rod installation. • Explain the cylinder head installation procedure. • Discuss torque-to-yield head bolts. • Explain valve train assembly and final assembly of an engine. • Explain dynamometer testing.

KEY TERMS: Assembly lube 498 • Clamping force 510 • Corrected torque 520 • Correction factor 520 • Dry bulb temperature 519 • Expansion plugs 499 • Fogging oil 498 • Freeze plugs 499 • Lash 514 • Piston ring compressor 506 • Soft core plugs 499 • Torque-to-yield (TTY) 511 • Transducers 520 • Welsh plugs 499

DETAILS, DETAILS, DETAILS

Successful engine assembly depends on getting all of the details right. Where to start? Start when all parts have been purchased or prepared for assembly.

When starting to assemble the engine, be sure to have all of the instructions from all of the parts used.

- **Read.** Read *all* instructions that are included with all new parts and gaskets. Often very important information or suggested specifications are included and may be at the end.

- **Understand.** Be sure to fully understand everything that is stated in the instructions. If unsure as to what is meant, ask a knowledgeable technician or call the company to be sure that all procedures are clearly understood. This is especially important if working on an engine that is not very common, such as the Audi/Volkswagen W-8. This engine has seven rotating shafts, including:

  - Four overhead camshafts
  - Two counterrotating balance shafts
  - One crankshaft

  A Ford 1.0 liter three-cylinder is also unique.
  ● **SEE FIGURE 34–1.**

- **Follow.** Be sure to follow *all* of the instructions. Do not pick the easy procedures and skip others.

FIGURE 34–1 A Ford 1.0 liter 3-cylinder engine is different than many small engines and may require detailed service information to be sure that all of the steps are taken for proper assembly.

SHORT BLOCK PREPARATION

ITEMS TO CHECK The following engine block details should be checked.

- All passages should be clean and free of rust and debris.
- All gasket surfaces are properly cleaned and checked for burrs and scratches.

FIGURE 34–53 Most adjustable valves use a nut to keep the adjustment from changing. Therefore, to adjust the valves, the nut has to be loosened and the screw rotated until the proper valve clearance is achieved. Then the screw should be held while tightening the lock nut to keep the adjustment from changing. Double-check the valve clearance after tightening the nut.

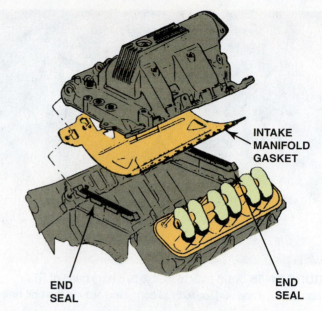

FIGURE 34–54 This intake manifold gasket includes end seals and a full shield cover for the valley to keep hot engine oil from heating the intake manifold.

FINAL ASSEMBLY

MANIFOLD INSTALLATION The intake manifold gasket for a V-type engine may be a one-piece gasket or it may have several pieces. V-type engines with open-type manifolds have a cover over the lifter valley. The cover may be a separate part or it may be part of a one-piece intake manifold gasket. Closed-type intake manifolds on V-type engines require gasket pieces (end seals) at the front and rear of the intake manifold.
● SEE FIGURE 34–54.

Inline engines usually have a one-piece intake manifold gasket. The intake manifold is put in place over the gaskets. Use a contact adhesive to hold the gasket and end seal if there is a chance they might slip out of place. Install the bolts and tighten to the specified torque following the correct tightening sequence.

Only some exhaust manifolds use gaskets. The exhaust manifold operates at very high temperatures, so there is usually some expansion and contraction movement in the manifold-to-head joint. It is very important to use attachment bolts, cap screws, and clamps of the correct type and length. ● SEE FIGURE 34–55.

They must be properly torqued to avoid both leakage and cracks.

NOTE: If the exhaust manifold gasket has a metal facing on one side, place the metal facing toward the head.

TIMING COVER INSTALLATION The timing cover with seal installed and gasket are placed over the timing gears and/or chain and sprockets. The attaching bolts are loosely

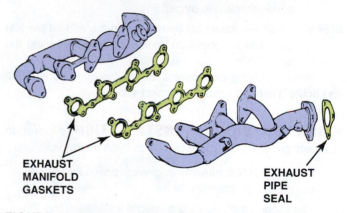

FIGURE 34–55 An exhaust manifold gasket is used on some engines. It seals the exhaust manifold to the cylinder head.

installed to allow the damper hub to align with the cover as it fits in the seal. The damper is installed on the crankshaft. On some engines, it is a press-fit and on others it is held with a large center bolt. After the damper is secured, the attaching bolts on the timing cover can be tightened to the specified torque.

Most timing covers are installed with a gasket, but some use RTV sealer in place of the gasket. A bead of RTV silicon 1/8 to 3/16 inch in diameter is put on the clean sealing surface.
● SEE FIGURE 34–56.

Sealing a cover using RTV silicon usually includes the following steps.

STEP 1 Encircle the bolt holes with the sealant.

STEP 2 Install the cover before the silicon begins to cure so that the uncured silicon bonds to both surfaces.

FIGURE 34–56 A 1/8 to 3/16 inch (3 to 5 mm) bead of RTV silicon on a parting surface with silicon going around the bolt hole.

STEP 3 While installing the cover, do not touch the silicon bead, otherwise the bead might be displaced and cause a leak.

STEP 4 Carefully press the cover into place. Do not slide the cover after it is in place.

STEP 5 Install the assembly bolts finger tight, and let the silicon cure for about 30 minutes before tightening the cover bolts.

When installing *cast covers*, anaerobic compound (such as Loctite®) is often used as a gasket substitute.

VIBRATION DAMPER INSTALLATION Vibration dampers are seated in place by one of three methods.

- The damper hub of some engines is pulled into place using the hub attaching bolt.

- The second method uses a special installation tool that screws into the attaching bolt hole to pull the hub into place. The tool is removed and the attaching bolt is installed and torqued.

- The last method is used on engines that have no attaching bolt. These hubs depend on a press-fit to hold the hub on the crankshaft. The hub is seated using a special tube-type driver. Check service information for the exact procedure and tool to use.

OIL PUMP INSTALLATION When an engine is rebuilt, the oil pump should be replaced with a new pump and oil pickup screen. Most vehicle manufacturers recommend that the oil pump and screen be replaced rather than cleaned. This ensures positive lubrication and long pump life. Oil pump gears should be coated with assembly lubricant before the cover is put on the pump. This provides initial lubrication, and it primes the pump so that it will draw the oil from the pan when the lubrication system is first operated. Torque the oil pump fasteners to factory specifications. ● **SEE FIGURE 34–57.**

FIGURE 34–57 A beam-type torque wrench being used to tighten the oil pump pickup assembly to factory specification.

TECH TIP

Check the Oil Pump Pickup to Oil Pan Clearance
Whenever installing the oil pan on a rebuilt engine, it is wise to check the clearance between the oil pump pickup and the bottom of the oil pan. This distance should be 3/16 to 3/8 inch (5 to 9 mm). To check the clearance, two methods can be used.

METHOD 1 With the engine upside down and the oil pump and pickup installed, measure the distance from the oil pan rail to the top (actually the bottom) of the oil pump pickup. Then measure the distance from the oil pan rail to the bottom of the oil pan and subtract the two measurements to get the clearance.

METHOD 2 Place about 1/2 inch (13 mm) of modeling clay on the pickup of the oil pump. Then temporarily install the oil pan with a gasket. Press down on the oil pan to compress the modeling clay. Remove the oil pan and measure the thickness of the clay. This thickness is the oil pan to oil pump pickup clearance. ● **SEE FIGURE 34–58.**

OIL PAN INSTALLATION The oil pan should be checked and straightened as necessary. ● **SEE FIGURE 34–59.**

With the oil pump in place, the oil pan gaskets are properly positioned. The oil pan is carefully placed over the gaskets. All oil

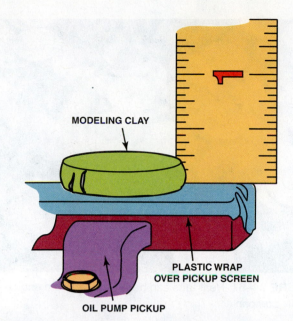

FIGURE 34–58 Using clay to determine the oil pan to oil pickup clearance, which should be about 1/4 inch.

MODELING CLAY

PLASTIC WRAP OVER PICKUP SCREEN

OIL PUMP PICKUP

FIGURE 34–59 Using a hammer to straighten the gasket rail surface of the oil pan before installing a new gasket. When the retaining bolts are tightened, some distortion of sheet metal covers occurs. If the area around the bolt holes is not straightened, leaks can occur with the new gasket.

pan bolts should be started into their holes before any are tightened. The bolts should be alternately snugged up and then they should be properly tightened to factory specifications. Always follow the instructions that come with the gasket for best results.

WATER PUMP INSTALLATION
A reconditioned, rebuilt, or new water pump should be used. Once gaskets are fitted in place, the pump is secured with assembly bolts tightened to the correct torque.

A new thermostat should be installed being careful to check that the wax pellet side of the thermostat faces toward the engine. The thermostat housing with the proper gasket is installed, and the retaining bolts are tightened to the proper torque.

 REAL WORLD FIX

The New Oil Pump That Failed
A technician replaced the oil pump and screen on a V-8 with low oil pressure. After the repair, the oil pressure returned to normal for two weeks, but then the oil pressure light came on and the valve train started making noise. The vehicle owner returned to the service garage where the oil pump had been replaced. The technician removed the oil pan and pump. The screen was almost completely clogged with the RTV sealant that the technician had used to "seal" the oil pan gasket. The technician had failed to read the instructions that came with the oil pan gasket. Failure to follow directions, and using too much of the wrong sealer, cost the repair shop an expensive comeback repair.

ENGINE PAINTING
Painting an engine helps prevent rust and corrosion and makes the engine look new. Standard engine paints with original colors are usually available at automotive parts stores. Engine paints should be used rather than other types of paints. Engine paints are compounded to stay on the metal as the engine temperatures change. Normal engine fluids will not dissolve or remove them. These paints are usually purchased in pressure cans so that they can be sprayed from the can directly onto the engine.

All parts that should not be painted must be covered before spray painting. This can be done with old parts, such as old spark plugs and old gaskets. This can also be done by taping paper over the areas to be covered. If the intake manifold of an inline engine is to be painted, it can be painted separately. Engine assembly can continue after the paint has dried.

PRELUBRICATING THE ENGINE
With oil in the engine and the distributor, if equipped, out of the engine, oil pressure should be established before the engine is started. This can be done on most engines by rotating the oil pump using an electric drive. This ensures that oil is delivered to all parts of the engine before the engine is started. Adapters are available that allow an electric drill motor to rotate the oil pump.

Engines that do not drive the oil pump with a distributor will require the use of a pressurized pre-lubing tool, such as the General Motor recommended J-45299 or the Goodson PL-40. ● **SEE FIGURE 34–60.**

SETTING IGNITION TIMING
After oil pressure is established, the distributor, if equipped, can be installed. Rotate the crankshaft in its normal direction of rotation until there is compression on cylinder 1. This can be done with the starter or by using a wrench on the damper bolt. The compression stroke can be determined by covering the opening of spark plug 1 with a finger as the crankshaft

FIGURE 34–60 Oil should be seen flowing to each rocker arm as shown.

FIGURE 34–61 Heat tabs can be purchased from engine supply companies.

 REAL WORLD FIX

"Oops"

After overhauling a big block Ford V-8 engine, the technician used an electric drill to rotate the oil pump with a pressure gauge connected to the oil pressure sending unit hole. When the electric drill was turned on, oil pressure would start to increase (to about 10 PSI), then drop to zero. In addition, the oil was very aerated (full of air). Replacing the oil pump did not solve the problem. After hours of troubleshooting and disassembly, it was discovered that an oil gallery plug had been left out underneath the intake manifold. The oil pump was working correctly and pumped oil throughout the engine and out of the end of the unplugged oil gallery. It did not take long for the oil pan to empty and the oil pump began drawing in air that aerated the oil which caused the oil pressure to drop. Installing the gallery plug solved the problem. It was smart of the technician to check the oil pressure before starting the engine. This oversight of leaving out one gallery plug could have resulted in a ruined engine shortly after the engine was started.

NOTE: Many overhead camshaft engines use an oil passage check valve in the block near the deck. The purpose of this valve is to hold oil in the cylinder head around the camshaft and lifters when the engine is stopped. Failure to reinstall this check valve can cause the valve train to be noisy after engine start-up.

 **TECH TIP**

Install Heat Tabs

The wise engine builder should install a heat tab to the back of the cylinder head(s). A heat tab uses a special heat-sensitive metal in the center of a mild steel disc. If the temperature of the cylinder head exceeds 250°F (121°C), the center of the tab will melt and flow out indicating that the engine was overheated. ● **SEE FIGURE 34–61.**

is rotated. Continue to rotate the crankshaft slowly as compression is felt, until the timing marks on the damper align with the timing indicator on the timing cover.

The angle of the distributor gear drive will cause the distributor rotor to turn a few degrees when installed. Before the distributor is installed, the shaft must be positioned to compensate for the gear angle. After installation, the rotor should be pointing to tower 1 of the distributor cap.

The distributor position should be close enough to the basic timing position to start the engine. If the distributor holddown clamp is slightly loose, the distributor housing can be adjusted to make the engine run smoothly after the engine has been started.

DYNAMOMETER TESTING

PURPOSES The purposes for using an engine dynamometer after an engine is assembled are varied. The testing:

1. Allows the completed engine to be started and run to operating temperature

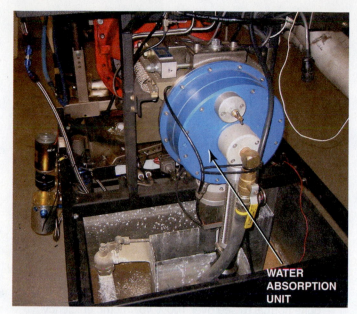

FIGURE 34–62 A dynamometer measures engine torque by applying a resistive force to the engine and measuring the force applied. Water is being used as the resistive load on this dynamometer.

2. Permits checking for possible problems or leaks before the engine is installed in a vehicle

3. Allows the piston rings to seat and the engine to be partially broken in before being installed in a vehicle

4. Permits the technician to determine the output of the engine

5. Allows the opportunity to maximize the engine output by changing air-fuel ratios and valve or ignition timing until the best performance has been achieved

TYPES OF DYNAMOMETERS
Basic types of dynamometers include:

- A *brake type,* where a variable load is applied to the engine and the computer calculates the power output based on the readings taken from the load cell or strain gauge and engine RPM. Most brake types use a water impeller to create the load on the engine. ● SEE FIGURE 34–62.

- An *inertia type,* which measures engine power by using the engine to accelerate a known mass load. An inertia type dynamometer is most often used to measure the power of an engine at the drive wheels of the vehicle. ● SEE FIGURE 34–63.

TERMINOLOGY
Numbers allow values to be assigned to virtually everything being measured or tested. The numbers help identify, quantify, and compare variables and performance. Two types of data include:

1. **Basic measured values.** Taken directly from the engine using sensors that read the actual data

2. **Calculated values.** Those found by using basic numbers and a formula to obtain them

FIGURE 34–63 A chassis dynamometer is used to measure torque at the drive wheels. There is a power loss through the drive train so the measured values are about 20% less than when measuring engine output at the flywheel using an engine dynamometer.

MEASURED VALUES
Measured units are those that are obtained directly from sensors and include:

- **Torque.** As the name implies, this is the amount of twisting force that the engine puts out at the crank flange. Typically this is measured in foot-pounds.

  NOTE: **Dynamometers only measure torque output of an engine. Horsepower is not measured directly but is instead a calculated value.**

- **Fuel flow.** Mass flow rate of fuel is calculated by the number of gallons per hour times pounds per gallon and is measured in pounds per hour. To determine this value, the specific gravity of the fuel has to be measured and entered into the computer prior to the engine tests so the program can calculate the fuel flow. Make sure there is enough fuel delivery for the engine by checking the gallons per hour prior to running each engine. Proper pressure (PSI) does not mean that there is enough volume being delivered to the engine especially under load conditions.

- **Manifold pressure.** Measured in inches of mercury (in. Hg), this value is called *manifold vacuum* in a normally aspirated engine.

- **Oil pressure.** This should be about 10 PSI per 1000 RPM.

- **Air inlet pressure.** Core value used to calculate the correction factor during the run, also referred to as dry bulb (DB) temperature. **Dry bulb temperature** is the temperature of a room where the thermometer is shielded from moisture. This reduces the effect of evaporation of moisture from the thermometer which could affect the temperature reading.

- **Fuel temperature.** Used to calculate the density of fuel for fuel flow values.

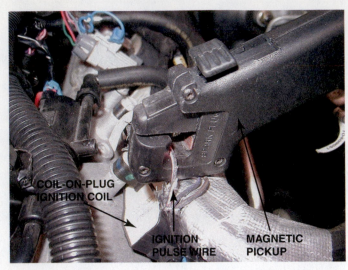

FIGURE 34–64 A magnetic pickup being used to monitor engine speed when the vehicle is being tested on a chassis dynamometer.

- **Oil temperature.** Very important in run-to-run comparisons. Typically, the hotter the oil, the more horsepower an engine makes (up to a point). Oil that is too hot loses its cooling capability as well as some of its lubricating properties.

- **Engine coolant temperature.** This reading is important to monitor as a safety limit to help prevent possible engine damage if it goes too high.

Transducers are needed to measure the basic values. A transducer is a device that is able to convert various input signals such as pressures and temperature into an electrical signal that a computer can recognize. Typical dynamometer transducers include:

- Magnetic pickups ● **SEE FIGURE 34–64.**
- Load cells
- Strain Gauge Flow meters
- Rotary potentiometers or rheostats
- Thermocouples
- Linear variable displacement transducers (LVDT)

CALCULATED NUMBERS   Calculated numbers are those that are obtained by using the measured values and processing them through software to obtain the following:

- **Corrected torque.** This is a calculated number determined by the actual torque multiplied by the correction factor. This is an important number and the reading should show a wide and flat band of torque over a broad engine speed range.

- **Corrected horsepower.** This is a calculated number showing the corrected observed horsepower.

 **TECH TIP**

Look at the Crossing Point

All dynamometers measure torque of an engine, then calculate the horsepower. Horsepower is torque multiplied by engine speed (RPM) divided by 5,252 (a constant). Therefore, all graphs should show that the two curves for horsepower and torque should be the same at 5252 RPM. ● **SEE FIGURE 34–65.**

- **Frictional horsepower.** This can best be thought of as the power required to rotate the engine over without firing and without pumping losses.

- **Volumetric efficiency.** This is a measure of the engine's cylinder filling efficiency; 100% represents filling a cylinder to its total swept volume. On a race engine, it is quite normal to see over 100% volumetric efficiency.

- **Mechanical efficiency.** This is the ratio of the engine's frictional torque divided by its corrected output torque. A value of 100% would indicate that the engine had no frictional losses.

STANDARDS   For best results, perform testing on nice days with low relative humidity and high atmospheric pressure. These factors have a huge effect on the amount of air that the engine can "breathe" in which in turn can dramatically affect horsepower readings. Testing on nice days is not always possible, so using corrected data allows the technician to compare test results from day to day and dynamometer to dynamometer. A **correction factor** is a value that is multiplied to the data values so that engine performance can be compared regardless of weather conditions. Over the years there have been many different correction factors specified by the Society of Automotive Engineers (SAE) including:

- SAE J606
- SAE J607 (Using this correction factor results in higher numbers than if using other correction factors mainly due to the higher barometric pressure standard used.)
- SAE J1349
- SAE J1739

There are subtle differences between each of the testing standards. The result after the correction factor has been applied is called **corrected torque.** From the corrected torque values the other units such as horsepower can be calculated.

FINAL NOTES

- Corrected numbers are to be applied to wide open throttle (WOT) runs only.
- Corrected numbers apply only to *normally aspirated* engines and are not to be used for turbocharged or supercharged engines.

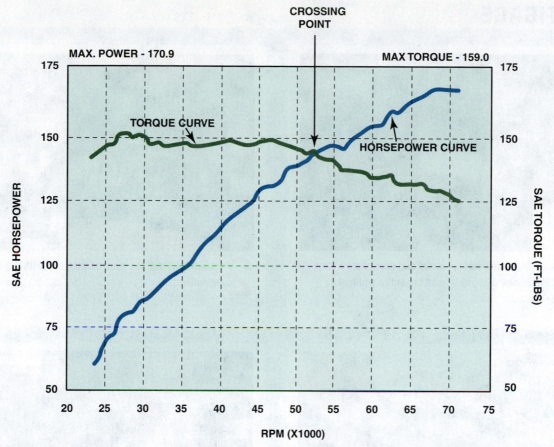

FIGURE 34–65 Because horsepower is calculated from measured torque, the horsepower and torque curves should always cross at exactly 5252 RPM.

 **TECH TIP**

Compare Dyno Results from the Same Dyno Only

There are too many variables between dynamometers to allow a fair comparison when testing an engine. If changes are made to the engine, try to use the same dynamometer and use the same correction factors. Using another dynamometer can result in readings that may not be equivalent when testing on the original tester.

- Double-check that the spark timing is set relative to top dead center (TDC).
- Double-check that the engine has good electrical grounds and adequate voltage.
- Be sure to have enough *good* fuel before starting to test an engine. Do not use any gasoline older than 90 days.

PLASTIGAGE

1 Clean the main bearing journal and then place a strip of Plastigage material across the entire width of the journal.

2 Carefully install the main bearing cap with the bearing installed.

3 Torque main bearing cap bolts to factory specifications.

4 Carefully remove the bearing cap and, using the package that contained the Plastigage strips, measure the width of the compressed material. The gauge is calibrated in thousandths of the inch. Repeat for each main bearing.

5 To measure rod bearing oil clearance, start by removing the rod cap.

6 Clean the rod bearing journal and then place a strip of Plastigage across the entire width of the journal.

7 Torque the rod bearing cap nuts to factory specifications.

8 Remove the rod cap and measure the oil clearance using the markings on the Plastigage package. The wider the compressed gauge material, the narrower the bearing oil clearance. Repeat for all rod bearings.

SUMMARY

1. Before assembling an engine, the technician should read, understand, and follow all instructions that came with the parts and gaskets to ensure proper assembly.

2. Assembling the short block includes preparing the block and installing the crankshaft and the piston/rod assemblies.

3. Cylinder head assembly includes checking valve spring tension as well as proper rocker arm and pushrod measurements.

4. A trial assembly should be performed before the final assembly.

5. All bearing oil clearances should be checked using a micrometer and telescoping gauges or Plastigage.

6. Piston ring end gap should be checked before the pistons are installed.

7. Cylinder head bolts should be properly tightened and in the specified sequence.

8. Timing chain or belt and all covers are installed using the specified gaskets or sealers.

9. Testing an engine on a dynamometer allows the engine to be tested before being installed in a vehicle.

REVIEW QUESTIONS

1. List the items that need to be installed as part of the short block assembly.

2. How is crankshaft end play measured?

3. Why should Teflon seals not be oiled prior to being installed?

4. List the measured and the calculated values as a result of testing an engine on a dynamometer.

1. About how much of the turning torque applied to a head bolt is lost to friction?
   a. 20%
   b. 40%
   c. 60%
   d. 80%

2. Service information states that SAE 30 engine oil should be used on the threads of the head bolts before installation and torquing. Technician A says that SAE 5W-30 will work. Technician B says that SAE 10W-30 will work. Which technician is correct?
   a. Technician A only
   b. Technician B only
   c. Both Technicians A and B
   d. Neither Technician A nor B

3. Technician A says that the torque applied to the head bolts is the same as the clamping force on the gasket. Technician B says that the clamping force is the force actually applied to the surfaces of the gasket. Which technician is correct?
   a. Technician A only
   b. Technician B only
   c. Both Technicians A and B
   d. Neither Technician A nor B

4. A coating often used to keep an engine from rusting during assembly is called _____.
   a. Engine oil
   b. Assembly lube
   c. Fogging oil
   d. Penetrating oil

5. Head gasket installation is being discussed. Technician A says that the surface finish of the cylinder head or block deck is very important for proper sealing to occur. Technician B says that if "front" is marked on a head gasket, the mark should be installed near the accessory drive belt end of the engine. Which technician is correct?
   a. Technician A only
   b. Technician B only
   c. Both Technicians A and B
   d. Neither Technician A nor B

6. Technician A says that studs should be installed finger tight. Technician B says that studs must be installed using a thread locker such as Loctite®. Which technician is correct?
   a. Technician A only
   b. Technician B only
   c. Both Technicians A and B
   d. Neither Technician A nor B

7. What can be used to check that heads are at the correct angle for the intake manifold on a V-type engine?
   a. Metal rule
   b. Angle gauge
   c. Tape measure
   d. Dial indicator

8. What is true about checking bearing clearance using Plastigage?
   a. The journal should be clean and oil free
   b. The cap should be torqued to factory specifications
   c. The wider the strip means the narrower the oil clearance
   d. all of the above

9. An engine dynamometer measures _____.
   a. Torque
   b. Horsepower
   c. Both horsepower and torque
   d. Fuel economy

10. If the torque and horsepower readings are graphed, where do the curves cross (equal each other)?
    a. Never
    b. At peak horsepower which can vary from engine to engine
    c. At peak torque which can vary from engine to engine
    d. At 5252 RPM

ENGINE INSTALLATION AND BREAK-IN

LEARNING OBJECTIVES: **After studying this chapter, the reader should be able to:** • Discuss the preinstallation checklist. • Explain the procedure for transmission installation. • Explain the process of dressing the engine and engine installation. • Explain engine start and discuss the break-in precautions of an overhauled engine.

KEY TERMS: Lugging 529 • Normal operating temperature 529

PREINSTALLATION CHECKLIST

NEED FOR A CHECKLIST   Engine installation must be thoroughly checked to ensure that it is in proper condition to give the customer dependable operation for a long time. Using a checklist guarantees that all accessories are correctly reinstalled on the engine.

ENGINE INSTALLATION CHECKLIST   Before installing or starting a new or rebuilt engine in a vehicle, be sure all of the following items have been checked.

1. Be sure the battery is fully charged.
2. Prelube the engine and check for proper oil pressure.
3. Check that all electrical wiring connecters and harnesses are properly installed. ● **SEE FIGURE 35–1.**
4. Check that all of the vacuum lines are correctly installed and routed.
5. Check that all fuel lines are properly connected and free from leaks.
6. Make sure all engine fluids are at the proper operating level such as coolant, engine oil, and power steering fluid.
7. Know the ignition timing specification and procedure.
8. Check that fresh fuel is in the fuel tank.
9. Be sure that the radiator has been tested, is free from leaks, and flows correctly.
10. Check that all accessory drive belts are routed and tensioned correctly.

CAUTION: Be sure to have a fire extinguisher nearby when the engine is first started.

FIGURE 35–1 A partially melted electrical connector indicates that excessive current flow was present. The cause of the excessive current should be located and corrected before the engine is started.

TRANSMISSION INSTALLATION

MANUAL TRANSMISSION INSTALLATION   If the engine was removed with the transmission attached, the transmission should be reinstalled on the engine before other accessories are added. The flywheel is installed on the back of the crankshaft. Often, the attaching bolt holes are unevenly spaced so that the flywheel will fit in only one way to maintain engine balance. The pilot bearing or bushing in the rear of the crankshaft is usually replaced with a new one to minimize the possibility of premature failure of this part.

ALIGNMENT
DOWEL PINS

FIGURE 35–2 Bell housing alignment dowel pins are used to ensure proper alignment between the engine block and the transmission.

The clutch is installed next and the installation usually includes the following steps.

STEP 1 Most experts recommend that a new clutch assembly or, at the least, a new clutch friction disc be installed.

STEP 2 The clutch friction disc must be held in position using an alignment tool (sometimes called a dummy shaft) that is secured in the pilot bearing. This holds the disc in position while the pressure plate is being installed.

STEP 3 The engine bell housing is put on the engine, if it was not installed before. The alignment of this type of bell housing is then checked. ● **SEE FIGURE 35–2.**

CAUTION: Perfectly round cylinders can be distorted whenever another part of the engine is bolted and torqued to the engine block. For example, it has been determined that after the cylinders are machined, the rear cylinder bore can be distorted to be as much as 0.006 inch (0.15 mm) out-of-round after the bell housing is bolted onto the block! To help prevent this distortion, always apply the specified torque to all fasteners going into the engine block and tighten in the recommended sequence.

STEP 4 The clutch release yoke should be checked for free movement. Usually, the clutch release bearing is replaced to ensure that the new bearing is securely attached to the clutch release yoke.

STEP 5 The transmission is installed by carefully guiding the transmission input (clutch) shaft straight into the clutch disc and pilot bearing. See the Tech Tip, "The Headless Bolt Trick." Rotate the transmission output shaft

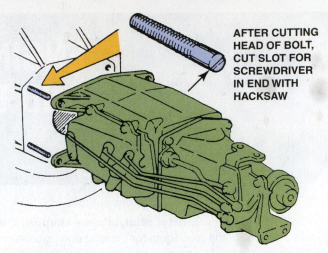

AFTER CUTTING HEAD OF BOLT, CUT SLOT FOR SCREWDRIVER IN END WITH HACKSAW

FIGURE 35–3 Headless long bolts can be used to help install a transmission to the engine.

TECH TIP

The Headless Bolt Trick

Sometimes parts do not seem to line up correctly. Try this tip the next time. Cut the head off of extra-long bolts that are of the same diameter and thread as those being used to retain the part, such as a transmission. ● **SEE FIGURE 35–3.**

Use a hacksaw to cut a slot in this end of the guide bolts for a screwdriver slot. Install the guide bolts; then install the transmission. Use a straight-blade screwdriver to remove the guide bolts after securing the transmission with the retaining bolts.

as needed to engage the splines of the clutch disc. The assembly bolts are secured when the transmission fully mates with the bell housing.

CAUTION: Always adjust the clutch free play *before* starting the engine to help prevent engine thrust bearing or clutch release bearing damage.

AUTOMATIC TRANSMISSION INSTALLATION

On engines equipped with an automatic transmission, the drive (flex) plate is attached to the back of the crankshaft. Its assembly bolts are tightened to the specified torque. The bell housing is part of the transmission case on most automatic transmissions. Installing an automatic transmission usually includes the following steps.

STEP 1 The torque converter should be installed on the transmission before the transmission is put on the engine.

STEP 2 Rotate the torque converter while it is pushed onto the transmission shafts until the splines of all shafts are engaged in the torque converter. ● **SEE FIGURE 35–4.**

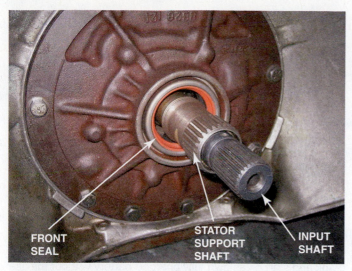

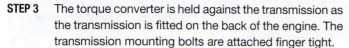

FIGURE 35–4 The internal splines inside the torque converter must be properly aligned with all of the splines of the automatic transmission.

STEP 3 The torque converter is held against the transmission as the transmission is fitted on the back of the engine. The transmission mounting bolts are attached finger tight.

STEP 4 The torque converter should be rotated to make sure that there is no binding. The bell housing is secured to the block and then the torque converter is fastened to the drive plate.

DRESSING THE ENGINE

"Dressing the engine" is a term used to describe the process of attaching all of the auxiliary items to the engine. The items include:

- Starter motor
- Fuel rail and related fuel system components
- New oxygen sensor(s), to ensure that the engine will be operating at the correct air-fuel ratio
- Engine/transmission wiring harness
- Ignition components, such the ignition coil(s) and spark plug wires, if equipped
- All belt-driven engine accessories, mounted on the front of the engine (Some engines drive all these accessories with one belt. Other engines use as many as four belts. Check service information or decals under the hood to determine the specific belt routing for the accessories used on the engine.) ● **SEE FIGURE 35–5.**
- Front accessories, such as the power steering pump, alternator, and air-conditioning compressor (These accessories may be installed before the engine is installed in the vehicle. On some vehicles it is easier to put the engine in the chassis before installing the front accessories.)

Always check service information for the exact procedure to follow.

FIGURE 35–5 It is often easier to install all of the accessory drive belts before the engine is installed in the vehicle.

FIGURE 35–6 A fixture installed that is used as a place to attach the hosting chains.

ENGINE INSTALLATION

SECURING THE ENGINE A sling, either a chain or lift cable, is attached to the manifold or head bolts or lifting brackets on the top of the engine. A hoist is attached to the sling and snugged up to take the weight and to make sure that the engine is supported and balanced properly. ● **SEE FIGURE 35–6.**

INSTALLING THE ENGINE

- **Rear-wheel drive.** The engine must be tipped as it was during removal to let the transmission go into the engine compartment first. The transmission is worked under the floor pan on rear-wheel-drive vehicles as the engine is lowered into the engine compartment. The front engine mounts are aligned and the rear cross-member and rear engine mount are installed. The engine mount bolts are installed, and the nuts are torqued. Then the hoist is removed.

- **Front-wheel drive.** Many engines for front-wheel-drive vehicles are installed from underneath the vehicle. Often the entire drivetrain package is placed back in the vehicle while it is attached to the cradle. The vehicle is positioned on a hoist and is lowered onto the engine cradle assembly to install. Always check the recommended procedure for the vehicle being serviced.

RECONNECTING COMPONENTS AND CONNECTORS
The following items should be connected to the engine assembly.

- Throttle and cruise control linkages or cables
- Exhaust system to the exhaust manifolds
- If any of the steering linkage was previously disconnected, it can be reattached while work is being done under the vehicle.
- After the engine is in place, the front engine accessories can all be installed, if they were not installed before the engine was put in the chassis.
- The air-conditioning compressor is reattached to the engine, with care being taken to avoid damaging the air-conditioning hoses and lines.

COOLING SYSTEM
The radiator is installed and secured in place, followed by the cooling fan and shroud. The fan and new drive belts are then installed and adjusted. New radiator hoses, including new heater hoses, and new coolant should be installed.

ELECTRICAL SYSTEM
Under the hood the following electrical components will need to be mounted and connected.

- Connect all wiring to the starter and alternator as required.
- Connect the instrument and computer sensor wires to the sensors on the engine.
- Double-check the condition and routing of all wiring, being certain that wires have not been pinched or broken, before installing a fully charged battery.

? FREQUENTLY ASKED QUESTION

What Is Break-In Engine Oil?

Many years ago, vehicle manufacturers used straight weight such as SAE 30 nondetergent engine oil as break-in oil. Today, the engine oil recommended for break-in (running in) is the same type of oil that is recommended for use in the engine. No special break-in oil is recommended or used by the factory in new vehicles. Always use the specified viscosity oil as recommended by the vehicle manufacturer.

- Attach the positive cable first and then the ground cable.
- Ensure that the starter will crank the engine.
- Install and time the distributor (if equipped), then connect the ignition cables to the spark plugs, again being sure that they are routed according to service information.

ENGINE START

PRECAUTIONS   The engine installation should be given one last inspection to ensure that everything has been put together correctly before the engine is started. If the engine overhaul and installation are done properly, the engine should crank and start on its own fully charged battery without the use of a fast charger or jumper battery. As soon as the engine starts and shows oil pressure, it should be brought up to a fast idle speed and *kept there* to ensure that the engine gets proper lubrication. The fast-running oil pump develops full pressure, and the fast-turning crankshaft throws plenty of oil on the cam and cylinder walls.

NOTE: In camshaft-in-block engines, the only lubrication sent to the contact point between the camshaft lobes and the lifters (tappets) is from the splash off the crankshaft and connecting rods. At idle, engine oil does not splash enough for proper break-in lubrication of the camshaft.

Maintaining engine speed above 1,500 RPM for the first 10 minutes of engine operation must be performed to break in a flat-bottom lifter camshaft. If the engine speed is decreased to idle (about 600 RPM), the lifter (tappet) will be in contact with and exerting force *on* the lobe of the cam for a longer period of time than occurs at higher engine speeds. The pressure and volume of oil supplied to the camshaft area are also increased at the higher engine speeds. Therefore, to ensure long camshaft and lifter life, make certain that the engine will start quickly after reassembly to prevent long cranking periods and subsequent low engine speeds after a new camshaft and lifters have been installed.

NOTE: Many molydisulfide greases used during assembly can start to clog oil filters within 20 minutes after starting the engine. Most engine rebuilders recommend changing the oil and filter after 30 minutes of running time.

After the engine has started, the following items should be checked.

1. Is the valve train quiet? Some engines will require several minutes to quiet down.
2. Record the engine vacuum. It should be 17 to 21 inch Hg (sea level).
3. Check for any gasoline, coolant, or oil leaks. Stop the engine and repair the leaks as soon as possible.
4. Check the charging system for proper operation. The charging voltage should be 13.5 to 15 volts.

As soon the engine is at operating temperature and running well, the vehicle should be driven to a road having minimum traffic. Perform the following during the test drive.

- The vehicle should be accelerated, full throttle, from 30 to 50 mph (48 to 80 km/h).
- Then the throttle is fully closed while the vehicle is allowed to return to 30 mph (48 km/h). This sequence is repeated 10 to 12 times.
- The acceleration sequence puts a high load on the piston rings to properly seat them against the cylinder walls. The piston rings are the only part of the modern engine that needs to be broken in. Good ring seating is indicated by a dry coating inside the tailpipe at the completion of the ring seating drive.

The vehicle is returned to the service area, where the engine is again checked for visible fluid leaks. If the engine is dry, it is ready to be turned over to the customer.

The customer should be instructed to drive the vehicle in a normal fashion, neither babying it at slow speeds nor beating it at high speeds for the first 100 miles (160 km). The oil and filter should be changed at 500 miles (800 km) to remove any dirt that may have been trapped in the engine during assembly and to remove the material that has worn from the surfaces during the break-in period.

A well-designed engine that has been correctly reconditioned and assembled using the techniques described should give reliable service for many miles.

NORMAL OPERATING TEMPERATURE **Normal operating temperature** is the temperature at which the upper radiator hose is hot and pressurized. Another standard method used to determine when normal operating temperature is reached is to observe the operation of the electric cooling fan, when the vehicle is so equipped. Many manufacturers define normal operating temperature as being reached when the cooling fan has cycled on and off at least once after the engine has been started. Some vehicle manufacturers specify that the cooling fan should cycle twice. This method also helps assure the technician that the engine is not being overheated. ● **SEE FIGURE 35–7.**

HOW TO WARM UP A COLD ENGINE The greatest amount of engine wear occurs during start-up. The oil in a cold engine is thick, and it requires several seconds to reach all the moving parts of an engine. After the engine starts, allow the engine to idle until the oil pressure peaks. This will take from 15 to 60 seconds, depending on the outside temperature. *Do not allow the engine to idle for longer than five minutes.* Because an engine warms up faster under load, drive the vehicle in a normal manner until the engine is fully warm. Avoid full-throttle acceleration until the engine is completely up to normal operating temperature. This method of engine warm-up also warms the rest of the powertrain, including transmission and final drive component lubricants.

FIGURE 35–7 Even though the dash gauge may show normal operating temperature, a scan tool or an infrared pyrometer can also be used to verify proper coolant temperature.

BREAK-IN PRECAUTIONS

Any engine overhaul represents many hours of work and a large financial investment. Precautions should be taken to protect the investment, including the following:

1. Never add cold water to the cooling system while the engine is running.
2. Never lug any engine. **Lugging** means increasing the throttle opening without increasing engine speed (RPM). An example where lugging an engine can occur is when the vehicle is driven at a low speed, such as 15 mph, with the manual transmission in third or fourth gear instead of in second gear as per the recommended speed for that gear as published in the owner manual.
3. Applying loads to an engine for *short periods* of time creates higher piston ring pressure against the cylinder walls and assists the breaking-in process by helping to seat the rings.
4. Change the oil and filter at 500 miles (800 km) or after 20 hours of operation.
5. Check for leaks after the engine has gone through several warm-up and cooling down periods.

SUMMARY

1. Carefully install all accessories.
2. When installing the transmission and other components on the engine block, be sure to use a torque wrench and tighten all fasteners to factory specifications.
3. Always adjust the clutch free play before starting the engine.
4. Change the engine oil after 500 miles (800 km) or sooner, and use specified engine oil.

REVIEW QUESTIONS

1. How are the clutch and bell housing installed?
2. What should be done to help prevent rear cylinder distortion when the bell housing is being installed on the engine?
3. Describe the engine break-in procedure.

CHAPTER QUIZ

1. "Dressing the engine" means _____.
   a. Installing all of the exterior engine components
   b. Cleaning the engine
   c. Changing the oil and oil filter
   d. Both b and c

2. If the bell housing is not properly torqued to the engine block, _____.
   a. The bell housing will distort
   b. The engine block will crack
   c. The rear cylinder can be distorted (become out-of-round)
   d. The crankshaft will crack

3. Break-in engine oil is _____.
   a. Of the same viscosity and grade as that specified for normal engine operation
   b. SAE 40
   c. SAE 30
   d. SAE 20W-50

4. Normal operating temperature is reached when _____.
   a. The radiator cap releases coolant into the overflow
   b. The upper radiator hose is hot and pressurized
   c. The electric cooling fan has cycled at least once (if the vehicle is so equipped)
   d. Both b and c

5. Lugging an engine means _____.
   a. Wide-open throttle in low gear above 25 mph
   b. That engine speed does not increase when the throttle is opened wider
   c. Starting a cold engine and allowing it to idle for longer than five minutes
   d. Both b and c

6. Which computer sensor should be replaced to help ensure that the engine will be operating at the correct air-fuel ratio?
   a. Throttle position sensor
   b. Oxygen sensor
   c. Manifold absolute pressure sensor
   d. Engine coolant temperature sensor

7. How should the vehicle be driven to best break in a newly overhauled engine?
   a. At a steady low speed
   b. At varying speeds and loads
   c. At high speed and loads
   d. At idle speed and little or no load

8. Which type of vehicle is the engine most likely to be installed from underneath the vehicle?
   a. Rear-wheel drive (RWD)
   b. Front-wheel drive (FWD)
   c. Four-wheel drive (4WD)
   d. Both a and c

9. Engine vacuum on a normal stock rebuilt engine should be _____.
   a. 10 to 15 inch Hg
   b. 12 to 16 inch Hg
   c. 17 to 21 inch Hg
   d. 19 to 23 inch Hg

10. Why must flat-bottom camshafts be broken in at a fast idle?
   a. Cam in a cam-in-block engine is only lubricated by splash oil.
   b. The flat-bottom of the lifters must become slightly concave in order to rotate
   c. Both a and b are correct
   d. Neither a nor b are correct

ENGINE REPAIR (A1) SAMPLE ASE-TYPE CERTIFICATION TEST AND ANSWERS

1. Two technicians are discussing the markings on the heads of bolts (cap screws). Technician A says the higher the number of lines, the higher the strength of the bolt. Technician B says the higher the number on metric bolts, the higher the grade. Which technician is correct?
   a. Technician A only
   b. Technician B only
   c. Both Technicians A and B
   d. Neither Technician A nor B

2. A metric bolt size of M8 means that _____.
   a. The bolt is 8 millimeters long
   b. The bolt is 8 millimeters in diameter
   c. The pitch (the distance between the crest of the threads) is 8 millimeters
   d. The bolt is 8 centimeters long

3. On a metric bolt sized M8 × 1.5, the 1.5 means that _____.
   a. The bolt is 1.5 millimeters in diameter
   b. The bolt is 1.5 centimeters long
   c. The bolt has 1.5 millimeters between the crest of the threads
   d. The bolt has a strength grade of 1.5

4. If the bore of an engine is increased without any other changes except for the change to proper-size replacement pistons, the displacement will _____ and the compression rate will _____.
   a. Increase; increase
   b. Increase; decrease
   c. Decrease; increase
   d. Decrease; decrease

5. A battery is being tested. Technician A says that the surface charge should be removed before the battery is load tested. Technician B says that the battery should be loaded to two times the CCA rating of the battery for 15 seconds. Which technician is correct?
   a. Technician A only
   b. Technician B only
   c. Both Technicians A and B
   d. Neither Technician A nor B

6. A starter motor cranks the engine too slowly to start. Technician A says that the cause could be a weak or defective battery. Technician B says that the cause could be loose or corroded battery cable connections. Which technician is correct?
   a. Technician A only
   b. Technician B only
   c. Both Technicians A and B
   d. Neither Technician A nor B

7. An engine uses an excessive amount of oil. Technician A says that clogged oil drain-back holes in the cylinder head could be the cause. Technician B says that worn piston rings could be the cause. Which technician is correct?
   a. Technician A only
   b. Technician B only
   c. Both Technicians A and B
   d. Neither Technician A nor B

8. Battery voltage during cranking is below specifications. Technician A says that a defect in the engine may be the cause. Technician B says that the starter motor may be defective. Which technician is correct?
   a. Technician A only
   b. Technician B only
   c. Both Technicians A and B
   d. Neither Technician A nor B

9. Two technicians are discussing torquing cylinder head bolts. Technician A says that many engine manufacturers recommend replacing the head bolts after use. Technician B says that many manufacturers recommend tightening the head bolts to a specific torque, and then turning the bolts an additional number of degrees. Which technician is correct?
   a. Technician A only
   b. Technician B only
   c. Both Technicians A and B
   d. Neither Technician A nor B

10. Two technicians are discussing the diagnosis of a lack-of-power problem. Technician A says that a worn (stretched) timing chain could be the cause. Technician B says that retarded ignition timing could be the cause. Which technician is correct?
    a. Technician A only
    b. Technician B only
    c. Both Technicians A and B
    d. Neither Technician A nor B

11. An engine equipped with a turbocharger is burning oil (blue exhaust smoke all the time). Technician A says that a defective wastegate could be the cause. Technician B says that a plugged PCV system could be the cause. Which technician is correct?
    a. Technician A only
    b. Technician B only
    c. Both Technicians A and B
    d. Neither Technician A nor B

12. Technician A says that coolant flows through the engine passages and does not flow through the radiator until the thermostat opens. Technician B says that the temperature rating of the thermostat indicates the temperature of the coolant when the thermostat is opened fully. Which technician is correct?
   a. Technician A only
   b. Technician B only
   c. Both Technicians A and B
   d. Neither Technician A nor B

13. Two technicians discuss the "hot" light on the dash. Technician A says that the light comes on if the cooling system temperature is too high for safe operation of the engine. Technician B says that the light comes on whenever there is a decrease (drop) in cooling system pressure. Which technician is correct?
   a. Technician A only
   b. Technician B only
   c. Both Technicians A and B
   d. Neither Technician A nor B

14. Two technicians diagnose an engine noise. Technician A says that a double-knock is likely to be due to a worn rod bearing. Technician B says that a knock only when the engine is cold is usually due to a worn piston pin. Which technician is correct?
   a. Technician A only
   b. Technician B only
   c. Both Technicians A and B
   d. Neither Technician A nor B

15. A compression test gave the following results:

   cylinder #1 = 155, cylinder #2 = 140, cylinder #3 = 110, cylinder #4 = 105

   Technician A says that a defective (burned) valve is the most likely cause. Technician B says that a leaking head gasket could be the cause. Which technician is correct?
   a. Technician A only
   b. Technician B only
   c. Both Technicians A and B
   d. Neither Technician A nor B

16. Two technicians are discussing a compression test. Technician A says that the engine should be turned over with the pressure gauge installed for "4 puffs." Technician B says that the maximum difference between the highest-reading cylinder and the lowest-reading cylinder should be 20%. Which technician is correct?
   a. Technician A only
   b. Technician B only
   c. Both Technicians A and B
   d. Neither Technician A nor B

17. Technician A says that the fuel or ignition system should be disconnected before taking a compression test. Technician B says that if the compression greatly increases when some oil is squirted into the cylinders, it indicates defective or worn piston rings. Which technician is correct?
   a. Technician A only
   b. Technician B only
   c. Both Technicians A and B
   d. Neither Technician A nor B

18. During a cylinder leakage (leak-down) test, air is noticed coming out of the oil-fill opening. Technician A says that the oil filter may be clogged. Technician B says that the piston rings may be worn or defective. Which technician is correct?
   a. Technician A only
   b. Technician B only
   c. Both Technicians A and B
   d. Neither Technician A nor B

19. A cylinder leakage (leak-down) test indicates 30% leakage, and air is heard coming out of the air inlet. Technician A says that this is a normal reading for a slightly worn engine. Technician B says that one or more intake valves are defective. Which technician is correct?
   a. Technician A only
   b. Technician B only
   c. Both Technicians A and B
   d. Neither Technician A nor B

20. Two technicians are discussing a cylinder power balance test. Technician A says the more the engine RPM drops, the weaker the cylinder. Technician B says that all cylinder RPM drops should be within 50 RPM of each other. Which technician is correct?
   a. Technician A only
   b. Technician B only
   c. Both Technicians A and B
   d. Neither Technician A nor B

21. Technician A says that black exhaust smoke is an indication of a too rich air-fuel mixture. Technician B says that white smoke (steam) is an indication of coolant being burned in the engine. Which technician is correct?
   a. Technician A only
   b. Technician B only
   c. Both Technicians A and B
   d. Neither Technician A nor B

22. Excessive exhaust system back pressure has been measured. Technician A says that the catalytic converter may be clogged. Technician B says that the muffler may be clogged. Which technician is correct?
   a. Technician A only
   b. Technician B only
   c. Both Technicians A and B
   d. Neither Technician A nor B

23. Two technicians diagnose a head gasket failure. Technician A says that an exhaust analyzer can be used to check for HC or CO when the tester probe is held above the radiator coolant. Technician B says that a chemical-coated paper changes color in the presence of combustion gases. Which technician is correct?
   a. Technician A only
   b. Technician B only
   c. Both Technicians A and B
   d. Neither Technician A nor B

24. Technician A says that pistons should be removed from the crankshaft side of the cylinder when disassembling an engine to prevent possible piston or cylinder damage. Technician B says that the rod assembly should be marked before disassembly. Which technician is correct?
   a. Technician A only
   b. Technician B only
   c. Both Technicians A and B
   d. Neither Technician A nor B

25. Before the valve is removed from the cylinder head, _____.
    a. The valve spring should be compressed and locks removed
    b. The valve tip edges should be filed
    c. The ridge should be removed
    d. Both a and b

26. Leaking intake manifolds can cause_____.
    a. An air (vacuum) leak
    b. A coolant leak
    c. An oil leak
    d. Any of the above

27. Technician A says that the purpose of the exhaust gas recirculation system is to re-burn the exhaust gases to reduce emissions. Technician B says that the exhaust in the EGR system helps prevent high combustion temperatures inside the combustion chamber thereby reducing NOx emissions. Which technician is correct?
    a. Technician A only
    b. Technician B only
    c. Both Technicians A and B
    d. Neither Technician A nor B

28. Technician A says that all valve train parts that are to be reused should be kept together. Technician B says that before testing valve springs for tension, the damper spring should be removed if used. Which technician is correct?
    a. Technician A only
    b. Technician B only
    c. Both Technicians A and B
    d. Neither Technician A nor B

29. A cast-iron cylinder head is checked for warpage using a straightedge and a feeler (thickness) gauge. The amount of warpage on a V-8 cylinder head was 0.002 in. (0.05 mm). Technician A says that the cylinder head should be resurfaced. Technician B says that the cylinder head should be replaced. Which technician is correct?
    a. Technician A only
    b. Technician B only
    c. Both Technicians A and B
    d. Neither Technician A nor B

30. Technician A says that a dial indicator (gauge) is often used to measure valve guide wear by measuring the amount by which the valve head is able to move in the guide. Technician B says that a ball gauge can be used to measure the valve guide. Which technician is correct?
    a. Technician A only
    b. Technician B only
    c. Both Technicians A and B
    d. Neither Technician A nor B

31. Technician A says that a worn valve guide can often be reamed and a valve with an oversize stem can be used. Technician B says that a worn valve guide can often be replaced with a bronze insert to restore the cylinder head to useful service. Which technician is correct?
    a. Technician A only
    b. Technician B only
    c. Both Technicians A and B
    d. Neither Technician A nor B

32. Technician A says that worn integral guides could be repaired by knurling. Technician B says that worn integral guides should be replaced with an insert or a new guide. Which technician is correct?
    a. Technician A only
    b. Technician B only
    c. Both Technicians A and B
    d. Neither Technician A nor B

33. Typical valve-to-valve guide clearance should be _____.
    a. 0.001 to 0.003 inch (0.025 to 0.076 mm)
    b. 0.010 to 0.030 inch (0.25 to 0.76 mm)
    c. 0.035 to 0.060 inch (0.89 to 1.52 mm)
    d. 0.100 to 0.350 inch (2.54 to 8.90 mm)

34. Before a valve spring is reused, it should be checked for _____.
    a. Squareness
    b. Free height
    c. Tension
    d. All of the above

35. Many manufacturers recommend that valves be ground with an interference angle. This angle is the difference between the _____.
    a. Valve margin and valve face angles
    b. Valve face and valve seat angles
    c. Valve guide and valve face angles
    d. Valve head and margin angles

36. To narrow and lower a 45 degree valve seat, the technician should use a _____.
    a. 30 degree stone
    b. 45 degree stone
    c. 60 degree stone
    d. 75 degree stone

37. To widen a valve seat without lowering or raising its position, the technician should use a _____.
    a. 30 degree stone
    b. 45 degree stone
    c. 60 degree stone
    d. 75 degree stone

38. Valve spring inserts are used _____.
    a. Under the valve spring
    b. To restore proper installed height
    c. To restore proper spring tension after the valves and valve seats have been reconditioned
    d. For all of the above

39. Technician A says that valve stem seals of the O-ring type are installed on top of the valve locks (keepers). Technician B says that a vacuum pump can be used to determine if the valve stem seal is correctly seated. Which technician is correct?
    a. Technician A only
    b. Technician B only
    c. Both Technicians A and B
    d. Neither Technician A nor B

40. A noisy valve train is being diagnosed. Technician A says that the rocker arm may be adjusted too tightly. Technician B says that the rocker arm may be

adjusted too loosely or may be worn. Which technician is correct?
   a. Technician A only
   b. Technician B only
   c. Both Technicians A and B
   d. Neither Technician A nor B

41. A cylinder is 0.002 inch out-of-round. Technician A says that the block should be bored and oversize pistons installed. Technician B says that oversize piston rings should be used. Which technician is correct?
   a. Technician A only
   b. Technician B only
   c. Both Technicians A and B
   d. Neither Technician A nor B

42. After the engine block has been machined, the block should be cleaned with _____.
   a. A stiff brush and soap and water
   b. A clean rag and engine oil
   c. WD-40
   d. Spray solvent washer

43. Technician A says that piston rings should be installed with the dot or mark facing up (toward the cylinder head). Technician B says that the mark on the piston rings is used to identify the position (groove) in which the ring should be installed. Which technician is correct?
   a. Technician A only
   b. Technician B only
   c. Both Technicians A and B
   d. Neither Technician A nor B

44. Two technicians are discussing ring gap. Technician A says that the ring should be checked in the same cylinder in which it is to be installed. Technician B says that the ends of the piston ring can be filed if the clearance is too small. Which technician is correct?
   a. Technician A only
   b. Technician B only
   c. Both Technicians A and B
   d. Neither Technician A nor B

45. Technician A says that connecting rod caps should be marked when the connecting rod is disassembled and then replaced in exactly the same location and direction on the rod. Technician B says that each piston should be fitted to each individual cylinder for best results. Which technician is correct?
   a. Technician A only
   b. Technician B only

   c. Both Technicians A and B
   d. Neither Technician A nor B

46. Two technicians are discussing bearing clearance measurement. Technician A says that the main and rod bearing clearance should be measured with plastic gauging material (Plastigage). Technician B says that the engine crankshaft should be rotated for two complete revolutions when Plastigage is used between the crankshaft and the main or rod bearings. Which technician is correct?
   a. Technician A only
   b. Technician B only
   c. Both Technicians A and B
   d. Neither Technician A nor B

47. When pistons are installed in the block, the notch on the piston should be facing _____.
   a. Toward the lifter side of the block
   b. Toward the front of the engine
   c. Toward the rear of the engine
   d. Away from the lifter side of the block

48. A bearing shell is being installed in a connecting rod. The end of the bearing is slightly above the parting line. Technician A says that this is normal. Technician B says that the bearing is too big. Which technician is correct?
   a. Technician A only
   b. Technician B only
   c. Both Technicians A and B
   d. Neither Technician A nor B

49. Two technicians are discussing the cause of low oil pressure. Technician A says that a worn oil pump could be the cause. Technician B says that worn main or rod bearings could be the cause. Which technician is correct?
   a. Technician A only
   b. Technician B only
   c. Both Technicians A and B
   d. Neither Technician A nor B

50. Break-in oil is_____
   a. The same oil as specified for us in the engine
   b. SAE 30
   c. SAE 40
   d. SAE 80W-90

ANSWERS TO THE ENGINE REPAIR (A1) SAMPLE ASE CERTIFICATION TEST

1.	c	14.	d	27.	b	40.	b
2.	b	15.	b	28.	c	41.	d
3.	c	16.	c	29.	d	42.	a
4.	a	17.	c	30.	c	43.	c
5.	a	18.	b	31.	c	44.	c
6.	c	19.	b	32.	c	45.	c
7.	c	20.	b	33.	a	46.	a
8.	c	21.	c	34.	d	47.	b
9.	c	22.	c	35.	b	48.	a
10.	c	23.	c	36.	a	49.	c
11.	b	24.	b	37.	b	50.	a
12.	a	25.	d	38.	d		
13.	a	26.	d	39.	b		

2013 NATEF CORRELATION CHART

MLR—Maintenance & Light Repair
AST—Auto Service Technology (Includes MLR)
MAST—Master Auto Service Technology (Includes MLR and AST)

ENGINE REPAIR (A1)

TASK	PRIORITY	MLR	AST	MAST	TEXT PAGE #	TASK PAGE #
A. GENERAL: ENGINE DIAGNOSIS; REMOVAL AND REINSTALLATION (R & R)						
1. Complete work order to include customer information, vehicle identifying information, customer concern, related service history, cause, and correction.	P-1		✓	✓	78; 85–89	15
2. Research applicable vehicle and service information, vehicle service history, service precautions, and technical service bulletins.	P-1	✓	✓	✓	85–89	17, 19, 20, 24, 25, 31, 42, 85, 86, 114, 124, 125, 132, 142, 149, 169
3. Verify operation of the instrument panel engine warning indicators.	P-1	✓	✓	✓	193; 305–306	45; 103
4. Inspect engine assembly for fuel, oil, coolant, and other leaks; determine necessary action.	P-1	✓	✓	✓	302–303	90, 91, 92, 93
5. Install engine covers using gaskets, seals, and sealers as required.	P-1	✓	✓	✓	476–480	170, 206
6. Remove and replace timing belt; verify correct camshaft timing.	P-1	✓	✓	✓	396–398; 411–417; 512–513	137, 172, 207, 208
7. Perform common fastener and thread repair, to include: remove broken bolt, restore internal and external threads, and repair internal threads with thread insert.	P-1	✓	✓	✓	27–30	4
8. Inspect, remove and replace engine mounts.	P-2		✓	✓	331	106
9. Identify hybrid vehicle internal combustion engine service precautions.	P-3	✓	✓	✓	179; 322–323	NA
10. Remove and reinstall engine in an OBDII or newer vehicle; reconnect all attaching components and restore the vehicle to running condition.	P-3		✓	✓	330–332; 525–529	104, 105, 205

TASK	PRIORITY	MLR	AST	MAST	TEXT PAGE #	TASK PAGE #
B. Cylinder Head and Valve Train Diagnosis and Repair						
1. Remove cylinder head; inspect gasket condition; install cylinder head and gasket; tighten according to manufacturer's specifications and procedures.	P-1		✓	✓	332–334; 497; 508–512	115, 171
2. Clean and visually inspect a cylinder head for cracks; check gasket surface areas for warpage and surface finish; check passage condition.	P-1		✓	✓	358–362	116, 123, 182
3. Inspect pushrods, rocker arms, rocker arm pivots and shafts for wear, bending, cracks, looseness, and blocked oil passages (orifices); determine necessary action.	P-2		✓	✓	399–403	133, 134
4. Adjust valves (mechanical or hydraulic lifters).	P-1	✓	✓	✓	508–509; 514–515	136
5. Inspect and replace camshaft and drive belt/chain; includes checking drive gear wear and backlash, end play, sprocket and chain wear, overhead cam drive sprocket(s), drive belt(s), belt tension, tensioners, camshaft reluctor ring/tone-wheel, and valve timing components; verify correct camshaft timing.	P-1		✓	✓	396–398; 411–417; 512–513	137, 172, 207, 208
6. Establish camshaft position sensor indexing.	P-1		✓	✓	413	141
7. Inspect valve springs for squareness and free height comparison; determine necessary action.	P-3			✓	384	129
8. Replace valve stem seals on an assembled engine; inspect valve spring retainers, locks/keepers, and valve lock/keeper grooves; determine necessary action.	P-3			✓	384–388	126
9. Inspect valve guides for wear; check valve stem-to-guide clearance; determine necessary action.	P-3			✓	362–364	118
10. Inspect valves and valve seats; determine necessary action.	P-3			✓	378–383	127, 128
11. Check valve spring assembled height and valve stem height; determine necessary action.	P-3			✓	384	129
12. Inspect valve lifters; determine necessary action.	P-2			✓	406–409	135
13. Inspect and/or measure camshaft for runout, journal wear, and lobe wear.	P-2			✓	410	138, 139
14. Inspect camshaft bearing surface for wear, damage, out-of-round, and alignment; determine necessary action.	P-3			✓	410	140
C. ENGINE BLOCK ASSEMBLY DIAGNOSIS AND REPAIR						
1. Remove, inspect, or replace crankshaft vibration damper (harmonic balancer).	P-2		✓	✓	335	165, 188
2. Disassemble engine block; clean and prepare components for inspection and reassembly.	P-1			✓	332–336	108
3. Inspect engine block for visible cracks, passage condition, core and gallery plug condition, and surface warpage; determine necessary action.	P-2			✓	346–347; 443–444	150

TASK	PRIORITY	MLR	AST	MAST	TEXT PAGE #	TASK PAGE #
4. Inspect and measure cylinder walls/sleeves for damage, wear, and ridges; determine necessary action.	P-2			✓	445	151
5. Deglaze and clean cylinder walls.	P-2			✓	447–448	152
6. Inspect and measure camshaft bearings for wear, damage, out-of-round, and alignment; determine necessary action.	P-3			✓	470–471	153
7. Inspect crankshaft for straightness, journal damage, keyway damage, thrust flange and sealing surface condition, and visual surface cracks; check oil passage condition; measure end play and journal wear; check crankshaft position sensor reluctor ring (where applicable); determine necessary action.	P-1			✓	462–463	161, 162, 183
8. Inspect main and connecting rod bearings for damage and wear; determine necessary action	P-2			✓	468–470	163, 173, 184
9. Identify piston and bearing wear patterns that indicate connecting rod alignment and main bearing bore problems; determine necessary action.	P-3			✓	432–433	143, 164, 185
10. Inspect and measure piston skirts and ring lands; determine necessary action.	P-2			✓	421–422	147
11. Determine piston-to-bore clearance.	P-2			✓	434; 505–507	154, 174, 186
12. Inspect, measure, and install piston rings.	P-2			✓	433–435	145, 146
13. Inspect auxiliary shaft(s) (balance, intermediate, idler, counterbalance, or silencer); inspect shaft(s) and support bearings for damage and wear; determine necessary action; reinstall and time.	P-2			✓	461–462	166, 187
14. Assemble engine block.	P-1			✓	494–508	189, 190

D. LUBRICATION AND COOLING SYSTEMS DIAGNOSIS AND REPAIR

TASK	PRIORITY	MLR	AST	MAST	TEXT PAGE #	TASK PAGE #
1. Perform cooling system pressure and dye tests to identify leaks; check coolant condition and level; inspect and test radiator, pressure cap, coolant recovery tank, and heater core; determine necessary action.	P-1	✓	✓	✓	171–172	32, 33
2. Identify causes of engine overheating.	P-1		✓	✓	173	41
3. Inspect, replace, and adjust drive belts, tensioners, and pulleys; check pulley and belt alignment.	P-1	✓	✓	✓	173–174; 527	34
4. Inspect and test coolant; drain and recover coolant; flush and refill cooling system with recommended coolant; bleed air as required.	P-1	✓	✓	✓	174–175	37
5. Inspect, remove, and replace water pumps.	P-2		✓	✓	168–169	38, 194
6. Remove and replace radiator.	P-2		✓	✓	164; 171	39, 195

TASK	PRIORITY	MLR	AST	MAST	TEXT PAGE #	TASK PAGE #
7. Remove, inspect, and replace thermostat and gasket/seal.	P-1	✓	✓	✓	162–163	36, 193
8. Inspect and test fan(s) (electrical or mechanical), fan clutch, fan shroud, and air dams.	P-1		✓	✓	170	40, 196
9. Perform oil pressure tests; determine necessary action.	P-1		✓	✓	305–306	103
10. Perform engine oil and filter change.	P-1	✓	✓	✓	186–190	209
11. Inspect auxiliary coolers; determine necessary action.	P-3		✓	✓	200–201	44
12. Inspect, test, and replace oil temperature and pressure switches and sensors.	P-2		✓	✓	193	45
13. Inspect oil pump gears or rotors, housing, pressure relief devices, and pump drive; perform necessary action.	P-2			✓	193–197	43, 191

GLOSSARY

Aboveground storage tank (AGST) A storage tank used to store oil that is above the ground.

AC ripple voltage The alternating voltage that is produced by an alternator. Some is normal and if there is a fault in the alternator the AC ripe voltage can be higher than 0.5 volt.

ACEA Association des Constructeurs European d'Automobiles represents most of the Western European automobile and heavy-duty truck market. The organization uses different engines for testing than those used by API and SAE, and the requirements necessary to meet the ACEA standards are different yet generally correspond with most API ratings.

Acetic acid Some RTV silicone sealers use the fumes from this acid. Use caution as this type can be drawn through the engine through the PCV system and cause damage to oxygen sensors.

Acid material Have pH numbers from 1 to 6.

Additive package Balanced additives.

Adjustable wrench A wrench that has a moveable jaw to allow it to fit many sizes of fasteners.

Adsorption A process where fuel vapor molecules adhere to the surface of carbon. This attaching force is not strong, so the system purges the vapor molecules quite simply by sending a fresh airflow through the charcoal.

Aerated Air mixed with the oil.

AFV Alternative fuel vehicle.

Agitation Keeps fresh cleaning solution moving past the soil to help it loosen.

AGST Above ground storage tank, used to store used oil.

AIR Air injection reaction emission control system; also called secondary air injection.

Air compressor A piece of shop equipment that uses an electric motor to power an air compressor, which is stored in a pressure tank for use in the shop.

Air drill A drill driven by the elastic pressure of condensed air; a pneumatic drill.

Air ratchet An air-operated hand tool that rotates a socket.

Air-blow gun A handheld nozzle attached to a compressed air hose to apply air pressure to a component or device.

Air-fuel ratio The ratio of air to fuel in an intake charge as measured by weight.

AKI (Anti-knock index) The octane rating posted on a gas pump, which is the average of the RON and MON octane ratings.

Alternator Is turned by the engine through an accessory drive belt. The magnetic field of the rotor generates a current in the windings of the stator by electromagnetic induction.

Aluminum bearing A type of engine bearing made from aluminum.

Ampere-hour The ampere-hour (Ah) battery rating is how many amperes can be discharged from the battery before dropping to 10.5 volts over a 20 hour period.

Ampere-hour rating An older type of battery rating.

Amplitude The difference between the highest and lowest level of a waveform.

Anaerobic sealers A type of sealer that cures in the absence of air.

Anhydrous ethanol Ethanol that has no water content.

Annealing Heat-treating process that takes out the brittle hardening of the casting to reduce the chance of cracking from the temperature changes.

ANSI (American National Standards Institute) An organization that publishes safety standards for safety glasses and other personal protective equipment.

Antidrainback valve Prevents oil from draining out of the filter when the engine is shut off.

Antiknock index (AKI) Another term for the octane rating of gasoline.

API American Petroleum Institute.

API gravity The density or specific gravity of diesel fuel is measured in units of API gravity, which is an arbitrary scale expressing the gravity or density of liquid petroleum products devised jointly by the American Petroleum Institute and the National Bureau of Standards.

Aqueous-based solutions Most aqueous-based chemicals are silicate based and are mixed with water.

Arithmetic average roughness height (RA) A method used to measure the roughness of a machined surface.

Armor Protects the fiber facing around the combustion chamber.

Asbestosis A health condition where asbestos causes scar tissue to form in the lungs causing shortness of breath.

ASD relay (Automatic shutdown relay) A main relay used to supply electrical power to the fuel pump, fuel injectors, and ignition system.

Assembly lube A lubricant designed for engine assembly. This lubricant is designed to remain on the parts and not drip or run.

ASTM American Society for Testing Materials.

Asymmetrical The amount of lift of a camshaft is often different for the intake and exhaust valves. If the specifications vary, the camshaft is called asymmetrical.

Aviation tin snips Cutters designed to cut sheet metal.

B5 A blend of 5% biodiesel with 95% petroleum diesel that can generally be used in unmodified diesel engines.

B20 A blend of 20% biodiesel with 80% petroleum diesel.

Babbitt Babbitt is the oldest automotive bearing material. Isaac Babbitt (1799–1862) first formulated this material in 1839. An excellent bearing material, it was originally made from a combination of lead, tin, and antimony.

Back clearance The space behind the piston ring.

Back flushing The use of a special gun that mixes air with water. Low-pressure air is used so that it will not damage the cooling system.

Back pressure The exhaust system's resistance to flow. Measured in pounds per square inch (psi).

Balancing bosses Balancing pad.

Bank Each group of four inline cylinders.

Bar When air is pumped into the cylinder, the combustion chamber receives an increase of air pressure known as boost and is measured in pounds per square inch (psi), atmospheres (ATM), or bar.

Barrel A part of a micrometer, which has 40 threads per inch.

Barrel face ring A piston ring that has a barrel shape.

Base timing The timing of the spark before the computer advances the timing.

Battery An electrical storage device that creates electricity through a chemical reaction.

Battery electrical drain A test to determine if a component or circuit is draining the battery.

Battery voltage correction The battery voltage correction factor occurs when the PCM senses low battery voltage and increases the fuel injector on-time to help compensate for the lower voltage to the fuel pump and fuel injectors. This increase in injector pulse time is added to the calculated pulse time.

BCI (Battery Council International) This organization establishes standards for batteries.

Beam-type torque wrench A type of wrench that displays the torque being applied to a fastener by the position of a deflective pointer and a scale, indicating the amount of torque.

Bearing crown The wall thickness of most bearings is largest in the center.

Bearing shell An engine bearing is called a bearing shell, which is a steel backing with a surface coating of bearing material.

Bearing splitter A two-part steel device used between a bearing and a gear or other component, which is used to remove the bearing using a hydraulic press.

Bedplate A structural member that attaches to the bottom of the block and supports the crankshaft.

Bench grinder An electric motor with a grinding stone and/or wire brush attached at both ends of the armature and mounted on a bench.

Bench vise A holding device attached to a workbench; has two jaws to hold work piece firmly in place.

Bend A turn of a fuel rail.

Billet A type of crankshaft made from a solid chuck of steel.

BIN number A United States federal rating of emissions. The lower the BIN number, the cleaner the exhaust emission is.

Biodiesel A renewable fuel manufactured from vegetable oils, animal fats, or recycled restaurant grease.

Biomass Nonedible farm products, such as corn stalks, cereal straws, and plant wastes from industrial processes, such as sawdust and paper pulp used in making ethanol.

Bleed hole Controls the oil flow through the bearing.

Block The foundation of any engine. All other parts are either directly or indirectly attached to the block of an engine.

Block deck The cylinder head is fastened to the top surface of the block.

Blood-borne pathogens Infections such as HIV and hepatitis B.

Blowby Combustion gases that leak past the piston rings into the crankcase during the compression and combustion strokes of the engine.

Blueprinting A process that is used to customize engine tolerances and clearances to match the intended use of the engine.

Bob weight The weight added to the rod journals of a crankshaft when balancing.

Bolt A fastener consisting of a threaded pin or rod with a head at one end, designed to be inserted through holes in assembled parts and secured by a mated nut that is tightened by applying torque.

Boost An increase in air pressure above atmospheric; measured in pounds per square inch.

Bore The inside diameter of the cylinder in an engine.

Bottom dead center (BDC) When the piston is at the bottom of the stroke.

Boundary lubrication When the oil film is thick enough to keep the surfaces from seizing, but can allow some contact to occur.

BOV Also called a dump valve or vent valve, the BOV features an adjustable spring design that keeps the valve closed until a sudden release of the throttle.

Box-end wrench A wrench with a closed loop (a socket) that fits over a nut or bolt head.

Boxer A type of engine design that is flat and has opposing cylinders; called a boxer because the pistons on one side resemble a boxer during engine operation. Also called a pancake engine.

Braided fabric seals Used as rear crankshaft oil seals.

Breaker bar A long-handled socket drive tool.

British Thermal Unit (BTU) A measure of heat energy. One BTU of heat will raise the temperature of 1 lb of water one Fahrenheit degree.

Bronze guide liners See Thin-Walled Bronze Alloy Sleeve Bushing.

Bucket Opens overhead camshaft valve trains.

Bump cap A hat that is plastic and hard to protect the head from bumps.

Bypass Allows a small part of the coolant to circulate within the engine during warm-up. It is a small passage that leads from the engine side of the thermostat to the inlet side of the water pump. It allows some coolant to bypass the thermostat even when the thermostat is open.

Bypass ignition A type of ignition system that uses the ignition control module to start the engine without the PCM but then switches to PCM control after the engine is running.

Bypass valve That allows intake air to flow directly into the intake manifold bypassing the supercharger.

CA (Cranking Amperes) A measure of battery capacity measured at 32°F (0°C).

CAA (Clean Air Act) Federal legislation passed in 1970 that established national air quality standards.

Calendar year (CY) A calendar year is from January 1 to December 31 each year.

Calibration codes Codes used on many powertrain control modules.

California Air Resources Board (CARB) A state of California agency which regulates the air quality standards for the state.

Cam chucking Is the movement of the camshaft lengthwise in the engine during operation.

Cam follower Opens overhead camshaft valve trains with a ratio similar to that of a rocker arm.

Cam ground Once a certain temperature is reached, the piston will have expanded enough across the piston pin area to become round.

Cam tunnel The cam bearings in an engine block or cylinder head.

Cam-in block Pushrod engines have the cam located in the block.

Cam-in-block design An engine where the camshaft is located in the block rather than in the cylinder head.

Camshaft A shaft with lobes which open valves when being rotated through a chain, belt, or gear from the crankshaft.

Camshaft bearings The camshaft is supported in the block by these bearings.

Camshaft duration The number of degrees of crankshaft rotation for which the valve is lifted off the seat.

Camshaft overlap The number of degrees of crankshaft rotation between the exhaust and intake strokes for which both valves are off their seats.

Capacity test Most automotive starting and charging testers use a carbon pile to create an electrical load on the battery. Also called a battery load test.

Cap screw A bolt that is threaded into a casting.

Capillary action The movement of a liquid through tiny openings or small tubes.

Case hardening Involves heating the crankshaft and adding carbon to the journals where it causes the outer surface to become harder than the rest of the crankshaft.

Cast iron guides A type of valve guide made from cast iron.

Casting number An identification code cast into an engine block or other large cast part of a vehicle.

Catalyst A catalyst is an element that starts a chemical reaction without becoming a part of, or being consumed in, the process.

Catalytic converter An emission control device located in the exhaust system that changes unburned hydrocarbons and CO into harmless H_2O and CO_2. In a three-way catalyst, NOx is divided into harmless, separate nitrogen (N_2) and oxygen (O_2).

Catalytic cracking Breaking hydrocarbon chains using heat in the presence of a catalyst.

Caustic material Chemical cleaners or strong soaps.

Cavitate A process of creating a cavity or void area.

Cavitation A process of creating a cavity or void area. Cavitation is usually used in the automotive field to describe what happens in the cooling system when water boils, creating a bubble in the system, and then cools below 212°F, which causes the bubble to collapse. When this event occurs, water rushes back into the void left by the bubble. The force of this moving water can cause noise as well as damage to cooling system parts such as water pumps.

CBV (Compressor bypass valve) A relief valve used in a turbocharger system. Also called *relief valve* or a *blow-off valve (BOV)*.

CCA (Cold Cranking Amperes) A measure of a battery tested at 0°F.

Cellulose ethanol Ethanol produced from biomass feedstock such as agricultural and industrial plant wastes.

Cellulosic biomass Cellulosic biomass is composed of cellulose and lignin, with smaller amounts of proteins, lipids (fats, waxes, and oils), and ash.

Centrifugal pump A rotodynamic pump that uses a rotating impeller to increase the velocity of a fluid.

Cerium An element that can store oxygen.

Cetane number A diesel fuel rating that indicates how easily the fuel can be ignited.

CFR Code of Federal Regulations.

Charging circuit Includes the alternator and related wiring used to keep the vehicle battery charged.

Cheater bar A pipe or other object used to lengthen the handle of a ratchet or breaker bar.

Check valves Contains a spring-type metallic disc or reed that closes the air line under exhaust backpressure.

Chisel A sharpened tool used with a hammer to separate two pieces of an assembly.

Christmas tree clips Plastic clips used to hold interior panels in place. The end that goes into a hole in the steel door panel is tapered and looks like a Christmas tree.

Clamping force The amount of force exerted on a gasket.

Clicker-type torque wrench A wrench that is first set to the specified torque and then it "clicks" when the set torque value has been reached.

Close-end An end of a wrench that grips all sides of the fastener.

Cloud point The low-temperature point at which the waxes present in most diesel fuel tend to form wax crystals that clog the fuel filter.

Coal to liquid (CTL) A method used to make synthetic fuel.

Coil by plug See Coil-on-Plug.

Coil near plug See Coil-on-Plug.

Coil over plug See Coil-on-Plug.

Coil-on-plug (COP) system Uses one ignition for each spark plug.

Cold chisel A type of chisel used to remove rivets or to break off fasteners.

Cold cranking amperes (CCA) The cold cranking performance rating.

Combination wrench A type of wrench that has an open end at one end and a closed end at the other end of the wrench.

Combustion The rapid burning of the air-fuel mixture in the engine cylinders, creating heat and pressure.

Combustion chamber The space left within the cylinder when the piston is at the top of its combustion chamber.

Combustion chamber volume The volume measured in cubic centimeters (CC) of the combustion chamber in the cylinder head.

Compacted graphite iron (CGI) Compacted graphite iron is used for bedplates and many diesel engine blocks. It has higher strength, stiffness, and toughness than gray iron. The enhanced strength has been shown to permit reduced weight while still reducing noise vibration and harshness.

Companion cylinders Cylinders of a V-6 or V-8 engine that have alternate firing.

Composite camshaft A lightweight tubular shaft with hardened steel lobes press-fitted over the shaft.

Compressed natural gas (CNG) A type of alternative fuel.

Compression ratio (CR) The ratio of the volume in the engine cylinder with the piston at bottom dead center (BDC) to the volume at top dead center (TDC).

Compression rings A compression ring is designed to form a seal between the moving piston and the cylinder wall.

Compression sensing ignition A software addition to a waste-spark ignition system that allows the PCM to determine which of the two cylinders that are fired at the same time is the one on the compression stroke.

Compression test Can be used to test the condition of valves and piston rings.

Compressor bypass valve This type of relief valve routes the pressurized air to the inlet side of the turbocharger for reuse and is quiet during operation.

Concentric Centered.

Conductance testing A tool that tests the capacity and the condition of a battery by measuring the conductance of the plates.

Conformability   The ability of bearing materials to creep or flow slightly to match shaft variations.

Connecting rod   A rod that transmits motion or power from one moving part to another, especially the rod connecting the crankshaft of a motor vehicle to a piston.

Connecting rod bearing journal   See Crank Throw.

Coolant recovery system   When the system cools, the pressure in the cooling system is reduced and a partial vacuum forms. This pulls the coolant from the plastic container back into the cooling system, keeping the system full.

Cooling fins   Fins that are exposed to airflow, which removes heat from the radiator and carries it away.

Cooling Jacket   Coolant passages around the cylinders are often called the cooling jacket.

Copper-lead alloy   Alloy is a stronger and more expensive bearing material than babbitt. It is used for intermediate- and high-speed applications. Tin, in small quantities, is often alloyed with the copper-lead bearings.

Core plugs   A subset of the plugs on a car engine cylinder block or cylinder head. The traditional plug is a thin, domed, disc of metal which fits into a machined hole in the casting and is secured by striking or pressing the centre to expand the disc.

Core tubes   Are made from 0.0045 to 0.012 inch (0.1 to 0.3 mm) sheet brass or aluminum, using the thinnest possible materials for each application. The metal is rolled into round tubes and the joints are sealed with a locking seam.

Cork rubber gaskets   Using synthetic rubber as a binder for the cork.

Corrected torque   The torque value determined by a dynamometer test after the testing parameters have been corrected to a standard value.

Correction factor   The factor that all measured results determined by a dynamometer test corrected to a standard value.

Corrosion resistance   The bearings' ability to resist attack from these acids in the oil.

Cotter key   A metal loop used to retain castle nuts by being installed through a hole. Size is measured by diameter and length (e.g., 1/8' × 1 1/2"). Also called a cotter pin. Named for the old English verb meaning "to close or fasten."

Cotter pins   A soft metal pin that is used to keep parts from loosening.

Counterweights   Weights used to balance the crankshaft.

Country of origin   The first number of the vehicle identification number (VIN), which identifies where the vehicle was assembled.

Cracking   A refinery process in which hydrocarbons with high boiling points are broken into hydrocarbons with low boiling points.

Crankpin   See Crank Throw.

Crank throw   The journals of the off-centre bearings of the crankshaft.

Cranking amperes   A battery rating tested at 32°F (0°C).

Cranking circuit   Includes the starter motor, stater solenoid and related components and wiring.

Cranking vacuum test   Measuring the amount of manifold vacuum during cranking is a quick and easy test to determine if the piston rings and valves are properly sealing.

Crankpin   See Crank Throw.

Crankshaft   A shaft that turns or is turned by a crank.

Crankshaft centerline   The center of a crankshaft as determined by drawing a line through the center of the main bearing journals.

Crankshaft end play   Thrust bearing clearance.

Creeper   A small platform mounted on short casters designed for a service technician to lie down and maneuver under a vehicle.

Crest   The outside diameter of a bolt measured across the threads.

Cross flow head design   By placing the intake and the exhaust valves on the opposite sides of the combustion chamber, an easy path from the intake port through the combustion chamber to the exhaust port is provided.

Crosshatch finish   The angled pattern left on a cylinder by honing.

Crowfoot socket   A type of socket that slips onto the side of the bolt or nut. Used where direct access from the top is restricted.

Crush   Occurs when the bearing cap is tightened, the ends of the two bearing shells touch and are forced together.

Cycle   A complete series of events that continually repeat.

Cylinder   The chamber in which a piston of a reciprocating engine moves.

Cylinder head cover gasket   A gasket that is used between the valve cover and the cylinder head.

Cylinder leakage test   Fills the cylinder with compressed air, and the gauge indicates the percentage of leakage.

Dampening   Reducing the vibration to an acceptable level.

DE (Drive end)   The end of an alternator that is driven by the engine.

Dead-blow hammer   A type of hammer that has lead shot (small pellets) inside a steel housing, which is then covered with a plastic covering. Used to apply a blunt force to an object.

Decibel (dB)   A measure of relative noise level.

Decking the block   A procedure where the block deck must be resurfaced in a surfacing machine that can control the amount of metal removed when it is necessary to match the size of the combustion chambers.

Deflector valve stem seals   See Umbrella Valve Stem Seal.

Detonation   A violent explosion in the combustion chamber created by uncontrolled burning of the air-fuel mixture; often causes a loud, audible knock. Also known as spark knock or ping.

DexCool   Extended life coolant.

DI (Distillation index)   A rating of the volatility of a fuel and how well it evaporates in cold temperatures.

Diagonal pliers   Pliers designed to cut wire and to remove cotter keys. Also called side cuts or dike pliers.

Die   A hardened steel round cutter with teeth on the inside of the center hole.

Die grinder   A handheld air-operated tool used with a grinding stone or a wire brush.

Diesel exhaust fluid (DEF)   Urea also called Adblue used in some diesel engines' exhaust system to reduce emissions.

Diesel exhaust particulate filter (DPF)   A filter that traps PM (soot) located in the exhaust system of most 2007 and newer diesel engines.

Diesel oxidation catalyst (DOC)   Consists of a flow-through honeycomb-style substrate structure that is washcoated with a layer of catalyst materials, similar to those used in a gasoline engine catalytic converter.

Diesohol   Standard #2 diesel fuel combined with up to 15% ethanol.

Differential pressure sensor (DPS)   Designed to remove diesel particulate matter or soot from the exhaust gas of a diesel engine.

Digital EGR The digital EGR valve consists of three solenoids controlled by the PCM.

Direct injection (DI) Fuel is injected directly into the cylinder.

Dish Pistons used in other engines may be provided with a depression.

Displacement The total volume displaced or swept by the cylinders in an internal combustion engine.

Distillation The process of purification through evaporation and then condensation of the desired liquid.

Distillation curve A graph that plots the temperatures at which the various fractions of a fuel evaporate.

Distortion A cylinder head should be checked for distortion using a precision straight edge.

Distributor cap A plastic cap with metal inserts used to distribute a high-voltage spark from a single ignition coil to multiple cylinders.

Distributor ignition (DI) Is the term specified by the Society of Automotive Engineers (SAE) for an ignition system that uses a distributor.

Divorced coil An ignition coil design where the primary and secondary windings are not connected.

Double knock The noise is created when the piston stops at top dead center and occurs again as it starts to move downward, creating a double-knock sound, which is also described as a rattling sound.

Double-cut file A file that has two rows of teeth that cut at an opposite angle.

Double overhead camshaft (DOHC) A type of engine that uses a camshaft located in the cylinder head.

Double roller chain A type of camshaft drive chain that are two chains used side by side.

DPFE Delta pressure feedback EGR sensor measures the pressure differential between two sides of a metered orifice positioned just below the EGR valve's exhaust side.

Dressed The act of cleaning or truing a grinding stone.

Drive size The size in fractions of an inch of the square drive for sockets.

Driveability index (DI) A calculated value from volatility tests that determines how a fuel will react in a cold engine.

Dry bulb temperature A method used to determine relative humidity. Used during dynamometer testing of an engine.

Dry cylinder sleeve Cast-iron dry sleeves are used in aluminum blocks to provide a hard surface for the rings.

Dry sump The oil pan is shallow and the oil is pumped into a remote reservoir. In this reservoir, the oil is cooled and any trapped air is allowed to escape before being pumped back to the engine.

Dry system A type of nitrous system that does not include additional gasoline.

Dual overhead camshaft (DOHC) An engine design with two camshafts above each line of cylinders; one for the exhaust valves and one for the intake valves.

Ductile iron Is very flexible and can be twisted without breaking, is also used as a piston ring material in some automotive engines.

Dump valve Features an adjustable spring design that keeps the valve closed until a sudden release of the throttle.

Dynamic compression test A compression test done with the engine running rather than during engine cranking, as is done in a regular compression test.

E10 A fuel blend of 10% ethanol and 90% gasoline.

E85 A fuel blend of 85% ethanol and 15% gasoline.

Easy out A tool used to extract a broken bolt.

E-diesel Standard #2 diesel fuel combined with up to 15% ethanol. Also known as diesohol.

EGR (Exhaust gas recirculation) An emission control device used to reduce NOx (oxides of nitrogen).

Elastic valve Type of poppet valve. The elastic valve is able to conform to valve seat shape. This allows it to seal easily, but it runs hot and the flexing to conform may cause it to break.

Elastomer Another term for rubber.

ELD Electrical load detector used to mange alternator output based on electrical demand.

Electrolysis A type of corrosion that requires the use of an outside voltage source. The source is usually due to a poor electrical ground connection.

Electromagnetic induction A voltage is produced in a wire if a changing electrical current flows through another close wire.

Electromagnetic interference (EMI) Causes problems to computer signals.

Electronic control unit Module for the electronic ignition system.

Electronic ignition (EI) The term specified by the SAE for an ignition system that does not use a distributor.

Electronic ignition module (or igniter) Opens and closes the primary ignition circuit by opening or closing the ground return path of the circuit.

Electronic ignition system The system consists of a pulse generator unit in the distributor (pickup coil and reluctor).

Electroplating A process of putting on an overplating layer onto the bearing.

Embedability The property that allows the bearing to fully embed the particle. The bearing material gradually works across the particle, completely covering it.

Embittered coolant Coolant that has been made bitter to deter ingestion by animals.

EMI Electromagnetic interference.

Engine stand A floor mounted-frame usually equipped with casters on which an engine can be attached and rotated.

EPA Environmental Protection Agency.

EREV Extended range electric vehicle.

Ethanol (grain alcohol) An octane enhancer added, at a rate of up to 10% to gasoline will increase the octane rating of the fuel by 2.5 to 3.0. Ethanol is a fuel oxygenate.

Ethyl alcohol see Ethanol.

Ethyl tertiary butyl ether (ETBE) An octane enhancer for gasoline. It is also a fuel oxygenate that is manufactured by reacting isobutylene with ethanol. The resulting either is high octane and low volatility. ETBE can be added to gasoline up to a level of approximately 13%.

Ethylene glycol-based antifreeze A type of antifreeze used by all manufacturers.

Ethylene glycol based coolant Contains 47% ethylene glycol (EG), 50% water and 3% additives.

EVP A linear potentiometer on the top of the EGR valve stem indicates valve position for the computer.

EVRV The computer pulses the solenoid to control the vacuum that regulates the operation of the EGR valve.

Exhaust gas recirculation (EGR) The process of passing a small measured amount of exhaust gas back into the engine to reduce combustion temperatures and formation of NOx (oxides of nitrogen).

Exhaust valve A valve through which burned gases from a cylinder escape into the exhaust manifold.

Exhaust valve cam phases (EVCP) Spline phaser system of variable valve timing system.

Expandable pilots A type of pilot used to guide a cutting stone for grinding valve seats.

Expansion plugs A type of plug that is adjustable.

Extension A socket wrench tool used between a ratchet or breaker bar and a socket.

External combustion engine Engine combustion occurring outside the power chamber.

Eye wash station A water fountain designed to rinse the eyes with a large volume of water.

Eyebrows Recesses machined or cast into the tops of the pistons for valve clearance.

Fatigue life The length of time before fatigue will cause failure.

Feeler gauge A set of precision thickness steel blades used to measure a gap. Also called a thickness gauge.

FFV Flex-fuel vehicles are capable of running on straight gasoline or gasoline/ethanol blends.

Fiber reinforced matrix (FRM) A ceramic material similar to that used to construct the insulators of spark plugs. The lightweight material has excellent wear resistance and good heat transfer properties making it ideal for use as a cylinder material.

Files A metal smoothing tool.

Finger follower See Cam Follower.

Finishing stone A fine grit stone used to finish honing a bore.

Fire blanket A fire-proof wool blanket used to cover a person who is on fire and smother the fire.

Fire deck The cylinder head surface that mates with the top deck of the block.

Fire ring See Armor.

Firing order The order that the spark is distributed to the correct spark plug at the right time.

Fischer-Tropsch A refining process that converts coal, natural gas, or other petroleum products into synthetic motor fuels.

Fitting wrench A wrench that is used to remove the fitting holding a brake line or other line.

Flare nut wrench A type of wrench used to remove brake lines.

Flash point The temperature at which the vapors on the surface of the fuel will ignite if exposed to an open flame.

Flat link type See Silent Chain type.

Flat-tip screwdrivers A screwdriver used to remove and insert screws that have a single slot.

Flat-top piston Are found in low-cost, low-performance engines.

Flex fuel An automobile that can typically use different sources of fuel, either mixed in the same tank or with separate tanks and fuel systems for each fuel.

Floor jack A hydraulic jack mounted on casters or steel wheels and used to lift a vehicle.

Flying web The flange between the splayed crankpin journals.

Fogging oil Coats metal parts to keep them from rusting.

Forced induction system A term used to describe a turbocharger or supercharger.

Formed in place gaskets (FIPG) A sealant that is extruded onto a sealing surface.

Forming stone See Roughing Stone.

Four-stroke cycle An internal combustion engine design where four strokes of the piston (two crankshaft revolutions) are required to complete one cycle of events. The four strokes include intake, compression, power, and exhaust.

Free rotators A type of valve retainer that allows the valve to be free to rotate when the valve is opening or closing.

Freewheeling engine An engine design that does not cause the valve to hit the position in the case of a broken timing belt or chain.

Freeze plugs See Core Plugs.

Frequency The number of times a waveform repeats in one second, measured in Hertz (Hz), frequency band.

Fretting A condition that can destroy intake manifold gaskets and is caused by the unequal expansion and contraction of two different engine materials.

Freshening A term used to describe the process of engine repair that usually includes only replacing the piston rings and rod bearings.

Frost plugs See Core Plugs.

FTD Fischer-Tropsch diesel process. See Fischer-Tropsch.

Firing line The vertical line of an ignition scope trace showing the voltage required to fire the spark plug.

Firing order The order of the spark plug firing as determined by engine design.

Fuel compensation sensor A sensor used in flex-fuel vehicles that provides information to the PCM on the ethanol content and temperature of the fuel as it is flowing through the fuel delivery system.

Fuel composition sensor Measures both the percentage of ethanol blend and the temperature of the fuel.

Fuel tank pressure (FTP) A sensor used to monitor the rate with which vacuum increases in the fuel tank.

Full round bearing Sleeve type bushing.

Full-floating A type of axle assembly where the weight of the vehicle is supported by the axle housing and not on the axle itself.

Fully counterweighted A crankshaft that has counterweights on both sides of each connecting rod journal.

Fungible A term used to describe that all fluids that meet the same grade can be intermixed.

Fusible link A type of fuse that will melt and open the protected circuit in the event of a short circuit, which could cause excessive current flow through the fusible link. Most fusible links are actually wires that are four gauge sizes smaller than the wire of the circuits being protected.

Gallery Longitudinal header. This is a long hole drilled from the front of the block to the back. Passages drilled through the block bulkheads allow the oil to go from the main oil gallery to the main and cam bearings.

Galvanic activity Is the flow of an electrical current as a result of two different metals in a liquid, which acts like a battery.

Gasoline Refined petroleum product that is used primarily as a gasoline engine.

GAWR (Gross axle weight rating) A rating of the load capacity of a vehicle and included on placards on the vehicle and in the owner's manual.

Generator The SAE term for alternator.

Gerotor   A design of oil pump.

Girdle   A one-piece unit that ties all main bearing caps together to increase strength.

Glow plug   A heating element that uses 12 volts from the battery and aids in the starting of a cold engine.

Grade   The strength rating of a bolt.

Grain alcohol   See Ethanol.

Grinder   Type of resurfacer that uses a large-diameter abrasive wheel.

Grit size   The size of the abrasive particles in the grinding and honing stones controls the surface finish.

Grooves   Piston ring grooves are located between the piston head and skirt.

GTL (Gas-to-liquid)   A refining process in which natural gas is converted into liquid fuel.

Gudgeon pins   A British term for pins used to attach the piston to the connecting rod.

Guttering   A type of valve failure often caused by a sticking valve. Results from poor seating that allows the high-temperature and high-pressure combustion gases to leak between the valve and seat.

GVWR (Gross vehicle weight rating)   The total weight of the vehicle including the maximum cargo.

Hacksaw   A saw that uses a replaceable blade and is used to cut a variety of materials depending on the type of blade used.

Half-shell bearing   The bearing is manufactured to very close tolerance so that it will fit correctly in each application.

Hall effect   A type of sensor that creates a square wave output signal.

Hangers   Are made of rubberized fabric with metal ends that hold the muffler and tailpipe in position so that they do not touch any metal part.

Hard seat stones   Hard seat stones are used to grind hard Stellite® exhaust seat inserts.

Harmonic balancer   See Vibration Damper.

Hazardous waste material   Material that requires special treatment and cannot be disposed of in regular trash.

Head gasket   Gaskets that are used between the cylinder head and engine block.

Heat dams   Most pistons have horizontal separation slots that act as heat dams.

Heat of compression   Incoming air is compressed until its temperature reaches about 1000°F.

Heavy metal   A tungsten alloy that is 1.5 times as heavy as lead used to balance crankshafts.

HEI (High Energy Ignition)   The brand name of an ignition system from General Motors.

Helical insert   A steel insert used to repair damaged threads.

Heli-Coil®   A brand name for a helical insert.

Helmholtz resonator   A resonance tube named for the discoverer of the relationship between shape and value of frequency Herman L. F. von Helmholtz (1821–1894) of the University of Hönizsberg in East Prussia.

HEPA vacuum   High efficiency particulate air filter vacuum used to clean brake dust.

HEV   Hybrid electric vehicle.

High energy ignition (HEI)   Use an air-cooled, epoxy-sealed E coil.

High pressure common rail (HPCR)   Newer diesel engines use a fuel delivery system referred to as a high-pressure common rail.

HO2S   Heated oxygen sensor.

HTHS (High temperature high shear)   An engine oil classification.

Hub   The center of a wheel or similar object.

Hybrid organic acid technology (HOAT)   A type of coolant that has organic acids and either no phosphates and some silicates, or no silicates and some phosphates. Coolants can be green, orange, yellow, gold, pink, red, or blue.

Hydraulic electronic unit injection (HEUI)   A type of diesel engine fuel delivery system that uses high pressure engine oil to create the high pressure needed to inject fuel into the cylinders.

Hydraulic lash adjusters (HLA)   Some newer engines have the hydraulic adjustment in the rocker arm called HLA.

Hydraulic lifter   A valve lifter that, using simple valving and the engine's oil pressure, can adjust its length slightly, thereby maintaining zero clearance in the valve train. Hydraulic lifters reduce valve train noise and are maintenance-free.

Hydraulic press   A piece of shop equipment usually mounted on the floor, which uses a hydraulic cylinder to remove and install pressed-on components, such as bearings.

Hydraulic valve lifter   A hydraulic valve lifter is a lifter with an automatic hydraulic adjustment built into the lifter body.

Hydrocracking   A refinery process that converts hydrocarbons with a high boiling point into ones with low boiling points.

Hydrodynamic lubrication   A wedge-shaped oil film is built up between the moving block and the surface. High oil pressure created between the crankshaft journal and the bearing created by the rotation of the oil film.

Hydroseal   A layer of water over the chemical to prevent evaporation of the chemical.

Hypereutectic   Pistons that are commonly used in the aftermarket and as original equipment in many turbocharged and supercharged engines.

IC   Ignition control.

ICM   Ignition control module.

Identification marks   For pushrod inline engines, they are normally placed on the camshaft side.

Idle stop   A condition when the engine stops when a hybrid electric vehicle comes to a stop.

Idle vacuum test   An engine in proper condition should idle with a steady vacuum between 17 and 21 in. Hg.

Igniter   A term used to describe an ignition control module.

Ignition coil   The coil creates a high-voltage spark by electromagnetic induction.

Ignition timing   The base timing when the spark occurs. Often adjustable on engines equipped with a distributor.

ILSAC (International Lubricant Standardization and Approval Committee)   Responsible for development of the ILSAC standard for motor oil performance.

Impact wrench   An air-operated hand tool used to install and remove threaded fasteners.

Impeller   The mechanism in a water pump that rotates to produce coolant flow.

Incandescent light   A type of light that uses an incandescent rather than a fluorescent or LED light source.

Inches of Mercury (in. Hg)   Unit of measure used to measure a vacuum.

Indirect injection (IDI) Fuel is injected into a small prechamber, which is connected to the cylinder by a narrow opening.

Inert Chemically inactive; not able to chemically combine with any other chemical.

Inertia friction welding A type of welding where the two parts to be joined are spun at high speed and then pressed together. The resulting friction creates the high temperatures needed and the two parts weld together.

Inertia ring The outer ring of a harmonic balancer.

Infrared pyrometer Measures the inlet and the outlet temperatures.

Initial timing The base ignition timing.

Injection pump A diesel engine injection pump is used to increase the pressure of the diesel fuel from very low values from the lift pump to the extremely high pressures needed for injection.

Inorganic additive technology (IAT) Conventional coolant that has been used for over 50 years. The additives used to protect against rust and corrosion include phosphate and silicates.

Insert seats An insert seat fits into a machined recess in the steel or aluminum cylinder head. Insert seats are used in all aluminum head engines and in applications for which corrosion and wear resistance are critical.

Insert valve seats A replaceable type valve seat.

Installed height The height of a valve spring as installed on a valve.

Intake centerline Point often located between 100 degrees and 110 degrees.

Intake lobe centerline method This method determines the exact centerline of the intake lobe and compares it to the specifications supplied with the replacement camshaft.

Intake valve The valve that is open during the intake stroke and allows air to entire the cylinder.

Integral seat The seat is generally formed as part of the cast-iron head of automotive engines.

Intercooler Is used on many turbocharged and some supercharged engines to reduce the temperature of air entering the engine for increased power.

Interference angle The difference between the valve seat angle and the valve face angle; usually about one degree.

Interference engine An interference engine will cause some of the valves that are open to hit the pistons, causing major engine damage.

Interference fit The modern method of retaining the piston pin in the connecting rod is to make the connecting rod hole slightly smaller than the piston pin. The pin is installed by heating the rod to expand the hole or by pressing the pin into the rod.

Internal combustion engine Engine combustion occurring within the power chamber.

Inertia forces A product of reciprocating action of the piston.

Inertial weight Also called reciprocating weight and includes the pistons and rods when balancing an engine.

IOD (Ignition off draw) Another term used to describe parasitic draw or key off battery electrical load.

Ion sensing ignition A type of coil-on-lag ignition that is capable of sensing the conditions inside the cylinder.

Intake lobe centerline method A method used to degree a camshaft using the center of the intake cam lobe as the basis.

Iridium spark plugs Use a small amount of iridium welded onto the tip of a small center electrode, 0.0015 to 0.002 inch (0.4 to 0.6 mm) in diameter.

Jack stand See Safety Stand.

Jam nut A second nut used to prevent the first nut from loosening.

JASO The Japanese Automobile Standards Organization (JASO) oil standards. The JASO tests use small Japanese engines, and their ratings require more stringent valve train wear standards than other countries' oil ratings.

Julian date The number of the day of the year.

Knock sensors An engine sensor that detects engine spark knock or detonation.

Labor guides A guide that shows the estimated labor times for each service or procedure.

Lands Area between the ring grooves.

Lash Valve clearance.

LED (Light-emitting diode) A high-efficiency light source that uses very little electricity and produces very little heat.

Left-hand rule A method of determining the direction of magnetic lines of force around a conductor. The left-hand rule is used with the electron flow theory (- flowing to +).

Lift pump The diesel fuel is drawn from the fuel tank by a lift pump and delivers the fuel to the injection pump.

Lifter preload The distance between the pushrod seat inside the lifter and the snap-ring of the lifter when the lifter is resting on the base circle (or heel) of the cam and the valve is closed.

Light off temperature The catalytic converter does not work when cold and it must be heated to its light-off temperature of close to 500°F (260°C) before it starts working at 50% effectiveness.

Linear EGR Contains a solenoid to precisely regulate exhaust gas flow and a feedback potentiometer that signals the computer regarding the actual position of the valve.

Liquefied petroleum gas (LPG) A type of alternative fuel usually used by small fleets.

Load test One of the most accurate tests to determine the condition of any battery.

Lobe A lobe is eccentric shape on a camshaft that opens the valve against the force of the valve springs.

Lobe centers Separation between the centerlines of the intake and exhaust lobes, measured in degrees.

Lobe displacement angle See Lobe Centers.

Lobe lift The lobe lift of the cam is usually expressed in decimal inches and represents the distance that the valve lifter or follower is moved. The amount that the valve is lifted is determined by the lobe lift times the ratio of the rocker arm.

Lobe separation See Lobe Centers.

Lobe spread See Lobe Centers.

LOC Light off converter.

Lock rings Retain full-floating piston pins in automotive engines.

Locking pliers Pliers that can be used to grasp an object and then be locked into position. Often called by a popular brand name VISE-GRIPS®.

Locks Also called valve keepers; retains the valve to the retainer.

Long block An engine block that has the pistons and crankshaft installed plus the cylinder head(s).

LP Gas Liquefied petroleum gas; another term for propane.

LRC (Load response control) A type of charging system that monitors the electrical load demands of the vehicle.

Lugging Increasing the throttle opening without increasing engine speed (RPM).

M85 Internal combustion engine fuel containing 85% methanol and 15% gasoline.

Magnetic pulse alternator The pulse generator consists of a trigger wheel (reluctor) and a pickup coil.

Magnetic sensor A type of sensor that uses a magnet wrapped with a coil of wire.

Major thrust surface The side of an engine cylinder that receives the greatest thrust or force from the piston during the power stroke.

Married coil An ignition coil that has one end of the primary winding electrically connected to the secondary winding.

MCA (Marine cranking amperes) A battery rating.

Mechanical force The pressure developed within the combustion chamber is applied to the head of a piston or to a turbine wheel.

Mechanical power The output of mechanical force.

Mercury A heavy metal.

Mesothelioma A lung disease contributed to asbestos.

Methanol (wood alcohol) Typically manufactured from natural gas. Methanol content, including co-solvents, in unleaded gasoline is limited by law to 5%.

Methanol to gasoline (MTG) A process of creating gasoline from methanol.

Methyl alcohol Another name for methanol.

Metric bolts Bolts manufactured and sized in the metric system of measurement.

Microbe A microorganism that is too small to be seen by the human eye.

Micron Is equal to 0.000039 in.

Milling Type of resurfacer that uses metal-cutting tool bits fastened in a disk.

Mini converter A small, quick heating oxidation converter.

Miscible Capable of mixing with other oils (brands and viscosities, for example) without causing any problems such as sludge.

Model year (MY) The year of a vehicle, which may be different from the calendar year when it is sold.

Monoblock The cylinder, water jacket, main bearing supports (saddles), and oil passages are all cast as one structure for strength and quietness.

Morse type See Silent Chain type.

MSDS Material safety data sheets.

MTBE Methyl tertiary butyl ether is an oxygenated fuel that is used as a gasoline additive to enhance its burning characteristics being phased out due to ground water contamination concerns.

MTG (Methanol-to-gasoline) A refining process in which methanol is converted into liquid gasoline.

MTHF (Methyltetrahydrofuron) A component of P-series nonpetroleum-based fuels.

Multi-groove adjustable pliers Pliers that are capable of grasping a wide range of object sizes; also called water pump pliers or by a popular brand name of Channel Locks®.

Multilayered steel The many layers of thin steel reduce bore and overhead camshaft distortion with less clamping force loss than previous designs.

Multilayered steel (MLS) gaskets Gaskets are constructed using three to five layers of stainless steel sheet are separated by elastomer (rubber) material. The elastomer material is between the layers of the sheet metal and on both surfaces.

Mutual induction Generation of an electric current in both coil windings.

Naturally aspirated Refers to an internal combustion engine that is neither turbocharged nor supercharged.

Necking Weakens the stem and leads to breakage.

Needle-nose pliers Pliers that are equipped with pointed jaws, which allow use in restricted areas or for small parts.

Negative back-pressure Some EGR valves react to this low pressure area by closing a small internal valve, which allows the EGR valve to be opened by vacuum.

Neutral safety switch A switch used in the cranking circuit that prevents the engine from being cranked unless the transmission is in neutral or park.

NGV Natural gas vehicle.

Nitriding The crankshaft is heated to about 1000°F (540°C) in a furnace filled with ammonia gas, and then allowed to cool. The process adds nitrogen (from the ammonia) into the surface of the metal-forming hard nitrides in the surface of the crankshaft to a depth of about 0.007 in. (0.8 mm).

Nitrous oxide A type of power adder that uses a gas containing oxygen along with additional fuel to increase engine power.

No-retorque-type gaskets A head gasket that does not require the cylinder head bolts to be torqued after the engine has been run for a while.

Non-principal end The front or the accessory drive belt end of an engine.

Normal operating temperature When the cooling fan has cycled on and off at least once after the engine has been started. Some vehicle manufacturers specify that the cooling fan should cycle twice.

Notch On the piston head indicating the "front."

NOx Oxides of nitrogen; when combined with HC and sunlight, form smog.

Nut splitter A hand tool designed to break a nut that is rusted onto a bolt or stud.

Octane rating The measurement of a gasoline's ability to resist engine knock. The higher the octane rating, the less prone the gasoline is to cause engine knock (detonation).

Offset aviation snip A tin snip that has curved jaws allowing it to make curved cuts either left or right.

Oil control ring Allows oil to return through the ring and openings in the piston.

Oil control valve Directs oil from the oil feed in the head to the appropriate camshaft position actuator oil passages.

Oil gallery An oil pump which is driven by the engine, forces the oil through the oil filter and then into passages in the crankshaft and block.

Oil gallery plugs Threaded plugs used to seal the ends of the oil galleries in an engine block.

Opacity The degree to which light is blocked.

Open circuit battery voltage test A test conducted with an open circuit—with no current flowing and no load applied to the battery.

Open end The end of a wrench that is open to allow the wrench to be inserted onto a fastener from the side.

Open end wrench A type of wrench that has an opening and can be placed on a fastener from the side.

Optical sensor A type of engine sensor that uses light and a disc with slits to determine engine piston position.

Organic A term used to describe anything that was alive at one time.

Organic acid technology (OAT) Antifreeze coolant contains ethylene glycol, but does not contain silicates or phosphates. This type of coolant is usually orange in color and was first developed by Havoline (called DEX-COOL) and used in General Motors vehicles starting in 1996.

OSC Oxygen storage capacity.

OSHA (Occupational Safety and Health Administration) Is the main federal agency responsible for enforcement of workplace safety and health legislation.

Overhead camshaft A camshaft that is either belt or chain driven from the crankshaft and is located in the cylinder head(s).

Overhead valve Is a type of piston engine that places the camshaft in the cylinder block (usually beside and slightly above the crankshaft in a straight engine or directly above the crankshaft in the V of a V engine) and uses pushrods or rods to actuate rocker arms above the cylinder head to actuate the valves.

Overlay Many of the copper-lead bearings have a third layer of metal. This third layer is usually of babbitt. Babbitt-overlayed bearings have high fatigue strength, good conformity, good embedability, and good corrosion resistance.

Oversize (OS) stems A valve that has a stem with a larger diameter than what came originally from the factory.

Oxygenated fuels Fuels such as ETBE or MTBE that contain extra oxygen molecules to promote cleaner burning. Oxygenated fuels are used as gasoline additives to reduce CO emissions.

Pal nut See Jam Nut.

Palladium An element that acts as a catalyst.

Pancake A pancake engine is an internal combustion engine that has the cylinders on a horizontal plane.

Paper test Hold a piece of paper or a 3" × 5" card (even a dollar bill works) within 1 in. (2.5 centimeters) of the tailpipe with the engine running at idle. The paper should blow out evenly without "puffing." If the paper is drawn toward the tailpipe at times, the exhaust valves in one or more cylinders could be burned.

Parallel flow system Coolant flows into the block under pressure and then crosses the gasket to the head through main coolant passages beside each cylinder.

Parasitic load A battery drain when the ignition and everything electrical in the vehicle is off.

Particulate matter (PM) Also called soot and an emission from diesel engines.

PASS A word used to help remember how to use a fire extinguisher; pull pin, aim, squeeze the lever, and sweep the nozzle from side to side.

Passivation A chemical process where a coolant adheres to and protects the metals in a cooling system.

PCV Positive crankcase ventilation.

Peened A process where metal is hit with steel shot and used to increase the strength of that area being treated.

Penetrating oil A thin oil that is designed to penetrate through rust and provide lubrication for the threads of a fastener.

Petrodiesel Another term for petroleum diesel, which is ordinary diesel fuel refined from crude oil.

Petroleum Another term for crude oil. The literal meaning of petroleum is "rock oil."

PFE Pressure Feedback EGR.

pH A measure of the acidity or alkalinity of a material. A pH of 7 is neutral, higher than 7 is alkaline, and lower than 7 is acidic.

Phosphate hybrid organic acid technology (PHOAT) A type of coolant that uses organic acids and some phosphate and is silicate free.

Pickup coil Also called a pulse generator. Used in distributor-type ignition system to trigger the ignition control module.

Piloting surfaces Closely fit reamed holes on the connecting rod bolts.

Ping Secondary rapid burning of the last 3 to 5% of the air-fuel mixture in the combustion chamber causes a second flame front that collides with the first flame front causing a knock noise. Also called detonation or spark knock.

Piston Forms a movable bottom to the combustion chamber.

Piston pin Attaches the piston to the connecting rod.

Piston ring Seals the small space between the piston and cylinder wall, keeping the pressure above the piston.

Piston ring compressor Holds the rings in their grooves.

Piston ring expander A tool that will only open the ring gap enough to slip the ring on the piston.

Piston ring expanding tool Piston ring removal tool.

Piston stroke Is a one-way piston movement between the top and bottom of the cylinder.

Pitch The pitch of a threaded fastener refers to the number of threads per inch.

Plain bearing A bearing such as an engine crankshaft bearing that does not have balls or rollers.

Plateau honing Honing leaves a plateau surface that can support the oil film for the rings and piston skirt. This plateau surface is achieved by first using a coarse stone followed by a smooth stone to achieve the desired surface.

Platinum An element that acts as a catalyst.

Platinum spark plugs Spark plugs that have a small amount of the precious metal platinum included on the end of the center electrode, as well as on the ground or side electrode.

Plenum A chamber, located between the throttle body and the runners of the intake manifold, used to distribute the intake charge more evenly and efficiently.

Polarity The polarity of an ignition coil is determined by the direction of rotation of the coil windings.

Pop rivet A type of fastener that uses a rivet gun to pull out the rivet until the end deforms, thereby creating a light clamping form.

Pop tester Is a device used for checking a diesel injector nozzle for proper spray pattern.

Poppet valve The valve is opened by means of a valve train that is operated by a cam.

Pop-ups Raised dome on the head of a piston.

Port An opening in a cylinder head where intake or exhaust gases flow.

Portable crane A piece of shop equipment that is used to lift and move heavy pieces of equipment, such as an engine.

Porting relieving The opening or enlarging the opening in a cylinder head where intake or exhaust gases flow.

Positive backpressure At low engine speeds and light engine loads, the EGR system is not needed, and the backpressure in it is also low.

Positive displacement A roots-type supercharger is called a positive displacement design, because all of the air that enters is forced through the unit.

Positive displacement pumps A type of pump where everything that enters the pumps, leaves the pump.

Positive twist ring A type of piston ring.

Power adder A unit such as a turbocharger, supercharger that is used to increase the power output of an engine.

Positive rotators A type of rotator that causes the valve to rotate in a controlled manner as it is opened.

Positive twist Will give the same wall contact as the taper-faced ring.

Pour point Coat the wax crystals in the oil so that they will not stick together. The oil will then be able to flow at lower temperatures.

Power balance test A test to determine if all cylinders are contributing power equally.

PPE Personal protective equipment, which can include gloves, safety glasses, and other items.

PPO Pure plant oil.

Precision insert-type bearing shells See Half-Shell Bearing.

Preconverter See Mini Converter.

Pressure regulating valve A valve that limits the pressure of the oil pump.

Pressure regulator A regulating device that maintains a specified pressure in a system.

Prevailing torque nut A special design of nut fastener that is deformed slightly or has other properties that permit the nut to remain attached to the fastener without loosening.

Primary ignition circuit The ignition components that regulate the current in the coil primary winding by turning it on and off.

Primary vibration A strong low-frequency vibration when pistons move up and down in the cylinders.

Primary winding The low-voltage winding of an ignition coil.

Principal end The end of the engine where the flywheel is attached.

Propane See LPG.

Pulse generator Another name for a pickup coil used to trigger an ignition control module in a distributor-type ignition system.

Pump-up Occasionally, engines are run at excessive speeds. This tends to throw the valve open, causing valve float. During valve float, clearance exists in the valve train. The hydraulic lifter will take up this clearance as it is designed to do. When this occurs, it will keep the valve from closing on the seat, called pump-up.

Punch A hand tool designed to be used with a hammer to drive out pins.

Pup converter A small catalytic converter that is used upstream from the main converter.

Push rod The link rod connecting the brake pedal to the master cylinder piston.

Push rod engine Also called an overhead valve engine or cam-in-block engine. The camshaft is located in the engine block and pushrods are used to operate the valves.

Putty knife A scraper with a broad blade that helps to avoid scratching the surface as it is used to clean the parts.

Pyrolytic High temperature oven.

Quench area See Squish Area.

Ramp A gradual rise in the cam contour.

Ratchet A handle used to rotate a socket, which is reversible and allows the socket to be rotated in one direction and then free movement in the opposite direction of rotation.

RCRA Resource Conservation and Recovery Act.

Rebuilding A process of replacing worn parts and restoring an engine or other component to useful service.

Recesses Cuts in the piston top for valve clearance.

Reciprocating weight Also called inertia weight which includes the pistons and rods when balancing an engine.

Reformulated gasoline (RG) Gasoline that has strict limits on chemicals that may be harmful to the environment.

Refractometer A test instrument used measures the extent to which light is bent (refracted) to determine the index of refraction of a liquid sample.

Regeneration A process of taking the kinetic energy of a moving vehicle and converting it into electrical energy and storing it in a battery.

Reid vapor pressure (RVP) A method of determining vapor pressure of gasoline and other petroleum products. Widely used in the petroleum industry as an indicator of the volatility of gasoline.

Relief valve Vents pressurized air from the connecting pipe between the outlet of the turbocharger and the throttle whenever the throttle is closed during boost, such as during shifts.

Removers This term is used to describe hand tools, which are designed to remove broken studs, bolts, and other fasteners.

Reserve capacity A battery rating.

Resonate Audible vibrations.

Restricted exhaust If the exhaust system is restricted, the engine will be low on power, yet smooth.

Retainer The upper support for a valve spring and held to the valve with keepers (locks).

Reverse capacity Is the number of minutes for which the battery can produce 25 amperes and still have a battery voltage of 1.75 volts per cell (10.5 volts for a 12-volt battery).

Reverse cooling The coolant flows from the radiator to the cylinder head(s) before flowing to the engine block.

Reverse twist Seals the lower outer section of the ring and piston ring groove, thus improving oil control.

Reverse twist ring A type of piston ring.

RFG Reformulated gasoline.

Rhodium An element that acts as a catalyst.

Right-to-know laws Laws that state that employees have a right to know when the materials they use at work are hazardous.

Rigid valve Type of poppet valve. The rigid valve is strong, holds its shape, and conducts heat readily. It also causes less valve recession. Unfortunately, it is more likely to leak and burn than other valve head types.

Ring gap Will allow some leakage past the top compression ring. This leakage is useful in providing pressure on the second ring to develop a dynamic sealing force.

Ripple current The alternating current (AC) produced by an alternator.

Rocking couple 90-degree V-6 engines use a split-crank journal to create an even-firing arrangement. As a result these forces cause the engine to rock back and forth.

Roller chain type A type of timing chain that is noisier but operates with less friction and stretches less than the silent type of chain.

Room temperature vulcanization (RTV) A type of sealer that cures in the presence of moisture at room temperature.

Root mean square (RMS) A mathematical method used to calculate a standard of measurement that is close to the average.

Roots type supercharger Is called a positive displacement design because all of the air that enters is forced through the unit.

Rotary engine An internal combustion engine in which power is transmitted directly to rotating components.

Rotating weight The big end of the connecting rod is considered to be rotating weight when balancing a crankshaft.

Rotor A part inside a distributor that conducts high voltage spark from the ignition coil to the terminals inside the distributor cap.

Roughing stone Used to rapidly remove large amounts of seat metal. This would be necessary on a badly pitted seat or when installing new valve seat inserts.

Rubber coated metal (RCM) A type of gasket.

Running compression test The running compression test can inform a technician of the relative compression of all the cylinders.

RVP (Reid Vapor Pressure) A measurement of volatility of gasoline.

Saddles Another term for bearing bores.

Safety stand A metal device with an adjustable vertical support that is designed to support a vehicle after it has been raised off the ground. Also called a *jack stand*.

SAI An abbreviation for the secondary air-injection system which provides the air necessary for the oxidizing process either at the exhaust manifold or inside the catalytic converter.

SAPS Sulfated ash, phosphorous, and sulfur.

Saturation The point at which a coil's maximum magnetic field strength is reached.

Scavenging partial vacuum created in the cylinders which helps bring in a fresh air-fuel charge into the cylinders.

Score resistance Prevents the bearing materials from seizing to the shaft during oil film breakdown.

Schmitt trigger An electronic device that changes analog signals into digital (on or off) signals.

Scraper ring Is usually recommended for use at the second compression ring.

Screwdriver A hand tool designed to remove or insert screws.

Scroll A smoothly curved passage that changes the fluid flow direction with minimum loss in velocity.

Scuff The valve stem temporarily welds to the guide when the valve is closed. The weld breaks as the valve is forced to open.

Seal driver A hand tool used with a mallet or hammer to seat seals into a seal groove.

Seal puller A hand tool designed to remove seals.

Sealed lead-acid battery (SLA) A battery that converts the released hydrogen and oxygen back into water instead of escaping as gasses.

Seat duration The number of degrees of crankshaft rotation that the valve is off the seat.

Secondary ignition circuit The components necessary to create and distribute the high voltage produced in the secondary windings of the coil.

Secondary winding The high-voltage winding of an ignition coil.

Secondary vibration A weak high-frequency vibration caused by a slight difference in the inertia of the pistons at top dead center compared to bottom dead center.

Selective catalytic reduction (SCR) A type of exhaust emission system that uses urea injection to reduce oxides of nitrogen emissions from diesel engines.

Self-induction When current starts to flow into a coil, an opposing current is created in the windings of the coil.

Self-tapping screw A screw that has a tapered tip which allows the screw to form threads in the metal.

Series flow system Coolant flows around all the cylinders on each bank. All the coolant flows to the rear of the block, where large main coolant passages allow the coolant to flow across the gasket.

Series-parallel flow system Some engines use a combination of the series and parallel flow system.

Service information Includes service manuals, owner's manuals, CD ROM discs, Internet sites, or other sources where vehicle information is found.

Short block An engine block that includes the pistons and crankshaft.

Siamese cylinder bores Engine cylinders that do not have cooling passages between the bores.

Siamese ports Name for when two cylinders share the same port because of the restricted space available.

Side clearance Space in the ring groove above the ring.

Silent chain type Camshaft chain drive that operates quietly but tends to stretch with use.

Silicone coupling A fan drive mounted between the drive pulley and the fan.

Single cut file A file that has just one row of cutting teeth.

Single overhead camshaft Is a design in which one camshaft is placed within the cylinder head.

Skewed Inaccurate information such as a skewed sensor that does not show the value of the conditions to the PCM accurately.

Skirt See Slipper Skirt.

Sleeve The part of a micrometer under the thimble that has the major segments marked.

Sleeve bearing Engine bearing.

Sleeving Cylinder blocks with deep gouges can be saved by boring the cylinder to a dimension that is greatly oversize to almost match the outside diameter of the cylinder sleeve. The sleeve is pressed into the rebored block, and then the center of the sleeve is bored to the diameter required by the piston.

Slip-joint pliers A hand tool which has two positions allowing the use of two different ranges of sizes.

Slipper skirt The cast-aluminum piston skirt has been reduced to a minimum by using an open-type slipper skirt.

Slots Act as heat dams.

Small-hole gauge A handheld measuring tool that is adjustable to fit inside small holes. A micrometer is then used to measure the gauge to determine the inside diameter of the hole. Also called a split-ball gauge.

Smog a word that combines two words: smoke and fog. Smog is formed in the atmosphere when sunlight combines with unburned fuel (hydrocarbon, or HC) and oxides of nitrogen (NOx) produced during the combustion process inside the cylinders of an engine.

Smog pump Pulls fresh air in through an external filter and pumps the air under slight pressure to each exhaust port through connecting hoses or a manifold.

Snap ring A spring steel clip that is used to retain an object in a bore by being inserted into a groove.

Snap ring pliers   A hand tool, which is designed to install or remove snap rings.

Society of Automotive Engineers (SAE)   A professional organization that sets standards for automotive systems.

Socket   A tool that fits over the head of a bolt or nut and is rotated by a ratchet or breaker bar.

Socket adapter   An adapter that allows the use of one size of driver (ratchet or breaker bar) to rotate another drive size of socket.

Soft core plugs   Also called core plugs or Welsh plugs.

Solid valve lifter   Assists in making sure that valve train clearance is not excessive.

Soluble   Dissolved with a chemical or solvent.

Solvent   Usually colorless liquids that are used to remove grease and oil.

Soot   Another name for particulate matter (PM).

Spark knock   Secondary rapid burning of the last 3 to 5% of the air-fuel mixture in the combustion chamber. Causes a second flame front that collides with the first flame front causing a knock noise.

Spark plugs   A plug used to transmit high voltage to ignite the air-fuel mixture in the cylinder.

Spark tester   A tester used to check for a spark from an ignition coil.

Specific gravity   Specific gravity is the ratio of the weight of a given volume of a liquid to the weight of an equal volume of water.

Spindle   The part of a micrometer that moves and contacts the object being measured.

Spiral bronze alloy bushing   Guide insert for guide repair.

Spit hole   Bleeds some of the oil from the connecting rod journal.

Splay angle   Angle between the crankpins on the crankshaft throws.

Split-ball gauge   See Small-Hole Gauge.

Split-type (half shell) bearing   See Full Round Bearing.

Spontaneous combustion   A condition that can cause some materials, such as oily rags to catch fire without a source of ignition.

SPOUT   Spark out connector used in some Ford ignition systems.

Spread   Holds the bearing shell in the housing while the engine is being assembled.

Spun bearing   Bearing shells that do not have enough crush may rotate with the shaft.

Squish area   An area of the combustion chamber where the piston nearly contacts the cylinder.

SRE (Slip ring end)   The end of the alternator that has the brushes and the slip rings.

Steam slits   See bleed holes.

Stellite   An alloy of nickel, chromium, and tungsten that is nonmagnetic.

Stoichiometric   An air-fuel ratio of exactly 14.7:1. At this specific rate, all the gasoline is fully oxidized by all the available oxygen.

Stone wheel   A grinding stone attached to a grinder used for cleaning, sharpening, or other similar operations.

Stop drilling   A hole drilled at each end of a crack to keep it from extending further.

Straight cut aviation snip   A tin snip that is designed with curved jaws that allow a straight cut through sheet metal.

Straightedge   Is a precision ground metal measuring gauge that is used to check the flatness of engine components when used with a feeler gauge.

State of charge (SOC)   It is the percentage of battery charge.

Stator   The stationary electrical winding inside an alternator.

Strip feeler gauge   Can be used to measure the piston-to-cylinder clearance.

Stroke   The distance the piston travels down in the cylinder.

Struts   A structural part of a suspension that includes the shock absorber.

Stud   A short rod with threads on both ends.

Stud removal tool   A hand tool used with a breaker bar or ratchet to remove what is left of a broken stud.

Stud remover   A stud removal tool grips the part of the stub above the surface and uses a cam or wedge to grip the stud as it is being rotated by a ratchet or breaker bar.

Sump   Another name for an oil pan.

Supercharger   Is a gas compressor that forces more air into the combustion chamber of an internal combustion engine.

Surface charge   A charge on the outer surface of the plates in the battery that is easily removed when the battery is connected to an electrical load.

Surface finish   Measured in micro-inches and the smaller the number, the smoother the surface. Where the surface finish of a machined block deck or cylinder head may range from 60 to 100 RA (roughness average), the typical specification for main and rod crankshaft journals is between 10 and 20 RA.

Surface grinder   A surface grinder uses a large-diameter abrasive wheel to restore the surface of a cylinder head.

Surface to volume ratio   An important design consideration for combustion chambers.

Surge tank   A reservoir mounted at the highest point in the cooling system.

SVO   Straight vegetable oil.

Switchgrass   A feedstock for ethanol production that requires very little energy or fertilizer to cultivate.

Switching   A power transistor used to control the primary current through an ignition coil.

Symmetrical   The amount of lift of a camshaft is often different for the intake and exhaust valves. If the specifications are the same, the camshaft is called symmetrical.

Syncrude   A term used to describe synthetic fuel base stock.

Syn-gas   Synthesis gas generated by a reaction between coal and steam. Syn-gas is made up of mostly hydrogen and carbon monoxide and is used to make methanol. Syn-gas is also known as town gas.

Synthetic fuel   Fuels generated through synthetic processes such as Fischer-Tropsch.

TAME (Tertiary amyl methyl ether)   TAME is an oxygenating fuel and is used as a gasoline additive similar to ETBE or MTBE.

Tap   A metal cutting tool used to create threads in metal after a hole of the proper size has been drilled.

Tap test   Involves tapping (not pounding) on the catalytic converter using a rubber mallet.

Taper face ring   Will contact the cylinder wall at the lower edge of the piston ring.

Tapered pilots   Locate themselves in the least worn section of the guide.

Tapped transformer   A transformer or ignition coil that has one end of the primary winding connected to the secondary winding.

Technical service bulletin When a problem has a correction, the vehicle manufacturer releases a technical service bulletin (TSB), which details the repair. Also called technical service bulletin information (TSBI).

TEL TEL was added to gasoline in the early 1920s to reduce the tendency to knock.

Tensile strength The maximum stress used under tension (lengthwise force) without causing failure.

Tetraethyl lead (TEL) A gasoline additive used to reduce engine knock and ping that was discontinued due to health concerns.

Thermactor pump See Smog Pump.

Thermal shock A sudden change in temperature. The shock will often cause radial cracks in the valve.

Thermostatic spring Operates a valve that allows the fan to free-wheel when the radiator is cold. As the radiator warms to about 150°F (65°C), the air hitting the thermostatic spring will cause the spring to change its shape.

Thick film integration This system uses a smaller control module attached to the distributor and uses an air-cooled epoxy E coil.

Thickness gauge See Feeler Gauge.

Thimble The part of a micrometer that is rotated to move the spindle.

Thin-walled bronze alloy sleeve bushing Guide insert for guide repair.

Threaded insert A type of thread repair where the original threads are replaced by an insert that contains the same size threads as the original on the inside of the insert.

Three-angle valve job A type of valve job that uses three angles; the seat angle; the topping angle; and the throating angle.

Throating This removes metal from the port side of the seat, raising the lower edge of the seat.

Throating angle The second angle uses a 60-degree stone or cutter to remove material right below the valve seat to increase flow in or out of the combustion chamber.

Thrust bearing Supports thrust loads and maintains the front-to-rear position of the crankshaft in the block.

Thrust plate Controls the shaft end thrust.

Tier A level of environmental regulation created by the EPA. Tier 1 is gradually being phased out in favor of stricter Tier 2 regulations.

Tin snips A hand tool used to cut sheet metal, thin cardboard, or similar material.

Top dead center (TDC) When the piston reaches the upper most position in the cylinder.

Topping angle The third angle uses a 30-degree stone or cutter and is used to smooth the transition between the valve seat and the cylinder head again to increase flow in or out of the combustion chamber.

Torque angle To have a more constant clamping load from bolt to bolt.

Torque-to-yield (TTY) See Torque Angle.

Torque wrench A wrench that registers the amount of applied torque.

Total indicator runout When measuring and regrinding camshafts the TIR should be less than 0.002 in.

Track An ignition coil that fails when a high voltage arc creates a low resistance path from the secondary winding of the coil to the primary winding of the coil to the steel core.

Tracked coil An ignition coil that fails when a high voltage arc creates a low-resistance path from the secondary winding of the coil to the primary winding of the coil to the steel core.

Transducers An electrical device that changes a varying pressure into a variable voltage.

Transformer An electrical device that has two windings of wire; a primary winding and a secondary winding.

Transistor An electronic switch.

Trigger A trigger is a device that signals the switching of the coil on and off. A trigger is typically a pickup coil in some distributor-type ignitions and a crankshaft position sensor (CKP) on electronic systems (waste spark and coil on plug).

Triggering A sensor that detects engine piston position and signals the ignition control module to fire the spark plug.

Trouble light A light used for close viewing of dark areas. Also called a work light.

Truing A process of making a surface straight and correct.

Tube-nut wrench See Fitting Wrench.

Tuftriding A trade name that General Motors Corporation uses for the process of heating the crankshaft in a molten cyanide salt bath.

Turbo lag The delay between acceleration and turbo boost.

Turbocharger An exhaust-powered supercharger.

Turns ratio The ratio between the number of turns in the primary and number of turns in the secondary winding of an ignition coil.

TWC Three-way catalytic converter, all three exhaust emissions (NOx, HC, and CO) are converted to carbon dioxide (CO_2) and water (H_2O).

Twist A cylinder head should be checked for twist using a precision straight edge.

UCG Underground coal gasification.

UCO Used cooking oil.

ULSD (Ultra-low-sulfur diesel) Diesel fuel with a maximum sulfur content of 15 parts per million.

Ultrasonic cleaning Parts are placed in a tank of cleaning solution which is then vibrated at ultrasonic speeds to loosen all the soil from the parts.

Umbrella valve stem seal Holds tightly on the valve stem and moves up and down with the valve. Any oil that spills off the rocker arms is deflected out over the valve guide, much as water is deflected over an umbrella.

UNC (Unified National Coarse) A type of thread used on fasteners.

Underground coal gasification (UCG) A type of synthetic fuel production process that is located underground.

Underground storage tank (UST) A type of oil storage container that is located underground.

UNF Unified national fine.

Universal joint A joint in a steering or drive shaft that allows torque to be transmitted at an angle.

Unshrouding A machining process used to remove metal from around the valves to increase airflow.

Up-integrated ignition A type of ignition system that does use a separate ignition control module. All functions of the ignition are included inside the PCM.

UREA A chemical used to reduce oxides of nitrogen emission on diesel engines that use an SCR emission control system.

Used oil   Any petroleum-based or synthetic oil that has been used.

Utility knife   A handheld knife that uses replaceable blades.

Vacuum test   Include testing the engine for cranking vacuum, idle vacuum, and vacuum at 2500 RPM.

Valve cam phases (VCP)   Another name for a spline phaser variable valve timing system.

Valve (camshaft) overlap   Is the number of degrees of crankshaft rotation during which both intake and exhaust valves are open.

Valve duration   The number of degrees by which the crankshaft rotates when the valve is off the valve seat.

Valve face   The location on a valve where the valve rests on the valve seat of the cylinder head.

Valve face angle   The angle that a valve grinder should be set to which is specified by the vehicle manufacturer.

Valve float   Occurs when clearance exists in the valve train.

Valve guide   Supports the valve stem so that the valve face will remain perfectly centered.

Valve guide knurling   A tool is rotated as it is driven into the guide. The tool displaces the metal to reduce the diameter of the valve guide.

Valve keepers   Secure the spring retainer to the stem of the valve.

Valve lash   Valve train clearance.

Valve lift   The amount of distance usually measured in thousandth of an inch that the valve is lifted off its seat.

Valve locks   A lock for engine valves.

Valve pockets   See Eyebrows.

Valve relief   See Eyebrows.

Valve resurfacer   A machine that is used to grind valves.

Valve seat   The place in the cylinder head where the valve rests when closed.

Valve seat inserts   Replaceable valve seats.

Valve shrouding   The valve is kept close to the walls of the combustion chamber to help increase mixture turbulence.

Valve spring   Holds the valve against the seat.

Valve spring inserts (VSI)   Also called shims and are used to adjust the installed height of valve springs.

Valve spring surge   The tendency of a valve spring to vibrate.

Valves stem height   The height of the stem of the valve from the spring seat.

Vapor lock   Vaporized fuel, usually in the fuel line, that prevents or retards the necessary fuel delivery to the cylinders.

Variable fuel sensor   See Fuel Compensation Sensor.

Variable rate springs   A type of valve spring that provides a variable force depending on how much it is compressed.

Variable valve timing   Uses electronically controlled, hydraulic gear-driven cam phaser that can alter the relationship of the camshaft from 15 degrees retard to 25 degrees advance (40 degrees overall) relative to the crankshaft.

VECI (Vehicle emission control information)   This sticker is located under the hood on all vehicles and includes emission-related information that is important to the service technician.

Vehicle identification number (VIN)   Alphanumeric number identifying vehicle type, assembly plant, powertrain, etc.

Vent valve   See Dump Valve.

V-FFV (Virtual flexible fuel vehicle)   This fuel system design does not use a fuel compensation sensor and instead uses the vehicle's oxygen sensor to adjust for different fuel compositions.

Vibration damper   Is a device connected to the crankshaft of an engine to reduce torsional vibration.

Viscosity   Resistance to flow of an oil. A high-viscosity oil is thicker than a low-viscosity oil.

Viscosity index   An index of the change in viscosity between the cold and hot extremes.

VISE GRIPS®   A brand name for locking pliers.

Volatility   A measurement of the tendency of a liquid to change to vapor. Volatility is measured using RVP, or Reid Vapor Pressure.

Voltage drop test   A test used to determine if there is resistance in an electrical circuit by measuring the difference in voltage between two points when the circuit is operating.

Volumetric efficiency   The ratio between the amount of air-fuel mixture that actually enters the cylinder and the amount that could enter under ideal conditions expressed in percent.

VTEC (Variable valve timing and lift electronic control)   A valve train control system developed by Honda Motor Company to enhance engine output and efficiency over a wide RPM range.

Wankel engine   See Rotary Engine.

Warpage   A distortion usually caused by excessive heat.

Washcoat   A porous aluminum material.

Washers   Flat or shaped pieces of round metal with a hole in the center used between a nut and a part or casting.

Wastegate   Is a bypass valve at the exhaust inlet to the turbine.

Water pump pliers   See Multiple-Groove Adjustable Pliers.

Water-fuel separator   Water is heavier than diesel fuel and sinks to the bottom of the separator.

Waste-spark system   A type of ignition system that uses one ignition coil to fire the spark plugs for two cylinders at the same time.

Welsh plugs   Core holes left in the external block wall are machined and sealed with this type of plug.

Wet compression test   When oil is used to help seal around the piston rings.

Wet cylinder sleeve   Coolant flows around this type of cylinder sleeve.

Wet holes   Head bolts that extend through the top deck of the block and end in a coolant passage.

Wet sump   A system where oil is held in the oil pan and the oil pump drains the oil from the bottom.

Wet system   A type of nitrous system that adds nitrous gas and gasoline at the same time.

WHMIS   Workplace Hazardous Materials Information Systems.

Windage tray   Tray that is sometimes installed in engines to eliminate the oil churning problem.

Wire brush wheel   A wheel attached to a motor usually at one end with a grinding stone on the other and part of a bench grinder.

Wood alcohol   See Methanol.

Work hardened   Flexing starts fatigue, which shows up as fine cracks in the bearing surface.

Work light   See Trouble Light.

Wrench   Any of various hand or power tools, often having fixed or adjustable jaws, used for gripping, turning, or twisting objects such as nuts, bolts, or pipes.

Wrist pin   See Piston Pin.

WVO   Waste vegetable oil.

WWFC (World Wide Fuel Charter)   A fuel quality standard developed by vehicle and engine manufacturers in 2002.

ZDDP   Commonly referred to as zinc dialkyl dithiophosphate. The use of ZDDP was intended to reduce sliding friction in an engine.

Zinc dithiophosphate (ZDP)   Antiwear additive.

Zyglo   A method where cracks show up as bright lines when viewed with a black light.

INDEX